Their Names Live On

Their Names Live On
Remembering Saskatchewan's Fallen in World War II

— Doug Chisholm —

Text by Gerald Hill

Introduction by Stewart Mein

2001

CANADIAN PLAINS RESEARCH CENTER, UNIVERSITY OF REGINA

Canadian Plains Research Center
University of Regina, Regina, Saskatchewan S4S 0A2 Canada
Tel: (306) 585-4758   Fax: (306) 585-4699
e-mail: canadian.plains@uregina.ca   http://www.cprc.uregina.ca

National Library of Canada Cataloguing in Publication Data

Hill, Gerald, 1951–
    Their names live on

    (Trade books based in scholarship, ISSN 1482-9886 ; 5)
    ISBN 0-88977-121-9

    1. World War, 1939–1945--Registers of dead--Saskatchewan. 2. War memorials--Saskatchewan. 3. War memorials--Saskatchewan--Pictorial works. 4. Soldiers--Saskatchewan--Biography. 5. World War, 1939–1945--Saskatchewan. I. Chisholm, Doug, 1953– II. University of Regina. Canadian Plains Research Center. III. Title.
    FC3512.H54 2001   940.54'677124   C2001-911458-3
    F1071.8.H56 2001

Cover Design: Brian Danchuk Design, Regina, Saskatchewan
Cover Photos: Aerial photo by Doug Chisholm, Woodland Aerial Photography, La Ronge, Saskatchewan. Ronald Dunbar, Shaunavon, Saskatchewan, is the serviceman on the far right in the photograph of airmen reflected in the lake. Warrant Officer Ronald Dunbar was assigned to Spitfire aircraft #BS196 and was shot down March 13, 1943 while flying a cross-channel escort mission with No. 403 Squadron. He was nineteen years old. He is buried at Blargies Communal Cemetery, France. In Saskatchewan, Dunbar Point (55°10' N 104°39' W) is named in his honour.
Editing and production: Donna Achtzehner

The publication of this book was made possible, in part, by a generous grant from the Saskatchewan Cultural Industries Development Fund.

Their Names Live On: Remembering Saskatchewan's Fallen in World War II is part of the Encyclopedia of Saskatchewan family of products.

Printed and bound in Canada by Houghton Boston, Saskatoon, Saskatchewan
Printed on acid-free paper

To
all of the families
including my own
who have
encouraged
and
supported
these
research activities

—Doug Chisholm

TABLE OF CONTENTS

Foreword

Saskatchewan's Geo-memorial Project

One important source of geographical names in Saskatchewan has been the roll of Saskatchewan military personnel who gave their lives in World War II. There are nearly 3,700 geographic features in Saskatchewan's northland named in honour of these men and women who enlisted for service in the province and subsequently lost their lives during their war service.

This was a provincial program between 1947 and 1965 under authority given by the Canadian Board on Geographical Names (CBGN) which, at the time, was the federal body responsible for approving all geographical names in Canada. The program evolved under the provincial director of surveying in Saskatchewan, Abraham Bereskin.

Names were taken from the official RCAF, Army, and Navy casualty lists. Initially, next of kin were encouraged to write to the Minister of the Department of Natural Resources requesting that a feature be named for their lost relative. A feature would then be selected by the Saskatchewan representative on the CBGN and submitted to that Board for final approval. Next of kin were notified, and a map showing the location of the feature was forwarded under cover of a letter of appreciation from the province.

As the program continued, the number of people writing to the Minister decreased sharply. Therefore, names were selected from Saskatchewan's casualty lists by the provincial representative on the CBGN to complete the program. Unfortunately, only in a few cases were next of kin known and notified. Yet, over the years, the provincial mapping office continued to identify and officially gazette the casualty names to lakes, islands, bay, and rivers.

This has been, and continues to be, a very timely and much appreciated program for recognizing and commemorating these servicemen.

David Arthur
Chair, Geographic Names Board

Preface

As a bush pilot in northern Saskatchewan, I have learned to study the maps, to find my way outbound, and to pick my return way home. The maps show the flow of the land, the waterways, and the many names and geographic features which become points of reference. On occasion, I have visited a site and come across a bronze plaque which had been placed by a family in memory of the person for whom the geographic feature is named. I had always been intrigued by these geo-memorial sites, but it was not until 1997 that a phone call led me to look into them further.

In August 1997, I received a call from a friend in Regina, asking me if I would take a photo from my aircraft of an island on Lac La Ronge. It was a simple request, since I have lived in La Ronge since 1975 and do love to fly my aircraft whenever I can find a good excuse. Apparently there was an elderly woman in a Regina hospital who had always wanted to visit Soutar Island, but who was now unable to make the trip. I was advised that Soutar Island had been named by our province in memory of her brother who had lost his life with the RCAF during World War II. I got out my map, and sure enough, there was Soutar Island, so away I went.

As I circled the island in my floatplane, I found myself wondering who Pilot Officer James Soutar really was and what his life was like. What circumstances had drawn this young man from Saskatchewan to enlist in the Royal Canadian Air Force in 1941? What about his surviving family?

The family was not sure if there was a commemorative plaque at Soutar Island, and as I circled I noticed a cabin with a boat at the dock. It was a lovely summer day, and I felt compelled to land my floatplane to find out more. When the cabin owner greeted me, I asked if he knew of any commemorative plaque on Soutar Island. After a cup of coffee, we explored the rugged Precambrian shoreline of the island and the lovely sand beach. We did not find a plaque, but I gathered a few rocks from the shoreline, some sand from the beach, and a few leaves from the trees— these were subsequently sent with the aerial photos to the family of Pilot Officer James Soutar.

That simple request from the Soutar family piqued my curiosity about many of the names which appeared on my maps. After a bit of initial research, I discovered how Soutar Island and many other geographic features had come to be named after men and women who, like James, had died during their service in the Second World War. Between 1947 and 1965, the province of Saskatchewan named nearly 3,700 geographic features after those Saskatchewan people whose names were found on the official RCAF, Army, and Navy casualty lists. Every name was officially gazetted at the provincial mapping office—the list included rank, casualty date, and regimental number, along with the geographic feature, its location, and the map sheet on which that feature could be found. The list did not include hometown, regiment, or family contact of the honouree. As the years went by, the origin of many of the names had become somewhat dormant. Families moved on, many unaware of the fact that a geographic feature had been named in memory of their son, daughter, father, or brother.

Since I first photographed Soutar Island in 1997, I have had the opportunity to record aerial photos of over 3,000 of these geo-memorial sites. Sometimes when I record an aerial photo of a particular lake or island, it is as a result of a specific request from family members; most times, I run merely on faith and the hope that at some time in the future, I will be contacted by a brother, sister, son or daughter, niece or nephew, someone who cares. I continue to be amazed by how many families are not aware that the province named a lake or island in memory of a long-lost brother or uncle, and it is enormously satisfying to be able to provide information when requested. Thus far, I have been able to provide aerial photo tributes to over five hundred families, and it has been through their encouragement and support that I have been able to continue my research.

Sometimes families request that I place a bronze memorial plaque at the site. On those occasions, I not only photograph the site, but land my 1954 Cessna 180 floatplane at a suitable location. After I mount the bronze plaque to the bedrock, I play an audio cassette of the Last Post and Reveille—the entire event recorded for the family with my video camera. Linton Lake on the Saskatchewan–Northwest Territories border was the site of one such visit in the year 2000.

Some family members want to visit the site themselves. My contact with the Bartlett family from Fort Qu'Appelle resulted in a visit to Bartlett Lake by fifteen relatives from all across Canada—a sister from Ottawa, a brother from Victoria, and one from Qu'Appelle. Together with children and grandchildren, they flew to the lake in July 1999, where a bronze plaque was placed in memory of Wing Commander Christopher Smales Bartlett, RCAF. As a guest of the family, I stopped in with my floatplane to share in the event and enjoy a wonderful lunch of fresh fish caught that day. For many family members the vastness and quiet beauty of the North brings a kind of peace to their memories of separation by war and death more than fifty years ago.

I was born in Scotland in 1953 and, coming from a British family, I always thought that I knew about the Second World War. My parents and all of my uncles and aunts had served their country in either the Air Force, Army or Navy. The same is true in the family of my wife Kathy, who was born in Estevan, where her father and his brothers had all enlisted during those war years. Although I thought I knew about the war, in reality, as a member of the post-war "baby boom" generation, my understanding of such matters took much for granted.

The post-war years were busy times for families, who earnestly tried to get on with their lives, work hard, and raise a family. Often families chose not to talk of the war, of the horrors they had experienced, and of the sacrifices which had been made. As my generation grew into early adulthood, images of our parents' military service were often distorted with images of the Vietnam War.

My research into Saskatchewan's geo-memorial sites has brought me in touch with hundreds of families who have shared their reflections of those war years and have taught me a lot. Saskatchewan young people enlisted from the cities, the universities, the farms, the Indian reserves, and the rural communities—91,000 in all, roughly ten percent of the province's population. Many were single and left behind parents and younger siblings. Some left fiancées, others left a young wife with a son or daughter. Each enlisted for his or her own reasons, but those were compelling times. The depression years had been tough, and the future seemed most uncertain. Recruitment posters called on everyone to serve King and Country, the uniforms were proud, and the money seemed good. The radio broadcasts from British Prime Minister Winston Churchill stirred a most powerful rally cry across the British Empire. For many, both the excitement and the sense of duty were irresistible.

For the groundswell of new recruits, Saskatchewan would become but a distant memory as they found themselves far from their hometowns. Once they enlisted, their training at bases across Canada changed keen young prairie boys into young men. When training in Canada was complete, they were off to England for more training or for duties in support of the war effort. Those who remained at home remember the fears and the tears, the prayers, cold winter nights, rations, nightly radio broadcasts, socks knitted, packages sent, and letters received from overseas. Some also received a telegram of regret from King George VI; some families would receive two such telegrams, and one Saskatchewan family would receive three.

In 1999, I visited the Canadian Plains Research Center at the University of Regina, and, there, a discussion about my research evolved into a discussion about a book. I feel honoured to share some of my aerial photo images of these geo-memorial sites, together with a collection of individual stories and family photos. It is hoped that these powerful images will reach beyond immediate family members, filtering out to extended families across the province and across the country. It is the younger generations who must be given these stories so that they, too, can remember. Written by Gerald Hill, the stories told in these pages are but seventy-eight of the hundreds of stories which families have openly shared with me. Indeed, for many families, even those who in earlier times chose not to discuss their experiences from the war years, it is now time to pass on these memories to future generations. Sadly, the stories of some of the 3,800 men and women will, in fact, never be told, because those who once remembered them are themselves gone. While their stories are gone, however, *their names live on*—in Saskatchewan's official gazetteer, on the province's map, and in the quiet beauty of our remote islands, lakes, and bays. Lest we forget.

—Doug Chisholm

Acknowledgements

Their Names Live On: Remembering Saskatchewan's Fallen in World War II is the result of the work, dedication, and support of many people.

****

The following people dedicated a number of days to a manual search of the card files at Information Services Corporation of Saskatchewan (Sask Geomatics) in order to update the province's World War II casualty list: Donna Achtzehner, Liese Achtzehner, Don Baron, Doug Chisholm, Pablo de Lucas, Hulme Henley, Jean Kempling, David Marshall, June Marshall, Bob Nelson, Dolores Nelson, Elizabeth Pederson, and Alice Reid. Thanks to David Arthur, Saskatchewan Geographic Names Board, for accommodating the work crew, and to his staff, especially Brian Hugel and Madoka Otani, for their assistance. Thank you to the individual Legion branches who provided honour rolls and information on servicemen.

Keith Inches and James O'Kane assisted with editing and proofreading. David McLennan proofread, researched additional photos, and assisted in updating the casualty list.

Donna Achtzehner, Canadian Plains Research Center, coordinated the production of *Their Names Live On.*

Les Allison, Will Chabun, David Marshall, Eric Nelson, Floyd Williston, and Garrett Wilson have provided support and encouragement along the way.

Thanks to all of the above, and I am especially grateful to the hundreds of families who continue to support my research and who have so generously shared their stories with me.

Doug Chisholm

****

For helpful background information and, in some cases, preliminary work on the stories, I thank Mark Bonokoski, Gordon Brown, Robert Cairns, Robert Calder, Will Chabun, Dennis Chisholm, Doug Chisholm, Pablo de Lucas, Joseph Flynn, Shirley Goodwin, Ralph Green, Maud Hale, Brent Hamre, Keith Inches, Robert McWillie, Doug Mullen, Barry Needham, Eric Nelson, Edward Neufeld, Reg Stead, Murray Straker, Stan Turner, Isaac Unger, Fred Wihak, and Gordon Wilson.

Above all, I am grateful to the numerous families who let me into their homes, into their personal documents, into their stories.

Gerald Hill

Photo Acknowledgements

All aerial photographs of the geographic features are by Doug Chisholm, Woodland Aerial Photography, Box 846, La Ronge, Saskatchewan, S0J 1L0.

Photographs were obtained from the following archives and are used by permission:
    Canadian Forces / Department of National Defense
    Commonwealth War Graves Commission
    Legion Magazine
    National Archives of Canada
    The Naval Museum of Alberta
    Saskatchewan Archives Board
    University of Regina Archives
We are grateful for the assistance of the staff at these institutions. Photographers are identified when they are known.

A number of other individuals provided photographs for use in the book. These are identified in the photograph credit line, and we are grateful for their contributions.

All other photographs have been provided by family members.

SASKATCHEWAN GOES TO WAR

An Introductory Essay by Dr. Stewart Mein

THE INTER-WAR YEARS, 1919–1939

WHEN THE BOYS CAME MARCHING HOME

Cheering crowds greeted returning soldiers in 1919 as they stepped off trains in cities, towns, and villages throughout Saskatchewan. The troops were coming home from the Great War, "the war to end all wars," to become civilians once again and to resume their peacetime lives.

The post-war world they returned to was a relatively affluent one. The province, along with the rest of the country, was soon caught up in the good times of the "Roaring Twenties," but all that would change within a decade.

DROUGHT AND THE GREAT DEPRESSION

The stock market came crashing down on "Black Thursday," October 24, 1929, and the bottom fell out of the wheat market. Then came a long and crippling drought. The double impact of drought and the Depression became the crucible that moulded Saskatchewan and its people as they faced, and eventually overcame, hardships unequalled in any other region of the country.

Men, looking for work, wandered the land in such great numbers that it soon became a concern. Work camps were set up across the country by the federal government through the Department of National Defence to alleviate the problem. The militia training area of Dundurn, south of Saskatoon, was one such camp. Here the men lived and worked on such projects as building railway spurs and airstrips. The camps were derisively named "Royal Twenty Centres" by their occupants, alluding to the twenty cents a day they received for their work.

Dissatisfaction with camp life produced political agitators who organised the unemployed into an army of the disaffected. Numbers grew as they rode the rails across Western Canada in the "on to Ottawa" trek. Alarmed, the federal government decided to stop the trek before it reached the national capital and ordered the R.C.M.P. to confront the men in Regina. The ensuing riot left a city policeman dead; however, the trek was stopped. A bitter solution finally relieved the problems of the Depression. The outbreak of World War II again brought the province and the nation a healthy economy and full employment.

SASKATCHEWAN AND THE PRE-WAR CANADIAN MILITARY

After World War I, Canada's armed forces were reorganised and all former military departments of the Canadian government were united into a Department of National Defence. As part of the reorganisation, two naval reserve half-companies were started in Saskatchewan, one in Regina, which became H.M.C.S. *Queen*, and the other in Saskatoon which became H.M.C.S. *Unicorn*. A new fledgling Canadian air force was also represented in the province. The militia in Saskatchewan was reorganised into two regions, one centred in Regina, the other in Saskatoon. Two infantry brigades were formed, one in each region, along with the necessary supporting cavalry, artillery, machine gun, army service corps, medical, and engineering units.

Work on a permanent military camp was begun in Saskatchewan in 1929 near the town of Dundurn. In the summer of that year and for each summer throughout the 1930s, special C.N.R. trains brought militia units from cities, towns, and villages across the province to the new camp for a week of training.

Because of the tremendous expansion of the Canadian armed forces during World War II, the Canadian military was again reorganised. Three separate defence departments were created: one each for the army, the navy, and the air force.

WAR CLOUDS GATHER—EUROPE TO 1939

EUROPE BETWEEN THE WARS

While Canada and Saskatchewan were desperately struggling through the Great Depression, Europe was witness to events which would again plunge the world into the darkness of war. The German people, embittered by defeat, and crippled by economic chaos and crushing repatriation payments, looked for a way to overcome their suffering. They turned to an obscure demagogue who seemed to have the answer to restoring German national pride. His name was Adolph Hitler.

In January 1933, Hitler was appointed chancellor of Germany and later that year, he withdrew his country from the League of Nations. Universal military service was instituted in 1935, and Germany began to rearm. At the same time, Italy, under another dictator, Benito Mussolini, invaded Ethiopia.

In 1936, Germany occupied the Rhineland and in 1938, formally abrogated the Treaty of Versailles. Alarmed, France set about its own rearmament. Germany then annexed Austria and in May, German troops marched into Czechoslovakia.

Attempting to avert total war, Prime Minister Neville Chamberlain of Britain flew to Munich to meet Hitler. Chamberlain returned home with the promise that there would be no more territorial demands by Germany. He was convinced that he had indeed achieved "peace in our time." Sadly, he was mistaken.

A year later, after formalising its alliance with Italy by treaty, Germany signed a non-aggression pact with the Soviet Union. Under the secret terms of the pact, Germany and Russia agreed to the partitioning of Poland between them. The British government, abandoning its policy of appeasement towards Hitler, warned

Nuremberg Rally, 1936: 140,000 political leaders gathered for the general assembly on Zeppelin Field in front of the *Führer*. As night fell, hundreds of spotlights provided illumination, creating an unforgettable sight.

Germany that if Poland were attacked, Britain would come to its aid.

THE SPANISH CIVIL WAR

In Spain, a bitter civil war broke out in 1936, and volunteers from all over the world joined international brigades to fight against the fascist forces of Francisco Franco. Included among them was a Canadian contingent of almost fifteen hundred men, known as the Mackenzie-Papineau Battalion. In its ranks were many of the unemployed from Saskatchewan who had taken part in the "on to Ottawa" trek four years earlier. Volunteers from Germany and Italy fighting alongside Franco's army perfected many of the land and air tactics of the Blitzkrieg, which would later be used so devastatingly throughout Europe in the spring of 1940.

CANADA AND THE BRITISH EMPIRE, A NEW RELATIONSHIP

After the First World War, Canada began to acquire an identity as an independent nation within the British Empire. This independence was given expression through the passing of the Statute of Westminster in 1931 by the British parliament. The dominions of the Empire had now become autonomous communities within the new British Commonwealth of Nations and were free to create their own foreign policy, even to the extent of exercising the right to declare war.

Although Canadians had achieved political autonomy, there was still a cultural affinity between themselves and the "Old Country." This was amply demonstrated when King George VI and Queen Elizabeth whistle-stopped across the country as part of their North American tour in May and June of 1939. Included in the tour was a three-day trip to the United States, in which the American people were charmed by the royal couple. Their visit went a long way towards influencing President Roosevelt's decision to help Britain at the outbreak of war.

THE BEGINNING—SEPTEMBER 1939

WAR IS DECLARED

Ignoring an ultimatum from Britain and France, Hitler invaded Poland on September 1, 1939. When German troops crossed the Polish frontier, Britain and France mobilised their armies and two days later, they declared war on Germany. Other dominions such as Australia and New Zealand immediately followed Britain's lead. Canada, however, emphasising its new-found status as an independent nation, declared war a week later. Southern Ireland, however, which had become the sovereign state of Eire within the British Commonwealth in 1937, remained neutral during World War II thereby denying the use of Irish ports to British shipping. Nevertheless, many Irish served voluntarily in the British armed forces.

MOBILISATION—CANADA ORGANISES FOR WAR

At the outbreak of war, Canada had only a minuscule navy and air force, a permanent army of slightly over four thousand, and a militia of about fifty-one thousand. Prior to the declaration of war, the defence budget had been raised, and an attempt had been made to modernise the military.

When war began, units of the Canadian army were quickly called up to guard harbours and other vital points throughout the country. In Saskatchewan, guards were hastily mobilised for airports, radio transmitters, and for "enemy alien" internment camps. A Saskatchewan Veterans' Civil Security Corps was activated to help safeguard rural areas.

A Canadian Active Service Force for home defence and for overseas service was authorised. However, unlike World War I, when the Canadian Expeditionary Force was raised independently from established military units, the Active Service Force in World War II was mobilised from existing units of the militia and the permanent force. By the end of December 1939, within three months of its mobilisation, the First Canadian Division, under the command of General A.G.L. McNaughton, from Moosomin, Saskatchewan, had been sent to Camp Aldershot in the United Kingdom.

SASKATCHEWAN ANSWERS THE CALL

In Saskatchewan the first unit to be raised for overseas service was the First Corps Ammunition Park, Royal Canadian Army Service Corps from Regina. The Saskatoon Light Infantry was mobilised into the First Canadian Division along with additional personnel recruited from all over the province.

The South Saskatchewan Regiment was mobilised into the Second Canadian Division and supplemented with men from Weyburn, Estevan, Moose Jaw, and the rest of southern Saskatchewan. When the division arrived in Britain in 1940, it became part of a newly formed Canadian Corps.

BRITISH COMMONWEALTH AIR TRAINING PLAN

Late in 1939 an agreement was made between Great Britain and the Dominions of Canada, Australia, India, and New Zealand to train their air force pilots and air crews in Canada under the British Commonwealth Air Training Plan.

The task of training so many airmen proved too great for the resources of the military alone, so the Royal Canadian Air Force turned to private flying clubs to administer the elementary flying training schools of the B.C.A.T.P.

In 1940, the British government developed its own plan to train Royal Air Force pilots in Canada. Over the next few years, a number of British flying schools were set up throughout the country. In Saskatchewan, these Royal Air Force stations were situated in Assiniboia, Estevan, Swift Current, North Battleford, and Moose Jaw.

British Commonwealth Air Training Plan (BCATP) graduates arrive in the United Kingdom.

About half the B.C.A.T.P. training establishments were on the prairies. In Saskatchewan, these schools were located in Regina, Saskatoon, Prince Albert, Weyburn, Davidson, Yorkton, Caron, Mossbank, and Dafoe, as well as in those communities hosting RAF stations.

Students from many dominions and colonies, and from other allied countries, including the United States, were sent to Canada for flight training. Some five thousand French, Czechoslovakian, Norwegian, Polish, Belgian, Dutch, and American students passed through the B.C.A.T.P. schools. In all, the project provided more than one hundred and thirty one thousand trained pilots, navigators, aerial gunners, bombardiers, and flight engineers for allied air forces.

The cost of funding the B.C.A.T.P. was over $2.25 billion; the accompanying infusion of money into the prairie economy helped boost the region out of the Depression.

THE OPENING PHASE IN EUROPE APRIL–JUNE 1940

THE PHONY WAR

The seven months after war had been declared was a period of relative calm in which little actual fighting took place. This "Phony War" ended abruptly when Germany invaded Denmark and Norway on April 9, 1940. Later that month, British forces were sent to Norway in an abortive attempt to counter the German invasion. In Britain, Chamberlain resigned as prime minister and Winston Churchill formed a coalition government on May 10.

MIRACLE OF DUNKIRK

The German "Blitzkrieg" rolled through Holland, Belgium and Luxembourg into France in May of 1940 and the First Canadian Division went to France to join the British Expeditionary Force in an attempt to stem the lightning advances of the Germans. Two weeks later, soldiers of the beleaguered British army stood stranded on the beaches of Dunkirk, seemingly doomed to surrender.

An appeal went out to the people of Britain, and from ports and waterways all around the country hundreds of private boats of every size and shape gathered to be towed across the English Channel to France to rescue the army. There, the men stood in long lines stretched along the beaches, waiting their turn to embark for the journey home. Altogether some three hundred and sixty thousand British, French, and Allied troops were evacuated in this "Miracle of Dunkirk." Four Canadian destroyers were included among the fleet of warships providing protection for the evacuation.

FALL OF FRANCE

France surrendered to Germany on June 22, 1940. In this, its "darkest hour," only Britain with the Dominions stood against the might of the German military forces that now occupied most of the Continent.

In response to events unfolding in Europe, the Canadian government authorised the raising of another division for overseas service. The Regina Rifle Regiment became part of this Third Canadian Division. Since many had already left the regiment to enlist in other active service force units, the Regina Rifles recruited men from all over Saskatchewan to fill its ranks. Companies were raised in Prince Albert and North Battleford to join those from Regina. In July of 1940, the regiment moved to Camp Dundurn for training and then proceeded to Debert, Nova Scotia, as part of the defence force for the east coast of Canada. The Regina Rifles finally embarked for Britain in August 1941.

THE BATTLE FOR BRITAIN

GERMANY PREPARES TO INVADE BRITAIN

After the evacuation at Dunkirk and the fall of France, Hitler, believing that Britain was defeated, proposed a plan for peace. When his overtures were rejected, he decided to invade the island.

Thus, the Battle of Britain began. The battle was fought in the air over the British Isles. Throughout the month of August the vastly superior German Luftwaffe sent its fighters and bombers to attack RAF airfields in an attempt to secure air superiority for the planned imminent invasion. The British fought to prevent a German landing.

Canadian airmen, including many from Saskatchewan, served in British squadrons of Fighter Command and were involved in the fighting from the very beginning. No. 242 (Canadian) Squadron, RAF, formed in early 1940 with all Canadian pilots, had flown cover over the beaches at Dunkirk. It went on to distinguish itself, under Squadron Leader Douglas Bader, during the Battle of Britain.

By February 1940, a Canadian unit, No. 110 Squadron, RCAF, had been formed overseas in Britain to act as air support for the First Canadian Infantry Division. In June, No. 1 Squadron, RCAF, arrived in England and went into action against the German Luftwaffe in late August. The unit was later renumbered 401 Squadron.

Prime Minister Winston Churchill paid tribute to the pilots who had so ably defended their island home throughout the Battle of Britain with the phrase: "Never have so many owed so much to so few."

THE BLITZ

Throughout September, in response to an air attack on Berlin, the German Air Force switched targets and began bombing London and other major British cities in an attempt to terrorise the British population into submission. These attacks became known as "the Blitz." The fateful decision by the Germans to concentrate on urban targets and away from airfields gave the Royal Air Force time to reorganise and re-equip Fighter Command.

Higher than expected casualties of both German aircraft and airmen forced the Luftwaffe to switch to night bombing. By mid-September the Germans realised that aerial bombing alone would not bring Britain to its knees, and the nightly bombings decreased. Although other British cities were bombed, the capital was again singled out for the last attack of the Blitz, in May 1941.

The Germans, unable to conquer Britain, turned their attention to the East. German aircraft were now diverted to the upcoming attack on Russia, which took place in June 1941.

THE AIR WAR OVER EUROPE

BOMBER COMMAND

During the Battle of Britain, the primary bombing missions of the RAF had been against the amphibious forces of the German army being assembled on the French coast for "Operation Sea Lion," the German code name for the invasion of Britain.

With the Battle of Britain over and Hitler's attention turned toward the invasion of Russia, RAF Bomber Command adopted a policy of raids on the continent designed to disrupt the German war effort.

In February of 1942, Air Marshal Arthur Harris took over Bomber Command. He would remain as its commander for the rest of the war. "Bomber" Harris, as he became known, implemented a new policy of "area bombing," the objective being to break the morale of the German civil population, particularly the industrial workers.

To initiate the new policy, on the night of March 3, 1942, two hundred and thirty-five aircraft took part in a bombing run on the Renault factory near Paris. Various other attacks were carried out over the next few nights, including a raid on the German town of Lubek on March 29. Two hundred and thirty-four aircraft carried out a successful attack goading Hitler into retaliatory attacks on Exeter and Bath. Attacks followed on Canterbury, Norwich, and York, producing a loss of over sixteen hundred lives. These became known as the "Baedeker raids," named after a German guidebook for travellers to Britain. With the exception of a period in January of 1943, this was to be the last serious German raid on Britain until the launching of the V1 rockets in June of 1944.

At the end of May 1942, plans were drawn up to conduct the first of the "thousand bomber" raids against the German town of Cologne. Aircraft were collected from all sources to make up the huge fleet. In the raid, code-named "Operation Millennium," all forms of bombs, including incendiaries, were dropped, killing some five hundred people and leaving a further forty-five thousand homeless. Two more thousand bomber raids were to follow, one over Essen and the other over Bremen. The thousand bomber raids were then discontinued until later in the war.

OPERATIONAL TRAINING UNITS

By 1940, the first of the British Commonwealth Air Training Plan graduates had begun to arrive in Britain and were posted to RAF units. Although trained, they had not been formed into aircraft crews. To further train the new airmen, operational training units were formed in which crews would complete some eighty hours of flying training as a team. Crews were then sent to heavy conversion units to train for planes such as the Wellingtons, Stirlings, Halifaxes, and Lancasters that they would fly in operational squadrons.

An Avro Lancaster bomber, used by RCAF squadrons in the bombing raids on Germany.

COURTESY OF THE CANADIAN FORCES / AEC 89-787B

THE RCAF IN BRITAIN

The first Canadian bombing unit, 405 Squadron, RCAF, came into existence in June 1941. Its first sortie was flown against railway marshalling yards in Germany. Seven more RCAF bomber squadrons were formed in 1942 and sixty-eight Canadian aircraft took part in the first of the thousand bomber raids.

On January 31, 1943, Canadian bomber squadrons in Britain were grouped together into Six (RCAF) Group. Although some of the squadrons had been sent to the Middle East to become part of the Desert Air Force during the Mediterranean and North African campaign, the Group continued to provide aircraft for British bombing raids over Europe. By June 24, 1943, Six Group had lost over one hundred aircraft.

THE UNITED STATES ARMY AIR FORCE IN BRITAIN

A number of American pilots had not waited for their country to declare war and had volunteered for service in the RAF. They were grouped into what became known as "Eagle Squadrons," where the pilots were American and the squadron commanders were British.

With the United States' entry into the war in December 1941, plans had been drawn up for a United States strategic bomber force to be based in the United Kingdom. The first operational mission by the United States Army Air Force was conducted on July 4, 1942, in conjunction with the RAF, on targets in Holland.

COMBINED AIR OPERATIONS

In 1943, a strategic directive was issued that called for a joint bombing offensive by RAF Bomber Command and the American army air force against Germany. The targets of the combined bombing campaigns were organised in such a way that the RAF would bomb at night and the American air force would bomb during the day.

United States tactics relied on bombing by B-17 "Flying Fortresses," which were protected by their own internal defensive gun armaments. However serious questions were raised about the tactics of daylight bombing after a raid on the Romanian oil refineries of Ploesti and later on the German town of Schweinfurt with its ball-bearing factory, in which the Americans suffered heavy losses.

British tactics relied on night bombing and advances in radar, which had improved navigational technology over the "GEE" system that had been used earlier. New squadrons called Pathfinders would now lead bombing formations to their targets carrying the improved systems.

THE DAMBUSTER RAIDS

On the night of May 16, 1943, the new British tactics using Pathfinder aircraft were brought into play in the air campaigns over the Rhur Valley. These became known as the "Dambuster" raids. No. 617 (Dambuster) Squadron, RAF, in which twenty-nine of the one hundred and thirty-three aircrews were Canadian, was especially trained in low-level bombing. With a specially designed "bouncing" bomb, the squadron flew against a series of dams in the Rhur Valley; the objective was to cut off the Germans' source of power for weapons production and transportation. The raid was successful in smashing two of the three objectives: the dams at Mohne and Eder. For his skill in leading the raid, the squadron commander, Guy Gibson, was awarded the Victoria Cross.

RAID ON HAMBURG

Bomber Command then switched its attention from the Rhur Valley to Hamburg. The bombing was so intense that the raids produced a firestorm that levelled the city and killed thirty thousand of its inhabitants. This was the first of the great fire storm raids that were to be inflicted on Germany for the remainder of the year. Seventy-two Canadian aircraft were among the seven hundred and ninety one bombers that took part in the raid. Attacks continued to be made against Hamburg until August 3, 1943.

The attacks on Hamburg became a prelude to raids on Berlin. The first of these attacks on the German capital took place in August 1943. Other American daylight raids and RAF night raids on Berlin took place continuously throughout 1944.

Just before the attacks on Berlin began, a raid was carried out on the Baltic Sea base of Peenemuende, where the Germans were developing their new terror weapons, the "V" rockets. Canadian bombers from Six Group took part in that raid.

The bombing of Germany reached its peak in August 1943 and continued into 1944. On February 21, for a full week, RAF Bomber Command and the Eighth and Fifteenth U.S. Air Forces targeted the south of Germany, concentrating on aircraft and ball bearing production factories. These attacks significantly damaged the Luftwaffe's fighter capacity to an extent from which it never fully recovered. The last of the large bombing raids against Germany took place in March 1944, over Nuremberg.

No. 42 Company, Canadian Women's Army Corps, Canadian Army Overseas, 1940s.

Because of upcoming D-Day operations, Bomber Command targets were switched to the destruction of German strongholds in France as the Allies prepared to open a second front in Europe at Normandy.

THE HALF MILLION—CANADIANS IN BRITAIN, 1940–1944

FORTRESS BRITAIN—CANADIANS DEFEND THE ENGLISH COAST

With the arrival of the First Canadian Division in December 1939, the Canadian army garrisoned Britain through 1940 until the invasion of France in June 1944. After the British losses in France in 1940, the only force capable of defending the British Isles was Canadian. Consequently, the Canadian Corps became the backbone of the defence of Britain throughout this period. In July 1940, the Canadian Corps joined units of the British army commanded by General Bernard L. Montgomery to help defend the southeastern coast of England. A decision was made to further increase the Canadian army contribution to the European war and so, in April 1942, the First Canadian Army was formed in Britain.

Along with the army, the Royal Canadian Air Force stationed squadrons in Britain throughout the war as part of Fighter, Bomber, and Coastal Commands, and the Royal Canadian Navy contributed ships to Royal Navy squadrons and flotillas. In all, some half million Canadians fought their war from the British Isles.

Dieppe, 1942

In addition to guarding the southeastern coast of Britain, the Canadian army spent considerable time in training for an eventual invasion of Europe. When Prime Minister Mackenzie King visited Canadian soldiers overseas, he was soundly booed by the troops, who were growing weary of training and impatient to see action. Their wishes were soon to be granted. The Canadians would be chosen to see fierce and bloody action.

In order to learn how to conduct a sea-borne assault against the mainland of France and to put pressure on German coastal defences, a plan was developed by Lord Louis Mountbatten, Chief of Combined Operations, to raid the small French port town of Dieppe. Code-named "Operation Jubilee," the plan was to launch attacks at five different points along a ten-mile front, with the main attack being on Dieppe itself. The operation was to be a "reconnaissance in force, "more than a raid, but less than a full-scale invasion.

The Second Canadian Division was to conduct the raid along with British commandos and a small group of American rangers. A large force of RAF aircraft, including eight Canadian squadrons, would maintain air superiority and protect the troops from enemy planes. Destroyers of the Royal Navy and the Royal Canadian Navy would also be in support.

The raid, originally to have been launched in July, had to be cancelled because of bad weather. The plan was revived, however, and in the early hours of August 19, 1942, some six thousand Allied troops set out for the beaches of Dieppe. As the assault force moved toward the French shore, it encountered a small enemy convoy and sank one of the German ships. This brief encounter may have alerted the German garrison on land.

With little support from naval gunfire, and sparse air cover, of the five thousand Canadians who stormed ashore on the beaches that morning, almost nine hundred were dead and one thousand wounded by the afternoon. Nineteen hundred more became prisoners of war.

To the west, on the beaches of Puys, the attacking force,

Bodies of Canadian soldiers lying among damaged landing craft and tanks following Operation Jubilee, Dieppe, France, August 19, 1942. This photograph was taken by the Nazis for propaganda purposes.

trapped by a heavily fortified sea wall and virtually decimated by enfilading machine gun fire, suffered the heaviest casualties. In the centre, the main attack on the town of Dieppe was a disaster. After a murderous dash across a shingle beach, continuously swept by enemy fire throughout the whole of the assault, very few of the troops managed to get to the town itself and the attack was brought to an abrupt standstill.

The South Saskatchewans at Green Beach

To the east, the South Saskatchewan Regiment from the Weyburn and Estevan area, together with the Cameron Highlanders of Canada, were able to achieve a limited success on "Green Beach" near Pourville by moving some distance further inland. The commanding officer of the South Saskatchewans, Colonel C.C.I. Merritt, won a Victoria Cross for his heroism in leading his regiment towards its objective. Merritt remained on the beach with the other members of his unit who could not be evacuated. He was captured and spent the rest of the war in a prisoner of war camp in Germany.

BATTLE OF THE ATLANTIC

The primary threat to Great Britain during the war was the attacks on British transatlantic shipping. Had the Germans been successful in choking off Britain's lifeline, the country would have had to capitulate for lack of food and materiel. The attempt to continue to re-supply Britain by sea, became known as the "Battle of the Atlantic."

THE U-BOAT THREAT

At the beginning of the war, Hitler was hesitant to engage in all out submarine warfare. He did not want to antagonise neutral nations and he expected to come to terms with Britain after Europe had been overrun. Instead, German "pocket" battleships and battle cruisers roamed the seas sinking allied merchant ships and generally causing havoc.

The problem of the U-boat became more acute after the fall of France. As new long-range submarines were introduced, all ocean shipping to Britain had to be routed north of Ireland through the Irish Sea but German "wolf packs" sank merchant ships faster than they could be replaced.

CONVOYS

To protect shipping, the convoy system was introduced. Blocs of merchantmen, some armed with a single gun, churned slowly across the ocean. Ahead, behind and on the flanks, "zig-zagging" around them, were the naval escort vessels. Ships and aircraft were placed in Newfoundland and Iceland to protect the western convoys, while the eastern Atlantic convoys were guarded by British Coastal Command. Although planes flying from both sides of the Atlantic and Iceland could patrol most of the sea-lanes, a gap of about three hundred miles existed in mid-ocean.

German U-boats began patrolling the North American coast from the Caribbean to Halifax and into the Gulf of St. Lawrence in early 1942. The United States had entered the war in December 1941, but their Atlantic fleet had been depleted when ships were sent to the Pacific to replace those lost during the bombing of Pearl Harbour. Weakened coastal defences drew German attacks on shipping, and more than two hundred ships, mostly tankers, were sunk within ten miles of North American shores.

Efforts were made by the Allies to cripple the U-boats by bombing their construction yards and bases in Germany and France. These efforts proved fruitless, however, because the massive concrete pens that were constructed to protect the boats in harbour were impervious to bombing.

By the winter of 1942, German submarine strength had grown, and attacks on convoys became more frequent. Support for the convoys was improved however, when the Canadian air force

The Canadian corvette HMCS *Battleford* escorting a convoy across the Atlantic, November 1941.

acquired long range Liberator bombers that could cover the mid-Atlantic gap. Also, more modern escort vessels, such as the corvette, had been developed. Designed on the pattern of the whaler, the corvette could be produced quickly and cheaply and, what is more, it could stay at sea for extended periods of time and could out-manoeuvre a submarine. With new equipment and better training, the allied navies eventually began to get the upper hand on German submarines.

PRAIRIE SAILORS

A surprising number of men from Saskatchewan served on the corvettes in the North Atlantic and in the destroyers and other ships in Canadian waters and in the British home fleet. These "prairie sailors" saw service with the R.C.N or the RN in almost every part of the world.

RUSSIA, THE EASTERN FRONT

With his plans for the invasion of Britain having been frustrated, Hitler had turned his attention eastward toward Russia. In June of 1941, he launched an massive attack under the code name "Operation Barbarossa." The German army achieved almost total surprise, striking deep into the heart of Russia, capturing three hundred thousand prisoners, and almost wiping out the Russian air force. After capturing Kiev the Germans moved on to Leningrad and to Moscow and rapidly moved into the Ukraine.

They had hoped for a quick victory and had not counted on a winter campaign. In December, the Russians counterattacked and broke the siege of Moscow and resupplied the besieged city of Leningrad.

In the summer of 1942 came the siege of Stalingrad. It was here that the German advance was stopped. The siege allowed Russian forces to regroup for a counteroffensive. Convoys of western supplies and equipment, delivered to Murmansk, helped the Soviets to re-arm.

WAR IN THE FAR EAST, DECEMBER 1941–1942

JAPANESE EXPANSIONISM AND MILITARISM

Throughout the decades preceding its involvement in World War II, Japan had embarked on a policy of economic and military expansionism in the Far East. Japanese forces overran Manchuria in 1931 and, by 1937, had occupied most of China. In 1940, under the influence of the "War Party" led by Premier Tojo, the country had formally allied itself with Germany. Basing its strategic war plans on the concept of surprise attacks, Japan went to war.

On December 7, 1941, planes from Japanese aircraft carriers launched a surprise attack against military airfields and the port of Pearl Harbor, Hawaii. Anchored there were ships of the United States Pacific Fleet. When the attack was over, most of the main battle fleet had been sunk at its moorings. A shocked American nation awoke the next morning to find that it was at war with Japan.

HONG KONG

Simultaneously with the attack on Pearl Harbor, Japanese land forces from China invaded the British colony of Hong Kong. The garrison was under-strength and poorly equipped; only a few Royal Navy ships and a small Royal Air Force contingent remained at the colony.

Among the British garrison forces were two Canadian infantry battalions, the Royal Rifles of Canada and the Winnipeg Grenadiers. Less than three weeks after landing at Hong Kong, they became the first Canadian troops to be engaged in battle. Both battalions had lately served as garrison troops in Newfoundland and Jamaica, respectively, and were supposed to receive the infantry training required for service in the front lines after their arrival in the colony. When the Winnipeg Grenadiers were brought up to war establishment in Canada, prior to leaving for Hong Kong, they were augmented by officers and men from the South Saskatchewan Regiment. They were also joined by a YMCA officer, George Porteous, who would become lieutenant governor of Saskatchewan in 1976.

After the initial clash with the Japanese, British forces were withdrawn from the mainland to the island of Hong Kong. During the desperate fighting, a farmer from Wapella, Sergeant Major John Osborn of the Grenadiers, was killed by throwing himself on an enemy grenade, thus saving the lives of the men around him. For this act of courage and self-sacrifice he was awarded the Victoria Cross.

After a spirited defence, the outnumbered garrison was forced to surrender on Christmas Day, 1941. Many of the Saskatchewan men, who had joined the Winnipeg Grenadiers, were killed. Those who survived the ensuing massacre after the surrender endured five long years of horrendous treatment, including starvation and torture in Japanese prison camps, before they were liberated in September 1945. Others had been sent to Japan to become slave labourers in mines. In all, of the nineteen hundred and seventy-five Canadians who left for Hong Kong, more than five hundred and fifty died in captivity.

JAPANESE CONQUEST OF SOUTH EAST ASIA

The Japanese juggernaut continued to roll over the rest of southeast Asia and the islands of the Pacific, but the Japanese advance was finally halted short of Australia in May 1942 with the battle of the Coral Sea, where American naval forces fought the Japanese navy to a standstill.

BURMA AND INDIA

After its conquest of Southeast Asia, the Japanese army turned westward, towards Burma, and by March had captured Rangoon. They then pushed northward to take the southern terminus of the Burma Road at Mandalay. India itself was now under threat.

In March of 1942, RCAF squadrons were moved to Ceylon to become air observers in the region. Canadian pilots in air transport squadrons supplied British and American forces in Burma, as well as flying over "the Hump," the Himalayan Mountains, along with American air forces, to re-supply the Chinese army.

The Japanese launched an attack against India in January 1944, but were repulsed and driven back into Burma. With the British attaining air superiority in the region and with the crippling reversals being suffered by Japan in the Pacific, there was no means of sustaining Japanese garrisons in Burma. By March 1944, British and Indian troops had recaptured Mandalay and by May 1945, Rangoon fell to the British. Japanese forces in Burma finally capitulated in August of 1945 as atomic bombs lay waste to their homeland.

SASKATCHEWAN AT WAR

THE RESERVE ARMY

After Canada went to war, plans for home defence were developed. Because a large percentage of reserve personnel had already enlisted for active service and recruiting had been slow, many reserve units had shrunk to little more than half their original strength. Recruiting for the Reserve Army, as the militia was now called, was stepped up. However, only those under twenty-one years of age or over the age limit or those unfit for active service could be recruited. In 1941 the Canadian government reduced the annual budget for the reserves to allocate resources to other areas of the war effort. Units were reduced in strength, and pay was drastically cut. Officers and men pooled their pay to provide extra funds so they could carry on training.

By 1941, the role of the reserve army had changed to home defence. It became responsible for the guarding of vital points and aid to the civil power. It also had to act as a recruiting ground for the active service forces of the army, navy, and air force.

TRAINING IN SASKATCHEWAN

A number of training centres were set up in Saskatchewan. No.120, Canadian Army Basic Training Centre was set up in Regina, No.121, C.A.B.T.C. in Maple Creek, and No.122, C.A.B.T.C. in Prince Albert. These units provided basic infantry training. Other training units were also formed in Saskatchewan by the army and air force. Among them were No.12, Vocational Training School in Saskatoon, No. 20, Pre-Aircrew Education Detachment of the RCAF, and training units at the University of Saskatchewan and Regina College. The cadet corps of the three services located in communities throughout Saskatchewan and units of the Veterans' Guard also contributed to the war effort.

CAMP DUNDURN

By far the largest military establishment in Saskatchewan was Camp Dundurn. After being turned back to the Department of National Defence as a military establishment from its previous role of housing homeless men in the Depression, Camp Dundurn was designated in 1940 as a basic training centre for overseas units. During the war years camp facilities were expanded to include a large hospital with nurses' residence, a Canadian Women's Army Corps barracks, and an extended training area.

Because of its largely sandy terrain, Dundurn became a major armoured corps training centre, and the camp later expanded to include an engineer training establishment. Some fifty thousand soldiers from across Saskatchewan and Canada were trained at Dundurn before deployment to permanent force units overseas.

Throughout the war, men of the reserve army in Saskatchewan took their compulsory training at Camp Dundurn. Most of the units were comprised of men who held essential service positions within the community but who were of a medical category that did not allow them to be employed overseas or were not old enough. Their officers and non-commissioned officers came from the local communities and were often veterans of World War I.

One such officer was the premier of Saskatchewan, T.C. Douglas. When war was declared, Tommy Douglas, then a member of the Federal Parliament, enlisted in the Second Battalion of the South Saskatchewan Regiment. When the Winnipeg Grenadiers were designated for duty in Hong Kong,

one hundred officers and men from Saskatchewan units were transferred to that regiment. Douglas was one of six officers of that group. After several weeks with the Grenadiers, he was returned to his own unit because of a medical condition. From then on, his military duties consisted of training reserve officers.

THE CIVILIAN WAR EFFORT—SASKATCHEWAN WAR INDUSTRY

After the Depression, war brought relative prosperity to Saskatchewan. The drought ended, bumper crops produced record yields, and Saskatchewan once again became the "bread basket" of the world. Along with agriculture came war industry. In Regina, the General Motors plant had been taken over by the government of

Interior of the largest munitions plant in Saskatchewan, Regina Industries Limited, taken over from Regina General Motors factory. Men and women working on the assembly line.

Canada. Instead of producing automobiles, the plant turned out anti-tank guns. The work force, which had been trained through a war emergency training program, included veterans, young tradesmen, and women. War related industries sprang up in other areas of the province, contributing to the overall rise in prosperity.

Women played their part in the war also. They worked in industry and on the farms and many joined the Women's Royal Canadian Naval Service, or the "Wrens," when they were formed in 1942. The army recruited women into the Canadian Women's Army Corps and the air force had its Women's Division.

CONSCRIPTION

Canada had two armies, the Canadian Active Service Force in which men voluntarily enlisted to serve overseas, and a home defence force created by the National Resources Mobilisation Act of June 1940, in which it was compulsory to serve. Although well-trained, the conscripts, known disparagingly as "Zombies," could not be used outside the continent of North America. Conscientious objectors were excused from service.

Pressure to require conscripts to go overseas began to mount as battle casualties increased. The turnover rate for front line units was so great that replacements were often poorly trained. At times, it was necessary for the wounded to return to service after treatment. Of the sixteen thousand conscripts who were eligible to be sent overseas, only thirteen thousand went and, of these, only twenty-five hundred served in field units on the Continent.

GUARDING THE WEST COAST

With the bombing of Pearl Harbor, the defence of Canada's West Coast became of vital concern. Japanese submarines ventured up and down the Pacific Coast of North America, surfacing to shell targets in California in February of 1942 and later to fire on a remote community on Vancouver Island.

Fear of a Japanese invasion of North America prompted two major responses—the building of the Alaska Highway, and the relocating of Japanese Canadians living on the West Coast to camps further inland. The RCAF patrolled, and the navy carried out coastal escort duties along the isolated and rugged coastline of Canada's Pacific Northwest.

Saskatchewan army units were sent to British Columbia to guard the Pacific coast as part of the home defence force. Regiments such as the King's Own Rifles of Moose Jaw and the Prince Albert Volunteers served on the west coast of Canada in the Sixth and Eighth Canadian Divisions respectively. A third battalion of the Regina Rifles also served on the West Coast, first as a coastal battery protection unit and then as an airfield defence unit. Armoured units such as the 14th Canadian Hussars (8th Reconnaissance) and artillery units from all over Saskatchewan played important roles as home defence forces.

THE ALASKA CAMPAIGN

In June 1942, Japanese forces occupied Attu and Kiska, two of the Aleutian islands off the coast of Alaska. In Alaska, a campaign to drive the Japanese from the Aleutian Islands was mounted. The RCAF had been flying reconnaissance missions through the latter part of 1942 as part of the United States air campaign against the Japanese, and by January of 1943 the American army had begun to build up its forces for an assault on Kiska and Attu for May 1943.

Canadians had been invited to be part of the assault force and it was decided to use the units from the Thirteenth Infantry Brigade of Pacific Command. The units of that brigade were conscripts who were only obligated to serve in the defence of North America. The Alaska Campaign fell within these parameters, but the men of Thirteenth Brigade did not agree, and many were reported "absent without leave" when it came time to embark.

Although American forces had been committed to battle earlier and had suffered heavy casualties, it was not until July that the combined Canadian and American forces gathered. With Thirteenth Brigade Group was the First Special Service Force, a combined Canadian and American unit. When the invasion force landed on August 15, 1943, the enemy had fled.

The Far East—The Tide Turns

The Pacific Theatre

In April 1942, aircraft flying from American aircraft carriers had bombed the home islands of Japan, forcing the Japanese to extend their defensive perimeter. The battle of the Coral Sea in May had stopped the Japanese advance to Australia.

In June of 1942, Japanese aircraft attacked the island of Midway. American aircraft, acting on intercepted intelligence, found the Japanese fleet and attacked, ultimately sinking four carriers. The loss of these carriers and their accompanying escorts effectively destroyed the Japanese navy and from then on, the Americans controlled the Pacific Ocean. This was to be the turning point for the war in the Pacific.

The spectacular success of Midway caught the American forces in the Pacific by surprise, and a major effort had to be undertaken to build up supplies and manpower to take advantage of the win and to pursue a series of counterattacks against the Japanese. What followed was a series of bloody campaigns in the Pacific as marine and army forces of the United States moved from island to island, dislodging their Japanese defenders.

The Mediterranean and North Africa, 1940–1943

The Balkans

In June of 1940 when the British army had evacuated France, Italy, which had formed an alliance with Germany, declared war on Britain. Italy's entrance into the war posed a serious threat for Britain since the Italian fleet could attack British shipping to the Middle East and threaten the Suez Canal. Various naval actions in the Mediterranean throughout 1940 and into the spring of 1941 eventually forced the Italian fleet into its main harbour at Taranto. The British sea-lanes to Egypt in the Mediterranean remained open.

With the invasion of Greece in October 1940 by the Italians, later strengthened by a German army in April 1941, the collapse of the country was inevitable. After a series of defeats, the British forces which had been sent to help the Greeks withdrew to the island of Crete. When the Germans invaded the island in June 1941, the British pulled back to North Africa. The whole of the Aegean area now lay under Axis domination.

Malta

The most critical point in the Mediterranean was the stretch of ocean between Tunisia and Sicily. The lynch pin was the island of Malta, held by the British. From Malta, British aircraft could disrupt Axis shipping. In March of 1942, a German air offensive was launched against the island in conjunction with an attack by the Italian fleet. In the ensuing battles, both sides lost many of their warships. The island, defended by the RAF, including Canadian pilots, held. The courage of the Maltese people was recognised when, on April 16, 1942, King George VI awarded the island of Malta the George Cross. The Cross appears on the flag of Malta to this day.

Germans in Africa

In North Africa, Italian troops invaded Egypt in September 1940. The British then counterattacked and drove the Italians out of Egypt and back through Libya, taking the port fortress of Tobruk along the way. Things changed with the arrival of the German general, Erwin Rommel. Armoured columns of the Afrika Korps pushed British forces out of Libya back toward Egypt in April 1941, but the fortress of Tobruk held. The Eighth Army counterattacked, forcing the Germans to retreat once again to Libya.

Rommel again went on the offensive in early 1942, pushing the British back from Libya to Egypt along the way capturing the fortress of Tobruk in June. Rommel's offensive had pushed the British back to a defensive position near El Alamein, threatening the Suez Canal. The tank battle of July and August by the Afrika

Korps failed to dislodge the British, and Egypt was saved.

In August a new commander took over the British forces in North Africa. General Bernard Montgomery, known as "Monty" to his troops, held off attacking Rommel until he had built up his recently formed Eighth Army—the "Desert Rats" as they called themselves—and thoroughly trained it. On October 23 he launched an overwhelming counterattack against Rommel and the Afrika Korps. Rommel, his supply lines stretched to the limit, could only withdraw. Meanwhile, the American army under General Dwight D. Eisenhower successfully landed in Morocco on November 8, 1942.

Rommel now faced the combined might of British and American forces, and in March of 1943, he left North Africa and abandoned the Afrika Korps in Tunisia to its fate. The next month British and American forces attacked, and by May all German resistance in Africa had ceased.

THE ITALIAN CAMPAIGN, 1943–1945

INVASION OF SICILY

To capitalise on the victory in North Africa, the Allies decided to continue their advance by crossing the Mediterranean to invade Italy. Sicily was chosen as the point of invasion. Canada was asked to contribute troops for the landings and the First Canadian Division, which included the Saskatoon Light Infantry, was selected to join the Eighth British Army. Eighth Army under General Montgomery and Americans under Lieutenant General George Patton were to become the invasion force.

When all was ready, Allied troops, preceded by airborne landings, waded ashore on Sicily on July 10, 1943. The First Canadian Division landed on the southern tip of the island at Pachino and moved inland, facing little resistance and sustaining few casualties. The American and British units were equally successful as they moved northward along the East Coast of the island.

As British and Canadian forces moved forward, the enemy continued to withdraw northward. The Canadians followed, capturing Piazza, Armerina, and Valgurnera until they were stopped at the town of Agira which they took after five days of fighting.

While the fighting was going on, a dramatic turn of events occurred in Italy. Rome had been bombed, Mussolini was overthrown and a new Italian government was formed by Marshal Pietro Badoglio. Germany, worried that a separate peace would be made with the Allies, sent troops into Italy and Sicily.

The Canadians came into contact with troops of the Hermann Goering division who were protecting the withdrawal of German forces from the island through the port of Messina. Although the Canadians had been tasked to prepare for the capture of the German stronghold of Adrano, they were withdrawn into reserve on August 7. By August 17 the Germans had been evacuated to the Italian mainland.

SOUTHERN ITALY

Beginning September 3, 1943, the Allies launched a two-pronged invasion of Italy. The landings were successful and by the end of September, they had occupied all of southern Italy. As the Allies moved forward from Naples and Foggia, they ran into the first serious resistance from the German army, and it was on October 1 that Canadians fought their first battle against elements of the German First Parachute Division. The Germans were making a tactical withdrawal to positions south of Rome; their line of defense ran from Cassino, on the Naples to Rome highway, across to Ortona on the Adriatic shore. It was here in the mountainous region at the narrowest part of Italy at what was called the "Gustav Line," that the Germans were determined to make their stand in the winter campaign of 1943.

Because a decision had been taken to strengthen the Canadian forces in the Mediterranean, the headquarters of First Canadian Corps, under Lieutenant General H.D.G. Crerar and the Fifth Canadian Armoured Division moved to Italy on November 5, 1943.

Canadians now had a full corps operating in Italy.

ORTONA

The First Canadian Division was selected to take the town of Ortona, which fell in the last action of Montgomery's assault on the Gustav Line. It was here that the Eighth Army stopped its advance in January 1944. Montgomery returned to Britain to prepare for the Normandy invasion.

There were now nearly seventy six thousand Canadians in Italy and the Corps had suffered almost ten thousand casualties of which two thousand one hundred and nineteen were fatalities. Through the winter of 1943-44, after Ortona, the Adriatic front saw little action and the area was reduced to the static warfare of patrolling. By May 1944, the Canadians had been taken out of the line.

MONTE CASSINO AND THE LIRI VALLEY

British and American forces had advanced to the German defences at Monte Cassino where they were stopped. Attack after attack by Allied forces could not dislodge the Germans from their mountain fortress stronghold. The Allies, hoping to force the German

These three photos of the war in Italy were taken by Terry Rowe, whose story begins on page 186.

Above left: Stretcher-bearers carrying a wounded soldier under enemy fire, Italy, October 1943.

TERRY F. ROWE / NATIONAL ARCHIVES OF CANADA / PA141662

Above: Refugees in a street, Ortona, Italy, December 30, 1943.

TERRY F. ROWE / NATIONAL ARCHIVES OF CANADA / PA163938

Left: An anti-tank gun in action during the battle with German paratroopers for control of Ortona, Italy, December 21, 1943.

TERRY F. ROWE / NATIONAL ARCHIVES OF CANADA / PA141671

army to withdraw from their positions at Monte Cassino and retreat towards Rome, decided to launch an amphibious landing behind the German lines on the coast at Anzio.

On January 22, 1944, British and American forces made an unopposed landing at Anzio, catching the Germans by surprise. However, the Americans did not move inland. Instead, they consolidated their beachhead position. German forces counterattacked but were unable to dislodge the Americans. For the next four months American forces sat immobile, unable to move forward, thereby making it necessary to continue the assault on Monte Cassino.

In April of 1944, the Canadians began their move across Italy from the Adriatic front to join the U.S. Fifth Army at Monte Cassino for the push to Rome. They were now facing a new set of fortifications that would become known as the "Adolf Hitler Line." After a number of assaults on the monastery fortress at Monte Cassino, Polish forces finally captured it.

This action opened the way for the First Canadian Corps to move across to the Liri Valley and break through the German defences at its mouth. On May 16, the First Canadian Corps advanced on the Hitler Line and, after heavy fighting, broke through, crossing the San Martino River on their way to the town of Ceprano. At this point the Canadians were withdrawn. Rome fell on June 4. Two days later allied forces would storm ashore at Normandy and open the second front.

THE GOTHIC LINE

After a period of time out of the line, the Canadians were sent back in August to the Adriatic Coast to take part in the operations to break through the Gothic Line, the last major German defence in Italy. It ran across Italy from Pisa over the Apennines to Pesaro on the Adriatic Sea.

On August 25, the three corps of British Eighth Army, including the Canadians, had moved to the Fogglia River to begin their assault. On August 30, they crossed the Foglia and by September 2, had broken though. It took three more weeks of heavy fighting for Canadian forces to reach the defences of the Rimini Line.

The Eighth Army again pushed forward in an attempt to reach the Lombardy Plain. The Canadians went into the line once more, fighting through the Romagna region, but became bogged down at the formidable defences of the Savio River. At this point the First Canadian Corps was withdrawn to Army Reserve. The Canadians returned to battle in December as the Eighth Army made its final attempt to break through to the Lombardy Plain. After capturing Ravenna the advance came to a halt at the end of December.

The First Canadian Corps did not participate in the final campaign in Italy. It was withdrawn to Army reserve in February, and in March, began its move to join First Canadian Army in Germany to take part in the final push into Holland.

EUROPE—THE SECOND FRONT, JUNE 1944–MAY 1945

RUSSIA AND THE EASTERN FRONT—THE TIDE TURNS

The Russian offensive of 1942 had managed to push back the Germans from Moscow, and by January of 1943, the Russians were mounting full-scale counterattacks against the German army on all fronts. The Russian winter offensive of early 1943 saw the entrapment and final surrender of the German army at Stalingrad and the eventual withdrawal of German forces from the Caucuses.

The last attempt by the Germans at an offensive on the eastern front took place at Kursk in July of 1943. "Operation Citadel" as the Germans named this action, was not successful, and with the Allied landings in Sicily, Hitler was now forced to divert some of his forces to meet this new Allied threat. The Germans were now on the defensive as the Russian armies began the advance westward.

In January of 1944, the Russians broke the siege of Leningrad in the north and steadily pushed the Germans on the Ukrainian front in the south. By spring, most of the Ukraine was liberated, and Finland came under attack. In June of 1944, the German eastern

Invasion craft en route to France on D-Day, June 6, 1944.

Canadian troops going ashore on Juno Beach at Bernières-sur-Mer, Normandy, France, June 6, 1944.

front disintegrated rapidly and Finland, Romania, and Bulgaria surrendered. As Allied armies fought through France, the Russians entered Poland and were poised to enter Germany itself.

D-DAY

While the Russian armies were steadily advancing toward Germany, plans were nearing completion for the opening of a second front in German-occupied Europe. Forcing Germany to fight on two fronts would deplete German resources by diverting men and materiel away from the Russians, thereby shortening the war.

The American general Dwight Eisenhower was appointed overall supreme commander of Allied forces in Europe and General Bernard Montgomery became the commander of the Allied invasion forces.

Montgomery planned to land in Normandy between Caen and the Cherbourg Peninsula. "Operation Overlord" as the assault plan was called, was put into effect on June 6, 1944. Throughout the night of June 5, Allied forces bombarded the assault areas around Normandy and in the early hours of the next morning five thousand ships began to move steadily toward the French coast. Among the Allied forces protecting this great armada were six RCAF coastal reconnaissance and strike squadrons as well as nine destroyers, eleven frigates, and nineteen corvettes of the RCN in flank positions. Canadian minesweepers also cleared lanes across the English Channel.

The landing area was divided into sectors and beaches, the flanks of which were secured by airborne units, one being the First Canadian Parachute Battalion. The assault force consisted of five infantry divisions, each assigned to its own shore area. The Third Canadian Division landed in the centre on Juno Beach.

Saskatchewan units of every arm and service made up portions of the Third Canadian Division with the primary infantry unit being the Regina Rifle Regiment. The Reginas stormed ashore near the town of Courseulles, and were the only unit of the invasion force to reach their designated positions on D-Day.

Of the approximately fourteen thousand Canadians who landed on D-Day, one thousand and seventy-four became casualties, three hundred and fifty-nine of them fatal.

GERMAN COUNTERATTACKS

Although in the Canadian sector there was light resistance to the initial landing, the next day, tanks of the Twelfth S.S. Panzer Division of the Hitler Jugend (Hitler Youth) attacked Third Canadian Division's positions, over-running the forward companies of the Regina Rifles. After a fierce battle, the Germans were beaten off and the Canadians continued to hold their positions astride the Caen–Bayeux road.

British and American units also faced fierce opposition to their landings, but after heavy fighting the Allies had firmly established their presence in France and the second front was a reality.

CAEN

Caen, the "hinge" on which the British and American forces were to swing through France, had to be taken. RAF Bomber Command and three divisions of First British Corps mounted a tremendous attack, and although Twelfth S.S. Panzer Division put up a fierce defence, Caen was taken on July 9 after a month of fighting. However, the troops still had to cross the Orne River and fight their way through the southern suburbs of the city.

With RAF Bomber Command delivering the heaviest attack of the campaign, British and Canadian forces crossed the Orne, capturing the suburbs of Faubourg de Vaucelles. It was the battle for the dominating high ground south of Caen, the Verrieres Ridge, that allowed the breakout to occur, but at great cost. Here, Canadians were to suffer the greatest number of casualties since Dieppe.

FALAISE

On August 4, 1944, the Canadian Army was ordered to move to the small town of Falaise to cut off the line of withdrawal of the German divisions in Normandy. The tanks of the Fourth Canadian Armoured Division and the Polish army division were mistakenly subjected to a tragic bombing by the United States Eighth Air Force that destroyed their advance. The second advance on Falaise saw the Canadians take the town on August 16.

The German army attempted to withdraw through the gap between the Canadian army at Falaise and the American army halted at Argentan. As the Canadians, Poles, and Americans moved to close the "Falaise Gap," the withdrawal of the Germans became a rout and a slaughter.

Major David Currie from Moose Jaw, an officer in the South Alberta Regiment, leading a small force of tanks, self-propelled guns and infantry, captured the village of Lambert-sur-Dives where he organised a defensive position that cut off one of the main German escape routes. Currie's force held the village for three days, destroying seven enemy tanks, killing three hundred and capturing twenty-one hundred enemy soldiers. For his actions Major Currie

A convoy moves along road through wrecked buildings, Falaise, France, August 17, 1944.

was awarded the Victoria Cross. On August 21, the Falaise Gap was finally closed.

ANTWERP AND THE SCHELDT

Through the months of August and September, the Canadian army moved along the coast through Dieppe, Boulogne, and Calais. While the Canadian army was engaged in liberating the channel ports, the Second British Army was moving swiftly northward into Belgium and Holland towards the port of Antwerp. On September 4, 1944, Antwerp fell.

Although Antwerp could handle many thousands of tons of cargo per day, it was useless to the Allies since it was located some fifty miles from the sea, and the Germans still occupied the estuary blocking its approaches. Capturing the Scheldt estuary was the next major Canadian operation.

At the beginning of October 1944, the Second Canadian Infantry Division began its advance north of Antwerp to close the eastern end of the south Beveland isthmus. Casualties were heavy as Canadian troops struggled over the open flooded ground. Meanwhile the British Second Army was attacking westward to clear the Germans out of the Netherlands and seal off the Scheldt region.

The Third Canadian Infantry Division then engaged in a bitter three-day battle to cross the Leopold canal and clear the Breskens pocket. By November 3, the south shore of the Scheldt had been taken. The way to Antwerp was now open, and after a mine-sweeping operation to clear the channel, the first Allied ships entered the port on November 28, 1944.

Canadian troops were now withdrawn to regroup in the Nijmegen area in Belgium to rest and take on reinforcements. For the next three months the Canadian army held this static centre and planned for its final major battle, the strike at Germany itself.

By January of 1945, the first of the Canadian conscripts had left Halifax for northwest Europe to bring Canadian units up to strength. The First Canadian Army was now at its greatest strength, having close to a half-million men.

AIR OPERATIONS

Through September of 1944, while the ground war continued, the RAF and the American Army Air Force kept up their bombing campaigns against European targets, concentrating on the coastal ports of France and the launching sites for V1 and V2 rockets. They also conducted a number of raids during the end of 1944 and the early months of 1945 in support of the Russian advances on Berlin and the final British and American crossing of the Rhine into Germany.

THE FINAL RUSSIAN ADVANCE

By 1945 the Russian forces were poised to strike at the heart of Germany. On January 17, 1945, Warsaw was captured and Russian troops poured across the Vistula Rive, moving deep into Germany. By the end of the month the Russians had reached the Oder River and were ready for their final assault on Berlin.

THE RHINELAND, THE FINAL PUSH INTO GERMANY

In February the Allies launched Operation Veritable, the final great offensive that would drive the German army back over the Rhine and bring about its defeat. The First Canadian Army advanced from the Nijmegan salient to clear a corridor on the West Bank of the Rhine between the Rhine and the Maas Rivers. As the Canadian troops moved forward, a strange new weapon attacked them. German jet planes had appeared for the first time in battle.

HOLLAND

The Canadian army then turned toward Holland, first to open the supply route to the north through Arnheim, and then to clear German forces from northeastern and western Holland. It was soon joined by the First Canadian Corps from Italy and, for the final campaign in Holland, First Canadian Army was now an all-Canadian force.

In the large cities of Amsterdam, Rotterdam, and the Hague, people were on the verge of starvation, and on April 28, 1945, fighting ceased while a truce was arranged with the German army so that food supplies could move through their lines to the civilians. On May 5, 1945, Lieutenant General Foulkes, commander of First Canadian Corps, accepted the surrender of all German troops in Holland. The war for the First Canadian Army was over.

VE Day, Germany Surrenders

By early April, American and British forces reached the Elbe and stopped. General Eisenhower had agreed that Allied forces would go no farther. The Russian armies reached the Elbe in April and the first contact between the Americans and Russians took place on April 25, 1945.

On April 21, the Russians had entered the outskirts of Berlin. Hitler committed suicide on April 30 and Berlin surrendered on May 2. Two days later, Montgomery accepted the surrender of all the German forces in northwest Germany, Holland, and Denmark. On May 7, at Reims, the Germans signed an unconditional total surrender to the Allies.

The next day was officially declared as Victory in Europe (VE) Day, and on that day the surrender ceremony was repeated in Berlin, this time including Russian representatives. Scattered resistance continued in Norway, Czechoslovakia, Austria, and Yugoslavia, but by May 23, all resistance had ceased. The war in Europe was now over.

Occupation, 1945–1946

At the end of hostilities, the Canadian government earmarked twenty-five thousand troops and eleven RCAF squadrons for the occupation of Germany. The troops remaining in Germany would

A Dutch girl places flowers on grave during the burial service for fifty-five members of "A" Company, the Black Watch (Royal Highland Regiment) of Canada, Ossendrecht, Netherlands, October 1944.

KEN BELL / NATIONAL ARCHIVES OF CANADA / PA176844

be those who volunteered to stay or were in the lower categories of an elaborate "point" system developed by the Canadian government to bring some order to repatriation to Canada.

The Canadian Army Occupation Force was established in June 1945, to garrison the British occupation zone in Germany and to enforce the rulings of Field Marshal Montgomery who had been appointed the British military governor. By March 1946, Canadian occupation duties in the British zone had ceased and the troops were returned to the repatriation depots in Britain. By June of that year the Canadians headed home and the occupation force ceased to exist.

The End in the Pacific

In the Pacific theatre, hostilities continued but were abruptly brought to an end with the dropping of atomic bombs on the cities of Hiroshima and Nagasaki in Japan. On August 15, 1945, Japan surrendered, and World War II was finally over.

New Beginnings—Saskatchewan Enters the Post-War World

Those who came Home

The servicemen who returned to Saskatchewan after the war came home to a province much different than the one they had left five years earlier. Some adjusted well to the transformation; others did not. In the post-war years, land was set aside for returned veterans under the Veterans' Land Act. Servicemen, taking advantage of educational and retraining schemes, filled the classes in the University of Saskatchewan and other provincial post-secondary institutions. In 1946, the former residence of the lieutenant governor of Saskatchewan, which was located in Regina, was leased to the Department of Veterans' Affairs to become a convalescent home for the province's veterans.

In Memorandum – Remembering the Sacrifice

After World War I, a number of monuments had been erected across the province and the country to commemorate the sacrifice of Canadians in that war. After World War II, those monuments were added to and others were built.

The Royal Canadian Legion played an important part in the life of each and every community across the province. With other veterans' organisations, it continued the annual Remembrance Day Ceremony, on November 11, to commemorate those who had laid down their lives for their country. Now, as the years go by, fewer and fewer Saskatchewan veterans remain to parade annually in November, and the memory of their deeds fades from the minds of the public, many of whom are too young to remember the Second World War as anything but a chapter in a history book.

The Saskatchewan government, realising that some permanent tribute must be made to honour those servicemen from the province who gave their lives in the war, named lakes, islands, and other geographic features after them. The names of those who fell in battle still live on… Lest We Forget!

Veterans Memorial Cemetery at Regina's Riverside Cemetery: Entrance (above) and monument (right).

DAVID MCLENNAN

Their Names Live On

Seventy-eight Stories, Eighty-nine Men

Anaka

Anaka Lake (55°49' N, 104°55' W), viewed here from the south, is located fifty air miles north of La Ronge. Just east of beautiful McIntosh Lake in the Boreal Shield ecozone, Anaka Lake is about one and a half miles in length.

Around the small town of Stenen, Saskatchewan, north of Yorkton, there are still a few friends and neighbours of Harry Anaka. "A darn nice fellow," one of them says. "The greatest—easygoing, soft-spoken. All the girls loved him," says another. Reg Stead and Murray Straker, in researching an RCAF book on Harry's brother Peter, report that "Harry's name came up often. He's remembered as a good lad, and smart." "Yes, all the Anakas were nice boys," remembers Elsie Anaka, Peter's widow. They all drove the family car, an Essex, Elsie adds. Every weekend, winter or summer, there was a dance in one of the district halls. Someone would play a violin, someone else a guitar or an accordion.

Three miles north and a mile east of Stenen, the farm of John and Zowie Anaka, immigrants from the Ukraine, is still operated by the Anaka family. John and Zowie raised six children there, Harry being the second youngest of their four boys. George Albert Public School, built right next to the Anaka farm on land donated by the Anakas, was where Harry began his education, finishing high school in Stenen. John and Zowie were as serious about religion as they were about education, for they also donated land on which the Assumption of the Holy Virgin Mary Orthodox Church was built.

After completing high school, Harry attended Saskatoon Technical College, graduating as a motor mechanic in 1938. He began work at a garage before following an older brother to work for a winter as a diamond driller with the Claw Bay Mining Company at Elbow Lake, Manitoba. Not long after the war started, Harry enlisted with the Edmonton Fusiliers, an infantry regiment, as a private. Basic training took him to Prince Rupert, B.C., and other training stops included Nanaimo and Vernon. Proving himself to be an excellent marksman, he earned his First Class Rifleman's Badge, and then, as the regiment became mechanized, he qualified as a driver, a section leader, and a weapons instructor. Before a personnel selection board in February 1943, he was judged to be "good officer material," and a promotion to the rank of first lieutenant soon followed.

Harry's life took another turn during his stint in Nanaimo. Dances were held on the base, and a group of girls would arrive by bus from downtown Nanaimo to share the fun. Viola Matson was only seventeen when she met Harry Anaka, who himself was a boyish, youthful-looking fellow, at one of the dances. They were married in August 1943, and enjoyed a brief honeymoon in Vancouver on one of Harry's leaves.

Harry Anaka never saw his son, Harry Jr., who was born the next year. By that time Harry had left for an officer training course in Sussex, New Brunswick. Lieutenant Anaka had volunteered for service in the British Army as part of the CanLoan program whereby Canadian officers would replace British officers lost in action. On April 26, 1944, Harry embarked for Britain,

posted to the Seventh Battalion of the Royal Hampshire Regiment, and was able to enjoy a reunion with his brother at Trafalgar Square. Just two weeks after D-Day, Harry—called Hank by his new British mates—was shipped with his regiment to Normandy.

Lieutenant Anaka's service was distinguished. Leading the Twelfth Platoon, he took two strategically vital objectives during the breakout from the Normandy beachhead. Later, during the battle to close the Falaise Gap, he commandeered a German amphibious Volkswagen. In this vehicle he led his men across France, across the Seine River, and on to the liberation of Belgium. On June 11, 1944, he was promoted to Captain.

The Hampshires reached the banks of the Neder Rijn near Arnhem in early October. On the fourth of October, Harry's platoon came under heavy fire in a brickwork. Cornered there with his sergeant, Captain Harry Anaka was killed. One of his men, Charles Reeves, would later write: "Captain Anaka was a brave and caring man and always looked after his men both in and out of battle. To me and all the others in the company he was a gentleman and a hero."

The brickwork in which Harry Anaka was killed was never repaired. It stands as a memorial to him and the other Hampshires. Buried in the Mook War Cemetery eleven kilometres south of Nijmegen, Captain Harry Anaka is memorialized in Saskatchewan by Anaka Lake. ✤

Below: The badge of the Royal Hampshire Regiment.

JAMES ROBINSON

Armstrong

SERGEANT MAJOR **WALTER DOUGLAS ARMSTRONG** • L27753 • 1919–1945

Armstrong Lake (56°27' N, 103°50' W), viewed here from the south, is located

120 miles northeast of La Ronge. Located in the Churchill River Upland ecoregion

of the Boreal Shield, Armstrong Lake is a body of clear water several miles long,

supporting an abundance of fish and wildlife. A trip by canoe from Brabant

Lake to Macoun Lake will pass through Armstong Lake.

In 1934 the Armstrong family packed up their possessions, gathered their livestock, and left the town of Elbow, Saskatchewan, on a horse-drawn wagon bound for Davidson. "I'm sure it made quite a hole in Elbow's population," Jack Armstrong remembers. "There were eight girls and three boys in the family." Walter Armstrong, the third oldest, impressed Jack by showing no fear of the coyotes the two of them could hear as they brought in the cows for milking. Walter, Jack, and the third brother, Bob, would all join the armed forces. In Walter's case, it was the Regina Rifles, which he joined after finishing high school and a stint in the Co-op butcher shop.

Walter Armstrong performed heroically on the Normandy beaches during the D-Day invasion. As the *Ottawa Citizen* reported in a 1994 retrospective on the fiftieth anniversary of D-Day, Sergeant Major Armstrong (then Lance Sergeant) while under heavy machine-gun fire crawled forward on the beach of Normandy. Assisted by two other infantrymen, he located and cleaned out an enemy machine gun position with his own light machine gun. This action enabled the rest of his company to take the buildings on the regiment's right flank.

It was afterwards discovered that Armstrong had been wounded, a bullet having passed right through one leg, grazing the other. Walter downplayed the wound by showing the leg that was not severely bleeding. He returned to the beach dressing station only when ordered to do so by his Company commander several hours later. Lance Sergeant Armstrong earned the Military Medal for his actions.

Throughout the war, Walter Armstrong exchanged letters with Jack, an air gunner with Bomber Command. In a letter dated October 1, 1944, Walter informs Jack about the situation in Calais, northern France. After seeing four years of cross-channel shelling, the town had at last been reclaimed by the French. According to the letter, Walter and his unit pushed into Calais—or at least "what was left of it"— with little opposition. In so doing, Sergeant Major Armstrong and his company had to be wary of booby traps and mines. As they infiltrated the southwest section of the village, they also had to wade through a mile of ice-cold water that reached to their armpits, while lugging seventy pounds of mortar bombs. The enemy had flooded the surrounding area in order to inhibit Allied troop movement.

In his letter, Walter attributes the success of the Calais campaign to the aid of bombers—the "Lancs" and "Hallies"—and heavy artillery that prepared the ground for the Allies and "softened things up." He tips his hat especially to those like his brother in the Air Force: "Believe me, we really appreciate the work you fellows [are doing] as it would be suicide to try and walk into some of these places without you fellows shaking them up so badly first."

The letter continues, giving an account of an amusing adventure in Calais. Lance Corporal Burton, Platoon Commander Pelletier and Sergeant Major Armstrong decided they would venture into the German-occupied section of town and try to seize a few prisoners. After coming across a truck with its motor still running, the three-man detachment checked the adjacent building, where they found an unlocked back door and heard muffled German voices on the other side. Figuring that they had a "good bag," Burton and Armstrong made their entry, grenades primed and automatics ready, as Pelletier covered them from behind.

To their disappointment, the only personnel behind the door were five Medical Corps officers attending to some forty wounded and sick Germans. Between speaking English and French, the two parties could communicate with each other. Before long, the German officers pulled out a few bottles of liquor to share with the Allied soldiers. Walter's letter continues:

So we sat around and had a very interesting time persuading them that the Allies weren't going to lose the war, that we wouldn't have to fight the Russians after we have finished with Germany and that we had several very good reasons for fighting with Britain and the Allies in this war. It was really funny and before we left we were even showing each other snapshots etc. After a two hour session…we shook hands all around [and] started back to our half of the city, feeling quite high.

Walter Armstrong's Silver Cross. The Silver Cross was awarded to mothers who lost their sons.

Above: Regina Rifle Regiment Badge.

COURTESY OF THE CANADIAN FORCES

Right: Members of the Regina Rifles waiting for the attack on Moyland Wood, February 16, 1945.

COLIN MCDOUGALL / NATIONAL ARCHIVES OF CANADA / PA177577

As it happened, Sergeant Major Armstrong and his comrades, not wanting to show up empty-handed, "pinched a Jerry car" on their way back. Since there was no key to be found, they resolved to push it all the way down the street and over the bridge to their

platoon's resting quarters. They awoke to find it stolen back by the Germans.

In February of 1945, the Allies launched their Rhineland offensive, Operation Veritable, the final push from the flooded lands of northern Holland into Germany. On February 16, the Regina Rifles, part of the Third Canadian Infantry Division, had the task of clearing the woods close to Moyland. The Reginas encountered heavy fire, and one of those killed that day was Sergeant Major Walter Armstrong.

Walter Armstrong is buried at the Groesbeek Canadian War Cemetery, ten kilometres southeast of Nijmegen. In Saskatchewan, Armstrong Lake is named in his memory. 🏵

Bartlett

There was plenty of Old England in the Bartlett family of Fort Qu'Appelle, Saskatchewan. Christopher Pennycuik Bartlett came to Canada from Kent, England, in 1910, heading to Calgary on the CPR but getting off the train at Fort Qu'Appelle to take a job as a cook. Soon he'd taken over a dairy farm at B-Say-Tah Point, met and married a local girl, Dolly Smales, and had begun to raise a family. He stayed close to the news in England by receiving the London *Times*, which, as the Second World War drew near, ran many Royal Air Force ads appealing for pilots. Mr. Bartlett, who encouraged several of his six children to join the armed services, may very well have brought such an ad to the attention of his eldest son, also named Christopher.

The younger Christopher Bartlett grew up enjoying all the pleasures of life in the Qu'Appelle valley—fishing and swimming in summer, skiing and tobogganing in winter. By the time he finished grade eleven, he knew what he wanted to do. He had prepared himself by acquiring a private pilot's license at the Regina Flying Club, boarding in the city while he did so. In July of 1937, just after school was out, he traveled to England and began training for a four-year Short Service Commission as a pilot officer with the RAF.

Early in 1939 Pilot Officer Bartlett was posted to No. 216 Squadron at Heliopolis, Egypt. No. 216 was a transport squadron, and Christopher Bartlett, flying old Vickers Valentias—described by one observer as

Fort Qu'Appelle •

Bartlett Lake (55° 30' N, 104° 59' W), viewed here from the south, is located thirty air miles northeast of La Ronge. A deep clear lake with excellent fishing, Bartlett Lake is accessible by canoe from the McKay Lake campground on Highway 102.

"museum pieces from the first world war"—flew troops and supplies to various trouble spots across North Africa and the Middle East. Soon he had extra duties—becoming the personal pilot for Viscount Wavell, the Commander-in-Chief, Middle East, and engaging in bombing operations on Tobruk, Libya.

On May 24, 1942, Christopher Bartlett, now a flight lieutenant, piloted one of the old Valentias on a special raid to destroy a strategic bridge in Syria. He had to land a demolition team of thirteen sappers in a rough field near the bridge. Les Allison describes the operation in *Canadians in the Royal Air Force*:

> The sappers would get only one chance. They packed enough charges around the bridge to guarantee demolition. Forty-five minutes later, Bartlett opened the throttle and the engines spoke up. As the aircraft rumbled along the ground picking up flying speed, an armoured car arrived and began firing with its machine guns. Too late, the aircraft was gone and so was the bridge.

Flight Lieutenant Bartlett won the Distinguished Flying Cross for that raid. "Much of the success of this daring and difficult operation," the citation said, "is attributed to F/L Bartlett's skill."

And that wasn't all in the career of this remarkable Canadian flyer. In August 1942 he returned to a series of hero's welcomes in Montreal, Regina, and, above all, at the Lion's Hall in Fort Qu'Appelle where he was presented with a gold signet ring. "It was a big affair," his sister Joan remembers, "and Dad was thrilled."

Fort Qu'Appelle flier wins praise of crew

WITH THE R.C.A.F. IN BRITAIN, March 11 (CP).—Sqdn. Ldr. C. S. (Chris) Bartlett, D.F.C., of Fort Qu'Appelle, Sask., has earned the plaudits of his crew for the way he handled his shell-blasted Ghost squadron Halifax after an attack on Berlin.

Most of the pilot's controls and navigator's instruments were shot away during two attacks by a twin-engine night fighter but Bartlett, a Middle East veteran, nursed the aircraft safely home.

The enemy fighter attacked just after the Halifax had unloaded its bombs.

"We saw him the first time," said PO. R. B. (Curly) Learn of New Westminster, B.C., the rear-gunner. "He came in from starboard and I opened fire with a four-second burst, at the same time directing the skipper to take evasive action. The fighter veered off below."

The second attack was launched from the starboard beam and from underneath, and none of the crew saw the fighter. He raked the mid-portion of the bomber with cannon shells and blew holes right through the mid-upper turret.

The second pilot was Sgt. S. Side of Dilke, Sask. Others were Sgt. C. H. Dyle, Moose Jaw, flight engineer, and FO. D. H. Crawford, of Portage la Prairie, Man., wireless operator.

After a few weeks on the farm, Bartlett was posted as chief instructor to No. 1 Bombing and Gunnery School in Jarvis, Ontario. But he was keen to get back into active operations, as many instructors were, and away from the war bonds drives that were part of his duties in Ontario. He flew a B-25 bomber back to England in May 1943, and began training in preparation for joining Bomber Command. His first posting was as squadron leader of RCAF No. 428 "Ghost" Squadron. On February 7, 1944, he was promoted to wing commander of No. 434 "Bluenose" Squadron.

During this time, tributes of various kinds continued to accrue to Christopher Bartlett. First there was the Distinguished Flying Cross (DFC) ceremony at Buckingham Palace, where he was decorated by King George VI. Then came several operations into Germany during the Battle of Berlin. "Fort Qu'Appelle flier wins praise of crew," proclaimed a Regina *Leader-Post* headline of March 11, 1944, over a report of how Squadron Leader Bartlett had nursed his shell-blasted Halifax home after a raid on Berlin. His gallantry in action earned him a Bar to his DFC.

Shortly after D-Day, No. 434 Squadron, flying out of Croft in Yorkshire, was part of a raid on railway yards in France on

June 12-13, 1944, that involved 671 aircraft. Wing Commander Bartlett, nearing the end of his second tour of operations, led the attack on the railway yards at Arras. His plane was one of twenty-three lost that night.

At home he was reported missing, but the elder Christopher Bartlett held out hope that his son had been rescued by the French Resistance and returned to his squadron. Another son, Dick—a prisoner of war in Germany—had to be the one to tell him his hope was in vain. As it happened, the only survivor of Chris's last flight had been taken prisoner and sent to the very camp where Dick had spent some five years as a POW. This chap told Dick that their bomber had collided with a German night fighter. As the crew prepared to bail out, the aircraft exploded in mid-air and crashed. Dick passed the sad news on to his family in Fort Qu'Appelle.

Wing Commander Christopher Bartlett is buried at the Calais Canadian War Cemetery. In Saskatchewan he is honoured by Bartlett Lake. Fifteen members of the Bartlett family visited there in 1999, enjoying some freshly caught pickerel and pike, erecting a plaque, and raising their glasses in a champagne toast to Christopher. ✤

Left: The plaque erected by the Bartlett family at Bartlett Lake.

DOUG CHISHOLM

Below: Dick Bartlett (far left) proposes a toast at Bartlett Lake, together with pilot and aerial photographer Doug Chisholm, two of Christopher's nieces, and other family members not shown in photo.

DOUG CHISHOLM

Bonokoski

PILOT OFFICER **DANIEL BONOKOSKI** • J90943 • 1920–1944

Daniel Bonokoski of Torquay, Saskatchewan, was paid tribute in a 1999 Remembrance Day feature in The Ottawa Sun. *The article, entitled "In memory of the valiant one," was written by Mark Bonokoski, Sun Media's national affairs columnist and relative of the World War II airman. Following is an abridged version of that article:*

Bonokoski Lake (59°44' N, 103°23' W), viewed here from the north, is located fifteen miles south of the Northwest Territories border and 320 air miles northeast of La Ronge, deep in the Taiga Shield ecozone of northern Saskatchewan. Twelve miles long, Bonokoski Lake is deep and clear with an abundance of lake trout, and its shoreline has numerous large sand beaches with glacial boulder deposits.

RCAF Pilot Officer Daniel Bonokoski's war ended in the early hours of January 29, 1944, during the Battle of Berlin when, bombing mission completed, German anti-aircraft fire blew off the tail section of his Halifax Bomber.

He was twenty-three when he died; my father Matt's first cousin. They were born in the same town, helped their fathers pioneer adjacent tracts of land, went to the same one-room school in the same horse-drawn buggy, went to the same tiny Roman Catholic Church, ate the same dust during the Depression years and, when the war cry was heard, they left the wheat fields together to enlist in the Royal Canadian Air Force. One never came back; the other could never talk about that loss without great sadness.

Daniel Bonokoski, coming from simple roots, grew up in a home with no running water and no electricity. His education stopped at grade ten, just after he learned enough reading and writing to manage the business end of farming—how to order seed, how to budget expenses, how to read the manuals.

And then the war came. Daniel was assigned to RCAF No. 431 "Iroquois" Squadron out of the English base at Croft, Yorkshire. He was trained to be a bomb aimer and, although he passed all his training, he was always near the bottom of his class.

One training report out of Halifax, dated February 27, 1943, said he was "quiet, tries hard and improved toward end of his course. Young but steady, good and honest."

Daniel Bonokoski's diary reflects that quiet honesty. It is simple and uncluttered. On New Year's Day 1944, for example, after celebrating the last New Year's Eve he would live to see, he wrote: "Drunk new years eve. Horrible way to start the new year. Went to 11:00 Mass." In another entry, dated January 20, Daniel describes his first bombing run over enemy territory: "Operation Berlin. Thought I'd be scared, funny but I wasn't even slightly scared. Guess we really banged them up." That was the last entry in his diary.

The pilot of the six-man Halifax bomber crew on the night of January 29, 1944, was a Canadian flight sergeant named Jack Maher who, after completing his mission over Berlin, was forced to push his plane to 20,000 feet in hopes of evading the heavy enemy flak they

were encountering. It soon became apparent, however, that the tail gunner, Sergeant J.R. Bothwell, had lost consciousness due to lack of oxygen at that elevation. Daniel Bonokoski left his position at midships, where he was positioned as bomb aimer, slid past gunner Sergeant B.S. Rowe, and was pulling Bothwell out of his turret to apply emergency oxygen when the tail section was taken out, killing all three men instantly. Maher, his engineer and his navigator somehow managed to bail out of the spiralling aircraft and were later taken prisoner-of-war by the Germans.

Today, the remains of Bonokoski, Bothwell, and Rowe share a collective grave in the British Military Cemetery in Berlin because individual identification of the three men was impossible.

After his release as a POW at war's end, Jack Maher wrote to Daniel's parents, Anton and Zita Bonokoski, from his parents' home in Chatsworth,

Below: Groundcrew working on the Merlin engines of a Halifax.

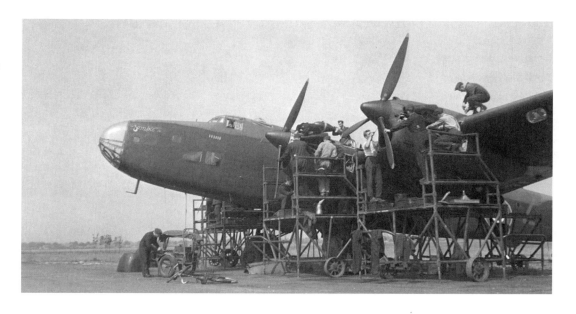

Ontario, to their home in Torquay, Saskatchewan. "This is the hardest letter I have ever written," he began. "Dan and I were great pals and I could not feel worse unless it was my own brother. We had bombed Berlin and were heading home when we had a direct hit from the flak shell. The two gunners and Dan, I think, were instantly killed because, after we were hit, they didn't answer me when I called them on the intercom. The aircraft went straight down in a violent spin, my controls were shot away, and it was only a miracle that the rest of us got out. It is certainly a bitter blow to you, I know," Maher continued, "but it will comfort you to know that Dan died in a state of Grace. He and I had been to Mass and had taken communion earlier that day."

After his death, Flight Sergeant Daniel Bonokoski was commissioned to the rank of Pilot Officer No. J90943, no doubt because his split-second decision to help his unconscious crewmate was not only heroic, but fatal.

****

Bonokoski Lake, Saskatchewan, is named to commemorate this RCAF pilot officer, "the valiant one." The remote location of Bonokoski Lake has not deterred family members from visiting the site; in addition to Mark Bonokoski, whose 1999 visit inspired the above story, Daniel's brother Gordon has made the trip twice, most recently accompanied by Gordon's daughter Anna. ✿

Right: Mark Bonokoski at Bonokoski Lake, August 19, 1999. He mounted the memorial plaque (detail above) for Daniel Bonokoski on a large boulder on the eastern side of the lake.

DOUG CHISHOLM

PILOT OFFICER CAMILLE ROBESPIERRE BONSEIGNEUR
• 42791 • 1918–1940

Bonseigneur

Not only his name but Camille Robespierre Bonseigneur's entire life was relatively exotic by depression-era Saskatchewan standards. The only son of a dentist who had served in the American military in World War I, Camille was born in Gull Lake but lived there only a short while. The family moved to Prince Albert, where Dr. Bonseigneur, originally from Washington State, died during the flu epidemic in 1918. His widow Irene (Laberge) Bonseigneur took their baby with her to Forget, Saskatchewan, then to Regina, where she worked at the Hotel Saskatchewan. Camille went to school at St. Joseph's Academy in Forget, a boarding school, and later finished his high school in Regina. When Irene remarried in Regina, he got a job in his stepfather's Chrysler dealership and was active in the Olympic Boxing and Wrestling Club.

Even before the war Camille was interested in military service. An early step in following that interest was to join the Royal Canadian Corps of Signals in Regina in 1937 and assume a posting in Barriefield, Ontario, near Kingston. During his work as a signalman he got a Meteorological Certificate (Distinguished), took some training as a wireless operator, and stood as part of the Guard of Honour during the Royal Tour to Kingston in 1939. He was described as having shown "very good character during his one year and 261 days service."

In June of 1939 he was discharged from the Signal Corps "by purchase"—he was bought out of his

Bonseigneur Lake (55°19' N, 104°31' W), viewed here from the west, is located thirty-six miles east of La Ronge in the Churchill River Upland ecoregion of the Boreal Shield. About one mile in length, Bonseigneur Lake is near the Rapid River portage to Iskwatikan Lake.

Gull Lake•

13

commitment by his stepfather, in other words—because what Camille really wanted to do was fly. A boarder with the family recalls that Camille "just wanted to go and help out before the Canadians over here were ready to go." In the summer of 1939, even before war was declared, he made his way over to England and joined the Royal Air Force. During training he enjoyed the sights of England, taking many photographs in London especially, and going with an English girl named Gwynneth. Becoming a pilot officer in the RAF in 1940, he joined No. 257 Squadron of Fighter Command.

"Death or Glory" was the motto of No. 257, and there was plenty of both during the Battle of Britain over southern England in 1940. Almost three thousand pilots took to the skies that summer to resist the Luftwaffe attacks that might have defeated Britain—these flyers were the "few" to whom, in Churchill's famous words, "so much [was] owed by so many." More than a sixth of them died. In a letter written in August, Camille described some of the action: "We spent a very hectic week in the big raids. They really kept us on the go. At times the sky was full of Huns, and we had some very exciting moments, but got through them all ok. We all take it as a matter of fact, all in a day's work."

For Camille Bonseigneur, flying a Hurricane Mk1 from No. 257 Squadron based in Martlesham Heath, Suffolk, the end came on September 3, 1940. The Battle of Britain campaign diary for that day shows enemy attacks, involving an estimated six hundred aircraft, on southeast England and the Thames estuary. Several Fighter Command squadrons, including No. 257, engaged them. Pilot Officer Bonseigneur, who had taken off at ten o'clock, was involved in combat with enemy raiders in the Chelmsford area. He was shot down and killed after bailing out at Ingatestone.

Irene Bonseigneur Craigen had now lost a husband and her only son, who was remembered as "a clean, wholesome young Canadian imbued with the highest ideals, who did not flinch at the call to arms." Camille Bonseigneur was buried at Saffron Walden Cemetery, Essex, and commemorated by the naming of Bonseigneur Lake in Lac la Ronge Provincial Park, twelve kilometres southeast of Stanley Mission.

A postscript to this story is provided by an account of an Essex Historical Aircraft Society archaeological dig carried out on August 11, 1974:

Below: Camille's boots, polished and ready for action.

The dig started at about 8:30 am and at a depth of one meter the smashed remains of the Rolls Royce Merlin [engine] came to the light of day for the first time in thirty-four years. Ravaged by corrosion, most of the outer casing had rotted away. Other finds include the gun firing button from the spade grip, engine mounts, Rotol propeller boss and the maker's plate, confirming this as the aircraft flown by Pilot Office Camille Robespierre Bonseigneur.

The site is now right beside the busy A12 Chelmsford by-pass. I very much doubt that people driving past know what history is matter of yards away. ✿

Left and below: Camille Robespierre Bonseigneur.

Below left: This photo (Camille at left) was published in the *Saturday Evening Post*, December 21, 1940. The caption reads, "They duel with death-dealing Nazi fighters one hour—and duel with each other at dominoes, their favorite game, the next."

Sat. Evening Post
Dec 21/40

They duel with death-dealing Nazi fighters one hour—and duel with each other at dominoes, their favorite game, the next.

Brière

Brière Lake (55°35' N, 106°42' W), viewed here from the west, is located sixty air miles west of La Ronge, near the community of Pinehouse. Situated in the Mid-Boreal Upland ecoregion, Brière Lake is about two miles long. Its relatively shallow depth makes it an ideal location for wild rice harvesting.

It was during a trip to Brière Lake in July of 2000 that the life and death of Sinai Thomas Brière, known to family and friends as Tommy, hit home to Marie Campbell, daughter of Tommy's sister Cécile. The trip was a challenging one for Marie and her fellow adventurers. They drove to the northern community of Pinehouse, where Marie's husband Jim had once been a teacher. Guided by a local man who reported that Brière Lake was well known in the area—a destination point for local fishermen and wild rice harvesters—Marie and company portaged to Yost Lake, canoed across it, then hiked to the lake named in honour of Tommy Brière. There they laid a plaque and set a flag and wreath afloat on the lake. "It was so important that we make the trip, especially to Mom and her sister Mary," Marie says.

For Cécile, the oldest of the seven children born to Isaie and Albina Brière, the death of her youngest brother Tommy in 1943 was one of several misfortunes to strike the family. The Brières had come from Québec via Manitoba in about 1912, and homesteaded in the Billimun district of southwest Saskatchewan. Soon after, Isaie and Albina lost a daugher, Antoinette. Albina herself died during the influenza epidemic of 1918, after which the six young Brière kids—including Tommy, age two months—went to live with their maternal grandparents, the Mongeons, while Isaie looked for work.

Tommy Brière grew up, then, in a little pioneer house in which eleven people shared a porch, kitchen, living room, and two bedrooms. Grandpa and Grandma Mongeon were caring but stern, and hard work was expected of all the kids: tending the cattle and the garden, gathering cow chips for fuel, picking rocks. Tommy attended MacDonald Dale school, about three miles from the farm, and got his grade eight there. A bilingual lad, he was well liked by family and friends who enjoyed his guitar playing or endured his playful teasing. He was popular with the girls in the area too.

By 1937, Tommy Brière, now twenty years old, had worked in the Val Marie and Ferland districts as a labourer and mechanic before taking over a butcher shop in Mankota with his brother-in-law and aunt. Tommy might have made a career of butchering. But war broke out, and Tommy became the first Mankota man to voluntarily enlist, travelling to Regina on June 6, 1940, to do so. People in the area thought he was crazy to volunteer for service when he didn't have to, and his family didn't really want him to go, but they must have been proud when he returned to Mankota in his uniform, posing for pictures in front of the town gas pumps. In July, Tommy went to the Engineer Training Centre in Petawawa, Ontario, and six months after that, in February of 1941, the young mechanic and butcher from Mankota was on his way overseas as a Sapper in the Royal Canadian Engineers (RCE).

According to the first letter Tommy sent home the moment he landed in Scotland, the eleven-day crossing of the Atlantic went without a hitch, other than the usual seasickness, and the subsequent train ride to England proved eventful and exciting for this young prairie boy. Tommy marvelled at the English countryside, the determination of the English people to carry on through the bombing, the wonders of London. In the next two years he transferred frequently as the Canadian forces slowly prepared for the inevitable invasion of Nazi-occupied Europe.

Posted with the Seventh Field Company, RCE, Tommy Brière, who reached the rank of Acting Corporal, had to endure periods of hospitalization. He'd had his appendix removed in 1940 while he was stationed in Ontario, and it seems that he was never quite right after that. While on duty June 4, 1943, he reported severe abdominal cramps and nausea and was sent to Canadian General Hospital in Horsham, west Sussex. His condition worsened over the following forty-eight hours, and just after midnight on June 6, exactly one year before D-Day, Tommy Brière died of an acute intestinal obstruction and was buried at Brookwood Military Cemetery near London.

Back home, a requiem high mass was held at St. Martin Roman Catholic Church in Billimun. And nearly fifty years later, on the shores of the lake in north-central Saskatchewan named in honour of Sinai Thomas Brière, Marie and the family said a prayer for him. ❀

Below: Tommy Brière while stationed at Petawawa in late 1940 or early 1941.

Brown

PRIVATE **MAX BRADIE BROWN** • L66655 • 1921–1945

Brown Bay (55°36' N, 102°2' W), viewed here from the south, is located one hundred air miles east of La Ronge at the north end of Wintigo Lake. This area of the Churchill River contains many rapids and some aboriginal pictographs, and it is in close proximity to a fur trading post from the 1800s. After much review, plans to construct a massive hydroelectric dam at Wintigo Lake were scrapped in 1979.

I n the blunt assessment of a fellow soldier who had known him since before the war, Max Brown was a "damn good guy." Born in Griffin, just east of Weyburn, he attended Dunreath School in Innes. His father Randolf had come up from Iowa to farm in the Griffin area, and Max, the youngest of a family of four, helped on the farm. He was known at that time as a friendly, soft-spoken fellow who was good-humoured and kind to children, even when he playfully threatened to kidnap his two-year-old niece in a duffel bag. One of Max's dreams was to go to British Columbia, so his father purchased a ten-acre orchard near Port Alberni, and Max hoped to return there after the war.

Max was preceded into service by his brother Wes, who was killed in action on the SS *Oklahoma* when the American Navy was attacked at Pearl Harbor December 7, 1941. Upon enlisting in the Canadian Army in the fall of 1942 at age twenty-one, Max trained at Camp Shilo, Manitoba. One of his letters speaks of the simple pleasures of life at Shilo: "We get plenty to eat, and good grub at that. Lots of jam and honey." Max was aware, of course, of what lay ahead. "It is pretty hard training here at Shilo," he wrote, "and from here you go overseas if you're a good enough man." His family remembers him crying as he readied to leave Canada. "I don't think I'll be coming back," he told them. They were to hear from him again once he arrived in Britain; he wanted his dad to send money to buy a kilt.

Although details of his service in Europe are

18

sketchy, we know that by July 1944, a month after D-Day, Max was in hospital and almost discharged from the army altogether, having been wounded in the thigh by a machine gun bullet. However, he was sent back into action with the Canadian Scottish Regiment, part of the Third Canadian Division, as it slowly pushed toward the Rhine and eastward into Germany. The particular task facing them was to clear the area west of the Rhine as part of Operation Veritable. It was "a difficult and disagreeable battlefield," according to C.P. Stacey's official history of the war. The Waal and Maas rivers were each "flanked by a wide flood plain in which backwaters, marsh and abandoned channels provided effective obstacles to movement. These flats were subject to inundation when excessive rainfall, such as had prevailed that winter [1944–45] produced an unusually high water level in the rivers." In fact, rising water levels and the enemy practice of breaching dykes meant that most of the Third Division's area of operations was submerged.

Nicknamed the "Water Rats," the Canadian Scottish had to ride to their objectives in amphibious vehicles known as "landing vehicles, tracked" (LVTs), or "Buffaloes." These vehicles could carry either thirty men with full gear or a Jeep and artillery, and could negotiate all manner of slopes, shallow water, or mud flats. In early February 1945, the Buffalo carrying Private Max Brown was hit by bazooka fire during an attack on the village of Niel, south of Nijmegen; two men were killed instantly. Max, however, stayed alive in the wreck of the vehicle for two more days. After the battalion had moved on, a young Dutch woman, looking for survivors, heard his moans from the LVT. She cared for him as best she could, but with severe burns to sixty percent of his body, he died soon thereafter, on February 9, 1945, his scorched dog tags evidence of the severity of the fire that killed him.

Max Brown was originally buried near Nijmegen in a simple grave marked by a wooden cross. Thelma

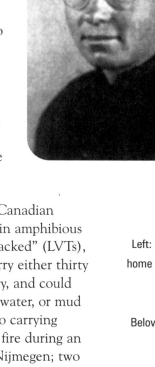

Left: Max Brown's letter home from Camp Shilo in August 1943.

Below: The badge of the Canadian Scottish Regiment.

Scheltes, the Dutch woman who had cared for him in his last days, corresponded with Max's family for several years. After his body was transferred to the Groesbeek Canadian War Cemetery in Holland, Mrs. Scheltes and her mother adopted the gravesite and visited it every Remembrance Day.

Max Bradie Brown, a "good enough man" indeed, is commemorated in Saskatchewan by Brown Bay, located on the Churchill River about 150 kilometres east of La Ronge.⊛

Above: Buffaloes of the Canadian army moving up to cross the Rhine, spring 1945.

BARNEY J. GLOSTER / NATIONAL ARCHIVES OF CANADA / PA137734

Right: Max Brown's gravesite.

Far right: The town of Kranenburg surrounded by floodwaters in February 1945. The "Water Rats" fought over this challenging terrain.

BARNEY J. GLOSTER / NATIONAL ARCHIVES OF CANADA / PA145752

Byers

When "The Dambusters" was showing at the Roxy Theatre in Nipawin in the summer of 1956, moviegoers would have known, thanks to an article in the *Nipawin Journal*, that a real Dambuster, Pilot Officer Vernon Byers, came from the nearby community of Star City.

Vernon's family had helped settle the Star City district, although his father Frank had quit farming in 1918 to become a grain buyer. Frank and Ruby moved around a lot after that, and, for a time, Vernon and a younger brother stayed in Star City with their Aunt Maggie, the postmistress. There wasn't much to do for young Vernon, but he liked to roam around the bluffs and streams of the countryside, play whatever sport was in season, maybe take in a Saturday night movie in town. He was good at anything he did, including school, and he had plenty of initiative, too. After graduating from high school, he went to work for Hudson Bay Mining and Smelting Company in Flin Flon—his cousin had married a fellow who got him the job. For two or three years, the future Dambuster pilot was an underground miner.

Vernon Byers didn't mind the mines but wanted more. The air force, he reasoned, would be a better life, and he went to Winnipeg in early 1941 to enlist. His parents were proud of him and of his brother, who also joined up, ready to go to war. Soon, it seemed, Vernon Byers was a pilot officer who had successfully completed a tour of thirty bombing operations overseas and was ready to come home, full of enthusiasm for

Byers Bay (55°39' N, 105°14' W), viewed here from the north, is located on the Churchill River about forty air miles north of La Ronge. A beautiful site, Byers Bay is about four miles in length, with many rock-terraced shorelines which are common in this area of the Boreal Shield. Byers Bay is a popular destination for anglers who fish for jackfish and pickerel in the Trout Lake area of the Churchill River.

how beautiful England looked from the air. "He promised to take the whole family over after the war and show us," his youngest brother Glenn remembers.

But Vernon wasn't going to be coming home just yet. Instead, he volunteered for one of the most famous operations of the war, the Dams raid of May 16–17, 1943. Virtually everything about this raid was extraordinary, according to Paul Brickhill's 1951 bestseller, *The Dam Busters*. The airmen, first of all, were selected from the best and most experienced in Bomber Command. Their Wing Commander, Guy Gibson—later played by Richard Todd in the movie based on Brickhill's book—had completed 172 operations and had earned both the Distinguished Flying Cross and the Distinguished Service Order and Bar. A special squadron was created: No. 617 "Dambuster" Squadron based in Scampton, Lincolnshire. And a special eight-week training program was undertaken to prepare the nineteen Lancaster crews for the low-level attack which would

be the most difficult and dangerous of their lives.

The target was also specialized. Instead of another in a series of conventional bombing raids on the German industrial heartland of the Ruhr Valley, this raid would attempt to destroy something all industries needed: the hydroelectric power produced by three dams on the Ruhr River. The problem of how to breach the mighty Möhne, Eder, and Sorpe dams required an inventive solution. These dams were heavily fortified with anti-torpedo netting and several anti-aircraft gun positions. They were so massive, furthermore, that no conventional bomb could cause serious damage even if it did strike home. And if a new, more powerful conventional bomb were built, its weight would mean that no bomber, even the mighty Lancs, could carry it. The solution, derived after months of research, was a bomb small enough for a modified Lancaster to hold it and powerful enough that, if dropped from low altitude, it could explode under water against the dam wall, thus breaching the dam.

One more ingenious feature was included. The bomb would be dropped with enough backspin— enabled by a special motor attached to the bomb—that when it hit the water it would bounce forward across the lake, and over the defensive netting, like a skipping stone. When it hit the dam wall, it would sink and detonate at a depth of thirty feet, activated by a pressure-sensitive fuse. The missions would be

Below: One of No. 617 "Dambuster" Squadron's specially modified Lancasters.

conducted at a 100-foot altitude at night with the bombs being released at sixty feet above the water.

Pilot Officer Vernon Byers and his crew took off at 9:30 p.m. on May 16, 1943. One of many international devotees of the Dambuster story, Alex Bateman of Middlesex, England, provides details of Byers' last flight:

> They were part of the reserve wave of aircraft, to be diverted en route as and where they were needed. It seems they had a quiet trip across the sea, but nearing the Dutch island of Vlieland, they climbed to around 450 feet, probably to try and identify landmarks. They flew on over the sea, but were engaged by German flak units based on the island of Texel, who hit them and shot them down. The aircraft crashed into the Waddenzee, 18 miles west of Harlingen at about 22:57.

Only one body was ever recovered, that of the tail gunner, who washed ashore over a month after the crash. The names of the rest of the crew, including that of Pilot Officer Vernon William Byers, are inscribed on the Runnymede Memorial in Surrey, England.

The raid itself was successful in damaging two of the three objectives: the Möhne and Eder dams were breached; the Sorpe dam was hit with bombs twice and, although damaged, it still held. An estimated 330 million tons of water poured through the Möhne and Eder valleys, flooding coal mines, factories, canal banks, industrial suburbs, power stations, foundries, waterworks, communications systems, and, it must be added, a Russian prisoner of war camp. The costs to No. 617 Squadron were considerable: fifty-six of the 133 airmen were missing, including thirteen of the thirty RCAF crew members.

Other than the telegram telling them that Vernon was missing in action, the Byers family knew nothing of the Dambuster raid until they read an account in *True* magazine. To this day they're proud of what Vernon accomplished with the RCAF. The movie may offer a glamorous way to remember the Dambuster story, but Glenn Byers prefers his visit on a perfect summer day to Byers Bay on the Churchill River, a country he knows very well. ✥

Above: The plaque at Byers Bay in memory of Vernon Byers.

DOUG CHISHOLM

Left: Glenn Byers and his sister Marjorie Temple visiting Byers Bay in 2000.

DOUG CHISHOLM

23

Calder ——————— CAPTAIN KENNETH ALEXANDER CALDER • L900179 • 1911–1945

Calder Lake (56°58' N, 102°08' W), viewed here from the north, is located about 175 air miles northeast of La Ronge, near the Manitoba border, deep in the Churchill River Upland region of the Boreal Shield. A serenely tranquil feature, Calder Lake is about two miles in length and is uniquely situated on Malcolm Island, one of the largest islands in the province. Malcolm Island itself is fifteen miles in length and located on Reindeer Lake, which at 120 miles, is one of the largest lakes in Saskatchewan.

⊕

●Moose Jaw

At the age of seven, Ken Calder and the other schoolchildren of Moose Jaw marched to the exhibition grounds to witness what must have been a glorious sight—the arrival home of the Forty-sixth Canadian Infantry Battalion, the famous "Suicide Squadron" (named after its 91 percent casualty rate during World War I). A few years later, Ken joined the volunteer militia himself, first the King's Own Rifles of Canada and then the Seventy-seventh Field Battery of the Royal Canadian Artillery, in which he eventually rose to the rank of captain.

Although Moose Jaw had been something of a boomtown in 1911 when Ken was born, by the time he reached his teens, the boom had collapsed. Despite the harsh economic conditions of the 1920s and 1930s, however, he got a job with the Co-op Creamery in Moose Jaw, and by the outbreak of war in 1939, he had risen to the position of foreman. Away from work, he enjoyed the outdoors, especially fishing on Last Mountain Lake. Socially, he was an affable, well-liked young man—a "man's man" who was also popular with the girls for his generosity and sense of humour.

On the weekend that Hitler marched into Poland in September 1939, Ken Calder volunteered for active service. "I don't feel I could run out on the Army now after 14 years of peace-time service," he wrote in a letter to an American cousin. In fact, Ken's years as a "Saturday night soldier" made him valuable as an experienced officer who could help train raw recruits as the Canadian Army hurried to mobilize for war after two decades of neglect. Also in 1939, Ken renewed a relationship with a girl named Margaret, whom he'd known since high school. They had gone together a few years earlier but had broken it off. Ken and Margaret were engaged at the beginning of November but then, like thousands of other couples, impulsively got married—on November 29, eight days before Ken went overseas.

Ken left for Britain with the Seventy-seventh Battery, then part of the Third Canadian Field Regiment, in December 1939, as Canada sent over its First Canadian Division. There followed nearly four years of training and various postings with anti-aircraft units, which were responsible for guarding the island fortress. After September 1940, he served with the Super-Heavy Railway Group, an elite Royal Artillery unit manning twenty-one-ton 9.2-inch railway guns in southern England. After one more transfer, to the Second Light Anti-Aircraft Regiment, Captain Ken Calder joined the Italian Campaign in October 1943.

The Canadians had landed in Sicily three months earlier. Still ahead were the Battle for Ortona, with its grim toll of casualties and battle exhaustion; the trench-bound winter of 1943-44 in which the Canadians endured conditions not unlike those in World War I; the spring 1944 offensive along the Liri Valley through the imposing defenses of the Gustav Line; and, finally, the advance along the Adriatic coast from Rimini to Ravenna, from August 1944 to February 1945. One description of the fighting in the Rimini-Ravenna sector suggests the difficulties faced during the entire twenty-month Italian Campaign: "Canadians fought a seemingly endless series of grueling struggles from one water obstacle to the next in that small triangle of land." All in all, Captain Calder endured some of the most difficult and demoralizing fighting of the war.

In the autumn of 1944, with the defeat of Germany only a matter of time, Ken turned his attention to Saskatchewan provincial politics as it pertained to the post-war lives of the troops. Tommy Douglas's CCF government, elected in June, called for the election of three servicemen MLAs, and Ken Calder ran for the seat allocated to the Mediterranean zone. His platform, printed in the Canadian Army newspaper, *The Maple Leaf*, focussed on pensions, employment, rehabilitation, education and training, disability allowances, and aid to those wishing to farm or start a small business. Though he did not win, Ken ran a respectable sixth out of fourteen candidates.

Ken spent the final months of the war in Holland, where the Second Light Anti-Aircraft Battery had been sent from Italy. Shortly after VE Day, he returned to England, sailed to Canada, and arrived home in Moose Jaw on June 19, 1945, five and a half years after he had left. After a week with his family—including a reunion with the family dog, a Boston terrier named Peggy who,

apparently, remembered Ken and made quite a fuss
over him—he went to Vancouver to be reunited with
Margaret, who was working there as a nurse. When she
told him, after three awkward days of hesitation, that
she was in love with another man and wanted out of
the marriage, he put on his best uniform one afternoon,
turned on the gas stove in the kitchen, and killed
himself.

The Department of National Defence rightly
considered Captain Calder to be a casualty of war,
someone confronted by an intense personal trauma too
soon after enduring the rigours of the Italian campaign
and seeing the horrors of the starvation of the Dutch.

Captain Kenneth Calder is buried at Rosedale
Cemetery in Moose Jaw. The beautiful Calder Lake,
named in his honour, lies within a large island on
Reindeer Lake, near the Manitoba border in northern
Saskatchewan. ✿

Chesney

Lorne Chesney was a fun-loving lad who made friends easily and lived life to the fullest. There are many stories that offer a glimpse of the spirit with which he lived his short life. While a high school student in his hometown of Wolseley, for example, he and a group of friends, none of them Roman Catholic, thought they would like to experience a Christmas Eve Mass. Becoming restless as he knelt for prayers that were long and in Latin, Lorne quietly unlaced the galoshes of the girls kneeling in front of him and tied them to the bench on which he knelt. The same spirit was evident some years later. When Lorne was stationed in North Africa and a male French officer (in keeping with his custom) greeted him with a kiss on the cheek, Lorne responded by kissing the officer's wife in the same manner. He wrote home, not entirely regretfully, that the French officer had taken "rather a dim view of it."

Nineteen forty-two was a pivotal year for Lorne. He celebrated his twenty-first birthday, graduated from the University of Saskatchewan with a degree in chemical engineering, enlisted in the armoured corps, and married his high school sweetheart, Vera Ingram. When his mother Isobel suggested that at twenty-one he was too young to marry, he replied, "If I'm old enough to lead men into battle, I'm old enough to get married." Of course, she agreed, and Lorne and Vera got married in Boharm on the tenth of October of that year.

Although Lorne's father Edward, who owned a hardware store in Wolseley, urged him to join the Royal

Wolseley•

Chesney Lake (60°01' N, 106°54' W), viewed here from the north, is located about 340 air miles north of La Ronge near the border between Saskatchewan and the Northwest Territories, fifty miles north of the community of Fond du Lac. Situated in the Taiga Shield ecozone, Chesney Lake is a distinct feature about four miles in length, with prominent islands, peninsulas, and bays.

Canadian Corps of Engineers, Lorne felt his place was with other Canadians on the battle line. He went overseas with the Governor General's Horse Guards (GGHG) in March of 1943, remaining in Britain—where he appreciated the hospitality of English families—until December, when he was sent to Algeria for further training. The invasion of Sicily had taken place earlier that year, and by the summer of 1944, the GGHG, part of the Third Canadian Armoured Reconnaissance Regiment, was active in the Italian campaign. In early October they had pushed up the boot of Italy and penetrated the Gothic Line, a heavily fortified belt extending across the mountains north of Rome.

Lieutenant Chesney's letters reveal the range of a soldier's emotions in the course of a long campaign. Christmas Day of 1943 had been a nostalgic occasion: "Last night we sang carols. Many of the men were back from the front and they seemed like the toughest fellows I'd ever met. Yet there wasn't a dry eye among us." The loss of his best friend and many of his other friends took its toll and the tone of Lorne's letters grew more somber: "Some fellows want to come home as heroes," he wrote. "I don't want to be a hero, I just want to learn how to be a man again." In his last letter, dated October 21, 1944, his fighting spirit was alive and well:

"We go in tomorrow at three," he wrote. "We intend to chase a few Germans from a town just ahead of us."

That town was Cervia. On October 24, Lorne Chesney died there: "Lorne's squadron was being harassed by an enemy machine gun. Lorne and his Sergeant brought up their tanks in order to destroy an enemy pillbox. They got up to within 100 yards of the enemy position when a burst of machine gun fire got both of them. They died instantly." That description, provided by Lorne's commanding officer, Lieutenant Colonel Jordan, goes on to tell of the gratitude of the Italian people and the esteem in which Lorne Chesney was held: "His grave is in the town square of the ancient town of Cervia. The people of the town keep fresh flowers on it every day and are working on a memorial stone on which will appear these words: *These Canadian soldiers gave their lives for the freedom of Cervia.* Lorne was a grand officer and his loss will be felt keenly in the regiment."

An Italian journalist, Franco Martinelli, offers this glimpse into the feelings of liberation Lorne Chesney and his men helped deliver to the people of Cervia: "After the last Germans were seen fleeing, there appeared the sight of the first liberators, and all the women and children, everyone happy and crying from happiness. Governor General's Horse Guards—Canada. That was all we could see through the tears of joy for being liberated. They have arrived. They have arrived."

On the fiftieth anniversary of Cervia's liberation, Lorne's widow, Vera—along with family members of all the other servicemen who died in this campaign—received a medal and plaque from Cervia's townspeople "in recognition of the ultimate sacrifice made by brave Canadian soldiers." At the time she noted that "What I remember most about Lorne was his love of life, his energy and intelligence, his concern and love for family and myself, his happy outlook—he wanted to come home and start our lives together. He would have made a great husband and father."

Lieutenant Lorne Chesney's final burial place is the Cesena War Cemetery, not far from Cervia. On his gravestone are the words: "TO LIVE IN HEARTS WE LEAVE BEHIND IS NOT TO DIE." After Chesney Lake, located in northern Saskatchewan near the Northwest Territories border, was named in Lorne's honour by his home province, Lorne's father wrote to A.G. Kuziak, who was the minister of natural resources. The last paragraph of the letter, dated January 31, 1957, reads: "Mrs. Chesney and I deeply appreciate the naming of Chesney Lake in honour of our son, James Lorne. He was a very fine son in every respect. He loved well his parents, home and country. There was no hesitancy on his part to give his life, if need be, for a duty he sincerely believed in." ✿

Dear Auntie —

Hospital
Sept 29/44

I thought that it was nearly time to write to you & let you know that I am well & am enjoying my little leave in Hospital. I am in a ward until I when officers who are feeling OK & so we have a fair amount of fun.

One is an medical officer until a bullet thru his arm. Most of the others are shrapnel wounds except one fellow who has asthma. At one had an arm & shoulder off. He has had it off for 2 weeks now & seems quite cheerful. They give him about 8 shots of Penicilon every day. They hauled my shrapnel out yesterday. It wasn't very much & I think that I shall be leaving here tomorrow.

It is sure nice to be sleeping in clean sheets & a nice building again. This place used to be a big Italian Sanitorium & it still has all the equipment. They have Italian girls working in there now. The one in our ward is called Tina. The food is very

Clarke

Clarke Island (55°09' N, 104°49' W), viewed here from the south, is located on beautiful Lac la Ronge about three miles from the entrance to Hunter Bay. About two miles in length, it is a popular summer destination, with numerous cabins surrounded by tall jack pines, white spruce, and birch trees.

For readers of the *Estevan Mercury* on Thursday, August 20, 1942, this was the beginning of the lead story: "Pulses quickened and pride surged through Estevan today when it was announced that the South Saskatchewan Regiment took part in the United Nations' smash behind a tank spearhead at the Nazi-held French harbour of Dieppe Wednesday." The *Mercury* and everyone else hoped for success, of course, but lack of artillery support, coupled with the strength of the German defenses, meant disaster for the attacking forces. Almost 5,000 Canadian soldiers landed; 901 of them, including Private James Clarke—Jim or Jimmy, as he was better known—died in the attack.

A few days later, back home on her family's farm near Estevan, Jim's wife Anne got the telegram saying her husband was missing. She had tried to talk him out of joining up in 1940. Their wedding and subsequent honeymoon in Minot in August of '39 must have seemed still fresh in her memory. In preparation for the big day, Jim had gone for his first barbershop haircut, instead of getting his dad to cut it. Anne remembered, too, driving around with Jim and her cousin Jack in Jack's Model T—the three of them (sometimes quite a few more) touring around, often going to Sunday afternoon concerts. Jim, who was a good enough swimmer to teach his younger brothers to swim, enjoyed a dip in the Souris River. If Jim and Anne and the gang felt like dancing, they would clear some space in someone's living room and turn on the gramophone.

Someone would play guitar, or perhaps Johnny Docherty would show up with his accordion. So life was for Jim and Anne, who went together for six or seven years before getting married. "He was a wonderful man," she remembers today.

Jim Clarke, being married and in his late twenties when war broke out, didn't have to enlist, but so many of the young men did anyway. Jim worked with his father, Sam, at Prairie Nurseries, taking care of the usual planting, packing, and shipping duties. "I thought we'd end up at the Nursery," Anne says. "Jim liked gardening and knew all the Latin names for the plants." His love of gardening continued after he went off for training to Winnipeg; he and Anne visited the greenhouse in Assiniboia Park during one of her visits there.

She last visited Jim in November and December 1940, during the final stages of his training in Toronto, although their time together was not as intimate as might have been expected. An outbreak of chicken pox had meant quarantine in the exhibition grounds for Jim and the rest of the company—Jim referred to their accommodations as a "horse palace in the fairgrounds." He couldn't even meet Anne at the train. With her friend Thelma, who also had a husband in the South Saskatchewan Regiment (SSR), Anne rented rooms near the exhibition grounds. Only occasionally were the two women able to have their husbands over for supper and the night.

On December 13, 1940, Jim boarded a train for Halifax and the trip overseas. *March of the Prairie Men*, the history of the SSR, describes the scene: "It seemed as if half of Toronto had come to bid us farewell. The march to the train with each man in full pack and two kit bags was a sight never to be forgotten. The streets were keenly iced with a freak rain, which had frozen. That, coupled with high spirits inside and out, made an ordinary military march into a three ring circus."

On board the troopship *Pennland*, with a Dutch captain and crew, the men of the SSR enjoyed some of the traditional pleasures of the season. The *Globe & Mail* reported that the celebration of Christmas "was not neglected as the ship plowed through buffeted seas. Padres in khaki held religious services. Carols rolled out over the

Below: Jim Clarke's script for his radio message home from England.

1939-1945

THE LAND
ON WHICH THIS
CEMETERY STANDS
IS THE GIFT OF THE
FRENCH PEOPLE
FOR THE PERPETUAL
RESTING PLACE
OF THE SAILORS
SOLDIERS AND AIRMEN
WHO ARE HONOURED
HERE

Above: The inscription at Dieppe Canadian War Cemetery.

Right: The beach where the South Saskatchewan Regiment landed in the Dieppe raid.

KEN BELL / NATIONAL ARCHIVES OF CANADA / PA137299

Atlantic in full-throated volume." The regiment landed in Scotland on Christmas Eve, 1940.

While in England over the next year and a half, Jim Clarke spent his leisure time enjoying shows, touring, visiting his brother Frank—generally making the most of his time there. He looked forward to shipments of cigarettes and cakes from home, and sent quite a few letters home, always reminding his folks to "give Anne a hug for me." On one occasion he was able to deliver his own message via radio broadcast from England. "Hello Anne, folks and Gang," reads his script. "How are things in Estevan. Not doing too bad over here. Keep that chin up, sugar. Our turn is coming. Be good to yourself. Wish I could give you a hug, lassie. So long for now."

Prior to the raid on Dieppe, the regiment established its headquarters in Norris Castle on the Isle of Wight, near what fifty years earlier had been one of Queen Victoria's favourite summer homes. Without knowing any exact details, the troops sensed that something was up, as exercises and drills intensified. On August 18, 1942, the troops moved to the south coast ports. Operation Jubilee, the raid on Dieppe, was about to begin.

Private James Clarke was buried in the Dieppe Canadian War Cemetery, and Clarke Island on Lac la Ronge, Saskatchewan, is named in his honour. ✿

Clarke

I f you were a boy living in a family of nine on a farm near Parkside, Saskatchewan, before World War II, chances are you'd be a hockey player—a goalie perhaps—and a softball and broomball player. You'd work hard on the farm, of course, and to help make ends meet, you'd take a job southwest of town picking raspberries and strawberries at A.J. Porter's horticultural farm known as Honeywood Nursery. You'd be a Boy Scout, and what you'd look forward to the most would be piling into a neighbour's truck that had hauled cattle all week, spreading out a few blankets, and heading down for a day at Emerald Lake.

Samuel Clarke, known as Ted, was all of the above. And there was another fellow very much like him—Leon Roberts (see his story on page 177). The two of them were best friends, fellow Scouts, and teammates throughout their childhood. Both boys were happy-go-lucky, popular with schoolmates and other Parkside residents. Ted was the musical one, like his mother. "He was a good singer," his sister Irene remembers, "who could sing any song. When it got dark, we would sit around and sing and sing and sing." He got as far as grade eleven in school. Because departmental exams cost a dollar each, Ted had to work extra hard at the nursery to pay for them, but he did it. He would have started grade twelve if World War II hadn't intervened.

"Ted was eager to go," Irene says. He followed in the footsteps of his father (also named Samuel), who had been in the army, and his older brother Jim, an airman. He enlisted on October 6, 1941, the day after

Clarke Lake (55°27' N, 105°37' W), viewed here from the south, is located about twenty-five air miles northwest of La Ronge. Situated just west of Nemeiben Lake and just south of the Churchill River, Clarke Lake is about two miles in length and hosts a healthy population of pickerel and jackfish.

Parkside●

his eighteenth birthday, and trained in Brandon, Edmonton, and Prince Albert—eventually receiving his wings in Saskatoon, graduating with highest marks in his class. Irene remembers the day Ted left Parkside for the last time. "It was darn cold, it must have been January. All the kids were let out of school. Family and neighbours gathered down at the station" as Ted boarded the North Battleford-Prince Albert train. He arrived overseas on January 18, 1943, posted to No. 419 "Moose" Squadron.

One of his early letters expressed regret at not being in one place long enough to send birthday greetings to Irene. "But please believe me," he wrote, "I thought of the cake that would be devoured by at least seven hungry mouths." He had always looked out for Irene. She recalls nearly drowning in Emerald Lake while swimming out to the floating diving board: "I got tired and sank. I could see the water above my head. Ted pulled me out." And when it came to war service, Ted did not want his sister to join up.

Another letter described happy visits to an uncle and aunt in Port Stewart, Northern Ireland, but by early October 1943, the dangers of a bomber pilot's life were becoming more evident. "We were night flying again last night," he wrote, "and it looks an awful lot like I will spend my twentieth birthday up there. Strange as it may seem, by adding just this one year to my age I seem at least four years older because when one passes the 'teen' age, there is nothing but worry and anxiety."

Just a few weeks before Ted died, his letter was again reflective in tone:

Last night I was going to hit the hay early but the mid upper gunner from Banff and I started talking of home and how little a young person appreciates home until he or she is at least twenty. Both of us think more of it now than we ever did. Even after the lights were out we lay in bed talking, the lighting supplied by the fireplace which kept the room lovely and warm all night.

At that time, No. 419 Squadron was an integral element in the first series of raids on the "big city," Berlin—about a 2000-kilometre round trip from the squadron base in Middleton St. George, Durham. On the night of November 26, 1943, a raid on Stuttgart was added to the Berlin attack in an effort to draw most of the German fighters away from the main attacking force. The plan was successful to that extent, but the Halifax Mark II bombers, capable of only a relatively low ceiling, were especially vulnerable to anti-aircraft flak. Six Halifaxes, including the one piloted by Flight Sergeant Ted Clarke, were lost that night.

Flight Sergeant Samuel Edward (Ted) Clarke is buried in Rheinberg War Cemetery, Germany. In Saskatchewan, Clarke Lake is named in his memory. ✿

Cockburn

When the mixed farm operated by Bill and Rachel Cockburn near Briercrest wasn't going so well in the 1930s, Bill started a dairy business to supplement the family income. So Jim Cockburn, the youngest of the three boys, had plenty of chores—delivering the milk to local homes twice a day for ten cents a quart and helping with the milking and barn duties. There was schoolwork to do also—Jim got all the way through high school at Briercrest School—and a lively array of more informal activities to enjoy. Jim would swim in the coulee with the Boothman boys, climb trees to rob crows' nests, or trap gophers for a penny a tail. For ten cents he could see a show in town on a Friday night. At home, often there was music. One of his three sisters, Peggy, remembers that "Jim played the guitar, and very often with mother on the violin, Vivian on the piano, and Archie on the mouth organ we enjoyed musical evenings. We all had a wonderful home life." The Cockburn home was something of a community gathering place as well. According to the town's local history book, the 1937 Sports Day Dance was held in the hayloft of the big Cockburn barn. So many people attended that the "barn swayed noticeably under the weight and motion of dancing to the Westrum Orchestra."

One of Jim Cockburn's passions as a boy was hockey. In his notebooks he kept careful records of NHL statistics—noting, for example, that the Boston Bruins finished on top of the final standings in 1938-39

Cockburn Lake (59°31' N, 105°32' W), viewed here from the south, is located three hundred air miles north of La Ronge, just twenty miles north of the community of Stony Rapids and thirty miles south of the border between the Northwest Territories and Saskatchewan. Cockburn Lake is two miles in length and is surrounded by the vast forests of the Taiga Shield ecozone. In fall, the colours are spectacular, as tamarack and birch stands contrast with black spruce.

Briercrest●

and that Toe Blake of the Canadians led the league in scoring. In October of 1939, he was able to see a pro game in Regina—the Rangers against the Americans—and he carefully noted the results in his book. Jim's own achievements as a player were considerable, his notebooks tell us, as he scored almost half his team's goals one season playing against teams from Avonlea, Hearne, Tilney, and the Bible College. He was a skilled and serious player, to be sure. In 1939-40 he spent more than twenty-four dollars on hockey equipment, and he was good enough to attract the attention of the Moose Jaw Canucks.

But war intervened. Jim enlisted in January of 1943, two years after his older brother Archie, while the eldest brother, George, stayed at home to operate the farm. At first Jim was attached to the Edmonton Fusiliers, but in a letter from Prince George, where his basic training took place, he expressed a hope to join Archie's unit. In the end, however, he joined The Black Watch (Royal Highland Regiment) of Canada—a unit, Jim's family proudly noted, with roots in eighteenth-century Scotland.

Before heading overseas, Private Cockburn was feted at a reception in the Briercrest town hall. Under the headline "Soldier Honored at Briercrest," the *Moose Jaw Times-Herald* reported on the spirit of the community and the esteem in which Jim Cockburn was held:

> Frank Arnold, in his address to Cpl. Cockburn, said that in all the years he had known him, he had always found him "tops" in curling, hockey, baseball, and in everything else. He extended the best wishes of the community as he presented an autograph book signed by about 125 people to Cpl. Cockburn, who expressed his appreciation by saying, "There is no place like home." A hearty applause was extended to Byron Jaques, who recently enlisted; to James Walker, home on leave; and to all the boys and girls in uniform from this district. After the singing of the National Anthem, lunch was served and a social hour enjoyed.

And there was another important matter to take care of before departure for England. In an earlier letter

Two of Jim's passions— playing guitar (above) and playing hockey (right).

Top right: The badge of the Black Watch (Royal Highland Regiment) of Canada.

home, Jim had written: "By the way, will you tell George if he has time to put my hockey stuff in a trunk in the bunkhouse so it won't get lost. Most of it is in one of them turkey sacks in there and I wouldn't want it to get lost because I'll be needing that again."

July 25, 1944, the day Jim Cockburn was killed, is an infamous date in Black Watch regiment history. As part of Operation Spring, the Second Infantry Division planned to take Verrières Ridge, near Caen. "From the moment of crossing the start-line," writes C.P. Stacey in his official history, "the [Black Watch] came under an intense and accurate fire…and men fell fast. The Black Watch nevertheless advanced with unwavering determination…. It appears that on or just beyond the crest they ran into a well-camouflaged enemy position strengthened with dug-in tanks. What

remained of the battalion was now 'pinned down' by intense close-in fire." Retreat was ordered, but only about five percent of the men who attacked made it back safely. "The 25th had been a bloody day," Stacey notes, and the Black Watch suffered more heavily—307 casualties, 123 of them fatal—than any other unit. Except for Dieppe, there was no other single day in which a Canadian battalion had so many casualties.

"Briercrest Man Reported Missing," proclaimed the *Times-Herald*. Private Jim Cockburn had been one of those killed at Verrières Ridge. Two French women, Mme. Bunel and her daughter, for many years tended his grave. The Cockburn family, in turn, sent parcels of food and other items to the Bunels.

Jim Cockburn is buried at Bretteville-sur-Laize Canadian War Cemetery; his brothers George and Archie were able to travel there in 1984. He is also honoured by Cockburn Lake, in Saskatchewan's far north. ❀

Left: Jim Cockburn's original gravesite at Bretteville-sur-Laize Canadian War Cemetery.

Conacher ————

Conacher Lake (57°20' N, 103°01' W), viewed here from the north, is located 190 air miles northeast of La Ronge. About four miles in length, Conacher Lake is connected to the west edge of Reindeer Lake by a four-mile creek. A bronze plaque was placed at Conacher Lake in September 2001.

Under a picture of her twin brother David in the living room of her home in Aylsham, Saskatchewan, Mary Conacher Valleau talks lovingly of her brother and of family life so many years ago in the Fairy Glen district. At that time, Fairy Glen, about forty kilometres southwest of Aylsham, was a vigorous community, at least as far as its sports teams were concerned. A baseball team did well at sports days throughout the northeast. And there were enough young men to form two hockey teams, the Hawks and the Owls, with an intense rivalry ongoing. David did play some hockey on the open-air rink, but he and his dad, John, especially enjoyed their hockey via the radio—a King model, with a big horn speaker and three dials on the front. It was on radio that they could hear of the exploits of their distant relatives, Lionel "Big Train" Conacher and his brother Charlie, who both played for the great Toronto Maple Leaf teams of the twenties and thirties. "They were glued to that radio," Mary remembers.

The Conacher family life was centered on the farm that John had started in the first decade of the century. He and his wife, also named Mary, had emigrated from Perthshire, Scotland, stopping first in Winnipeg, where John worked as a carpenter. "The whole family was involved in the work of the farm," Mary Valleau says, "especially at haying time." Work or not, the kids found time to play, too—tumbling, romping, playing hide and seek around the hay coils, occasionally having a nap there. "It was a real picnic," Mary remembers. "Mom would bring cakes and cookies, sandwiches, lemonade to be shared by all."

Farm life, in fact, was David's passion. It was tough going on the Conacher farm, but David and his brother John became full working partners with their dad. David looked forward to some day owning his own farm. First, though, came school—David got as far as grade eight before staying home to work on the farm. "We had to sit in the same double desk at Fairy Glen School," Mary says, admitting that her brother was not much of a scholar. "He wasn't crazy about going to school. One day he hid in the ditch instead of going. He got a spanking from Dad and was sent to bed without his supper, although when Dad went out to do the chores, Mom took supper up to him."

No matter how strongly attached David Conacher was to the farm life, it was a foregone conclusion that he would enlist in the army sooner or later. He did so in Melfort in December of 1942, a time made even more difficult by the fact that his father was just getting over a major heart attack. After training at Regina and Shilo, he became Private David Conacher of the Highland Light Infantry of Canada. In Mary's words, "He went off sadly but bravely to perform his duty in a war, a way of preserving his future and fulfilling his dream."

By the last weeks of August 1944, the Highland Light Infantry of Canada had participated in what military historian C.P. Stacey called "two and a half months of the most bloody fighting since D-Day." In

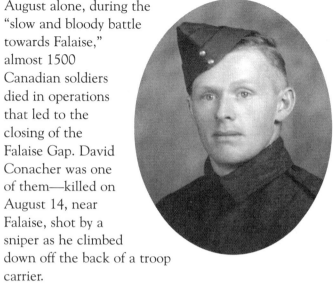

August alone, during the "slow and bloody battle towards Falaise," almost 1500 Canadian soldiers died in operations that led to the closing of the Falaise Gap. David Conacher was one of them—killed on August 14, near Falaise, shot by a sniper as he climbed down off the back of a troop carrier.

Back home, as Mary, his twin sister, recalls it, things "felt strange and different. We didn't know what the 'different feeling' was." Then they got the news: *The Minister of National Defense deeply regrets to inform you....*

Private David Conacher is buried in the Bretteville-sur-Laize Canadian War Cemetery near Cintheaux, France. His name, as the cemetery dedication reads, "liveth for ever more." In Saskatchewan, too, David's name lives on—Conacher Lake was named in memory of the man his sister calls this "quiet, unassuming lad with no great aspirations to greatness or visions of grandeur, a farm boy doing his duty." ✤

Below: David Conacher's gravesite at Bretteville-sur-Laize Canadian War Cemetery. When his nephew Wayne Valleau visited there in 1961, he described the experience in these words: "It was a beautiful warm spring evening, a gentle breeze rustled the leaves on the trees, the air was filled with the sweet fragrance of lilacs in blossom, the muted sounds of birds could be heard as they nestled down for the night in the soft glow of the setting sun. As I knelt by my uncle's grave, I was surrounded by a feeling of peace and tranquility. I could sense God's presence: his sadness for lost sons and daughters who would never again return to homes and families."

Cove

Cove Lake (57°55 N, 108°24' W), viewed here from the south, is located 220 air miles northwest of La Ronge. Distinct in shape, Cove Lake is about four miles in length, its waters clear and deep. The surrounding terrain is consistent with the Athabasca Plain ecoregion of the Boreal Shield. Old-growth forest at Cove Lake is limited due to the forest fires which have exposed the glacial sandstone deposits.

For some men, serving one's country meant service in both world wars. Thomas Austin Cove, a farmer near Grenfell in the period between wars, was one such man.

Thomas was decorated with the Military Medal for bravery during World War I. A member of the Lord Strathcona's Horse regiment, Thomas Cove had, in fact, been around horses all his life. His father, a gentleman farmer near Reading, England, had owned and raced them. Thomas, however, left England in 1910 at the age of eighteen for a new life as a farmer in Canada, a life he resumed after his World War I service. He married Alice Ainger of Grenfell, honeymooning at Crooked Lake, Saskatchewan.

He never strayed far from the military life, maintaining his affiliation with the Army Reserves in the Grenfell area in the years before the Second World War. His experience overseas made him a valuable instructor for his younger Reserve recruits, one of whom was his eldest son, Ted. "He used his World War I maps to teach us map-reading," Ted recalls. "And it was Dad who got me into the army."

For Thomas himself, almost fifty years old as World War II began, a return to active duty called for some creative disclosure of information. "He kind of lied about his age," his son says, "and claimed he only had two kids instead of nine." Years later, some of Ted's siblings still chuckle that their father never admitted to the Army the exact size of his family.

Remembering his father now, Ted recalls a man

who was a strict disciplinarian; a man who enjoyed the pleasures of a MacDonald's roll-your-own cigarette or, after a day in the fields, a brisk bath in the horse trough; a man whose handwriting was particularly elegant and whose skill at fishing would later keep the Sergeants' Mess of the Twentieth Company Canadian Forestry Corps well stocked with salmon. Physically, Thomas Cove was sturdy of build. As the legacy of a mustard gas incident during World War I, he had a "hole under his chin," as Ted calls it, which leaked saliva when he ate, requiring the dignified application of a fine white handkerchief at meal times. For years he wore a tiny moustache to counter the effects of having no upper teeth, a condition that existed until the Army gave him a set of dentures just before World War II.

Both of the Coves were based in Britain during the war, Thomas with the Forestry Corps and his son Ted as an NCO in the Army. For Thomas, service in England provided an opportunity to visit his parents and family who had never left England. For young Ted, being stationed in England meant he could spend time on leaves—one of them in Scotland—with his father. Ted remembers the last time they saw one another:

> It was after Christmas. I put him on the train at Burnham Junction, Sussex. As the train pulled away, he stuck his head out the window and waved. I remember thinking that was odd, because he never used to wave goodbye when he'd left the farm from time to time in the Thirties to work in Manitoba.

Some time later, after Ted had met and married an English girl, Anne, and they had their first child, Ted sent a letter to his Dad, inviting him to the christening. The letter was returned, marked DECEASED. That was the first Ted heard of his father's death.

After a life of distinguished, heroic military service, Thomas Austin Cove died far from the front lines. One day when he was excused from exercises at a Field Craft School in Caernarvon, Wales, Thomas volunteered to do some tree trimming. He may have suffered a heart attack while he was up there; in any case, at about 11:00 on the morning of June 11, 1943, he fell from the tree onto a rock and died. A few days later he was buried at Brookwood Military Cemetery in Surrey. One of the sergeants of his company, Arthur Ogden, paid tribute to Thomas Cove: "He taught us all we know about soldiering from the days of recruithood to our present stage, and without boast we are known to be the best all round men in the Canadian Forestry Corps, all due to his hard work."

In northern Saskatchewan, Cove Lake is named in honour of Warrant Officer Thomas Cove. ❀

Left: Thomas Cove's whistle used in World War I— now treasured by son Ted—was carried and used by Ted in World War II.

Center of page: Thomas Cove in uniform, World War I (upper); World War II (lower).

Below: Thomas Cove, right, and son Ted, embarking on service in World War II.

Danielson

Danielson Bay (56°53' N, 103°08' W), viewed here from the north, is located 140 air miles northeast of La Ronge. Situated at the south end of Nokomis Lake, Danielson Bay is over three miles in length, while Nokomis Lake itself is over twelve miles in diameter.

Melvin Danielson was raised on a farm in Stockholm, Saskatchewan, one of five brothers who served their country in World War II. Their parents, Peter and Hildur, had emigrated from Sweden. As a boy, Melvin had dabbled in a variety of hobbies that included stamp collecting, hunting, and playing the violin. He was a good softball player, too—not only the starting pitcher for his school team but also a trusty home-run hitter.

Melvin's exceptionally retentive memory allowed him to score 92.5 percent on his grade nine exam without ever once studying for it; his mother would find his scribbler untouched in his lunch box every morning. Although army records confirm that he had "well above average mental ability" and was possibly NCO material, what earned this lad a reputation in his pre-military years was his brawn. Local boys often gathered at the Danielson farm to watch him take on challengers in friendly wrestling matches. When opponents were selected, it was agreed that two at a time were permitted to wrestle against Melvin. Regardless of the advantage, the match seldom lasted more than one or two minutes.

Yet anyone who knew Melvin Danielson would attest that his physical ruggedness belied his gentle nature. He was not one to ever seek out a fight, but neither did he back down when challenged. A message he later had tattooed on his arm expressed his fighting spirit: *I shall never surrender.* For all his strength, this Stockholm native who would become a respected heavyweight boxer in the Canadian Army weighed in at a bare 162 pounds.

Melvin left school at age sixteen in order to take over the farming operation after four older brothers had joined the Canadian Army. He was glad to step in and assist his aging parents, but when it finally became apparent that the war situation was not improving, he was faced with a dilemma: whether to stay at home and lend support to his parents, or fight in the war and serve his country. In the end, his country took precedence, and he joined the South Alberta Regiment.

On Melvin's last leave just prior to going overseas, he had a premonition. To the friends who were seeing him off at the train station, he said, "I will not come back." Martin Danielson vividly recollects his brother's parting look through a car's rear window—a look of resignation. On October 25–26, 1944, when Trooper Danielson was mortally wounded in action, something out of the ordinary happened to Martin. While on the farm in Saskatchewan, Martin experienced a disturbing vision of his brother's final moments on the battlefield in Belgium:

> I was terribly restless and became more emotional as the day progressed, went to town to watch a movie, and was so disturbed by something unknown that it was necessary to leave midway through it. The car became balky, and I finally arrived home at about 10 p.m., went to bed and was suddenly aroused by a vision of riding in a tank, peering over Melvin's shoulder. As the tank approached the edge of a large [grove] of trees, I could see the enemy loading artillery…next I saw a soldier on the ground outside the tank and Melvin standing beside [him] firing his pistol deliriously in the air.

The South Alberta regiment, part of the Fourth Armoured Division, landed in Normandy on July 24, 1944. Equipped with the versatile American-built Sherman medium tank, the South Albertas acted as reconnaissance, armoured, infantry support, artillery or other roles as required during the breakout from Normandy and subsequent actions across northern Europe. At the battle for Bergen-op-Zoom, October 25–27, 1944, the regiment got the job of providing flank protection while the remainder of the Fourth Division attacked Bergen itself.

The details of Melvin Danielson's death in that battle are mentioned in *The South Albertas: A Canadian Regiment at War* by Donald E. Graves. After having been rendered unconscious and taken captive, Danielson was transported under a flag of truce, once firing had subsided, safely across Allied lines. He passed away at 3:45 a.m. after an operation to amputate his leg. His death was a result of shell-fragment wounds and a compound fracture to his upper left femur.

Trooper Melvin Danielson lies buried at the Canadian War Cemetery, Bergen-op-Zoom, Holland. In Saskatchewan, Danielson Bay on Nokomis Lake has been named in his honour. ✿

Above: The badge of the South Alberta Regiment.

Below: Melvin (left) and his younger brothers, Oliver and Martin, hauling wood about 1942.

Dermody ———

Dermody Lake (59°29' N, 108°43' W), viewed here from the south, is located about three hundred air miles north of La Ronge on the Crackingstone Peninsula, just ten miles south of the community of Uranium City near the old road to the Lorado minesite. Dermody Lake is one mile in length and is situated in a rugged and beautiful area of the Tazin Lake Upland ecoregion.

●Kennedy

Much of the life and times of Bernard Dermody—known as Barney (or as "Red," for his auburn hair)—is conveyed in stories told by his brother Len or by his cousin John.

One night, for instance, there was a dance at the Belleville School, in the countryside near Kennedy, Saskatchewan, where Barney's father Selby ran a real estate agency. Barney and a couple of pals wanted to get out there—he was popular with the girls, after all—but the only means of transportation was the team of horses, Dick and Lady, owned by his grandparents, the Donnellys. After dark, Barney and the boys caught the horses, hitched them to a lumber wagon, and headed out to the dance. Hours later, they rode the wagon back, unharnessed the horses, and turned them loose. In the morning, when Grandpa Donnelly went out to get Dick and Lady for the day's work, he couldn't figure out why they were sweated up.

John Dermody tells another story about his cousin Barney. One afternoon at recess at Kennedy School, some of the boys went out behind the biffy in the schoolyard to have a smoke. Unfortunately, Principal Elliott spotted the smoke from a second-storey window. He asked for a confession and got one. The boys were expelled and had to go to a school board meeting that night with their dads, at which Selby Dermody said, "If you'd like, I'll take Barney home and give him a damn good whipping."

His sternness aside, Selby Dermody clearly admired

Barney, the eldest of his nine children—even if Barney "would sooner play ball than hoe the garden," as Len puts it. Barney finished his high school in the early 1930s and soon thereafter went out to St. Thomas, Ontario, to take a job in a factory making car mufflers. He found time to play hockey with the St. Thomas team, earning the Most Gentlemanly Player Award. When the war came along, Barney was "raring to go," as Len says, and he joined the RCAF in Ontario.

Barney's Initial Training School stop was in Regina. When it came to being granted leaves, it may have helped that Barney's uncle was W.J. "Billy" Patterson, the premier of Saskatchewan. In any case, Barney was soon heading east and across to England, arriving there in May of 1941. Sergeant Dermody was posted with RAF No. 99 Squadron based in Waterbeach, near Cambridge, as a wireless operator in a Wellington bomber.

He and his cousin John, who was in England with the South Saskatchewan Regiment, spent three or four leaves together. On May 10, 1941, they happened to be staying at the YMCA across from Westminster Abbey. It was the night of a German bombing blitz and, as John Dermody tells the story, the two men answered an unexpected call to action:

I think we went to bed shortly before midnight and shortly thereafter, the call for volunteers came from the Abbey. The Jerries had dropped incendiary bombs. Upon reaching the Abbey, we learned that a number of incendiaries had hit the lead dome of the structure, had ignited, and the dome was burning. The red-hot lead was falling on the Coronation Altar. We were asked to place sandbags on the altar to prevent as much damage as possible. It didn't matter much that the hot lead was falling on the volunteers but "God save the altar."

Some 3,000 Londoners died that night. In a letter to his aunt, Barney Dermody understated his own impressions of the incident: "None of us was hurt, and we had our first real taste of war. It was sure a thrilling experience and I don't care to be in too many air raids."

John remembers another weekend he and Barney spent together in London. On this occasion, the two Kennedy men could not get a bed for the night—there were thousands of service personnel in London each weekend—so after midnight they strolled into a park, settled on two wrought iron benches under some trees, and went to sleep. About 6:00 a.m. they were woken by a Bobby, who informed them that they were cluttering the park and would have to move on. Years later, John recognized the "hotel room" he and Barney had shared that night. It was in Leicester Square.

During his training in England, Barney told John that he'd been in

Below: Unveiled September 21, 2000, this plaque at the College Building in Regina (the former Regina College) commemorates No. 2 Initial Training School which was housed at Regina College from 1940–1945. No. 2 I.T.S. was where Barney Dermody first trained.

DOUG MULLEN

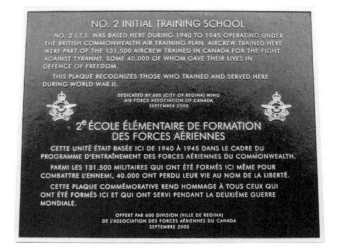

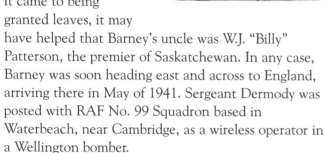

two accidents, the first a crash landing after a training flight and the other, a training flight during which a motor had come loose and gone through the fuselage of the aircraft. "Being a ball player, I know you only get three strikes," Barney told John. "I don't know when the third one is coming up." Strike three would come on November 15, 1941, when Sergeant Bernard Dermody did not return from his very first operational flight, a raid on Germany. A few days later, his wing commander wrote to Selby and Agnes Dermody: "Your son was very popular and hard-working, and although fairly new had all the markings of a certainly valuable wireless operator. We have very little information, I am afraid, as to what happened that night. We know that the aircraft in which your son was flying attacked its target but the weather got very bad later on and I think they probably got lost." In fact, his body was never

recovered, and Sergeant Dermody is honoured at Runnymede Memorial, overlooking the Thames in Surrey.

Back home in Kennedy, the telegram reporting that Barney was missing was followed by another telegram from Barney himself saying everything was fine. Of course, Barney's had been sent earlier, but for a while the family thought he was okay. "In a small town," notes Len Dermody, "if you saw the station agent coming to the door, you knew there was bad news." Indeed, a third telegram confirmed that Barney had died. In Saskatchewan's far north, Dermody Lake is named in his honour. ❀

Right: Barney at his parents' home in Kennedy, Saskatchewan, in December 1940.

Below: the Runnymede Memorial.

JOHN YEOMANS

46

Dmytruk

The remarkable story of Peter Dmytruk, from RCAF tail gunner to hero of the French Resistance, has been ably told in media such as *Reader's Digest* and the CBC television program *Man Alive*. The story begins like many others. He was born in Radisson, the only son of Ukrainian immigrants, on May 27, 1920. His father ran a Massey-Harris dealership there, later moving to Kamsack, then Wynyard. Leaving high school after grade ten, Peter, too, started work at Massey-Harris as a repairman, meanwhile earning a reputation as a popular, easygoing, well-mannered young man who enjoyed his hockey.

In the summer of 1941 he joined the RCAF, and a year later, after graduating from Bombing and Gunnery school, he was assigned to No. 405 "City of Vancouver" Squadron, flying from the bases of Topcliffe and Leeming, Yorkshire. Returning from a raid on Stuttgart, March 12, 1943, the Lancaster on which Flight Sergeant Dmytruk was the rear gunner (one of the most dangerous positions for any flier) was attacked by a German fighter. According to the navigator on the flight:

> The Messerschmitt pummeled us with 20 mm cannon shells, some of them containing phosphorus which set the tail of our plane on fire. This made Pete a sitting duck for the fighter. We heard him say he was hit but he kept telling us which way the fighter was coming in and his voice grew dimmer and dimmer. After the second attack, the fighter opened us right up from the nose to the stern and I

Dmytruk Lake (57°47' N, 106°58' W), viewed here from the east, is located 190 air miles north of La Ronge, just twenty-five miles north of beautiful Cree Lake. Dmytruk Lake is two miles long, surrounded by sandy glacial deposits and pine and spruce forests, terrain which is typical of the Cree Lake Upland of the Athabasca Plain ecoregion.

Wynyard ●

was wounded and bleeding badly. We then received the order to bail out.

For all his surviving crewmates knew, that was the end of Peter Dmytruk. Back home in Wynyard, the only news his parents received was that he was missing in action.

But the Dmytruk story continues. We don't know the precise circumstances of his 30,000-foot parachute drop into occupied France, or how he managed to travel undetected the four hundred kilometres to the Auvergne region. But it was standard procedure for all air crew to carry money, cloth maps to guide them to the Spanish border, and instructions to contact the French underground. Once in neutral Spanish territory, some airmen were able to return to their squadrons. Peter Dmytruk, however, apparently decided that he would rather fight his war where he was than return to get shot up in the tail of a Lancaster. He earned the trust of the Resistance members, made an immediately positive impression on them, and for ten months joined them in their guerilla operations of resistance to the Nazi occupiers.

It was a dangerous time; they lived in constant fear. But constant, too, was the determination and resourcefulness of the French Resistance. Hiding in the hills of the Auvergne, Dmytruk and his French mates stole supplies, hijacked ammunition trucks, blew up railroads, hid other fallen Allied airmen, and did whatever else the secret life of the Resistance operation required. No raid or ambush was ever too risky for this popular and charismatic man, Peter Dmytruk, who became known as Pierre le Canadien. "The work was tough," one of his comrades, Abel Martinon, recalled after the war. "We slept little in between attacks on French army depots, picking up supplies from parachute drops and provisioning maquis [resistance] groups in the hills. But Pierre was strong, mentally and physically, and he never complained. After a while, we almost stopped thinking of him as Canadian. He was one of us." And Peter, or Pierre, picked up the language too, while he courted a young hairdresser. "The more she talked, the more his French improved," says Monsieur Martinon.

On December 9, 1943, Peter Dmytruk and another man were returning to the village of Martres-de-Veyre after picking up some fuel when they encountered a German roadblock, set up because an ammunition train at the village had been destroyed. Peter and his companion tried to run straight through it in their Citröen but were gunned down, Dmytruk dying instantly. Convinced that they had eliminated the leader of the premier Resistance corps in the area, the Germans spared the village the usual reprisals, including mass executions, often meted out for acts of sabotage. For the people of Martres-de-Veyre, then, Peter Dmytruk's sacrifice of his life earned their eternal gratitude. "The town exists only because Pierre died," one of the townspeople says, many years later.

And these many years later, Peter Dmytruk remains a local and national hero to the French, who have erected a monument to him on the spot where he was killed and have named a street after him. In 1947 the people of France awarded him the Croix de Guerre, and the anniversary of his death is commemorated at his gravesite. He is buried in the communal cemetery in Martres-de-Veyre, located in a valley in mountainous central France. In Saskatchewan he is memorialized by Dmytruk Lake.

Although the story of Peter Dmytruk is taught in French schools, little of it was known in Canada until 1972, when at the initiation of the French, the towns of Wynyard and Martres-de-Veyre were twinned. In the years since, there have been frequent triumphal exchanges of visits by the people of one town to the other. They've learned each other's language, formed enduring friendships and bonds, and, together, celebrated the life and sacrifice of a hero, Peter Dmytruk. ❀

Left: Wynyard Mayor Walter Goodyear and Martres-de-Veyre Mayor Paul Brun at Martres-de-Veyre Cenotaph.

BARRY NEEDHAM

Below left: The monument in Martres-de-Veyre to the memory of Peter Dmytruk (Demytruck)—"Pierre le Canadien."

Below: In honour of hometown hero Peter Dmytruk, Wynyard's Legion displays this plaque and a painting of the French monument.

BARRY NEEDHAM

Dreaver

Dreaver Lake (55°53' N, 104°47' W), viewed here from the west, is located fifty-six air miles north of La Ronge. Located in the Churchill River Upland ecoregion of the Boreal Shield, Dreaver Lake is four miles at its longest point, with deep, clear waters and numerous islands. Its shoreline features many rugged bedrock outcrops. Over the past thirty years, several families have continued to make summer visits to their secluded cabins at Dreaver Lake.

●Mistawasis

The will to serve their country ran strong in two generations of the Dreaver family. Harvey Dreaver's father, Chief Joe Dreaver of the Mistawasis Band, had served in World War I, receiving the Military Medal for his service. Two of Chief Dreaver's brothers also fought in the Battle of Vimy Ridge; one was killed in action as a result, the other died later from his wounds.

As soon as World War II broke out, Chief Dreaver took seventeen young men from his reserve, including three of his own sons, to sign up in Prince Albert. Two daughters were also among the Dreavers that enlisted. Too old himself for overseas service at age forty-eight, Chief Dreaver joined the Veterans Guard to watch over German prisoners of war at Medicine Hat.

Harvey Dreaver, fluent in Cree and English, joined D (code name "Dog") Company of the Regina Rifles when it was first mobilized in June of 1940. Four years later, after training at Dundurn, Saskatchewan, and Debert, Nova Scotia, and at various bases in the Sussex countryside of southern England, he landed on the beaches near the French town of Courseulles-sur-Mer on D-Day.

As Captain (later Lieutenant Colonel) Gordon Brown notes, the landing was difficult for Dog Company, even though the first wave of infantry had already broken through the landing area defenses. The English Channel had never been so bumpy, and many of the men were seasick. Obstacles blocked the paths of the landing crafts, two of which struck mines and exploded. Several soldiers were killed in other landing craft as well, but Harvey Dreaver made it ashore— fewer than half of his company of about 120 men did—to join the rest of the regiment in clearing Courseulles. The Regina Rifles continued inland, taking the village of Reviers about four kilometres south of the beaches and capturing thirty-five enemy prisoners. Harvey Dreaver and his men, notes Captain Brown, had "won their first fire fight with the enemy."

As a lance corporal on D-Day, Harvey Dreaver had responsibility for about five other soldiers. Later, promoted to corporal, that number increased to about ten men. Later still, when he became a platoon sergeant, he often commanded thirty men, as he did in late June and early July when the Regina Rifles prepared to join the assault on Caen. Between Caen and the Canadian front on the morning of July 7 lay the thirteenth-century Abbaye d'Ardenne that, when finally captured at one minute before midnight, would become the scene of one of the Regina Rifles' most famous and costly victories.

Amid the heavy fighting around the abbey and subsequent battles for Falaise, Elbeuf, and Calais, among others, Harvey Dreaver "made a great name for himself," in Gordon Brown's words. "Harvey never

faltered and had become a real Canadian hero. His cool and courageous leadership had helped his Company and the Regina Rifle Regiment to win several key battles."

One such key battle was the battle at the Leopold Canal, described in *Look To Your Front: Regina Rifles, A Regiment at War, 1944-45,* written by Gordon Brown and Terry Copp, as "the worst of the actions the Reginas were in." As part of the battle to clear the Scheldt Estuary and open the port of Antwerp, the particular role of the Seventh Brigade, including the Regina Rifles, was to stage an assault crossing of the Leopold Canal, behind which an experienced and well-equipped German infantry division was garrisoned. Once the crossing was achieved, a relentless counterattack ensued. The situation was "a literal hell," Brown and Copp write. "Both Charlie and Dog companies were attacked with what appeared to be at least a company." Losses were heavy on both sides: "So many dead

Below: D "Dog" Company of the Regina Rifles leaving the Prince Albert train station, July 6, 1940.

and wounded were on Dog company's front that a half-hour truce was called at the Germans' request."

"Canucks Storm Over Canal," declared the headline of the Prince Albert *Daily Herald* for Friday, October 6, 1944. Sergeant Harvey Dreaver was killed that day, the first day of the assault. According to an eyewitness account, Harvey "was looking over a parapet with binoculars when a [sniper's] bullet hit him in the forehead." The account concludes, "Dreaver was a hell of a nice fellow."

Dennis Chisholm, a former comrade, remembers Harvey Dreaver as "a steady and quiet gentleman. He always wore a grin and was never pushy, but he commanded respect from all his men." Harvey's sister Gladys remembers him fondly too. "He always kept an eye on me," she says. "Only now am I accepting his death." Harvey left a widow, Louise, who never remarried, and a daughter, Doris, who was about a year old when he left. Both were present at the memorial service held on the Mistawasis Reserve church in late October 1944. Louise and Doris also took a trip to Europe in 1993 and visited Harvey's grave, an experience that Doris says gave her mother a sense of closure.

Sergeant Harvey Dreaver is buried at Adegem Canadian War Cemetery in Belgium. The Belgian government posthumously awarded him the Belgian Croix de Guerre avec Palme, and Saskatchewan honoured him by naming Dreaver Lake in his memory. Harvey Dreaver also has a place of honour in Buckingham Palace. Gordon Brown recalls that during the Regina Rifle Regiment's training period in England, King George VI and Queen Elizabeth commissioned portraits of aboriginal servicemen from the British Commonwealth. Their request to the Regina Rifle Regiment was reviewed by Brown himself and Colonel Foster Matheson from Prince Albert. Sergeant Harvey Dreaver was chosen. His portrait was prepared, framed, and sent to Buckingham Palace, where it hangs with other portraits from Australia and New Zealand. ✿

Dreger

I n June of 1944, Freddie Dreger's sister Anna went down to the post office in Woodley, Saskatchewan, to mail him a parcel. As usual, it contained candy, soap, and the thing Freddie looked forward to the most in these parcels Anna mailed every two or three weeks—his favourite homemade fudge. A half-hour later came the telegram reporting that Freddie's Canso had been shot down by a U-boat in the North Atlantic. Anna went to the post office to retrieve the parcel, but they wouldn't give it back.

His sister remembers Fred, the youngest of four children, as a kind and gentle boy, a bit of a clown, whom everyone liked. He was happy-go-lucky as a youth, although his freckles apparently caused him so much grief, especially at the hands of the schoolgirls at Minard School, that Freddie went to the doctor to have them removed. According to Dr. Corrigan's playful diagnosis, the freckles were only beauty spots, and Freddie needn't worry.

One of young Dreger's passions in the years before the war was training his dog, Prince, and his pony, Sally, to do tricks. Fred would tie a rope to sawhorses across the driveway and get Sally to jump. Sally could lift a front leg to "shake hands" too, and if the kids stood too close she might grab their toques with her teeth and give them a mighty shake. Another animal around the farm was Fred and Anna's pet heifer. On Sundays in winter they would put harness and sleigh bells on her and hitch her to a sleigh. It took plenty of tugging and persuasion to travel the quarter of a mile to town for a

Woodley

Dreger Lake (55°45' N, 106°45' W), viewed here from the north, is located seventy air miles west of La Ronge. Situated on the Churchill River, Dreger Lake is over four miles in length, and can be accessed from Highway 914, upriver from Sandy Lake.

53

Above: Fred Dreger with childhood companions, Prince and Sally.

Right: Fully amphibious, the Canso could take off or land on ground or water, and could patrol for up to eighteen hours without refueling.

five-cent chocolate bar, but they'd manage it. And if they turned the heifer loose on the way back, she knew how to get home in a hurry.

Anna remembers many other instances of mischief and joy—climbing the roof of the barn, using the lightning rod guy wires for support; or milking the cows and giving most of the cream to the cats; or letting the air out of the elevator man's tires at Hallowe'en. The inevitable scolding in each case hardly deterred them. "It's all a sad memory now," Anna says, "those days Freddie and I got into trouble." Trouble or not, Fred completed grade twelve at Lampman High School. Jobs were hard to come by after that. He worked as a farm labourer in Manitoba and kept up his main hobby, carpentry.

His skills and resourcefulness with wood were remarkable. He'd often go down to the railway tracks and salvage

wood from the grain cars (which were made of wood in those days) to use for the end tables and flower stands he liked to make. A bedroom chair he made for his sister remains a cherished possession to this day, as does a Plexiglas heart he engraved with her initials. But carpentry was not the answer in the scarce-money days before the war, and Freddie wanted to enlist.

He left home to join the air force in September of 1939. "It was a sad day when he left me and Dad and the family," his sister recalls, "even though he would get home for a visit." Fred often sent presents home, too, including a porcelain doll for his goddaughter. After training at Camp Shilo he was stationed at St. Thomas, Ontario, as a navigator. By early 1944 he had re-mustered to flight engineer and was stationed in Reykjavik, Iceland, with RCAF No. 162 Squadron. From there, he and the crew flew hundreds of hours in his Canso aircraft, patrolling for U-boats across the North Atlantic.

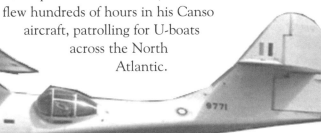

After D-Day, June 6, 1944, U-boats were forced to vacate their French ports in favour of Norwegian ports. Accordingly, No. 162 Squadron of Coastal Command sent some of its Cansos on temporary detachment to Wick, Scotland. From there, Warrant Officer Dreger's Canso, piloted by Flight Lieutenant L. Sherman, sank one U-boat on the eleventh of June, during a twelve-hour operation, and attacked another on the thirteenth of June. Fred Dreger's logbook for that day ends with the ominous words: "A/C/ MISSING." It was learned later that the Canso had been shot down near Alesund, Norway.

Warrant Officer Fred Dreger is commemorated at Runnymede Memorial in Surrey, England, in a spot on Cooper's Hill overlooking the Thames. In Saskatchewan, Dreger Lake is named in his honour. ❀

Above: A humorous certificate presented to airmen who flew in the far north of Europe.

Left: Fred Dreger's logbook, opened to the last page.

Dupré ————————————

Dupré Lake (57°08' N, 109°15' W), viewed here from the north, is located two hundred air miles northwest of La Ronge, about two miles north of the community of Descharme Lake. A shallow lake about three miles long, Dupré Lake is part of the Descharme River, which flows from the Firebag Hills to the mighty Clearwater River.

One of the first jobs Fred Dupré had after finishing his grade thirteen in Kingston, Ontario, was working as a guard at the Kingston Penitentiary. But he didn't much like that kind of work and, being an adventurous soul, went out to Saskatchewan in the 1930s even though he didn't know anyone there. You had to be adventurous to make a go of it in the frontier outpost that was La Ronge, Saskatchewan, at that time. Fred not only found a job, he found a wife, Louise, the daughter of a fur trader manager in La Ronge. They would have two sons—George, born 1933, and William, 1939.

Fred had been a signalman with the active militia in high school, and later served as a radioman/telegrapher in the Royal Canadian Signals Corps. But he was not a man to suffer fools gladly, according to his surviving son, Bill, and he received a discharge from the militia, apparently following an altercation with an officious sergeant. "I think he punched the sergeant," Bill says. Ever willing to try something new, Fred got a job at the gold mining settlement of Goldfields on the north shore of Lake Athabasca near the present-day town of Uranium City, starting as a mucker before qualifying as a miner.

When war broke out, Fred thought he had a duty to go. Better to fight the enemy over there, he reasoned, before they got over here. Furthermore, his father, who had been a sergeant in World War I but did not see any action, had felt badly about not going overseas, and Fred now viewed his own service opportunity as a way to see action for both of them. Too old at thirty-one to be a pilot, Fred trained at No. 2 Bombing and Gunnery School in Mossbank and eventually was posted overseas as a bomb aimer in the crew of a Wellington bomber with RAF No. 166 Squadron.

Louise and the two boys stayed behind, of course, having followed Fred as far as Kingston, where they lived with Fred's mother. All of this was confusing for the youngest boy, Bill, who was two or three when his father went overseas. They'd been close, Fred and his boys. When Fred was building a porch, young Bill helped by carrying nails. Occasionally, Fred would playfully hang him up on a nail. Another time, Bill accidentally bopped his father in the eye, giving him a black eye. After Fred had gone overseas, Bill remembers being told by his mother to "be good, because Dad's coming home."

The pilot of Fred's crew was an Englishman, Bob Hodgson. In his memoir, Hodgson's brother David offers this view of Fred Dupré, who often stayed with the Hodgson family on leave:

At age 34 he was the oldest of the crew, and his experience and maturity must have been a steadying influence on them. He had worked as a radio operator…and could do Morse at a colossal speed. He was about five feet nine tall, and was fast losing his hair. He was a charming avuncular man who had come across to serve in Bomber Command because "the job had to be done."

The memoir goes on to note that the Hodgson crew "remained together as a crew for the whole of their service," developing "enormous personal loyalty to each other, and a remarkable faith in their collective ability to face the inevitably terrifying risks."

Fred Dupré was able to send a couple of letters to his family in Kingston a few days before his death. To his son George, he wrote "Here is ten shillings, which our mother will have changed to Canadian money for you. I thought you might like to buy her a little present for her birthday, on the 16th of April. You can have any

money left over." And on the first day of spring, 1943, he wrote to Louise, telling of some leisure time:

> Went into Grimsby last night with Bob Hodgson. We cycled four or five miles to a station and caught the train. It's better than hitchhiking. Especially for coming back. Saw a show, had supper and a couple of beers and came home. Seems there is nothing to do in any town after about nine thirty. Guess the blackout has something to do with it.

> There's not much more to say, darlin, except thanks for the smokes. I love you, Louise dear. Remember me to the folks and kiss the babies for me.

The Hodgson crew, including Fred Dupré, died on the night of March 29, 1943. They were one of six planes lost that night when seventy-five Wellingtons attacked the industrial centre of Bochum, Germany. A German night fighter intercepted the bomber stream and shot down Hodgson's aircraft near the Dutch village of Schaarsbergen. Initially, the crew was buried in the Moscowa Municipal Cemetery at Schaarsbergen. In 1945, Fred Dupré and the other Canadian in the crew were moved to the Canadian War Cemetery at Groesbeek, ten kilometres southeast of Nijmegen, close to the German border. A Dutch woman, Riny Palm, has cared for the grave for many years.

The inscription on No. 166 Squadron memorial plaque in Kirminton, Lincolnshire, reads: "Ye that live mid England's pastures green, think on us and what might have been." Another memorial is Dupré Lake, located in northwest Saskatchewan and named in honour of Pilot Officer Fred Dupré. ✿

Below: This twin-engined Wellington bomber photographed in 1941 at Pocklington, Yorkshire, would have been much like the Wellington that Fred Dupré flew on with No. 166 Squadron.

LANCE BOMBARDIER **HEINRICH GEORGE DYKE** • L62103 • 1919–1944
PRIVATE **VICTOR EDWARD DYKE** • L92901 • 1921–1944

Dyke

The Dyke boys, Henry and Victor, came from a Lutheran family of six children, five of them boys. Their parents, Jacob and Katharina, had come from Austria in 1911 to homestead in the Oakshela area. Like their siblings, Henry and Victor attended public school at Oakshela and later completed grade twelve at Grenfell, Henry often driving a Model A Silver Coupe to and from school. At the same time, all the kids helped their mother work the farm while Jacob ran a store in Oakshela, just a few miles down the highway.

Henry and Victor were both easygoing boys who got along well with everyone. Victor would take the younger ones to a show in town or for a ride in his '39 Dodge in which he was a bit of a daredevil at times. Henry, red-haired like his brother, was mechanically inclined, able to overhaul a tractor or build a radio (a skill he acquired through a correspondence course). He was a good athlete too, a pitcher who could "throw the ball pretty damn fast," his brother Ernie remembers. Henry's plan was always to take over the home place once his dad and mom retired.

But the war years intervened. Henry enlisted in October 1941, and went overseas about a year later attached to the Forty-fifth Canadian Medium Battery of the Seventh Canadian Medium Regiment. His many letters reflect his thoughtfulness and compassion.

on Christmas in England: "Sure brings back memories, like singing in the choir Christmas eve, setting up the tree and decorating it and the church

Dyke Lake (59°40' N, 108°06' W), viewed here from the west, is located twenty-two air miles northeast of Uranium City, about 320 miles north of La Ronge. Dyke Lake is about one mile in length, and is part of the spectacular Oldman River which descends through the Tazin Lake Upland ecoregion of the Taiga Shield, flowing into Lake Athabasca. Areas ravaged by fire in 1978 are now being rejuvenated with fresh forest growth of spruce and birch.

Oakshela●

a few days before, the happy and expectant look on the children's faces. Seems that's the way it should be, and I hope it will when this is over."

on receiving a parcel from home: "I have a few cookies left but with so many friends, a parcel don't go too far and a person just can't go ahead and eat with all the others sitting around licking their lips."

on visiting relatives in England: "I had breakfast in bed for 7 days. Eggs and all. I said they would spoil me but I must admit it was wonderful."

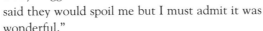

on his unit: "We have a good outfit, proved on schemes to be as good and better usually than any other outfit we've come up against. It's an old outfit—have been organized since '39 and know their work. I'm proud to be one of their members."

on drinking: "Don't worry, Mom. I'm no drunkard— yet, ha ha. No, it's only natural here. Everyone drinks a little, women and all. And they don't behave any worse than back home where they have to sneak it out and drink it on the sly."

on Christianity: "A Christian can be a manly person, not a weakling or a softie."

on worry: "You'd please me a lot if you didn't worry about me. I'll take good care of myself. And

worrying isn't going to do me or you any good. I never worry here. Makes a person too morose and irritable."

on surviving in an artillery unit in France: "I've learned how to dodge and what it is to be scared—things you learn very fast."

Although the exact details of Henry Dyke's death on August 10, 1944, are not known, it likely occurred during Operation Totalize, the Allied offensive designed to break through German positions astride the Caen-Falaise road. A few months later, one of his comrades wrote to Henry's mother: "Henry and I met nearly two years ago in Borden, England. We came to this regiment together and worked, ate and slept together ever since. He was certainly a grand partner and N.C.O. He was indeed a true friend and if we were all like him there would be no more wars." Henry Dyke was buried in the Bretteville-sur-Laize Canadian War Cemetery in France.

Victor enlisted about a year after Henry, travelling to Moose Jaw with a pal from Grenfell to join the RCAF. "Next thing we heard," Ernie Dyke recalls, "he's in Regina and signed up for the army. Perhaps his eyeglasses prevented him from becoming a pilot." Joining the Royal Canadian Engineers, Victor was posted overseas in June 1943 and transferred to the South Saskatchewan Regiment which was short of infantrymen. In a letter home, Victor told of an unexpected family reunion during his ocean voyage:

> Boy was I ever glad and also surprised when one morning I was up on the deck strolling around, and somebody called me by my first name. So I turned around and lo and behold there was Uncle Oscar. Well you could have knocked me over with a feather.

In England Victor bought himself a bicycle and had a girlfriend and, like his brother, enjoyed parcels from home. Cigarettes, toothpaste, soap, and baking were the favourite items to receive. He did make contact with Henry in England, and judging by Henry's letters, Victor seemed "to be getting fed up" by what must have seemed to be endless waiting to see action.

But by October of 1944, Victor's regiment, now in the thick of the action, had moved into Holland as part of the general operation known as The Battle of the Scheldt, designed to open the port of Antwerp. Victor Dyke was killed on October 13, when he and a comrade tried to get close enough to a machine gun emplacement to toss a grenade at it. He was buried at Bergen-Op-Zoom Canadian War Cemetery just a few kilometres inside the border of the Netherlands from France.

In northwestern Saskatchewan, Dyke Lake is named in honour of brothers Henry and Victor Dyke. 🏵

Left: Bombing on the Caen–Falaise road during Operation Totalize, August 1944.

Einarson

FLIGHT SERGEANT **HAROLD BJORN EINARSON** • R87296 • 1920–1942

FLIGHT LIEUTENANT **JOHANN WALTER EINARSON** • J17276 • 1920–1944

Einarson Lake (57°21' N, 106°06' W), viewed here from the north, is located 160 air miles northwest of La Ronge. Situated just ten miles east of beautiful Cree Lake in the Athabasca Plain ecoregion of the Boreal Shield, Einarson Lake is four miles in length, with clear blue waters and sandy shores.

L ike many in the area around Wynyard, Saskatchewan, the Einarson twins, Harold and Walter, came from an Icelandic-Canadian family. Both parents had been born in Iceland; the twins were born in Wynyard on November 20, 1920. During the 1920s, the family lived in Elfros, operating a hardware and furniture store. When the store went bankrupt in 1930, the family moved back to Wynyard, where the boys finished their secondary schooling. By 1935, both parents had died, and Walter and Harold moved in with a sister and her husband.

"The twins were inseparable during those years," remembers a boyhood chum, Barry Needham (himself a Spitfire pilot during World War II). "They were very close, almost identical in appearance. You had to get to know them to tell them apart." They were teammates in hockey, competitors in track and field—always ready for sporting events of any kind. Another interest the twins shared was in flying. Barry Needham recalls taking his first airplane ride in a farmer's field. The Einarsons, too, may have been boyhood aviators. In any event, after two years at the University of Saskatchewan, they both enlisted in the RCAF in 1940.

The twins' logbooks, compiled from the time of their very first training flight on a Tiger Moth to their last on a Lancaster bomber, give us the details of their service careers. These careers were, not surprisingly, closely intertwined in the beginning. Both trained at No. 15 Elementary Flight Training School in Regina, beginning in May 1941; both moved up to the Harvard trainers at No. 11 Service Flying Training School in Yorkton in July. By November 1941 they were stationed at Honington, Suffolk, flying the Oxfords, and a month later they were both posted to No. 19 Operational Training Unit (OTU) in Kinloss, Morayshire, training on the Whitley V. The final stop in the training process for the twins, as for many other fliers, was the Heavy Conversion Unit, the finishing school in which they trained on the mighty four-engine Lancasters they would use on operations.

Harold Einarson was killed in action September 10, 1942, while flying with No. 207 Squadron. His Lancaster bomber had taken off from the RAF station at Syerston. Flight Sergeant Harold Einarson has no known grave, but other members of his crew are buried in Jutland, Denmark.

Walter Einarson, posted to RAF No. 44 Squadron, flew his first operation, a raid on Bremen, in July of 1942. Many more successful operations followed; "above average," reads the "Assessment of Ability" in his log book. In the spring of 1943, during the early days of No. 6 Group, the only RCAF Squadron Group within RAF Bomber Command, Walter was back at OTU, this time as an instructor. At about the same time, he was awarded the Distinguished Flying Medal:

This pilot has displayed the greatest possible determination to locate and bomb his target on all possible occasions. He has taken part in many long and dangerous raids on a variety of targets in Germany and Italy including the recent raids on Berlin. He has also secured good photographs. His calmness and courage have inspired great confidence in his crew and contributed to the success of many missions.

Later that year Walter received his commission and embarked on another tour of duty, flying a Lancaster from the Waddington base in Lincolnshire. His logbook entry from November 26, 1943, notes "collided with Lanc, severely damaged." Soon thereafter came another award citation, this one for the Distinguished Flying Cross:

This officer has completed a very large number of sorties, including five attacks on Berlin. On the last occasion, one night in November, 1943, his aircraft was hit by anti-aircraft fire and sustained damage. Nevertheless, Flying Officer Einarson pressed home his attack. Soon after the bombs had been released the aircraft was struck, the starboard wing tip and part of the aileron were torn away and the aircraft went into a steep dive. Flying Officer Einarson succeeded in regaining control and afterwards flew safely to an airfield in this country. Throughout his

The Einarson twins: Harold on the left, and Walter on the right.

tour of operations, this officer has invariably displayed a high degree of skill, courage and determination.

By late 1943 and early 1944, Bomber Command had intensified its focus on Berlin. Flight Lieutenant Einarson's Lancaster, flying from his base in Waddington, was a frequent participant in operations on Germany, including raids on Stettin, Leipzig, and Stuttgart, in addition to those on the "big city" of Berlin. By the time the focus of Bomber Command had shifted from the Battle of Berlin to D-Day invasion support, about five hundred bombers and their crews had been lost. One of these was Flight Lieutenant J. Walter Einarson and crew, lost over Augsburg on

February 25, 1944. The last entry in his logbook, an entry inevitably made by someone else, says simply "Missing."

Walter Einarson is buried in the Choloy War Cemetery in France; his brother Harold is memorialized at the Runnymede Memorial in Surrey. Although there are no family members left to remember the Einarson twins, in Saskatchewan, Einarson Lake is named in honour of Harold and Walter Einarson. ❀

64

Fleury

The L27 prefix to his service number signifies that Conrad Fleury was one of the original Regina Rifles to enlist when the regiment was raised in the summer of 1940. Conrad's father ran a timber mill in Green Lake, but the family, including Conrad and his four sisters, moved around to various communities in the Meadow Lake area. Conrad would have joined D (Dog) Company of the regiment in Prince Albert, or B (Baker) Company in North Battleford.

The original recruits, about one thousand in total, trained together at Dundurn, Saskatchewan, through the summer of 1940. In September they boarded the trains for the long trip cross-country to Debert, Nova Scotia, and a brand new base they helped build, clearing seven square miles of land and constructing barracks. The big Debert air base was right next door.

In August of 1941 it was time to ship out overseas. The *Empress of Russia*, still smelling of the over-ripe sugar cane it had been carrying, carried the "Johns," as the Regina Rifles were known, to Glasgow, Scotland. A train ride later they'd arrived at the huge Ramillies Barracks at Aldershot in the south of England and the beginning of almost three years of exercises in preparation for the inevitable invasion of mainland Europe. As vital as the basic battle drill and battalion training was, "much of it was of a dreary, monotonous and repetitive nature," according to one description.

Sergeant Conrad Fleury landed in Normandy with the Regina Rifles on D-Day. Over the next ten months,

Green Lake

Fleury Creek (54°36' N, 108°34' W), viewed here from the south, is located 130 air miles southwest of La Ronge in Meadow Lake Provincial Park. Accessible from Highway 904 at Flotten Lake, Fleury Creek flows for fifteen miles from the Mostoos Escarpment of the Boreal Plain.

Sergeant Fleury, in charge of a Support Company anti-tank platoon—a half-dozen men and a carrier pulling a six-pound gun—fought in all the regiment's battles from the tentative beachhead on the Green sector of Nan beach all the way to Germany. Bretteville-l'Orgeuilleuse, Carpiquet, the Abbey of Ardenne, Calaise, The Scheldt, Moyland Wood, the clearing of western Holland—Conrad Fleury served in all those actions, and survived them.

"He was my Sergeant," says Gordon Wilson. "We dug a lot of slit trenches together. With me at six feet three inches and Fleury at about five foot three, it was a Mutt and Jeff deal." Wilson tells a couple of stories about the good buddy he calls simply "Fleury." Alternating two-hour shifts on guard duty one night, Wilson would light a match in Fleury's face to wake him up. Fleury's response

would be to stick his revolver—the only weapon he ever carried—into Wilson's face, saying he couldn't ever be too sure who it was waking him up. On another occasion, at Leopold Canal, with the bullets flying every which way over their slit trench, the two of them got ready to move to a safer position. That was an easier matter for Fleury, armed only with his Smith & Wesson handgun, than it was for Wilson, with his rifle and Bren gun and related gear. He asked Fleury for a little help, but the only response was a suggestion to throw the rifle in the canal if he couldn't carry it. "That's what I did. It's there still," Wilson says. And near Nijmegen, the two of them kept warm one morning with some sparring. "He gave me a belt on one arm and I gave him one. I could see he'd done some boxing," Wilson says.

Eventually Gordon Wilson was wounded and left the regiment. He never did hear for sure what happened to Conrad Fleury. But in 1995 while strolling through the Holten Canadian War Cemetery in Holland, Wilson saw Fleury's gravestone. Remembering the happy-go-lucky, likeable, French-speaking "little squirt" he'd served with, Wilson laid a flag and poppies on Fleury's grave.

In April 1945, the Regina Rifles, part of the Third Canadian Infantry Division, had the task of clearing

Below: King George VI and Queen Elizabeth review the Regina Rifle regiment, 1940s.

the area from Deventer north to Steenweik, Holland, and beyond to the North Sea. It was the final fortnight of the war; the end was clearly in sight. Still, as historian C.P. Stacey notes, there were "spasmodic exchanges of machine gun, mortar and artillery fire." One such exchange claimed the life of Conrad Fleury on April 22, 1945. Robert McWillie, who served as a dispatch driver attached to Sergeant Fleury's platoon, recalls that the platoon had taken up a position in the southeast edge of the town of Scheemda. Setting up a six-pounder anti-tank gun in the yard of a house and using a stone shed as an observation post, they could see smoke rising from the enemy's position in a field adjacent to the town. "We also realized," McWillie says, "that the enemy had us under surveillance."

Conrad Fleury was manning the observation post while the others ate lunch. Moments later three enemy eighty-eight shells struck the anti-tank gun, the shed just above the observation window, and the house. "Conrad was in the stone shed with field glasses watching the terrain through a small window," McWillie recalls. "We carried him to a nearby first aid station but it was already too late."

Fleury Creek in Saskatchewan is named in honour of Conrad Fleury, one of the last Canadians to die in the liberation of Holland. ❁

Flynn

Flynn Lake (56°07' N, 103°38' W), viewed here from the west, is located one hundred air miles northeast of La Ronge. Accessible by canoe from Brabant Lake, which is located on Highway 102, Flynn Lake is almost two miles in length. Dense forests stand green and tall, evidence that in recent times forest fires have not occurred here.

John Flynn, a man of dual citizenship, had roots on the Canadian prairies but served in the United States army. John's parents, Sarah and John, had met in Crosby, North Dakota. Sarah McGough was a schoolteacher there, and John had moved to Crosby in 1915 to work as a bricklayer. In 1916, shortly after their marriage, they moved north to Canada to the Flynn homestead near Seven Persons, Alberta, south of Medicine Hat. The younger John Flynn, the eldest of six boys and two girls in the family, was born at Manyberries in 1917. It was tough to make a go of a southern Alberta farm in those dry years before irrigation. Drought conditions forced the family to move to Creighton and finally to Aylesbury, Saskatchewan, where they farmed throughout the war years.

John took his grade eight at Boule Creek School south of Creighton and finished his high school in St. Paul, Minnesota. He had moved down there to live with his grandmother and work in the family construction business, McGough Construction. The business was successful enough that John was able to continue with the company after high school until he was drafted and, in April of 1941 at the age of twenty-four, inducted into the U.S. army as a rifleman in the 164th infantry. Three of his brothers would later serve in the war, their dual allegiances reflected in the fact that two of them served in the Canadian forces.

After basic training at Camp Clarborne, Louisiana, Private John Flynn shipped out for action on

Guadalcanal—a small, mountainous island, covered in rainforest, near the southern end of the Solomon Islands in the South Pacific. Guadalcanal was of significant strategic importance to both the Japanese and the Americans as they fought for control of the entire South Pacific area. The Japanese had established bases in the northern Solomons and had built an airfield on Guadalcanal. No further expansion of the already formidable Japanese position could be permitted. Accordingly, on August 7, 1942, the U.S. marines invaded the island. The army, which landed two months later, was given the job of protecting a newly constructed airfield, Henderson Field. The six-month Guadalcanal campaign—consisting of seven major naval engagements, dozens of clashes ashore, and almost daily air combat—would eventually result in the first major U.S. victory against the Japanese after a succession of defeats following Pearl Harbor. But the cost in human lives was high. Some 24,000 ground troops were killed on the island. One of these was

Private John Flynn, killed in action on October 25, 1942, during the Battle for Henderson Field. He'd been on the island for less than two weeks.

John Flynn spent only a single harvest season in the Aylesbury area. But his family was established there, and the town remembers John as one of its own, having included his photograph in the Aylesbury Community Hall among those of other casualties of war. The Aylesbury community would have been aware of the telephone call that John Flynn Sr. received in late 1942 as he supervised his threshing crew, getting the crop off one last farm. He was called into town to pick up a telegram with the news of his eldest son's death far away in the South Pacific.

A military Guard of Honour was present at the burial of his son in Eckelson, North Dakota, his paternal grandparents' home. In Saskatchewan, Flynn Lake, located northeast of La Ronge, honours the memory of Private John Flynn. ❀

Fontaine

Fontaine Island (57°45' N, 102°28' W), viewed here from the south, is located near the northwest shore of Reindeer Lake, 220 air miles northeast of La Ronge. Fontaine Island is four miles long and Reindeer Lake is 120 miles long.

●Claydon

During the first ten days that followed the Normandy landings [June 6, 1944]," writes Howard Margolian in his 1998 book, *Conduct Unbecoming,* "156 Canadian officers, NCOs, and rank-and-file troops, all members of the 3rd Canadian Infantry Division, were deliberately and brutally murdered after capture by elements of the German formation that opposed them, the 12th SS Panzer Division [known as] 'Hitler Youth.' " Thirty of the Canadian POWs were murdered near the French villages of Authie and Buron on June 7, according to the Supreme Headquarters of the Allied Expeditionary Force (SHAEF) Court of Inquiry. One of those men, a tank driver/mechanic with the Twenty-seventh Armoured Regiment, the Sherbrooke Fusiliers, was Trooper George Fontaine.

In the Occupational History form he completed upon enlisting in March of 1942, George Fontaine described himself as having been a farm labourer ever since he'd completed grade twelve at the school near Dollard, in southwestern Saskatchewan, where his family farmed. His hobby was "training horses," he noted on the form, adding that he "plays most games, reads a good deal, fiction adventure, gets along well with people, has five brothers and four sisters, is the seventh in the family." His strengths, according to his self-assessment, were those appropriate to a farm labourer. He was a truck driver and tractor operator. He could drive a car and repair a motor. And he had nine years of farm working experience at the home farm and in southern Alberta. Did he feel competent to operate a farm? Yes. Did he wish to engage in farming after the war? Again, yes.

But first came the war. George "wishes to take up mechanics in the army," notes one of his enlistment forms, and in early 1942 he was sent to a basic training course in Camrose, Alberta. By the end of the year he'd been attached to the Sherbrooke Fusiliers—a suitable posting for the bilingual farmer from Saskatchewan—and had made the voyage overseas. "I had a real nice trip over," he wrote in November, soon after arriving in Gourock, Scotland. "I should have been a sailor because I was never even seasick." And once a farmer, always a farmer: "How's good old western Canada these days?" he writes. "Even if this country is awfully pretty, the rolling prairie looks darn good too."

The plan of attack for the Sherbrooke Fusiliers on D-Day was to land on the White sector of Nan beach and press inland as far the high ground and airfield at Carpiquet, about ten kilometres from the beach. Part of the Ninth Brigade Group, the Sherbrookes with their armoured carriers and Stuart tanks (an American-built lightly armoured reconnaissance tank known as the swiftest on the Normandy battlefield) got as far as Villons before dark. By early afternoon next day the advance guard had taken Buron and Authie and was in sight of Carpiquet, but the expected counterattacks finally materialized in the form of the Twelfth SS Panzer Division. So successful were these counterattacks that the Canadians were driven back from Buron and Authie, with the result that the primary objective of Carpiquet would remain in German hands for another month. The Sherbrooke Fusiliers suffered twenty-six casualties on the seventh of June and the loss of twenty-five to thirty tanks. The survivors would live to fight another day, but "for their comrades who had

been captured during the battle for Authie," writes Howard Margolian, "the afternoon and evening hours of June 7 would bring horrors greater than anything they had experienced on the battlefield."

The exact circumstances of the murder of George Fontaine, taken prisoner near Authie on June 7, 1944, are not known. According to Howard Margolian, the murder took place during one of two incidents. In one incident, six prisoners were taken into the kitchen of Mme. Godet, a resident of Authie, and shot execution-style in the back of the head. In the other, the officer at the head of an SS detachment opened fire on a column of prisoners he encountered on the road between Authie and Cussy. All that the Fontaines back in Claydon, Saskatchewan, knew, until many years later, was that George had been killed in action the day after D-Day.

Upon hearing the news of her son's death, George's mother, Delia Fontaine, was so distraught that another son, home on leave from his own army training, did not tell her of his own imminent trip overseas. Fortunately, the war ended before he had to go.

Trooper George Fontaine, first buried in a mass grave at Authie, now lies buried at the Beny-sur-Mer Canadian War Cemetery northwest of Caen, near the road on which he travelled the last day of his life. Fontaine Island, on Reindeer Lake in northern Saskatchewan, is named in his honour. ✿

Below: The badge of the Sherbrooke Fusiliers Regiment.

COURTESY OF THE CANADIAN FORCES

Gedak

Gedak Lake (57°43' N, 109°25' W), viewed here from the north, is located 230 air miles northwest of La Ronge. Almost three miles in diameter, Gedak Lake is accessible from Highway 955, about fifty miles south of the Cluff Lake mine site. This is a sandy area of the Athabasca Plain ecoregion, where vast stands of black spruce are prominent.

●Estevan

The Gedak family, like many on the prairies, had roots in Europe—Romania in the case of Anton Gedak, a blacksmith. It was April of 1912, the night the *Titanic* sank, when Anton crossed the Atlantic on a ship that passed within fifty miles of the *Titanic*, close enough to detect its SOS signals. Anton eventually settled in Estevan, Saskatchewan, where he worked on the CPR and for another blacksmith before setting up his own business. His family grew to eight children, five of them boys. The youngest of the eight was Joseph. Years later, as the pilot of a Stirling bomber, Joseph was sensitive to the fact that many of his parents' relatives would be on the receiving end of the bombing operation. "It was like dropping bombs on my own people," he said.

In Estevan in the early 1940s, all the young guys had been joining the Forces and heading overseas, so that's what young Joseph did. He had been an above-average student at Estevan Collegiate Institute and before that at Valleyview Public School, an altar boy for years, and generally a popular, athletic fellow (although not a big man—about 5'10" or so) who enjoyed hockey, boxing, and ball. His nickname was "Babe" but, as his brother Matt remembers, he couldn't hit the ball quite like Babe Ruth.

Dances, run by the Green brothers, were popular social events. The Estevan Pavilion in River Park hosted many of the finest orchestras of the day. Better yet, the dances attracted carloads of girls from Crosby, North Dakota, just across the line. Five or six girls would come up, or Joe and his pals would drive their '29 Oldsmobile to Crosby for dances down there. "The dances were once a week. Several marriages resulted," Matt Gedak says now, nodding at his wife Lillian, one of those Crosby girls. Joseph Gedak, too, had a girlfriend in Crosby. "I don't know if it would have worked out or not," Matt says, but Joe continued to visit her even after he joined up, each time requesting the standard permission at the border to enter the United States "for the purpose of visiting friends and relatives."

Joe worked at Oliphant's grocery store before he enlisted, then at the Jesse Brothers meat market. He joined the army first, switching to the air force later, training at Yorkton, Brandon, Prince Albert, and Edmonton. By his twentieth birthday, May 11, 1942, Joseph Gedak was posted to RCAF No. 90 Squadron in England. His letters home told of leaves spent in London, "where I pounded the pavement," he wrote to Matt and Lillian, "until my shoes wore out, so I had to scrounge a new pair, without coupons at that." He was able to spend at least one of his leaves in London with some of his old pals from the Crosby dances, Jimmy and Barney. It was "just like the old days," he wrote, "but we missed the rest of our gang." And he congratulated Matt and Lillian on the birth of their son Vince, noted that he was "still waiting for that cigar from Mutzy [Matt]," and promised to see his new nephew soon.

One of Joe's letters enclosed a clipping from the London *Evening Standard*:

> Flight Sergeant Joseph Gedak has good excuse for throwing a party in the sergeants' mess at his bomber station on May 11. That day is his 21st birthday. But Gedak has something more than that to celebrate, for he survived the mid-air collision when his big four-engine Stirling, in the RAF raid

on southwest Germany on Saturday night, collided with a Junkers 88.

The *Standard* story went on to provide more details of the dramatic scene:

> "'We're done for,' the Rear Gunner yelled down the intercom to Flt. Sgt. Gedak. Though he thought so, he poured bullets in the Junkers, and watched it go down. The Stirling kept aloft. Gedak wobbled the control column to see whether the aircraft would answer. It did. 'It's Ok,' he said. 'We're going on.'"

Gedak and his crew successfully completed its operation that night.

A few nights later, Bomber Command attacked Duisburg, in the German Ruhr Valley. Although the raid was so successful that no further raids on the city were considered necessary, the costs were high. Thirty-four of the 572 bombers failed to return that night, May 12–13, 1943. One of them was Joe Gedak's Stirling.

"Everybody lived in hope that we'd hear from him," Joe's brother Matt says. "We didn't believe he wouldn't show up." But his brother's body was never recovered. Pilot Officer Joseph Gedak is commemorated at the Runnymede Memorial in Surrey, England, and by Gedak Lake north of Meadow Lake in Saskatchewan. He is remembered, too, by Stacey Gedak, age twelve, who after seeing his name on the cenotaph in Estevan wrote a poem for "my great uncle Joe." "It was kind of neat to know about him," Stacey says. ⊛

Gordon—

LEADING SICK BERTH ATTENDANT **CYRIL JAMES ALBERT GORDON** • V47603 • 1914–1943
FLIGHT SERGEANT **MILTON GEORGE GORDON** • R120737 • 1921–1943

Gordon Lake (55°50' N, 106°28' W), viewed here from the north, is located seventy miles west of La Ronge, just five miles north of the Churchill River. The lake is about six miles long, and its clear waters provide excellent trout and jackfish habitat. Gordon Bay is about four miles in length and is situated at the south end of Gordon Lake. Since 1980, when Highway 914 to the Key Lake mine site was opened, there has been boat access at Gordon Bay.

The Gordon family was well-known in the Webb district, where Francis and Ethel had moved from New Brunswick in 1909. The farm was the family's main focus, but all seven children were also encouraged to become involved in the life of the community—church, town, and school. Certainly Francis and Ethel did. Ethel became known as an expert seamstress and, later in her life, a member of the Remembrance Association of Silver Cross Women of Canada. Francis, or Frank as he was better known, served as leader of the Junior Grain Club, an elder and steward at the United Church, a councillor in the Municipality of Webb, and for many years a trustee on the local school board.

For the children, life followed the usual seasonal cycles. Summer would bring strawberry and ice cream socials and baseball—the Gordon boys often comprising most of a team. Winter meant hockey and the annual Christmas concert. The Gordons were all educated at Prosperous Valley School, a couple of miles from the farm, and Webb School in town. Cyril, the fourth oldest, left the farm at age twenty-three to seek work in Ontario, eventually settling at Whitby, where in 1939 he started nurse's training with one of his sisters, Alma. Milton, seven years younger than Cyril and the youngest in his family, stayed at home until 1941, when at age twenty he joined the RCAF and went off to Regina to begin Elementary Flying Training School.

Milton's career in the air force was relatively brief. Going overseas in 1942, he was posted as an observer with No. 21 Operational Training Unit and had acquired the nickname "Flash" after the comic strip action hero Flash Gordon. Like many other young airmen, Milton was killed before seeing action in an operational unit. On June 6, 1943, just before his twenty-second birthday, Milton Gordon died in a Mitchell bomber taking off on a training flight. The unit had just received the Mitchells to replace the Venturas they had been using; June 6 was the day of the first instructional flight— take-offs and landings only. The lone survivor of

the crash, Gordon Hewatt, described what happened:

> Flash and I asked if we could go along just for the ride. The runway was the shortest on the field but we should have cleared the field with many feet to spare. For some reason we did not get airborne soon enough with the result that when we reached the edge of the field our wheels caught a small hedge. This in itself would have meant nothing had there not been a Ventura parked in a dispersal point beyond the hedge. The port half of the tail surface was completely severed by the Ventura propeller. This sent us into a spin and after that I know nothing else except that when I did escape it was too late. The others had all been killed.

Flight Sergeant Milton Gordon was buried in the nearby town of Swanton Morley, Norfolk, in the All Saints Churchyard.

Cyril Gordon, meanwhile, graduated as a registered nurse in 1942 and immediately joined the Royal Canadian Navy Volunteer Reserve. Promoted and given charge of a ward in the Halifax naval hospital, he chose duty at sea and soon found himself as a leading sick berth attendant on HMCS *St. Croix*. The doctor on board was Surgeon Lieutenant William Lyon Mackenzie King, nephew and namesake of the prime minister.

The *St. Croix* was one of seven over-age destroyers that had been loaned to the Canadian Navy by the United States. Built for World War I conditions, these destroyers, in the words of Joseph Schull's account of Canadian naval operations, *Far Distant Ships*, "were to remain to the end of their not inglorious careers seagoing purgatories of which those who sailed in them still speak with mingled horror and affection." It was a useful ship, nonetheless—an important component in the six-year battle along the convoy routes in the North Atlantic. In the summer of 1942 it had earned praise for its pursuit and sinking of one of the U-boats that, in the words of the Regina *Leader-Post*, "preyed on trans-ocean convoys."

On September 12, 1943, the *St. Croix* set out from Britain as one of eleven ships in support of a sixty-three-ship convoy. As usual, the ships attracted what Schull calls "a growing swarm" of U-boats. When the

Upper left: Milton Gordon

Lower left: Cyril Gordon

St. Croix detached from the support group to investigate an aircraft sighting southwest of Iceland on the twentieth of September, it was fatally wounded by two torpedoes. "Am leaving the office" was the cryptic message received by the British frigate *Itchen* a few miles away. That was the last message the *St. Croix* sent. As it took on a heavy list, preparations for abandoning ship were carried out. "But a third torpedo struck the stern of the ship," Schull writes, "and there was a terrific explosion. Flames vaulted skyward; and within three minutes the destroyer was gone, taking with her the commanding officer and many of the crew." Before eighty-one survivors could be rescued by the *Itchen*, they had spent thirteen hours in the freezing waters of the North Atlantic. Their rescue lasted only a few hours until the *Itchen* was also sunk by a U-boat.

Cyril Gordon was one of 147 men from the *St. Croix* lost at sea. "Their graves are unknown but their memory shall endure," says the engraving on the Halifax monument. In northern Saskatchewan, Gordon Lake and Gordon Bay were named in honour of Milton and Cyril Gordon, respectively. ✿

Right: HMCS *St. Croix*

NAVAL MUSEUM OF ALBERTA

Below: Mitchell bomber

SASKATCHEWAN ARCHIVES BOARD / RA9613 (2)

Graham

MAJOR **KENNETH LAURIE GRAHAM** • 1920–1944

Kenneth Graham's leadership qualities would have been apparent to the people who knew him in Maple Creek. For one thing, his father Melvyn had been a career army man, an officer in World War I who had received the Military Cross and been mentioned in Dispatches. Like his sisters Jeanne and Maureen, who played women's hockey on the outdoor rink at the south end of town, Ken was athletic. A popular, smart young fellow, Ken had not only completed high school in Maple Creek, where his mother Margaret ran the post office after his father died in 1930, but had also taken some post-secondary studies at Notre Dame College and a radio course in Toronto. "He was probably headed for university eventually," says his nephew, Graham Heard. Or he might have become a writer; during his teenage years, he wrote many humorous stories about cowboys or soldiers for his mother.

Whatever the future might have held for Ken Graham, first came military service. He was in a hurry to join up, so he chose the army over the air force, and his service record details a rapid rise. Before his twentieth birthday, he was commissioned as second lieutenant with the 16th/22nd Saskatchewan Horse; he was promoted to lieutenant later in 1940 and to captain in 1942. He was appointed adjutant to the regiment in July 1942 and embarked for Britain on June 16, 1943. The fact that he was selected as adjutant provides further evidence of his capabilities as an officer. As chief administrative officer, Captain Graham

Graham Lake (58°27' N, 102°04' W), viewed here from the north, is located 260 air miles northeast of La Ronge, near the Saskatchewan/Manitoba border. Situated in the Neultin Lake Plain of the Taiga Shield, Graham Lake is over five miles long and is connected by numerous creeks to other large bodies of water.

Maple Creek

77

was responsible for meeting all regimental needs in terms of personnel, supplies, and equipment, mail service, recovery of the wounded, officers' conduct and discipline, and so on. In short, he made the 16/22 run.

His first impressions of England were most favourable: "I used to think the English poets thought a little too highly of their country, but England really did knock me for a loop. The variation in the country is wonderful and all the people have been more than swell to us." During his leisure time, Captain Graham preferred the company of a family of English nobility to the nightlife of London. Perhaps it was his love of horses—his love of all animals, in fact—that cemented his relationship with the family that informally adopted him. His father had raised sulky horses, and young Ken was a fine horseman himself in the English tradition. In any case, he spent many of his leaves in the south of England in the company of nobility, at one point riding a polo pony belonging to the cousin of the Duke of Gloucester. "So I feel quite snobbish these days," he told his mother.

Major Graham, as he was entitled to be addressed after January of 1944, was attached to the Seventy-ninth British Armoured Division in the months before D-Day. The British were short of officers at the time,

Right: Ken Graham in 1939 with his sister Jeanne (left) and his mother Margaret (right).

and they frequently borrowed Canadian officers, especially those as proven as Ken Graham. At home, a newspaper report later described the importance of Major Graham's particular abilities:

> Tens of thousands of Canadian, British and American troops were trained for the D-Day amphibious landing by two Saskatchewan officers [including Major Ken Graham]…who were recognized experts in warfare over sea, river and other water obstacles. "They were the brains behind successful river crossings by amphibious craft," said the military affairs branch of the ministry of information. For nine months they trained Allied forces for the D-Day operation. They made an intensive study of tides, embankments, winds and currents which all had to be taken into account.

That D-Day operation was ultimately a success, of course, and soon thereafter Major Graham's service career took another turn.

He was attached to the Staffordshire Yeomanry—

its origins as a cavalry regiment must have seemed particularly appropriate to the horseman, Ken Graham—and on September 8, 1944, he landed in continental Europe, something he'd been yearning for since the Second Front had opened three months earlier. Soon he was part of the Battle of the Scheldt, the difficult struggle to secure access to the port of Antwerp for the Allies. In a letter home, he marveled at "the endless stream of tanks, guns, and vehicles moving up and…the constant drone of our aeroplanes overhead all day, the full meaning of the words 'mechanization and mobility.' " Major Graham himself was mechanized and mobile, for the Staffordshire Yeomanry was an armoured regiment now, the so-called "mailed fist" of the British army.

A month later he was attached to the Thirtieth Armoured Brigade headquarters in a staff position he held until the time of his death. Major Graham was killed on November 1, 1944, while riding in an amphibious vehicle that struck a land mine near the Holland-Belgium border. "During the time he was with us," wrote his commanding officer, "he did a great deal of invaluable work for us and had made a great many friends in the regiment."

Like hundreds of others who died in northwest Belgium, Major Kenneth Graham is buried in Adegem Canadian War Cemetery, Belgium. In the extreme northeast corner of Saskatchewan lies Graham Lake, named in his honour. ✿

Left: Ken Graham's original gravesite at Adegem Canadian Cemetery.

Grant

Grant Bay (55°17' N, 104°12' W), viewed here from the south, is located forty-five air miles east of La Ronge. The bay is situated at the north end of Big Whitemoose Lake; from here, the Whitemoose River flows for another fifteen miles to the Churchill River. This area is rich in wildlife, with excellent pickerel fishing. In 1964, members of the Grant family visited Grant Bay and participated in the filming of a CBC documentary. At that time, a memorial plaque was placed at the site.

Duncan Grant was something of a movie star on Canadian theatre screens in the summer of 1943. A series of films called "Canada Carries On, " produced by the National Film Board, was being shown to boost the war effort. Because he had achieved an international reputation—and a Distinguished Flying Cross—for his successful attacks on the Nazi railroad system in occupied France, Flying Officer Grant was a natural for a segment in one of the films, the one called "Train Busters." His blonde good looks were an asset too. "Champion Train Buster on Local Screen," boasted a headline of the *Watrous Manitou*. And there he was, on the screen of the Roxy Theatre in Watrous: Duncan Grant in a briefing session, chatting with his colleagues, climbing into his Mustang—all narrated with appropriate urgency by Lorne Greene.

Among the audience in Watrous was a girl named Norma. She and Duncan (who was known as "Bitsy" for his diminutive stature) had gone together before he left high school to join the air force in September of 1940. Norma had given him a cameo ring, which he wanted for good luck, and she could see the ring on his finger as he waved from the cockpit of his Mustang. Seeing him on the screen at the Roxy surely reminded her of many happy times together—playing tennis, cycling to Manitou Beach, dancing at Danceland, strolling through the gardens behind the Bessborough Hotel in Saskatoon when Duncan went in to enlist. Many years later she still remembers Duncan as a handsome, active, easygoing fellow—a sportsman, photographer, artist.

The Grant family hadn't been long in Watrous. Duncan's father, William, who worked as a radio engineer for CBK, had moved his two youngest children there— Duncan and his younger sister Barbara—in 1939, after having spent the previous sixteen years in Calgary in private broadcasting. By the time war broke out, a tradition of military service had long been established in the Grant family. Duncan's father, a veteran of the Royal Flying Corps in World War I, would re-enlist in World War II and serve as a signals expert for the RCAF in Ottawa. Duncan's two brothers, William and Robert, had already enlisted in the army before the family moved to Watrous. Both served overseas with the Canadian Signal Corps. And Duncan himself had been a sea cadet in Calgary.

Early in 1941, Duncan, just eighteen years old, was off to Elementary Flying Training School in Regina and, shortly thereafter, to Service Flying Training School in Yorkton. "I guess I finally reached one of my great ambitions," he wrote to his dad, referring to flying the new Mark II Harvard trainers. "I sure hope I'll show a pair of wings on my left chest," he added. Indeed, by the end of the summer of 1941 he had received his wings, had been newly commissioned as a pilot officer, and had been posted with No. 400 Squadron in Odiham, Hampshire.

No. 400 was an Army Co-operation Squadron. At first, its operations consisted mainly of photo reconnaissance sorties, and the first opportunity to perform its support role with the Canadian Army under operational conditions came during the ill-fated Dieppe Raid in August of 1942.

Once the P51A Mustang aircraft were acquired by the squadron, daylight intruder operations, known as "rhubarbs," were commenced. The low-flying Mustang fighters, flying in pairs, would attack enemy railways, damaging or destroying dozens of locomotives, dealing a significant blow to the efficiency of the Nazi railway network throughout Europe. Other targets included barges, military vehicle convoys, and enemy aircraft on the ground or in the air. Later, night operations called "rangers" became part of the unit's tactics, and Flying Officer Grant carried out the first of these operations, which entailed flying over France well beyond Paris.

By all accounts, Duncan Grant was a remarkably effective pilot. His logbook suggests part of the story: April 9, 1943—"damaged fifteen locomotives"; April 13—"destroyed Dornier 217 ten miles south of Paris"; May 9— "damaged six locomotives and three aircraft on the ground"; May 14—"damaged five locomotives, one automobile"

Below: P51 Mustang Fighter.

SASKATCHEWAN ARCHIVES BOARD / RA17455 (1)

and so on. "Awarded DFC" gets only a casual mention in his logbook for May 26, but the official citation for the medal is more forthcoming: the Distinguished Flying Cross is awarded "for an act or acts of valour, courage or devotion to duty performed whilst flying in active operations against the enemy." Newspapers from the *Watrous Manitou* to the *Ottawa Citizen* and the *New York Times* carried accounts of his train-busting successes—as many as sixty locomotives put out of commission, and seven enemy planes shot down or damaged. In a letter to the family after Duncan's death, his squadron leader called him: "our very best pilot, a very fine officer, a fine example to all pilots and very good friend of everyone both in and out of the Squadron." It was said that all the pilots would sooner go on a job with him than with anyone else.

Above: Duncan and his sister Barbara, taken in Calgary, 1935.

Right: Duncan Grant in 1942 or 1943, Odiham, England.

By late September 1943, some six weeks had passed since Duncan Grant's last action. He had been sick, and what flying time he did accumulate was spent in formation practices. One reconnaissance operation was cancelled because of poor weather. Duncan's brother Bob, many years later, speculates that Duncan's impatience for action may have contributed to his death. On September 28 Duncan and another pilot—a young flyer on his first operation—set out on a typical rhubarb to France. "The weather was poor that day," Bob says, "and Duncan had waited off-shore for the weather to clear enough to make his attack. He may have been picked up by German radar and thus they were waiting for him and his partner." Duncan's Mustang was hit by flak, and he was killed when the plane crashed in a woods near Dieppe.

Flight Lieutenant Duncan Grant is buried in the Dieppe Canadian War Cemetery. In Saskatchewan, on the shore of Grant Bay in Whitemoose Lake is a plaque, set there by Duncan's brother Bill and his son, also named Duncan, in memory of Duncan Grant.

Hale

I n 1937, Earl Hale, the fourth child and second son of Robert and Maud Hale, left the family farm near Lemsford, Saskatchewan, riding the rails west to look for work. He was quite a well-educated young man, having attended Nutana Collegiate in Saskatoon and having finished his grade twelve in Lemsford, where he was active in young peoples' groups and as a Sunday school teacher at the United Church. That winter, 1937-38, he earned a living partly as a freelance writer in Vancouver, working for various newspapers, including *The Vancouver Province*. "He had a natural talent that way," his sister Alice says, remembering how Earl earned praise for his essays in high school. One of his articles in the *Province* affirmed the optimistic mood of prairie wheat farmers in the face of drought and economic despair.

In August of 1938, Earl applied to the RAF in Calgary for Officers Training before returning home to help out with the harvest. It was not until the following March that he was instructed to report for duty in Ottawa. On the twenty-eighth, a day so rainy that the grid roads were impassable for cars, the Hales took Earl to the train station in Lemsford by wagon. They never saw him again, although Ralph, a brother working in Perron, Quèbec, was able to visit Earl for a few days in Ottawa.

In early April 1939, Earl set sail for England aboard the *Duchess of Richmond*. In those days before the British Commonwealth Air Training Plan, all aircrew training took place in England—Middlesex,

Hale Lake (55°21 N, 104°31' W), viewed here from the north looking towards Diefenbaker Bay on Lac la Ronge, is located thirty-five air miles east of La Ronge. Waters from Lac la Ronge drain at Diefenbaker Bay through a small water control dam at Rapid River, descending into Hale Lake. From here, the flow of water continues through Iskwatikan Lake, then over Nistowiak Falls to the Churchill River. Located in the rugged landscape of the Boreal Shield ecozone, Hale Lake is about two miles in length. A bronze plaque in memory of Pilot Officer Earl R. Hale has been placed at the site by the family.

Gloucestershire, and Oxfordshire, in Earl's case. Earl received his wings on May 26, 1939, and was posted to RAF No. 82 "United Provinces" Squadron based in Watton, Norfolk. The advent of war a few months later led to some personal reflection: "I was wrong about the war coming—some ideas changed—perhaps a different set of values, but I'm not sorry I came over. I'm just another little pin in a little wheel in a big machine and so the best I can do is try not to shear off."

Below: Earl Hale, age 23, leaving Lemsford, Saskatchewan, March 28, 1939, an RAF recruit headed for England.

Returning from a daylight shipping search over the North Sea on March 27, 1940, Earl's Blenheim bomber crashed into an unlit ammunition dump, seriously injuring him and his crew. He was treated for a skull fracture at Halton Hospital in Buckinghamshire and later sent to Torquay, Devon, for convalescence. After his recovery, he was assigned to aerial photography duties, but it was not long after that he was back in the pilot's seat with No. 82 Squadron.

In a draft broadcast for the BBC, Pilot Officer Hale told of one dramatic escape. When a protective cloud cover cleared away during one of his daytime operations, making his Blenheim bomber an easy target for anti-aircraft guns, Hale and his crew

aborted a morning raid and headed for home. Five miles north of Amsterdam, both a Messerschmitt 109 and Heinkel 112 attacked. Earl maneuvered his plane downward to just above sea level, forcing the two enemy aircraft to come at them from overhead. The rear gunner, Sergeant Boland, directed him either to "turn port" or to "turn starboard," as required, to elude gunfire. Boland managed to shoot down the Messerschmitt, but the Heinkel persisted in the attack. Opening fire with its cannon and machine gun, the German warplane knocked out both the bomber's intercommunication and hydraulic systems. Sergeant Oliver, the observer, had to indicate with hand signals which way to turn. For thirty-five minutes the chase continued, until the Heinkel turned away.

In his BBC report, Earl goes on to tell about the end of that flight:

We knew we were in for what we call a "belly-landing"—that is to say, landing on the body of the machine with the wheels up, because with the hydraulic system out of action, the undercarriage wouldn't come down. We therefore jettisoned a few things that might have added to the danger of the landing, and I circled the aerodrome a few times to

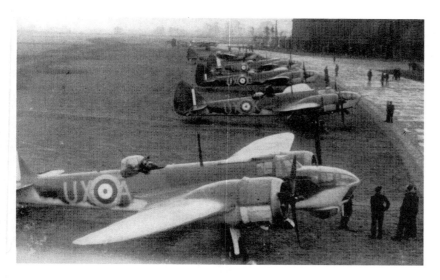

recovered and cremated, the ashes were buried in the collective grave at Vadum Churchyard, six kilometres north of Aalborg, to the sound of "The Last Post."

Maud Hale was awarded the RAF Silver Memorial Cross in November 1941, and Robert Hale received a certificate commemorating "the gratitude of the Government and People of Canada for the life of a brave man freely given in the service of his country, Pilot Officer Earl Robert Hale, R.A.F. His name will ever be held in proud remembrance."

The remembrance took other forms as well. In May 2000, a Blenheim bomber returned to Aalborg to commemorate the liberation of Denmark and to pay tribute to the crew of the eleven bombers shot down that night in August 1940. Furthermore, the Battle of Britain Memorial Chapel in Westminster Abbey bears the name of Pilot Officer Earl Robert Hale, and in Saskatchewan, Hale Lake is named in his memory. ✥

warn the ground staff to have the ambulance and fire engine ready. However, they weren't needed, for she parked down all right.

Earl's story, intended for the BBC Overseas Service, never got to air. On the thirteenth of August, 1940, eleven Blenheims attacked the airfield outside Aalborg in northeastern Denmark. The plan was to catch the Germans off guard, but the anti-aircraft artillery and the ME-109s were waiting. All eleven bombers were shot down, killing twenty crew members, including Pilot Officer Earl Hale. Earl's aircraft was not found until 1995, when excavations at Aalborg Airport uncovered his Blenheim R3821. After the remains of Earl Hale, Rear Gunner Alfred Boland, and Navigator Ralson Oliver were

Heard

Heard Lake (59°20' N, 106°04' W), viewed here from the south, is located 290 air miles north of La Ronge, only ten miles west of the northern community of Stony Rapids. Rugged Taiga Shield terrain surrounds Heard Lake. Irregular in shape and almost two miles long, it is connected by creek the short distance to Axis Lake.

A painting on the side of Stan Heard's Halifax Mark II bomber announced the nickname of the aircraft and crew: "The Thundering Heard," complete with an image of stampeding steers charging over everything in their path.

The image evokes Stan Heard's home in the ranch country of southwest Saskatchewan where the schools Stan attended had names like Skull Creek, Stoney Knoll, Beaver Dam. His parents, Wesley and Rosanna, who had gone to school together in Maple Creek, made their first home of a log house on the Fleming ranch before they homesteaded near Piapot, west of Swift Current. Stan, born in 1920, was one of nine children, all born on the farm with the help of midwives. They were a musical family, the Heards. Wesley liked to sing, play mouth organ, and call square dances. Young Stan, too, was a performer—in debates, talent shows, concerts, the glee club.

At the age of twenty, Stan began his training at No. 15 Elementary Flying Training School (EFTS) in Regina, taking his first training flight on a Tiger Moth one winter day early in 1941. Nine months later, after completing Service Flying Training School in Dauphin and Flying Instructor's School in Trenton, Ontario, he was back in Saskatchewan, instructing on Tiger Moths at an EFTS.

Pilot Officer Heard didn't want to be an instructor—was furious about it, in fact. He wasn't the only one. As Spencer Dunsmore observes in *Wings For Victory*, many young men "had volunteered for the air force, dreaming of flying Spitfires and graduating with shining pilot's wings, only to find themselves at a flying instructor's school sentenced to serve their country in Tiger Moths or Finches." Many instructors, as Dunsmore notes, were "trapped in work that few of them wanted and from which few would soon escape." Within a year, however, Stan Heard, promoted to Flying Officer, made his "escape." In an October 1942 letter home, he writes, "I'm on the right track at long last." And by Christmas of that year he had completed his conversion training at Rockcliffe, Ontario, and had embarked for Britain.

His training in England culminated with his posting to RCAF No. 419 Squadron in May 1943, flying Halifax bombers out of the base at Middleton St. George. No. 419 "Moose" Squadron was front and centre in the Battle of the Ruhr in the spring and summer of 1943. For his part, Flight Lieutenant Stan Heard participated in eight operations over the industrial heartland of Germany. This sustained campaign encountered stiff resistance in the form of the most experienced German night fighter units and most extensive flak and searchlight capabilities. In his letters home during this period, Stan invented some ranchland code to convey to his brother what he and his crew had been up to. "The four horses are behaving nicely," he wrote after his first few operations to the Ruhr.

Then Bomber Command turned its attention to Hamburg, home of the famous shipyard where the Bismarck and hundreds of U-boats had been built. A half-dozen operations in late July and early August 1943, consisting of more than 700 aircraft each time,

devastated the German city. Stan Heard expressed his role in the success of those operations by telling his brother: "I have had the four horses out for a couple of trips recently and they brought us safely home OK."

The next target would be Berlin, but first there was a special job to do. The Germans had built a top secret, experimental rocket research station at Peenemünde on Germany's Baltic coast. The deadly V2 rockets were being built and tested there by a sizable organization of scientists, engineers, and production staff. What was required was a forceful and precise raid on that specific target. Part of the unusual danger of that operation was that it had to occur in moonlight so that the individual targets—the experimental site, the workshops, and the living quarters—could be correctly identified.

After a leave in Scotland, including a day at Loch Lomond, Stan Heard was back at the base ready to go on August 17, 1943, when the weather conditions were finally right for the raid on Peenemünde to proceed.

Stan's "Thundering Heard" and sixteen other bombers from No. 419 Squadron took off from Middleton St. George that night. An eighth crew member was aboard—a young pilot flying as an observer on his first operational flight. Flying east across the North Sea, over southern Denmark, then southeast toward Peenemünde, Flight Lieutenant Heard dropped his bombs over the target and turned for home—just as the German night fighters arrived. As it happened, many of the fighters were equipped, for the first time in the war, with twin upward-firing guns fitted into the cockpit of their Me110s. Spencer

Dunsmore's account of the Peenemünde Raid in *Reap the Whirlwind* notes that "conditions could hardly have been better for the fighters. They arrived just as the last waves of bombers were leaving the target area, labouring as they climbed to cruising altitude for the trip home. Silhouetted against bright flames on the ground and bathed in brilliant moonlight, the bombers were perfect targets. The fighters waded in, cannons and machine guns blazing."

Halifax JD158, the "Thundering Heard" piloted by Flight Lieutenant Stan Heard, was one of three from his squadron, one of forty altogether, shot down that night. His plane went down in the sea off what is now the German-Poland border. Thousands of miles away on the small Heard family farm in southwest Saskatchewan, Stan's dog Ring, somehow sensing his master's death, could not be consoled.

Stanley Heard is commemorated by the Runnymede Memorial overlooking the River Thames in England, and by Heard Lake, Saskatchewan. ✿

Right: Stan Heard's Halifax Mark II bomber.

Below: This telegram notified the Heard family that Stanley was missing in action.

Far right: Stan Heard with his beloved dog Ring in about 1937.

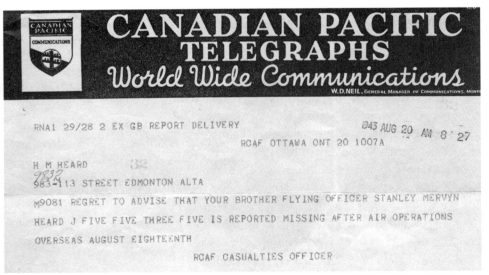

Hillis

William Hillis was the eldest of seven children of Samuel and Lily Hillis, Irish emigrants who farmed just north of Semans. He was good with horses at a time when it took a week with two horse-drawn ploughs to cultivate eighty acres. Usually the outfits of heavy horses, Percherons, pulled the plough. But if William got a bronc that wasn't fully broke, he could break it, even hitch it to a plough, reasoning that it could do the job just as well as a heavy horse and was a lot smarter. To this day, his brothers marvel at his way with horses. "We brought some wild horses in from Alberta," Lawrence remembers. "One of them kicked like blazes, but William wasn't scared of them. He could walk into the stable and stand between them."

William was handy in other ways. As the farm gradually got out of horses, he proved mechanically resourceful as well—helping Samuel to fix up the Model T and then, when it became too costly to run, helping to convert the car into a milk wagon for the family dairy business. The kids would sell twelve quarts for a dollar in Semans, or trade milk for bread. Although he never did have a car of his own, William could keep the family's '27 Chevy tuned up and in good shape. A few years later, while home on leave, he was full of enthusiasm for the family's plans to buy a tractor and, his brother Walter recalls, "would have loved the John Deere we bought for $1600 in '44."

As dull a life as farming may have been for a young man on the farm, there were always some fun times as

Hillis Island (55°16' N, 104°55' W), viewed here from the southwest, is located on Lac la Ronge, twenty miles from the townsite. Together with the adjacent Bear Island, Hillis Island provides spendid shelter for summer residents and visitors to this tranquil site. In 1988, a plaque was placed at Hillis Island by Mr. Joe Anderson and his late wife Louise, who undertook to place plaques at every geographic feature named in memory of servicemen from Semans, their hometown.

well—Saturday night, for instance, when everybody went to town. If they got in early, there'd be a good parking space in front of the café or pool hall. The men would shoot some pool, have a drink. At eleven o'clock it would be time for a banana split or sundae at Woo's. At other times William could play all the old tunes on a mouth organ—Lawrence remembers "Roll Out the Barrel" in particular—or carve a top for the kids, or hunt rabbits, or curl. "He was just a big brother you respected," Lawrence says.

William was already a kind of hero, then, by the time he joined the army in November of 1942, first with the Saskatoon Light Infantry then the South Saskatchewan Regiment (SSR). William's parents didn't want him to join up—already one son, Victor, had joined the air force—and after William shipped out overseas in early 1944, his mother sent him a letter a day, and box after box filled with all the good things she could think of. The boxes and letters never reached William, who was on the move with his regiment across Belgium and into Holland in early October 1944, serving as a stretcher-bearer.

The SSR was part of the Fourth Infantry Brigade during the Battle of the Scheldt. At issue was the port of Antwerp, the importance of which was clearly stated by Field Marshal Montgomery: "The opening of the port is absolutely essential before we can advance deep into Germany." The Allies controlled Antwerp, but much of the surrounding territory—the banks of the East and West Scheldt—was still in German hands. Lasting almost two months, the battle for that territory was both vital and costly to the Allies. The SSR role in the battle in mid-October was to push northeast from the Antwerp-Bergen road, north of Antwerp. Fighting was heavy, the counterattacks severe. As the Fourth Brigade regrouped for an attack on Woensdrecht on October 14, the SSR shifted its ground to allow the Royal Regiment to come in on their right. Another enemy counterattack hit at that time, causing a two-day delay in the proposed SSR attack, and Private William Hillis was among those killed in action that day.

SSR Medical Officer Captain I.S. Robb, noting Private Hillis's "high devotion to duty and disregard for personal safely," wrote to the Hillis family with details of William's death:

> I have just been talking to Pte. H.D. Martin, another of our stretcher-bearers, who was with your son on October 14th. Martin saw him start out to collect the casualties in the face of heavy artillery and mortar fire. When he learned that there was only one wounded man to be brought in, he waved Martin and the other stretcher-bearers back and

Below: William Hillis, his father Samuel Victor Hillis Sr., and brother Samuel Victor Hillis Jr. at the Hillis farm in the winter of 1942/43.

went forward alone. He was carrying the wounded soldier out when a mortar barrage fell, and your son was killed instantly.

In another letter, Captain C.M. Ballem reinforced the reputation by which William Hillis was known: "I grew to admire and respect him very highly, as he at all times placed the need of a wounded man above his own safety."

Private William Hillis is buried in Bergen-Op-Zoom Canadian War Cemetery in northern Holland. In Saskatchewan, Hillis Island on Lac la Ronge is named in his honour. ✿

Left: Original gravesite of William Hillis, Bergen-Op-Zoom Canadian War Cemetery.

Above: Joe Anderson and Ron Mackay prepare the concrete for the plaque.

Right: Louise Anderson, Ev Mackay, and Joe admire the finished product.

Far right: Thirteen years later, in August 2001, Doug Chisholm stops at Hillis Island to see the plaque.

THE SEMANS SERVICEMEN REMEMBERED

Between 1988 and 1992, war veteran Joseph Anderson and his late wife Louise committed themselves to placing plaques at the sites named for the young men from their hometown—Semans, Saskatchewan. This labour of love took them to eighteen sites named for World War II casualties and two sites named for peacetime casualties. One of the first sites they visited was Hillis Island, named for William Hillis. Designed and created by Joe Anderson, the metal plaques set in concrete are both a reminder for those who visit these sites and a tribute to those for whom they are named.

Hutchings

FLYING OFFICER **CYRIL GEORGE HUTCHINGS** • J16294 • 1922–1944

Hutchings Lake (55°52' N, 104°16' W), viewed here from the north, is located sixty-five miles northeast of La Ronge. Hutchings Lake is accessible from the McLennan Lake Provincial Campground on Highway 102. A four-hour paddle by canoe through pristine waters (plus a few short portages) leads to this area of abundant wildlife and fish habitat. Hutchings Lake is a point of entry for a nearby eco-tourist camp, and there is a retired couple who live at the lake year-round.

⊛

•Biggar

Cyril Hutchings seemed headed for a career in the banking or teaching professions. He did well in school, skipping grades and finishing his grade twelve early, and when barely seventeen years old he was off to university in Saskatoon, staying in residence and studying general arts. A year later he worked in a bank at Eston. His father George was well educated, too, progressing up through the Education system as he moved his family of three children around Saskatchewan—Swift Current, Elrose, Humboldt, finally to Biggar, where George was Superintendent of Schools.

George and Margaret Hutchings enforced firm guidelines, not just about education but also about the Sabbath. Cyril was an athletic lad who enjoyed hockey particularly, but he wasn't allowed to attend practices on a Sunday morning. And if one of the Saturday night dances extended past midnight, Cyril could be sure he would hear about it from his dad.

His sister Elaine, only a year younger, often accompanied Cyril in whatever was going on. Skating parties, excursions to Stony Lake where the family had a cottage, music-making—Cyril on cornet or trombone, Elaine on piano—whatever the occasion, it seemed, Cyril and Elaine enjoyed plenty of good times together. "He was always my best friend," she says. She helped see him off at the CNR train station in Saskatoon one bitterly cold night in November of 1941. "Cyril and his two buddies looked so young and full of hope," Elaine remembers, "but none of them would survive the war."

Cyril Hutchings was a fighter pilot whose service career took a number of turns. First, in 1942, he was posted to RCAF No. 421 Squadron flying Spitfires from Digby, Lincolnshire. Mainly a training squadron, No. 421 did fly many coastal convoy patrol and army reconnaissance operations, sometimes two or three a day, and the occasional bomber escort. In February 1943, as the Allies intensified their efforts in North Africa prior to the invasion of Italy, Cyril transferred to No. 93 Squadron based in Tunisia. From there he frequently escorted bombers or took part in patrols over Malta and Sicily. June 20, 1943, his logbook notes, was an extraordinary day: "King [George VI] here today on inspection," he wrote. During the Italy invasion itself, July 10–14, 1943, Cyril's Spitfire was one of many to provide cover for the troops landing at Pachino. By October 1943 he'd completed his tour of operations and returned to Canada.

But Cyril's service career wasn't over yet. He was posted as an instructor to an RCAF training depot at Mt. Jolie and, later, Bagotville, Québec. Before reporting to Québec he spent a good part of a month-long leave in Saskatchewan with his family. "He took me out to dinner and bought me some winter clothes," Elaine recalls. "I was shocked when I saw him. He had aged ten years. He was a very weary and war-shocked man, not the youthful nineteen-year-old I remembered."

In Québec, Flying Officer Hutchings—like many instructors, especially those who had already seen action overseas—was dissatisfied with the routine at the training base. And he had another reason for wanting to return to England. He'd met a Welsh girl, Connie Lewis, shortly after first arriving in England in 1942, most likely when No. 421 Squadron was based in Fairwood Common, South Wales. They had apparently kept in touch and were quite serious about one another—so much so that in Cyril's view Connie belonged with his mother and Elaine as "the three best girls in the world," and he sent a dozen roses to each of them. After a month's leave in Québec, Cyril was back in England, where he and Connie were married on July 7, 1944. Not long after that Cyril was back in the cockpit of a Spitfire, attached to No. 401 Squadron.

No. 401 "Ram" Squadron, using the motto "Very Swift Death to the Enemy," was engaged in "taking the fight to the Luftwaffe over France, Britain, Holland and Germany" after D-Day, as the RAF website tells us. By the time Cyril joined the squadron in August of 1944, it was based in Beny-sur-Mer, France, and patrolled the front lines in support of the advancing Allied forces. Flying Officer Hutchings was reported missing on September 29, 1944;

Below: Cyril, on the wing of a Spitfire, takes a break with his buddies.

Saskatchewan Spitfire Men

Above: The caption under this Saskatoon *Star Phoenix* newspaper clipping identifies these men as "some Western Canadian members of a Royal Canadian Air Force Spitfire squadron in Britain." Cyril is sitting on the wing, wearing the white scarf his sister Elaine had given him. Around the marker that the Dutch farmer put up at Cyril's original gravesite, there was a white scarf wrapped, along with Cyril's dog tag.

Right: A map drawn by Squadron Leader Roderick Smith, in a letter to Cyril's father. Smith had joined the squadron only the day before Cyril's death.

a January 1945 letter from his squadron leader to Cyril's father describes in detail the events of that day:

We took off on a morning patrol of twelve aircraft, a full squadron, from a base in Belgium to patrol the Nijmegen-Arnhem area. We were at a low altitude and we were keeping an eye on the vital Nijmegen bridge across the Rhine as it was frequently attacked by the German Air Force. Towards the end of our patrol we were over the Reichswald Forest and just about ready to come home when we saw a dogfight between a few Typhoons and a lot of Messerschmidt 109s. The cloud was low (3–4000 ft.) and was completely overcast. The fight was taking place just north of the Reichswald Forest and two or three miles East of Nijmegen Bridge. We turned towards the fight and engaged. As there were thirty or forty 109s, some above the cloud, some in it, and many below we became split up as we always do and everything became very confused. Aircraft, mostly enemy, were falling and crashing in many places. Hutch said nothing on the radio to us…. When we landed we noticed that Hutch was missing. That was three and a half months ago now…. I do not wish to give you any false hopes for your son's safety as I think there is little chance of his safety now.

A Dutch farmer found Cyril's body in his field and buried it there. Flying Officer Cyril Hutchings—"an experienced, dependable and utterly fearless pilot," in the words of his squadron leader—was later reburied in the Reichswald Forest War Cemetery in Germany, four kilometres from the Dutch border. When George and Margaret Hutchings visited their son's gravesite years later, they remarked that "no quieter or more beautiful place could be found anywhere."

Elaine Hutchings, with whom Cyril had kept in such faithful touch throughout his years overseas, received the news of her brother's death while she was studying nursing at City Hospital in Saskatoon. "It was terrible news, but I knew I wasn't alone," she says.

Hutchings Lake in northern Saskatchewan, also a quiet and beautiful place, is named in honour of Flying Officer Cyril Hutchings. ❀

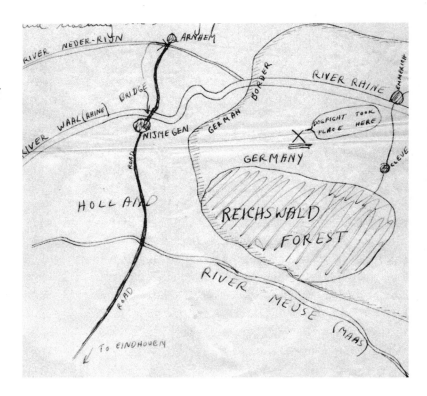

Imrie

There wasn't much to do for a young fellow growing up in Herbert, Saskatchewan, in the 1930s. Jim Imrie, the youngest of eight children, did have his siblings to play hide-and-seek and kick-the-can and other games with, and the neighbour's dogs were always around, but Jim was "a restless kid," his sister Anne remembers, and a bit of a handful for his parents. "It was easier for them to raise the six girls than the two boys," Anne says, adding that she was often the one in charge of Jim, the one to make sure that he got home before nine o'clock on a summer evening. The family lived in town where Jim and Anne's dad, Andrew Imrie, ran the Dominion Power plant across from the old mill. A warning bell in the bedroom was connected to the plant, and Jim and Anne and the other children often heard it ring, signaling that power levels were low, and that their dad would have to go over to the plant to make adjustments.

School didn't seem to offer much to young Jim. He was taking his grade nine in 1941 when, after a confrontation with his teacher which led to her smacking him with a hardcover book, Jim walked out of the school, never to set foot inside the red brick building again. Around that time, he decided to run away from home with a friend, Jack French, and hitchhike to the west coast. Anne, perhaps not taking his decision seriously, packed a lunch for them. Jack's mother reported the runaways, however, and the adventure abruptly ended when the gentleman who

Imrie Lake (59°59' N, 102°51' W), viewed here from the south, is located 340 air miles north of La Ronge on the border between Saskatchewan and the Northwest Territories. A distinct, almost round-shaped feature, Imrie Lake is about one mile in diameter, surrounded by a mixture of stunted black spruce and birch, typical of the Selwyn Lake Upland ecoregion of the Taiga Shield.

Herbert

Above: Young Jim in one of his less "restless" moments.

Below: Jim and his sister Agnes

picked them up heard a news bulletin over his car radio. The teenage runaways got as far as Gull Lake.

Given Jim's restless nature and the fact that a decent job was hard to come by in the late 1930s, Andrew and Agnes Imrie would have been somewhat relieved when an army recruiting team rolled into Herbert in 1941. They knew their youngest was only sixteen, too young to enlist, but they'd rather see him in the army than roaming the countryside. Jim, tall for his age, claimed he was eighteen, and that was good enough. "Mom didn't worry about him as long as he was in the army," Anne says, "and she would never have let him go overseas until he was of age."

That time came two years later when Jim Imrie went overseas with the South Saskatchewan Regiment and took part in the push across northern Europe. His letters express confidence that the Allies would soon win the war. In a letter he sent in December of 1944, Jim noted that he expected to spend the next Christmas at home, assuming "that dope Hitler and all his henchmen come to their senses and realize that they're fighting a losing battle." To his sister Flo he confided that one day in Europe he had butchered a couple of goats he'd found in an abandoned house. He felt somewhat guilty about killing someone's goats, and he discovered that he couldn't stand the taste of goat meat anyway. In fact, he swore that for as long as he lived, he would never again eat it.

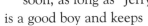

Other letters were casual about the risks of a soldier's life. "Friends back in Canada," he wrote, "are always telling me to keep my chin up, but just between you and me a fellow lives longer if he keeps it down over here." He closes another of his letters by saying that he'll try to write soon, as long as "Jerry is a good boy and keeps his bullets and shells to himself which he hates doing—he'd rather let you carry them around inside your body."

Jim Imrie was also capable of careful reflection. Just one month prior to his death, he speaks of how war had changed him:

Out here is one place where a fellow thinks of things and does things that he normally wouldn't think of doing in civil life such as saying the odd prayer. Just put yourself in my place for a little while and you'll know the reason. Another thing you don't worry about is the shell that has your name on it, it's the one that has "to whom it may concern" that you worry about mostly.

As one family member put it, this passage now seems so sadly foreboding. On January 12, 1945, an enemy mortar shell claimed this young man's life, as well as the lives of two fellow machine-gunners.

The following day, Captain A.M. Matheson wrote to Andrew Imrie, affirming that his son's "personal courage and fortitude was a great inspiration on many occasions." Private James Imrie is buried at Groesbeek Canadian War Cemetery in Holland. Imrie Lake, located near the Northwest Territories border in northern Saskatchewan, is named in his honour. ❦

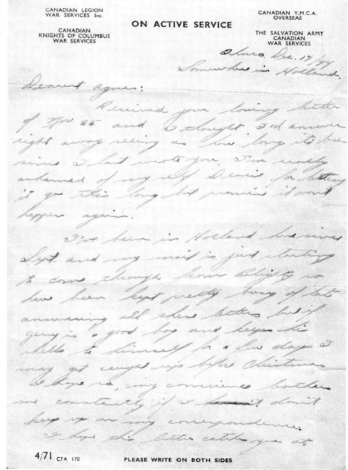

Far left: Jim Imrie and his father Andrew

Top left: Jim with his mother Agnes

Below: First page of Jim's letter to his sister Agnes, written less than a month before his death, from "Somewhere in Holland."

Isbister

RIFLEMAN **ARCHIE ISBISTER** • L105938 • 1906–1944
RIFLEMAN **RUSSELL ISBISTER** • L105571 • 1918–1944
RIFLEMAN **VERNON COLIN ISBISTER** • L27546 • 1921–1944

Isbister Lake (52°32' N, 101°46' W), in memory of Rifleman Archie Isbister, viewed here from the north, is located 240 air miles southeast of La Ronge, one of the most southerly geo-memorial locations in the province. Approximately one mile in diameter, Isbister Lake is accessible from Highway 980.

n the summer of 2000, about 150 people from all across Canada and from as far away as Hereford, England, crowded into the Mont Nebo Community Hall, west of Prince Albert, to celebrate. In addition to being simply a reunion of current and former district residents, the occasion was to dedicate the newly renovated hall and to honour the district's war veterans, many of whom were there to enjoy the potluck picnic. A prominent feature in the hall, and a focal point of the proceedings that afternoon, were the more than one hundred photographs that lined the walls. Included among them are pictures of the Isbister boys, Archie, Russell, and Vern (better known as Tony), three cousins born and raised in the district.

Archie Isbister, the oldest of the three, had been a farmer a few miles north of Mont Nebo in the Debden district. He and his wife Edith and their four kids had big gardens, chickens, and a few head of cattle on the farm. Russell Isbister, born at the Sandy Lake Reserve and raised in the Shell lake district west of Mont Nebo, was a quiet lad, the oldest of eight kids in his family, who got his grade eight at Camp Lake School. A hard worker, he was a farm labourer over the years, mostly for his uncle. Before he went off to begin his basic training in 1942 he got married, and he and his wife Helen had one daughter, Velma, who was only six months old when Russell went overseas. The third Isbister cousin, Tony, was the youngest but biggest of the three. Only seventeen when he joined up, he too had spent most of his working life as a farm labourer, mainly on the farm of his father, Jack, near Mont Nebo.

For all three of the Isbisters, then, life on a small farm—a half-section at most, mixed farms, all work done with horses—was what they knew best. In the winter there'd be work at a logging camp near Big River, further north, when there was less to do on the home farm. And all three were avid hunters and fishermen. Archie was a musician too. He and his brothers performed occasionally in a band with guitar and violin.

In the early 1940s, all three became infantrymen—Russell with the Royal Winnipeg Rifles, Archie and Tony with the Regina Rifles. In the organizational hierarchy of the Canadian Army, both regiments were part of the Seventh Canadian Infantry Brigade of the Third Canadian Infantry Division. And on D-Day, June 6, 1944, the two regiments would land side by side on a four-mile stretch of French beach code-named "Juno."

The general objective of the Seventh Brigade was to penetrate about ten miles inland as far as the Caen-Bayeux road. Specifically, according to Army historian C.P. Stacey, the Royal Winnipeg Rifles were to overwhelm beach defences, clear the hamlet of Vaux and its chateau, and seize both Graye-sur-Mer and a nearby "island" formed by locks at the mouth of the Seulles. Reserve companies of the Winnipegs would then advance and take the village of Ste. Croix and Banville, nearly two miles inland. Meanwhile, on the left flank…the Regina Rifle Regiment was to land immediately east of the Seulles, clear Courseulles and seize crossings over the river at Reviers.

And that was the just the first of a three-phase objective for the day.

Both Archie and Russell were killed that day. The precise circumstances are unknown, but we do know that both regiments came under heavy fire as they landed at about 7:45 in the morning and had a difficult time, though ultimately successful, of achieving their objectives. In finally achieving the deepest penetration of any Allied forces on D-Day, the Canadians lost 335 officers and men, Rifleman Archie Isbister and Rifleman Russell Isbister among them. Russell's regiment, the Royal Winnipegs, suffered particularly heavy casualties. Archie is commemorated by the

Top: Archie Isbister

Centre: Russell and Helen Isbister

Below: Vernon (Tony) Isbister

Isbister Lake (56°27' N, 102°01' W), in memory of Rifleman Russel Isbister, viewed in the photo below from the east, is located 160 air miles northeast of La Ronge at the Manitoba border. Quite a large lake, Isbister Lake contains several arms which are three miles in length, as well as Isbister Island (right), named in memory of Rifleman Tony Isbister, located at 56°26' N, 102°02' W.

• Mont Nebo

Bayeux War Memorial and Russell is buried at Beny-sur-Mer Canadian War Cemetery, Reviers, Calvados, France.

For Tony, the war continued for another two days as the Regina Rifles—their motto was "Swift and Bold"—pressed south from the beach toward their D-Day objective, becoming the first unit to reach it (although the Royal Winnipegs arrived at the same time). The eighth of June, however, saw a series of violent German counterattacks directed against the Regina Rifles which held the village of Bretteville-l'Orgueilleuse. German tanks approached to within three hundred yards of battalion headquarters in the village, but the Reginas withstood the attack. Among the casualties was Rifleman Tony Isbister, buried at Brookwood Military Cemetery near Woking, Surrey, in England.

"It was really a sad thing," remembers Ollie Dreaver, Russell's sister, referring to the news of the boys' deaths in France. They were never too far apart in life, whether growing up in the Mont Nebo district or fighting on the battlefields of Normandy. Isbister Lake near the Manitoba border southeast of Hudson Bay is named in memory of Archie Isbister. Farther north, but also on the Manitoba border, is another Isbister Lake, named in memory of Russell Isbister, and Isbister Island, named in memory of Tony Isbister. ✤

Bayeux War Memorial, France.

Jackson

Jackson Lake (58°43'N, 109°41'W), viewed here from the east, is located three hundred air miles northwest of La Ronge, just twenty miles southwest of the vast Athabasca Sand Dunes. Plans are underway for the placement of a bronze memorial plaque on the shore of Jackson Lake in 2002.

• Valparaiso

The blacksmith on HMCS *Prince Robert* was part of the first Allied landing party on the island of Hong Kong in August of 1945. "When we got in there we had to get up to the high part of the shore to the hospital to let the Canadian POWs out. I had to take a cutting torch and cut through the steel fences while our guys were coming behind me. I cut a way through to let our guys in to release these fellows. Many of the prisoners were in very bad shape."

The blacksmith understates the situation, for the 1500 prisoners liberated from the hospitals and Sham Shui prison camp had endured generally horrific treatment since Christmas Day of 1941, the day Hong Kong fell to the Japanese. The defense of Hong Kong had begun on the lower Kowloon peninsula on December 8, 1941 after the attack on Pearl Harbor. In the face of the Japanese advance, the combined British Commonwealth forces retreated to the island of Hong Kong five days later; the Japanese landed there on the eighteenth. The Winnipeg Grenadiers, forming the bulk of the Fortress Reserve company in the middle of the island, were thus the first Canadian forces to see action in World War II as they resisted the powerful invasion force that killed, or took prisoner, every member of the regiment. One of the Grenadiers, Sergeant Major John Osborn, earned a Victoria Cross for his actions on December 19. Another, Corporal Kenneth Jackson, was wounded but still fighting on Christmas Day, the day of surrender.

Kenneth Jackson's daughter Shirley remembers that

day. "We sat at the radio all day. What a sad day it was. I cannot find the words to describe it." Memories of the ensuing four years are no easier: "We heard from him twice while he was a prisoner of war—very short letters, but certainly not written by my Dad. They spoke of returning home and killing the fatted calf. Also how well he was being treated. The only real thing was his signature, 'Slow.' We heard many horror stories. I never talked about them and I still don't."

The Jacksons lived in Valparaiso, Saskatchewan, in 1939 when Kenneth enlisted, giving up his job as a grain buyer and the company of workmates around the elevator who had affectionately given him the nickname "Slow," for his easygoing nature. Kenneth and his two children lived with his in-laws, the Milnes, after his wife left the family a few years before. Jessie and Finlay Milne were wonderful grandparents for the two children, Shirley and Morley. Together they saw Kenneth off at the CNR train station in Valparaiso when he went off to Jamaica to serve on garrison duty, guarding German prisoners, in the summer of 1940. And together they enjoyed the messages he sent home at birthdays and other special occasions. They also shared their worries, although the children less so, over news that the Winnipeg Grenadiers were being sent to Hong Kong—the regiment was escorted there by the *Prince Robert*—without much proper training or preparation.

After almost four years of horrific treatment in Japanese prison and slave labour camps, Kenneth and his fellow POWs who had survived were finally released in September of 1945. Kenneth was to arrive in Vancouver, and Shirley and Jessie began to make plans to meet him there. Two days later, Roy Harper—a family friend who was to become Shirley's father-in-law—delivered a telegram with the heartbreaking news that Kenneth had died on board the VSS *Gosper* off the coast of Manila.

Later the following story emerged: the Japanese, in an apparent show of celebration, had given saki to some of the prisoners in the hospital in Hong Kong. The saki, however, was poisoned. Some of the men survived, but Kenneth Jackson did not. It was only his personality and acceptance of things, a chaplain told the family, which had enabled him to survive the years as prisoner of war. But too weak to survive a poisoning, he died on September 29, 1945. Corporal Jackson, buried at sea, is named on one of the bronze panels of the Halifax Memorial. In Saskatchewan, Jackson Lake is named in his honour.

Upon returning to Hong Kong in 2000 to dedicate a memorial, one of the Hong Kong veterans offered an informal prayer to his

Below: Kenneth Jackson and his children, Morley and Shirley.

old mates: "Sleep well, young buddies, and keep a place for us, because we'll be joining you." Shirley Goodwin's reflections about her father, Kenneth Jackson, are equally poignant: "One never gets over the loss of a parent," she writes. "On every special occasion—births, graduations, weddings, even funerals—I think of him. Every time I hear John McDermott sing 'Dance With Me, Daughter' I think yes—I would love to have danced with my Dad, 'Slow.'" Both she and her brother Morley named sons after their father, Kenneth Royden Jackson. ❀

Kidd

I n the summer of 1962, the family of Pilot Officer Leonard Kidd made a trip north to Lac la Ronge to visit the island named in his honour. They used a cement drill and hammer to lay a plaque on the "sunset" side of the island—"a lovely island," Fred Kidd remembers, "with a beautiful sand beach."

Fred and another brother had preceded Leonard into service—the Regina Rifles, in Fred's case—but Leonard chose the air force, joining right out of high school. Their father, also named Fred, worked as a machinist for CN in Humboldt, and Leonard, too, seemed destined for a career with the railroad until war intervened. "I held him in high esteem," says Fred of his younger brother (by fifteen years). "He was a nice fellow all the way around." He was only about five and a half feet tall, "but you didn't want to cross him," Fred says. "He was an independent guy."

Some of that independence showed up after an incident at No. 16 Elementary Flying Training School in Edmonton in the spring of 1942. Instead of bailing out of his Tiger Moth when a prop blew off during a solo flight, Leonard managed to land the plane safely in a farmer's field. "An officer chewed him out pretty good," Fred says, resuming the story. "So Leonard went AWOL for a while. 'I saved him a plane, but all he did was go up one side of me and down the other,' he told us." Nevertheless, Leonard's training proceeded without further major incident, although he did lose his logbook in Saskatoon while attending No. 4 Service Flying Training School. He received his wings on

Kidd Island (55°12' N, 105°03' W), viewed here from the south, is located on Lac la Ronge. A beautiful place where sand beaches and rocky Precambrian shoreline prevail, Kidd Island, which is situated off the tip of Nut Point Peninsula, serves as a key navigational landmark for boat travellers. In 1962, a permanent memorial plaque was placed by the family on the sunset corner of Kidd Island.

September 11, 1942, and within two months was overseas, based in Dalcross, Scotland.

At both the Advanced Flying Unit in Dalcross and, later, the Beam Approach Training School in Dishforth, England, Leonard was flying two-engine Oxford trainers and following the training path that usually would lead straight to Bomber Command. His next training stop, an Operational Training Unit (OTU) in Osworth, was another step along that path, but then came an odd step sideways to a different OTU in April of 1943—this one for fighter pilots; Leonard was now flying Spitfire fighters. Such a shift from bombers to fighters was rare indeed. "He didn't want to be responsible for a whole crew, so he asked for a transfer to fighters," his brother Fred says. Although such personal preferences would not normally be accommodated in wartime, perhaps in this case they were. It may be that suddenly more fighter pilots were needed for the war effort, although by the summer of '43, the Battle of Britain was over, and losses in Fighter Command were relatively low.

Pilot Officer Kidd's first operations with No. 124 "Baroda" Spitfire Squadron were in the Spitfire VII, a stripped-down version of the fighter. Without armaments, and with a pressurized cabin, it was capable of high altitude flying—as high as 35,000 feet—for weather or other reconnaissance purposes. As D-Day approached, Leonard Kidd was posted to No. 602 "City of Glasgow" Spitfire Squadron, flying the Mark IX model and engaging in various dive bombing or strafing sorties along the coast of occupied Europe. The day after D-Day he was forced to land amid heavy action near a beach in France, but a week later he was back in the air, providing low cover to assault forces as they consolidated the Normandy beachhead. Pilot Officer Kidd's logbook for this period shows a typical range of fighter operations, often several per day. He patrolled the beachhead, escorted 100 Halifax bombers in a daylight raid, destroyed a Focke-Wulf 190 and damaged an Me109, patrolled for the deadly V1 rockets (which a skilled pilot could fly alongside and nudge off course), fired on lorries, and generally "attacked anything that moved," as another Spitfire pilot puts it.

On July 7, 1944, Pilot Officer Leonard Kidd did not return from an armed reconnaissance sortie near Caen. His brother Fred, who landed in Europe with the Regina Rifles that very day, did not find out until the war was over how Leonard had died. Inquiring in London on behalf of his mother, Fred found out that a Frenchman had retrieved Leonard's body from the downed plane and buried it in his backyard. The burial was not reported until the war was over, at which time the body of Leonard Kidd was moved to the Banneville-La-Campagne War Cemetery, some ten kilometres east of Caen. Fred Kidd, who had never managed to connect with his brother to share a leave in England, did manage to find his gravesite, where he added a brass plaque to the gravestone. "It was a relief to know where he was," Fred says.

In Saskatchewan, Kidd Island on Lac la Ronge, honours the memory of Pilot Officer Leonard Kidd. ✿

King

The dozens of letters George King wrote home from England during the last nine months of his life tell us much about that life, both before he enlisted and while in service.

He'd grown up a farm boy first of all—although his brother Bill was the one to stay home from the war and help their parents, William and Agnes, run the family farm in the Summerberry district near Wolseley. In his letters home, George is ever-sensitive to the rhythms of the life and work on the farm—the stock ("are the two white heifers still milking?"), the wheat and hay crops, the wood hauling, the endless cycles of chores. He asks after the old family dog, Major, and the four workhorses—Harry and Daisy, Beaut and Doc. "Nothing will ever take the farming out of a person's blood," he observes in one letter. In August 1943—just one month before he died—he declares to Bill: "you'll have help next year. That's a promise."

George's letters provide glimpses, too, of his old social life around Summerberry. He reminisces about the games of hockey, ball, and curling; swimming in the town dam; hunting; the picnics and dances, and buggy or sleigh rides; the Saturday trips to Grenfell or even Saskatoon. Generally, he speaks fondly of all manner of fun and activities with family and "the old gang," among whom George was known as a colourful, playful character.

The letters also show us George King the family man, who is generous with his expressions of love and gratitude on occasions such as birthdays and Mother's

King Creek (59°18' N, 106°11' W), viewed here from the west, is located about twelve miles west of the northern community of Stony Rapids. Commencing about one mile west of Heard Lake, King Creek flows for about five miles through several small lakes, eventually connecting to Neufeld Creek, where the water drains into Lake Athabasca. This is rugged country; here the glaciers carved steep ridges into the landscape.

Summerberry•

Day. His father had left Henley-on-Thames, England, for Canada and the homestead in 1890 and was never to return, but George did. During his leaves he made several visits to his Uncle George, after whom he was named, and Aunt Sallie in Henley. Dutifully, he notates for his father the details of the sights and sounds of the area:

> We went down and looked over the regatta course and all that. The hills on the far side of the river are really beautiful now. There was sure a crowd there on Sunday afternoon—hundreds of people were rowing. We watched them let some boats through the lock. There are still lots of swans on the river there, too. I always remember you telling us about the swans.

On one occasion in Henley, the elder George, a shoemaker, took one look at the sorry condition of his nephew's shoes and "in no time at all he had a new pair of heels put on," George reports.

Below: The King children, ca. 1928. Left to right: James, Bill, George, and Jeannie.

Of course, the letters of Flight Sergeant George King also trace his air force career. He had left the farm to enlist in November of 1941, had trained in Regina

and at No. 3 Air Observer's School in Pearce, Alberta, and had arrived in England before Christmas of 1942. For the next few months his letters express considerable discontent with the slow pace of training. It's "slow for the air crews," he observes in January 1943, and "I've yet to see a German aircraft." A month later he admits that seeing no action "gets pretty tiresome." In early April he still feels "pretty much unemployed," but that feeling would soon end with his posting to an Operational Training Unit (OTU).

His letters acknowledge the change of pace: "We're flying twice a day now," doing "quite a bit of training." At OTU he crewed up with three other Canadians and a Welshman. "They sure are a fine bunch of fellows," he writes in late May. "We should do really good, because there isn't one man who would cause trouble in the crew." In a later letter he offers further affirmation of the cohesion of his crew: "We all know just what one another is like in the air now, and it is easy to fly when you know the other chaps." A month before he died, he tells his Mom, "I'd never want to fly with anyone else."

It was at that time that George King and his crewmates, now seven in number, began operational flying, posted with RAF No. 218 Squadron at Downham Market, Norfolk. Flight Sergeant King was the navigator of their Stirling bomber. The first two operations consisted of "gardening"—laying mines in coastal waters. Soon the crew joined raids deep into Germany. By September 19, 1943, the crew had completed nine such ops "and really blasted the hell out of them," as George writes to his brother, Jim, who was also in the RCAF. The next day he writes to his mother for the last time, telling her only that "we have our own aircraft now and it is getting its decoration today—just a wolf painted on the outside."

That's the plane that crashed on September 23, 1943, during the homeward leg of a raid on Hanover. It would be nearly two years before William and Agnes King would learn the cause of the crash from one of the two crew members to survive it:

The controls and two engines went out of order, and we had a fire in the nose. George and Doug managed to extinguish the fire, but we also had another one in the rear of the machine. We all fixed on our chutes, but we found out we were cut off from the escape hatches by fire, as the nose went on fire again. The aircraft blew up in mid-air, causing me to be blown out. Bill also was blown out of the turret, as he was getting out of it at the time.

The bodies of the other five crewmen, including George King, were found near the wreckage.

George King—"a great favourite of everyone," as his obituary in the *Wolseley News* stated—is buried in the Hanover War Cemetery. King Creek, named in his honour, is situated about seventy kilometres east of Fond du Lac in northern Saskatchewan. ✿

Left: The "fine bunch of fellows" that George King flew with, taken at O.T.U. in the summer of 1943. Standing, left to right: Doug Wylie, Norm Spencer, and George. Kneeling, left to right: Harold Hicks and Bill Baker. Of these five, Bill Baker was the only survivor. Flight Sergeant W. Morement, who joined the crew after this photo was taken, also survived. Both were sent to prisoner of war camps. A seventh member of the crew, Ray Eberle, also perished.

Below: Stirling bomber.

COURTESY OF THE CANADIAN FORCES / PL4960

Knight

Knight Lake (55°39' N, 104°07' W), viewed here from the south, is located sixty air miles northeast of La Ronge in the Churchill River Upland ecoregion. Knight Lake has three distinct bays, each about two miles in length, containing many bedrock outcrops. The family visited Knight Lake in 1972, placing a permanent marker in memory of William J. Knight. Although the entire area was impacted by a massive forest fire in 1981, fresh growth of jack pine, spruce, and birch are returning.

Estevan

The bigger they are, the harder they fall," Billy Knight liked to say. And he must have known from experience, being only 5'4" tall himself and weighing in at just 145 pounds. But apparently he was as tough as nails. "Nobody could lick him," says his son Don, one of three of Billy's sons to serve in the war. "He used to arm wrestle against the Mounties, and he could beat them all right-handed and all but one left-handed."

That kind of toughness was forged over a lifetime of work and action. Born in a sod house near Roche Percee, just southeast of Estevan, Bill Knight was the eldest of twelve children. Eventually, his father Mathew built a stone house, and a hotel with bar and pool room. On the side, Mathew broke and dealt horses, keeping a herd of about 250. Young Bill helped with all of that and enjoyed hunting coyotes on horseback with a pack of hounds. He went to school in town up to grade four and took grades five to eight by correspondence. But schooling had to wait for war; Bill served with the Lord Strathcona's Horse (Royal Canadian) regiment for two years, despite a lifelong affliction with psoriasis that threatened to cut short his army career altogether. After the war, in 1921, he got married to Daisy Mathieson and lived in Ogema. There he farmed a half-section of land and worked as a pumpman for the CPR, until electrification of the pump system put him out of work. He built a reputation as a fine sportsman there—"a good hockey player, fast," Don recalls—and coached gymnastics, wrestling, and boxing, which was a passion he'd developed in the army. "He had an awful strong punch," Don Knight says, remembering the days he and the other boys were coached by his dad, "and if the boys got too tough, he'd add a little more to his punch."

Returning to Estevan in 1931, Bill found himself in the middle of the action, as usual: he became one of the first organizers for the United Mineworkers of America in the coal mines near Estevan. The difficult fight for certification of the union lasted throughout the 1930s, culminating in a three-week strike in 1938 after which certification of the UMWA was achieved. Bill had to hold union meetings in the trees near the mine, hiding from the mine operators. Needless to say, not everyone was friendly to the union, and Bill managed to get himself onto a blacklist or two.

We can add horse trainer to Bill Knight's slate of activities during the 1930s. In the thriving cross-border circuit of thoroughbred races, Bill's horses—going by names such as Lady Light, Bienfait Kate, Cop the Coin, and Black Bird—were frequently among the winners. And the boxing gloves were always close at hand. As one of his exercise boys, Harvey Boles, recalls: "Billy would get us squared off in the horse barn with instruction that boxing was a sport and all in fun. Eventually you would get popped in the beak and forget about the good sportsmanship."

Then it was time for a new challenge: World War II. One day in June 1940, Bill got a ride to Regina with

the mayor of Estevan, Harry Nicholson, to join the South Saskatchewan Regiment (SSR), not telling his family until a week later. He was thirty-nine years old at the time. Arriving in Cove, England, with the regiment shortly after Christmas Day, 1940, soon Bill Knight was second in charge of the SSR boxing team, a squad of seven or eight boxers, including Bill's son Don, the Battalion boxing champ in the 160-pound division. There they were, father and son—boxers, both of them—in the same platoon of the SSR. Another son, Jim, was also with the SSR for a time before he transferred to the RCAF and served in India and Ceylon (now Sri Lanka).

Bill enjoyed the army life, although like many men he'd rather have seen action other than the endless rounds of fieldwork. By May 1942, the regiment had begun special training for what would turn out to be the raid on Dieppe. According to the regimental history, "Rugged assault training…consisted of forced speed marches, cliff and wall climbing, unarmed combat, breeching wire obstacles, street fighting, night compass work, and countless hours of practicing landings from landing craft." That summer of 1942, Bill knew action would come soon. Shortly before the raid, Bill told his son Don, who at the time was laid up with blood poisoning: "There's something in the wind. I'm glad you're not going. You look after your mother."

Bill Knight was listed as "missing in action" from August to December. After four difficult months of waiting and hoping, his wife Daisy and his son Ken received official word of his death. The regiment had

Right: The boxing team of the South Saskatchewan Regiment, England, 1942. Back row, left to right: Pte. Billy Knight, coach; Pte. Johnny Frazze, Pte. Don Knight (160 lb. Champion, 6th Canadian Infantry Brigade); L/Cpl Frank Nieviadomy (Heavyweight Champion, 6th Canadian Infantry Brigade); Pte. Kelly Webb, Trainer; Pte. Stu Leader (160 lb. Champion, 2nd Canadian Division); Pte. Paul Delorme; Cpl. Joe Gregory, head coach. Front row, left to right: Pte. Howie Phillips (147 lb. Champion, 6th Canadian Infantry Brigade); Major H.T. Kempton, 2 I/C; Lt. Col. Sherwood Lett, M.C., E.D. Officer Commanding; Lieut. Tommy Gentles, o/c training; Pte. Norm Dingwall.

pushed about five to six miles inland before the order to fall back. Fighting a rearguard action as they pulled back to the beach, Bill was killed by an artillery shell landing nearby, the shrapnel tearing him in half. On Major Lefty White's recommendation, Bill Knight received official notice from British Secretary for War J.J. Lawson: "By the King's order, the name of Lance-Cpl. W.J. Knight, Canadian Infantry Corp, was published in the London Gazette on March 14, 1946 as mentioned in a Despatch for distinguished service. I am charged to record His Majesty's high appreciation."

William Knight is buried in the Dieppe Canadian War Cemetery. Thirty years after his death, in the summer of 1972, William's son, James Knight, along with James's wife Lillian and son Harold, travelled to northern Saskatchewan, where they canoed, camped, and fished for five days at Knight Lake, named in honour of Lance Corporal William J. Knight. ✿

Labbee

I n the years before the war, a curly-haired young fellow named George Labbee often rode horseback into Radville from the farm with his suit over his back. "He spent a lot of time at our place in town," remembers his nephew, Mel Van de Sype. "I always thought he was a giant." George would hand over the suit for cleaning to his sister, one of many ways, as Mel remembers, that "my mother spoiled him." Later, when George came home on leave, "she probably ironed his uniform twice a day." He always looked "distinguished and dignified" in that uniform, Mel adds.

The second youngest of sixteen children in a Roman Catholic family that had emigrated from Québec via Maine, George was in many ways a typical rural Saskatchewan lad. He helped his parents Frederick and Melina (who was a midwife) and the rest of the family work hard to make a living on the farm, first in the Lacadia district, then in the Brokenshell district. At school, he wasn't that strong a student but did get as far as grade eight. During the summer he liked to play ball; he'd play in one town one Sunday, in another town the next. His social life included a girlfriend, Rosalie, the cousin of one of his good friends in the Radville area. Generally, George liked to have a good time, and he "was a good chum," one of his pals recalls, "who never gave anyone a problem." His hobbies were mechanical, as George indicated later on his service enrolment form, and he was bilingual.

George—"a man with a lot of guts," says his nephew—wanted to make his contribution to the war

Labbee Lake (55°43' N, 102°32' W), viewed here from the north, is located 120 air miles east of La Ronge in the Churchill River Upland ecoregion of the Boreal Shield. About four miles in length, Labbee Lake is situated eight miles north of the Churchill River, on the old winter road between the Island Falls hydroelectric dam and the Whitesand Falls dam site on the Reindeer River. This winter road was cleared in 1937 and was used until construction of the Whitesand Dam was completed in 1942.

Radville

effort like his brother Germaine, a tank commander, who would survive the war. George Labbee reported for training in Regina on January 23, 1942. In the evenings he and his old pal, Henry Mazenc, would quite often walk over to his sister's place for coffee or a meal, the two of them making sure they got back to the camp on time. His route overseas was a circuitous one: basic training in Regina, advanced training in Winnipeg, transfer to the Rocky Mountain Rangers in Nanaimo with training in Field, B.C., another transfer to the Sault Ste. Marie and Sudbury Regiment. There were a couple of AWOL incidents. Finally, having renewed his enrolment and attestation and having been granted a new regimental number, George Labbee, now attached to the South Saskatchewan Regiment, arrived overseas in June of 1944.

Labbee's regiment arrived in France soon after D-Day, in time to participate in the latter stages of the Battle of Normandy. Allied forces were pushing southwards from Caen in an attempt to trap German

Below: George Labbee during his training in Field, British Columbia, May 1943.

divisions west of the Seine. The heavily reinforced village of Tilly-la-Campagne proved particularly resilient to Allied assaults, and Canadian losses were heavy. George Labbee died in the assault operation of July 25, 1944.

Like thousands of other families, George's family at home received two Canadian National telegrams. The first reported that George was missing in action, the second that he "has now been officially reported killed in action." One of George's sisters, however, contacted a psychic in Winnipeg named Dr. Hugh J.

CLASS OF SERVICE SYMBOL
Full-Rate Message
Day Letter — D L
Night Message — N M
Night Letter — N L
If none of these three symbols appears after the check (number of words) this is a full-rate message. Otherwise its character is indicated by the symbol appearing after the check.

CANADIAN NATIONAL TELEGRAM

W. M. ARMSTRONG, GENERAL MANAGER, TORONTO, ONT.

Form 6123
Exclusive Connection with
WESTERN UNION TELEGRAPH CO.
Cable Service to all the World
Money Transferred by Telegraph

STANDARD TIME
GS WS 43 GB DL 2 Extra   Repbrt Deleivery Via Regina   930pm
Ottawa Ont August 8.44

Mr Fred Labbee
Radville Sask

3644 Minister Of National Defence Deeply regrets to inform you that L 154237 Private George Joseph Labbee has been officially reported missing in action twenty fifth July 1944 stop when further information becomes available it will be forwarded as soon as received

Director Of Records

1030PM

CANADIAN NATIONAL TELEGRAM

W. M. ARMSTRONG, GENERAL MANAGER, TORONTO, ONT.

STANDARD TIME

49DL. GB 2 EXA.
OTTAWA ONT 302 PM.24
FRED LABBIE
REPORT DELIVERY
RADVILLE SASK.

12840 MINSTER OF NATUONAL DEFENCE DEEPLY REGRETS TO INFORM YOU THAT L 154237 PRIVATE GEORGE JOSEPH LABBIE PREVIOUSLY REPORTED MISSING IN ACTION HAS NOW BEEN OFFICIALLY REPORTED KILLED IN ACTION DATE NOT KNOWN STOP. IF ANY FURTHER INFORMATION BECOMES AVAILABLE IT WILL BE FORWARDED AS SOON AS REQEIVED

DIRECTOR OF RECORDS.

440P.

Radville soldier killed in action

Pte. George Labbee, son of Mr. and Mrs. Fred Labbee, Radville, has been killed in action in France. He was 25 years old, born at Radville, and enlisted there Sept. 15, 1942. Besides the parents he leaves eight sisters and three brothers. One brother, Germain, is with theh Canadians in Italy.

Pte. G. Labbee

Opposite page, bottom right: This telegram notified the Labbee family that George is missing in action.

Left: This telegram officially reported that George was killed in action.

Below: Dr. Munro's letter asserting that George was still alive gave the family hope for a time.

Munro and sent him a photo of George. In February 1945, Munro wrote, "I do not think there is any doubt that your brother is alive and in fairly good health," and he suggested that George "belongs to the Commandos." The family remembered George's training with the Rocky Mountain Regiment. Could there be anything to the psychic's pronouncement? By January of 1946, however, even Dr. Munro had conceded, in a letter to George's niece in Radville, that "your uncle has passed away."

Today George Labbee is remembered in various ways, official and unofficial. For many years, his nephew's son carried hockey equipment in one of George's duffel bags. In France, he is buried in the Bretteville-sur-Laize Canadian War Cemetery where some three thousand other Canadians were also laid to rest. And in northern Saskatchewan, Labbee Lake is named in his honour. ❀

DR. HUGH J. MUNRO

928 SOMERSET BLOCK
WINNIPEG
MAN.

TELEPHONE 21 179

February 8, 1945.

Mrs. Remie Van De Sype,
Radville, Sask.

Dear Madam:

I regret the necessary delay in replying to your letter, which was due to the large amount of correspondence, and the many patients coming to our office.

I do not think there is any doubt that your brother is alive and in fairly good health, although he may have some trouble in the right knee in the form of arthritis. I am under the impression that he is in England--it may be that the reason you do not hear from him is that he belongs to the Commandos; I give this only as a suggestion and not as a definite fact. If he did belong to this organization he would not be allowed to write home. However, I do believe my first suggestion that he is alive and in fairly good health is quite correct.

I hope this information will be of some comfort to you, and that the ultimate outcome will reveal the truth of what I have said.

I am,

Sincerely yours,

Hugh J. Munro

Dr. Hugh J. Munro.

HJM:JE

Labrecque

Labrecque Bay (55°30' N, 104°57' W), viewed here from the east, is located on Welk Lake, thirty-two air miles north of La Ronge. Over a mile long, Labrecque Bay is connected by creek to Bartlett Lake, about one-half mile to the west. This popular area is accessible by canoe and short portages from the MacKay Lake campground on Highway 102.

Growing up on a farm east of Rosetown, the second oldest boy in a large French-speaking family of eight, Hervé Labrecque was "everyone's favourite, even as a baby," remembers his sister Marie. He was a happy-go-lucky boy, full of energy and humour. Physically very strong, perhaps aided by a set of barbells he and a chum used, Hervé was also known as a kind boy who would defend the little people at Hillside School from the occasional rough treatment at the hands of the older ones. Devout and studious, he lived a life of faith. Hervé's studies toward the priesthood at St. Thomas College, Battleford, where he had finished high school, would have exempted him from military service (which would have been fine with his father, who didn't want him to go) but he chose to enlist in the army anyway, intending to resume religious studies after the war. His mother would observe, after seeing Hervé off, that you lose half of your son when he gets on the train, and the other half when he dies.

One of Hervé's letters from England to the Bechard family, neighbours at home, reveals a reflective young man who was appreciative of the scenery in eastern Canada, during that train ride east from Winnipeg, and of the pastoral settings of rural Scotland, where he thought perhaps he could hear "the distant lament of bagpipes." For good luck he carried with him a penny Denis Bechard had given him. Hervé was sensitive, of course, to the realities of war, hinting that "I wouldn't be a bit surprised to see another front open from this side in a short time."

That other front would be the Normandy front, opened on D-Day, June 6, 1944. Hervé and his regiment, the Royal Winnipeg Rifles, were among the western flank of the Canadian forces landing on Juno beach. Just two days later, Hervé Labrecque died during one of the most chilling episodes of the war, the Bremer Murders. While in the battle for control of the Caen-Bayeux railway line, Canadian troops deployed around the town of Putot were

captured in a German counterattack. The prisoners were escorted to German battalion headquarters, under the command of SS Major Gerhard Bremer, and directed onto the grounds of the Chateau d'Audrieu. Interrogation at the hand of the SS ensued, the Canadians revealing only name, rank and service number. According to Howard Margolian's *Conduct Unbecoming: The Story of the Murder of Canadian Prisoners of War in Normandy*—between 4:30 and 5:00 in the afternoon, thirteen prisoners, including Private Hervé Labrecque, were lined up before a firing squad in the orchard of the chateau, and executed. Details of the atrocity were not to reach the Labrecque family in Rosetown, Saskatchewan, until after the war was over.

Sent home by the nuns at the convent school in Rosetown just when she was getting ready for June exams, Marie Labrecque arrived to find everyone crying. All they knew at the time was what the June 27

telegraph told them: Hervé had been killed in action on June 8. That week's Rosetown *Eagle* reported that Hervé "is the first of our Rosetown lads to die in the French invasion." A requiem high mass, as the *Eagle* noted, was said on July 3 at St. Theresa's Catholic Church for the repose of his soul.

Young Alfred Labrecque, fourteen years old when his cousin was killed, was attending boarding school in Gravelbourg and could not attend the mass. He said his own prayers for Hervé, his hero. "So big and strong, he was," says Alfred, who remembers visiting Hervé at the farm during his last furlough before heading overseas in 1943. On that occasion, Hervé's soldierly skills were on full display for his admiring cousins. "He took us around the corner of the barn. First thing we knew, he was behind us. He showed us how he could scout around the yard without us seeing him. He showed us how he could scale a wall, too, by throwing a rope up." Many years later, Alfred paid his respects at Hervé's gravesite in the Beny-sur-Mer Canadian War Cemetery near Caen. "I broke down," Alfred says. "It had never really hit me until I saw that grave. He died at such an early age. We all looked up to him."

Labrecque Bay, on Welk Lake in northern Saskatchewan, honours the memory of Hervé Labrecque. ✿

Leboldus

FLYING OFFICER **PETER JOHN LEBOLDUS** • J15034 • 1918–1943
SERGEANT **MARTIN BENEDICT LEBOLDUS** • R61333 • 1921–1944
FLIGHT SERGEANT **JOHN ANTHONY LEBOLDUS** • R155568 • 1922–1943

Leboldus Lake (56°15' N, 107°51' W), Leboldus Islands (56°15' N, 107°52' W), and Leboldus Channel (56°16' N, 107°52' W) are seen here from the west—looking down Leboldus Channel, where Leboldus Islands open to Leboldus Lake. Situated 125 air miles northwest of La Ronge in the Frobisher Plain area of the Churchill River Upland ecoregion, Leboldus Lake is eight miles in length and is connected to Frobisher Lake and the Churchill River through Leboldus Channel. A sandy terrain supports black spruce, jack pine, and tamarack forest growth, while the waters provide excellent pickerel and jackfish habitat.

● Vibank

Father Bernie Leboldus, the youngest in his family, remembers a stormy, wintry day just before Valentine's Day in 1943. He had been to see "Yankee Doodle Dandy" at the Capitol Theatre in Regina. Returning to Vibank by train that evening after his father and mother had gone to bed, he found on the kitchen table a telegram with the terrible news that his brother Peter was missing in action. The family would receive similar telegrams two more times—Peter, John, and Martin all died within a twelve month period in 1943-44. One other son survived his war service.

Before the war, Peter Leboldus worked as a service man for the John Deere dealer in Yorkton, but he was in love with aviation, having taken an aeronautical course at Balfour Tech in Regina in 1936. He enlisted in February of 1940 and several months later achieved some national prominence for a note-dropping episode in Ottawa. At the end of a twelve-week observer training course in Malton, Ontario, Pete (as he was known) flew in one of fifteen RCAF Avro-Anson trainers on a flight from Toronto to Montreal. At noon one August day in 1940, dozens of notes fell to the streets of Ottawa from one of the aircraft: "Lonesome flier wishes to correspond with a young lady," the message said. Peter Leboldus's name and address were attached, although he was quick to deny responsibility for the prank:

> In the first place, I am not lonely. I have a steady girl with whom I am perfectly satisfied. In the second place, I didn't write the note. It was written

by a fellow airman in a frisky mood. I guess I'll get some answers to the message, though. I'll certainly have lots of time to read them. I might answer some of the good ones.

Indeed, Peter received dozens of letters.

A few months later, Peter was in the north of Scotland, stationed with No. 418 "City of Edmonton" Squadron, a fighter squadron flying Douglas Boston aircraft. His letters home— this time there was no doubt that he was the author— spoke of his appreciation for the natural beauty of the countryside, for the courage of the British people in the midst of their many perils. On one occasion he had tea at Windsor Palace with the Queen and the two Princesses, Elizabeth and Margaret. Now commissioned as a Flying Officer, he participated in numerous operations over Europe, including a successful attack on a German battleship in the Skagerrak Channel between Norway and Denmark. He was killed in action on February 13, 1943, his Boston shot down while engaged in night operations over France. Peter Leboldus is buried in France at Grandcourt War Cemetery, about thirty kilometres east of Dieppe.

Like everyone else in his family, Martin Leboldus was a musical fellow who at home had frequently performed with one or more of his siblings on guitar and piano. Martin had followed his brother Peter to Balfour Tech, into the RCAF, and into active service.

On one occasion, he even seemed to follow his brother to a dance in London when they were both stationed in Britain. Each of the two brothers didn't know the other was at the dance until they met when they were leaving. And they were to meet at least one more time. When Peter embarked on the mission from which he never returned, it was his brother Martin who had helped him into his parachute harness. Later Martin remustered to air crew as a flight engineer in No. 419 "Moose" Squadron. On February 20, 1944, Martin's Halifax was one of 823 aircraft in a raid on Leipzig. It was a difficult operation. The bomber stream was under attack from night fighters all the way to the target, and wind and cloud conditions were unsuitable for accurate bombing. Seventy-nine aircraft— one of them carrying Sergeant Martin Leboldus and his crewmates—did not return that night, the heaviest Bomber Command loss of the war to that point. Martin Leboldus is commemorated by the Runnymede Memorial in Surrey.

John Leboldus was sent to the Middle East in April 1943, an Air Gunner in RAF No. 142 Squadron. Before enlisting, however, his education had taken

Left: Peter Leboldus

Below: Martin Leboldus

119

him to St. Peter's College in Muenster, Saskatchewan, where he studied Arts in 1940–41 and, as often as he could, played hockey. The most outgoing of the boys, he, too, had sung in the church choir, conducted by his father, and had the added distinction of being American by birth, having been born in Yakima, Washington, where his mother was visiting his aunt. In the Middle East, John's squadron was active in operations over Italy. During a raid on Turin in northwest Italy on November 24, 1943, his plane crashed on a hillside. It had been flying low in foggy conditions. Flight Sergeant John Leboldus is buried at Stagliano Cemetery in Genoa.

Twelve years later, the boys' mother, Mrs. Regina Leboldus from Vibank, placed a wreath on the National War Memorial during the Remembrance Day service in Ottawa. She was the Silver Cross Mother for 1955, the first to be chosen from outside Ontario. Reports of the service noted that as she came down the granite steps of the Memorial after laying the wreath, Mrs. Leboldus paused, turned, and looked up to the bronze figures at the top of the column. She bowed her head and, for a time, did not move.

The flight to Ottawa was the first she'd ever taken. "I swore that I would never go up in a plane," she said at the time, "but now they want me, so I guess I will have to go." Her husband John confirmed that "Yes, she will go, for she has the courage of her sons."

As if to signify the bond of the three Leboldus brothers in life, in death they are memorialized by three linked geographical features in Saskatchewan's north. Leboldus Channel, named after John, connects Frobisher Lake to Leboldus Lake (named after Peter) around Leboldus Islands (named after Martin). ✿

MOTHERHOOD OF CANADA

Leskiw

The Halifax Memorial, a granite cross more than twelve metres high located in Point Pleasant Park, is clearly visible to all ships approaching Halifax harbour. Its podium contains inscriptions of the names of nearly 2,000 members of the Royal Canadian Navy who were lost at sea in World War II. One of these names is Anthony Leskiw.

Born in Saskatoon on May 12, 1920, the only boy and the youngest of three children, Tony Leskiw came from a proud Ukrainian-Canadian family. Both pairs of grandparents had emigrated from Ukraine to Dauphin, Manitoba, around the turn of the century. By the 1930s, in the Pleasant Hill district of Saskatoon, young Tony was involved in all the usual school activities, as well as being an active member of the St. Thomas Wesley Young Boys' Club and the Ukrainian National Youth Federation (UNYF). His sister Anne remembers that "everything we did at the UNYF hall had to be blended in some way with the larger Canadian community." Tony Leskiw was loyal to Canada and to his Ukrainian heritage and, as Anne says, "too bad for anybody who said anything against either one."

Emily and Anne "thought the world" of their brother, and so, apparently, did many outside the Leskiw family. He was a good-looking boy, full of personality, including a vigorous repertoire of jokes. Fluently bilingual, Tony was in demand as an actor in Ukrainian plays, despite his playful threats to jump up on stage and say his own little bit before retreating into his character. Choir practice was another forum for

Leskiw Lake (54°35' N, 102°38' W), viewed here from the north, is located 115 miles southeast of La Ronge. A shallow feature, Leskiw Lake is about two miles in length and is characteristic of the wetlands which attract waterfowl to the Mid-Boreal Lowland ecoregion of the Boreal Plain.

Saskatoon•

some Leskiw mischief. Tony had the knack for planting an elaborate yawn in the midst of the choir. Soon it would spread throughout the whole group, disrupting the rehearsal plans of the harried conductor. Tony did have a wonderful voice, though, and was a keen participant in all voice, drama, and sports activities. Dance was the one thing Tony *didn't* do.

All in all, the UNYF hall was a home away from home for Tony and his sisters and friends, prompting his mother to exclaim: "Why don't you kids just get your beds and take them over to the hall and sleep there." The janitor at the hall could testify to the vigour of the youth community. For hours the kids would play and sing— Tony accompanying on mouth organ— around the furnace at the hall. When the janitor chased them out, they'd continue outside on the front steps. "If we ran out of Ukrainian songs," Anne says," we'd sing anything at all."

Tony attended Saskatoon Technical Collegiate taking art as well as typing. Instead of completing high school, he took a job as a typesetter at New Pathway Publishers, helping to produce a Ukrainian-language newspaper which is still publishing today. His sister Emily remembers that her daughter Lorette used to run to the corner to meet him after work. He would carry her home on his shoulders.

As a young man Tony had wanted to be a Cossack; what he did become was a member of Royal Canadian Navy Volunteer Reserve *Saskatoon*, Saskatoon, in 1938 and then the Royal Canadian Navy. He enlisted in the navy in June of 1940, just after his twentieth birthday. His training took him eventually to Esquimalt, British Columbia, where he trained as an anti-aircraft machine gunner. Tony saw his family for the last time during a twenty-minute stopover at the CNR train station in Saskatoon. Then he was on to Halifax.

Tony had always wanted to go overseas, believing that nothing could be more fulfilling than naval service. He was not afraid to die, he told his former colleagues at New

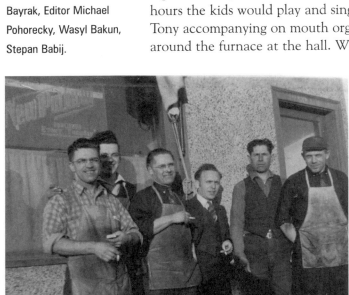

Upon hearing of Tony's death, his father took his Bible and went upstairs. "He seemed to turn white overnight," Tony's sister Anne recalls, "and Mother simply went to bed." Emily, the one who answered the knock on the door and first read the telegram, "still shivers when she thinks of it," she

admits. Grandfather Chimboryk, who had visited the Leskiw home every day, could no longer bring himself to come into the house. Even the beloved pet dog, Brownie, seemed to sense the loss. Brownie had been devoted to Tony, and died not long after he did.

The memory of Anthony Leskiw is honoured in Saskatchewan by Leskiw Lake. By the sea in Halifax, the dedication on the Halifax Memorial reads: "In honour of the men and women of the navy, army and merchant navy of Canada whose names are inscribed here. Their graves are unknown but their memory shall endure." ❀

Pathway, and if he was to die, he would die as a Ukrainian. "I still believe Ukraine will be a free country," he wrote, underlining it three times. Death came early in Ordinary Seaman Leskiw's service career, during his very first voyage on active duty aboard the S.S. *Whitford Point*. The ship, one in a convoy of forty-nine ships crossing the North Atlantic bound for England, was sunk by a U-boat torpedo on the night of October 20, 1940.

Above: Tony (left) in 1923 with his grandfather, Harry Chimboryk, and cousin Steven Chimboryk.

Tony during training: far left, at Mount Robson, left, at Stanley Park.

Linton

Linton Lake (60°00' N, 103°17' W), viewed here from the northwest, is located 340 miles northeast of La Ronge, on the border between Saskatchewan and the Northwest Territories. Deep in the Selwyn Lake Upland ecoregion, Linton Lake is about four miles long with a prominent presence of black spruce, lichens, and sandy glacial deposits.

The Alameda *Dispatch* printed this "Tribute from a Friend" after Leonard Linton was reported killed in action in 1944:

> Leonard Linton was a fine type of manhood and a general favourite. He took part in the work of the church, and other phases of community life. He was truly an asset to any district.
>
> In his educational career he showed remarkable ability, and in attaining his goal, he applied the spirit of the noble Roman who said, "I'll find a way or make it."
>
> In the tragic passing of Leonard, Douglaston mourns the death of one of her best and bravest souls.

The eldest of five children born to Mary and Edward Linton, Leonard was indeed active in all phases of the life of the Douglaston district in southeast Saskatchewan. Friends and family would see him playing guitar with his brother Dave on fiddle, enjoying a swim and a picnic up at Carlyle Lake, or joining a Young People's Club activity in Douglaston. Always the type to do the driving, he would take children to school in the cutter pulled by the school horse, Dan (one time tipping the cutter and breaking the family's Hallowe'en pumpkin), or he'd drive the Model T to a rodeo in Oxbow. Once he drove the family car full of Douglaston youngsters to see the King and Queen in Regina during the Royal Tour of 1939. He enjoyed sports of all kinds, excelling at any of several events during sports days or, with Dave, shooting pucks against a wall of bales at home, using his sisters—Mary, Edith, or Helen—as helpless goalies.

Of course, there was some schooling to take care of, and Leonard, always the head of his class, got as far as grade ten at Douglaston before taking a year off to work. Soon the war had started, and Leonard was determined to be a pilot. Thinking he'd need his grade twelve, Leonard boarded with his Uncle Ralph (owner of the famous Linton round barn two miles northwest of Willmar) and finished his high school in Willmar. He did chores to pay for his board—milking, harvesting, hauling wood— becoming ever handier with wood and metal like his Grandpa Linton, a blacksmith, who showed him how to make skis, kites, and hockey sticks.

Leonard enlisted in December of 1941 with the support of his parents, whose loyalty to the Crown was always strong. Beginning in Brandon, his training included a six-week stint at No. 3 Bombing and Gunnery School in MacDonald, Manitoba, in the summer of 1943. During his embarkation leave after finishing the course at MacDonald, he returned home to marry his long-time girlfriend Velma Woods. After their wedding on the Woods farm, there was just enough time for a short honeymoon at Carlyle Lake, and Leonard was off by train for eastern Canada and then to England. He did stop in Montreal, where his mother had been a nurse, and took a side trip to visit his maternal grandparents in Sutton, Québec.

Flying with a Wellington bomber crew piloted by a Sergeant Jarvis, Leonard progressed through No. 14 Operational Training Unit at Bosworth and Market Harbord and 1661 Heavy Conversion Unit at Winthorpe. In late December of 1943, his crew was posted to RAF No. 207 Squadron. Now they were flying a Lancaster, mixing further training exercises with operations during the Battle of Berlin. In fact, one of the crew's operations was a seven-hour and forty-minute raid on the Big City itself. Meanwhile, as Leonard reported in a letter home, "I got my second

Opposite page: Leonard Linton on guitar with brother Dave on fiddle.

Bottom left: Leonard and Velma.

Centre: Leonard's dogtag.

125

uniform today so now I have twice as many buttons to shine."

Leonard Linton received his commission as a Pilot Officer the day he was killed in action, February 18, 1944. Eight hundred and twenty-three aircraft attacked Leipzig that night, and almost ten percent of them did not return, as the bomber stream was under attack all the way to the target. *The Bomber Command War Diaries* reports further difficulties: "Winds were not as forecast and many aircraft reached the Leipzig area too early and had to orbit and await the Pathfinders [to pinpoint the target]. Four aircraft were lost by collision and approximately twenty were shot down by flak." As the *Diaries* concludes, "it was an unhappy raid for Bomber Command."

Pilot Officer Leonard Linton is buried at Becklingen War Cemetery, Germany. In the extreme northeast of Saskatchewan lies a four-mile-long body of water named Linton Lake in Leonard's honour. ❀

MacMillan

In many ways William Russell MacMillan was well-suited for his work as a Stoker on HMS *Bramble*. He had "considerable experience along mechanical lines," as his Naval Reserve Commanding Officer noted in recommending Russell for a Stoker I (Mechanic) rating with the Canadian Navy. His civilian experience, as Russell himself noted on an enlistment form, included "ten years experience in operation and maintenance of tractors"; his present employment was "working at Nutana service station," an Esso station near his home in Saskatoon. And his father, also named William, was a steam engineer by trade, although he'd become a farmer after moving to Saskatchewan from Ontario.

William and Nettie had seven children, of whom Russell was the second oldest. "Dad and Russell were the greatest of pals," says his sister Doris. "Russell loved to farm, and he was his Dad's main helper." He was able to sharpen his mechanical aptitude by working on his brother-in-law's International 1530 tractor—Russell knew it inside out—or by driving and maintaining, always carefully, his father's Studebaker, which he drove to dances. The mixed farm the MacMillans rented was located just east of Saskatoon in the district of Floral (birthplace of hockey great Gordie Howe). William operated a threshing outfit, travelling around the district with his thresher, bunkhouse, and cookhouse. In 1940 the family moved into Saskatoon, and William was employed by No. 7 Training School (Air Force) as steam engineer.

MacMillan Lake (56°51' N, 103°32' W), viewed here from the south, is 145 air miles northeast of La Ronge. Situated in the Athabasca Plain ecoregion, MacMillan Lake, which is four miles long, is part of an extended waterway that drains from Reindeer Lake. This flow of water, over twenty miles in total length, can be navigated through a series of short portages. Accessible from Highway 905 at the Kane Lake outfitters camp, MacMillan Lake is surrounded by rugged and rocky country that supports abundant wildlife and various fish species. In the summer of 2001, the family of W.R.E. MacMillan visited MacMillan Lake and placed a bronze plaque in his memory.

Saskatoon●

Russell had begun his school education in the one-room schoolhouse at Floral and obtained his grade nine in 1930. He was active in athletics—hockey and softball especially. Once he broke his arm playing ball during the Saskatoon Exhibition and, somewhere along the line, acquired a scar above his left eye.

Russell was the kind of friendly, thoughtful guy who wouldn't hurt human or animal. Good with horses, and careful with them, if he had a team out on a winter day hauling wood or pulling the cutter, he wouldn't risk their well-being by racing them simply to get himself out of the cold. Everybody liked him, especially his brother Lorne, who would also join the Navy, and his five sisters, who knew that whenever they needed a lift somewhere, Russell would be ready to help. "I never heard him swear," Doris says.

Russell was also ready to help his country during wartime. Joining the Navy on May 12, 1941, within a year he was sent "on loan" to the Royal Navy after training stops in Pictou, Nova Scotia, and the famous Devonport Royal Navy dockyard in Plymouth, England. Partly to compensate Britain for its support of the Canadian effort in the Atlantic in the early years of the war, and partly to accumulate a fund of experience

from which Canadians could draw later in the war years, the loan program sent hundreds of Canadians to British ships of all types. Stoker MacMillan was assigned to HMS *Bramble*, an Algernine-class minesweeper. Fitted with mechanical, acoustic, and magnetic minesweeping equipment, the *Bramble* had the job of clearing shipping lanes of mines of various kinds—some were moored to the sea floor, others would float below the surface—and marking the cleared lanes with buoys.

His letters home report his observations on the currency, the costs and rationing of food and gasoline, his purchase of some blue serge he wants to have tailored into a suit, and the pleasures of Scotland: "if it were not for Scotland we would have no place to go for our leaves." He inquires after everyone at home, and requests "a thousand cigarettes" and a lighter. And for

Right: HMS *Bramble*.

NAVAL MUSEUM OF ALBERTA

128

his brother Lorne he has a special reminder "to have the car in tip-top shape when I get back there as we might happen to go on a little trip." He seems lonely at Devonport, wishing he were somewhere else, and in his last letter, dated December 21, 1942, he hopes " to be in harbour somewhere for Christmas instead of out to sea so we will have some peace eating our Christmas dinner."

As it happened, the next day Convoy JW 51B sailed from Loch Ewe in Scotland bound for Russia. Guarding the fourteen merchant ships were six destroyers, two corvettes, two trawlers, and one minesweeper, the *Bramble*. At first the passage was

uneventful, but at noon on the thirtieth of December, a U-boat spotted the convoy, reporting it as "weakly protected." A squadron of German destroyers was dispatched from Altenfiord in northern Norway, and at 10:47 a.m. on December 31, the over-matched *Bramble*, firing only a single gun, was damaged by the *Hipper* and sunk. Despite the loss of the *Bramble* and one other British ship, the convoy remained intact, and the Germans had to retreat to Altenfiord.

The news of Russell's death was devastating to his friends and family. "Russell used to fight my battles at school," wrote an old friend from Floral to Russell's brother, "and I always thought of him when word would come of some big convoy movement. He had a big job and it ended like it has for so many others. God, let's hope something worthwhile comes from this awful mess."

Stoker William Russell Elwood MacMillan's name is among the thousands of names inscribed on the Halifax Memorial at Point Pleasant Park, Halifax. He is also commemorated in Floral, Saskatchewan, by a plaque beside the grave markers of his parents and sisters—and in northern Saskatchewan by MacMillan Lake. ✿

Above: Doris Pope, Russell MacMillan's sister, and her husband Bert, along with other family members, visited MacMillan Lake in July 2001. There they put up a plaque in memory of Russell.

DOUG CHISHOLM

Left: Veterans' Memorial, Point Pleasant Park, Halifax, Nova Scotia

ANNE SELLER, EARTHEN FOCUS IMAGES

MacPherson

MacPherson Bay (55°21' N, 104°28' W), viewed here from the west, is almost four miles long and is located thirty-five air miles east of La Ronge on Iskwatikan Lake. Situated in the Churchill River Upland ecoregion, Iskwatikan Lake flows through Nistowiak Falls into the Churchill River. This area is a popular summer and winter destination for northern travellers.

Growing up in Regina in the 1920s and 1930s, Ian MacPherson was a bright, active young man. An accomplished figure skater, he competed annually in a show held by the Wascana Winter Club. He also exhibited his athletic skills on the football field, where he was an all-star on Central Collegiate's senior football team. And true to his Scottish roots, he played the bagpipes, joining the Regina Boys Pipe Band. At home he often practiced the pipes in the company of his younger brother's cocker spaniel, Laddie, who would sit at his feet and howl along to the music.

One of his favourite activities was sailing. He built a sailboat in his parents' basement, forgetting only to consider the size of the boat in relation to that of the doorway. To his parents' displeasure, a basement wall had to be demolished before the boat could be taken down to Wascana Lake for its launch. Out at Katepwa, where the family had a cottage, he capsized his boat one cold spring day. A priest from the nearby Oblate seminary summer camp came to his rescue, offering a brandy to reduce the chill. His brother Donald recalls that such tipping incidents happened frequently thereafter, often just in front of the priest's camp.

A tradition of military service had been established in the MacPherson family. Ian's father Murdoch, a prominent Regina lawyer, had served overseas in the First World War, seeing action at Vimy Ridge and surviving serious wounds received at Arleux. He was invalided home where he was assigned, while on crutches, to sell war bonds. After the war, he headed the Soldier Settlement Board. For Ian, then, it was a natural move from high school at Central to the Royal Military College (RMC), where he completed officer's training in 1940. At this point he requested permission to serve with the Indian Army, thus fulfilling a long-time fascination with eastern culture—one stimulated by the many books on India that his father had provided.

By July of 1940, he received orders to sail on a merchant vessel to England from where, after a brief period, he boarded another ship for India. Just off the coast of Ireland, however, the ship was torpedoed. The attack brought down the ceiling of Ian's cabin, rendering him unconscious. He would have surely drowned but for an old Regina and RMC friend who helped him to a lifeboat. Captain MacPherson required three months in a London hospital to recover from his head wound. During his out-of-hospital convalescence, he helped fight fires in London during the Blitz. In the end, the worst misfortune to have befallen him to this point in his military life was that he'd lost his bagpipes when his ship went down in the Irish Sea.

Upon arriving in India he served with the Seventh Gurkha Rifles in the course of the British retreat from Singapore to northern Burma in 1942, during which he was twice mentioned in Dispatches. After returning to India for jungle training and refitting, he was recruited into the Seventy-seventh Brigade of the Long Range Penetration Force as part of the allied offensive through north Burma. Known as the second Wingate expedition, this operation sent glider-borne troops into what its commander, Brigadier Michael Calvert, called "the heart of Burma" behind enemy lines. Establishing a stronghold called Broadway and later a second called White City, these troops, Captain Ian MacPherson among them, engaged two infantry and one artillery battalions of the Japanese army which would have otherwise fortified Japanese forces at the front line further north. Captain MacPherson performed admirably in the fierce fighting around White City. In *Prisoners of Hope*, his account of the Wingate expedition, Brigadier Calvert describes MacPherson as "one of the finest men I have met. Skilful, fearless, quiet, with tremendous energy and endurance, he was a proud and worthy soldier."

Brigadier Calvert's book includes an account of Ian MacPherson's death, April 18, 1944, near Mawlu, Burma:

I asked Francis, "Where is Ian?" "He is dead." I said, "He can't be." He said, "I saw him shot through the forehead." I said that I was going back to see. I could not leave anyone like that without knowing for certain. I started to go back into the fight. Quite a lot of fire was still taking place. As I went into the jungle alone I must have had a crazy look about me, for Francis rushed up and told me I must not go on, my duty was with my brigade. I said, "I don't believe

Ian is dead." Francis heaved out his revolver, stuck it in my stomach and said, "I'll shoot you if you don't go back. I was with him when he was killed." With a heavy heart I retraced my steps.

In a letter written to Murdoch MacPherson a month after Ian was killed, Major-General W.D. Lentaigne confirms the merits of Ian MacPherson's conduct in Burma: "Your son undertook cheerfully, and with no thought of self, a task that ranks with the most difficult and hazardous asked of any man in this war. Nothing can compensate you for his loss, but I can assure you that no father has cause to be prouder of his son's courage."

Captain Ian Edgar MacPherson's name is engraved on the Rangoon Memorial in Myanmar (formerly Burma). MacPherson Bay in northern Saskatchewan is named in memory of this man who, in Calvert's words, "lived for his Gurkhas and for soldiering." ✿

Mandel

Captain Jacob Mandel, one of two Saskatchewan doctors to be killed during World War II, came from Estevan. His father Max, who had immigrated to the area from Russia in 1908, ran a clothing store, M. Mandel & Co., on Main Street. Jake was an outstanding student at both elementary and high school in Estevan—a champion public speaker and winner of the Governor General's Medal. He also won a scholarship to the University of Saskatchewan, and after taking his pre-med studies there, Jake went on to medical school at the University of Alberta, graduating in 1939. In the next two years he interned in Edmonton, joined the staff of St. Paul's Hospital in Saskatoon, married his childhood sweetheart, Pearl, and seemed destined for a career as a prairie doctor.

But it was wartime, and Jake joined the Royal Canadian Army Medical Corps in February 1941. He served in the Halifax Military Hospital at Lawlor's Island before being placed in charge of a thirty-five-bed hospital in New Glasgow, Nova Scotia. In late 1942 he went overseas, attached to the Governor General's Foot Guards in England, transferring later to the Twelfth Light Field Ambulance Unit of the Fourth Armoured Division.

The precise circumstances of his death on August 14, 1944 are uncertain. The Fourth Canadian Armoured was part of Operation Tractable across the valley of the Laison River toward Falaise. "The 14th of August was a beautiful summer day," notes C. P. Stacey

Mandel Island (55° 06' N, 105° 01' W), viewed here from the east, is located on Lac la Ronge, ten boat miles from the community. About two miles in length, Mandel Island is a popular summer destination for cabin owners and visitors to Lac la Ronge, who enjoy its peaceful beauty.

Estevan

in his official army history. "Those who saw it were to remember long the sight of the great columns of armour going forward 'through fields of waving golden grain.'" As a medical doctor, Captain Mandel would have been stationed at the aid post, located close to the front line but protected from small arms fire, where he would tend to the wounded brought there by stretcher-bearers. One version of Captain Mandel's death has him riding a jeep near the front lines, as medical officers did from time to time, and striking a land mine; another has him taking a bullet intended for someone else. Whatever the exact circumstances, Jake's medical school pal from Edmonton, Dr. Elliot Corday, was with him at the time, and for the rest of his life, including many years as a renowned cardiologist in the United States, Dr. Corday attributed his own survival to the courage of Captain Mandel.

Below: Canadian tanks and armoured vehicles taking part in Operation Tractable. This photo was taken on the day Captain Mandel was killed, August 14, 1944.

DONALD I. GRANT / NATIONAL ARCHIVES OF CANADA / PA116525

The strength of the bond between these two Medical Corps comrades became apparent to the Mandel family years later. In 1978, Gertrude Brookler, Jake's sister, went to France to visit her brother's gravesite at Beny-sur-Mer Canadian War Cemetery near Caen. It was the anniversary of Jake's death, and someone had placed a beautiful wreath on his grave. Curious, Mrs. Brookler inquired after the anonymous wreath-layer and eventually discovered that it was none other than the famed American general, Omar Bradley. It happened that General Bradley's personal physician had been Dr. Corday, who over the years, especially while accompanying General Bradley on trips back through the Normandy battlegrounds, had told the general all about Captain Jacob Mandel, about how Jake had in effect saved Dr. Corday's life. Perhaps feeling as if Jake Mandel had touched his own life, General Bradley had arranged for a wreath to be laid at the gravesite every year on the fourteenth of August.

Captain Jacob Mandel is remembered in other ways as well. To a wartime mate, Captain Hardy, Jake will forever be "William Tell" Mandel because he was an outstanding marksman. A generation of high school students at Estevan Collegiate Institute remembered Jacob Mandel for the Mandel Memorial Award, an annual award established by his family in 1946 and presented for many years for proficiency in English. The

province of Saskatchewan's way of remembering Jake was to name Mandel Island, a popular cabin area on Lac la Ronge, in his honour. Finally, Jake's cousin Eli, one of Canada's most important poets of the last fifty years, remembers Jake with poetry. Eli had visited Jake in Europe three weeks before Jake's death, and upon returning home to visit Gertrude, Jake's sister, and share her grief after her brother's death, Eli wrote what he claimed to be his first poem. A later poem,

"returning from war: (for jbm 1918 [sic]–1944), ends with this eloquent simplicity:

in the estevan summer
hazardous as desert hear
gopher squeaks momentary hawks
lean in the pushing and shoving
wind   the sun breathing
heat

and the impossibility of death ❀

Below far left: The cenotaph in Estevan, Saskatchewan, honouring Estevan sons killed in the two world wars, includes the names of Jacob Mandel, James A. Clarke (page 30), Joseph Gedak (page 72), William Knight (page 110), and David Murray (page 151).

DON HALL

Left: U.S. General Omar Bradley in 1978 at Mandel's gravesite.

Mason

Mason Island (54°55' N, 102°50' W), viewed here from the south, is located on Jan Lake, one hundred air miles east of La Ronge. A popular recreational site, Jan Lake is a large feature, reaching sixteen miles at its longest point. Jan Lake is accessible from Highway 135, and Mason Island is only two miles from the provincial campground. As boat traffic ventures out onto Jan Lake, all must pass Mason Island on the way north. In June 2001, Glen Mason travelled to Mason Island and placed a bronze plaque in memory of his brother Earl.

● Elrose

As the son of the CNR station agent in Elrose, Saskatchewan, Earl Mason had quite a few things going for him as he was growing up in the 1920s and 1930s. The Mason family, parents Nathan and Agnes and nine children—Earl was the second oldest—had free electricity and water and better access to coal and ice than did many others in the town. And it was easy for Earl to take advantage of a CNR pass to travel down to Minnesota to visit his grandfather. He spent the whole summer after grade eleven working in his grandfather's store, in fact. More importantly, Earl was the kind of fellow people liked. Relatively short in stature, he drew upon a winning personality and a good sense of humour to resist the occasional teasing because of his height, although once in a while he'd apply his "hit first, talk later" policy. He was a good ballplayer—a strong-armed pitcher—and a happy-go-lucky boy often in the centre of fishing and swimming excursions to Clearwater Lake.

Like his brothers, Earl became an expert telegraph operator—his family lived in the train station, after all—and thought he might take up such work as a career. Meanwhile, he finished his grade twelve at the four-room Elrose School and pumped gas for the Hunt and Graber car dealership. By that time he'd picked up the nickname "Tootie," although no one can remember how; the garage owner's dog had the same name.

When Earl enlisted in the RCAF in June of 1940, he specified "pilot only," as many would-be flyers did,

and soon had achieved a small degree of fame, coming second in a "forced landing" competition in his Tiger Moth at No. 6 Elementary Flying Training School in Prince Albert. He was further immortalized, this time in verse form, when J.G. Wilson, a training mate, composed "Rhymes of the Terrible Twenty-Three" about a few of the trainees at EFTS:

> Mason E., stands five foot three,
> He's called the might atom.
> With a voice of scorn, he says each morn:
> Let me up and at 'em.

Coming home to Elrose on leave, Earl made quite an impression on his family with how good he looked in his uniform and how briskly he could snap off a salute. Once he drove an old motorcycle home. It was such a wreck that his father wouldn't let him drive it back, instead loading the bike into the trunk of his brand new Pontiac and letting Earl drive back to the base in style.

Prior to the United States' entry into World War II, many Americans volunteered for service with one of three Eagle squadrons of the Royal Air Force. The Battle of Britain through the summer of 1940 had left RAF pilot ranks depleted, and the Eagle Squadrons, manned entirely by American pilots but commanded by Englishmen, were welcome additions to Fighter Command. Trained in Canada, the pilots would be posted to an Operational Training Unit in England before joining one of the squadrons. For Earl Mason, who had dual citizenship—before moving to Elrose, his father had been a station agent in Roosevelt, Minnesota, and Earl was born in Pitt—an Eagle Squadron was the way to go. The Battle of Britain was over, but Sergeant Mason, not yet a pilot officer, could fly both a Spitfire and a Hurricane, and when No. 121 Squadron was formed in May of 1941, he was one of the first to join.

Below: A Hurricane IIb, the same type of aircraft that Earl Mason flew on various escort operations and raids.

Flying a Hurricane IIb, Sergeant Mason took part in a variety of operations, including convoy escort patrols, bomber escort, and low-level ground attack raids on railroads, troops, tanks, or anything else of military value on the continent. Encounters with enemy aircraft were minimal. September 15, 1941, was a "non-operational" day—"just a day," wrote Flight Lieutenant George Brown, "of mock strafing attacks on British Army units practicing maneuvers." Flying from their base at Kirton-in-Lindsey, Earl "Tootie" Mason and Bert Stewart finished their army co-operation duties for the day and started playing what Stewart would call a kind of follow-the-leader:

> We were doing some aerobatics over the tanks—rolls, and just generally cutting up. I went down and did a slow roll maybe fifty feet off the ground, and slipped out of the roll and almost hit the ground myself. I came very close to writing myself off.
>
> It crossed my mind immediately to call Tootie and tell him, "Don't do it." Before I could call him, I saw him roll into the ground.

Sergeant Mason had crashed into a tree and was killed instantly. He had been commissioned as a pilot officer less than a month earlier.

Nathan Mason received the casualty telegraph himself, transcribing the Morse code message in his office at the CNR station in Hanley, where he had been recently transferred. He delayed going into the kitchen to tell his wife, Agnes, until another message came a few hours later confirming their son's death.

"As you can well imagine," wrote Earl's squadron leader, "English people are slow to make up their minds about people coming from other parts, but we didn't take very long to realize that Earl was definitely what we call over here a 'good type.'" Buried with full military honours at Brookwood Military Cemetery near London, Pilot Officer Earl Mason is honoured by a memorial to the Eagle squadrons in Grosvenor Square, London, and by the naming of Mason Island in Saskatchewan. 🏵

Right: In June 2001, Glen Mason of Burnaby, British Columbia, placed a bronze plaque at Mason Island, in memory of his brother, Pilot Officer Earl W. Mason.

DOUG CHISHOLM

138

Maxmen

Edythe McDonald effortlessly recites the service number of her first husband, Stan Maxmen. Out on her balcony, she has set a thirty-seven-pound rock from the shores of Maxmen Lake, the lake in northern Saskatchewan named in Stan's honour. Inside on a shelf she has placed two smaller rocks from the same location. Each bears a small plaque inscribed *Maxmen Lake, Sept.1, 2000.*

Stan and Edythe had gone together at Central Collegiate in Moose Jaw, where Stan was very good in school. "A young man with excellent ability," noted Principal Ballard. "He is conscientious and industrious. He is especially good in Science and Math." Edythe remembers him as a quiet man who "wasn't one to push himself ahead." Stan's father, Ole Maxmenko—later the family surname was legally changed to Maxmen— had come from the Ukraine and had married an Eyebrow girl, Annabelle Booth, in 1921. Stan, born the next year, was the eldest of their four children. Ole worked at Swift Canadian, and Stan got a job there too after graduating from Central. He didn't have a car, but he and Edythe enjoyed walks together or swimming at River Park in summer or skating in winter. "Once in a while, six of us would pile into a friend's car and go places," Edythe says. Stan's hobbies were photography—he had even built his own darkroom— and lacrosse.

Stan didn't want to work in the smoked meats department of Swift Canadian for the rest of his life. He took several machine shop courses at Moose Jaw

Maxmen Lake (59°21' N, 104°45' W), viewed here from the north, is located about sixteen miles east of the community of Stony Rapids, about three hundred air miles north of La Ronge. Maxmen Lake is only about two hundred yards wide for most of its three-mile length, and its deep clear water is sheltered by some rugged two-hundred-foot rock cliffs which are dominant features in the Taiga Shield ecozone. At each end of Maxmen Lake, there is an abrupt change in waterflow direction and elevation, producing spectacular waterfalls and rapids.

Technical School and went east to Fort William to take a job in an aircraft factory. But he found work boring, he told Edythe, and, as she remembers, "he just wrote and said he was joining up."

At each step of his training Stan seemed to make a positive impression. "Keen and alert. Should make excellent fighter pilot," noted an instructor at Initial Training School in Regina. The next stage was No. 19 Elementary Flying Training School in Virden, Manitoba, where Stan was described as "an excellent apt student." At No. 1 Service Flying Training School (SFTS) in Ontario, he was seen as a "very good student who wants to fly night fighters."

After Stan received his wings in March 1942, he and Edythe made a decision. "He was going over, and we both wanted to get married," she remembers. "We didn't have time to arrange much of a wedding. He came home on leave on a Wednesday and we got married on the Saturday at St. Andrew's Church. We had to back-date the marriage license at the jewelry store." There was no time for a honeymoon; Stan was off to Halifax. Then Edythe got an odd telegram: Stan had been sent to the west coast. Could she meet him in B.C.? Uttering a silent thanks that her

Below: Edythe and Stan on their wedding day.

husband would be all right, now that he was staying on this side of the Atlantic, Edythe joined him at Patricia Bay on Vancouver Island. The newlyweds, living in a rented log cabin near Sydney, would enjoy less than three months together.

Stan had been posted to RCAF No. 111 Squadron, a coast artillery co-operation squadron that had been hastily sent west after the Japanese bombed Pearl Harbor in December 1941. Since most of the pilots had, like Stan, just finished their SFTS training and were not yet ready to fly the high-performance P-40E Kittyhawk fighters, the aircraft had to be shipped to the west coast by train. But by spring of 1942, the squadron was up and flying a regular pattern of coastal patrols. When the Japanese established bases on the outer Aleutian Islands, No. 111 made a corresponding move to the north, to Elmendorf Air Base, the major U.S. airforce base at Anchorage, Alaska. It was June 1942.

In July, part of No. 111 Squadron transferred to Umnak Island, further out in the Aleutians, to support the American squadrons there. It seemed an ill-fated operation from the start. Bad weather postponed departure several times until finally, on July 13, seven

Kittyhawks were able to leave Elmendorf. One aircraft was lost when its engine caught fire on the first leg of the journey; the pilot bailed out and was rescued. Another P-40 suffered a bad landing at Naknek, and was grounded while repairs were being made. On July 16 the weather cleared enough to fly the next leg to Cold Bay, and although weather was reported as marginal at Umnak, the seven fighters (two had been added to replace the two lost) continued their journey. Encountering severe fog near Unalaska Island, the island just east of Umnak, the pilots lost visual contact with one another. Wing Commander McGregor ordered a return to Cold Bay and was able to do so himself only after narrowly missing a cliff on the north side of the island. One other pilot found clear air between layers of cloud and was able to land safely. The five other pilots crashed into the mountains of Unalaska.

Back in Moose Jaw, the telegram reporting that Sergeant Stan Maxmen was missing in action arrived via CP where, as it happened, Edythe's father worked. He got the word first and went home to tell his daughter. Four days later, the telegram reporting that Stan had been killed was sent via CN, and Edythe received the telegram herself. "The word 'killed' jumped out at me," she remembers.

"It's almost like a dream after all these years," says Edythe McDonald, who was only nineteen when she was widowed, "but very emotional." In 1996, Edythe visited Stan's gravesite for the first time. As she arrived at Fort Richardson Post Cemetery, near Anchorage, a military funeral was taking place. Thus Edythe heard "The Last Post" as she approached Stan's grave. ✿

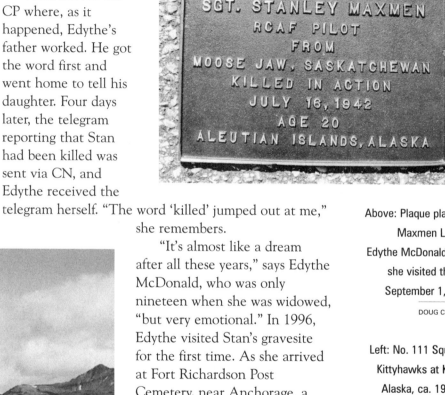

MAXMEN LAKE
NAMED IN MEMORY OF
SGT. STANLEY MAXMEN
RCAF PILOT
FROM
MOOSE JAW, SASKATCHEWAN
KILLED IN ACTION
JULY 16, 1942
AGE 20
ALEUTIAN ISLANDS, ALASKA

Above: Plaque placed at Maxmen Lake by Edythe McDonald when she visited the lake September 1, 2000.

DOUG CHISHOLM

Left: No. 111 Squadron Kittyhawks at Kodiak, Alaska, ca. 1942–43

COURTESY OF THE CANADIAN FORCES / PMR80-197

McKee

McKee Island (55°08' N, 105°01' W), viewed here from the south, is located on beautiful Lac la Ronge. Situated in a popular recreational area, McKee Island is in a central position among three parallel islands, about two miles in length. In 1966, Mr. Abraham Bereskin, the provincial director of surveying who initiated the geo-memorial naming program in Saskatchewan, travelled to McKee Island with the widow of Sergeant Gordon McKee, where a bronze plaque was placed in memory. This site is well known to those who frequent the area, and visitors often pause for reflection at the memorial plaque.

●Creelman

G ordon McKee left the farming life of the Creelman district of Saskatchewan not long after completing his grade ten by correspondence. He was destined for the west coast, and he found a variety of jobs out there, all in the logging industry. When war broke out he joined the army, mobilizing with the Seaforth Highlanders in Vancouver. Among the first Canadians to go overseas, the Seaforths embarked from Halifax aboard the *Andes* on December 20, 1939. More than two years of training and exercises in England followed before the regiment finally got word of where exactly they would see action. It would be Italy. There was another voyage, this time aboard the *Circassia*, and on July 10, 1943, the Seaforth Highlanders, Gordon McKee among them, landed on Sicily as part of Operation Husky.

While he was stationed in Great Britain, Gordon had made a significant personal decision. Having met one Rose Miskelly in Scotland when he and a friend had the opportunity to escort her to a bus, Gordon claimed to his friend, "I'm going to marry that girl"— and he did just that. On January 17, 1941, Gordon and Rose were married in Rose's hometown of Dundry, near Bristol, England. It was the second marriage to a military man for Rose, whose first husband, a flying instructor with the RAF, had been killed in action.

The Seaforth Highlanders were part of Montgomery's Eighth Army that pursued the enemy some 125 miles across Sicily and then, in September of 1943, up the boot of Italy. They advanced north into increasingly mountainous terrain and stiff resistance as far as the town of Baranello. As for Gordon McKee in particular, the events surrounding his death have been documented by Gordon Cameron in the January 3, 1945 issue of the *Leader-Post*, as well as in a short story by the same writer entitled, "No Surrender: A True Story." The story that follows has been adapted primarily from these two sources.

According to Cameron's accounts, Sergeant McKee had the duty, as sergeant of a scouts and snipers platoon, to gather information on the number and disposition of German soldiers in enemy-occupied territory. On the night of October 18, 1943, while independently reconnoitering the area of Baranello, McKee was captured in an ambush. But he escaped and sought refuge in a home, where he was received and offered food by an Italian family. His meal, however, was interrupted by German intruders, one of whom hollered, "You are my prisoner!" McKee, who had sworn he would never surrender to the Nazis, retorted, "Prisoner, hell!"

As the German soldier trained his revolver on Sergeant McKee, the twelve-year-old boy of the Italian household smashed a wine bottle on the German's head. The boy scurried past the Germans and down the street, while McKee fled in the opposite direction.

Coming to the village square, the Creelman soldier was surrounded by an estimated thirty German soldiers. When asked again to surrender, he responded by shooting five of his would-be captors. Taking a bullet in return, Sergeant McKee retreated into a stairwell. Before he could reach the door, he was shot for the second time in the chest. His comrades later found his body, propped against the wall.

When the officer commanding the German company was later captured by Allied infantry, he confirmed the events leading up to Gordon McKee's death. "The sergeant was a brave man. I regret we had to shoot him," he said.

In addition to his widow, Sergeant Gordon Kenneth McKee left behind his stepdaughter, Dianne Miskelly, and a Sicilian boy named Paolo, whom McKee had informally adopted. Gordon and a fellow soldier named Testawich had rescued the eight-year-old boy in Italy when they found him clinging to his dead mother. The Seaforth Highlanders decided to care for the boy, who grew particularly attached to McKee and Testawich. According to a *Leader-Post* article in 1943, after both soldiers were killed, Paolo was so grieved that "it took days for the men of the Seaforth Highlanders to compose him sufficiently so that he might continue with the troops."

Gordon's youngest brother Howard was also serving overseas at the time, and back in Canada, his mother, sister Myrtle, and brother Lyall received the news of Gordon's death. A letter from Lieutenant Colonel Douglas Forin to Gordon's mother provides another indication of the esteem in which he was held. "I have known your son for a long time in the unit," he wrote.

Below: Gordon McKee's wife, Rose, and stepdaughter, Dianne.

Right: Gordon's widow placed this plaque on the southeast tip of McKee Island.

Below right: Gordon plays guitar with his band called the Seaforth Hillbillies. The band was formed to help entertain the unit in their off-hours during two years of training for combat before embarking for Sicily. Note the "blacked out" windows.

Below: Gordon, shortly before he left for Sicily.

"Always he has been an outstanding soldier and leader, full of worth, efficient and quietly determined. The men in his platoon thought very highly of him." Forin went on to tell her of her son's funeral: "He was buried in a quiet park nearby, with the sound of guns still heard, and the Pipe Major played the lament *The Flowers of the Forest* at the service. Our cross marks where he fell, and daily Italian women keep it fresh with flowers.

Your loss and ours is a common and great one. Some consolation lies in the fact that he went as he would have wished."

Sergeant Gordon Kenneth McKee is buried at the Moro River Canadian War Cemetery near Ortona, Italy, on elevated land overlooking the Adriatic Sea. In Saskatchewan, a commemorative plaque lies on the southern tip of McKee Island on Lac la Ronge, named in honour of this worthy soldier.

McKEE ISLAND
NAMED IN MEMORY OF
SGT. GORDON KENNETH McKEE
1ST DIV. SEAFORTH HIGHLANDERS OF CANADA.
KILLED IN ACTION OCT. 18, 1943.

"THE LIFE GIVEN BY NATURE IS SHORT,
BUT THE MEMORY OF A WELL SPENT LIFE
IS ETERNAL."   CICERO.

1966

DEVONSHIRE COTTAGE

McLaren

Despite missing the odd term at school because of harvest or other farm duties, Jack McLaren always did well in school. "He could read anything and tell you about it," his sister Alice says, recalling scenes of Jack reading an encyclopedia or bringing home another glowing report card. "He was the smartest in any school," she says. Indeed, Jack was able to finish high school at the age of sixteen by combining grades eleven and twelve at Battleford High School.

Education around the home was more informal. It was a storytelling family—at home by firelight, usually about animals. Jack's father Ewing would start by sharing some story he had read, and Alma and the kids (nine, eventually) would take their turns in the storytelling role. Ewing and Alma encouraged their children's wide general knowledge and were themselves precise in the knowledge and use of the English language. A second-hand piano, purchased in 1917, also featured prominently in the family gatherings. Ewing could play a little, and liked to get his family singing around the piano on Sunday afternoons. Jack, too, was a piano player, taking lessons from Mr. Hurnard-Smith.

There was no chance for Jack, being the eldest, to pursue post-secondary education, despite his intelligence and academic abilities. "Hard times were a fact of life" on the farm, as his brother Harry says today. Because Jack was a farmer first, he answered the call to arms only in 1941 when he was nearly thirty years of

Named for Jack McLaren, McLaren Lake located at 60°01' N, 105°45' W and viewed here from the west, is located 330 air miles north of La Ronge, just beyond the border between Saskatchewan and the Northwest Territories. About four miles wide, the lake has many distinct bays and small islands. As is typical for the Taiga Shield, there is an abundance of lichen growth and cranberries among the black spruce and birch trees. Caribou are common in this habitat, as are wolves and bears. A description and photo of McLaren Lake named for Lewis McLaren (and indicated on the map left by the more southerly poppy) can be found on page 147 below.

Maidstone

Opposite page, centre: Lewis McLaren.

Opposite page, bottom: Lewis McLaren with his sister Eleanor before he left for service.

Right: Jack McLaren.

Below: Jack, Betty, and Martyn McLaren.

age. He'd married Elizabeth, a local girl, by that time. Betty, as she was known, accompanied Jack as he progressed through the RCAF Observor's course—a course that enabled him to apply his considerable mathematical aptitude. Jack McLaren received his Observor's wing in March of 1942, four days after Betty gave birth to their son Martyn back in Maidstone. Martyn was only a few months old when Jack went overseas.

Lewis McLaren had gone to school long enough to get his grade eight, but didn't care nearly as much for it as his oldest brother, Jack, had done. In fact, he didn't mind staying home from school, his sisters remember, to sleep all day. Lewis's talents lay in other areas. He could make a tune out of anything, for instance—a mandoline or mouth organ, a saw, the family piano. "He always had to be doing something," Alice says, and you could

count on Lewis to be the one goofing around whenever someone took out a camera. Although the McLarens, good Presbyterians, wouldn't play games on Sundays, they'd be busy most Saturdays—in the winter, skating on Silver Lake, and in the summer, playing ball or swimming—and Lewis would be one of the more active ones among them. He was active in looking for work, too, even riding the rods to do so. What he found was military service, becoming Private Lewis McLaren of the Saskatoon Light Infantry.

Lewis's sister Eleanor, a very young girl at the time, remembers the day Lewis got on the train at Maidstone to go off to war. There was a large crowd at the station, and Eleanor still remembers the feel of his rough greatcoat as he hugged her that wintry day. She remembers, too, that Lewis, who was normally such a happy fellow, seemed unusually sober before he left. In fact, he broke into tears, apologizing to his mother for doing so.

Lewis and Jack McLaren had a single visit together in England when Jack was posted to No. 22 Operational Training Unit. But by that time Jack was ill with the latest in what had been a string of illnesses throughout his life. An emergency tonsillectomy in Winnipeg had been required in 1919 during a visit to his grandparents' home in Pipestone, Manitoba. He'd had to spend several weeks recovering from a heart condition during his high school years. And now he was severely ill with meningitis. He died of the disease in hospital at Stratford-on-Avon in October of 1942, only a few weeks after arriving in England. He was buried in the Stratford-on-Avon Cemetery in Warwickshire.

Lewis McLaren landed in Sicily at the beginning of the Italian campaign in July of 1943. The landing was largely successful, but the subsequent northward push up the boot of Italy was difficult. Bill McAndrews' *The Italian Campaign* offers this blunt assessment: "It was as unpleasant a campaign as any in modern history. The weather was unvaryingly cruel. The mud was as devouring as anything on the Somme. The mountains were stony and bare of cover." Five months later, roughly halfway up the Adriatic coast of Italy, the Canadians were to cross the Moro River and take the city of Ortona. But an anticipated one-day march took three weeks. Said one Canadian general, "all the fighting before then [the Battle of Ortona] had been a nursery tale in comparison." Private Lewis McLaren, who died from his wounds after being shot, was one of over five hundred Canadians killed in that bitter December struggle that finally culminated in the taking of Ortona. Private McLaren was buried in the Moro River Canadian War Cemetery.

At home in the McLaren district, things were never the same. Ewing and Alma, who had listened to the radio day in and day out for news of their boys,

moved to Victoria in 1942, leaving the family farm to Harry. "They were unsettled after Jack's death," Alice McLaren says. Both Jack and Lewis left widows—Lewis had married an English girl—and young sons. And the rest of the family was left with their memories of their two beloved brothers. The memory of each man was honoured by the naming of a lake in northern Saskatchewan—McLaren Lake on the Northwest Territories border for Jack, and McLaren Lake about 220 kilometres north of La Ronge, for Lewis. ✹

Named for Lewis McLaren, McLaren Lake at 57°05' N, 104°31' W and viewed here from the south, is located about 140 air miles north of La Ronge. About six miles long, this lake is situated in an area of the Boreal Shield that supports an abundance of fish and wildlife through a series of connecting lakes.

Mullen

The Mullen Islands site (55°16' N, 104°41' W), viewed here from the north, is located on Lac la Ronge. Situated in the northeast corner of the lake, this site is a close cluster of several islands near the entrance to Diefenbaker Bay, about thirty miles from the townsite of La Ronge.

Albert Mullen (who went by his second name, Lorne) made quite the positive impression on those who knew him during his high school days at Scott Collegiate in Regina. He was a solid student—achieving grades of over 80 percent in geometry and physics, although not as good in literature and composition. However, it was for less academic activities that he made his mark. For instance, he played the lead role in the school's 1939 presentation of "Bits O' Blarney: Tom Brown's School Days." The following year his schoolmates affectionately cast him, along with a pal, Bruce Lehman, as "our jitterbugs from 1940" in the high school yearbook. The yearbook also reported that Lorne and his girlfriend Erna Leib could often been heard and seen "yacking at one another." In fact, it must have been Erna on whom Lorne made a most positive impression during their time together at school or, with Lorne's pal Hugh Middlemas, visiting her house to listen to records. A few years later, in a letter to Lorne's family, Principal Reid of Scott Collegiate summed up the impression Lorne made at Scott: he "would always be held in affectionate memory by all of us who knew him while he was a student here."

Lorne had to leave his high school sweetheart and the rest of his high school education behind when he enlisted in the RCAF in September of 1942, following in the footsteps of his older brother Doug. Both boys were, in turn, following the example of military service set by their father, Leslie, who had served in the 195th

Battalion Canadian Expeditionary Force in World War I. Later, Leslie farmed just northwest of Regina near his parents' homestead.

Training in different locations, the two Mullen brothers saw each other only once during those years.

In September 1943, they met at the pier in Vancouver and took a tram to their parents' new home in Burnaby. At that time, Lorne confided to his brother that the life expectancy of an air gunner on active service was six weeks. Only a wide grin on Lorne's face could put Doug at ease after that information. It would be the last Doug saw of his younger brother, although they continued to correspond with one another regularly.

Sergeant Lorne Mullen was ultimately posted to Dishforth, Yorkshire, England, as an air gunner in the 1664 Heavy Conversion Unit of Bomber Command. According to one of his letters, Dishforth was located "miles from somewhere but I haven't found out just where as yet." Another letter to Doug, dated September 28, 1943, speaks of the extreme cold Lorne and his crewmates suffered in their Quonset hut: "'England their England' as the saying goes and they can keep it. It's a nice enough country and people but right now it's unbearably cold in our huts and classes with no wood or coal till 24th October." With only galvanized steel as their

Above: Lorne (second from right) with his father Leslie (far left), sister Joan, brother Doug, and childhood chum, Hugh Middlemas.

Left: Lorne's September 28, 1943, letter to brother Doug.

149

Bottom right: Lorne's crew, all under twenty years, all killed in the training accident, from left to right: Sergeant Bob Rahn, bomb aimer; Warrant Officer Bill King, wireless operator; Sergeant Lorne Mullen, mid-upper gunner; Sergeant Ed Martin, rear gunner; Sergeant Lew Riggs, navigator; Flight Sergeant Mac McLeod, pilot.

Below: Young Lorne at his great-aunt's home, the original Mullen homestead.

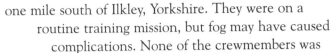

insulation, Mullen and his crew resorted to sleeping in their flying suits at night for extra warmth.

Lorne's many letters provide a glimpse of his experience overseas. In a letter to his parents dated January 11, 1944, Lorne recounts the pleasant Christmas and New Year's Eve he celebrated at his grandparents' home in Rothesay on the island of Bute, Scotland (at which time his grandmother was careful to scrutinize Lorne's social calendar). Another letter requested a record: "Pistol Packin' Momma" by the Charioteers. He asked for cigarettes, too ("300's only"), which arrived in the mail without delay. Generally, however, he admitted to a dislike for letter writing, only doing it, "when I feel it is absolutely necessary to keep up the morale of the folks on the home front."

A freak air crash on January 31, 1944 claimed the lives of Lorne Mullen and his crew. The last entry in the mid-upper gunner's logbook records Sergeant McLeod as pilot of the Halifax Bomber which struck a hill and disintegrated at 1,300 feet,

one mile south of Ilkley, Yorkshire. They were on a routine training mission, but fog may have caused complications. None of the crewmembers was any older than nineteen years of age. Blame was not assigned to anyone.

On August 20, 1946, the RCAF posthumously awarded Sergeant Mullen the Operational Wings in recognition of the gallant services rendered by "a young life offered on the altar of freedom in defence of his Home and Country," as his Air Marshal put it.

Albert Lorne Mullen is buried at RAF Stonefall Cemetery, Harrogate, England. In Saskatchewan, Mullen Islands are named in his memory. ❀

Murray

Growing up on the farm south of Estevan, the four Murray boys knew all about military service. Their father, Alexander, who had come over from England in 1903, had served in World War I; his farming career began when he'd received some land as part of the post-war Soldiers Settlement Plan. And Alexander was a charter member of the Estevan branch of the Royal Canadian Legion formed after World War I. No wonder, then, that as soon as he could in 1939, David Murray joined the army, the first of his brothers to do so. He joined up so promptly once war was declared, in fact, that at first he wore a World War I uniform, the only one available.

As much as his father's example, it might also have been the circumstances of the times that motivated David Murray to join up. He had been working at Perry Motors for five dollars per month doing whatever general duties needed doing. There just weren't many jobs around, and prospects on the farm, or perhaps working for Prairie Nursery at potato harvest season, didn't seem too promising. Despite the hard times, the Murray boys—David, his twin brother Doug, Archie, and young Bud—made their own fun when they could. On the twins' birthday, February 28, they'd clear a patch of bare ground for a game of marbles. A couple of Model Ts provided much entertainment. The boys would drive them around for something to do, having to block up the rear end, Bud recalls, and then drop it down once the motor started.

David had finished his grade eight at Valleyview

Murray Island (55°14' N, 105°02' W), viewed here from the west, is located on Lac la Ronge about six miles from the Wadin Bay campground. A rugged feature about two miles in length, Murray Island has extensive Precambrian shoreline so typical of Lac la Ronge. In the summer of 2001, a bronze memorial plaque was placed on the sunset side of Murray Island.

Estevan•

School, walking the four kilometres between the farm and the school, which was in the east end of Estevan. One of his schoolmates, Art Densley, remembers him as being an ordinary fellow, fairly easygoing. Like David, some of the Valleyview boys—the Pow boys, for instance—later went over to the International Harvester Building in Weyburn to join the South Saskatchewan Regiment. By October of 1939, David Murray was one of six hundred men to have

volunteered for active duty with the SSR, the only Saskatchewan infantry regiment to become part of Canada's first two divisions.

Early in his training, David Murray got sick. The regimental doctor, Captain Millions, who had known the Murrays in Estevan, reassured them that David was all right. But when family members got a ride with a cousin to see David at the Weyburn Hospital, the nurses reported that he had been delirious, not sure of where he was. David recovered, however, and the rest of his early army career unfolded through the winter of 1939–40 without further medical incident. By May the unit was off to Camp Shilo to join the rest of the Sixth Canadian Infantry Brigade. The months at Shilo included the standard course of training: night compass marches, range work, trench digging, bayonet practice, route marches, and company tactics in attack and defense. After a stay in barracks in the livestock barns of the Canadian National Exhibition Grounds in Toronto, the regiment made its way to Halifax, boarding the SS *Pennland* for the ten-day voyage overseas. They arrived in Scotland on Christmas Day, 1940, and a few days later began settling in at Morval

Barracks in Cove, Hants. Like all the men of the SSR, David Murray, who had so impressed his family during trips home on leave, felt sure he'd see action soon.

Meanwhile, the time in England was a chance for David to visit his relatives, including his father's twin brother in Newcastle. There was a fellow from Bienfait who had no relatives to visit, so David would always take him along on leave. When action did come for the regiment, it was the ill-fated raid on Dieppe, August 19, 1942. As luck would have it, David Murray missed the raid, having become involved in a traffic accident with a civilian while driving a transport truck in Supply Company. Two summers later, Sergeant Murray was with the regiment as it consolidated in Normandy after D-Day.

Left: The original gravesite of David Murray.

Below left: This bronze plaque was placed at Murray Island in 2001.

DOUG CHISHOLM

The breakout from Normandy took place during the last week of July in 1944. Operation Spring, as it was called, pushed south from Caen and encountered heavy resistance. David Murray, sergeant in an anti-tank platoon, was among those killed by mortar fire on July 27. Receiving the news in Brandon, where he was training with the RCAF, David's youngest brother Bud took a train home. There he walked with his dad for a while—to visit another veteran and to stroll around Woodlawn Park on the Souris River south of Estevan. "He just wanted to walk," Bud says.

Sergeant David Murray is buried in Bretteville-sur-Laize Canadian War Cemetery about fourteen kilometres south of Caen in France and commemorated by Murray Island in Lac la Ronge, Saskatchewan. ❁

Neufeld

Neufeld Bay (55°29' N, 104°32' W), viewed here from the north, is located forty air miles northeast of La Ronge, eight miles upstream from the community of Stanley Mission. This is a secluded bay about two miles in diameter. The family of Private Leslie Neufeld has placed a bronze plaque to his memory in the peaceful atmosphere of Neufeld Bay's Precambrian shoreline.

In 1906, a few pioneering Mennonite families moved to a remote district of northeastern Saskatchewan later called Lost River. The first to arrive in that bush-covered area, these families faced challenges to simply survive, particularly in winter. They gradually succeeded in clearing the land by axe and oxen, however, and a farming community emerged. The parents of Leslie Neufeld, Henry and Anna, part of that pioneer community, got married in 1917, cleared their own field, built a one-room house of logs, and began a family. Leslie, born January 17, 1922, was the third of ten children.

Over the years, Henry Neufeld became a registered seed grower and operated a seed cleaning and seed merchandising business. The family subsequently moved from Lost River to Codette and then to Nipawin to facilitate the growth of the business. Young Leslie, benefiting from his family's emphasis on education, took a year of high school in Winnipeg and another in Altona, Manitoba. A good student with an inquiring mind, he was active in sports, and his high school poetry gave signs of intellectual maturity. The future seemed bright—especially since Leslie, it seemed, might be the one to take over the family farming and seed business.

But then came the war, and the Neufeld sons had to resolve the conflict between the tenets of the Mennonite religion and the duty to serve their country. Like his older brothers, Richard and Leonard, and later his younger brother Arthur, Leslie made the decision to enlist, and on January 13, 1942, just four days before his twentieth birthday, Leslie joined Leonard in the Royal Canadian Army Medical Corps (RCAMC). Exactly eleven months later, he and Leonard boarded the *Queen Elizabeth* for England.

The next thirteen months were filled with intensive training in the RCAMC. But in early 1944 the Canadian army called for volunteers for the First Canadian Parachute Battalion. For a young man of Leslie Neufeld's character and temperament, the challenge was irresistible. Parachutists, he knew, would most likely play an important and early role in the invasion of Europe, which was not far off. Barely twenty-two years old, he joined the Battalion on February 26, 1944. Training was intensive—there was not much time—and for Leslie this training included handling the PIAT gun, a light rocket launcher. On April 8th he qualified as a parachutist and became a member of C Company of the Battalion.

In late May came the exciting news that not only would C Company be dropped into Normandy on the eve of the invasion but that it would be the first company to jump, paving the way for the rest of the allied parachutists in their area of the attack. In a letter home written on June 4, two days before D-Day, Leslie let his family know "how things are going":

Dad, the time has come for that long awaited day, the invasion of France. Yes, I am in it. I'll be in the first one hundred Canadians to land by parachute. We know our job well. We have been trained for all conditions and circumstances. We have a fair chance.

To go in as a Paratrooper was entirely my own choice. I am in no way connected with any medical work. This job is very dangerous. If anything should happen to me, do not feel sad or burdened by it, but take the attitude of "He served his country to his utmost." With that spirit I am going into battle. And let it be known that the town of Nipawin did its share to win the war. I have full expectations of returning and with God's strength & guidance I'm sure he will see me through all peril. My trust is in God.

He and his comrades, each loaded down with arms, ammunition, and supplies weighing nearly one hundred pounds, jumped into enemy territory just after midnight of the fifth of June. Their objective was to secure and protect the dropping zone near Varaville which was planned for the main body of the Third Parachute Brigade. Badly scattered in landing, almost disastrously so, the paratroops essentially achieved their objective, but with a very high cost in lives and injuries.

Leslie and a small number of his comrades participated in all this, ending up at the gatehouse of the enemy-occupied Chateau of Varaville in the early morning of June 6. One of their targets was a 75-mm German gun in a nearby concrete bunker. Corporal

Oikle, in charge of the PIAT gun, took Leslie with him to the second floor of the gatehouse for a better view of the German gun. They fired at the gun in its concrete emplacement, but failed to destroy it. The German gun replied, hitting the gatehouse and causing the extra PIAT rocket shells to explode. Leslie Neufeld was among those mutilated beyond recognition in the explosion.

Leslie's parents heard the news of his death a month later. It was a devastating blow. A younger brother, Edward, recalls that it was the only time in his life that he saw his father weep. The family gradually learned to live with the tragedy of losing such a promising son, but they could never forget what they had lost.

Far right: The First Canadian Parachute Battalion prepares for D-Day. This mass drop from Douglas "Dakota" aircraft was over Salisbury Plain, England, February 1944.

STRATHY SMITH / NATIONAL ARCHIVES OF CANADA / PA132785

Right: Edward and Arlette Neufeld visited Neufeld Bay in July 2001. The plaque had been placed there in 2000, and the event was filmed for a Discovery Channel documentary about the Churchill River. Edward and his brother Leonard, who had been a stretcher bearer in France during the war, visited the site that same summer, an experience which brought back many memories of the war years for Leonard.

DOUG CHISHOLM

A large monument in Bayeux, France, honouring British Commonwealth servicemen who were killed but have no known graves includes Private Leslie Neufeld's name. He is further honoured in Saskatchewan by the naming of Neufeld Bay on the Churchill River. ✿

Okemasis

The tradition of military service by men and women of the Muskeg Lake Cree Nation is an impressive one through two world wars and the conflicts in Korea and Vietnam. During World War I, the connection between First Nations peoples and the monarchy, formalized by Treaty 6 in 1876, may have stimulated the sense of patriotic duty that led so many Muskeg Lake people to volunteer for service.

By 1939, a different set of factors affected the rate of volunteering. Like so many other areas in the province, Muskeg Lake, a somewhat isolated reserve 150 kilometres northwest of Saskatoon, had to endure relatively harsh economic conditions in the years between the wars. There were few jobs, few everyday conveniences for the community of several hundred people. The area is a strong farming and livestock community now, but in the 1920s and 1930s, feeding your family was a challenge no matter how hard you worked. Trapping prairie chicken and rabbit, hunting geese on Salt Lake, chopping fence posts for sale— those were some of the means of economic survival, "survival of the fittest," as one Elder says.

For youngsters like Joe Okemasis, son of Andrew and Jane, life centred around the school—St. Michael's Residential School, run by Roman Catholic missionaries—or the church, built by community volunteers, where families would meet and visit after Sunday Mass or enjoy the annual picnic. And when the older kids at the school went off to join the army rather than go back to the reserve, the younger ones were

Okemasis Lake (59°23' N, 104°39' W), viewed here from the south, is located forty miles east of the northern community of Stony Rapids, about three hundred air miles north of La Ronge. Set in the ruggedness of the Taiga Shield ecozone, Okemasis Lake is deep and clear, about four miles in length, and surrounded by massive hills up to two hundred feet high.

tempted to follow them. Joseph Okemasis was barely seventeen years old when he ran away from school to Prince Albert to enlist in the Saskatoon Light Infantry on October 14, 1941.

Two years later, Private Okemasis was in the thick of some of the most difficult fighting of the war. By the end of September 1943, the Allies had taken southern Italy and were driving north from Foggia and Naples into the central mountain range. Resistance was stiff. October brought a series of "brief but bloody actions," as the Veterans Affairs website account describes them. The Allies had advanced 725 kilometres in sixty-three days, but Rome, the objective, was not yet in sight. The First Canadian Infantry Division, including the Saskatoon Light Infantry, would drive the Germans from one deep river valley only to find the same task awaiting them a few kilometres further north. It was December now, and snow was falling. The Veterans Affairs account continues: "Along the line of the Moro River, some of the bitterest fighting of the war took place. The Germans counter-attacked repeatedly, and often the fighting was hand-to-hand as the Canadians edged forward to Ortona on the Adriatic coast." Two thousand one hundred and nineteen Canadians were killed in the Italian campaign to that point. One of them, on December 7, 1943, was Joseph Okemasis.

At home, a Canadian Pacific telegram arrived with the official news: "Regret deeply—L2987 Private Joseph Okemasis officially reported killed in action, seventh December 1943. Director of Records, Ottawa." Private Okemasis was buried with some 1,600 other war casualties in the Moro River Canadian War Cemetery near the sea close to Ortona.

Joseph Okemasis is one of forty-five names engraved on three monuments outside the band office at Muskeg Lake, which "show appreciation," as the Muskeg Lake website tells us, "for what the veterans have done for Canada and the native community." The flags of Canada, Saskatchewan, and Muskeg Lake fly overhead. *Nikiskisinan: We remember them*, they say at Muskeg Lake. In northern Saskatchewan, Okemasis Lake is named in honour of Joseph Okemasis. ❀

Below right: Three monuments to Muskeg Lake Cree Nation war veterans, Muskeg Lake.
JOI ARCAND

Below: Detail of the monument to W.W. II Veterans.
JOI ARCAND

W. W. II VETERANS
1939-1945

ARCAND, ALBERT
ARCAND, CLEMENT
ARCAND, COLLIN
ARCAND, FRANCIS X.
ARCAND, GEORGE
ARCAND, JOSEPH
ARCAND, JOSEPH T.
ARCAND, LOUIS D.
ARCAND, MAURICE
GREYEYES, DAVID
GREYEYES, ESTHER (MOWAT)
GREYEYES, FLORA
GREYEYES, GERTRUDE (LLOYD)
GREYEYES, JOSEPH
GREYEYES, JOSEPHINE
GREYEYES, MARY (REID)
GREYEYES, STANLEY
GREYEYES, THOMAS
GREYEYES, WILLIAM C.
GREYEYES, WILLIAM R.
LAFOND, ALBERT
LAFOND, BEATRICE
LEDOUX, VINCENT
LONGNECK, FELIX
OKEMASIS, JOSEPH
SANDERSON, FRANCIS X.
SANDERSON, WILLIAM
TAWPISIM, ALEXANDER
VENNE, BEATRICE (LUCIER)
VENNE, EMILE
VENNE, HARRY

Piprell

In the years before the war, Halcyonia School truly was a "place of peace" for the families of the countryside north and east of Borden, Saskatchewan. It was a busy, active kind of peace. In addition to school functions—John Diefenbaker had been a student there—Halcyonia hosted young people's community club events, card parties, dances and concerts, weddings and holiday events, and programs to raise money for the Red Cross. Kids got their immunization shots at Halcyonia, and the Anglican Church, which held joint services there with the United Church, often included in its congregation the Piprell and Walker boys, home on leave.

Gordon Piprell's family farm was located just a short horse and buggy ride straight east of the school. The Piprells had been there since 1905, and Gordon was the third oldest of the family of five, four of them boys. Gordon's dad Charles had come from the English Channel island of Guernsey, and it would be a great delight for Flying Officer Piprell when, during a daylight operation to Blaye, France, the route of his Lancaster took him over Guernsey, then occupied by the Nazis, and allowed him a brief view of his father's family home. "Dad, I've seen your greenhouses," Gordon wrote in a letter.

It was a long way to the controls of a heavy bomber from life on the Piprell farm. Seventy-five percent of the farmers in the area were still using horses, Gordon's brother Gerry estimates, and Gordon had never operated machinery more complicated than a binder.

Piprell Lake (54°09' N, 104°54' W), viewed here from the north, is located seventy air miles south of La Ronge. Accessible by road from Highway 913, Piprell Lake is a popular destination for campers and anglers who enjoy clear waters, vast forests, and rainbow trout.

Below: The Piprell brothers and Walker brothers, cousins posing on the steps of Halcyonia School on a Sunday after church, circa June 1943. From left to right, Cliff Piprell, Gordon Piprell, Art Walker, and Frank Walker.

Before leaving home he'd almost certainly never flushed a toilet or turned on an electric light switch—activities uncommon in rural Saskatchewan at that time. Once in a while he did hop into the family's '29 Chev, or maybe his cousins' Model "A" Ford, for a movie in Radisson. And he knew how to handle a .22 rifle, judging by the time he stood up in his sleigh in the middle of winter on the way to Borden from the farm and shot an eagle he thought was a hawk. He enjoyed hunting, in fact—first gophers, later ducks, geese, and rabbits. Always resourceful, Gordon could build a bobsleigh for the kids to pull around, and he carved a comical attachment for his brother's wooden flute: a pipe, in case he wanted to have a smoke while he played.

As the war years approached, Gordon finished his schooling at Halcyonia, completing most of his high school by correspondence, and the rest of it during a pre-enlistment course in Regina. Gordon's brother Cliff had joined up first, cursing the thirties and the dirt of the farm, and that helped motivate Gordon, although, as Gerry reports, Gordon seemed to have his own vision that there was work to be done over in Europe. And the RCAF was the means of doing it. Flying was the elite service,

the boys reckoned, and Gordon enlisted in June of 1942, receiving his wings in Dauphin, Manitoba, on August 4, 1943. Before heading overseas, he made a surprise visit to the farm, one forever vivid in the memory of young Gerry, who was thirteen at the time:

Taking the cream from the morning milking to the ice house out by the old windmill at the end of the garden path, I just got to the garden gate, and there was Gordon, with a big grin on his face. We did not know he was coming home. He'd caught a ride from the railway station in Borden with a neighbour who'd just dropped him in our yard. I turned on my heels, yelling "Gordon's home, Gordon's home." It's a wonder I didn't spill the cream.

As Gerry remembers now, "That's just the way he did things."

Gordon sent weekly letters home from England to his mom and dad, and to his girlfriend, reporting on visits with a cousin, Alice Walker, and hunting trips with the family of a crewmate. Meanwhile his service career followed the usual course, leading to his posting with No. 101 Squadron. The Lancasters that Gordon Piprell flew with No. 101, however, were not the ordinary ones. They were fitted with radio-jamming equipment code-named ABC, or Airborne Cigar, and carried an eighth crew member, usually a German-speaking airman whose job consisted of scanning the airwaves for German transmissions, tuning his transmitter to the same frequency, and sending out a jamming signal. Because No. 101 Squadron was the only squadron so equipped, its bombers were dispersed throughout the bomber stream on operations.

The night of August 30, 1944, Gordon Piprell, recently promoted to Flying Officer, embarked on his twelfth operation from Ludford Magna (sometimes called Mudford Magna) in Lincolnshire. The target this time was the Baltic port of Stettin, Germany, a nine-hour operation. In fact, there were two related operations that night. The first operation stirred up heavy fighter opposition, still in effect when the second group, including Flying Officer Piprell's Lancaster, followed the same route south over neutral Sweden

into Germany. Piprell's Lancaster was attacked and damaged so severely that it finally went into a steep dive and crashed.

There was a funeral in Sweden, "a solemn and impressive ceremony," as a Swedish newspaper reported, and burial at the Halsingborg Municipal Cemetery. Back in Saskatchewan, people gathered once more at Halcyonia school, this time for a memorial service. It was a sad affair, Gerry Piprell remembers. "Mom got emotional at the number of neighbours there," he says. Gordon Piprell is also memorialized by Piprell Lake, "in the heart of fishing country" not far northeast of Prince Albert. ✿

Above: Prince Albert airport, where Gordon Piprell trained, as it was in the early 1940s.

Left: L.A.C. Gordon Piprell (standing second from left) in front of a Cessna Crane at No. 40 Service Flying Training School at Dauphin, Manitoba, July 1943.

Platana

Platana Lake (55°10' N, 104°10' W), viewed here from the southeast, is located

forty-five miles east of La Ronge in the Boreal Shield. About five miles in length,

the southern half of Platana Lake hosts rich forests of jack pine, spruce, and

poplar over granite hills and shorelines. Although the area surrounding the

northern half of Platana Lake was burnt by forest fire in 1995, new growth

is now returning.

Dan Platana's dream was to become a pilot. "He read a lot of magazines, everything he could get his hands on about flying," his sister Jacqueline remembers. Dan and Sis, as he called her, would often see aircraft in the skies above the Assiniboine and Pasqua Reserves, where the five Platana children lived while their father, Antoine, worked as a farming instructor for Indian Affairs. "He wanted to stay in the Air Force after the war," Jacqueline says.

She and Dan, only twenty-one months apart in age, were especially close, sharing interests in music and sports. Dan taught his sister how to dance, a skill he'd learned from his mother, Martha. In fact, the last time the two of them spent together was a Saturday night dance at the Trianon Ballroom in Regina. Dan was home on leave—the family lived in Regina by that time—and Sis was his "date" for the evening. Remembering him now, Jacqueline still remarks on his compassion and sensitivity.

The wartime RCAF fulfilled Daniel Platana's desire to fly—if not as a pilot, at least as a member of aircrew, a tail gunner. His first tour of thirty operations was completed with No. 425 "Alouette" Squadron, flying in Wellington bombers from Tunisia in the summer and autumn of 1943. Part of 331 Wing, No. 425 provided heavy bombardment of airfields, harbours, freight yards, and rail junctions in preparation for, and support of, the Allied landings in Sicily and mainland Italy. Flying Officer Platana was shot down during one such operation but was rescued at sea, returning with the rest of his squadron to a hero's welcome in England in October 1943.

He served as an instructor there before joining the RAF's famed No. 156 Pathfinder Squadron— a specialist squadron, part of Number 8 Group in Bomber Command, whose job was indicated both by the squadron's motto—"We Light the Way"—and by its official badge, an image of Mercury holding a torch. The Pathfinder squadrons' job was simple but deadly: mark enemy targets for the bulk of the Bomber Command force that would follow on any given raid.

The obvious dangers of such work were not apparent in Daniel Platana's diary entry of June 5, 1944, two days before D-Day: "Got married in Felling. Happiest man in the world." At age twenty-one, he had married a Newcastle girl, Sarah—a clerk for the RAF. Six weeks later, she was a widow, and although her husband hadn't known, Sarah was pregnant when he died. Their son Terrence would one day become a judge for the Ontario Superior Court of Justice.

Flying Officer Platana flew in one of 242 Lancasters that attacked the railway yards at Revigny, France, on the night of July 14, 1944. The last contact No. 156 Squadron had with the mission chief was logged at 1:53 a.m. as the marker bombs were being dropped to illuminate the targets. Sustaining an attack by a German night-fighter, Platana's bomber attempted

unsuccessfully to make an emergency landing just outside the village of Ancerville. The aircraft went down in the forest of Valtiermont. Only two crew members survived and safely escaped. Flying Officer Daniel Platana did not.

The news reached Jacqueline during a workday at the Massey-Harris plant in Regina. A branch manager took the call, and told her she was wanted at home. Although her brother had survived the earlier crash off North Africa, "I had a feeling," Jacqueline says, "that this time he would not make it back."

For his "varied operational career," Flying Officer Daniel Platana was awarded the Distinguished Flying Cross. As the citation noted:

This officer is a keen operational gunner with a zest for operations. He is cool and consistently reliable, and his alertness has been largely responsible for many successful evasions of enemy aircraft. His coolness and determination in carrying out his duties and his high sense of devotion to duty make him very worthy of the award of Distinguished Flying Cross.

In 1949, Daniel's widow, Sarah Platana, travelled to the residence of the Governor General in Ottawa to receive the medal. Sarah had come to Canada after the war with her infant son, arriving in Halifax on February 14,

Below: The Platana family in the summer of 1935 at their Latreille grandparents' farm, situated in the Qu'Appelle Valley, twelve miles south of Indian Head. Back row: Daniel, his mother Martha, his father Antoine, sister Jacqueline; in front, brothers Gaston and Hervé.

his mother's wishes and took Sarah's ashes to the Ancerville Communal Cemetery. Many of the townspeople of Ancerville joined Justice Platana and his wife Madeleine for the burial service, and a poster bearing a picture of Daniel Platana hung above the altar. In French, an inscription read: "In Your goodness Lord welcome Sarah into this ground of Ancerville, where her husband Daniel has been buried since July 1944." Among those in attendance were several people who witnessed the plane crash, including the secretary to the mayor and council in 1944, Mme. Claude. It was

1946, and then travelling by train to Regina, where the Platanas were to become her new family.

Sarah died in March of 1996. One of her final wishes was that her ashes be buried with her husband in France. In August 1997, fifty-three years after his father's death, Mr. Justice Terrence Platana carried out

she who had recorded the details of the Lancaster's crash that night in 1944 and who had made handkerchiefs from the parachutes found at the crash site. When Mr. Justice Platana expressed his gratitude to the French villagers, one man replied, "Unless you have lived under oppression, you will never know what it is like to experience freedom. It is we who thank you."

Flying Officer Daniel Platana, then, is buried with his four crewmates and his wife near the war memorial at the Ancerville Communal Cemetery in Ancerville, France. Platana Lake, Saskatchewan, is named in his honour. ✿

Popplewell

A wedding took place at St. Michael's Church, Aylsham, Norfolk, on August 10, 1943. Flying Officer Chetwin Popplewell of Dinsmore, Saskatchewan, married Eileen Mary Howard of Aylsham. They had met, we assume, at one of the many social events held at Blickling Hall, a large Tudor hall where Chet Popplewell was billeted while stationed at Oulton, about four miles from Aylsham. Eileen and her friends often attended such events. Reporting on the wedding, the local newspaper noted that a "short honeymoon was spent in London" and that the "bridegroom is a member of the Royal Canadian Air Force." Indeed, after the honeymoon, Flying Officer Popplewell returned to his new posting with No. 434 "Bluenose" Squadron at Tholthorpe, in Yorkshire. Eileen went along, staying with some people up there, and despite the uncertainties of the time, the couple was extremely happy together.

By that time, Chet had been in England some eighteen months and had participated in his first operation with RAF No. 88 Squadron in November of 1942, flying a Boston light bomber on reconnaissance over North Sea shipping lanes. Other operations followed during the winter of 1942–43, many of them on docks or Luftwaffe fighter bases in France. Popplewell received this assessment from his Wing Commander: "A sound, average pilot and officer who will be useful with more experience." In May of 1943, that new experience began when Chet was posted to No. 22 Operational Training Unit for training on

Popplewell Island (56°24' N, 108°11' W), viewed here from the south, is located 135 miles west of La Ronge in the Churchill River Upland ecoregion. A large feature two miles in diameter, Popplewell Island is situated in Frobisher Lake, near where it joins the Churchill River system.

Dinsmore●

Wellington heavy bombers and, later, on the Halifax bombers that would carry him and his crew on operations deep into enemy territory. At the end of this training course, he received a further assessment: "An experienced pilot who has done several daylight sorties on Boston aircraft. He has had no difficulty with the Halifax and should do well on night bombing operations with experience. Good, average crew." In late August of 1943, Chet Popplewell, now married for only a week or two, was ready for his first raid on a German target—Nuremberg.

The spectre of high-risk night operations into Germany must have seemed a stark contrast to the open skies of his home—Dinsmore, a small town southwest of Saskatoon. The only boy in a family of five kids, all of whom were active in the musical and church life of the community, Chet had enjoyed the usual pleasures of boyhood on the prairies. He was keen on baseball, tennis and hockey, and his tall, lanky frame enabled him to excel at high jump on sports days. "He used to tuck his big long legs under him when he jumped," his sister Joy remembers. "We couldn't figure out how he could jump as high as he did." In school he did well, especially in mathematics. Chet completed his grade twelve in Dinsmore, and in the short time before enlisting he worked as a truck driver for the local B.A. Oil company and as a clerk in the local Red & White store (a career pursued by several of his uncles). The war was on, however, and Chet chose to enlist in the RCAF in Saskatoon, perhaps wishing to avoid the trench-bound realities of infantry service. After the usual course of training, Chet was awarded his wings on December 5, 1941.

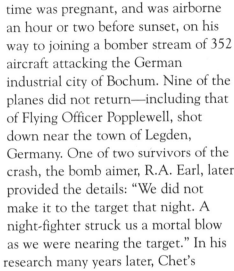

His last mission began in the late afternoon of September 29, 1943, as he and the crew prepared for a raid—their third—deep into the Ruhr Valley. Chet had said his goodbyes to Eileen, who by this time was pregnant, and was airborne an hour or two before sunset, on his way to joining a bomber stream of 352 aircraft attacking the German industrial city of Bochum. Nine of the planes did not return—including that of Flying Officer Popplewell, shot down near the town of Legden, Germany. One of two survivors of the crash, the bomb aimer, R.A. Earl, later provided the details: "We did not make it to the target that night. A night-fighter struck us a mortal blow as we were nearing the target." In his research many years later, Chet's cousin Brent Hamre was able to determine that the fighter pilot who had managed to shoot down two Halifax bombers in a ten-minute span that night was none other than Major Egmont Prinz zur Lippe-Weissenfeld, one of the Luftwaffe's greatest night-fighter aces.

Flying Officer Chet Popplewell lies buried in Reichswald Forest War Cemetery near Kleve, Germany, not far from the Dutch border, and Popplewell Island on Frobisher Lake in northern Saskatchewan is named in his memory. Years after the war, Chet's daughter Annette visited his gravesite at Reichswald: "On reaching the graves of my father's crew, I had a feeling of sadness that they were all so young and that I never knew my father." About her mother, Annette adds: "She said that her life was never the same after losing Chet." ✾

Anderson Point, located on Lake Athabasca at 59°35' N, 109°33' W, is named in memory of Rifleman Harry Earl Anderson, Regina Rifle Regiment, from Prince Albert, Saskatchewan.

Corner Lake, located at 55°57' N, 105°57' W, is named in memory of Corporal Roy H. Corner, RCAF, from Lac Vert, Saskatchewan.

Derbyshire Lake, located at 56°14' N, 108°38' W, is named in memory of Flight Sergeant George Edward Derbyshire, RCAF, from Willows, Saskatchewan.

Drever Island, located on Reindeer Lake at 56°47' N, 102°28' W, is named in memory of Rifleman Roland Armstrong Drever, Royal Winnipeg Rifles, from Meskanaw, Saskatchewan.

Dunbar Point, located on Lac la Ronge at 55°10' N, 104°39' W, is named in memory of Spitfire Pilot Ronald Dunbar, RCAF, from Shaunavon, Saskatchewan.

Jepson Lakes, located at 55°21' N, 104°52' W, is named in memory of Alan Arthur Jepson, RCAF, from Atwater, Saskatchewan. In the summer of 2001, twelve family members visited Jepson Lakes and placed a plaque.

Upon the request of families, Doug Chisholm prepares framed tributes like these, each with a photo of the geo-memorial, its location, the serviceman's photo, and details of his service, age, casualty date, and place of rest.

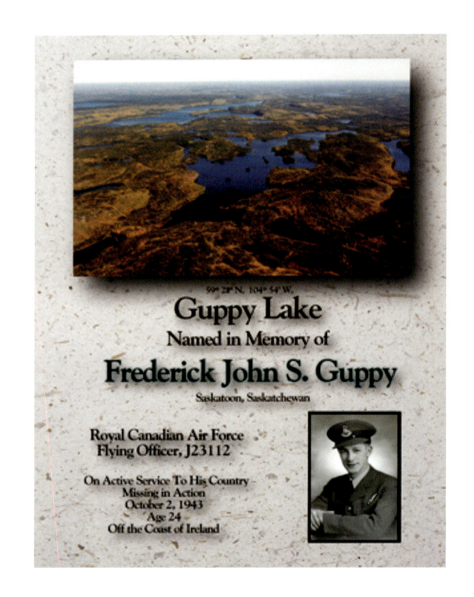

59° 29' N, 104° 54' W.

Guppy Lake
Named in Memory of

Frederick John S. Guppy
Saskatoon, Saskatchewan

Royal Canadian Air Force
Flying Officer, J23112

On Active Service To His Country
Missing in Action
October 2, 1943
Age 24
Off the Coast of Ireland

55° 32' N, 106° 14' W.

Moloski Lake
Named in Memory of
Harvey Thomas Moloski

Esterhazy, Saskatchewan

Regina Rifle Regiment
Rifleman, L107950

On Active Service To His Country
Killed in Action
February 17, 1945
Age 20
Buried at
Groesbeek Canadian War Cemetery
Holland

56° 21' 105°27'

Sommerfeld Lake
Named in Memory of
Samuel Whitney Sommerfeld

Saskatoon, Saskatchewan

Royal Canadian Navy
Volunteer Reserve
Able Seaman, V32952

On Active Service To His Country
H.M.C.S. Athabaskan
Lost at Sea
April 29, 1944
Age 20
Torpedoed in the English Channel

MacLean Islands, located on Pipestone Lake at 57°54' N, 106°36' W, is named in memory of Pilot Officer WIlliam Osborne MacLean, RCAF, from Regina, Saskatchewan.

McMahon Lake, located at 55°43' N, 108°25' W, is named in memory of Stoker Jack Bernard McMahon, Royal Canadian Navy, from Melfort, Saskatchewan.

Rehill Lake, located at 59°24' N, 106°32' W, is named in memory of Pilot Officer Donald Ross Rehill, RCAF, from Kamsack, Saskatchewan.

Sebestyen Island, located on Waskamio Lake at 56°43' N, 108°47' W, is named in memory of Pilot Officer Denis Sebestyen, RCAF, from Saskatoon, Saskatchewan.

Stephens Lake, located at 55°36' N, 103°32' W, is named in memory of Captain Roger L. Stephens, Royal Canadian Infantry Corps, from Oxbow, Saskatchewan.

Wood Island, located on Grollier Lake at 59°43' N, 105°27' W, is named in memory of Sergeant William G. Wood, RCAF, from Brancepeth, Saskatchewan.

Reid

Bill Reid "had to be good-natured," his sister Gladys says, "to get along with his older siblings." There were five kids older and only one younger than Bill on the farm near Cymric, Saskatchewan, which the Reids had worked since 1908. Growing up on a farm meant that Bill, born August 23, 1923, had horses, cattle, and poultry "to chase around," as Gladys puts it. There certainly wasn't much to do in the hamlet of Cymric, which even in its prime didn't take up much space on the prairie north of Regina close to Last Mountain Lake. Depending on the season, there were ball games in the pasture, or shinny on the slough. Bill took his elementary schooling at Mountain View School before finishing his high school in Govan. Around that time his mother died, and big sister Vera took on the job of looking after Bill and Gladys. The family home was located near the railroad tracks, and Gladys remembers many a transient coming to their door requesting food.

Bill Reid wasn't a big man, well under six feet tall, but that wasn't going to stop him from joining the Air Force in January of 1942. Two of his older brothers, Joe and Gordon, may have inspired him. Living with relatives in Ontario, they had joined the army two years earlier. The three of them were eventually able to spend some leave time together in England. Bill and Gordon spent a week in London together on leave, sightseeing at Westminster Abbey and St. Paul's Cathedral and observing the bomb damage around the city. His brothers "adopted a fatherly attitude and had a

Reid Island (54°58' N, 102°22' W), viewed here from the south, is situated at the entrance to Long Bay at the south end of Wildnest Lake, 120 air miles east of La Ronge. Precambrian outcrops and clear waters provide excellent fish and wildlife habitat. Vast stands of mature forest prevail in this area, with massive white spruce, jack pine, poplar, and birch trees. The Reid family has visited here and placed a memorial plaque.

Cymric

167

big time showing me a good time," Bill reported to his aunt in a letter from England.

Of course, prior to his arrival in England there had been the usual training process, from Manning Depot through to graduation as an observer. By November of 1942 he was sent overseas, posted to RCAF No. 429 "Bison" Squadron based at East Moor, Yorkshire. And the training continued, as he reported in another letter home: "I am still training to be a navigator, which in my opinion is the hardest job in aircrew. It seems we are always working. The rest of the crew are all Canadian Sergeants and we get along well together, which helps a lot." The norm for forming aircrews at Operational Training Units (OTU) was to allow pilots, bomb aimers, navigators, wireless operators and air gunners to make their own decisions about whom to crew up with. If that didn't work, OTU staff would make the crew decisions. However it was done in Flight Sergeant Reid's case, he

appreciated the value of a good set of crew mates: "I have been crewed up, so from now on everyone ceases to work as an individual but rather as a man with the interest of the crew at stake. We are all Sergeants and, except for the Pilot who is thirty, are a bunch of youngsters age 19 or 20. The Pilot does not drink or smoke, so he serves as a steadying influence on the rest of us."

Not yet twenty years old himself, Bill Reid was killed on his first operation over Germany, part of the Bomber Command assault on the Ruhr Valley. On the night of May 12, 1943, a force of 572 heavy bombers, including Wellingtons from No. 429 Squadron, attacked the German city of Duisberg. The raid was so successful, from the perspective of Bomber Command, that no further bombing of Duisberg would be required. But thirty-four bombers and crews were lost. Flight Sergeant Reid was buried near the spot where his Wellington went down, near Munchen Gladbach, Germany. Later he was reburied at the beautiful Rheinberg War Cemetery.

Back in Govan, a memorial service was conducted for Sgt. William John Reid. Reverend Passmore cited Psalm 110: "The young warriors shall gather to thee as the dew of the morning." A memorial gravestone for Bill was laid between those of his parents in the Govan cemetery. Many years later, Bill's family flew into Wildnest Lake in northern Saskatchewan. There they visited Reid Island, named for William, and the family has placed a plaque there in his memory. ✥

Reisner

A t 12:57 hours on May 19, 1943, a Halifax bomber co-piloted by Flying Officer Russell Melvin Reisner of Limerick, Saskatchewan, took off from Holmsley South airfield in England, towing a Horsa Glider, the huge attack glider weighing three and a half tons with a wingspan of some eighty feet. This was a common sight at Holmsley, the base of RAF No. 295 Squadron. Glider towing, flying training, paratroop and supply dropping, and leaflet raids were all part of squadron life at the base. "Aid from the Skies" was the squadron motto.

The RAF Air Historical Branch describes the rest of what was to be Reisner's last flight:

> During the flight the aircraft carried out a diving circuit from which the Horsa Glider was successfully cast off. However, shortly after this the Halifax is believed to have suffered an engine failure and was unable to pull out of the dive. The Halifax was later reported to have crashed into the ground at Damerham, near Fordingbridge, Hampshire, killing three of the six-man crew. F/O Reisner, seriously injured in the crash, was taken to the Tower House Emergency Hospital in Salisbury, Wiltshire, where two days later he succumbed to his injuries.

Melvin Reisner, then, was one of forty-six names on a casualty list, one of 588 such lists reported by the RCAF up to May of 1943.

Back home in Limerick, Melvin Reisner was considerably more than a name on a list or in an official description. His memorial service packed the

Reisner Lake (57°47' N, 103°35' W), viewed here from the southwest, is located 190 air miles northeast of La Ronge, near the south end of Wollaston Lake, one of Saskatchewan's largest lakes. Reisner Lake is about five miles long and is accessible either by canoe through a series of lakes and creeks from Wollaston Lake or from Highway 905.

United Church, where Melvin had been a member. Reverend Kelmo conducted the service; two Limerick girls sang "We'll Never Know How Much We Owe." Melvin's brother Cecil remembers that "one of his chums drove the car for us that day." He adds, "We still go to the same church."

Born March 27, 1922, Melvin Reisner, the eldest of three children, two of them boys, took all his schooling in Limerick. His grandfather had homesteaded in the area in 1908. Melvin was a high-spirited fellow who was interested in the ladies and liked to go to dances. Occasionally he chafed against the necessary restrictions— whether or not he could take the car on one of his outings, for example—of a farm family during the depression. "He wanted to do it all," his brother remembers, "but couldn't." He attended a post-secondary school in Regina and worked at Mossbank during construction of the British Commonwealth Air Training Plan facility, later known as the Mossbank Bombing and Gunnery School. In a period of economic desperation—no jobs, no prospects—Melvin wanted to be a flyer. "He couldn't wait to go," says Cecil. "It was better than being a hired hand for no money." And off he went,

enlisting in the RCAF in September 1941.

For his younger brother Cecil, these were exciting times. "I remember Melvin coming home with paycheques, which he never had before. I wished I was old enough to join up." In the meantime, there was a special present from Melvin. "Here's a dollar," Melvin wrote from Dauphin. "You can get whatever you like with it." Melvin graduated at Dauphin on October 22, 1942. Receiving his wings and commission as Pilot Officer, he immediately proceeded overseas, stuffing his belongings in a six-square-foot trunk that weighed 110 pounds. "I was afraid of it splitting," he later wrote, "but it held up alright." At home, the Reisner family became substantial boosters of the war effort. Adolph, Melvin's father, went into hogs in order to support the "Bacon for Britain" program. He was barely making money on the farm, but he would spend whatever he could on Victory Bonds.

Melvin's letters from overseas report a series of minor, not altogether unpleasant, misadventures. He experienced his first blackout: "I got lost last night trying to find my way home from the show as it was pitch black out and I didn't have my flashlight. But I finally made it after making quite a few inquiries." He seemed less lost when it came to female companion-ship: "I've been to two dances and find the English girls interesting to chat with. I usually have to ask them to

Cecil Reisner remembers being picked up at school by his father and sister the day the telegram came reporting that Melvin had died in England. "He was kind of a hero in my eyes," Cecil says, and hero he remains. Today, Cecil is a proud supporter of the Halifax Restoration Project, the plan to restore the world's only remaining Halifax bomber, one retrieved in 1995, well preserved, from seven hundred feet of water in a Norwegian lake. His brother flew a plane like that.

repeat what they say as it's hard to understand them." And during his first solo flight he "got lost and had to land at a strange aerodrome and spend the night there." He was a good pilot, though. By April of 1943 he'd been promoted to Flying Officer.

Flying Officer Reisner was buried at St. Mary's Churchyard, Hampshire, United Kingdom. Reisner Lake, named in Melvin Reisner's honour, is located south of Wollaston Lake in northern Saskatchewan. ✿

Riches

Riches Lake (59°46' N, 102°15' W), viewed here from the south, is located 340 air miles northeast of La Ronge, not far from Saskatchewan's borders with Manitoba and the Northwest Territories. About six miles in length, Riches Lake contains many distinct peninsulas and bays. In the winter, this area of the Selwyn Lake Upland ecoregion of the Taiga Shield hosts vast herds of caribou as they migrate south.

●Aberdeen

Thirty-nine years after his death in 1944, Bill Riches was remembered fondly by his mother, Clara, Silver Cross Mother for 1983. "Bill was an awfully good boy, in the flower of manhood when he was lost like so many others," she said at the time.

Bill was the older of two boys born to Clara and Russell Riches in Yorkton, Saskatchewan. His brother Bob would become a navigator in the RCAF and complete a tour of operations with Bomber Command. Before Bill was school age, the family moved to Aberdeen, where Russell was the manager of the Bank of Commerce. A natural leader even as a boy, Bill was active in sports and quite athletic. In the late 1930s he would drive the family's '33 Plymouth to sports days in the nearby towns of Vonda, Prud'homme, and Elstow, often in the company of one of the Aberdeen girls among whom he was popular. He attended the same school in Aberdeen for twelve years, doing well enough to earn admittance into Engineering at the University of Saskatchewan in Saskatoon.

An active officer's training program at the university may have indirectly curtailed Bill's studies there. In his mother's view, the officers made the boys want to enlist. "I begged Bill not to enlist until he was finished his course," she said, "but he felt he couldn't wait any longer because the war would be over." In the spring of 1942 he joined the army, and after basic training he headed out to Gordon Head, on the outskirts of Victoria, for a three-month officer's training course. From the formal ceremony at the conclusion of the course Bill emerged as Lieutenant William Riches of the Royal Canadian Artillery.

The Riches brothers, who corresponded with one another regularly, shared only one leave together while they were based in England. Meeting in London, "we went up to Aberdeen, Scotland, for a week together," Bob remembers. "While we were there we called at the Mayor's office and introduced ourselves as coming from Aberdeen, Saskatchewan, in Canada. Naturally, we were well received and entertained that day and evening." That was the last time the two Riches boys saw one another. When Bob eventually received word of his brother's death, he was devastated. "He had such promise," Bob says.

Lieutenant Bill Riches was attached to the Fifth Anti-Tank Regiment of the Fourth Armoured Division that pursued the retreating Germans toward the River Seine in late August of 1944. The general objective of the Second Corps, which included the Fourth Armoured, was to cross the Seine, clear the Le Havre peninsula and capture the port of Le Havre. In particular, Bill Riches' unit was to push through the village of Bernay toward Pont de l'Arche on the Seine south of Rouen. The Canadians encountered relatively insignificant resistance to their advance. Most remarkable was the welcome they received, according to official army historian C.P. Stacey:

> The historian of the Tenth Brigade [part of the Fourth Armoured Division] wrote later, "Will Bernay ever be forgotten? Bernay where the people stood from morning till night, at times in the pouring rain and at times in the August sun. Bernay where they never tired of waving, of throwing flowers or fruit, of giving their best wines and spirits to some halted column." But in every town and hamlet the reception was much the same. It was an experience to move the toughest soldier.

The Fourth Division began to cross the Seine on the twenty-seventh of August. For Lieutenant Bill Riches, the end came when he was wounded on the afternoon of the twenty-eighth. He was helping to dig a foxhole after his unit had advanced through the night. "He always said he wouldn't send his men where he wouldn't go himself," his mother observed. Mentioned in Dispatches for leadership and bravery, Bill died the next day. He is buried at Bretteville-sur-Laize Canadian War Cemetery south of Caen.

When Clara and Russell received the telegram, "we knew in our own minds that he had gone," as Clara said in 1983. The Riches and another family who had lost two boys arranged for a reproduction of Da Vinci's "Last Supper" to be hung in the Aberdeen United Church as a memorial. Another memorial is Riches Lake, north and west of Wollaston Lake, named in honour of William Riches. ✿

Robb

FLIGHT SERGEANT **GEORGE "JOE" BARCLAY ROBB** • R107812 • 1914–1942
CORPORAL **ROBERT "BERT" BARCLAY ROBB** • L12173 • 1916–1944

Robb Lake (54°30' N, 105°08' W), viewed here from the south, is located forty-five miles south of La Ronge in the Boreal Plain ecozone. About three miles in length, Robb Lake is shallow with a good flow of water, making it an ideal habitat for wild rice which is harvested each September from a local cabin. Healthy stands of spruce and poplar grow in the surrounding forest, and pickerel, jackfish, and waterfowl are abundant.

When George and Janet Robb immigrated to Canada in 1924, buying a farm near Expanse, Saskatchewan, they brought with them the five sons and a daughter who had been born in county Fife, Scotland. The family also carried the military traditions of two uncles from World War I—Robert Barclay who had died at Passchendaele while attached to the Canadian Corps, and Barclay Robb who had served with the British forces in Egypt.

In order to be distinguished from his uncles, young Robert Robb, born in 1916, was called simply "Bert" by close friends and family (and later "No Legs," for his short stature, by his army mates). Bright enough to get his grade twelve at age fifteen, Bert was known for his nimble wit and wry sense of humour. He liked to dress well and, as his younger brother Alex remembers, "usually contrived to be neatly turned out even when dollars for duds were scarce."

A couple of Alex's fondest memories of brother Bert involve hockey. On occasion, Bert would take him on CPR-organized hockey excursions to Moose Jaw:

> This involved boarding the train in Expanse in late afternoon or early evening, travelling to the city, walking from the station to the rink, enjoying the game, walking back to the station to catch the train home, arriving in Expanse near midnight and walking the mile and a half to the farm. But it was well worth it because the competing teams included many future NHL stars such as the Bentley brothers.

Shorter hockey trips would be to Mossbank. "To get there," Alex remembers, "we walked the two miles to Ardill then travelled in open sleighs the six miles to Mossbank. After the games we were treated to apple pie à la mode and coffee at the café. Then home again. We considered ourselves lucky to have this opportunity."

A few years later, the two shared memorable meetings in England. In 1942, Alex, himself in the army, travelled from Aldershot to join his brother who was on leave from the South Saskatchewan Regiment (SSR). Alex and his brother had a somber conversation in a London hotel room about the disastrous Dieppe raid that had taken place in August. So many of Bert's friends had died, or been wounded or taken prisoner. Dieppe was the reason for another meeting between Alex and Bert. Bert invited his younger brother to the ceremony in early 1944 when the King and Queen presented the SSR with colours commemorating the regiment's part in that Dieppe raid.

Rather than pursue officer training when the opportunity arose, Corporal Bert Robb opted to remain in combat with his regiment. On July 20, 1944, the SSR moved south across the Orne River south of Caen, attempting to take the important tactical position of Verrières Ridge. Encountering considerable opposition, including heavy artillery barrage from west of the Orne, and without the expected air support, two companies of the SSR nonetheless managed to achieve their objectives by late afternoon. Among those who died in the day's advance was Bert Robb, in charge of a Bren gun carrier, who was killed instantly when struck by an artillery shell. Corporal Robert Barclay Robb is buried at Bretteville-sur-Laize Canadian War Cemetery in Calvados, France.

George "Joe" Barclay Robb, born two years before Bert, began his formal education in infant and primary schools in Scotland. By the time he finished his grade

Above: Corporal Robert "Bert" Barclay Robb.

Left: Canadian Bren carriers preparing for the D-Day invasion. This photo was taken in southern England in May 1944.

HAROLD G. AIKMAN / NATIONAL ARCHIVES OF CANADA / PA154974

175

twelve in Expanse, he'd been elected secretary on the student council, a job he took seriously. When composing letters to neighbouring towns, inviting them to the Expanse sports day, he debated over how to sign his letters—George B. Robb, or Geo. B. Robb, or Joe Robb—finally settling on simply George Robb. Joe's education served him well during the wintry nights by a coal heater when he and his brothers would engage in discourses on such diverse topics as the outlook for the Depression, the controversy over the Doukhobors in Saskatchewan, and the poetic grandeur of Keats or Shelley.

Around the farm, Joe could handle any task. When the family acquired a young filly named Queen, Joe undertook to break her. He was thrown so often that his mother Janet anticipated that he would be seriously injured. But Queen was broke eventually, and she became a valuable saddle horse on the farm. Indeed,

horses were an important part of the farm operation, and Joe was constantly involved in their care and use—seeding, summerfallowing, harvesting, hauling grain, hauling coal, and even hauling youngsters to school on cold winter days. Joe was the one who seemed destined to take over the farm.

That would have to come after air force service, however, into which Joe Robb enlisted in 1941. Trained as an observer, he was sent to England in the spring of 1942. A letter dated February 17, 1942, from Flight Sergeant Robb to his parents describes the exhilaration he discovered in flying, particularly the thrills of "hedge hopping" at 300 miles per hour: "It means you're crossing a road allowance about every twelve seconds so you just more or less hop along over the ground. We were so low most of the time we would see trees between the wing tips of the two planes and trees are not very big in this country."

Flight Sergeant George Barclay Robb's plane crashed and burned during a training flight on September 7, 1942, near Oxford. He was laid to rest at Bicester Cemetery, Oxfordshire, England.

Robb Lake in northern Saskatchewan honours the memories of Corporal Robert Robb and Flight Sergeant George Robb. ✿

Centre: Flight Sergeant George "Joe" Barclay Robb.

Right: Alex Robb wrote these verses on September 13, 1996, as he thought about the fifty-two years between July 20, 1944, when his brother Bert (Robert) was killed in action near Caen, France, and September 13, 1996, when Bert would have been eighty years old.

LOST YEARS

We still recall with grief and pride
The sacrifice of those who died;
The ones by early death denied
So many years of life.

Proud to serve though loath to die,
Knowing the risks they chose to try
For a better world. Now we sigh
For years with them we've lost.

Roberts

The first Christmas Leon Roberts ever spent away from his hometown of Parkside, Saskatchewan, was "somewhere on the Atlantic" on the way to Belfast and his posting in Britain in 1942. He'd just graduated from No. 1 Air Observers' School in Malton, Ontario, after enlisting in the summer of 1941. "I was listening to carols today and it really made me homesick," he wrote, "Imagine, a man of my age talking about being homesick—disgusting, isn't it? No fooling, I *do* wish I were home for Christmas at least but it can't be helped. There's a big job to be done and it's up to us to get in there and finish it."

Of course, he wasn't alone in doing that job. Even in his hometown there were others joining up, including Leon's best friend, Ted Clarke (see his story on page 33). Although it would prove to be difficult for the two of them to stay in touch while stationed with their squadrons—especially since Leon had (by his own reckoning) been at fourteen different stations in Canada and the British Isles—they had spent plenty of time together as youths. The school in Parkside was one centre of many of the boys' activities. The Scout troop and hockey rink were two of the others. The church was part of their lives as well; the fourth of five children of the Parkside blacksmith, Leon was confirmed as a Lutheran. "It wasn't an option, not to go to church," his sister Lorraine remembers. Perhaps best of all among the childhood activities was swimming at Emerald Lake, the closest summer resort. The kids went down there by the truckload, often stopping at

Roberts Lake (59°29' N, 107°58' W), viewed here from the south, is located 320 air miles north of La Ronge. Situated in the rugged Tazin Lake Upland ecoregion of the Taiga Shield, Roberts Lake is just ten miles from the north shore of Lake Athabasca.

Parkside●

the Chinese café in Leask after a day at the lake.

Leon was "a real clown," as Lorraine puts it. One day his mother had finished making another batch of dandelion wine and gone out for a visit. Leon and a pal decided to pretend they'd gotten into the wine. They staggered around downtown, acting drunk, to the horror of his mother, who promptly headed straight home, went down into the basement, and emptied all the wine down the drain.

From overseas, every letter Leon sent home seemed happy. Whether it was describing the elaborate steps needed to procure a couple of eggs in egg-deprived England, or the regret at having to cancel a date because he had to fly that night, or his playful self-assessment as a "good bombardier"—each letter gave his family at home a reason to appreciate his positive outlook. These thoughts are typical: "I have been lucky all the way through, no really hard luck. I'm in with a swell bunch and all that, and have a swell crew to fly with. It makes a difference if you make up your mind to take what comes and like it. As you know, I've liked this life right from the start." The same letter, written in September of 1943, a month before he died, expresses his patriotism: "In this last nine months I have really found out and realized what a swell place Canada is, maybe a bit hard at times, but you are your own boss and I honestly would sacrifice a lot to keep it that way."

He was determined to make it home: "If you ever get word that I'm missing, just keep praying, but don't worry. I'll be back if I have to walk every step." Soon, the family did get word that Leon was missing in action. Flying with RAF No. 207 Squadron, Leon Roberts' Lancaster was shot down at Nettersheim, Germany, during the second of two daylight raids on Kassel, October 22, 1943. Sixteen other aircraft and crews were lost in the two raids. In his short time with the squadron, Leon "had impressed everyone with his ability as an Air Bomber and his terrific keenness to fly," wrote the Wing Commander in a letter to the family in Parkside. "He was very popular with his Flight

Below: Leon (centre) boarding the train at Parkside after his last trip home.

named after her son. She remembered the sight for the rest of her life.

A poem George Greening wrote, in the voice of Mrs. Roberts, concludes:

> So rest my boy and so will I,
> Remembering nature's shrine,
> An everlasting memorial to
> That darling boy of mine.

Roberts Lake, named in honour of Leon Roberts, lies near Lake Athabasca, in Saskatchewan's far north. Flying Officer Roberts is buried in Rheinberg War Cemetery, Germany. 🌸

Commander, who was his captain, and the other Squadron boys and had the makings of one of our best air bombers."

The day Leon had left for Britain was the day his grandmother died. The juxtaposition of the two events was hard on Leon's mother. She found some relief twenty-five years later when, during a DC-3 flight from Prince Albert to Fond du Lac to visit her granddaughter, Mrs. Roberts met the legendary bush pilot George Greening, another passenger on the flight. Upon meeting her, Greening had the pilot fly over Roberts Lake so Mrs. Roberts could at last see the lake

ROBERTS LAKE

Here on Athabasca's shore,
A symbol of bravery lies,
A lake named after my airman son,
Imagine my surprise.

After all these years now, eighty one,
I should fly this way today,
And pass by chance the memorial
Of a Son so far away.

So rest my boy and so will I,
Remembering nature's shrine,
An everlasting memorial to
    That darling boy of mine.

Top: Leon Roberts, taking a break at the creamery in Parkside, where he was working.

Left: "Roberts Lake," the poem written by George Greening for Leon's mother.

Robertson

ABLE SEAMAN **DONALD MORRISON ROBERTSON** • 3302 • 1920–1941

Robertson Point (56°50' N, 103°43' W), viewed here from the south, is located about 145 air miles northeast of La Ronge on beautiful Davin Lake. A popular destination for anglers, Davin Lake is accessible through the airstrip at the tourist camp, or through road access at a point fifty miles along Highway 905. Deep into the Boreal Shield, Davin Lake is a ruggedly beautiful feature about twelve miles in length, centrally separated through a narrows at Robertson Point. All boats which journey the length of Davin Lake must pass Robertson Point, a significant landmark which is clearly marked on the 1:50,000-scale provincial map.

onald Robertson was the first young man from Watrous to be killed in World War II. He had been working as a jeweler in a store next door to his dad's when he got the urge to join up after seeing another Watrous boy home on leave from the navy. Despite the fact that Donald hadn't been a great scholar in school, he managed to provide appropriate certification of education. By the time war broke out, he'd already been training at the naval base in Esquimalt on Vancouver Island, and had served there on the Honour Guard for the Royal Visit of 1939. But he was neither the first nor the last of this Robertson family to join the military. His father, James, had served with the Kings' own Scottish Borderers in World War I, an uncle had been the first Watrous boy killed in that war, and three of Donald's brothers followed him into service in World War II.

The Robertson family had been in Watrous since 1910, although James and his wife Jessie didn't arrive until 1919, when they came over from Scotland with their four children to take over the tailor shop from James's father, David. Jessie, who was pregnant with Donald at the time, was sick throughout the fourteen-day voyage across the Atlantic. Once established in Watrous, James Robertson proved to be generous and resourceful in providing leadership for Donald and the other children. He formed a gymnastics club in the old Brown Drygoods store and helped to build a Scouts hall out of a couple of CNR cabooses. For the young people of the town, the social life included movies, curling, skiing up and down the hills around Manitou Beach, and hockey on Stacey's Dam about a mile and a half out of town, where Donald earned a reputation as a good goalie. "We were a poor family," Donald's younger brother Stewart recalls, "and a humble one. We were taught good manners in the home."

Stewart remembers Donald as being both "my protector and my tormenter." One instance of brotherly torment took place along a dark road on the way home from Manitou Beach. "He promised he wouldn't leave me alone," Stewart says, "but sure enough, he ran ahead just when we were about to pass the cemetery." But no amount of tricks or teasing would diminish his brother's stature in Stewart's eyes. "With one bullet he could get a rabbit for supper," Stewart says, "and he had a bit of the daredevil in him." Apparently at the old pool at Manitou Beach you could climb out on some high beams, if you were fearless like Donald, and dive in from way up there. "After sixty years, he's still my big brother," Stewart says today.

The last time the two brothers saw each other was when Donald was home on the leave he'd earned for serving on the Honour Guard. His train arrived in Watrous late at night when the family was asleep in their home at the back of the store. His knocking on the door frightened them at first, until everyone realized, in Stewart's words, that "it was nobody breaking in, it was Donald home from the navy." Soon he was gone again, heading to Halifax and off to war. A letter would later confirm the Robertson family bond: "When this war is over," Donald wrote, "we'll have a family reunion because we haven't been together for a while." The letter arrived after he'd been killed in action.

Donald served on HMCS *Trillium*, an anti-submarine corvette used throughout the war for the escort of merchant ship convoys between North America and Great Britain. The *Trillium*, commissioned at Montreal in 1940, assumed its escort duties in April of 1941, the month Donald Robertson was killed. On the twelfth of April, as a German fighter aircraft attacked the ship off the coast of

Below: HMCS *Trillium*

Scotland, the four-inch anti-aircraft gun jammed. One of Donald's chums had to get out from under cover to try to fix it, and Donald, in turn, risked his own life in an attempt to save the other man. Donald was hit, and he died a short time later, one of three Canadians killed that day. Able Seaman Robertson was mentioned in Dispatches for his bravery. Later in the war, Stewart Robertson, by that time a radar technician in the navy, serviced the radar on the *Trillium* and stood in the very spot where his brother had been mortally wounded.

Right: William Robertson at the grave of his uncle Don, Stornoway, Isle of Lewis, Scotland, May 2000.

MARY MAXWELL

The initial telegram to the Robertson family when Donald died said only the usual "missing in action." Stewart remembers being handed the telegram by his father, who had been rendered speechless by his grief. There was a memorial service in the United Church in Watrous, and Donald's mother Jessie hoped that he had been buried at sea so that she could visit his gravesite at any seashore. In fact, Donald Robertson is buried at Sandwick Cemetery on Stornoway, an island in the Outer Hebrides, Scotland. Stewart's son, Bill, visited his uncle's gravesite in 2000, and "broke into tears," he wrote in an account of his visit, as if "carrying all the grief of the family to this place." Later that year, Bill visited Robertson Point, Saskatchewan, too—a prominent landmark named in honour of his Uncle Donald. The point extends into Davin Lake, northeast of La Ronge.

There is a remarkable postscript to this story. A few years ago, Stewart Robertson sat down to watch a film on CBC television called "War At Sea: U-boats in the St. Lawrence." Expecting to view background on the campaign that had claimed his brother, he was astounded to see, halfway through the film, a detailed account of Donald's death as told by a medical aide from HMCS *Trillium*. The film included scenes from the gravesite, which Stewart was seeing for the first time. The man in the film wept as he read from the words on the stone: "In the sweet by and by we shall meet on that beautiful shore." ✿

Robertson

Three of Forbes Robertson's nieces—Pat, Peggy and Mary—who were raised with him at the Robertson home in Saskatoon looked up to him as a big brother. Therefore, his mother Sarah, conscious of his influence on them, insisted he model proper manners. If she asked, "More pie, Forbes?" and Forbes answered simply "No," she would say, "No *what*, Forbes?"—to which he would reply, "No more pie." So perhaps it wasn't proper manners, precisely, that impressed the three nieces, who were not that much younger than Forbes. What they remember is that he was very good to them—taking them to parades (tying them together with scarves to better keep track of them) and generally sticking up for them when needed. He was the one who started the girls reading, giving them *Uncle Wiggily* books. And if he was the babysitter, the girls could count on being able to pull the mattresses off the bed and really have some fun.

Attending first Mayfair Public School then Bedford Road Collegiate, Forbes got his grade twelve in 1938. He had been a Boy Scout for a few years and an active sportsman. For a time he delivered groceries with his bicycle and did other odd jobs, also working for a tire rubber company in the city. Right after high school he joined a militia unit, the Saskatoon Light Infantry (SLI), and helped form one of the guards of honour during the Royal Visit to Saskatoon. On April 1, 1940 he asked for his discharge from the SLI in order to join the air force and become a pilot. Forbes' training culminated at No. 2 Wireless School in Calgary, from

Robertson Bay (55°47' N, 104°47' W), viewed here from the east, is located fifty-five air miles northeast of La Ronge at the southern corner of Forbes Lake. Spectacular scenery throughout this area of the Churchill River Upland ecoregion of the Boreal Shield makes Forbes Lake a popular destination for tourist anglers and voyageurs. Forbes Lake can be carefully navigated by canoe to surrounding lakes via small portages. Robertson Bay supports a healthy pickerel and jackfish population.

Saskatoon•

where he graduated as a wireless operator in August of 1941.

During his training, there were frequent trips home on leave. Often he brought a couple of his mates with him. There were always great festivities—plenty of special baking and other preparations—when he came home, his nieces remember. Borrowing his brother George's dark blue Ford, he'd say "Let's take the kids for a ride," and off they'd go. Forbes always had lots of friends around. By the time he was finishing his training in Calgary he had a special friend, a girl named Thelma, to whom he became engaged.

By the end of 1941, Sergeant Robertson had completed a course at No. 5 Bombing and Gunnery School at Dafoe. Soon thereafter he was sent to England and from there, in August of 1942, to North

Africa on loan to the United States Army Air Force. He was attached to No. 434 Squadron of the Twelfth Medium Bombardment Group as a radio gunner. "It was a happy day when your son and five other boys of the RCAF were sent to us," his commander would later write to Forbes' parents, William and Sarah. "They proved to themselves worth their country and of the affection and esteem which they earned in the hearts of all of us."

Generally, the Twelfth Bombardment Group was engaged in all manner of army support operations during the Anglo-American pursuit of General Rommel across North Africa in 1942–43: attacks on storage areas, transport and communication facilities, troop concentrations, and other targets in Egypt, Libya, Tunisia, and Crete. Forbes assured his family that he was nowhere near "the skirmish out here in the western desert." But the logbook of Forbes Robertson, who since December 1942 was Pilot Officer Forbes Robertson, shows that he took part in more than two dozen missions, flying an American B-25 Mitchell bomber, a two-engine medium bomber with a crew of six. One of his last raids was on the Mareth Line, Rommel's last defense which, once broken, as it was in April of 1943, paved the way for the final surrender of

Below: Forbes Robertson.

all Axis forces in North Africa and the subsequent invasion of Italy.

Pilot Officer Robertson's B-25 was returning from a mission on April 29, 1943, when it exploded upon touching down at El Mour Airfield in Sfax, Tunisia.

"Evidently one of the bombs had failed to release over the target, and unknown to the crew, was still aboard the aircraft," wrote Major George Gutru, until mid-March the pilot of that crew and now commander of the squadron. "It is doubtful that we shall ever know exactly the cause of the tragedy. It may have been a mechanical failure, but I am inclined to believe that the malfunction was caused by damage sustained through enemy fire over the target."

Pilot Officer Forbes Robertson, posthumously awarded the Purple Heart and United States Air Medal, was buried near Sfax with full military honours. "We shall not forget 'Robbie,'" wrote Major Gutru. "I, for one, shall find his memory a constant inspiration. He was a gentleman and a man of honour, a gallant soldier, and

our cherished friend." Back in Saskatoon, all the kids were gathered together at home and told the terrible news. The three nieces remember their grandparents' grief:

A PYRAMID OF GREETINGS

"Grandpa shoveled coal from one side of the bin to the other, and Grandma carried the sadness on her face for years." They all attended the ceremony at the training depot when a special delegation of American officials presented the Purple Heart to William Robertson, who proudly accepted on behalf of his son. It was probably the first time the prestigious American tribute had been awarded in Canada. Sarah Robertson, too, was proud in 1949 when the Government of Saskatchewan asked her permission to name a geographic feature after Forbes—it would be Robertson Bay—which, as she wrote, is "an honour offered to my son's memory." ✿

Above: A card Forbes sent to his family from North Africa.

Top left: Forbes Robertson's Purple Heart, awarded posthumously in January 1944.

Left: B-25 Mitchell bombers.

SASKATCHEWAN ARCHIVES BOARD / RA17453(1)

185

Rowe

Rowe Island (55°11' N, 104°53' W), viewed here from the west, is located on Lac la Ronge. About one mile in length, Rowe Island is situated roughly halfway along the main twenty-five-mile boat route between La Ronge and Hunter Bay.

Terry Rowe, a Canadian army photojournalist, died at Anzio, Italy, on February 6, 1944, the very day his baby son was christened in Winnipeg. Almost as if he sensed something, the baby, also named Terry, cried through the whole service. Nine years later, when an island in Lac la Ronge, Saskatchewan, was named in honour of Lieutenant Rowe, his father W.H. Rowe wrote to J.H. Brocklebank, the provincial minister of natural resources, acknowledging the government's gesture: "Terry was very fond of that district and I have had the pleasure of fishing in that lake."

The Rowes—Terry, his sister Katherine, his mother and father (a retired druggist)—enjoyed the outdoors. They had a cottage at Round Lake, and one of Terry's neighbours, Kay Mahon, remembers Terry in a canoe playing a musical instrument, a saxophone perhaps. He certainly had talent for writing, which showed itself during his school years in his hometown of Prince Albert, first at King George Public School, then at Prince Albert Collegiate Institute, from which he graduated in 1929. In 1934 he got a job with the Regina *Star* as a reporter, remaining in that position until the *Star* closed a few years later. In August 1935 he married Margaret Shaw of Winnipeg, who at the time was librarian for the Regina *Leader Post*. The couple was able to move to Winnipeg in 1938 when Terry was offered the position of photographer with the Winnipeg *Tribune*. During the Royal Tour of 1939, Terry took a pair of photographs of the King and

Queen called "Sympathy" and "Understanding" that hung in Windsor Palace for many years.

As photographer for the *Tribune* Terry was assigned to take pictures of the Canadian troops as they left Winnipeg for Halifax and embarkation to Britain. According to biographical information accompanying the Rowe Island memorial certificate, the notion of service overseas "proved too much for the young photographer to resist. So as soon as an opening occurred he was one of the first to join up as Public Relations Officer."

"He was commissioned as a First Lieutenant," the biography continues, "and left for overseas in the early spring of 1943. In July 1943, his only child, Terry, was born in Winnipeg. After some time in England, Terry was sent to North Africa, and from there to Sicily and Italy to cover the Canadian landings and the sieges of Ortona and Foggia." The sparse prose of the biography obscures the difficult fighting Lieutenant Rowe would have witnessed. The twenty-month Italian campaign, consisting of one agonizingly slow and difficult ridge or valley after another, resulted in more than 25,000 Canadian casualties, including more than 5,900 deaths.

In early 1944, the Allied amphibious landing near Anzio on the west coast was designed as essentially a shortcut to Rome, one that would avoid the costly and difficult step-by-step progress toward the liberation of Italy. The landing was successful, but the expected German counterattack a week later was ferocious, threatening the beachhead. Lieutenant Rowe, his biography informs us, "volunteered to go to Anzio and it was there that he was killed by a bomb February 6, 1944."

Terry Rowe is buried at the Anzio War Cemetery, seventy kilometres south of Rome. His son Terry, a computer consultant, made the trip to see the gravesite. "We lived in England for a year in '55 or '56," he says, "and during Easter holidays we made a sort of pilgrimage across Europe, and among other things went to Anzio." There the teenager stood by his father's grave and wished he knew who his dad was. "I never saw him. I never had a father, so in a sense it was easier than somebody who loses a parent at twelve or thirteen. That can be really traumatic, but I never knew what a father was."

Margaret Rowe never remarried. Living until the 1980s, she had requested that her ashes be put on her husband's grave. With the help of the Canadian and Italian governments, her son made certain her wishes were fulfilled. ✿

Above: Terry Rowe

WESTERN CANADA PICTORIAL INDEX
11326-39638

Left: "Understanding" and "Sympathy"—Terry Rowe's striking photographs of the Royal Couple taken during their Royal Tour to Canada in 1939.

COURTESY TERRY ROWE JR.

Senton

Senton Lake (60°00' N, 108°02' W), viewed here from the south, is located 340 air miles north of La Ronge on the border between Saskatchewan and the Northwest Territories. Over a mile in length, Senton Lake is situated in the Tazin Lake Upland ecoregion of the Taiga Shield.

Growing up near Simpson, Saskatchewan, Claude and Glen Senton "were just a normal pair of farm kids with dogs and barn cats for company," Glen says. "The economy was terrible. We had years of drought and couldn't grow a crop." The fun times during those hard years included skating, baseball, horseshoes, or dances at Flanderdale School with the boys' father, Joseph Senton, calling the square dances. But the main responsibility for Claude, as the eldest of three children, was helping his dad. Often the boys would be alone with the chores on weekends while Joseph went to Saskatoon to visit his wife, Jennie Mae, who was ill with tuberculosis. Sometimes Claude and Glen would drive the horse and stoneboat to visit their sister Lillian, who was being raised at their grandparents' while Jennie Mae was ill, and enjoy Sunday dinner, which their grandma would always serve early so the boys could get home to do the chores.

After harvest one year, Claude and a friend rode the rails to Ontario, looking for work but finding none. They had to return in the dead of winter, walking the last sixteen miles from Young and almost freezing to death. Next year Glen made the trip with Claude, the two of them given twenty dollars each by their father, and they found work building prisoner of war barracks at Ignace, Ontario. These episodes on the rails taught Glen Senton much about his big brother: "Claude would always make sure that I got on a train before he did, that he carried the heaviest backpack, and that he chose the right men to associate with."

It was partly to earn a more secure, if dangerous, living that Claude Senton joined the army in late March 1941. Enlisting in Regina and training in Claresholm, Alberta, Claude soon tired of the army life and transferred to the air force three months later, just days before his nineteenth birthday. He trained at No. 3 Bombing and Gunnery School in MacDonald, Manitoba, and No. 3 Wireless School in Winnipeg, received his air gunner's badge, and shipped out for overseas on the *Queen Elizabeth* on October 27, 1942.

Claude was posted to RCAF No. 422 Squadron of Coastal Command. Winston Churchill, in assessing the importance of No. 422 Squadron's anti-submarine patrols, stated that "unless the war in the North Atlantic was won, the invasion and liberation of Europe could not take place." Accordingly, No. 422 helped patrol, over and over again, sea lanes leading to Great Britain. For weeks on end they'd not spot a U-boat but, as Coastal Command headquarters reminded them, "the value of these continuous patrols is considerable, and crews should know that their apparently unprofitable patrols have contributed greatly."

Claude Senton was an air gunner on one of the most famous aircraft of World War II, the Short Sunderland Flying Boat—the largest operational aircraft in the war and one of the few to remain in service throughout. Moored in the harbour of one of several bases in Ireland, Scotland, or Wales, a Sunderland—a huge plane with a crew of as many as thirteen—could range as far as 2,500 miles on patrol operations that could last fourteen hours.

Heavily armoured, carrying as many as twenty-one guns and eight depth charges, the Sunderland was known as "The Flying Porcupine" to its enemies.

Quite often, the gunners served as third pilots and would stand between the pilot and second pilot, observing the operation of the aircraft. With the galley close at hand, the gunners often became cooks as well, serving as many as three meals to the crew in the course of an operation. Claude Senton, already a good cook from his years looking after his brother on the farm, would have been especially well-suited for that job. In his letters he could not, of course, say much about his work, except "I get around plenty" and "everything is going ok." On September 28, 1943, however, his Sunderland crashed during entry to a fjord near Reykjavik. The aircraft was lost, but the crew was saved. At home in Simpson,

Below: One of No. 422 Squadron's Short Sunderlands

Joseph and Jennie Mae Senton found out by telegram that Claude, suffering from exposure, had spent four days in a U.S. air force hospital but had returned to duty.

About eight months later, a more devastating telegram was delivered to the Senton farm. On May 24, 1944, Claude Senton, newly commissioned as a pilot officer, took off from Castle Archdale, Scotland, as part of a crew of twelve on an anti-submarine sweep north of the Shetland Islands to approximately one hundred miles west of Norway. At 14:19 hours, a weak SOS was received. A minute later a second Sunderland sighted a large puff of smoke or splash and, when it went to investigate, a U-boat. Aircraft wreckage was seen about five hundred yards from the U-boat. "It is believed that the aircraft was so badly damaged in attacking the submarine that it crashed shortly after the attack," wrote Wing Commander J.R. Frizzle to Joseph Senton. He added: "Claude has been with the squadron some considerable time and was considered a very valuable Air

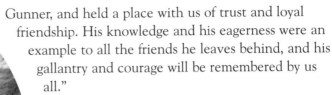

Gunner, and held a place with us of trust and loyal friendship. His knowledge and his eagerness were an example to all the friends he leaves behind, and his gallantry and courage will be remembered by us all."

"This time next year I hope I'm home," Claude had written on the back of the last picture he sent home. His mother saved it in her trunk with all the other pictures and letters. He was twenty-four years old when he died.

Buried in Stavne Cemetery in Trondheim, Norway, Claude Senton is memorialized by Senton Lake on the Saskatchewan-Northwest Territories border. ✿

Shorten

Except for his service years, Albert Shorten lived his entire life in the family house his father Joseph had built in what was the extreme southwest corner of Regina. A patch of prairie separated Little England, as the area was known, from the rest of the Lakeview district of the city. Although the depression meant that the possibility of achieving one's dreams seemed distant, for Albert a tangible reminder of his personal dream was close at hand. From the kitchen window of the Shorten house, he could see the Regina airport—the planes taking off and landing—and Albert knew he wanted to be a pilot. He was fascinated by the sheer number of planes and by the new models showing up that were ever faster and better looking.

At about the same time at Lakeview School, Albert was showing some of the same aptitude for woodworking that his father possessed. The family still uses a lamp Albert made for them in grade eight. His specialty, though, was aircraft. Grabbing a log of firewood from the coal pail, he would carve an airplane, complete to the tiniest detail on the tail, wings and landing gear. It would take about a week to finish the carving and painting. If the model didn't turn out just right, he would burn it and start again. Other than that hobby, which he continued throughout his life prior to enlisting, Albert was an ordinary boy. A bicycle was a prize possession. Games of tag on the open prairie, horsing around with his brother and sister, hours of play with his pals out in the garage (re-imagined as a

Shorten Lake (59°49' W, 108°01' W), viewed here from the south, is located 340 air miles northwest of La Ronge, in the rugged Taiga Shield ecozone, just ten miles south of the border between the Northwest Territories and Saskatchewan. Part of the mighty Tazin River, Shorten Lake is about two miles in length. Although a forest fire rolled through the area in the summer of 2000, a trapper's cabin remains standing on a sandy point at Shorten Lake.

Regina•

fabulous circus tent), spending his allowance of five cents a week—these and other everyday activities filled his boyhood. He enjoyed all sports equally, not excelling in any one in particular. At school he took part in all the usual school activities and achieved average marks. He played trumpet in the YMCA band and enjoyed trips to his uncle's farm where he could take a rifle and do some shooting.

In the words of Albert's brother Roy, as Albert became interested in airplanes, countries became interested in war. Albert completed his grade eleven at Central Collegiate in Regina, where he had a job washing glassware in the lab, then joined the RCAF in the spring of 1941. "He really wanted to go," Roy remembers, "but he didn't know what he was getting into." He had never been away from home. But after training at Penhold, Alberta, and graduating from the No. 3 Bombing and Gunnery School in Macdonald, Manitoba, as an air gunner, Albert Shorten was sent very far from home indeed—to Bournemouth, England, in March of 1942, assigned to RAF No. 199 Squadron of Bomber Command. "Let Tyrants Tremble" was the squadron motto, and their

almost nightly raids to Essen, Hamburg, and Cologne lived up to that motto.

The danger and stress of the operations, combined with a shortage of food and coal for heat at the base in Ingham, Lincolnshire, made for difficult conditions for Albert Shorten and his mates. The mixture of Canadian boys with British officers wasn't always a happy one either. Parcels from home, one a month, often saved the day. And Albert's excursions on leave to meet relatives in Norfolk were a blessing too. He could shoot rabbits with his cousins, enjoy plenty of food (but no eggs), and return to duty—"an ordinary guy," his brother says now, "doing his job."

On March 13, 1943, Albert Shorten's Wellington bomber took off on a test flight. The aircraft suffered structural failure, exploded in mid-air, and crashed near Newport Cemetery, where Albert Shorten was laid to rest in a section reserved for Canadian servicemen. The Shorten family was never the same after Albert's death, and his mother Victoria never achieved personal peace when the war ended. The eldest of the three Shorten kids, Albert had barely turned twenty when he died. In the family's memory he remains a good, kind, and gentle son and brother who will never be forgotten. Just south of Saskatchewan's northern border lies Shorten Lake, named in Albert's honour. ✿

Below: Albert Shorten sent home this photo of himself looking a little disheveled. On the back he wrote: "This one isn't too good. just came down. Felt kind of tired."

Taylor

O n March 15, 1944, a Lancaster bomber crashed in a field near the village of Hilsenheim, France. RCAF Flying Officer William Taylor was among the crew. Fifty years later, some of the families of the crew members gathered for a memorial service at the gravesites in the Hilsenheim Communal Cemetery. In the words of William's sister Edna,

> It was a moving experience for all that attended. The Canadian family was greeted very warmly by the British family of the crew member, Hudson. Later they met and were treated very warmly and graciously by the French family, Steydli, who had taken care of the graves of all of the crew members through the years. A bond was created that day among the Canadian, English, and French families that is in itself a fitting tribute to a young life, cut off before he had a chance to really live.

William Taylor's "young life" had begun in Nottingham, a hamlet north and east of Carnduff, Saskatchewan, on April 20, 1920. His parents, homesteaders in the area, had emigrated to Canada from England and Ireland, and William was the eighth of what was eventually a family of nine. His school years, during which William had the same teacher in a one-room school for grades one through ten, provided a few special family memories. William and the other young ones of the family used to make their own stilts. (One brother, Ernest, claims to have walked one and a half miles to school on them.) And William, a

Nottingham●

Taylor Bay (57°24' N, 105°22' W), viewed here from the north, is four miles in length. It is located on Russell Lake, 150 miles north of La Ronge and fifteen miles north of the Key Lake mine site. A large lake fifteen miles in length, Russell Lake flows with the Wheeler River and is a popular destination for angler tourists and paddling voyageurs.

vigourous, good-natured boy, loved to wrestle in the house, especially putting on a show in the kitchen, where most of the spectators could be found. "I thought the house was going to get wrecked," one of his sisters recalls. Another time, William was out hunting for crows' eggs, keen to collect the bounty of two cents an egg (more if it was a live bird) the government had placed on the pests. After the successful hunt, William rode his horse home, the eggs stashed safely in his hat. But the horse began to gallop, and soon William had crow egg running down his face, to the everlasting mirth of his siblings. He loved to ride horses, though—egg hunting or not.

Eventually he got his grade twelve at the high school in Carievale by boarding near town and riding his bicycle to and from school, meanwhile keeping an eye open for employment opportunities. Once during another wrestling session with his brother, William saw a fellow named Jim Murray walk by the house. In an instant the boys tidied their clothes, straightened their hair, and dashed out the door after Mr. Murray. Soon thereafter, William was off to Manitoba to work on the Murray farm.

By that time William wanted earnestly to enlist in the RCAF, which he did. He'd always had a good, strong will. His sister relates that, during his first solo flight while training, William "had difficulty bringing the plane down. Wind kept bouncing it back up. He decided that he would land that plane if it were the last thing he would ever do, so through determination and patience, he eventually landed safely."

There was a spell of crying when William was sent to England and he said his goodbyes to his family in Carnduff, including a sister who was about to give birth. He was assigned in 1943 to No. 408 "Goose" Squadron, the second Canadian bomber squadron formed overseas. Whenever he could, William visited his Uncle Will and other relatives in England. "Sorry to say," he wrote in a letter home dated March 14, 1944, "I can't tell you much about what I'm doing or what targets I have been on." The next day, William Taylor's Lancaster was bound for Stuttgart when, apparently, the plane collided with another of the same squadron. The plane crashed in Monsieur Steydli's field in France, and the crash site became a monument of its own. You could see the indentation in the field, and nothing grew there for twenty years. Mr. Steydli respectfully preserved whatever pieces of the plane he could find.

The family's visit there fifty years later was "a simple meeting without tambourines or trumpets, but nevertheless imprinted with melancholy, memories, and emotions" of the kind evoked by this verse written by William's sister Isabel shortly after his death:

Last night a star fell from the sky,
It seemed so sad its light had gone,
Till I looked overhead and saw
A million others shone.

In northern Saskatchewan, William Taylor is memorialized by Taylor Bay, located on Russell Lake.

ABLE SEAMAN **ABRAHAM UNGER** • V39733 • 1923–1944 ———————————————— # Unger

oming from a Mennonite farming family in the McMahon district southeast of Swift Current, Able Seaman Abe Unger needn't have gone to sea at all. Granted a dispensation from Queen Victoria, the Mennonites and their descendants were absolved from military service in order to live their pacifist beliefs. Nevertheless, "these were different times," as Abe's brother Isaac wrote many years later. "Now, along with reciting the Lord's Prayer during morning exercises, our small schoolful of Mennonite children stood at attention before the Union Jack, confirming each day, aloud and in unison, our allegiance to all that we could understand the flag to represent." In all, six brothers and one sister-in-law out of the Unger family's eleven siblings served in the armed forces in the war years or in subsequent peacetime. Jacob and Judith Unger, then, accepted the decision of Abe, the seventh oldest of their ten boys, to join the Royal Canadian Navy Volunteer Reserve at HMCS *Queen* in Regina on May 19, 1942. He had just turned nineteen.

After finishing public school he'd stayed to help on the home farm for several years, hiring out his services as a labourer to other farmers on occasion. Left-handed, six feet tall, Abe called himself a "fair" swimmer when he volunteered for the Navy, although the body of water with which he was most familiar was the dugout on the farm. He was given agricultural leave during harvest season in 1942 before resuming his Navy career. Becoming Able Seaman in September 1943—

Unger Lake (59°47' N, 109°59' W), viewed here from the north, is located 370 air miles northwest of La Ronge, only one mile from the Alberta border and fifteen miles south of the border between the Northwest Territories and Saskatchewan. Situated in the Tazin Lake Upland ecoregion of the Taiga Shield, Unger Lake is over one mile in length and is part of an extensive series of creeks and lakes flowing into Lake Athabasca.

McMahon●

his character rating at each evaluation was "Very Good"—he was soon thereafter assigned to HMCS *Skeena*, a destroyer.

The *Skeena* had been part of the Canadian naval force from the very beginning of the war. Based in Halifax, its main function was to patrol the convoy routes back and forth across the North Atlantic. Joseph Schull's *Far Distant Ships* describes the routine of convoy escort:

> [Escort ships] slogged on day after day by the side of the crawling convoys, sometimes without any break in the monotony, sometimes pursuing a sighting or an echo with no result, returning again to the merchant ships and slogging on. A convoy or a series of convoys might cross entirely without incident…. Then, suddenly, about a succeeding convoy the U-boats would gather….

Routine or not, it was dangerous, vital work. There had been many tense nights for the *Skeena*, including its sinking of a U-boat in 1942, pre-invasion operations in the English Channel in the spring of 1944, and several anti-U-boat operations off the French province of Brest.

The *Skeena* was patrolling south of Iceland in the afternoon of October 23, 1944, the day before Abe Unger died. After several stormy days, an intense gale had developed, and the ships were ordered to Reykjavik. By half past nine that evening, the *Skeena* was anchored near Videy Island, a location that offered little shelter from the heavy seas and wind or from continual snow squalls that reduced visibility to almost zero. Around midnight, the officer of the watch

discovered that the ship had been dragging her anchor and had run aground. It was in grave danger of breaking in two and capsizing. The order to abandon ship was first given, then cancelled a few minutes later.

Between the giving and the canceling of the order to abandon ship, Able Seaman Unger had been set adrift in one of three carley floats that held in total about thirty men. In spite of the fact that the beach was less than one hundred yards away, fifteen men drowned as the floats drifted, carried by an ebb tide, into open sea before dawn the next morning, October 24.

A board of enquiry was convened. Isaac Unger, in his research conducted years later, summarizes part of the board's conclusion:

Although the shore was only a few yards from the fore part of the ship, the first order to abandon ship was given without due regard to this fact, and without sufficient preparation. The fact that three floats, in spite of having been fitted with extra tails for veering ashore, were cut adrift, was the indirect cause of practically all the deaths, and no death can be attributed to the negligence of anyone. The Board allowed for confusion aft, bearing in mind the constant pounding and the heavy seas. Under the circumstances, the Board believed that an organized unhurried evacuation of the ship would have met the situation very much better.

Skeena Aground, the book in which Isaac Unger comes to terms with the circumstances and meaning of his brother's death, details a variety of responses to Abe's death. Jacob and Judith Unger responded with quiet acceptance. Men who served with Abe paid their respects "the navy way"—holding an "auction sale" of clothing and assorted items left behind by their fifteen friends. Abe's collar, for example, a ninety-cent item, sold for twenty-one dollars to a shipmate, Fredrick Fear. Altogether, $150 was raised for the Unger family, and a similar amount for the other fifteen families.

At Fossvogur Cemetery south of Reykjavik, Able Seaman Abraham Unger was buried with full military honours. Shipmates dug the grave, built the wooden cross, and saluted it. In 1951, a Cross of Sacrifice was unveiled there. And in 1960, Unger Lake north of Lake Athabasca, Saskatchewan, was named in his memory. 🏵️

Left: HMCS *Skeena* aground at Videy Island.

Above: The memorial cross that marks the graves of HMCS *Skeena's* dead in Fossvogur Cemetery, December 1945. The cross was designed by *Skeena* shipwright George Duncan.

Wallace

FLIGHT LIEUTENANT **DONALD WALLACE** • J17372 • 1912–1944
FLIGHT SERGEANT **JOHN WALLACE** • R176389 • 1921–1943

Wallace Bay (59°28' N, 108°03' W), viewed here from the east, is four miles in length and is located on the rugged north shore of Lake Athabasca, twenty miles east of Uranium City. In this spectacular setting near the mouth of the Oldman River, Wallace Bay hosts excellent jackfish habitat and is a popular location providing shelter and beauty for voyageurs and anglers.

All eight of the Wallace boys of Lang, Saskatchewan were in uniform in 1943. A *Leader-Post* article reported that Mrs. Jessie Wallace—whose husband Thomas had died in 1941—"misses her sons, but since they are doing their patriotic duty, she is content to wait till hostilities cease and they once more gather at her home." Two of the boys, however, did not come home: Donald, and her second youngest boy John, known as Jack.

Jessie and Thomas Wallace had lived around Lang since coming from Ontario in 1901. Their homestead was established about three miles northwest of Lang, and at the same time Thomas operated a livery and dray business in Milestone, ten miles west of the homestead. When Thomas would ride home every Saturday night, Jessie knew he'd arrived when she could hear the traces on the horses. As to the general state of the family farm, the youngest son, Jim Wallace, remembers that "Dad had money in the 1920s, but the 30s was tough on all the farmers."

Most of the time, Don and Jack and the others walked into town to school. Sometimes their dad would hitch the school horse, Belle, to a buggy in summer or a sleigh in winter, and then stay in town playing bridge at the café until school was out. Horses were always a prominent part of the Wallace farm operation. At one time they had thirty-three workhorses in the barn. A boxing ring was set up in that same barn—a way for the boys to learn to look after themselves, their dad reckoned. On Sundays, neighbour kids would come over too.

Don Wallace was not much for school. He did get his grade twelve, at one point paying two dollars to appeal his literature grade of 43, getting it raised to a 50. And he did begin, without finishing, some post-secondary studies at Regina College in 1930. He had enough of a knack for languages that a few years later, on his Record of Service, he was able to claim "some knowledge of the French and German languages." But mainly he worked on the home farm and other farms in the area, always seeming to have a job even when jobs were hard to come by. For several years he headed up to the Peace River country to work for the Bailey family. Once in a while he'd ride the train back home, sewing some precious cash into patches on the knees of his jeans.

Don was working for the Baileys in the spring of 1941 when he decided to join the air force. First he finished the seeding, then made the trip into Edmonton to enlist. He was sent directly to Manning Depot in Brandon, necessitating some quick instructions to his mother to unpack some extra clothes he'd sent home: "as soon as you can," he wrote, "because some of them

are still damp. So if you will dry out everything before you pack it away I will be much obliged." Careful with his money, he reminded his mother that "if anything should happen" she was to retrieve the money he'd deposited in a half-dozen different banks.

His training as an air gunner concluded at No. 5 Bombing and Gunnery School in Dafoe. Then there was time for an embarkation leave spent with his family on the farm and with his sister Katie Jean at Fort San, where she worked as a nurse, before he was off to England, arriving there in May of 1942. Promotions followed—to flight sergeant, September, 1942; pilot officer, March 1943—and by June, 1944, he reported to his mother the "good news" that he'd been promoted to flight lieutenant.

That was his last letter, one that asked about the well-being of his brothers and whether or not Jessie had received the Mother's Day flowers he'd cabled. "I'm terrifically busy right now," he told her, referring, no doubt, to the flurry of D-Day invasion support operations the RCAF was involved in—raids on German troop and gun positions, ammunition and oil dumps, and rail and road communications to the battle front in France.

Attached to RAF No. 172 Squadron, Flight Lieutenant Wallace was an air gunner in a Wellington bomber that took off in the late evening of June 14, 1944 on anti-submarine patrol. Its last known location was over the Bay of Biscay, approximately forty miles south of St. Nazaire, France. The Wellington did not return, and Don Wallace's body was not recovered. He was "an extremely popular member of the Squadron, and always carried out his duties in an efficient and praiseworthy manner," wrote the Squadron Leader. "His

Above: Don Wallace at Fort San, 1942.

Left: Don Wallace, standing far right, with fellow airmen.

Above: John "Jack" Wallace.

Right: This identification tag accompanied Jack's personal effects which were sent to his mother after his death.

presence, and cheerful personality, will be missed by all ranks." Flight Lieutenant Donald Wallace is memorialized at Runnymede, Surrey, wherein "are recorded the names of 20,000 airmen who have no known grave." As his mother said, "Where his grave is, we do not know. He was always alone."

Jack Wallace also chose the RCAF as his branch of the Armed Forces. The second youngest in the family, Jack was an active lad. He wouldn't shy away from a scuffle with anyone, including his brothers, and was "always doing some stunt," his niece remembers, "like standing on the horse, or hanging from the door jamb at the farm." He got as far as grade nine in school at Lang, having to repeat his algebra/geometry along the way, and enlisted in Regina in July 1942. Training as an air gunner, as Don had done, Jack graduated from No. 3 Bombing and Gunnery School in MacDonald, Manitoba, and was sent overseas in early 1943. After a time with an Operational Training Unit in Worcestershire, he was posted to No. 1664 Heavy Conversion Unit based at Croft, Yorkshire, the last stage of training on the heavy bombers before being posted to an operational squadron.

Michael Millar was a schoolboy attending Applegarth Junior School in Northallerton, North Yorkshire, on December 2, 1943, when a Halifax bomber crashed just two hundred yards away. It was a Halifax piloted on a training flight by Pilot Officer W.J. Taylor. All seven crew members, including Jack Wallace, the tailgunner, were killed in the crash. "We were told to go home," Michael Millar writes. "My route took me very close to the scene of the crash. I remember seeing aircraft parts strewn all over the place and burning, including part of the landing gear. I hurried on home, humming 'O Come, O Come Emmanuel' to myself." The scene stayed with Millar, and years later he conducted research into the crash.

His research revealed that "rudder stall" was a factor in many of the crashes of early versions of the Halifax bomber. "When the aircraft was put into a tight turn," Millar explains, "the airflow through the gap between the tail fins and the rudders was so great that the pilot was unable to get the rudders back into a central position to come out of the turn. This resulted in the aircraft going into a fatal spiral." At high enough altitudes, the crew might be able to bail out. But at the low altitude of the training flight, the crew had no chance to save themselves on that December day in Yorkshire. After a full military funeral, Flight Sergeant Wallace was buried in the Air Forces section of the Harrogate Cemetery. With understated humour that accompanied their affection for Jack Wallace, his friends allowed that they'd miss his mouth organ playing more than anything else.

Wallace Bay on Lake Athabasca is named in honour of Donald and Jack Wallace. In further honouring her sons, and all mothers who had lost sons in the war, the Canadian government named Jessie Wallace one of the Silver Cross Mothers after the war. "She was a real soldier, the way she took everything," Jim Wallace says. ✿

Welsh

The Welsh brothers, Victor and Lawrence, two of six boys in the family of seven children, earned money as teenagers in Regina by delivering telegrams on bicycle. As the war years progressed, a messenger's job became more stressful than it may have appeared because of the large number of casualty notices which had to be delivered. Watching one family after another receive the dreadful news of a lost loved one exacted a heavy toll on the telegraph messengers. One bereaved Regina woman reportedly suffered a stroke and died before the very eyes of a young messenger, the casualty notice still clenched in her hand.

The Welsh family had already experienced its own losses. One son, Billy, had died of a heart condition at age four after a long illness. The family had moved from Nokomis to Regina so that William and Claire Welsh could visit their son at the Grey Nuns' Hospital. Another son, Leonard, six years old, was playing with firecrackers one day when they exploded, catching him on fire. Leonard died as a result of his severe burns. The incident seemed particularly traumatic for Victor, who had been present at the time but unable to save his brother. Already known to be relatively private and reserved in character, Victor grew even more so during his visits to the site of the accident.

But there were happier times as well. Victor was a skilled ballroom dancer. Every weekend he and his girlfriend Victoria frequented The Silver Dell, a nightspot opposite the CNR station, where they fox-

Welsh Bay (56°26' N, 105°28' W), viewed here from the north, is located one hundred air miles north of La Ronge on Foster Lake, not far from Welsh Rapids (photo and description on the following page). Located in the rugged country of the Churchill River Upland ecoregion of the Boreal Shield, the Foster Lakes and River system experiences numerous elevation changes as it flows south to the Churchill River.

Regina

Top: John Victor Welsh

Centre: Lawrence Albert Welsh

Below: Welsh Rapids (56°26' N, 105°35' W), viewed here from the south, is located one hundred air miles north of La Ronge, situated on the Foster River about five miles downstream of Foster Lake.

trotted and swing-danced to all the hit songs of the 1930s, his personal favourite being "In the Mood." Victor and Victoria were to be married upon his return from service.

Lawrence Welsh was an athlete, a quarterback for the Campion College team on which he was nicknamed "Huck" after the Canadian football player Huck Welsh. And like his brother, Lawrence enjoyed female companionship, giving rise to the following story. After

one evening out, Lawrence was invited back to the young woman's home where the two sat together on the living room sofa. Throughout their entire time together, his date's father paced back and forth before them in his long johns, winding an alarm clock. He neither made any eye contact with Lawrence nor muttered a single word. The pacing and clock winding proceeded for about an hour until Lawrence got the hint and, somewhat spooked, raced all the way home from the opposite end of town. His family was quite surprised to see him arrive home so early on a Saturday night.

Education was important in the Welsh family—so much so that Claire Welsh washed clothes for the boarders at Campion College to pay her sons' way through that highly regarded high school. During the years after high school and before the war, Victor and Lawrence managed to find work when work was difficult to come by. Victor trained as a machinist apprentice. He used to tell Lawrence, who worked as a bookkeeper for Toronto General Trust, to work with his brain, while Victor would work with his hands. At wartime, both boys chose to serve in the air force, Victor serving as a wireless air gunner with RAF No. 13 Squadron. The last his family saw of him was when he and his mates waved goodbye at the train station. Warrant Officer Victor Welsh was killed in

action on December 18, 1942, when his Blenheim bomber failed to return from operations while based in the Mediterranean region. With no known grave, he is commemorated by the Malta Memorial in Floriana, Malta. His fiancee, Victoria, never did marry.

Lawrence Welsh, who had joined the air force although technically underage, received word of his brother's death while he was training in Trenton, Ontario. The news was a setback, of course, and it delayed his training, but Lawrence carried on and was eventually posted overseas as a bomb aimer with RAF No. 78 Squadron. Returning from a raid on the synthetic-oil refinery in Sterkrade, Germany, his Halifax Mark III bomber appeared to run out of fuel before reaching the aerodrome in Breighton, Yorkshire, on November 21, 1944. The port wing clipped the treetops, causing the bomber to spiral and collide with a brick building not far from the village of Goole. The aircraft disintegrated upon impact, instantly killing Pilot Officer Welsh and five crewmates. Lawrence Welsh is buried at Stonefall Cemetery, Harrogate, England.

The Welsh family's distress at the news of the boys' deaths was exacerbated after the war upon receipt of boxes supposedly returning their sons' belongings. Victor's contained only a mismatched pair of shoes, not the wellingtons that he always wore and that the family periodically sent from home. Lawrence's box contained only a tunic and some pictures. The family also felt that errors were made in the dispersal of the boys' pension funds after the war. However, both William and Claire, who lived well into their eighties, were proud when Welsh Rapids and Welsh Bay in Saskatchewan were named in honour of their two airmen sons, Lawrence and Victor, respectively. ✿

Photos counterclockwise from top: Victor and a fellow trainee while training in Dafoe; Victor and an unidentified buddy at Dafoe; Lawrence disembarking from his plane at his base in England; Lawrence relaxing.

White

White Lake (55° 54′ N, 106° 22′ W), viewed here from the west, is located seventy-five air miles northwest of La Ronge. Its irregular shorelines and rocky islands are characteristic of the ruggedness of the Churchill River Upland ecoregion. The deep clear waters of White Lake are accessible by canoe from Highway 914 at Gordon Bay through Gordon Lake.

Wilmotte McCallum of Saskatoon tells her children and grandchildren that her brother Lisle "would have loved you all and brightened your lives." He was, by all accounts, a remarkably kind and able man. Having known Lisle when he was a member of an Honour Guard on the occasion of the Royal Visit to Regina in 1939, Father Athol Murray saw Lisle White as "a grand chap—full of personality and unique delightfulness," adding that "all the Notre Dame Hounds loved Lisle White." From overseas, Lisle's padre in the Regina Rifle Regiment reported that "Lisle did a grand job. He was perfectly fearless, very much loved and admired by his men, whose confidence he held." Wilmotte, his only sister, says simply: "He was my best friend all my life."

They had grown up together in Regina and shared a childhood filled with activities and achievements— everything from snaring gophers to fishing, hunting, sports, and stamp collecting. Lisle, the big brother, took his "Sis" to her first day of kindergarten, and generally was always looking after her as they were growing up. Together they won figure skating competitions in Regina, and many junior badminton awards. Lisle played the drums, too—for that he was banished to the garage by his mother during practice times—and built a sailboat in the basement. In order to get the boat to water at the Regina Boat Club, where he and others won rowing events, all the doors and jambs of the White house had to be temporarily removed.

At Lakeview School and later Campion College in

Regina, Lisle was more interested in doing extracurricular things than in being a great student, but he always got through. During his high school days he sold *Liberty* and *Maclean's* magazines door to door. The proceeds helped him buy a Harley-Davidson motorcycle that he drove to Port Hope, Ontario, over gravel roads most of the way, for studies at Trinity College School. Later he studied a year of Arts at the University of Minnesota.

The day war was declared—September 3, 1939—was the day Lisle White enlisted with the Regina Rifle Regiment, the sixteenth man to do so. He trained in Regina and eventually Debert Military Camp at Truro, Nova Scotia. Wilmotte and their mother drove to Nova Scotia and stayed there until the regiment shipped out for England in September of 1941. Only a few weeks later, a letter home offered evidence that Lisle's sociability and organizational skills had made the ocean crossing intact: "Last Saturday night we held a dance in our mess, and invited quite a few of the girls in the area to it. It was grand, and I think that all of them had a grand time. I was in charge of it, and it kept me pretty busy for some days." The same letter reported that Lisle had qualified as a class three driver, enabling him to "drive any military vehicle or motorcycle on duty."

His main duty, however, was as a specialist in "dealing with gas," as he put it in another letter. "We have to know the various types, and what to do to treat them so that they become harmless, and therefore cannot inflict casualties on our own troops. We also have to know how to throw, spray, and send out gas, and all the safety precautions that come with it. We are equipped with special outfits, and if the Regiment gets into gas, we are the first there." So knowledgeable was Lisle about gas warfare that in 1942 he returned to Calgary to teach the subject to new recruits.

A year later he was back with his regiment overseas. "They don't come any better in any man's army than these men of the Regina Rifles," reported the Saskatoon *Star-Phoenix* War correspondent in August of 1944. The regiment, part of the Third Canadian Infantry Division assault of Juno Beach on D-Day, had continued to figure prominently in the subsequent Battle of Normandy. On July 8, the Regina Rifles attacked the Abbey of Ardenne, which was the command post of an S.S. Panzer Grenadier Regiment, and met heavy resistance. Captain Lisle White's C company, of which he was second in command, held the most forward position of the most forward sector of the attack on the Abbey. When Major Stuart Tubb, commanding officer of the company, was hit in the leg by machine gun fire, Lisle White came running over to help. Just as he got a few feet away, he too was hit in the chest by a machine gun burst and died instantly. Padre Jamieson provided further details to the family in a letter written a few months later:

Lisle made me promise one time in England, in his usual breezy manner, that if ever he were killed that I would bury him myself. I personally attended to him, helping, shortly after the engagement, to carry his body to the vehicle in which it was transported to the Canadian Military Cemetery at Beny-sur-Mer, a little village north-west of Caen, France. I conducted his funeral service myself.

Wilmotte McCallum honours her brother's memory by attending reunions of the Regina Rifle Regiment, visiting the Normandy battlefields in France, and, in 1979, by flying up by float plane to White Lake, Saskatchewan, named after Lisle. On that day, in the absolutely beautiful setting of water and trees, she and her family laid a plaque, had a picnic, swam, caught a fish, and brought back three small spruce trees, still growing in her family's yards. In her own quiet words: "He meant a lot to me." ❀

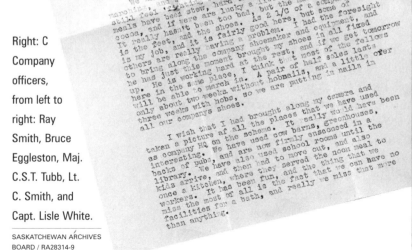

Wick

Flying out of RCAF No. 429 Squadron base in Leeming, Yorkshire, in 1943 and 1944, Flight Sergeant Stan Wick and his crew had done well. They had been rated above average at their Operational Training Unit and had made the transition to the four-engine heavy bombers smoothly. Not long after they began taking part in operations over Germany, Stan Wick's Commanding Officer recommended him for a commission, noting that here was "a steady and reliable captain and a first class operational pilot." The crew's sixteen operations through the winter of 1943-44 included sorties to Frankfurt, Dusseldorf, Stuttgart, Hanover and Leipzig as well as four ops to the Big City, Berlin. The crew had even managed to survive being mistaken for an enemy fighter and shot at by the tail gunner of another Halifax. But then came what was later known as "The Night of the Big Wind"—March 24, 1944.

That night the more than eight hundred aircraft that attacked Berlin encountered a jet stream with winds of over 220 kilometres per hour. Aircraft were blown far off course to the south, away from the cohesion of the bomber stream, over heavily-defended areas below, resulting in what was by any measure a disastrous operation for Bomber Command. Although Pilot Officer Wick and his crew managed to drop their bombs and head for home, they soon ran into trouble. *Reap the Whirlwind: The Untold Story of 6 Group, Canada's Bomber Force of World War II* includes an account of what happened:

Wick Rapids (55°30' N, 104°07' W), viewed here from the south, is located fifty-five air miles east of La Ronge, a lovely set of rapids in the Churchill River Upland ecoregion of the Boreal Shield. Here the waters of Irving Lake descend through numerous rapids and small lakes, finally draining eight miles south into the historic Churchill River.

Conquest•

'I received a wireless message from HQ giving details of wind directions and speed' [reported the crew's wireless operator, Stan Boustead].... 'We were pointing directly towards heavy flak and searchlights, obviously Magdeburg. The navigator said we would track south of Magdeburg due to the heavy winds. I turned back to the wireless.' At that instant flak smashed into the Halifax. To Bob Kift, the mid-upper gunner, it sounded as if someone was hitting the aircraft with a heavy hammer. The Halifax staggered, mortally wounded. Flames streamed back from the overload fuel tank amidships. Boustead heard the three or four thuds of direct hits plus the sound of tearing metal. He quickly switched back to intercom. The skipper, Wick, seemed remarkably sanguine about the situation, asking each crew member in turn for his opinion of damage. It rapidly became apparent that the situation was hopeless.

Not all of the crew was able to bail out. The Halifax exploded, killing Stan Wick and three of his crew instantly. That "Night of the Big Wind," the total death toll among Bomber Command aircrew was 382.

It was "quite a jolt back home," his brother Gordon says about the news of Stan's death reaching the town of Conquest, Saskatchewan, south of Saskatoon. Peter and Olufine Wick, both born and raised in Norway, had settled in Conquest in the early part of the century and raised a family of eight kids. Peter, a building contractor, had to break the news of Stan's death in a letter to one of Stan's five sisters. "It is such a terrible shock that I can hardly write or do anything else. Yes, it is a very sad home tonight. War has come to our house and taken our dear boy away."

Stan had been a sportsman whose passion for curling and whose prowess on the curling ice, often teamed-up with his father, was well known in the area. He was not too bad a hockey player either, Gordon suggests, and with his school chums loved hiking and hunting. In the school band he played bass horn and showed a fondness for music, often singing to himself, one of his sisters recalls. Generally, this handsome, blond-haired young man had a happy disposition, but he could have a bit of a temper at times.

He had finished high school in Conquest and had a couple of jobs before enlisting. One was planting shelter-belt trees on the outskirts of town. He also worked for one of the town's bankers, a job that may have continued after the war. Leaving behind his family and a girlfriend in Conquest, Stan was inducted into the RCAF in September of 1941, training in Edmonton, High River, and McLeod before receiving his wings in November of 1942 and heading overseas soon thereafter. "He's in a little town, then all of a sudden he's in the middle of a war," as Gordon puts it.

Pilot Officer Stan Wick is buried in the Berlin 1939-1945 War Cemetery alongside the three crewmates who died with him. His mother composed the text on his headstone: *Not just today but every day in silence we remember*. Stan Wick is remembered, too, on the map of Saskatchewan; Wick Rapids east of La Ronge are named in his honour. ✿

WARRANT OFFICER CLASS II GORDON WALTER WILDFONG • R151070 • 1921–1944 — Wildfong

For a young man near Cut Knife, Saskatchewan, during the early days of World War II, the desire to join the RCAF would have been fueled by the sight of numerous aircraft flying out of the base at North Battleford, a few miles to the east. Dorothy Stewart remembers that her cousin, Gordon Wildfong, was inspired in just that manner. "We'd look out the school windows and see them fly by," she says.

For a time, the Wildfongs lived on the family farm of Gordon's mother, Mae, in the Gallivan area south of Cut Knife. Later, Gordon's father, Walter, established his own farm nearby. He was an Ontario man who had trained as a stretcher-bearer in World War I. While he was in Halifax, somehow he missed the ship that was to take him overseas and was reassigned to the military police. In fact, during the famous Halifax explosion of the munitions ship in December 1917, Walter Wildfong was standing in front of City Hall on Barrington Street. Upon his discharge from the army, Walter rekindled his friendship with Mae Hardy in Winnipeg, where she worked for Birks Jewelers. The two of them had first met during their high school years in North Battleford. They married, began raising a family (Gordon was born in Winnipeg in 1921), and then moved to the Hardy farm to help out, intending to stay only a short time.

That short time turned into twenty years, during which time Gordon, the eldest of three children, took ten years of schooling in a country school three and a half miles from the farm, before finishing high school in Cut Knife. It was a happy time, Dorothy Stewart

Cut Knife●

Wildfong Lake (54°49' N, 102°27' W), viewed here from the north, is located 120 air miles east of La Ronge, twenty-five miles west of Flin Flon, and just six miles south of Highway 106. A shallow, circular-shaped body of water, Wildfong Lake is situated in the Mid-Boreal Lowland ecoregion. This is a transitional area: just ten miles to the north is the rugged Boreal Shield while, to the south, the landscape is dominated by wetlands, with open stands of tamarack and black spruce.

remembers. There were sports days in Gallivan, featuring ball games against teams from surrounding districts. Gordon Wildfong earned a reputation as one of the best ballplayers around and as a prize-winning pole vaulter. In winter, the kids took full advantage of the farm's location on a bend of Cut Knife Creek surrounded by steep banks and high hills. "Often cousins and friends would clear snow off the creek for a skating rink," Dorothy says. "We would gather wood for a bonfire. Or we would toboggan and ski on Island Hill. When we were all played out we would climb the hill to Grandma's house where Gordon's Mom would serve us hot chocolate." No matter what the time of year, Christian faith was an important part of family life, and Christmas and Easter family gatherings at the Hardy farm were always highlights.

Gordon was known as a gentle, quiet fellow—a good family boy. His thoughtful manner served him well in school, where he was a solid student. "I don't think he had any enemies at all," Dorothy says. Later, she and her husband Russ, with whose family Gordon stayed during his two years of high school in Cut Knife, named their eldest son after Gordon.

Gordon returned to the east and took a job working for International Nickel in a mine near Sudbury. He enlisted and trained in Ontario, and his family moved to Waterloo County to be closer to him. But the Gallivan–Cut Knife area seemed more like home to him. During leave he'd travel all the way from the east by train to visit his grandparents, cousins, and friends. "He looked very handsome in his uniform," Dorothy Stewart recalls. He reinforced his family connections during leaves in England, too, visiting Grandma Hardy's sister Ada in London—part of his delight with this country "I like very much," as he wrote in a letter home.

On one visit to his aunt's, he laid out all the contents of his pack at her request and demonstrated the correct procedure for packing it all up again. Then his cousin came in and asked him to do it all over again, which he did. After he had it repacked the second time, a neighbour girl came over and Gordon obliged with a third demonstration.

Gordon Wildfong served as a navigator with RAF No. 100 squadron based in Grimsby, Lincolnshire. In the weeks before D-Day, many operations of Bomber Command focused on railway targets near the proposed invasion landing areas—operations designed to hinder the enemy's ability to bring up reinforcements and supplies once the invasion occurred. On the Thursday night of March 15, 1944, 140 aircraft attacked the railway yards at Amiens, France. Including a major raid on Stuttgart, operations for that night used over 1,100 aircraft, a new record for Bomber Command.

One of the crews that did not return that night included Warrant Officer Class II Gordon Wildfong, who is buried beside his crewmates in the sixteenth-century churchyard of Poix-de-Picardie, twenty-eight kilometres southwest of Amiens. In Saskatchewan, Wildfong Lake, named in his honour, lies just west of the Hansen Lake Road. And at home, in the Cut Knife area, his name is read on the Honour Roll every November 11 and is included on the cenotaph at Rockhaven Cemetery, where his grandparents and extended family members are buried. ❁

Wilson

By the time Kevin Wilson joined the air force in 1941, he had established a successful career with Wilson Brothers Insurance Agents, a company formed in 1912 by his father Charles in Limerick, Saskatchewan. No wonder that Kevin, when the RCAF recruiting officer suggested he was "just another unemployed bum looking for a pay cheque," could pull a ten-dollar bill from his pocket and offer to wager that he had left a better job than the officer had.

A few months later, Kevin was eloquent in explaining to his sister his reasons for leaving such a job:

> to preserve a way of life in which we all believe and which has given us everything we have; to make it possible for our mother and father to spend the last years of their life in peace, freedom, and comfort, as they so richly deserve; to make it possible for our younger brother and sister to receive the same education we received; to enable a sister who has started a career with great brilliance to pursue that career to the much greater heights of which we all believe her capable.

Accordingly, he had embarked on the usual course of pilot's training, beginning at Initial Training School in Regina.

Kevin, a fellow with a winning personality, had always been one to make things happen. With his friend Johnny, he'd organized a carnival to raise money for the war effort. The D&R Garage was the hub of the

Wilson Lake (57°16' N, 105°31' W), viewed here from the north, is located 150 air miles north of La Ronge, only four miles from the airstrip at the Key Lake mine site. Situated near the northern edge of the Churchill River Upland ecoregion, where it merges with the Athabasca Plain, Wilson Lake has large bays and peninsulas which give it a unique and pronounced shape. Vast stands of black spruce and birch trees line the shore amidst glacial sandstone deposits and extensive sand beaches. The clear waters of Wilson Lake host a significant population of lake trout and jackfish.

Limerick●

day's activities, but the main street of town was blocked off, too. The carnival featured a small midway, games of chance, and a raffle for a small Massey tractor. Kevin and Johnny also supervised tree planting bees, and the poplars still line Limerick streets.

Kevin Wilson was educated at Limerick Public School, at Mathieu College in Gravelbourg (becoming fluent in French), and at Success Business College in Regina. By the time he was nineteen, he ran the Limerick office of the Wilson Brothers firm, supervising two secretaries. One of them, Olive Keating from Regina, eventually became his wife. They married at St. Chad's chapel in the city, with a reception at the Hotel Saskatchewan and a honeymoon at Banff.

Below: Kevin Wilson and Olive Keating in front of Wilson Bros. in 1940. On Olive's arm is Kevin's crow, Dick, who lived with the family for three or four years.

It had become apparent to Kevin that pilot's training was not for him—his eyesight wasn't good enough. At the time of his marriage, therefore, he was on leave prior to re-mustering as an observer, a course of training that would take him through Air Observer's School in Regina and Bombing and Gunnery School in Mossbank. In the summer of 1942 he said goodbye to Olive in Halifax—"the toughest job I ever undertook in my life," he wrote—and was posted to an Operational Training Unit, training as a navigator.

His letters of that period express spells of homesickness and loneliness: "a combination of worry, wondering, discouragement and longing." England was "almost 5000 miles too far east of western Canada, and something should be done about the weather," he stated. But there were many pleasures as well. On one of his leaves he visited his aunt and uncle in County Wicklow, Ireland, and the house wherein his father Charles was born. On another occasion he celebrated his twenty-fifth birthday in style: "the whole town of Leamington," he wrote, "gathered around to watch a bunch of Canadian officers on a bender." In November of that year, 1942, he bought a second-hand set of the complete Charles Dickens, sixteen bound volumes, for £2.

November of 1942 was also when he was posted to No. 420 "Snowy Owl" Squadron based at Middleton St. George in Durham. Their first operation was to Lorient, a French port used as a U-boat base. Several more operations during the Battle of the Ruhr followed: Oldenburg, Cologne, Hamburg, Essen, Stuttgart, Mannheim. Amid the dangers of those operations, Kevin in his letters would frequently express his love for Olive, "the grandest girl in the world." And he would

pause to consider a time after war when, as he wrote, "a fire to warm my feet, a chair big enough for both Olive and I, my pipe and bottle of beer will represent to me heaven itself."

In the meantime, three squadrons, including No. 420, were ordered to stand down from 6 Group in preparation for a move to the Middle East. Upon his arrival in Tunisia in June 1943, Kevin told his sister that "we like Africa. It is almost like home." His was an experienced, all-commissioned crew at that point, which was "not bad," as Kevin put it, and with more than a dozen operations under his belt, he expected to be home before Christmas. However, on its first Italian operation, the "tropicalized" Wellington bomber carrying Kevin Wilson failed to return from a raid on

San Gionvanna, part of the RCAF support for the impending invasion of Sicily. The date was June 27, 1943. No trace of the aircraft was ever found.

In 1954, Mr. and Mrs. Charles Wilson attended the unveiling of the Malta War Memorial by Queen Elizabeth II and Prince Philip. The name of Flying Officer Kevin Wilson is inscribed on it and a plaque at the base of the fifteen-metre marble column reads: "Over these and neighbouring lands and seas, the airmen whose names are recorded here, fell in raid or sortie, and have no known grave. An island resolute of purpose remembers resolute men." Kevin Wilson is also memorialized by Wilson Lake, named in his honour in northern Saskatchewan. ✿

Far left: Kevin Wilson, Christmas 1940.

Centre: The Malta Memorial.

COMMONWEALTH WAR GRAVES COMMISSION

Below: Kevin's brother, Garrett Wilson, Q.C., and Garrett's son Kevin (named for his uncle) placed a plaque at Wilson Lake on August 25, 2001, in honour of Flying Officer Kevin Davies Wilson. Garrett and Kevin also camped overnight at Wilson Lake.

DOUG CHISHOLM

Wood

Wood Bay (56°10' N, 104°40' W), viewed here from the north, is located on Jewett Lake, eighty air miles north of La Ronge. About five miles long, Wood Bay is narrow and lined with high granite hills and dense forests. This tranquil place is deep within the Churchill River Upland ecoregion. In 1994, the Wood family placed a memorial plaque at Wood Bay.

rt Wood of North Battleford, Saskatchewan, knows well the significance of the sacrifice made by his older brother Jim, who was killed in action in Italy in late 1944. Art served overseas himself, as did two other brothers, Fraser and Bill. "Jim was the only one who didn't come back," he says.

Art and Jim, who always got along well, used to talk about joining up while they were out shooting rabbits in the Glaslyn district. The bounty of ten cents a rabbit skin represented real income for the Wood boys at a time when there just wasn't much money around. (They did manage to scrape twenty dollars together to buy a '32 Model A, however). Likewise, the army, in addition to its patriotic appeal, represented economic opportunity, and a chance for something more than picking rocks or shoveling manure for five dollars a month. Inevitably, then, talk on the hunting trips would turn to joining the army. Art (nicknamed "Beans") would say something like, "I'm tired of working. I'm going to join up," to which Jim would reply, "I thought I might too, Beans." Soon Beans and Jim were on the train to Regina to enlist (although an intestinal condition for which surgery was required delayed Jim's eventual departure for overseas).

The Wood farm, which is still in the family, is located just east of Glaslyn. For Samuel and Susan Wood and their nine kids, the farm in the decades before World War II was a tough go, but Samuel wouldn't accept government relief. All of the family helped out on the farm and the older ones worked for neighbours as well. School, for Jim, meant Glaslyn Rural School for the primary years, and grade twelve at the school in town. But his real love at that time was horses. He'd ride Kit to school but could handle any horse and train it for saddle or harness.

There were other pleasures during those years. Music, for one. Jim's dad liked to sing and had a button accordian which Jim learned to play by ear, often accompanied by his brothers on banjo or violin. "Listen to the Mockingbird" and "Snow Deer" were two favourites, as was the old wartime standard "We're Going to Hang Out the Washing on the Siegfried Line." In the late thirties and early forties, Jim even had a small band that played at schoolhouse dances in the surrounding area for one dollar a night. The community held sports days with games and sports for all ages. And when the cinema would arrive by train, a special treat was in store. Silent movies were shown inside a coach, with the occasional voice-over provided by a man with a megaphone. "It was quite a thing for the village," Art Wood remembers.

Samuel Wood was killed in a car accident in 1939; after that, Jim helped his mother in the home and with the farm until he was able to join up in 1943. That year, Jim and his girlfriend Agnes, who was from nearby Medstead, got married at Glaslyn Anglican Church. A few months before Jim left for overseas, Jim and Art had a few last hours together during Art's fourteen-day embarkation leave in Halifax. He had hitchhiked the last bit home, and Jim, who was with an outfit in the field, was the first to see his arrival. As Art remembers it, "Jim dropped everything and ran over to me. Together we took the horses home and turned them loose. We had about a half a day together before I had to head back and I didn't quite get back to Halifax on time." The two brothers never saw each other again.

When he was stationed in England, Art did get one letter from Jim. It was sent from "somewhere in Italy," where Jim had landed in the summer of 1943 with the Princess Louise Dragoon Guards, an infantry regiment. The letter remarked on the heat, but the weather was only one of the difficulties the Canadians faced in the twenty-month Italian campaign. Those final months, late 1943, were "worse than those they had spent a year before in the Ortona salient," writes Bill McAndrews in *The Italian Campaign, 1939-1945*. "In places only the width of a river dyke separated them from the Germans. Each side did what it could to at least give an appearance of holding the initiative." The Battle of Ravenna, along Italy's north Adriatic coast, was more or less a stalemate a year later when both sides settled in for the winter in December 1944.

Jim Wood was killed during those final days of the campaign, as were about 2,500 other Canadian troops. Art Wood learned some of the details later in England from one of the Princess Patricias who had served alongside his brother. Jim had moved away from the action for a short rest, the soldier told Art. Then a

German counterattack required an immediate return to action. Jim was killed instantly when hit by machine gun fire. "The boys were played out," Art concludes, "and short of ammunition." He adds: "Just another day or week and he would have come through."

Private John James "Jim" Wood is honoured by the inclusion of his name on the Cassino Memorial, a series of marble pillars below the Benedictine Monastery in the valley of the River Liri, 140 kilometres southeast of Rome. In Saskatchewan, Wood Bay, located on Jewett Lake, was named in his honour. Thirteen members of the Wood family flew to Wood Bay in 1994 to lay a plaque for Jim. There they enjoyed coffee and cookies and memories of the brother they still miss. ❀

Right: The Wood family gathered in honour of Jim at Wood Bay in 1994—back row from left to right: Raymond Allen, Bill Wood, Kathy Fahr, Agnes Wood, Betty Monsebroten, Alice Wood, and Art Wood; seated in left foreground: Aggie, Jim's wife.

Far right: Aggie, Jim's wife, takes a turn at drilling during the plaque installation at Wood Bay. Looking on, and waiting their turn, right to left, are Jim's sisters Betty and Kathy and Jim's nephew Raymond.

Near right: Art and Alice Wood in Italy at the Cassino Memorial.

Their Names Live On

Saskatchewan's World War II
Honour Roll

The following list of Saskatchewan's World War II casualties is the most comprehensive honour roll available to date. Based on a database generously provided by the Government of Canada, it has been further supplemented by research of various kinds: by a manual check of the card files held by the provincial department responsible for naming geographic sites, by reference to the Commonwealth War Graves Commission website, the Veterans Affairs Canada website and Allison and Hayward's RCAF casualty list in *They Shall Grow Not Old*, and also by the author's research and contacts with Saskatchewan people over the past four years.

Considerable effort was made to include hometowns when possible; otherwise census division numbers from 1-18 (as indicated on the accompanying map) are provided according to the original war casualty list. In some cases, hometowns could not be determined (indicated so by "UNKNOWN"), and readers are invited to contact the author with any additional information about hometowns.

The Saskatchewan government undertook to designate a geo-memorial site for every Saskatchewan casualty and, in essence, completed its task during the 1960s; yet the project continues to be an ongoing one. Saskatchewan families continue to bring forward names of World War II casualties who have not had sites named for them; when this happens, the Geographic Names Board assesses the request and, when legitimate, assigns a site. Likewise, the research undertaken in order to provide this printed list brought to light a number of casualties who as yet do not have a geo-memorial designation. These names are therefore currently under consideration by the Geographic Names Board and the geo-memorial site is listed as "PENDING." Because compiling a truly complete "World War II Honour Roll" for Saskatchewan is an ongoing process, the author and publisher welcome additions and corrections to the list below.

Saskatchewan's World War II Honour Roll

Name	Branch	Rank	Hometown	Casualty Date	Latitude	Longitude	Geo-memorial
AADLAND, RICHARD	ARMY	RFN	CHAMBERY	12/02/45	59°25'	108°43'	AADLAND LAKE
AASTROM, THOMAS F.	ARMY	PTE	BJORKDALE	27/02/45			PENDING
ABBOTT, ARTHUR W.	RCAF	FO	HERSCHEL	05/04/42	54°46'	102°28'	ABBOTT LAKE
ABBOTT, WALTER J.	ARMY	GNR	RICHLEA	11/06/44	56°47'	102°26'	ABBOTT ISLAND
ABEL, JOHN J.	ARMY	PTE	PERDUE	21/07/44	54°28'	107°13'	ABEL LAKE
ABRAM, ALLAN F.	ARMY	LIEUT	REGINA	13/05/44	55°23'	104°24'	ABRAM ISLAND
ABRAMS, ROBERT W.	RCAF	PO	ROCKHAVEN	06/03/45	55°02'	104°49'	ABRAMS BAY
ACASTER, DOUGLAS HAIG	NAVY	L CK 2	NORTH BATTLEFORD	13/07/44	55°54'	109°51'	ACASTER LAKE
ACORN, WILFRED L.	ARMY	PTE	DAVIS	18/02/45	55°47'	105°57'	ACORN LAKE
ACTON, GEORGE N.	RCAF	PO	MEADOW LAKE	26/06/43	59°18'	104°56'	ACTON LAKE
ADAIR, ARTHUR D.	RCAF	FS	FAIRLIGHT	21/06/42	59°24'	108°50'	ADAIR LAKE
ADAM, GEORGE FRANK	NAVY	MECH 1	REGINA	18/03/45	56°26'	105°19'	ADAM LAKE
ADAMS, ARTHUR K.	ARMY	SIGMN	SASKATOON	19/08/42	56°06'	104°34'	ADAMS LAKE
ADAMS, CLARENCE	ARMY	PTE	SINTALUTA	19/12/44	53°54'	103°15'	ADAMS CREEK
ADAMS, HUGH A.	RCAF	PO	DAFOE	29/07/44	59°41'	108°21'	ADAMS RIVER
ADAMS, LLOYD H.	ARMY	LIEUT	BATTLEFORD	06/06/44	57°38'	106°08'	ADAMS PENINSULA
ADAMSON, JOHN W.	RCAF	WO2	HINCHLIFFE	14/10/43	55°04'	104°47'	ADAMSON BAY
ADDIE, JOHN A.	ARMY	PTE	REGINA	21/06/44	59°42'	106°18'	ADDIE LAKE
ADILMAN, BERNARD M.	RCAF	FL	SASKATOON	06/01/45	55°19'	104°23'	ADILMAN LAKE
AGNEW, DAVID R.	RCAF	FO	WEYBURN	29/06/43	54°44'	102°50'	AGNEW BAY
AHRENS, WALTER C.	RCAF	FL	ROSETOWN	16/07/44	54°50'	102°17'	AHRENS LAKE
AIRRIESS, FRANK H.	ARMY	PTE	TOGO	15/09/45	55°38'	106°18'	AIRRIESS LAKE
AITKENHEAD, WILFRED J.	ARMY	CPL	UNKNOWN	13/12/43	59°38'	105°48'	AITKENHEAD LAKE
ALBERTS, EDWARD L.	RCAF	PO	BREDENBURY	23/04/42	54°54'	109°29'	ALBERTS LAKE
ALBRECHT, OSCAR	ARMY	SIGMN	LEADER	17/07/44	59°37'	103°38'	ALBRECHT LAKE
ALDER, WILLIAM L.	RCAF	PO	PRINCE ALBERT	25/02/44	54°48'	102°11'	ALDER LAKE
ALDRIDGE, KENNETH C.	ARMY	PTE	REGINA	14/07/44	59°35'	105°31'	ALDRIDGE LAKE
ALEXANDER, EDWARD S.	RCAF	SQ/LDR	REGINA	14/01/44	55°25'	105°59'	ALEXANDER ISLAND
ALEXANDER, GEORGE L.	RCAF	CPL	TURTLEFORD	05/10/43	55°28'	104°07'	ALEXANDER BAY
ALEXANDER, ROBERT G.	RCAF	LAC	SASKATOON	05/06/41	57°11'	104°38'	ALEXANDER LAKE
ALLAN, GEORGE I.	RCAF	FO	IMPERIAL	22/01/45	55°51'	108°20'	ALLAN ISLAND
ALLAN, JAMES L.	RCAF	FO	TISDALE	05/11/44	55°57'	105°22'	ALLAN LAKE
ALLAN, JOHN J.	RCAF	LAC	REGINA	25/10/42	57°53'	107°47'	ALLAN RAPIDS
ALLCOCK, NELSON S.	ARMY	GNR	KERROBERT	20/07/41	55°50'	106°39'	ALLCOCK LAKE
ALLEN, ARTHUR P.	ARMY	L CPL	REGINA	10/01/44	52°32'	102°02'	ALLEN LAKE
ALLEN, FRANK	RCAF	FS	PLEASANTDALE	12/12/42			PENDING
ALLEN, HERBERT JOHN	RCAF	LAC	LONE SPRUCE	07/07/43	55°37'	104°38'	ALLEN BAY
ALLEN, HUGH G.	RCAF	WO2	GOODWATER	30/03/43	54°44'	102°50'	ALLEN PENINSULA
ALLEN, JOHN	ARMY	PTE	MACKLIN	13/02/44	57°23'	103°29'	ALLEN LAKE
ALLEN, KENNETH G.	ARMY	PTE	INDIAN HEAD	03/05/45			PENDING
ALLEN, THOMAS P.	ARMY	CFN	TISDALE	08/02/45	59°40'	106°35'	ALLEN RAPIDS
ALLNUT, ALASDAIR M.	ARMY	LT	UNKNOWN	18/06/44	58°58'	102°01'	ALLNUT LAKE
ALTERSON, JOHN	RCAF	SGT	PUNNICHY	13/10/41	52°21'	102°58'	ALTERSON LAKE
AMUNDSON, SAMUEL	ARMY	L CPL	ROBSART	03/03/45	55°12'	105°25'	AMUNDSON LAKE
AMY, HARRY T.	RCAF	FL	SASKATOON	11/05/44	54°49'	102°13'	AMY LAKE
ANAKA, HARRY J.	ARMY	A CAP3	STENEN	04/10/44	55°49'	104°55'	ANAKA LAKE
ANDERSON, CLARENCE C.	ARMY	CPL	ELSTOW	22/09/44			PENDING
ANDERSON, CLARENCE H.	RCAF	PO	PALMER	31/08/43	59°24'	108°33'	ANDERSON ISLAND
ANDERSON, DAVID M.	RCAF	FO	YORKTON	24/05/43	59°52'	102°26'	ANDERSON CHANNEL
ANDERSON, DONALD D.	RCAF	FS	LAFLECHE	29/11/42			PENDING
ANDERSON, FLOYD R.W.	RCAF	FS	PUNNICHY	07/04/43	55°15'	108°18'	ANDERSON BAY
ANDERSON, G.J.	RCAF	LAC	SASKATOON	20/12/44			PENDING

Name	Branch	Rank	Hometown	Casualty Date	Latitude	Longitude	Geo-Memorial	Name	Branch	Rank	Hometown	Casualty Date	Latitude	Longitude	Geo-Memorial
ANDERSON, HARRY E.	ARMY	RFN	PRINCE ALBERT	09/06/44	59°35'	109°33'	ANDERSON POINT	BAKER, DOUGLAS H.	RCAF	FO	REGINA	24/06/44	55°00'	109°35'	BAKER ISLAND
ANDERSON, PATRICK L.	ARMY	RFN	REGINA	18/06/44	59°26'	108°45'	ANDERSON LAKE	BALDHEAD, JAMES L.	ARMY	PTE	DUCK LAKE	20/07/44	55°26'	104°52'	BALDHEAD LAKE
ANDERSON, RITCHIE	ARMY	TPR	LESTOCK	04/04/45	59°54'	108°46'	ANDERSON BAY	BALDWIN, ROBERT W.	RCAF	FS	REGINA	16/12/43	55°26'	104°06'	BALDWIN LAKE
ANDERSON, ROBERT C.	ARMY	PTE	SOUTHEY	13/09/44	59°49'	108°49'	ANDERSON PENINSULA	BALDWINSON, WALTER B.	RCAF	WO2	WYNYARD	25/04/44	57°10'	106°51'	BALDWINSON LAKES
ANDERSON, SETH B.	ARMY	SPR	DIVISION 15	10/08/44	53°48'	103°03'	ANDERSON ISLAND	BALL, ELLRY E.	ARMY	TPR	YORKTON	09/07/44	55°28'	105°10'	BALL LAKE
ANDERSON, SYDNEY A.	RCAF	WO2	RADVILLE	18/11/43	56°22'	108°03'	ANDERSON PENINSULA	BALL, WILLIAM S.	RCAF	PO	VALJEAN	20/02/44	55°34'	104°38'	BALL ISLAND
ANDERSON, WILLIAM O.	RCAF	FS	UNKNOWN	10/09/42			PENDING	BALLANTYNE, WALLACE B.	RCAF	FS	UNITY	09/10/43	57°11'	107°32'	BALLANTYNE LAKE
ANDERSON, WILLIAM G.	RCAF	SGT	MARYFIELD	08/03/45	57°21'	106°08'	ANDERSON RAPIDS	BALLER, LLOYD G.	ARMY	GNR	GRENFELL	14/07/44	54°58'	102°20'	BALLER ISLAND
ANDRES, ARNOLD R.	ARMY	A SGT	SASKATOON	28/08/44	57°20'	107°12'	ANDRES LAKE	BALLIET, THOMAS A.	ARMY	PTE	YORKTON	08/12/43	59°25'	105°00'	BALLIET LAKE
ANDREW, CARL A.	ARMY	PTE	DIVISION 12	21/04/42	59°28'	108°20'	ANDREW LAKE	BALTUS, JOHN H.	ARMY	C S M	REGINA	01/05/41	59°20'	103°49'	BALTUS LAKE
ANDREW, ELMER R.	ARMY	PTE	DIVISION 16	19/04/45	58°12'	104°38'	ANDREW LAKE	BANCESCU, GEORGE	RCAF	WO2	FLINTOFT	24/05/43			PENDING
ANDREW, WALTER H.	ARMY	TPR	MAYMONT	18/09/44	55°34'	106°13'	ANDREW LAKE	BANCESCU, WILLIAM	ARMY	GNR	FLINTOFT	17/04/45	55°55'	105°57'	BANCESCU LAKE
ANDREWS, ROBERT E.	ARMY	TPR	KERROBERT	31/08/44	59°28'	108°08'	ANDREWS ISLAND	BANDUR, SIGMUND B.	RCAF	PO	BRODERICK	28/05/44	55°43'	104°39'	BANDUR LAKE
ANEY, ROY L.	RCAF	LAC	REGINA	08/06/42	59°28'	107°56'	ANEY LAKE	BANYARD, WILLIAM E.	ARMY	PTE	DARMODY	29/07/44	56°02'	104°54'	BANYARD LAKE
ANTON, LEE	ARMY	TPR	DIVISION 8	12/04/45	57°06'	108°08'	ANTON LAKE	BAPTISTE, EDGAR H.	ARMY	PTE	RED PHEASANT	19/12/41	56°58'	103°02'	BAPTISTE ISLAND
ANTONY, THOMAS	ARMY	PTE	SASKATOON	14/08/44	56°12'	103°31'	ANTONY LAKE	BARABONOFF, JOSEPH A.	RCAF	WO2	SASKATOON	20/10/43	57°14'	107°26'	BARABONOFF LAKES
APPLEBY, FLOYD A.	ARMY	RFN	PINKHAM	16/02/45	57°56'	106°57'	APPLEBY RIVER	BARBER, WILLIAM A.W.	ARMY	PTE	CRESTWYND	19/02/45	59°51'	109°19'	BARBER POINT
ARCHIBALD, LEWIS P.	RCAF	PO	MOOSE JAW	16/12/43	56°06'	105°16'	ARCHIBALD LAKE	BARIBEAU, GERARD C.	ARMY	PTE	DOMREMY	28/04/44	59°58'	109°47'	BARIBEAU LAKE
ARCHIBALD, VIVIAN G. H.	RCAF	WO1	NORTH BATTLEFORD	07/02/45	59°47'	102°07'	ARCHIBALD LAKES	BARKER, G.A.	RCAF	FL	REGINA	06/04/45	55°40'	104°48'	BARKER LAKE
ARCHIE, STEVE	RCAF	SGT	WYNYARD	17/04/43	59°28'	107°45'	ARCHIE LAKE	BARKER, KENNETH H.	RCAF	FO	KILDEER	21/11/44	55°40'	104°48'	BARKER ISLAND
ARMATAGE, LINTON C.	ARMY	CPL	LANIGAN	06/06/44	57°41'	106°19'	ARMATAGE BAY	BARKER, LAURENCE S	RCAF	WO1	SASKATOON	11/03/44	56°23'	107°18'	BARKER BAY
ARMBRUSTER, PETER	ARMY	L CPL	DUFF	12/09/44	59°26'	108°41'	ARMBRUSTER LAKE	BARKER, LLOYD R.	RCAF	PO	KILLDEER	15/03/44	59°40'	108°16'	BARKER LAKE
ARMITAGE, IRVING	RCAF	FO	WAWOTA	23/11/43	54°59'	109°13'	ARMITAGE LAKE	BARKWELL, JOHN H.	RCAF	FS	PRINCE ALBERT	12/11/43	57°37'	106°06'	BARKWELL BAY
ARMOUR, WILTON G.	RCAF	PO	FOAM LAKE	11/11/44	54°45'	109°05'	ARMOUR LAKE	BARNES, RAYMOND J.	RCAF	WO2	BATTLEFORD	17/04/43	55°58'	104°31'	BARNES ISLAND
ARMSTRONG, GERALD G.	RCAF	FS	WEYBURN	27/11/41	55°53'	107°27'	GERALD LAKE	BARRETT, ERIC H.	RCAF	FS	CORONACH	02/11/42	55°59'	103°43'	BARRETT ISLAND
ARMSTRONG, IRVINE C.	NAVY	TEL	DRIVER	26/03/41	55°36'	109°53'	ARMSTRONG CREEK	BARRETT, FREDERICK H.	RCAF	FS	YOUNG	27/01/43	57°56'	106°28'	BARRETT LAKE
ARMSTRONG, JOHN E.	RCAF	FO	ROCANVILLE	29/10/42	57°42'	102°11'	ARMSTRONG ISLAND	BARRITT, GEORGE R.	ARMY	PTE	RUNCIMAN	26/01/45	59°20'	108°59'	BARRITT BAY
ARMSTRONG, LEONARD W.	RCAF	FO	AUBURNTON	15/03/45	59°17'	106°46'	ARMSTRONG POINT	BARROWMAN, ARCHIBALD	RCAF	PO	TISDALE	15/03/44	55°37'	105°20'	BARROWMAN LAKE
ARMSTRONG, WALTER D.	ARMY	C S M	DAVIDSON	16/02/45	56°27'	103°50'	ARMSTRONG LAKE	BARTKO, MIRO G.	ARMY	PTE	WEEKES	14/12/44	55°44'	104°29'	BARTKO LAKE
ARN, HERBERT W.	ARMY	A SGT	KINISTINO	08/07/44	55°05'	103°31'	ARN LAKE	BARTLAM, KENNETH J.	ARMY	A L CPL	GRENFELL	19/08/42	54°58'	102°07'	BARTLAM BAY
ARNER, LAWRENCE A.	RCAF	FO	CECIL	06/02/44	54°48'	102°03'	ARNER LAKE	BARTLETT, CHRISTOPHER S.	RAF	WC	FORT QU'APPELLE	13/06/44	55°30'	104°59'	BARTLETT LAKE
ARNFIELD, HERBERT V.	ARMY	SPR	REGINA	12/03/41	52°20'	102°44'	ARNFIELD LAKE	BARTLETT, RALPH H.	ARMY	L BDR	WALDRON	21/02/45	58°35'	109°51'	BARTLETT LAKE
ARNOLD, VERNON C.	RCAF	FS	REGINA	26/10/43	58°06'	105°33'	ARNOLD RIVER	BARTS, ROY J.	RCAF	SGT	REGINA	19/12/43	59°59'	109°35'	BARTS LAKE
ARNOLD, VICTOR C.	RCAF	PO	SASKATOON	05/05/41	54°46'	109°03'	ARNOLD LAKE	BASARABA, MIKE W.	ARMY	L CPL	SHIPMAN	24/11/44	56°19'	105°17'	BASARABA LAKE
ARONSON, KENNETH J.	RCAF	FS	MAZENOD	30/07/42	55°16'	104°48'	ARONSON ISLAND	BASSETT, GEORGE H.	ARMY	PTE	CORONACH	19/08/42	55°35'	104°59'	BASSETT LAKE
ARPS, LYSLE RALPH	RCAF	SGT	TISDALE	06/12/42	52°23'	102°45'	ARPS LAKE	BATEMAN, ALBERT L.	RCAF	FS	BATEMAN	01/03/43	55°54'	104°39'	BATEMAN LAKE
ASHDOWN, HENRY	ARMY	TPR	SASKATOON	12/08/44	59°30'	106°03'	ASHDOWN LAKE	BATTY, ARCHIE V.	RCAF	FO	LIMERICK	14/10/44	54°48'	102°14'	BATTY LAKE
ASHLEY, RUTH L.	ARMY	LT N 2	SASKATOON	06/06/43	58°07'	103°33'	ASHLEY PENINSULA	BATYSKI, JOHN J.	ARMY	PTE	ITUNA	28/04/45	55°43'	107°27'	BATYSKI LAKE
ASHWORTH, JAMES R.	ARMY	CPL	ELBOW	10/06/44	59°26'	104°53'	ASHWORTH BAY	BAXTER, ARIE G.	RCAF	PO	MOOSE JAW	05/12/44	54°10'	106°53'	BAXTER LAKE
ASKEW, RICHARD G.	RCAF	FO	MOOSE JAW	25/07/44	54°47'	109°02'	ASKEW LAKE	BAXTER, HENRY G.	ARMY	TPR	WEYBURN	30/10/44	57°46'	104°47'	BAXTER LAKE
ASPHOLM, REUBEN L.	ARMY	SIGMN	NORQUAY	13/02/45	57°11'	107°54'	ASPHOLM LAKE	BAYARD, JOHN WILLIAM	RCAF	FO	REGINA	14/09/44	53°36'	103°41'	BAYARD ISLAND
ASSAF, GEORGE	RCAF	FS	MCCORD	23/05/43	59°23'	108°56'	ASSAF ISLANDS	BAYARD, RICHARD L.	RCAF	FO	REGINA	10/10/43			PENDING
ASTLEFORD, STEWART S.	ARMY	PTE	MOOSE JAW	09/03/42	56°34'	105°10'	ASTLEFORD LAKE	BAYLEY, SAMUEL M.	RCAF	CPL	ASSINIBOIA	06/11/44	59°04'	108°37'	BAYLEY LAKE
ATCHISON, RICHARD E.	ARMY	PTE	MAWER	28/10/44	55°26'	103°08'	ATCHISON ISLAND	BEALE, WALTER S.	RCAF	FS	BETHUNE	09/11/42	59°22'	108°57'	BEALE LAKE
ATTREE, EARL R.	RCAF	WO2	PRINCE ALBERT	19/12/44	54°43'	102°40'	ATTREE LAKE	BEAR, THOMAS	ARMY	FUS	MEADOW LAKE	13/01/45			PENDING
ATTREE, VINCENT E.	RCAF	FS	PRINCE ALBERT	25/08/43	54°43'	102°40'	ATTREE LAKE	BEARDALL, ROBERT H.	RCAF	SGT	PRINCE ALBERT	24/11/41	57°02'	106°24'	BEARDALL LAKE
AURIAT, JEAN M.J.	ARMY	PTE	SAINT FRONT	07/06/44	57°28'	106°32'	AURIAT ISLAND	BEATON, JOHN G.	ARMY	L CPL	PRINCE	25/06/45	53°48'	102°11'	BEATON LAKE
BABCOCK, ROY F.	ARMY	PTE	DIVISION 16	12/04/45	59°35'	104°22'	BABCOCK BAY	BEATTY, ALVIN M.	RCAF	FO	TISDALE	23/05/44	54°51'	102°03'	BEATTY LAKE
BACHELU, JOHN H.L.	ARMY	PTE	MONTMARTRE	19/08/42	57°26'	103°31'	BACHELU LAKE	BEATTY, HAROLD C.	RCAF	FS	MOOSE JAW	06/07/42	58°25'	103°21'	BEATTY POINT
BACHMAN, EDDY	ARMY	RFN	PADDOCKWOOD	09/07/44	57°27'	105°44'	BACHMAN LAKE	BEATTY, MELVILLE D.	ARMY	PTE	CARLYLE	19/08/42	55°52'	104°41'	BEATTY BAY
BACHMEIER, VALENTINE J.	ARMY	PTE	PRELATE	26/07/44	56°35'	104°56'	BACHMEIER LAKE	BEATTY, WALTER E.	ARMY	PTE	CARLYLE	19/08/42	55°52'	104°39'	BEATTY ISLAND
BACKES, ORVAL G.	RCAF	PO	ARCOLA	06/12/44	54°58'	109°42'	BACKES ISLAND	BEATTY, WILLIAM WESLEY	ARMY	GNR	SYLVANIA	13/10/44	57°26'	102°16'	BEATTY ISLAND
BACKUS, JOSEPH	ARMY	A CPL	NORTH BATTLEFORD	06/10/44	59°36'	105°26'	BACKUS LAKE	BEAUDRY, ELOI J.E.	RCAF	FS	CUT KNIFE	18/08/43	55°35'	105°00'	BEAUDRY LAKE
BADER, JOHN	ARMY	PTE	DIVISION 8	28/08/44	57°41'	108°33'	BADER LAKE	BEAULIEU, ALEXANDER	ARMY	PTE	FORT QU'APPELLE	26/07/44	58°21'	106°53'	BEAULIEU LAKE
BADGER, GEORGE C.	ARMY	PTE	KAMSACK	05/11/43	55°57'	104°33'	BADGER LAKE	BECK, ALBERT J	RCAF	FO	SIMPSON	21/02/45	55°44'	104°53'	BECK ISLAND
BAHNUICK, WILLIAM	ARMY	PTE	WEYBURN	19/08/42	59°36'	108°48'	BAHNUICK LAKE	BECK, JOHN D.	RCAF	LAC	MAWER	12/10/44	54°20'	109°58'	BECK LAKE
BAHT, RALPH E.	RCAF	FO	IMPERIAL	09/10/43	54°50'	102°21'	BAHT LAKE	BECKER, JOHN H.	ARMY	PTE	DIVISION 14	20/07/44	54°43'	101°57'	BECKER BAY
BAILEY, DENNIS H.	RCAF	FO	DEMAINE	22/03/44	54°59'	109°41'	BAILEY ISLAND	BECKETT, GERALD A.	RCAF	SGT	GLENAVON	03/01/44	57°22'	104°24'	BECKETT LAKE
BAILEY, JOHN C.	ARMY	SPR	SONNINGDALE	06/09/44	53°41'	103°36'	BAILEY CREEK	BECKWALL, AUGUST L.	RCAF	FS	RADVILLE	05/12/42	59°41'	108°29'	BECKWALL LAKE
BAILEY, THEODORE R.	RCAF	FO	ROADENE	19/11/44	54°54'	103°02'	BAILEY LAKE	BEDARD, LEO L.	ARMY	PTE	DIVISION 11	08/07/44	56°57'	102°27'	BEDARD ISLAND
BAILEY, WESLEY G.	RCAF	FS	ALIDA	29/09/43	57°10'	104°26'	BAILEY LAKE	BEECH, PERCY C.	ARMY	PTE	BIGGAR	18/10/44	59°27'	105°30'	BEECH LAKE
BAIRD, FRANCIS V.	ARMY	SGT	MOOSE JAW	10/08/46	53°56'	103°51'	BAIRD LAKE	BEECHING, CHARLES F.	RCAF	SGT	REGINA	23/08/42	57°34'	103°28'	BEECHING LAKE
BAKALAR, PETER P.	ARMY	GNR	MELVILLE	10/08/44	59°34'	102°55'	BAKALAR LAKE	BEECHINOR, THOMAS J.	RCAF	WO2	SASKATOON	11/01/44	59°31'	108°16'	BEECHINOR LAKE
BAKER, DOUGLAS C.	RCAF	WO2	MANOR	09/10/43	57°09'	107°09'	BAKER CREEK	BEED, CECIL E.	ARMY	L CPL	DIVISION 16	20/07/44	59°34'	105°20'	BEED LAKES

Name	Branch	Rank	Hometown	Casualty Date	Latitude	Longitude	Geo-Memorial
BEEDS, ALFRED E.	ARMY	PTE	SHELL LAKE	21/07/44	55°31'	106°08'	BEEDS LAKE
BEISE, JAMES A.	RCAF	LAC	SASKATOON	13/11/40	59°24'	108°46'	BEISE LAKE
BELANGER, JOHN G.	ARMY	RFN	BATTLEFORD	12/02/45	56°54'	103°23'	BELANGER ISLAND
BELL, ANGUS F.	RCAF	FO	ADANAC	02/10/43	56°31'	104°08'	BELL FALLS
BELL, ANGUS H.	RCAF	PO	REGINA	04/07/43	55°27'	104°37'	BELL LAKE
BELL, CHARLES H.L.	RCAF	SGT	REGINA	10/09/42	53°02'	109°48'	BELL COULEE
BELL, CHESTER H.	ARMY	PTE	PENNANT	20/07/44	59°12'	102°35'	BELL LAKE
BELL, DANIEL	NAVY	AB	LANG	09/05/45	56°54'	103°59'	BELL RAPIDS
BELL, FRANK G.	RCAF	WO2	DIVISION 10	12/11/43	59°27'	106°03'	BELL BAY
BELL, FRANK H.C.	ARMY	LIEUT	SWIFT CURRENT	05/05/41	55°16'	105°23'	BELL BAY
BELL, GEORGE B.	ARMY	L CPL	LANDIS	09/09/41	58°58'	102°35'	BELL CREEK
BELL, GORDON R.	RCAF	LAC	SASKATOON	01/05/45	53°12'	102°36'	BELL LAKE
BELL, HAROLD C.	RCAF	PO	SCOTT	16/03/44	57°22'	106°09'	BELL RAPIDS
BELL, JAMES F.	ARMY	PTE	NIPAWIN	13/09/44	59°14'	102°29'	BELL BAY
BELL, LAWRENCE R.	ARMY	TPR	BATTLEFORD	19/02/45	55°27'	102°08'	BELL ISLAND
BELL, RUEL	ARMY	CPL	ROCANVILLE	10/12/44	53°55'	102°20'	BELL ISLAND
BELLA, JULIUS	ARMY	TPR	MCKIM	02/06/44	55°15'	107°27'	BELLA LAKE
BELLAMY, GLENN C.	RCAF	FO	SYLVANIA	14/10/44	54°49'	102°07'	BELLAMY BAY
BELLEGARDE, MAURICE	ARMY	RFN	FILE HILLS	03/11/44			PENDING
BELLOWS, EDWARD L.	ARMY	L SGT	BEECHY	18/05/45	55°44'	104°53'	BELLOWS LAKE
BELLS, ROBERT W.	ARMY	LIEUT	QUILL LAKE	11/04/45	59°23'	107°46'	BELLS ISLAND
BELOUS, WESLEY L.	RCAF	WO2	STENEN	19/07/42	59°27'	108°04'	BELOUS ISLAND
BELTON, FRANCIS E.	ARMY	A CPL	STAR CITY	09/04/45	55°32'	107°15'	BELTON LAKE
BENJAMIN, EARL R.	ARMY	GNR	GAINSBOROUGH	22/05/43	55°44'	104°46'	BENJAMIN LAKE
BENNETT, CLIFFORD W.	RCAF	FS	SASKATOON	18/12/43	57°02'	105°25'	BENNETT BAY
BENNETT, HARRY C.	RCAF	FL	MOOSE JAW	13/08/43	55°35'	104°38'	BENNETT ISLAND
BENNETT, HARRY M.	NAVY	AB	SASKATOON	01/12/40	55°05'	108°27'	BENNETT BAY
BENNETT, WILFRED H.	ARMY	GNR	SASKATOON	28/01/45	56°18'	102°17'	BENNETT LAKE
BENSON, OLIN	ARMY	TPR	PORCUPINE PLAIN	06/08/44	57°32'	105°54'	BENSON LAKE
BENTLEY, PHILIP A.	ARMY	CPL	SHAUNAVON	30/03/45	58°51'	103°22'	BENTLEY LAKE
BENTLEY, THOMAS L.	RCAF	WO2	MOOSE JAW	27/05/43	56°24'	108°14'	BENTLEY PENINSULA
BENTLEY, THOMAS ALISON	ARMY	BDR	SWIFT CURRENT	12/12/46	55°49'	106°53'	BENTLEY BAY
BENTZ, GEORGE P.	ARMY	PTE	PUNNICHY	02/12/45	55°06'	102°25'	BENTZ BAY
BERANEK, STANLEY J.	RCAF	PO	SASKATOON	19/06/42	55°33'	104°56'	BERANEK LAKE
BERG, GEORGE T.	RCAF	FL	VALPARAISO	03/10/43	55°33'	104°52'	BERG LAKE
BERGEN, SIMON	ARMY	PTE	HUDSON BAY	15/08/44			PENDING
BERGER, EDWARD J.E.	ARMY	S SGT	LANGENBURG	10/12/44	59°29'	102°16'	BERGER LAKE
BERGLAND, NORVAL	RCAF	PO	MOOSE JAW	25/02/44	55°31'	104°44'	BERGLAND LAKE
BERGLUND, JOHN R.	RCAF	AC2	SONNINGDALE	14/12/42	59°53'	102°31'	BERGLUND ISLAND
BERNARD, FRANCIS J.	ARMY	PTE	PRINCE ALBERT	28/08/44	56°21'	102°18'	BERNARD LAKE
BERNASKI, LADIMER J.	RCAF	FO	ESTERHAZY	01/07/44	55°12'	104°59'	BERNASKI BAY
BERNETT, NEVILLE	RCAF	FO	BOUNTY	04/03/43	55°32'	104°37'	BERNETT LAKE
BERNHARDT, PHILIP	ARMY	A L SGT	DIVISION 10	07/06/43	56°50'	102°08'	BERNHARDT LAKE
BERNICK, LLOYD A.	RCAF	WO2	HAWARDEN	26/02/43	57°56'	104°28'	BERNICK LAKE
BERTRAND, GERALD C.	ARMY	A BDR	RADVILLE	03/09/43	59°41'	106°33'	BERTRAND BAY
BERVEN, BRUCE M.	RCAF	WO1	QU'APPELLE	17/09/43	55°47'	104°33'	BERVEN LAKE
BESSE, CLAUDE A.	RCAF	FS	DIVISION 12	16/12/43	56°41'	105°17'	BESSE LAKES
BESSETTE, BERTIE J.A.	RCAF	FS	WAWOTA	16/04/43	59°42'	108°27'	BESSETTE LAKE
BEST, FREDRICK T.	ARMY	RFN	MAYMONT	08/07/44	55°44'	106°14'	BEST LAKE
BETTIN, WENDELIN B.	RCAF	SGT	WATSON	28/08/43	55°23'	104°19'	BETTIN ISLAND
BEWLEY, DONALD G.	RCAF	FS	GRENFELL	19/12/44	53°49'	102°12'	BEWLEY LAKE
BICKLER, JOHN G.	ARMY	PTE	LEADER	18/07/44	59°49'	103°31'	BICKLER LAKE
BIDEN, BYRON S.	RCAF	PO	WOLSELEY	28/08/42	55°38'	104°43'	BIDEN LAKE
BIELBY, KEITH T.	RCAF	PO	RAPID VIEW	17/08/44	55°33'	104°48'	BIELBY LAKE
BIELBY, TERENCE J.F.	ARMY	PTE	MELVILLE	07/11/43	56°57'	108°36'	BIELBY RAPIDS
BILLESBERGER, HERBERT H.	ARMY	L CPL	CUDWORTH	22/09/44	56°47'	103°52'	BILLESBERGER LAKE
BILLINGS, HERBERT L.	ARMY	GNR	SASKATOON	26/07/44	57°06'	107°34'	BILLINGS LAKE
BING, GERRARD R.	RCAF	FO	REGINA	15/10/42	55°32'	104°55'	BING LAKE
BINGHAM, JAMES M.	ARMY	PTE	MANKOTA	31/12/43	55°13'	105°23'	BINGHAM LAKE
BINKLEY, ROBERT E.	ARMY	PTE	HUDSON BAY	28/04/45	57°23'	106°15'	BINKLEY BAY
BINNIE, COLIN M.	RCAF	PO	TULLIS	29/07/43	55°38'	107°05'	BINNIE LAKE
BINNS, RONALD	ARMY	PTE	MEOTA	03/09/44	53°35'	102°33'	BINNS LAKES
BIRBAN, HARRY	ARMY	L SGT	PRINCE ALBERT	06/06/44	60°01'	106°43'	BIRBAN LAKE
BIRD, BENJAMIN H.	ARMY	A CPL	TIGER HILLS	11/09/44	57°52'	104°21'	BIRD LAKE
BIRD, CHARLIE	ARMY	RFN	FOXFORD	06/06/44	58°26'	102°56'	BIRD ISLAND
BIRD, COLIN R.	RCAF	FS	LASHBURN	04/03/43			PENDING
BIRD, SIDNEY D.	RCAF	FS	LASHBURN	15/06/43			PENDING
BIRD, THOMAS V.	ARMY	RFN	RED DEER HILL	06/06/44	58°29'	102°51'	BIRD LAKE
BIRKBECK, ALBURN F.	RCAF	FS	WELWYN	26/05/43	58°40'	106°41'	BIRKBECK LAKE
BIRKETT, THOMAS P.	ARMY	TPR	BLAINE LAKE	25/04/45	55°08'	103°40'	BIRKETT LAKE
BIRNEY, JAMES F.	ARMY	GNR	GLASNEVIN	13/08/44	58°45'	107°35'	BIRNEY LAKE
BIRNIE, GEORGE A.	ARMY	RFN	LUCKY LAKE	15/08/44	55°29'	106°14'	BIRNIE LAKE
BISH, JOHN	ARMY	PTE	DIVISION 6	19/08/42	58°28'	107°49'	BISH LAKE
BISSCHOP, JOSEPH C.	ARMY	RFN	SHEHO	12/05/45	59°28'	108°45'	BISSCHOP LAKE
BISSON, ROGER J.	ARMY	PTE	REGINA	01/01/45	59°19'	103°14'	BISSON ISLAND
BITSCHY, EUGENE E.	ARMY	TPR	CLIMAX	14/08/44	57°45'	108°26'	BITSCHY LAKE
BLACHFORD, GLEN H.	RCAF	FO	COLONSAY	17/06/44	55°46'	103°17'	BLACHFORD LAKE
BLACK, ALVIN H.	ARMY	SIGMN	RALPH	14/11/44	54°49'	102°01'	BLACK LAKE
BLACK, JAMES C.	RCAF	FS	REGINA	08/06/42	55°06'	104°48'	BLACK ISLAND
BLACK, KENNETH A.	ARMY	PTE	SHELLBROOK	10/03/44	59°24'	103°44'	BLACK RAPIDS
BLACK, ROBERT J.	ARMY	GNR	KAMSACK	08/10/44	58°09'	103°36'	BLACK ISLAND
BLACK, THOMAS STEWART	ARMY	LT	UNKNOWN	07/04/45	59°42'	108°01'	BLACK CREEK
BLACKMAN, DESMOND H.	ARMY	PTE	UNKNOWN	24/07/43	56°28'	103°48'	BLACKMAN ISLAND
BLACKMORE, GEORGE R.	RCAF	SGT	YORKTON	10/09/41	55°14'	104°06'	BLACKMORE LAKE
BLADON, JAMES S.	RCAF	PO	REGINA	24/07/42	57°19'	102°39'	BLADON ISLAND
BLAIR, GILBERT THOMPSON	ARMY	CAPTAIN	DRAKE	03/11/44	59°22'	108°55'	BLAIR CHANNEL
BLAIR, JOHN L.	RCAF	FS	REGINA	10/09/42	56°08'	104°26'	BLAIR LAKE
BLAIR, TIMOTHY C.	RCAF	FS	DRAKE	24/07/42	59°22'	108°55'	BLAIR CHANNEL
BLAIS, EDWARD L.	ARMY	GNR	ROSETOWN	13/07/44	56°52'	107°31'	BLAIS LAKE
BLAIS, RAYMOND L.	ARMY	RFN	ROSETOWN	08/07/44	56°27'	103°54'	BLAIS LAKE
BLAKE, LEONARD H.	RCAF	FS	SASKATOON	05/05/42	57°46'	108°28'	BLAKE LAKE
BLAKELY, ROBERT A.	RCAF	AC1	KAMSACK	21/12/41	59°59'	105°39'	BLAKELY LAKE
BLANCHARD, ARTHUR J.	ARMY	PTE	HUDSON BAY	02/02/44	57°18'	106°24'	BLANCHARD LAKE
BLANCHARD, HUBERT A.	ARMY	PTE	REGINA	16/02/42	55°15'	104°47'	BLANCHARD ISLAND
BLAZEIKO, PANKO P.	RCAF	WO2	WEST BEND	02/09/43	57°11'	107°20'	BLAZEIKO LAKE
BLIGHT, HENRY T.	ARMY	PTE	BANKEND	14/07/44	55°03'	102°08'	BLIGHT LAKE
BLIXRUD, ALBERT L.	ARMY	A CPL	NORTH BATTLEFORD	17/09/44	58°08'	104°49'	BLIXRUD LAKE
BLONDEAU, ANTHONY W.	ARMY	RFN	ESTEVAN	10/06/44	57°34'	103°02'	BLONDEAU RIVER
BLONDEAU, LOUIS	RCAF	AC1	ESTEVAN	14/03/45	55°07'	104°44'	BLONDEAU ISLAND
BLOUDOFF, STEVE	ARMY	GNR	KAMSACK	01/06/44	56°39'	107°56'	BLOUDOFF LAKE
BLOW, FRANK E.	ARMY	PTE	DAVIDSON	22/03/42	59°35'	108°52'	BLOW LAKE
BLYTH, JOHN W.	RCAF	FO	NORTH BATTLEFORD	07/07/44	59°02'	102°17'	BLYTH ISLAND
BODDY, GEORGE W.	ARMY	TPR	MAIDSTONE	30/09/42	56°13'	104°16'	BODDY LAKE
BODDY, HUTSON A.	RCAF	CPL	ROSETOWN	27/01/44	59°26'	108°05'	BODDY POINT
BOE, RUSSELL M.	RCAF	AC2	BATEMAN	27/05/43	55°29'	104°15'	BOE LAKE
BOEHLER, STANLEY WILLIAM	NAVY	STO 1	CHOICELAND	17/08/43	56°15'	104°26'	BOEHLER BAY
BOEHM, JOSEPH	ARMY	RFN	PRINCE ALBERT	17/02/45	55°11'	103°55'	BOEHM LAKE
BOHONIS, KORNELIUS	ARMY	TPR	HATHERLEIGH	04/10/44	60°01'	108°09'	BOHONIS LAKES
BOIRE, LEO A.	RCAF	FS	GRAVELBOURG	03/06/43	54°27'	108°09'	BOIRE LAKE
BOISSIERE, ETIENNE	ARMY	PTE	ST. BRIEUX	11/12/42	55°45'	105°47'	BOISSIERE LAKE
BOKITCH, MICHAEL J.	ARMY	RFN	REGINA	30/03/45	59°13'	103°17'	BOKITCH ISLAND
BOLAN, MORRIS V.	ARMY	RFN	DIVISION 16	06/06/44	55°34'	106°02'	BOLAN LAKE
BOLAND, RALPH A.	ARMY	A L SGT	DIVISION 14	05/07/44	57°52'	103°50'	BOLAND LAKE
BOLDING, STANLEY F.	ARMY	CPL	DIVISION 16	03/09/44	57°53'	107°00'	BOLDING RIVER
BOLL, RODERICK J.J.	RCAF	AC1	VICEROY	25/12/40	58°41'	109°20'	BOLL LAKE
BOLSTAD, KENNETH W.	RCAF	FO	BENGOUGH	24/11/43	59°41'	102°48'	BOLSTAD LAKE
BOLSTER, CYRIL L.	RCAF	FO	CUPAR	29/03/43	59°24'	106°36'	BOLSTER PENINSULA
BOLTON, EDWARD W.R.	RCAF	LAC	LLOYDMINSTER	06/04/43	57°34'	108°41'	BOLTON LAKE
BONAZEW, PETER	ARMY	PTE	YORKTON	08/09/44	57°39'	107°44'	BONAZEW LAKE
BOND, WALTER FREDERICK	RCAF	PO	CUPAR	12/02/42	59°15'	106°30'	BOND ISLAND
BONNEVILLE, JOHN R.	RCAF	PO	SWIFT CURRENT	20/02/44	56°05'	102°01'	BONNEVILLE LAKE
BONOKOSKI, DANIEL	RCAF	PO	TORQUAY	29/01/44	59°44'	103°23'	BONOKOSKI LAKE
BONSEIGNEUR, CAMILLE R.	RAF	PO	GULL LAKE	03/09/40	55°20'	104°32'	BONSEIGNEUR LAKE
BONVILLE, ANDREW	ARMY	RFN	ZENON PARK	04/07/44	56°41'	105°30'	BONVILLE LAKE
BOOTH, ROBERT GORDON	NAVY	AB	SASKATOON	20/09/43	55°06'	108°17'	BOOTH BAY
BOOTH, WALTER J.	ARMY	RFN	RITCHIE	08/06/44	55°37'	102°03'	BOOTH BAY
BOOY, HARRY	ARMY	SPR	BATTLEFORD	13/05/44	53°33'	102°48'	BOOY LAKE
BORYS, STEVEN	ARMY	PTE	YORKTON	19/08/42	55°43'	104°59'	BORYS LAKE

Name	Branch	Rank	Hometown	Casualty Date	Latitude	Longitude	Geo-Memorial
BOTHAM, CHARLES R.	ARMY	PTE	PLATO	23/05/44	57°15'	106°30'	BOTHAM LAKE
BOTHAM, ROBERT JOHN	NAVY	AB	PLATO	20/09/43	54°43'	102°46'	BOTHAM BAY
BOUCHARD, V.J.	RCAF	FO	MOOSE JAW	22/12/44	59°44'	103°16'	BOUCHARD LAKE
BOUCHER, ARTHUR A.	ARMY	PTE	BIGGAR	21/04/45	56°55'	102°17'	BOUCHER ISLAND
BOUGHNER, LYSLE S.	ARMY	PTE	ZEALANDIA	06/08/44	59°36'	105°50'	BOUGHNER LAKE
BOULDING, ALBERT E.	ARMY	PTE	RADISSON	07/01/44	58°12'	105°14'	BOULDING LAKE
BOURASSA, CLARENCE O.	ARMY	PTE	LAFLECHE	20/07/43	57°43'	109°58'	BOURASSA CREEK
BOURASSA, PAUL A.	ARMY	SPR	DIVISION 16	09/10/44	53°37'	102°54'	BOURASSA LAKE
BOURGEAULT, JOHN A.	RCAF	PO	BLAINE LAKE	23/04/44	57°47'	107°57'	BOURGEAULT RAPIDS
BOURGET, ANTOINE P.	ARMY	PTE	DIVISION I	13/12/44	55°59'	102°32'	BOURGET LAKE
BOURNE, CECIL D.	ARMY	GNR	KINDERSLEY	13/10/44	57°20'	106°25'	BOURNE BAY
BOURNE, KENNETH R.	RCAF	PO	SUMMERBERRY	13/08/43	59°40'	103°28'	BOURNE LAKE
BOUSFIELD, GEORGE R.	RCAF	FO	CEYLON	04/07/43	55°33'	104°43'	BOUSFIELD LAKE
BOUSQUET, ELBERT C.	RCAF	PO	WILKIE	02/03/44	54°23'	109°21'	BOUSQUET LAKE
BOUVIER, MAURICE A.	ARMY	GDSM	GRAVELBOURG	15/04/45	55°17'	106°08'	BOUVIER LAKE
BOUVIER, THEODORE J.	NAVY	SIG	GRAVELBOURG	07/05/44	55°04'	109°39'	BOUVIER CREEK
BOVAIR, DOUGLAS J.	ARMY	TPR	DIVISION 13	28/02/45	57°57'	108°37'	BOVAIR LAKE
BOWERING, HENRY T.	ARMY	PTE	MOOSOMIN	13/10/44	55°27'	104°17'	BOWERING ISLAND
BOXALL, GILBERT D.	ARMY	RFN	CANWOOD	09/06/44	55°53'	105°55'	BOXALL LAKE
BOYCE, JOHN W.	RCAF	FS	SASKATOON	01/09/41	59°55'	105°04'	BOYCE ISLAND
BOYCE, REGINALD S.	ARMY	A CAPT	ANEROID	26/02/45	55°40'	104°11'	BOYCE LAKE
BOYD, FRANCIS E.	ARMY	L BDR	MOOSE JAW	02/12/45	55°16'	104°59'	BOYD ISLAND
BOYD, LORNE G.	RCAF	FS	LLOYDMINSTER	15/09/43	56°24'	105°10'	BOYD LAKE
BOYER, GEORGE C.	ARMY	RFN	DIVISION 5	04/07/44	59°16'	102°36'	BOYER LAKE
BOYES, HARRY T.	RCAF	FO	SASKATOON	21/12/42	55°41'	104°59'	BOYES ISLAND
BOYLE, HARRY V.	RCAF	FO	GRANDORA	17/08/44	55°41'	104°58'	BOYLE ISLAND
BRAATEN, STERLING LORNE	RCAF	PO	LANCER	23/08/44	55°18'	104°50'	BRAATEN ISLAND
BRACEY, MAURICE J.	RCAF	FS	REGINA	30/09/42	55°49'	104°31'	BRACEY LAKE
BRACKEN, WILLIAM H.	RCAF	FS	MOOSE JAW	20/05/42	55°56'	104°34'	BRACKEN LAKE
BRACKENRIDGE, DOUGLAS	RCAF	SGT	ABERNETHY	07/02/43	55°34'	103°03'	BRACKENRIDGE ISLAND
BRADFORD, ROY	ARMY	PTE	SALTCOATS	24/09/44	60°02'	103°06'	BRADFORD LAKE
BRADLEY, ALLEN C.	RCAF	FO	GOVAN	29/11/42	55°39'	104°17'	BRADLEY BAY
BRADLEY, FRANK	RCAF	PO	SASKATOON	16/08/44	57°56'	107°01'	BRADLEY RAPIDS
BRADLEY, HOWARD E.	RCAF	WO2	MOOSE JAW	13/07/43	59°27'	106°05'	BRADLEY LAKE
BRADLEY, JOHN E.	RCAF	WO2	REGINA	09/01/43	57°24'	102°13'	BRADLEY ISLAND
BRADSHAW, ROBERT A.	RAF	SGT	SASKATOON	26/12/40	55°25'	104°37'	BRADSHAW BAY
BRADSHAW, SIDNEY V.	RCAF	FS	SASKATOON	29/03/43	55°25'	104°37'	BRADSHAW BAY
BRAGER, KENNETH L.	RCAF	PO	WATSON	20/12/43	59°21'	106°56'	BRAGER LAKE
BRAITHWAITE, GEORGE R.	ARMY	RFN	TRAYNOR	07/06/44	56°54'	103°11'	BRAITHWAITE LAKE
BRAKEWELL, RICHARD	ARMY	B Q M S	PRINCE ALBERT	01/09/44	57°30'	103°43'	BRAKEWELL LAKE
BRANDSER, RAYMOND A.	RCAF	FO	GLENBAIN	15/09/46	57°56'	103°21'	BRANDSER ISLAND
BRAY, ERIC WILLIAM	RCAF	PO	NOKOMIS	22/04/43	57°27'	109°22'	BRAY LAKE
BRAZIER, AUSTIN W.	ARMY	TPR	QUILL LAKE	05/10/44	57°22'	103°49'	BRAZIER LAKE
BRAZIER, GEORGE H.	RCAF	PO	ARBUTHNOT	20/12/42	57°23'	109°29'	BRAZIER LAKE
BREBBER, JOHN GRANT	NAVY	LDG S36	SHAUNAVON	22/10/40	55°01'	104°49'	BREBBER ISLAND
BREMNER, LAURENT E.	ARMY	PTE	DOMREMY	26/08/44	59°46'	107°58'	BREMNER LAKE
BRENNAND, GEORGE F.	ARMY	PTE	MOOSOMIN	01/09/42	56°29'	103°45'	BRENNAND BAY
BRENTON, EDWIN SWAYNE	RCAF	FO	WILKIE	15/08/43	56°32'	102°47'	BRENTON ISLAND
BRENTON, KENNETH S.	RCAF	PO	WILKIE	16/03/45	56°32'	102°47'	BRENTON ISLAND
BRENTON, LEO A.	RCAF	PO	NORTH BATTLEFORD	25/04/44	57°04'	107°31'	BRENTON LAKE
BRETT, WALTER B.	NAVY	ERA 3	REGINA	20/09/43	55°01'	109°40'	BRETT CREEK
BRETTELL, AUBREY L.E.	ARMY	PTE	INDIAN HEAD	26/12/43	59°17'	103°25'	BRETTELL LAKE
BREWER, WILLIAM D.	ARMY	A CPL	BORDERLAND	08/07/44	55°25'	107°13'	BREWER LAKE
BRIAN, JOHN C.	ARMY	TPR	TOMPKINS	22/07/45	55°49'	104°53'	BRIAN LAKE
BRIDGEMAN, ROBERT V.	RCAF	WO2	TURTLEFORD	08/01/43	55°33'	104°46'	BRIDGEMAN LAKE
BRIÈRE, SINAI T.	ARMY	SPR	BILLIMUN	07/06/43	55°35'	104°42'	BRIÈRE LAKE
BRIESE, RICHARD G.	RCAF	WC	LANIGAN	22/10/41	55°50'	105°40'	BRIESE LAKE
BRIGGS, THOMAS A.P.	ARMY	PTE	MAPLE CREEK	14/04/45	57°53'	104°38'	BRIGGS LAKE
BRIGGS, THOMAS S.	RCAF	PO	VENN	18/02/43	60°00'	109°55'	BRIGGS LAKE
BRIGHTWELL, RUSSELL H.	ARMY	RFN	MOOSE JAW	16/05/42	59°38'	106°33'	BRIGHTWELL BAY
BRINK, GLEN A.	ARMY	A CPL	GRONLID	11/12/43	57°37'	102°15'	BRINK ISLAND
BRINSDON, NORMAN E.F.	ARMY	PTE	MOOSE JAW	20/07/44	56°08'	104°08'	BRINSDON LAKE
BRINSON, FRED JOHN DAVID	NAVY	STO 2	LIVELONG	18/12/42	59°25'	108°08'	BRINSON POINT
BRISBIN, GERALD GISE	ARMY	PTE	HARRIS	13/04/44	55°58'	105°54'	BRISBIN LAKE
BRISTOW, MORRIS	ARMY	TPR	SASKATOON	31/08/44	56°48'	102°05'	BRISTOW LAKE
BRITTIN, ROBERT HENRY	NAVY	AB	MOOSE JAW	15/07/44	56°11'	104°26'	BRITTIN BAY
BRITTS, ALFRED J.	RCAF	PO	LAKE LENORE	21/07/44	57°23'	109°31'	BRITTS LAKE
BROADBENT, ROBERT C.	RCAF	SGT	PRINCE ALBERT	31/07/43	56°39'	108°20'	BROADBENT LAKE
BROCHU, ARMAND J.	ARMY	MAJ	COLONSAY	01/03/45	55°56'	104°37'	BROCHU LAKE
BROCK, RONALD A.	ARMY	FS	PRINCE ALBERT	06/02/45	54°52'	103°01'	BROCK BAY
BROCKBANK, HAROLD M.	ARMY	PTE	OUTLOOK	23/11/44	57°58'	102°12'	BROCKBANK LAKE
BROKENSHIRE, EDWARD D.	RCAF	FS	LUCKY LAKE	06/08/43	58°15'	102°26'	BROKENSHIRE LAKE
BROOKS, DENZIEL	ARMY	PTE	MOOSE JAW	21/10/42	59°23'	105°58'	BROOKS LAKE
BROPHY, JOHN L.D.	RCAF	FS	BEECHY	16/08/42	60°01'	105°23'	BROPHY LAKE
BROWN, ALFRED L.B.	ARMY	TPR	PORTAGE CREEK	11/06/44	56°15'	109°48'	BROWN CREEK
BROWN, ARTHUR J.	ARMY	SPR	SWIFT CURRENT	17/05/40	53°46'	102°34'	BROWN BAY
BROWN, CHARLES G.	ARMY	SIGMN	SASKATOON	12/07/43	56°04'	109°45'	BROWN LAKE
BROWN, CHARLES H.	ARMY	RFN	REGINA	18/06/44	56°21'	103°54'	BROWN FALLS
BROWN, CHARLES T.	ARMY	L BDR	YORKTON	10/11/44	58°03'	104°27'	BROWN BAY
BROWN, CLAYTON P.L.	RCAF	WO1	MOOSE JAW	07/07/42	55°32'	104°06'	BROWN RAPIDS
BROWN, DAVID O.	RCAF	FO	REGINA	21/07/44	55°37'	106°26'	BROWN CHANNEL
BROWN, DOUGLAS W.	RCAF	FO	TANTALLON	15/08/44	55°46'	106°02'	BROWN BAY
BROWN, EDWARD J.	RCAF	FO	BJORKDALE	09/11/44	57°29'	102°37'	BROWN POINT
BROWN, GEORGE A.	ARMY	A CPL	BALDWINTON	08/06/44	56°49'	102°51'	BROWN LAKE
BROWN, GEORGE H.	ARMY	PTE	BIENFAIT	06/01/44	55°32'	102°47'	BROWN PENINSULA
BROWN, GILBERT J.	ARMY	CPL	ARTLAND	05/04/43	56°11'	104°22'	BROWN RIVER
BROWN, GORDON S.	ARMY	PTE	ELDERSLEY	28/02/45	57°52'	106°58'	BROWN LAKE
BROWN, HAROLD N.	ARMY	BDR	REGINA	14/08/44	59°20'	108°59'	BROWN LAKE
BROWN, JAMES C.	ARMY	SGT	WATROUS	16/12/43	56°11'	104°26'	BROWN CREEK
BROWN, JAMES H.	ARMY	SGT	SASKATOON	24/06/43			PENDING
BROWN, JOHN A.C.	ARMY	SGT	UNKNOWN	30/11/41			PENDING
BROWN, JOHN A.C.	RCAF	FO	YORKTON	12/05/44	58°38'	105°44'	BROWN CREEK
BROWN, JOHN H.	ARMY	PTE	FAIRHOLME	20/07/44	57°41'	102°37'	BROWN CHANNEL
BROWN, MAX B.	ARMY	PTE	GRIFFIN	09/02/45	55°36'	102°52'	BROWN BAY
BROWN, NORMAN A.	ARMY	LIEUT	HAWARDEN	14/08/44	59°57'	103°45'	BROWN LAKE
BROWN, ORLAN R.	RCAF	FO	PALMER	16/02/43	57°16'	105°53'	BROWN LAKE
BROWN, REGINALD W.	RAF	SQ/LDR	ANTLER	24/06/44	55°41'	106°29'	BROWN ISLAND
BROWN, ROBERT G.	RCAF	CPL	REGINA	14/08/40	53°03'	109°40'	BROWN COULEE
BROWN, ROBERT J.	RCAF	FO	LANGHAM	14/09/44	55°25'	106°42'	BROWN PENINSULA
BROWN, ROBERT J.	ARMY	L/SGT	TANTALLON	08/08/44	56°47'	102°51'	BROWN CREEK
BROWN, ROSS A.	ARMY	RFN	SWIFT CURRENT	26/02/45	59°45'	109°22'	BROWN POINT
BROWN, THEARON	ARMY	PTE	ANTELOPE	03/03/45	53°45'	102°34'	BROWN LAKE
BROWN, THOMAS L.	RCAF	FS	WOLSELEY	06/05/42	59°37'	106°25'	BROWN FALLS
BROWN, VERNON E.	ARMY	PTE	QUILL LAKE	21/07/44	58°05'	104°25'	BROWN ISLANDS
BROWN, WALTER G.	RCAF	PO	LANGHAM	16/03/45	55°23'	106°40'	BROWN ISLAND
BROWN, WALTER J.	NAVY	AB	SPRINGSIDE	19/10/40	56°56'	103°41'	BROWN NARROWS
BROWN, WILLIAM E.	RCAF	WO2	COPPEN	22/05/44			PENDING
BROWN, WILLIAM J.	ARMY	SGT	THEODORE	14/05/43			PENDING
BROWNFIELD, OSCAR D.	RCAF	AC1	BIG RIVER	10/06/40	57°17'	106°37'	BROWNFIELD LAKE
BROWNRIGG, JOHN W.	ARMY	GNR	MOOSE JAW	14/05/43	56°33'	105°51'	BROWNRIGG LAKE
BRUCK, JOHN J.	ARMY	BDR	FLAT VALLEY	26/02/45	59°58'	109°39'	BRUCK LAKE
BRUNELLE, ARTHUR L.	ARMY	A SGT	ALBERTVILLE	06/09/44	55°41'	107°23'	BRUNELLE LAKE
BRUNNING, LOUIS G.	ARMY	RFN	PRINCE ALBERT	06/06/44	55°46'	105°59'	BRUNNING LAKE
BRYAN, GERALD G.	RCAF	FO	LOCKWOOD	23/09/44	55°51'	104°20'	BRYAN LAKE
BRYANS, ROBERT J.	RCAF	PO	MAIDSTONE	13/05/43	54°50'	102°56'	BRYANS LAKE
BRYANT, WILLIAM J.	ARMY	PTE	KAMSACK	28/08/44	56°30'	102°02'	BRYANT LAKE
BRYDE, NELSON	ARMY	L BDR	CRANE VALLEY	08/09/45	59°60'	102°25'	BRYDE LAKE
BRYDEN, GEORGE S.	RCAF	CPL	SHELLBROOK	12/05/44	58°44'	103°16'	BRYDEN LAKE
BRYER, EDWARD	ARMY	PTE	MARCHWELL	03/08/44	59°26'	108°09'	BRYER ISLAND
BRYKSA, STEVE	ARMY	RFN	WEST END	29/03/45	59°27'	106°06'	BRYKSA LAKE
BUCHANAN, ALEXANDER G.	RCAF	FS	NORTH BATTLEFORD	06/01/42	55°58'	104°02'	BUCHANAN LAKE
BUCHANAN, BORDEN	ARMY	PTE	MOOSE JAW	28/02/45	55°06'	107°23'	BUCHANAN PENINSULA
BUCHANAN, DAVID	RCAF	FL	NORTH BATTLEFORD	27/03/45	55°58'	104°02'	BUCHANAN LAKE
BUCHANAN, GEORGE H.P.	RCAF	SGT	SASKATOON	16/08/41	57°54'	107°54'	BUCHANAN LAKE
BUCHNER, JOSEPH P.	ARMY	A CPL	MACKLIN	23/07/43	55°43'	104°14'	BUCHNER LAKE
BUCK, ALFRED W.	ARMY	PTE	MOOSOMIN	18/03/42	55°41'	106°21'	BUCK ISLAND
BUCKMAYER, WENDELIN	ARMY	SPR	DIVISION 6	15/08/44	53°04'	102°56'	BUCKMAYER LAKE
BUDD, GEORGE L.	ARMY	PTE	CUMBERLAND HOUSE	20/07/44	56°26'	102°38'	BUDD LAKE

NAME	BRANCH	RANK	HOMETOWN	CASUALTY DATE	LATITUDE	LONGITUDE	GEO-MEMORIAL
BUDD, HENRY E.	RCAF	WO2	REGINA	15/04/43	55°05'	104°39'	BUDD LAKE
BUDD, MALCOLM H.	ARMY	A L SGT	SOMME	17/08/44	53°51'	102°57'	BUDD ISLAND
BUGG, CHARLES H.	ARMY	PTE	MOZART	28/07/44	55°44'	108°05'	BUGG LAKE
BULLER, EDWARD M.	ARMY	TPR	SASKATOON	26/02/45	56°33'	107°46'	BULLER LAKE
BULMER, NORMAN C.	ARMY	LIEUT	REGINA	18/07/44	59°54'	108°09'	BULMER LAKE
BUNN, JAMES E.	RCAF	WO2	BROADVIEW	24/03/45	55°39'	104°02'	BUNN LAKE
BURGESS, RAYMOND R.	RCAF	FL	BIGGAR	25/07/44	55°41'	104°49'	BURGESS BAY
BURGESS, WILLIAM	ARMY	L CPL	DIVISION 9	10/12/44	55°22'	105°10'	BURGESS LAKES
BURGETT, GEORGE A.	ARMY	SIGMN	DIVISION 16	13/08/44	59°32'	105°26'	BURGETT LAKE
BURKE, WILLIAM J.	ARMY	LIEUT	EARL GREY	19/02/45	55°41'	104°44'	BURKE CREEK
BURKOSKY, JOHN	ARMY	SGT	PRINCE ALBERT	12/08/44	57°12'	106°15'	BURKOSKY LAKE
BURMAN, WALTER A.	ARMY	PTE	MARYFIELD	19/09/44	57°59'	103°37'	BURMAN ISLAND
BURNARD, HARVEY S.	ARMY	LIEUT	THEODORE	25/07/44	56°51'	105°18'	BURNARD ISLAND
BURNARD, MELVIN E.	RCAF	SGT	THEODORE	25/03/44	56°40'	105°18'	BURNARD LAKE
BURNETT, DAVID M.T.	RCAF	PO	REGINA	13/05/44	59°02'	102°18'	BURNETT LAKE
BURNS, EDGAR J.	ARMY	RFN	SASKATOON	06/06/44	59°25'	108°46'	BURNS LAKE
BURNS, JOHN A.	ARMY	SGT	REGINA	01/05/41	58°48'	108°22'	BURNS BAY
BURNS, OWEN K.	ARMY	SIGNM	ALIDA	09/03/45	55°30'	105°44'	BURNS ISLAND
BURNS, ROBERT G.	ARMY	PTE	WEYBURN	19/08/42	55°09'	105°04'	BURNS ISLAND
BURRELL, HERBERT T.	ARMY	PTE	SASKATOON	18/12/43	55°31'	106°06'	BURRELL LAKE
BURRILL, WILBERT I.	ARMY	PTE	ARCOLA	27/08/44	58°46'	102°57'	BURRILL BAY
BURRISON, REGINALD M.	ARMY	A SGT	BIGGAR	13/11/44	54°18'	102°06'	BURRISON CREEK
BURRISON, RICHARD L.	ARMY	L SGT	BIGGAR	25/04/45	54°18'	102°06'	BURRISON LAKE
BURTON, EARL A.	RCAF	FO	ZEALANDIA	26/11/43	57°16'	102°32'	BURTON ISLAND
BURTON, FLOYD W.	ARMY	L SGT	GLENBAIN	04/01/45	54°35'	102°21'	BURTON LAKE
BUSH, HERBERT R.	ARMY	GNR	ESTON	18/12/44	59°35'	108°40'	BUSH LAKE
BUSHELL, CHRISTOPHER	RCAF	SL	FORT QU'APPELLE	08/11/41	59°30'	108°45'	BUSHELL INLET
BUSS, ARTHUR	ARMY	RFN	WEYBURN	04/07/44	55°53'	105°53'	BUSS LAKE
BUTLER, EARLE NELSON	ARMY	SGT	KAMSACK	09/02/44	55°39'	106°56'	BUTLER CREEK
BUTLER, JOHN H.N.	ARMY	RFN	MOOSE JAW	08/06/44	56°50'	102°19'	BUTLER BAY
BUTLER, NORMAN A.	RCAF	PO	BLADWORTH	06/01/45	55°31'	104°33'	BUTLER BAY
BUTULA, WILLIAM	ARMY	PTE	STRONG PINE	16/08/44	59°29'	106°02'	BUTULA LAKE
BUZIK, JOSEPH P.	RCAF	AC2	PRINCE ALBERT	11/07/42	58°07'	108°28'	BUZIK LAKE
BYERS, GORDON L.	ARMY	PTE	DIVISION 15	08/05/45	59°44'	108°24'	BYERS BAY
BYERS, VERNON WILLIAM	RCAF	PO	STAR CITY	17/05/43	55°39'	105°14'	BYERS BAY
BYKLUM, ARNE	ARMY	PTE	SWIFT CURRENT	19/08/42	54°36'	101°53'	BYKLUM LAKE
CABLE, GEORGE V.	ARMY	A CPL	HUDSON BAY	13/09/44	57°21'	107°07'	CABLE BAY
CAIRNS, LEONARD MELVILLE	NAVY	OS	SASKATOON	19/03/42	56°46'	103°44'	CAIRNS BAY
CAIRNS, RICHARD FOOTE	RCAF	SGT	SASKATOON	15/02/43	59°30'	108°59'	CAIRNS ISLAND
CALDER, GORDON A.	RCAF	PO	NIPAWIN	13/05/43	56°27'	104°29'	CALDER ISLAND
CALDER, KENNETH A.	ARMY	CAPT	MOOSE JAW	06/07/45	56°58'	102°08'	CALDER LAKE
CALDWELL, ALEXANDER P.	ARMY	RFN	SALTCOATS	30/03/45	55°43'	106°43'	CALDWELL PENINSULA
CALDWELL, CLARENCE C.	ARMY	TPR	TISDALE	07/12/44	59°27'	108°21'	CALDWELL BAY
CALDWELL, JAMES G.	ARMY	PTE	CARRUTHERS	07/03/45	57°06'	103°32'	CALDWELL LAKE
CALLIN, WILLIAM E.	ARMY	GNR	TISDALE	04/07/45	56°46'	104°34'	CALLIN LAKE
CALQUHOUN, CARMAN M.	RCAF	PO	MAPLE CREEK	22/09/43			PENDING
CALVERT, ROBERT W.	RCAF	FS	NORTH BATTLEFORD	15/09/43	59°03'	105°26'	CALVERT LAKE
CAMERON, DUNCAN J.	RCAF	FO	HUMBOLDT	29/03/44	56°50'	102°26'	CAMERON ISLAND
CAMERON, HILLARD J.	ARMY	PTE	SASKATOON	01/06/41	59°55'	108°48'	CAMERON LAKE
CAMERON, JOHN E.	RCAF	FS	SASKATOON	28/08/43			PENDING
CAMERON, LLOYD W.	ARMY	SIGMN	CARLYLE	09/07/43	55°33'	102°41'	CAMERON FALLS
CAMERON, MORLEY L.	RCAF	FO	SASKATOON	30/06/44	59°08'	102°02'	CAMERON BAY
CAMERON, PHILIP G.	RCAF	LAC	CODERRE	15/08/42			PENDING
CAMERON, WILLIAM	RCAF	FS	SASKATOON	12/06/42			PENDING
CAMPBELL, ALEXANDER G.	RCAF	PO	REGINA	11/04/44	55°15'	104°36'	CAMPBELL BAY
CAMPBELL, ALLAN P.	RCAF	FO	MELVILLE	02/01/44	57°16'	103°17'	CAMPBELL RIVER
CAMPBELL, COLIN H.	ARMY	PTE	NESTLEDOWN	25/10/44	58°17'	105°26'	CAMPBELL BAY
CAMPBELL, DONALD E.	RCAF	FS	ZEALANDIA	26/06/43			PENDING
CAMPBELL, DONALD J.	RCAF	PO	BROCK	16/02/45	55°51'	105°06'	CAMPBELL RAPIDS
CAMPBELL, DONALD J.M.	ARMY	A SGT	MOOSE JAW	17/09/44	56°59'	103°39'	CAMPBELL BAY
CAMPBELL, DOUGLAS A.	RCAF	FS	RUSH LAKE	28/01/42	59°18'	106°40'	CAMPBELL POINT
CAMPBELL, DUNCAN A.	RCAF	FS	SOMME	25/06/42			PENDING
CAMPBELL, EDWIN R.	ARMY	PTE	LACADENA	13/12/44	59°07'	108°10'	CAMPBELL LAKE
CAMPBELL, GORDON KEITH	NAVY	OS	ESTON	13/09/42	56°59'	103°40'	CAMPBELL NARROWS
CAMPBELL, HUDSON C.	RCAF	FO	KAMSACK	24/02/44	55°10'	105°08'	CAMPBELL CHANNEL
CAMPBELL, JAMES D.	ARMY	PTE	ARCOLA	19/08/42	58°43'	138°05'	CAMPBELL PENINSULA
CAMPBELL, JOSEPH W.	RCAF	FS	YORKTON	16/07/43			PENDING
CAMPBELL, RICHARD A.	RCAF	FL	ASSINIBOIA	10/10/44	57°07'	105°37'	CAMPBELL CREEK
CAMPBELL, ROBERT R.	RCAF	FO	REGINA	13/05/44	55°15'	104°36'	CAMPBELL BAY
CAMPBELL, RUSSELL J.	ARMY	RFN	KINISTINO	08/07/44	58°52'	103°54'	CAMPBELL LAKE
CAMPBELL, WILLIAM F.	NAVY	L CR	SASKATOON	06/02/43	56°59'	103°40'	CAMPBELL ISLANDS
CANN, GEORGE G.	RCAF	FO	BALCARRES	03/11/42	55°23'	103°02'	CANN LAKE
CAPRARU, VASIL	ARMY	RFN	REGINA	08/06/44	59°54'	108°26'	CAPRARU LAKE
CAREFOOT, GARNET O.	RCAF	FO	CANTUAR	19/11/43	57°47'	103°25'	CAREFOOT LAKES
CAREFOOT, HERBERT R.	RCAF	GC	ESTON	25/04/42	57°47'	103°25'	CAREFOOT LAKES
CAREY, PERCIVAL GEORGE	NAVY	AB	REGINA	07/05/44	54°53'	103°14'	CAREY ISLAND
CAREY, ROBERT W.B.	RCAF	PO	ESTEVAN	30/07/44	55°02'	104°33'	CAREY LAKE
CARL, CHARLES GORDON	NAVY	SIG	MEADOW LAKE	04/10/44	54°32'	108°38'	CARL CREEK
CARLETON, GLEN I.	ARMY	L CPL	DIVISION 4	03/02/45	58°03'	102°01'	CARLETON ISLAND
CARLEY, JOHN W.	RCAF	FS	SASKATOON	28/04/43	60°00'	109°08'	CARLEY LAKE
CARLSON, ELMER K.	RCAF	FS	PLEASANTDALE	12/09/44	57°02'	108°34'	CARLSON LAKE
CARLSON, HENRY I.	ARMY	PTE	RADVILLE	10/10/40	57°47'	104°47'	CARLSON CREEK
CARLTON, DOUGLAS A.	NAVY	AB	BRADWELL	25/06/40	55°01'	109°07'	CARLTON LAKE
CARLYLE, WALTER B.	RCAF	PO	SUTHERLAND	21/07/42	55°50'	104°40'	CARLYLE LAKE
CARNEY, HARRY	ARMY	PTE	REGINA	19/08/44	59°32'	108°40'	CARNEY LAKE
CAROL, ROY F.	RCAF	PO	STORTHOAKS	06/06/44	56°33'	107°48'	CAROL LAKE
CARPENTER, E.C.	RCAF	FL	SASKATOON	23/12/42	57°14'	107°21'	CARPENTER LAKE
CARR, LESLIE E.	ARMY	PTE	GRENFELL	01/10/44	54°56'	102°04'	CARR LAKE
CARRAGHER, JAMES C.	ARMY	TPR	STURGIS	21/08/44	55°01'	106°48'	CARRAGHER LAKE
CARRIERE, JOSEPH D.	ARMY	GNR	JACKFISH LAKE	26/06/46	56°48'	102°53'	CARRIERE LAKE
CARRUTHERS, HAROLD A.	RCAF	PO	BIGGAR	12/01/45	55°42'	103°25'	CARRUTHERS LAKE
CARSON, FRANCIS W.	NAVY	SLE	UNITY	18/11/43	56°57'	103°46'	CARSON PENINSULA
CARSON, MORLEY	NAVY	O SIG	SASKATOON	05/11/40	56°55'	103°47'	CARSON BAY
CARSON, WILLIAM A.	RCAF	SGT	LLOYDMINSTER	28/08/42	58°42'	103°12'	CARSON LAKE
CARSWELL, ARTHUR R.	ARMY	GNR	CONGRESS	26/08/44	58°48'	109°14'	CARSWELL RIVER
CARSWELL, JAMES R.	RCAF	FO	TURTLEFORD	15/08/43	58°37'	109°20'	CARSWELL LAKE
CARSWELL, NELSON A.	ARMY	PTE	HARRIS	08/12/44	57°04'	103°25'	CARSWELL LAKE
CARSWELL, ROBERT L.	ARMY	PTE	MOOSOMIN	19/08/44	55°48'	106°30'	CARSWELL PENINSULA
CARTER, HENRY W.T.	RCAF	PO	REGINA	30/08/44	56°13'	104°50'	CARTER RAPIDS
CARTER, STEWART M.	ARMY	A CAP3	PRINCE ALBERT	03/03/45	54°57'	102°41'	CARTER BAY
CARTWRIGHT, DOUGLAS C.	ARMY	RFN	COLEVILLE	09/06/44	59°23'	105°20'	CARTWRIGHT LAKE
CASAT, IVIE F.	ARMY	PTE	MAPLE CREEK	01/11/45	54°48'	105°42'	CASAT LAKE
CASCON, DANIEL J.R.	ARMY	PTE	REGINA	11/02/44	59°26'	106°13'	CASCON LAKE
CASE, THOMAS E.	RCAF	PO	KELVINGTON	19/02/43	53°11'	102°44'	CASE LAKE
CASSIDY, LORNE F.	RCAF	PO	REGINA	29/07/44	54°20'	108°27'	CASSIDY LAKE
CASTON, THOMAS W.	RCAF	PO	MACKLIN	28/02/42	59°32'	102°44'	CASTON LAKE
CAUSIER, RUSSEL G.	RCAF	SGT	REGINA	14/12/42	57°31'	103°49'	CAUSIER LAKE
CAWSEY, AUBREY C.	ARMY	CAPT	MOOSE JAW	07/08/44	55°07'	102°15'	CAWSEY LAKE
CAYEN, ADELORD	ARMY	PTE	REGINA	19/08/42	60°02'	102°34'	CAYEN LAKE
CAYFORD, MAX H.	ARMY	L CPL	DIVISION 13	14/09/44	53°09'	104°02'	CAYFORD LAKE
CEGLARZ, JOSEPH	ARMY	TPR	HUMBOLDT	25/07/44	55°28'	107°15'	CEGLARZ LAKE
CHABAN, MICHAEL	ARMY	PTE	SASKATOON	12/01/44	59°30'	104°37'	CHABAN LAKE
CHADBOLT, DONALD D.	ARMY	LIEUT	WILKIE	26/02/45	56°47'	107°02'	CHADBOLT LAKE
CHALK, ARTHUR E.	ARMY	RFN	MEDSTEAD	12/10/44	55°57'	105°51'	CHALK LAKE
CHALUS, PETER	ARMY	PTE	GRONLID	23/10/44	60°01'	109°28'	CHALUS LAKE
CHAMBERLAIN, ERNEST C.	ARMY	PTE	NORTH BATTLEFORD	04/03/44	59°24'	105°07'	CHAMBERLAIN LAKE
CHAMBERS, RICHARD E.	RCAF	PO	LLOYDMINSTER	29/09/44	59°36'	104°23'	CHAMBERS ISLAND
CHAMBERS, WILLIAM M.	RCAF	SGT	ROULEAU	08/11/41	59°27'	106°09'	CHAMBERS LAKE
CHAMNEY, BURNET M.	RCAF	FS	SASKATOON	26/02/43	54°36'	102°10'	CHAMNEY ISLAND
CHAMPAGNE, WILLIAM J.	ARMY	L CPL	DIVISION 10	04/07/44	55°45'	104°54'	CHAMPAGNE ISLAND
CHANCELLOR, LESLIE T.	ARMY	A CPL	LUCKY LAKE	01/07/46	56°41'	102°03'	CHANCELLOR LAKE
CHAPMAN, EARL W.	RCAF	FO	MARSHALL	29/07/44	55°56'	104°08'	CHAPMAN LAKE
CHAPMAN, JACK	ARMY	L CPL	ROCANVILLE	12/09/44	55°17'	104°43'	CHAPMAN BAY
CHAPMAN, LLOYD E.	RCAF	FO	RIDGEDALE	30/08/44	59°55'	107°55'	CHAPMAN LAKE
CHAPMAN, RICHARD H.	ARMY	PTE	ESTEVAN	03/03/45	55°48'	102°04'	CHAPMAN ISLAND
CHAPMAN, ROBERT E.	ARMY	L CPL	MOSSBANK	12/04/45	59°24'	108°40'	CHAPMAN BAY
CHARANDUK, ANTONY	ARMY	PTE	ITUNA	27/04/43	56°20'	109°26'	CHARANDUK LAKE
CHARBONNEAU, LAWRENCE	ARMY	TPR	BATTLEFORD	29/01/45	58°48'	108°21'	CHARBONNEAU RIVER

Name	Branch	Rank	Hometown	Casualty Date	Latitude	Longitude	Geo-Memorial	Name	Branch	Rank	Hometown	Casualty Date	Latitude	Longitude	Geo-Memorial
CHARBONNEAU, LEO J.	ARMY	PTE	GRAVELBOURG	14/12/44	55°14'	102°24'	CHARBONNEAU ISLAND	COCKBURN, JAMES W.	ARMY	PTE	BRIERCREST	25/07/44	59°31'	105°32'	COCKBURN LAKE
CHARTIER, JOSEPH L.T.	RCAF	FS	RABBIT LAKE	28/09/42	56°04'	103°45'	CHARTIER RIVER	COCKS, BARRY		PTE	LEADER	18/07/44	59°50'	103°37'	COCKS LAKE
CHARTIER, WELLWOOD E.	ARMY	SPR	GARRICK	30/07/44	53°12'	102°40'	CHARTIER LAKE	COCKWILL, WILFRED G.	RCAF	FO	BALGONIE	03/01/44	55°49'	104°35'	COCKWILL LAKE
CHASE, GEORGE R.	ARMY	PTE	MILESTONE	03/02/42	54°39'	102°07'	CHASE ISLAND	CODE, HARRY R.	ARMY	PTE	ESTON	20/02/45	55°12'	104°10'	CODE LAKE
CHEDISTER, WARD DONALD	NAVY	LDG S45	CADILLAC	22/10/40	55°35'	109°04'	CHEDISTER CREEK	COE, GEORGE R.	ARMY	RFN	WAWOTA	09/07/44	59°38'	108°35'	COE LAKE
CHEESEMAN, EDWIN L.	ARMY	SPR	SHELLBROOK	21/07/44	53°50'	102°18'	CHEESEMAN LAKE	COFFIN, ROY W.	ARMY	PTE	NOKOMIS	16/04/45	55°50'	106°36'	COFFIN LAKE
CHERMISHNUK, SAM R.	ARMY	PTE	MAPLE CREEK	10/08/44	56°14'	104°18'	CHERMISHNUK LAKE	COFLIN, JOHN G.	RCAF	PO	BLAINE LAKE	20/01/44	57°50'	109°13'	COFLIN LAKE
CHERCPITA, WILLIAM T.	RCAF	FS	THEODORE	27/08/43	60°01'	105°20'	CHEROPITA LAKE	COGGER, WALTER L.	RCAF	WO2	PRINCE ALBERT	18/08/43	59°25'	108°44'	COGGER LAKE
CHERPETA, JOHN EDWARD	NAVY	AB	REGINA	07/09/42	55°35'	109°03'	CHERPETA CREEK	COGHILL, CLARANCE M.M.	RCAF	WO2	TANTALLON	03/04/43	55°26'	104°23'	COGHILL LAKE
CHERVEK, LOUIS E.	ARMY	PTE	REGINA	29/08/44	59°07'	103°38'	CHERVEK ISLAND	COHEN, CYRIL B.	RCAF	FO	SWIFT CURRENT	07/49	57°49'	108°54'	COHEN LAKE
CHESNEY, JAMES L.	ARMY	LIEUT	WOLSELEY	24/10/44	60°01'	106°54'	CHESNEY LAKE	COJOCAR, DAN	ARMY	PTE	OGEMA	08/08/44	55°48'	106°30'	COJOCAR BAY
CHESTER, JOHN W.	RCAF	WO1	MOSSBANK	03/09/43	59°25'	108°47'	CHESTER LAKE	COJOCAR, GEORGE	RCAF	PO	REGINA	23/03/43	54°15'	104°48'	COJOCAR LAKE
CHESTNUT, GUY A.	RCAF	SGT	MOOSOMIN	11/06/41	59°25'	104°43'	CHESTNUT LAKE	COLBRIDGE, REGINALD	ARMY	A SGT	MAIDSTONE	14/02/44	58°37'	105°34'	COLBRIDGE CREEK
CHEVALIER, MARCEL J.	ARMY	CAPT	ST. BRIEUX	23/08/44	59°48'	109°53'	CHEVALIER LAKE	COLE, CHARLES V.	ARMY	SIG	CUPAR	18/05/43	59°17'	106°28'	COLE LAKE
CHEYNEY, ALBERT J.	ARMY	CPL	PADDOCKWOOD	06/09/43	55°43'	104°28'	CHEYNEY LAKE	COLE, JOHN WARD	NAVY	SIG	REGINA	22/10/40	55°06'	108°21'	COLE BAY
CHILTON, LEONARD R.	ARMY	A L CPL	REGINA	19/08/42	55°26'	107°23'	CHILTON LAKE	COLE, STANLEY H.	ARMY	RFN	RESOURCE	06/06/44	57°25'	103°43'	COLE LAKE
CHILWELL, THOMAS	ARMY	PTE	WILKIE	29/10/44	59°27'	108°05'	CHILWELL BAY	COLE, WILLIAM ARTHUR	NAVY	CPO	SASKATOON	29/09/45	55°08'	108°20'	COLE ISLAND
CHISHOLM, ROBERT D.	NAVY	AB	RHINELAND	13/09/42	54°38'	102°58'	CHISHOLM LAKE	COLEBOURNE, WALTER G.	ARMY	PTE	REGINA	25/03/45	58°06'	106°59'	COLEBOURNE LAKE
CHOBANIUK, NICHOLAS	RCAF	FO	REGINA	14/01/45	59°40'	102°10'	CHOBANIUK LAKE	COLEMAN, E.L.J.	RCAF	FS	MELFORT	10/05/42	59°42'	105°43'	COLEMAN LAKE
CHOBOTUK, MICHAEL	ARMY	A CPL	SNOWDEN	08/10/44	55°43'	105°19'	CHOBOTUK LAKE	COLLARD, JOHN A.	ARMY	GNR	LANGBANK	08/08/44	56°40'	105°52'	COLLARD LAKE
CHOMYN, JOHN P.	ARMY	PTE	CARPENTER	19/02/45	55°22'	102°07'	CHOMYN LAKE	COLLEY, ROBERT C.	RCAF	PO	DENZIL	26/09/41	57°53'	109°10'	COLLEY LAKE
CHORNEYKO, ATHANAZIE	RCAF	FO	ARRAN	22/10/43	54°58'	104°57'	CHORNEYKO LAKE	COLLIER, JAMES E.	ARMY	PTE	PRINCE ALBERT	12/01/45	57°24'	103°28'	COLLIER LAKE
CHRISTIE, HARRY D.	RCAF	FO	RAYMORE	12/01/45	57°38'	105°02'	CHRISTIE LAKE	COLLINS, GEORGE	ARMY	PTE	REGINA	27/04/45	56°46'	103°15'	COLLINS LAKE
CHRISTIE, JAMES OLIVER	RCAF	PO	DYSART	03/04/44	55°47'	104°31'	CHRISTIE ISLAND	COLLINS, MELVIN W.	RCAF	FO	SASKATOON	16/05/43			PENDING
CHRISTIE, MALCOLM LESLIE	ARMY	PTE	WATSON	05/08/45			PENDING	COLLINS, RICHARD	ARMY	PTE	ARCOLA	19/08/42	59°50'	107°45'	COLLINS LAKE
CHRISTOPHERSON, C.T.	RCAF	CPL	NEILBURG	26/10/42	59°40'	105°35'	CHRISTOPHER LAKE	COLLINS, WILLIAM	ARMY	PTE	BIG RIVER	17/01/44	56°46'	103°56'	COLLINS RAPIDS
CHUDYK, STEVE	ARMY	RFN	OAKSHELA	25/04/45	55°16'	107°40'	CHUDYK LAKE	COLVIN, DAVID A.	RCAF	FO	PRINCE ALBERT	08/07/43	53°44'	102°03'	COLVIN LAKE
CHURCH, HAROLD W.	RCAF	FL	PRINCE ALBERT	18/01/44	54°40'	102°57'	CHURCH LAKE	COLVIN, RICHARD J.T.	RCAF	FS	PRINCE ALBERT	10/10/42	53°44'	102°03'	COLVIN LAKE
CHURCH, JAMES M.	RCAF	FS	DILKE	30/07/43	57°55'	106°25'	CHURCH RAPIDS	COLWELL, ROBERT E.	RCAF	CPL	PORTREEVE	07/07/44	55°05'	104°41'	COLWELL LAKE
CHURCH, MAURICE G.	RCAF	WO2	CHAMBERLAIN	03/04/43	56°19'	104°24'	CHURCH ISLAND	COMBRES, MAURICE E.	RCAF	FS	RICHARD	04/07/43	59°59'	102°29'	COMBRES LAKE
CHUTE, CLINTON M.	RCAF	FS	REGINA	30/05/42	53°48'	107°19'	CHUTE LAKE	CONACHER, DAVID B.	ARMY	PTE	FAIRY GLEN	14/08/44	57°20'	103°01'	CONACHER LAKE
CHVALA, WILLIAM P.	ARMY	CPL	NORTH BATTLEFORD	06/12/44	59°35'	105°27'	CHVALA LAKE	CONLEY, ROBERT	ARMY	LIEUT	HUMBOLDT	01/11/44	60°00'	109°00'	CONLEY CREEK
CHYMKO, WALTER D.	ARMY	PTE	SEMANS	19/08/42	57°21'	107°32'	CHYMKO LAKE	CONN, JOHN K.	RCAF	WO2	ABERDEEN	11/12/42	59°24'	108°45'	CONN LAKE
CIOCIA, ANTONE	ARMY	PTE	FLINTOFT	23/10/44	59°59'	105°31'	CIOCIA LAKE	CONNELL, MATTHEW	ARMY	RFN	MOOSE JAW	17/11/44	55°08'	105°06'	CONNELL ISLAND
CLAMPITT, EDWARD B.	RCAF	FS	WOODROW	12/03/43	57°55'	109°55'	CLAMPITT LAKE	CONNOR, GEORGE R.	RCAF	FS	MOOSE JAW	18/07/43	55°42'	103°21'	CONNOR LAKE
CLARK, CYRIL B.	ARMY	SGT	WEYBURN	19/08/42	55°43'	104°52'	CLARK FALLS	COOK, BENJAMIN D.	RCAF	LAC	BRADWELL	07/03/42			PENDING
CLARK, DONALD	ARMY	PTE	SASKATOON	01/08/44	59°51'	108°45'	CLARK CHANNEL	COOK, GILBERT L.	ARMY	PTE	PRINCE ALBERT	10/10/44	57°31'	103°27'	COOK LAKE
CLARK, JOHN F.	ARMY	TPR	MITCHELLTON	25/11/45	58°38'	102°01'	CLARK LAKE	COOK, HOWARD J.	RCAF	PO	HILLMOND	25/11/44			PENDING
CLARK, LESLIE W.	ARMY	TPR	SASKATOON	06/10/43	59°50'	108°44'	CLARK ISLAND	COOK, JOHN EDWARD	NAVY	STO1	LAFLECHE	25/06/40	56°57'	103°43'	COOK PENINSULA
CLARK, NEIL N.	ARMY	SGT	AVONLEA	27/02/45	55°27'	102°10'	CLARK BAY	COOK, R.J.	ARMY	GNR	UNKNOWN	25/02/45	55°19'	105°42'	COOK BAY
CLARK, ROBERT G.	ARMY	PTE	CHELAN	20/12/44	53°47'	102°28'	CLARK BAY	COOK, RUSSELL G.	RCAF	FO	HAZENMORE	09/04/43	55°04'	104°58'	COOK ISLAND
CLARK, SAMUEL S.	RCAF	PO	RADISSON	29/11/42	59°39'	108°36'	CLARK LAKE	COOK, VICTOR E.	RCAF	WO1	UNKNOWN	08/10/43	59°56'	109°27'	COOK LAKE
CLARK, WALLACE E.	ARMY	CFN	PONTEIX	29/10/44	59°23'	107°28'	CLARK ISLAND	COOK, WILLIAM H.	RCAF	FS	MOOSE JAW	03/02/45	55°37'	106°28'	COOK ISLAND
CLARK, WESLEY M.	ARMY	GNR	REGINA	05/05/45	56°57'	103°24'	CLARK ISLAND	COOKE, DWIGHT RUSSEL	NAVY	STO PO	SASKATOON	07/05/44	56°17'	105°17'	COOKE LAKE
CLARKE, DONALD M.	RCAF	PO	HAZENMORE	22/04/43	54°44'	103°33'	CLARKE POINT	COOKE, JAMES R.	ARMY	PTE	DIVISION 8	25/07/44	56°59'	102°18'	COOKE ISLAND
CLARKE, JAMES A.	ARMY	PTE	ESTEVAN	19/08/42	55°09'	104°49'	CLARKE ISLAND	COOMBE, ROY F.	ARMY	CPL	PRINCE ALBERT	21/03/44	55°48'	103°48'	COOMBE LAKE
CLARKE, SAMUEL E.	RCAF	FS	PARKSIDE	26/11/43	55°27'	105°37'	CLARKE LAKE	COOPER, ALLAN E.	RCAF	SGT	FORT QU'APPELLE	07/11/44	55°49'	107°12'	COOPER CREEK
CLARKE, THOMAS H.	ARMY	PTE	DAVIDSON	29/10/44	59°03'	103°34'	CLARKE ISLAND	COOPER, ARTHUR D.	RCAF	FS	REGINA	15/09/42	57°50'	105°03'	COOPER LAKE
CLARKE, WILLIAM R.	RCAF	WO2	WATROUS	02/12/43	56°03'	102°24'	CLARKE RAPIDS	COOPER, EUGENE J.	RCAF	FS	SASKATOON	23/09/43			PENDING
CLAVELLE, ALFRED F.	ARMY	GNR	WHITEWOOD	06/06/44	59°36'	108°55'	CLAVELLE LAKE	COOPER, WILFRED H.	ARMY	PTE	BRADDOCK	18/12/43	59°10'	102°51'	COOPER LAKE
CLEARWATER, RAY L.	RCAF	FL	WEYBURN	14/10/44	59°41'	108°38'	CLEARWATER BAY	COOPER, WILLIAM R.	ARMY	CAPT	MOOSE JAW	15/01/45	54°58'	102°42'	COOPER LAKE
CLEMENT, HARRY	RCAF	SGT	MARCELIN	16/08/43	55°42'	103°20'	CLEMENT LAKE	COPELAND, BEN B.	RCAF	SGT	MOOSE JAW	01/10/42	60°00'	105°06'	COPELAND LAKE
CLEMENTS, DESMOND B.	RCAF	FO	SWIFT CURRENT	09/11/42	57°03'	107°28'	CLEMENTS LAKE	COPELAND, MELVILLE	ARMY	PTE	SENLAC	20/07/44	55°13'	103°40'	COPELAND LAKE
CLEVELAND, ARCHIE V.	RCAF	SGT	NIPAWIN	26/07/43	58°27'	103°12'	CLEVELAND ISLAND	COPPIN, CLIFFORD S.	RCAF	FO	KAMSACK	15/09/46	57°51'	109°02'	COPPIN LAKE
CLINE, WESLEY R.	RCAF	SGT	ZELMA	22/08/44	55°20'	104°05'	CLINE LAKE	CORCK, ARTHUR G.	RCAF	FO	REGINA	08/07/44	59°06'	105°15'	CORCK LAKES
CLOSE, KEITH C.	ARMY	PTE	MORSE	08/02/44	57°53'	104°57'	CLOSE LAKE	CORMAN, JOHN R.M.	RCAF	SGT	WILLOWS	01/07/44	55°37'	105°32'	CORMAN ISLAND
CLOUT, HARRY C.	ARMY	PTE	SALTER	26/10/44	55°26'	104°12'	CLOUT LAKE	CORNELL, JOHN L.	RCAF	SGT	MOOSE JAW	28/12/42	56°07'	105°32'	CORNELL CREEK
CLOWES, FRANK	ARMY	CPL	REGINA	19/08/42	57°20'	107°39'	CLOWES LAKE	CORNELL, WILLIAM F.	ARMY	GNR	NORTH BATTLEFORD	14/09/44	55°13'	102°18'	CORNELL BAY
CLUFF, JOHN M.	RCAF	FS	SASKATOON	22/12/41	58°22'	109°34'	CLUFF LAKE	CORNER, ROY H.	RCAF	CPL	LAC VERT	12/12/42	55°57'	105°57'	CORNER LAKE
COADY, JOHN A.	ARMY	PTE	LUSELAND	09/10/42	55°24'	104°44'	COADY LAKE	CORNWELL, GEORGE F.	RCAF	FL	WATROUS	06/09/44	56°18'	105°54'	CORNWELL LAKE
COATES, ALLAN C.J.	RCAF	CPL	MELFORT	01/06/43	57°17'	102°14'	COATES ISLAND	CORSON, WILLIAM	ARMY	SGT	WAWOTA	19/08/42	58°44'	103°45'	CORSON LAKE
COATES, PERCY H.	RCAF	FO	SENLAC	04/09/43	57°53'	108°41'	COATES LAKE	COSFORD, JOHN E.	RCAF	WO1	SIMPSON	08/06/43	55°52'	104°45'	COSFORD LAKE
COBB, FLOYD B.	RCAF	PO	OUTLOOK	17/03/42	54°33'	104°52'	COBB LAKE	COSGRAVE, FRANCIS W.G.	RCAF	FS	WHITEWOOD	26/11/44	57°17'	107°17'	COSGRAVE LAKE
COCHRANE, ARNOLD W.	RCAF	WO2	CREELMAN	02/03/43	55°17'	104°58'	COCHRANE BAY	COSLETT, THOMAS O. D.	ARMY	PTE	DIVISION 5	03/03/45	57°46'	108°09'	COSLETT LAKE

Name	Branch	Rank	Hometown	Casualty Date	Latitude	Longitude	Geo-Memorial
COTE, EDWARD G.	ARMY	A CPL	DELMAS	26/02/45	55°27'	104°53'	COTE LAKE
COTE, JOSEPH R.	RCAF	FS	LAMPMAN	02/10/43	60°01'	103°48'	COTE LAKE
COTTER, DAVID GRENFELL	RCAF	PO	WILKIE	13/01/45	55°31'	106°18'	COTTER LAKE
COUBROUGH, GEORGE T.	RCAF	FS	CORONACH	30/11/42	55°04'	104°35'	COUBROUGH LAKE
COUGHLIN, JAMES T.	ARMY	SGT	VANSCOY	15/07/44	59°23'	105°36'	COUGHLIN LAKE
COULTER, HARVEY A.	ARMY	L CPL	ROCANVILLE	19/08/42	56°25'	103°29'	COULTER LAKE
COUPLAND, THOMAS K.	RCAF	PO	GOLDEN RIDGE	07/08/41	54°42'	108°57'	COUPLAND LAKE
COURTENAY, KENNETH W.	ARMY	PTE	REGINA	12/01/45	57°24'	103°58'	COURTENAY LAKE
COVE, THOMAS A.	ARMY	C S M	GRENFELL	11/06/43	57°55'	108°24'	COVE LAKE
COWAN, CHARLES W.	ARMY	L CPL	SHAND	08/08/44	55°11'	104°47'	COWAN ISLAND
COWAN, MURRAY ALLAN	NAVY	LDG STO	YORKTON	10/02/42	56°54'	103°54'	COWAN RAPIDS
COWARD, WILLIAM J.	RCAF	WO1	REGINA	11/11/44	59°39'	108°32'	COWARD ISLAND
COWIE, DONALD M.	ARMY	CAPT	SASKATOON	18/09/44	57°10'	102°43'	COWIE LAKE
COYLE, ALFRED S.	ARMY	GNR	PLEASANTDALE	26/08/44	56°45'	103°34'	COYLE LAKE
CRAIG, DOUGLAS E.	RCAF	CPL	SASKATOON	04/06/41	57°22'	108°33'	CRAIG LAKE
CRAIG, JOHN F.	ARMY	PTE	TISDALE	03/11/44	57°17'	103°02'	CRAIG ISLAND
CRAIG, LORNE W.	ARMY	CPL	STAR CITY	25/09/44	54°39'	102°06'	CRAIG ISLAND
CRAIG, LYLE L.	ARMY	TPR	PADDOCKWOOD	19/04/45	54°38'	101°52'	CRAIG LAKE
CRAIK, DAVID S.	RCAF	SGT	MOOSE JAW	15/01/41	55°36'	105°24'	CRAIK ISLAND
CRAMPEAN, NEIL G.	ARMY	GNR	WAWOTA	27/09/44	58°15'	102°54'	CRAMPEAN LAKE
CRANE, WILBURT M.	RCAF	FS	WEYBURN	15/05/42	57°50'	102°23'	CRANE ISLAND
CRANG, WILLIAM REGINALD	NAVY	AB	WILKIE	14/02/45	54°33'	102°44'	CRANG LAKE
CRATTY, THOMAS B.	ARMY	L CPL	ANGLIA	04/07/44	55°41'	104°16'	CRATTY LAKE
CRAWFORD, GEORGE W.	ARMY	RFN	TURTLEFORD	27/09/44	53°14'	108°48'	CRAWFORD CREEK
CRAWFORD, THOMAS A.	RCAF	FS	HARRIS	06/05/42	57°25'	105°50'	CRAWFORD LAKE
CRAWFORD, WILLIAM B.	ARMY	B S M	PRINCE ALBERT	22/06/42	54°49'	102°54'	CRAWFORD LAKE
CREIGHTON, ALLAN D.	RCAF	PO	LUSELAND	22/06/44	55°12'	104°47'	CREIGHTON ISLAND
CRELLIN, CHARLES M.	ARMY	PTE	WELWYN	20/12/44	57°58'	108°36'	CRELLIN LAKE
CREMER, EDWARD B.	RCAF	LAC	DIVISION 5	17/02/41	59°59'	109°52'	CREMER LAKES
CRESSMAN, CHARLES H.	RCAF	FO	CEYLON	21/09/44	59°59'	109°08'	CRESSMAN LAKE
CRESWELL, GEORGE E.	RCAF	FO	WADENA	21/02/45	56°34'	103°12'	CRESWELL BAY
CREW, BASIL G.	RCAF	SL	WAWOTA	05/01/45	55°39'	105°08'	CREW LAKE
CRICH, HARVEY L.	ARMY	SGT	GRIFFIN	19/08/41	55°01'	104°45'	CRICH LAKE
CRICHTON, CHARLES W.D.	RCAF	FS	MOOSE JAW	07/03/42	58°44'	106°59'	CRICHTON LAKE
CRICHTON, DONALD J.	ARMY	PTE	REGINA	28/02/45	58°46'	108°17'	CRICHTON CREEK
CRIMES, RICHARD G.	ARMY	CAPT	MAPLE CREEK	24/05/44	57°58'	102°17'	CRIMES LAKE
CROCKETT, WILLIAM V.	RCAF	WO2	RIDGEDALE	13/11/43	57°16'	107°36'	CROCKETT LAKE
CROMPTON, RICHARD C.	RCAF	FO	REGINA	29/01/44	60°00'	107°14'	CROMPTON LAKE
CROSS, ALBERT JAMES	NAVY	AB	YORKTON	14/02/45	59°21'	105°16'	CROSS LAKE
CROSS, ARTHUR L.	RCAF	WO2	MELVILLE	29/01/43	57°52'	102°41'	CROSS ISLAND
CROSS, HERBERT H.	ARMY	PTE	GLENAVON	13/12/44	56°47'	103°02'	CROSS LAKE
CROSS, STANLEY N.	ARMY	L BDR	SALTCOATS	01/09/44	56°46'	103°04'	CROSS BAY
CROWE, LEO R.	RCAF	WO2	CARLETON	08/04/43	55°59'	104°44'	CROWE LAKE
CROZIER, LLOYD D.J.	RCAF	SGT	CARNDUFF	23/03/42	56°42'	108°12'	CROZIER BAY
CROZIER, WILLIAM J.	RCAF	FS	EDAM	03/08/43	58°32'	103°11'	CROZIER ISLAND
CRUMP, EDWARD R.	RCAF	LAC	REGINA	05/02/43	56°19'	108°02'	CRUMP ISLAND
CRUMP, JOHN C.	RCAF	SGT	REGINA	24/07/41	58°27'	106°02'	CRUMP LAKE
CULHAM, ANDREW N.	ARMY	SGT	UNITY	29/01/44	55°29'	104°25'	CULHAM LAKE
CUMING, LLOYD W.	RCAF	PO	GLENAVON	27/01/44	60°00'	108°48'	CUMING LAKE
CUMMINE, GORDON	RCAF	FS	SASKATOON	29/12/43	59°57'	108°59'	CUMMINE LAKE
CUMMING, ALISTER G.	RCAF	FS	FOAM LAKE	06/11/42	55°16'	104°05'	CUMMING LAKE
CUMMING, ROBERT M.	ARMY	GNR	DIVISION 9	25/04/43	56°13'	103°02'	CUMMING LAKE
CUMMING, ROBERT S.	ARMY	RFN	SASKATOON	29/03/45	59°21'	105°28'	CUMMING LAKE
CUNNING, WALTER A.	ARMY	A Q M S	REGINA	06/11/44	56°21'	103°22'	CUNNING LAKE
CUNNINGHAM, FRANCIS L.	RCAF	PO	NORTH BATTLEFORD	01/10/42			PENDING
CUNNINGHAM, FRANK	RCAF	FS	NORTH BATTLEFORD	22/10/43	57°29'	105°51'	CUNNINGHAM LAKES
CUNNINGHAM, MERL	ARMY	A CPL	BIRCH HILLS	14/08/44	55°03'	102°16'	CUNNINGHAM LAKE
CUNNINGS, RONALD E.	RCAF	SGT	MAJOR	29/02/44	55°07'	107°50'	CUNNINGS LAKE
CURRIE, ARCHIEBALD W.	ARMY	TPR	MORIN CREEK	11/08/45	56°10'	102°03'	CURRIE LAKE
CURRIE, ARTHUR A.	RCAF	PO	NETHERHILL	31/07/42	57°35'	106°15'	CURRIE ISLAND
CURRIE, GORDON	RCAF	PO	SONNINGDALE	21/01/44	59°40'	108°36'	CURRIE LAKE
CURRIE, STANLEY K.	ARMY	PTE	SASKATOON	18/09/44	56°50'	103°39'	CURRIE BAY
CUSHING, CLIFFORD J.	ARMY	L CPL	REGINA	30/07/44	58°14'	104°41'	CUSHING CREEK
CUSHON, GEORGE R.	RCAF	PO	OXBOW	17/06/41	55°52'	104°19'	CUSHON BAY
CUTHILL, EDWIN O.	RCAF	LAC	FLEMING	06/09/44	59°40'	108°39'	CUTHILL LAKE
CUTLER, RONALD A.J.	ARMY	RFN	MOOSOMIN	06/06/44	59°38'	108°28'	CUTLER LAKE
CYBULSKI, STANLEY J.	RCAF	FL	REGINA	21/12/42	59°59'	103°43'	CYBULSKI LAKE
DAGG, ARCHIE	ARMY	SPR	NORTH BATTLEFORD	04/10/44	53°09'	102°44'	DAGG LAKE
DAHL, CALVIN W.	RCAF	FS	MELVILLE	02/04/43	58°25'	103°15'	DAHL POINT
DAHL, CARL M.	ARMY	SPR	LOVERNA	18/09/44	53°10'	102°34'	DAHL LAKE
DAHL, WILLIAM E.	ARMY	PTE	BIRCH HILLS	23/12/43	57°30'	106°12'	DAHL ISLAND
DAHLE, TRUMAN H.	RCAF	FO	ATWATER	17/08/44	57°32'	109°13'	DAHLE LAKE
DAKIN, THOMAS D.	RCAF	SGT	REGINA	23/03/42	54°42'	109°46'	DAKIN LAKE
DALGLIESH, LLOYD G.	RCAF	PO	GOODWATER	06/01/44	60°01'	108°57'	DALGLIESH LAKE
DALSHAUG, ERNEST W.	ARMY	RFN	BUCHANAN	06/06/44	56°45'	106°16'	DALSHAUG LAKE
DALTON, GORDON E.	RCAF	FS	REGINA	03/10/43	60°00'	104°37'	DALTON ISLAND
DALY, JAMES T.	RCAF	FO	REGINA	29/07/44	55°51'	104°07'	DALY ISLAND
DALY, PATRICK M.	ARMY	RFN	PRINCE ALBERT	08/06/44	59°36'	109°36'	DALY LAKE
DANCHUK, WILLIAM	ARMY	PTE	REGINA	19/08/42	58°43'	106°56'	DANCHUK LAKE
DANFORTH, GORDON A.	ARMY	PTE	FILLMORE	19/08/42	60°01'	102°53'	DANFORTH LAKES
DANIELS, BILL A.	ARMY	RFN	BALCARRES	06/06/44	59°37'	108°18'	DANIELS LAKE
DANIELS, EDWARD J.	RCAF	LAC	LAFLECHE	16/01/43	58°53'	102°38'	DANIELS BAY
DANIELS, WILLIAM	ARMY	RFN	DIVISION 16	22/04/45	56°07'	102°03'	DANIELS LAKE
DANIELSON, DANIEL G.	RCAF	FO	STRASBOURG	30/08/44	56°23'	107°37'	DANIELSON LAKE
DANIELSON, MELVIN A.	ARMY	TPR	STOCKHOLM	27/10/44	56°53'	103°08'	DANIELSON BAY
DARBY, ALAN	RCAF	FS	WEYBURN	07/05/43	57°22'	106°22'	DARBY BAY
DARLING, SIDNEY	ARMY	LIEUT	REGINA	07/06/43	59°52'	103°37'	DARLING LAKE
DARNELL, RALPH V.	ARMY	RFN	DIVISION 16	18/09/44	55°58'	105°57'	DARNELL LAKE
DASCHUK, BILLY	RCAF	SGT	PREECEVILLE	13/07/43	58°50'	102°11'	DASCHUK LAKE
DAUK, HIRONIMUS D.A.	RCAF	FS	ANNAHEIM	02/10/43	58°12'	102°13'	DAUK LAKE
DAUTREMONT, LOUIS S.	ARMY	PTE	ALIDA	21/04/45	58°17'	107°00'	DAUTREMONT LAKE
DAVENPORT, HAROLD	RCAF	SGT	SASKATOON	30/03/43	59°39'	106°17'	DAVENPORT LAKE
DAVENPORT, JOHN J.	RCAF	FS	SASKATOON	13/04/42	56°24'	108°15'	DAVENPORT BAY
DAVID, JOHN M.	RCAF	FO	SASKATOON	18/10/43	56°27'	106°25'	DAVID RAPIDS
DAVIDSON, KEITH B.	RCAF	FS	LUSELAND	12/06/43	57°42'	109°48'	DAVIDSON RIVER
DAVIDSON, LEONARD H.	RCAF	LAC	REGINA	21/08/42	53°03'	109°31'	DAVIDSON COULEE
DAVIDSON, MARVIN	ARMY	TPR	WYNYARD	01/10/44	57°34'	106°38'	DAVIDSON ISLAND
DAVIE, JOHN	ARMY	CPL	REGINA	02/04/46	59°28'	109°02'	DAVIE ISLAND
DAVIES, ANTHONY J.	RCAF	FO	LLOYDMINSTER	17/12/43			PENDING
DAVIES, CHARLES	ARMY	SPR	QU'APPELLE	19/02/45	59°28'	108°17'	DAVIES BAY
DAVIES, EDMUND A.J.	RCAF	PO	TISDALE	17/12/44	54°36'	106°43'	DAVIES LAKE
DAVIES, LEONARD G.	ARMY	CPL	YORKTON	09/04/45	59°17'	102°49'	DAVIES LAKE
DAVIES, LEONARD O.	ARMY	PTE	ABERNETHY	19/08/42	57°36'	106°09'	DAVIES ISLAND
DAVIES, LESLIE J.	ARMY	PTE	SPRINGSIDE	15/01/41	56°28'	103°58'	DAVIES LAKE
DAVIES, WALTER C.	RCAF	FO	ASQUITH	16/06/43	57°16'	105°50'	DAVIES CREEK
DAVIS, ERNEST L.	RCAF	PO	WEBB	16/01/45	56°24'	107°21'	DAVIS ISLAND
DAVISON, WILLIAM W.	ARMY	PTE	DIVISION 4	19/08/42	59°29'	105°46'	DAVISON LAKE
DAVY, HENRY W.	RCAF	WO1	PRINCE ALBERT	24/06/44	58°53'	108°18'	DAVY LAKE
DAW, LAURENCE F.	RCAF	WO2	KELLIHER	01/06/43	59°28'	108°46'	DAW LAKE
DAWSON, CHARLES	ARMY	PTE	DIVISION 12	06/05/43	57°26'	103°33'	DAWSON LAKE
DAYMAN, GEORGE H.	ARMY	RFN	WINDTHORST	06/06/44	57°58'	108°30'	DAYMAN LAKE
DE ARMOND, GORDON LEE	NAVY	LDG SMN	SASKATOON	29/04/44	56°01'	104°27'	DE ARMOND LAKE
DE BALINHARD, JOHN S.C.	ARMY	LIEUT	YORKTON	28/07/43	54°29'	109°11'	DE BALINHARD LAKE
DE LA RONDE, PAUL	ARMY	CPL	MEADOW LAKE	18/05/44	54°33'	108°37'	DE LA RONDE CREEK
DE NEVERS, FRANK H.	RCAF	PO	VANDURA	14/09/42	60°00'	106°59'	DE NEVERS LAKE
DEACON, DONALD J.	ARMY	RFN	REGINA	01/08/43	59°18'	103°16'	DEACON ISLAND
DEATHERAGE, GEORGE E.	RCAF	PO	SMILEY	17/12/44	59°50'	102°31'	DEATHERAGE BAY
DEATHERAGE, WALTER D.	RCAF	SGT	SMILEY	10/09/44	59°50'	102°31'	DEATHERAGE BAY
DEBUSSAC, GEORGE H.	RCAF	PO	LYDDEN	22/06/43	59°02'	109°39'	DEBUSSAC CREEK
DEERING, VERNON J.	RCAF	SGT	COLGATE	01/05/43	58°24'	102°05'	DEERING LAKE
DEGRYSE, ERNEST N.	ARMY	GNR	LANGENBURG	28/08/44	55°35'	106°57'	DEGRYSE LAKE
DEITSCH, LAWRENCE H.	ARMY	PTE	ROSETOWN	31/07/43	56°51'	103°09'	DEITSCH LAKE
DELAMERE, EDWARD J.	ARMY	PTE	HAGUE	25/06/44	59°58'	109°56'	DELAMERE LAKE
DELHAYE, ROGER A.	RCAF	AC	REGINA	18/11/44	59°07'	103°02'	DELHAYE LAKE
DELL, RONALD F.	RCAF	FO	CHAPLIN	30/08/44	57°36'	108°51'	DELL LAKE
DELMAGE, RAY J.	RCAF	PO	HAZEL CLIFFE	24/09/44	60°03'	102°57'	DELMAGE RIVER
DELORME, JOHN B.	ARMY	RFN	PRINCE ALBERT	06/06/44	57°14'	103°51'	DELORME BAY
DELORME, LOUIS T.	RCAF	SGT	LEBRET	31/05/43	54°50'	102°53'	DELORME LAKE

Name	Branch	Rank	Hometown	Casualty Date	Latitude	Longitude	Geo-Memorial
DEMCHENKO, MAX E.	ARMY	L CPL	MAPLE CREEK	31/08/44	55°03'	105°18'	DEMCHENKO LAKE
DEMPSEY, DAGNALL T.	ARMY	PTE	NEVILLE	19/08/42	59°22'	107°26'	DEMPSEY BAY
DEMPSTER, RICHARD	RCAF	SGT	MELVILLE	23/09/43	57°50'	106°58'	DEMPSTER LAKE
DENNIS, FRANCIS B.	RCAF	WO2	MOOSE JAW	18/04/44	59°40'	108°42'	DENNIS ISLAND
DENNIS, RUSSEL E.	RCAF	PO	PARKMAN	10/06/44	57°37'	109°06'	DENNIS LAKE
DENNISON, GORDON J.	RCAF	PO	WILLOWS	16/09/44	54°05'	102°10'	DENNISON BAY
DEPPER, CLIFFORD L.	RCAF	PO	SASKATOON	22/01/44	57°33	109°06'	DEPPER LAKE
DERBYSHIRE, GEORGE E.	RCAF	FS	WILLOWS	04/09/44	56°14'	108°38'	DERBYSHIRE LAKE
DERKSON, WILLIAM E.	ARMY	PTE	RADISSON	27/07/44	57°42'	109°01'	DERKSON LAKE
DERMODY, BERNARD	RCAF	SGT	KENNEDY	15/11/41	59°29'	108°43'	DERMODY LAKE
DESCHAMPS, JOSEPH A.	RAF	PO	ARDATH	17/01/41			PENDING
DESJARDINS, JOSEPH E.	RCAF	SGT	CLIMAX	17/10/42	59°58'	109°38'	DESJARDINS LAKE
DESJARDINS, MARCEL E.	ARMY	A CPL	PASCAL	08/10/44	55°C9'	103°25'	DESJARDINS LAKE
DESJARLAIS, MATHEW J.	ARMY	RFN	DIVISION 6	06/06/44	59°41'	108°35'	DEJARLAIS LAKE
DESNOMIE, JOSEPH N.	ARMY	PTE	FILE HILLS	29/09/44	56°58'	106°46'	DESNOMIE LAKES
DEVLIN, LOUIS J.	RCAF	FS	DRUID	30/05/42	59°25'	108°21'	DEVLIN ISLAND
DEWAR, FRANCIS I.	ARMY	PTE	MELVILLE	08/06/44	59°37'	108°32'	DEWAR ISLAND
DEWAR, MURRAY S.	RCAF	SGT	HOOSIER	11/01/43	57°47'	107°47'	DEWAR LAKE
DEWAR, PETER	RCAF	PO	MOOSE JAW	13/05/44			PENDING
DEXTER, STAN. R.	ARMY	LB	MOOSE JAW	25/10/40	55°24'	105°36'	DEXTER LAKE
DEZALL, ARTHUR E.	ARMY	A SGT	MONT NEBO	15/12/43	59°45'	108°15'	DEZALL LAKE
DEZALL, RAYMOND P.	RCAF	PO	MONT NEBO	29/05/42			PENDING
DEZORT, OTTO L.	ARMY	L CPL	DINSMOFE	10/03/44	55°06'	102°17'	DEZORT LAKE
DICKIN, GLEN D.	ARMY	LIEUT	MANOR	06/06/44	53°35'	104°19'	DICKIN ISLAND
DICKIN, LEONARD L.	ARMY	MAJ	SASKATOON	31/10/44	55°57'	104°44'	DICKIN LAKE
DICKSON, HARRY E.	ARMY	CAPT	SWIFT CURRENT	13/08/44	56°34'	103°49'	DICKSON ISLAND
DICUS, HARVEY E.	ARMY	PTE	LEASK	19/08/42	56°06'	104°03'	DICUS LAKE
DILWORTH, GORDON A.	RCAF	AC1	RUSH LAKE	03/06/41	58°16'	107°25'	DILWORTH LAKE
DILWORTH, JAMES R.	ARMY	PTE	GULL LAKE	13/09/44	52°46'	101°59'	DILWORTH CREEK
DIMICK, HAROLD W.	ARMY	PTE	HARRIS	15/08/44	57°01'	107°34'	DIMICK LAKE
DINGWALL, FRED T.	RCAF	PO	ASQUITH	30/05/44	55°29'	104°36'	DINGWALL LAKE
DINNIE, ALEXANDER	ARMY	C S M	LLOYDMINSTER	04/07/46	60°01'	107°08'	DINNIE LAKE
DIONNE, EDMOND	ARMY	GNR	MEADOW LAKE	19/07/42	59°59'	102°20'	DIONNE LAKE
DIRKS, WILLIAM M.	ARMY	A CAPT	PRINCE ALBERT	06/06/44	53°57'	103°57'	DIRKS LAKE
DIXON, ALBERT	RCAF	SGT	MOOSE JAW	13/06/43	59°23'	108°48'	DIXON BAY
DIXON, ALFRED R.	RCAF	FS	NEUDORF	03/07/43	57°13'	102°36'	DIXON ISLAND
DIXON, CHESTER B.	RCAF	PO	MAPLE CREEK	27/04/43	57°29'	109°11'	DIXON LAKE
DIXON, GARTH L.	RCAF	SGT	TOMFKINS	13/09/42	57°22'	106°51'	DIXON ISLAND
DMYTRUK, PETER	RCAF	FS	WYNYARD	09/12/43	57°47'	106°58'	DMYTRUK LAKE
DOBSON, WILLIAM A.	ARMY	TPR	MELFORT	20/10/41	57°42'	102°49'	DOBSON LAKE
DOCKERILL, FREDERICK J.	ARMY	CPL	FENWOOD	22/05/44	55°38'	107°14'	DOCKERILL LAKE
DOCKERILL, JOHN P.	RCAF	PO	FENWOOD	22/06/43	59°42'	108°18'	DOCKERILL LAKE
DODD, THOMAS W.	RCAF	PO	SINNETT	22/01/44	59°40'	109°10'	DODD LAKE
DODDS, GILBERT D.	RCAF	SGT	NORTH BATTLEFORD	01/08/41	59°34'	108°03'	DODDS LAKE
DODDS, ROLAND	ARMY	PTE	ANEROID	28/08/44	55°14'	104°40'	DODDS ISLAND
DOERKSEN, ABRAHAM W.	ARMY	PTE	RUSH LAKE	26/03/43	55°57'	103°43'	DOERKSEN BAY
DOHOO, ERNEST G.	RCAF	LAC	DELISLE	14/08/45	59°28'	108°41'	DOHOO LAKE
DOMINAS, EDWARD R.	ARMY	PTE	NIPAWIN	13/10/44	60°01'	109°33'	DOMINAS LAKE
DONALDSON, JAMES	RCAF	WO2	REGINA	05/02/44	55°41'	104°49'	DONALDSON LAKE
DONNELLY, EARL B.	RCAF	WO2	MACKLIN	22/09/43	59°45'	106°18'	DONNELLY LAKE
DORRELL, MATTHEW	RCAF	PO	BULYEA	02/11/44	60°00'	106°47'	DORRELL LAKE
DORWARD, HENRY D.	ARMY	A SGT	RIDGEDALE	08/04/45	57°50'	103°57'	DORWARD BAY
DOUCET, JOACHIM R.	ARMY	PTE	REGINA	14/08/44	56°54'	102°25'	DOUCET LAKE
DOUGHERTY, FRANKLIN E.	ARMY	TPR	DAFOE	23/02/45	55°04'	102°18'	DOUGHERTY LAKE
DOUGLAS, HARRY L.	RCAF	SGT	HERSCHEL	07/09/01			PENDING
DOUGLAS, WILLIAM E.	RCAF	WO2	BALCARRES	26/05/43	57°39'	104°28'	DOUGLAS LAKE
DOWD, MORTIMER J.	RCAF	FO	DENZIL	25/09/43	54°36'	104°41'	DOWD LAKES
DOWD, PHILIPP	RCAF	FO	DENZIL	22/03/44	54°32'	104°30'	DOWD CREEK
DOWLER, NORMAN G.	RCAF	WO2	SASKATOON	20/01/44	58°53'	109°50'	DOWLER LAKE
DOWNTON, JOHN E.L.	RCAF	FS	WILCOX	25/06/42	55°08'	105°14'	DOWNTON LAKE
DOWSON, JAMES C.	ARMY	L CPL	WHITEWOOD	12/02/45	59°31'	108°57'	DOWSON BAY
DRAKE, JAMES M.	RCAF	PO	MEDSTEAD	26/12/44	52°27'	109°56'	DRAKE LAKE
DRAMNITZKE, ELDORE	RCAF	PO	WILLOWBROOK	20/02/44	59°24'	104°51'	DRAMNITZKE BAY
DRANSFIELD, HARRY C.	ARMY	RFN	CARLYLE	05/07/44	58°22'	103°11'	DRANSFIELD ISLAND
DRAPER, ROBERT A.C.	RCAF	FO	REGINA	18/04/42	59°31'	109°02'	DRAPER LAKES
DRAPER, THOMAS W.	RCAF	SGT	SASKATOON	18/09/43	56°13'	106°19'	DRAPER BAY
DREAVER, HARVEY	ARMY	A SGT	MISTAWASIS	06/10/44	55°53'	104°47'	DREAVER LAKE
DREGER, FREDRICH R.	RCAF	WO2	WOODLEY	13/06/44	55°45'	106°45'	DREGER LAKE
DREVER, ROLAND A.	ARMY	RFN	MESKANAW	27/08/44	56°47'	102°28'	DREVER ISLAND
DREW, WENDELL P.	RCAF	FO	RADISSON	29/07/44	55°59'	105°31'	DREW LAKE
DREYER, RAYMOND W.	RCAF	FS	YORKTON	15/05/42	56°20'	106°06'	DREYER LAKE
DRISCOLL, STANLEY ALBERT	RCAF	PO	SHAUNAVON	09/10/43	55°10'	104°40'	DRISCOLL ISLAND
DRISCOLL, THOMAS J.	RCAF	FS	COLEVILLE	06/08/43	55°36'	104°13'	DRISCOLL LAKE
DROPE, WILLIAM J.	RCAF	FL	REGINA	07/06/44	55°26'	104°28'	DROPE LAKE
DRUMMOND, NEVILLE S.	ARMY	LIEUT	MOOSOMIN	04/01/45	55°51'	104°35'	DRUMMOND LAKE
DUBE, LAURENZO J.	ARMY	TPR	MELFORT	30/03/44	58°35'	105°04'	DUBE LAKE
DUBETS, JOHN	ARMY	PTE	SASKATOON	21/04/41	57°53'	108°20'	DUBETS LAKE
DUBOIS, WILLIAM	ARMY	SPR	TURTLEFORD	09/09/43	59°42'	108°10'	DUBOIS LAKE
DUCKER, BENJAMIN V.L.	RCAF	WO2	LASHBURN	27/03/43	55°39'	104°33'	DUCKER LAKE
DUCKETT, DENYS R.	ARMY	PTE	KERROBERT	25/07/43	59°41'	105°46'	DUCKETT BAY
DUFFIELD, MURRAY D.	ARMY	PTE	SEMANS	22/09/44	56°53'	103°02'	DUFFIELD LAKE
DUFFY, FRANCIS J.	RCAF	FS	ROSTHERN	27/04/43	59°23'	108°52'	DUFFY ISLAND
DUKART, JOHN	ARMY	PTE	ESTEVAN	28/08/44	54°03'	106°56'	DUKART LAKE
DUMAS, MAURICE G.	ARMY	PTE	SPIRITWOOD	24/04/45	59°34'	105°28'	DUMAS LAKE
DUMMER, HENRY	ARMY	L CPL	REGINA	31/12/44	56°59'	107°47'	DUMMER LAKE
DUMONT, JOHN D.	ARMY	TPR	FILE HILLS	11/06/44	56°49'	107°07'	DUMONT FALLS
DUMVILLE, GORDON	RCAF	FO	ROCANVILLE	06/07/44	59°03'	109°38'	DUMVILLE CREEK
DUNAE, ALEXANDER	RCAF	WO2	RABBIT LAKE	23/05/44	59°27'	106°02'	DUNAE LAKE
DUNAJSKI, FRANCIS X.J.	RCAF	FS	DILKE	13/01/42	55°00'	104°37'	DUNAJSKI LAKE
DUNAND, EMILE J. F.	RCAF	FO	VAL MARIE	02/02/43	59°18'	103°54'	DUNAND LAKE
DUNAND, MARCEL J.F.	ARMY	PTE	VAL MARIE	24/09/44	58°06'	102°00'	DUNAND ISLAND
DUNBAR, EDGAR J.	ARMY	L CPL	EATONIA	20/03/45	59°28'	108°18'	DUNBAR BAY
DUNBAR, RONALD	RCAF	WO2	SHAUNAVON	13/03/43	55°10'	104°39'	DUNBAR POINT
DUNBAR, WILLIAM P.	RCAF	SGT	BIGGAR	16/03/44	57°24'	107°10'	DUNBAR FALLS
DUNCAN, GEORGE RUSSELL	ARMY	SAPPER	SEMANS	07/11/44	56°05'	105°11'	DUNCAN LAKE
DUNCAN, MERVYN	RCAF	FS	MOOSE JAW	26/03/42	55°34'	102°46'	DUNCAN ISLAND
DUNCAN, WILLIAM WALTER	RCAF	WO1	LEASK	16/02/44	57°34'	104°15'	DUNCAN LAKE
DUNLOP, JAMES MATHER	RCAF	FS		07/09/42			PENDING
DUNLOP, JOHN G.	RCAF	PO	GRONLID	15/11/41	57°27'	102°23'	DUNLOP ISLAND
DUNLOP, LAWRENCE G.	RCAF	FO	MAZENOD	07/09/43	57°34'	107°02'	DUNLOP BAY
DUNN, DENNIS C.	ARMY	PTE	KERROBERT	24/07/45	58°33'	105°01'	DUNN LAKE
DUNN, EDRIC L.	RCAF	SGT	KINCAID	24/09/44	56°23'	102°05'	DUNN BAY
DUNN, EUSTACE H.	RCAF	SGT	BURNHAM	23/07/42	56°11'	105°11'	DUNN LAKE
DUNN, GORDON M.	RCAF	WO2	REGINA	13/12/42	55°31'	104°34'	DUNN ISLAND
DUNN, LORNE S.	ARMY	PTE	CORNING	08/08/44	55°53'	102°20'	DUNN LAKE
DUPRÉ, FREDERICK L.E.	RCAF	PO	GOLDFIELDS	29/03/43	57°08'	109°15'	DUPRÉ LAKE
DUPUEIS, CHARLES G.	RCAF	WO2	REGINA	20/01/44	54°20'	104°32'	DUPUEIS LAKES
DURK, NORMAN A.	RCAF	CPL	BLADWORTH	06/11/43	60°01'	105°09'	DURK LAKE
DURRANT, JOHN C.	RCAF	FO	REGINA	08/08/44	58°34'	104°25'	DURRANT LAKE
DUSYK, MICHAEL	ARMY	SPR	MONTMARTRE	27/09/44	59°45'	108°06'	DUSYK LAKE
DUTERTRE, JOSEPH R.P.	ARMY	GNR	PORCUPINE PLAIN	27/06/42	55°37'	106°46'	DUTERTRE LAKE
DUTTON, THOMAS A.	RCAF	WO2	SWIFT CURRENT	03/03/43	59°41'	102°22'	DUTTON LAKE
DWYER, FRANCIS D.	RCAF	FO	CORNING	29/09/43	55°46'	104°06'	DWYER ISLAND
DYCK, JOHN	ARMY	RFN	SASKATOON	03/03/45	57°35'	108°49'	DYCK LAKE
DYE, JACK E.	RCAF	FO	SASKATOON	03/06/44	55°57'	105°23'	DYE LAKE
DYER, HAROLD G.	RCAF	FS	LEBRET	08/01/43	55°31'	104°42'	DYER LAKE
DYKE, HENRY G.	ARMY	L BDR	OAKSHELA	10/08/44	59°40'	108°06'	DYKE LAKE
DYKE, VICTOR E.	ARMY	PTE	OAKSHELA	13/10/44	59°40'	108°06'	DYKE LAKE
DZIKOWICZ, ADOLF	ARMY	TPR	DIVISION 14	03/01/45	57°46'	103°56'	DZIKOWICZ LAKE
EADIE, CLIFFORD JOHN	NAVY	AB	SASKATOON	16/04/45	55°38'	108°52'	EADIE LAKE
EAGLES, PHILIP B.	RCAF	PO	SASKATOON	29/07/44	54°10'	106°56'	EAGLES LAKE
EAGLESTONE, WALTER R.	RCAF	FO	READLYN	21/08/44	56°35'	107°01'	EAGLESTONE LAKE
EARL, WILLIAM H.	RCAF	PO	SASKATOON	05/10/43	55°55'	104°14'	EARL BAY
EARLY, JAMES W.	RCAF	SGT	SEMANS	15/11/41	55°32'	104°35'	EARLY BAY
EASTER, REGINALD	RCAF	LAC	DAVIDSON	15/05/45	59°29'	109°04'	EASTER HEAD
EASTERBY, LEROY H.	ARMY	L CPL	MOOSE JAW	28/07/44	55°34'	105°28'	EASTERBY LAKE
EASTLEY, FREDERICK C.	RCAF	FO	GLENTWORTH	09/08/44	57°52'	109°29'	EASTLEY LAKE
EASTMAN, GARNET R.	NAVY	TEL	NIPAWIN	13/01/45	55°52'	108°03'	EASTMAN LAKE

Name	Branch	Rank	Hometown	Casualty Date	Latitude	Longitude	Geo-memorial
EATON, LLEWELLYN E.	ARMY	TPR	UNKNOWN	04/09/44	54°38'	102°11'	EATON ISLAND
ECCLES, NORMAN CLEARY	ARMY	SGT	ISLAND FALLS	21/12/41	55°06'	101°59'	ECCLES LAKE
EDELMAN, GEORGE M.	ARMY	SGT	SASKATOON	12/03/42	57°35'	108°58'	EDELMAN LAKE
EDGAR, JOSEPH W.	RCAF	FS	MOOSE JAW	25/05/44	59°23'	108°46'	EDGAR BAY
EDGELOW, DOUGLAS G.	ARMY	A SGT	CAVALIER	15/08/44	54°24'	105°54'	EDGELOW LAKE
EDWARDS, DAVID E.	ARMY	LIEUT	SWIFT CURRENT	27/06/44	59°06'	103°12'	EDWARDS LAKE
EDWARDS, REGINALD	ARMY	PTE	LANIGAN	09/12/43	55°30'	104°30'	EDWARDS ISLAND
EDWARDS, ROBERT E.	ARMY	GNR	PRINCE ALBERT	10/06/44	59°07'	103°12'	EDWARDS BAY
EDWORTHY, JOHN D.	RCAF	SGT	STAR CITY	25/08/41	59°40'	108°00'	EDWORTHY LAKE
EFRAIMSON, ARNOLD M.	ARMY	PTE	MARGO	03/03/45	56°19'	108°23'	EFRAIMSON ISLAND
EHNISZ, BENNIE E.	RCAF	FO	BURSTALL	13/02/43	55°51'	104°02'	EHNISZ ISLAND
EICHENDORF, BERTHOLD	ARMY	PTE	WALDHEIM	05/03/45	55°57'	105°59'	EICHENDORF LAKE
EICHLER, JOHN	ARMY	PTE	SONNINGDALE	26/10/44	56°32'	102°13'	EICHLER LAKE
EICHLER, RUDOLPH	ARMY	PTE	SONNINGDALE	14/09/44	56°57'	103°03'	EICHLER ISLAND
EINARSON, HAROLD B.	RCAF	FS	WYNYARD	10/09/42	57°21'	106°06'	EINARSON LAKE
EINARSON, JOHANN W.	RCAF	FL	WYNYARD	25/02/44	57°21'	106°06'	EINARSON LAKE
EISLER, LEO J.M.	RCAF	FO	VIBANK	31/05/45	55°37'	103°25'	EISLER LAKE
ELDRIDGE, EDGAR M.	ARMY	A BDR	PRINCE ALBERT	01/06/41	55°12'	103°57'	ELDRIDGE LAKE
ELEFSON, GEORGE H.	ARMY	PTE	ORDALE	27/08/44	56°24'	102°05'	ELEFSON LAKE
ELL, CANISIUS J.	ARMY	RFN	SEDLEY	10/04/45	58°02'	107°08'	ELL LAKE
ELLARD, WILLIAM CAMERON	RCAF	SGT(FE)	MORTLACH	05/05/43	55°46'	104°14'	ELLARD LAKE
ELLEFSON, EDWARD M.	ARMY	PTE	KINDERSLEY	26/02/45	59°48'	108°49'	ELLEFSON BAY
ELLEFSON, ORLANDO M.	ARMY	PTE	SASKATOON	06/06/44	56°50'	103°02'	ELLEFSON LAKE
ELLERAAS, GORDON A.	ARMY	L CPL	PREECEVILLE	08/09/44	56°51'	106°37'	ELLERAAS LAKE
ELLIOTT, HOWARD LEE	RCAF	SGT	FORGAN	15/10/41	56°27'	102°43'	ELLIOTT LAKE
ELLIOTT, LEONARD A.	ARMY	L SGT	ST. WALBURG	20/07/44	55°38'	106°29'	ELLIOTT ISLAND
ELLIOTT, TARLTON A.	ARMY	PTE	WELWYN	25/07/44	56°51'	103°06'	ELLIOTT BAY
ELLIS, DONALD W.	ARMY	PTE	MONTMARTRE	20/07/44	55°36'	106°31'	ELLIS PENINSULA
ELLIS, HERBERT C.D.	RCAF	CPL	BIENFAIT	30/03/44	55°05'	104°29'	ELLIS LAKE
ELLIS, JOHN W.	RCAF	SGT	ELROSE	07/08/44	54°53'	103°13'	ELLIS ISLAND
ELLIS, STANLEY	ARMY	PTE	REGINA	27/04/45	59°36'	109°12'	ELLIS BAY
ELLIS, STANLEY F.	RCAF	PO	QUILL LAKE	12/05/44	56°54'	103°18'	ELLIS BAY
ELRICK, KEITH	ARMY	TPR	RUNCIMAN	12/01/45	54°14'	104°49'	ELRICK LAKE
EMERSON, ROBERT C.	ARMY	LIEUT	MOOSE JAW	23/12/43	54°41'	102°52'	EMERSON BAY
EMERSON, THOMAS H.N.	RCAF	PO	MOOSE JAW	14/07/43	59°42'	102°57'	EMERSON LAKE
EMMERSON, HOWARD G.	ARMY	GNR	ABERNETHY	01/05/45	57°26'	106°12'	EMMERSON ISLAND
EMPERINGHAM, ARTHUR J.	ARMY	PTE	BORDER ROAD	19/08/42	56°35'	102°07'	EMPERINGHAM LAKE
ENGLUND, SIGVARD D.	ARMY	PTE	KELLIHER	20/12/43	52°25'	103°22'	ENGLUND LAKE
ENNIS, WALTER J.	ARMY	SGT	MANOR	03/05/43	54°38'	105°06'	ENNIS LAKE
ENS, FRANK	ARMY	PTE	DIVISION 14	20/07/44	57°56'	105°05'	ENS LAKES
EPP, PETER B.	ARMY	RFN	ROSTHERN	28/03/45	57°47'	105°24'	EPP LAKE
ERICKSON, DONALD L.	RCAF	FS	SASKATOON	22/12/42	54°02'	103°06'	ERICKSON LAKE
ERICKSON, GEORGE K.	ARMY	SPR	FRENCHMAN BUTTE	30/05/41	59°31'	108°47'	ERICKSON INLET
ERICKSON, GORDON B.	ARMY	PTE	MOSSBANK	11/09/44	56°45'	103°54'	ERICKSON LAKE
ERICKSON, LAWRENCE	ARMY	PTE	HENDON	24/09/44	59°11'	103°04'	ERICKSON LAKE
ESMAY, ROBERT S.W.	RCAF	WO2	DAVIDSON	14/09/43	55°46'	104°44'	ESMAY LAKE
ESSAR, ELMER	ARMY	PTE	THEODORE	19/09/44	59°30'	108°27'	ESSAR LAKE
ESTABROOKS, WILLIAM L.	ARMY	TPR	GULL LAKE	28/08/42	55°57'	106°21'	ESTABROOKS LAKE
ETTINGER, EVERETT E.	RCAF	FL	SASKATOON	03/04/45	59°22'	102°04'	ETTINGER LAKE
ETTLE, WILLIAM	ARMY	PTE	REGINA	07/07/40	57°33'	103°07'	ETTLE CREEK
EVANS, ALLAN L.	RCAF	FO	REGINA	28/01/45			PENDING
EVANS, ARTHUR L.	ARMY	L CPL	ALSASK	25/07/44	58°33'	103°38'	EVANS CREEK
EVANS, DONALD J.	ARMY	RFN	NORBURY	18/02/45	56°12'	102°21'	EVANS BAY
EVANS, JOHN W.	RCAF	PO	RICHLEA	23/05/43	56°24'	106°26'	EVANS RAPIDS
EVANS, LEWIS BRYCHAN	NAVY	OS	SASKATOON	24/11/44	56°55'	103°31'	EVANS LAKE
EVERNDEN, LYNN B.	ARMY	PTE	GRIFFIN	19/08/42	53°44'	104°35'	EVERNDEN LAKE
EWEN, FRANK M.	ARMY	GNR	GLEN EWEN	07/09/44	55°12'	105°15'	EWEN BAY
EWEN, JOHN W.	ARMY	A CPL	ASQUITH	15/12/44	55°05'	102°25'	EWEN LAKE
EWERT, HENRY	ARMY	TPR	DRAKE	08/10/44	55°36'	105°11'	EWERT LAKE
EWONUS, FRED	ARMY	GNR	MELVILLE	22/07/44	56°55'	108°20'	EWONUS LAKE
EYAHPAISE, EDWARD S.	ARMY	PTE	DUCK LAKE	21/07/44	55°35'	103°35'	EYAHPAISE LAKE
EYRE, JOHN C.	RCAF	FS	WADENA	21/04/43	59°50'	106°39'	EYRE LAKE
FAGAN, WILLIAM H.	RCAF	SGT	MOOSE JAW	05/09/41	59°32'	106°47'	FAGAN LAKE
FAGRIE, HAROLD	ARMY	PTE	BIRCH HILLS	24/07/44	55°57'	105°53'	FAGRIE LAKE
FAHLMANN, ANDREW C.	ARMY	GNR	MINTON	24/11/43	56°50'	107°46'	FAHLMANN LAKE
FAHSELT, RICHARD E.	RCAF	SGT	CABRI	02/11/44	55°34'	104°18'	FAHSELT LAKE
FAIBISH, JACK	ARMY	L SGT	MARKINCH	28/07/44	55°54'	107°17'	FAIBISH BAY
FAIR, THOMAS W.	RCAF	PO	SASKATOON	25/04/44	55°40'	104°36'	FAIR LAKE
FAIRBAIRN, ALFRED D.	ARMY	RFN	SASKATOON	16/08/44	56°52'	103°03'	FAIRBAIRN LAKE
FAIRHEAD, CYRIL	ARMY	TPR	DIVISION 10	30/05/44	55°18'	104°39'	FAIRHEAD ISLAND
FAIRLEY, WILLIAM I.	RCAF	FS	REGINA	12/01/42	59°48'	109°40'	FAIRLEY LAKE
FALARDEAU, ARTHUR M.	ARMY	PTE	SOMME	23/05/44	56°15'	103°22'	FALARDEAU LAKE
FALHUN, ISADORE L.	ARMY	SGT	WHITE STAR	06/06/44	55°53'	105°46'	FALHUN LAKE
FANNON, CHARLES L.	ARMY	PTE	HIGH TOR	01/03/45	56°22'	105°23'	FANNON LAKE
FANSHER, HARRY F.	RCAF	PO	GOVAN	18/01/43	57°29'	106°55'	FANSHER LAKE
FANSON, GORDON W.N.	RCAF	FL	REGINA	18/08/43	59°15'	103°43'	FANSON LAKE
FARROW, DAVID G.	ARMY	L BDR	REGINA	08/08/44	59°31'	108°48'	FARROW INLET
FAST, WALTER H.	ARMY	CPL	REGINA	16/07/44	59°59'	108°15'	FAST LAKE
FAWLEY, JAMES P.	ARMY	LIEUT	NORTH BATTLEFORD	23/11/40	56°48'	102°24'	FAWLEY ISLAND
FEAREY, CHARLES EDGAR	NAVY	OS	REGINA	22/10/40	59°27'	108°01'	FEAREY BAY
FEARNSIDE, JAMES	RCAF	WO2	BOUNTY	19/11/42	55°44'	104°24'	FEARNSIDE LAKE
FEAVIOUR, WILLIAM M.	ARMY	RFN	CUPAR	08/06/44	57°51'	102°13'	FEAVIOUR PENINSULA
FEDORCHUK, WOLODEMIR	RCAF	PO	INSINGER	15/02/45	58°48'	107°02'	FEDORCHUK CREEK
FEDUN, WILLIAM	ARMY	PTE	YORKTON	22/09/44	56°43'	106°03'	FEDUN LAKE
FEHR, JOHN	ARMY	PTE	DIVISION 15	23/10/43	59°18'	105°18'	FEHR LAKE
FEIL, EDWARD G.	RCAF	LAC	MAPLE CREEK	14/11/44	59°32'	108°55'	FEIL LAKE
FEINDELL, LEWIS L.	RCAF	PO	SEMANS	27/04/44	59°19'	102°07'	FEINDELL LAKE
FEIST, OTTO V.	ARMY	TPR	WILKIE	15/08/44	59°20'	106°12'	FEIST LAKE
FENNELL, EMERY ORVILLE	RAF	FO	CANORA	10/03/40	59°31'	108°03'	FENNELL LAKE
FENNELL, LLOYD R.	RCAF	FO	SHAUNAVON	19/07/44	55°10'	104°38'	FENNELL ISLAND
FENTON, GEORGE	RCAF	SGT	TISDALE	09/04/43	54°38'	102°05'	FENTON ISLAND
FENUIK, JOHN	ARMY	PTE	YORKTON	20/07/44	59°26'	105°54'	FENUIK LAKE
FERCHUK, NICKOLAS	ARMY	PTE	WHITE STAR	18/08/44	55°53'	106°00'	FERCHUK LAKE
FERGUSON, DONALD A.	RCAF	FS	WEYBURN	28/02/43	54°04'	103°04'	FERGUSON LAKE
FERGUSON, FRANK G.	ARMY	RFN	NORTH BATTLEFORD	12/01/42	59°05'	103°24'	FERGUSON BAY
FERGUSON, JOHN H.	RCAF	PO	KEDLESTON	04/05/44	55°16'	104°49'	FERGUSON POINT
FERGUSON, LAWRENCE A.	RCAF	FS	LIPTON	29/06/43	55°49'	105°04'	FERGUSON BAY
FERGUSON, ROBERT G.	ARMY	PTE	DIVISION 4	19/08/42	58°14'	102°00'	FERGUSON LAKE
FERGUSON, ROBERT SCOTT	NAVY	OS	REGINA	22/10/40	59°18'	107°26'	FERGUSON BAY
FERN, RAYMOND J.	RCAF	FO	CHRISTOPHER LAKE	11/03/45	54°49'	108°12'	FERN LAKE
FERNER, PETER	RCAF	AC2	SEDLEY	13/11/41	55°11'	104°07'	FERNER LAKE
FEW, THOMAS H.	RCAF	SGT	MOOSOMIN	10/07/42	55°14'	104°16'	FEW LAKE
FICHTNER, JAMES R.	RCAF	FO	YORKTON	28/10/44	59°05'	102°22'	FICHTNER LAKE
FIDLER, CECIL	ARMY	RFN	PRINCE ALBERT	26/08/43	57°19'	103°47'	FIDLER LAKE
FIELD, WALTER H.G.	RCAF	SGT	SASKATOON	14/01/45	58°31'	108°53'	FIELD LAKE
FIELDS, WILLIAM R.	RCAF	WO2	ARBORFIELD	25/02/45	56°20'	104°23'	FIELDS LAKE
FIEST, MICHAEL HUBERT	ARMY	PTE	ESTEVAN	19/08/42	56°02'	105°40'	FIEST LAKE
FIFE, FREDERICK J.	RCAF	FO	KERROBERT	05/09/42	58°28'	103°15'	FIFE ISLAND
FIGGITT, WALTER	ARMY	PTE	BALCARRES	14/08/44	55°34'	105°13'	FIGGITT LAKE
FILE, FREDERICK K.	ARMY	GNR	UNITY	08/08/44	55°04'	102°21'	FILE BAY
FINCH, GLEN ALLEN	ARMY	PTE	TOGO	07/08/44	57°38'	106°48'	FINCH BAY
FINDLAY, BRUCE E.	RCAF	FS	GIRVIN	20/01/44	59°58'	105°10'	FINDLAY LAKE
FINDLAY, JOHN	ARMY	TPR	DIVISION 14	21/10/44	57°19'	103°57'	FINDLAY LAKE
FINDLAY, ROBERT H.	ARMY	PTE	INVERMAY	24/07/44	57°23'	102°25'	FINDLAY ISLAND
FINES, EDGAR S.	ARMY	SGT	DIVISION 16	28/05/44	56°33'	102°21'	FINES ISLAND
FINLAY, THOMAS B.G.	RCAF	FS	SASKATOON	04/07/42	56°10'	109°54'	FINLAY LAKE
FINLAYSON, GEORGE	RCAF	WO2	REGINA	06/12/43	56°20'	108°00'	FINLAYSON ISLAND
FINNIE, JAMES C.	ARMY	A L SGT	KAMSACK	08/10/44	56°33'	107°00'	FINNIE LAKE
FIRNEISZ, ELMER A.	ARMY	PTE	WAKAW	15/09/42	57°38'	105°17'	FIRNEISZ LAKE
FISH, HAROLD	ARMY	PTE	WEYBURN	23/05/44	55°24'	102°05'	FISH LAKE
FISHER, CHARLES H.	RCAF	FL	WATROUS	17/08/44	55°20'	104°41'	FISHER LAKE
FISHER, DUNCAN	ARMY	L CPL	REGINA	19/11/44	56°46'	102°48'	FISHER LAKE
FISHER, JACK G.M.	RCAF	FO	SHAUNAVON	27/11/44	59°17'	106°30'	FISHER CREEK
FISHER, JOHN AGNEW	NAVY	AB	BIGGAR	13/09/42	57°01'	103°45'	FISHER PENINSULA
FISHER, PERCY K.	ARMY	SIGMN	CRYSTAL SPRINGS	08/08/44	56°12'	105°02'	FISHER LAKE
FISHER, RALPH G.H.	RCAF	FO	SHELLBROOK	12/06/45	54°45'	103°28'	FISHER BAY
FISHER, WARREN J.K.	RCAF	FO	INDIAN HEAD	03/02/45	57°39'	104°38'	FISHER RIVER
FISHLEY, CLARENCE W.	ARMY	TPR	BETHUNE	09/10/44	59°43'	105°50'	FISHLEY LAKE

Name	Branch	Rank	Hometown	Casualty Date	Latitude	Longitude	Geo-Memorial
FITCH, JAMES H.	RCAF	FS	SASKATOON	17/04/43	58°46'	102°40'	FITCH RAPIDS
FITCH, MAURICE S.	ARMY	TPR	QUILL LAKE	19/07/43	55°23'	108°21'	FITCH LAKE
FITZGERALD, TERENCE C.	RCAF	FS	GRENFELL	27/09/41	54°58'	102°08'	FITZGERALD LAKE
FITZPATRICK, JAMES M.E.	ARMY	RFN	SINTALUTA	10/06/44	55°34'	105°16'	FITZPATRICK LAKE
FLACK, CARL T.	RCAF	WO2	RADISSON	04/12/43	59°35'	108°21'	FLACK LAKE
FLAMMAND, JOSEPH	ARMY	RFN	MEADOW LAKE	06/06/44	58°33'	108°48'	FLAMMAND RIVER
FLATT, JOHN M.	ARMY	RFN	FENWOOD	30/04/45	55°49'	105°57'	FLATT LAKE
FLATT, WILLIAM H.	RCAF	FO	LEMBERG	23/06/43	59°12'	103°04'	FLATT LAKE
FLAVELLE, ROBERT E.	RCAF	FS	SASKATOON	21/10/42	59°39'	102°29'	FLAVELLE BAY
FLEMING, DOUGLAS	RCAF	SGT	KINISTINO	23/11/41	56°30'	102°45'	FLEMING BAY
FLEMING, ERNEST C.	ARMY	RFN	WOLSELEY	11/06/44	56°53'	103°19'	FLEMING BAY
FLEMING, KENNETH G.	ARMY	TPR	MEACHAM	08/08/44	57°23	106°53'	FLEMING ISLAND
FLEMING, WALLACE	RCAF	FO	KINISTINO	28/01/45	55°05'	108°15'	FLEMING CREEK
FLETCHER, GRANT A.	RCAF	PO	LANIGAN	03/04/43	55°12'	103°45'	FLETCHER LAKE
FLETCHER, JAMES L.	RCAF	SGT	NORTH BATTLEFORD	18/08/44	55°41'	104°55'	FLETCHER ISLAND
FLETT, WESLEY JOHN	ARMY	PTE	MELFORT	17/02/44			PENDING
FLEURY, CONRAD R.	ARMY	L SGT	GREEN LAKE	22/04/45	54°36'	108°34'	FLEURY CREEK
FLOREN, HAROLD A.	RCAF	PO	WEYBURN	14/01/44	54°20'	104°07'	FLOREN LAKE
FLYNN, DOUGLAS W.	ARMY	PTE	KINDERSLEY	26/07/43	59°55'	108°38'	FLYNN LAKE
FLYNN, JOHN JOSEPH	USA	PTE	AYLESBURY	25/10/42	56°07'	103°38'	FLYNN LAKE
FOGG, EDGAR D.	RCAF	FO	UNITY	18/11/43	54°51'	104°51'	FOGG ISLAND
FOLK, MIKE	ARMY	A CPL	LIEBENTHAL	13/02/44	59°36'	108°43'	FOLK LAKE
FOLKERSEN, VICTOR R.	RCAF	FO	KAMSACK	05/09/43	54°58'	104°22'	FOLKERSEN LAKE
FONTAINE, GEORGE	ARMY	TPR	CLAYDON	07/06/44	57°45'	102°28'	FONTAINE ISLAND
FOOKES, DAVID	ARMY	SPR	RHEIN	26/08/42	59°33'	108°25'	FOOKES LAKE
FORBES, ALLAN L.	RCAF	FO	MAPLE CREEK	30/07/43	59°27'	104°50'	FORBES BAY
FORBES, ALLAN P.	RCAF	FL	MORTLACH	30/08/44	56°55'	107°44'	FORBES ISLAND
FORD, CLARENCE W.	ARMY	L CPL	SASKATOON	29/08/44	59°12'	103°05'	FORD LAKE
FORD, EDGAR I.	RCAF	FO	GILROY	24/04/45	59°13'	107°50'	FORD BAY
FORD, GEORGE E.	RCAF	WO2	REGINA	01/08/42	55°05'	104°23'	FORD LAKE
FORD, HUBERT V.	RCAF	LAC	KINLOCH	07/03/42			PENDING
FORD, JOHN E.	RCAF	WO1	READLYN	14/06/44	57°19'	105°53'	FORD LAKE
FORD, LEONARD J.	ARMY	CPL	REGINA	19/08/42	5E°12'	106°34'	FORD FALLS
FORD, LINDSAY G.	ARMY	GNR	PAYNTON	14/08/44	53°14'	108°39'	FORD LAKE
FORD, MALGWYN CHARLES	NAVY	AB	SUCCESS	25/06/40	55°54'	107°33'	FORD LAKE
FORDE, HAROLD R.	ARMY	A CPL	SWIFT CURRENT	15/04/45	56°22'	105°20'	FORDE LAKE
FORDHAM, LEONARD BASIL	RAF	FO	PRINCE ALBERT	17/07/41	57°39'	103°13'	FORDHAM LAKE
FOREST, JOHN K.	RCAF	PO	PRINCE ALBERT	09/12/43	56°37'	107°55'	FOREST ISLAND
FORRESTER, ROBERT L.	RCAF	WO2	BROMHEAD	22/11/43	55°28'	104°22'	FORRESTER LAKE
FORSACHUK, NICK	ARMY	PTE	DIVISION 9	17/04/45	59°27'	105°58'	FORSACHUK LAKE
FORSBERG, MORRIS S.	RCAF	PO	DUNBLANE	06/06/44	54°50'	102°50'	FORSBERG LAKE
FORSETH, KENNETH G.	RCAF	FO	KINGSFORD	06/02/45	55°44'	104°05'	FORSETH LAKES
FORSYTH, HAROLD E.	RCAF	PO	REGINA	14/05/43	58°37'	104°42'	FORSYTH LAKE
FORSYTH, JOHN H.	RCAF	FS	CARNDUFF	02/06/42	57°26'	102°28'	FORSYTH ISLAND
FOSKETT, CHARLES R.	RCAF	PO	SASKATOON	06/09/42	59°36'	106°03'	FOSKETT LAKE
FOSTER, ALLAN G.	RCAF	WO1	WHITEWOOD	12/08/43	59°23'	108°49'	FOSTER LAKE
FOSTER, EMERSON J.	ARMY	L CPL	NORTH BATTLEFORD	13/07/44	55°16'	104°59'	FOSTER ISLAND
FOSTER, JAMES E.	ARMY	PTE	DIVISION 17	20/12/44	57°13'	103°12'	FOSTER LAKE
FOSTER, LESLIE C.	RCAF	FO	SOUTHEY	27/06/43	59°28'	108°15'	FOSTER CHANNEL
FOSTER, OSCAR F.	ARMY	SPR	NORTH BATTLEFORD	04/08/43	59°16'	108°48'	FOSTER ISLAND
FOSTER, PHILIP H.	RAF	SL	BROOKSBY	26/05/42	55°10'	102°00'	PHILFOSTER LAKE
FOSTER, THOMAS	RCAF	FO	ARCOLA	30/08/44	56°51'	107°48'	FOSTER BAY
FOULDS, RODERICK P.	RCAF	FL	PRINCE ALBERT	12/07/45	59°12'	103°00'	FOULDS LAKE
FOURNIER, JOSEPH W.R.	RCAF	WO1	PRINCE ALBERT	16/07/44	57°04'	108°26'	FOURNIER LAKE
FOWELL, ALBERT EDWARD	RCAF	WO2	UNKNOWN	12/06/43	55°53'	104°17'	FOWELL LAKE
FOWLER, DOUGLAS G.	ARMY	PTE	PRINCE ALBERT	11/09/44	55°11'	105°10'	FOWLER ISLAND
FOX, ALEXANDER A.	ARMY	PTE	SWIFT CURRENT	09/03/44	56°56'	102°25'	FOX ISLAND
FOX, ERWIN A.	ARMY	PTE	SEMANS	16/02/43	55°08'	104°48'	FOX ISLAND
FOX, HAROLD B.	ARMY	L BDR	INDIAN HEAD	27/07/44	57°45'	105°12'	FOX LAKE
FOX, RONALD G.	RCAF	SGT	LLOYDMINSTER	30/10/44	55°44'	104°32'	FOX RAPIDS
FRAMPTON, JOHN A.	RCAF	FO	REGINA	20/02/44	60°00'	103°19'	FRAMPTON LAKE
FRANCIS, GEORGE L.	ARMY	A L BDR	BATTLEFORD	21/07/44	55°03'	102°02'	FRANCIS BAY
FRANCIS, RICHARD WILLIAM	RCAF	PO	PRINCE ALBERT	13/06/44	54°58'	109°32'	FRANCIS BAY
FRANK, MICHAEL	RCAF	FS	PRUD'HOMME	16/01/45	55°32'	104°38'	FRANK BAY
FRASER, ALEXANDER M.	RCAF	FO	REGINA	20/11/43	56°07'	106°16'	FRASER LAKE
FRASER, ARTHUR R.	ARMY	GNR	CHURCHBRIDGE	02/12/44	56°46'	102°39'	FRASER BAY
FRASER, JOHN M.	RCAF	FS	OXBOW	01/07/44	57°02'	104°56'	FRASER LAKES
FRASER, ROBERT A.	RCAF	SGT	UNKNOWN	31/08/43			PENDING
FRASER, ROBERT W.	ARMY	PTE	DIVISION 5	23/10/44	56°49'	102°37'	FRASER CREEK
FREDERICKSON, VADN L.	ARMY	GNR	PRINCE ALBERT	10/06/44	57°42'	105°42'	FREDERICKSON LAKE
FREEMAN, ELTON E.	RCAF	FO	FOSTERTON	26/08/44	59°56'	102°34'	FREEMAN BAY
FREEMAN, JAMES H.	RCAF	FL	FLEMING	29/01/45	56°53'	107°22'	FREEMAN CREEK
FREESTONE, JOHN H.	RCAF	PO	WALDRON	03/09/42	55°27'	104°45'	FREESTONE LAKE
FRETWELL, JOHN A.	RCAF	AC2	LLOYDMINSTER	06/12/43	59°30'	108°27'	FRETWELL LAKE
FREWEN, STANLEY D.	RCAF	FS	SONNINGDALE	22/05/43	54°11'	101°51'	FREWEN LAKE
FREYSTEINSSON, HARRY	RCAF	FS	CHURCHBRIDGE	29/07/42	57°17'	105°07'	FREYSTEINSSON LAKES
FRIEDT, JOSEPH	RCAF	WO2	MERID	28/05/44	59°30'	108°25'	FRIEDT LAKE
FRIESEN, JOHN	RCAF	LAC	WYMARK	07/08/45	57°32'	105°46'	FRIESEN LAKE
FRIESEN, PETER	ARMY	TPR	SOMME	19/08/42	56°01'	103°32'	FRIESEN CREEK
FRIESEN, WILMER J.	RCAF	FO	LAIRD	07/07/45	59°33'	108°49'	FRIESEN LAKE
FRIGON, OLIVER J.	ARMY	GNR	ST. LOUIS	04/12/43	55°32'	106°06'	FRIGON LAKE
FROOM, GEORGE E.	ARMY	A SGT	CHELAN	09/01/44	54°58'	102°29'	FROOM LAKE
FROOM, JAMES A.	ARMY	L CPL	CHELAN	05/04/45	57°18'	103°40'	FROOM LAKE
FROST, GORDON J.	RCAF	FO	IMPERIAL	27/11/43	59°18'	103°56'	FROST LAKE
FROST, JOHN B.	RCAF	SGT	LLOYDMINSTER	18/02/43	56°14'	102°02'	FROST ISLAND
FROUD, DENIS P.	RCAF	LAC	REGINA	20/12/41	59°07'	106°33'	FROUD ISLAND
FUCHS, FRANK L.	ARMY	RFN	REGINA	09/06/44	55°34'	105°56'	FUCHS LAKE
FULCHER, LOUIS T.	RCAF	SGT	REGINA	03/04/43	54°53'	109°52'	FULCHER POINT
FULLER, CHARLES R.	ARMY	RFN	EARL GREY	19/02/45	55°16'	104°50'	FULLER ISLAND
FULTON, DANIEL	ARMY	SPR	MEADOW LAKE	08/07/44	59°33'	108°25'	FULTON LAKE
FULTON, DOUGLAS B.	RCAF	SGT	BIENFAIT	09/10/43	55°16'	104°21'	FULTON ISLAND
FULTON, ROY O.	RCAF	SGT	SASKATOON	05/03/43	56°15'	108°10'	FULTON BAY
FUNK, MERVIN	RCAF	FS	DRAKE	11/11/42	54°45'	107°55'	FUNK LAKE
FURMAN, STANLEY A.	ARMY	PTE	MIKADO	08/08/44	56°20'	102°53'	FURMAN LAKE
FURULIE, TRYGVE	ARMY	PTE	DIVISION 2	20/07/44	59°38'	108°45'	FURULIE LAKE
FYSH, HARRY O.	ARMY	PTE	MOOSE JAW	25/11/44	56°33'	103°32'	FYSH RAPIDS
FYSON, GORDON RICHARD	NAVY	A CK 2	ARELEE	04/04/44	53°39'	104°38'	FYSON LAKE
GAGNON, CLOVIS A.J.	ARMY	PTE	DIVISION 3	23/02/45	57°57'	107°54'	GAGNON LAKE
GALBRAITH, WILLIAM D.	ARMY	CPL	QUILL LAKE	20/11/44	55°09'	102°24'	GALBRAITH LAKE
GALE, GEORGE C.	RCAF	FS	RAVENSCRAG	09/04/43	56°14'	107°32'	GALE RAPIDS
GALE, WALTER J.	ARMY	L SGT	RIDGEDALE	26/10/44	59°33'	108°07'	GALE LAKE
GALGAN, PETER E.	RCAF	SGT	DANA	26/11/43	57°09'	107°23'	GALGAN LAKE
GALL, RODERICK M.	ARMY	CPL	ROSE VALLEY	23/09/44	57°40'	108°58'	GALL LAKE
GALLAGHER, HOWARD J.	NAVY	LDG S45	MELVILLE	13/09/42	55°26'	106°21'	GALLAGHER LAKE
GALLAGHER, JAMES	RCAF	PO	SWIFT CURRENT	24/02/45	58°32'	102°47'	GALLAGHER LAKE
GALLANT, ANTHONY E. J.	ARMY	PTE	WAWOTA	19/08/42	55°39'	102°39'	GALLANT BAY
GALLANT, JOHN	RCAF	FS	ITUNA	12/09/43	54°44'	107°57'	GALLANT LAKE
GALLOP, CHARLES S.	ARMY	PTE	DIVISION 12	06/06/42	56°51'	102°54'	GALLOP LAKE
GAMBLE, CAMERON C.	RCAF	FS	REGINA	23/03/43	55°46'	104°09'	GAMBLE LAKE
GANNAW, PETER E.	ARMY	LIEUT	LASHBURN	28/09/44	59°55'	109°34'	GANNAW LAKE
GARDIPEE, VINCENT J.	ARMY	GDSM	ESTEVAN	30/10/44	58°53'	106°49'	GARDIPEE LAKE
GARES, ERNEST J.	RCAF	PO	DUFF	19/04/44	59°59'	109°37'	GARES LAKE
GARNER, JOHN G.	ARMY	LIEUT	REGINA	09/06/44	59°58'	108°04'	GARNER LAKE
GARNER, ROBERT C.	ARMY	PTE	WEYBURN	29/07/44	54°53'	102°47'	GARNER LAKE
GARTNER, MICHAEL	ARMY	RFN	LANDIS	15/06/44	57°53'	109°48'	GARTNER LAKE
GASS, LEONARD KEITH	ARMY	A MAJ	REGINA	06/10/44	59°58'	108°40'	GASS LAKE
GATTINGER, JACOB P.	ARMY	PTE	BATEMAN	23/05/44	56°08'	107°20'	GATTINGER LAKE
GATZKE, KURT H.	ARMY	RFN	WEYBURN	18/02/45	59°44'	108°31'	GATZKE LAKE
GAUCHER, JOSEPH L.	RCAF	WO1	CODERRE	23/12/42	57°19'	107°11'	GAUCHER LAKE
GAUDRY, ORVILLE G.	RCAF	LAC	WILLOW BUNCH	30/05/45	54°27'	108°12'	GAUDRY LAKE
GAUTHIER, JOSEPH O.R.	RCAF	FS	TISDALE	19/02/43	54°38'	102°09'	GAUTHIER ISLAND
GAVAN, CLARENCE G.	RCAF	FO	MOOSE JAW	06/11/44	59°36'	102°46'	GAVAN LAKE
GAVEL, ARTHUR D.	RCAF	FO	WALDECK	17/04/44	55°43'	106°51'	GAVEL LAKE
GAWTHROP, KENNETH G.D.	RCAF	FO	RADVILLE	18/38/43	56°38'	102°39'	GAWTHROP ISLAND
GEBERT, JOHN CASPER	ARMY	PTE	KAYVILLE	10/12/44	54°57'	102°07'	GEBERT BAY
GEBHARD, CLAUDE W.	RCAF	FO	LIBERTY	27/04/43	59°50'	103°20'	GEBHARD LAKE
GEDAK, JOSEPH	RCAF	PO	ESTEVAN	13/05/43	57°43'	109°25'	GEDAK LAKE
GEE, ALAN J.	ARMY	TPR	CARLEA	05/03/45	55°11'	103°23'	GEE LAKE

Name	Branch	Rank	Hometown	Casualty Date	Latitude	Longitude	Geo-Memorial
GEIZE, MARTIN	ARMY	PTE	YORKTON	05/02/44	52°47'	101°47'	GEIZE CREEK
GENTLES, THOMAS P.	ARMY	CAPT	MOOSE JAW	18/10/44	59°44'	103°12'	GENTLES LAKE
GEORGE, ALAN B.	RCAF	FO	WAPELLA	14/11/44	55°21'	104°22'	GEORGE ISLAND
GEORGE, GILBERT L.	RCAF	FS	PRINCE ALBERT	16/04/45	59°18'	106°10'	GEORGE CREEK
GEREIN, ADAM J.	RCAF	FS	ODESSA	12/07/42	55°13'	104°17'	GEREIN LAKE
GERGLEY, STEVE J.	RCAF	FS	REGINA	21/01/43	54°35'	107°56'	GERGLEY LAKES
GERLITZ, ALEXANDER	ARMY	PTE	REGINA	06/10/40	55°59'	104°58'	GERLITZ LAKE
GERMANN, VINCENT F.	ARMY	A CPL	QU'APPELLE	24/03/45	56°27'	103°27'	GERMANN LAKE
GERMIQUET, GEORGE E.	RCAF	PO	PRINCE ALBERT	17/08/44	58°43'	103°29'	GERMIQUET LAKE
GEROW, GLEN T.	RCAF	FS	LLOYDMINSTER	29/12/43	59°58'	103°55'	GEROW LAKE
GIBBENS, JOHN P.	ARMY	GNR	ESTEVAN	13/11/44	54°41'	107°25'	GIBBENS BAY
GIBBONS, FRANCIS E.	RCAF	FS	GRAY	10/08/42	55°56'	104°30'	GIBBONS LAKE
GIBBONS, THOMAS	RCAF	FS	SALTCOATS	02/07/42	59°17'	105°57'	GIBBONS CREEK
GIBBS, MERVYN S.	ARMY	L CPL	REGINA	08/07/44	59°34'	108°14'	GIBBS LAKE
GIBSON, ALBERT G.	RCAF	FS	PENSE	21/07/42	57°20'	102°45'	GIBSON ISLAND
GIBSON, ALEXANDER C.	RCAF	FS	SASKATOON	17/07/42	58°43'	102°25'	GIBSON LAKE
GIBSON, ARTHUR L. P.	RCAF	FS	UNKNOWN	20/01/44			PENDING
GIBSON, HARRY F.	RCAF	LAC	RIVERHURST	16/01/42	59°07'	107°25'	GIBSON LAKE
GIBSON, STANWILL J.	RCAF	FO	CODERRE	29/01/44	54°58'	104°38'	GIBSON ISLANDS
GIBSON, WILLIAM D.	RCAF	FO	SASKATOON	19/09/42	55°38'	104°10'	GIBSON LAKE
GIESEN, RAYMOND W.	ARMY	SPR	RADVILLE	21/05/44	59°32'	108°24'	GIESEN LAKE
GIFFORD, JOHN H.	ARMY	CPL	GLENSIDE	30/07/44	60°01'	107°29'	GIFFORD LAKE
GIFFORD, STANLEY	ARMY	GNR	IMPERIAL	24/01/43	55°06'	102°19'	GIFFORD BAY
GILCHRIST, H.G.	RCAF	FO	FOAM LAKE	14/08/44	55°39'	103°10'	GILCHRIST BAY
GILCHRIST, WILLIAM C.	RCAF	SGT	CHIPPERFIELD	18/11/43	57°29'	106°06'	GILCHRIST BAY
GILES, DAVID HENRY	NAVY	AB	HUDSON BAY	07/05/44	58°55'	105°48'	GILES LAKE
GILES, JAMES R.	RCAF	PO	RED DEER HILL	26/07/44	54°58'	104°45'	GILES CREEK
GILLATT, WILLIAM H.	RCAF	FS	LILAC	06/02/44	53°54'	107°21'	GILLATT LAKE
GILLESPIE, HUGH GORDON	RCAF	FS	LEMBERG	14/11/42	57°07'	103°29'	GILLESPIE LAKE
GILLESPIE, ANDREW P.	ARMY	PTE	ROCANVILLE	20/04/45	56°53'	103°05'	GILLESPIE BAY
GILLIES, DONALD J.	RCAF	FS	BLAINE LAKE	03/07/43	59°18'	106°11'	GILLIES CREEK
GILLIES, KENNETH M.	RCAF	FS	PRINCE ALBERT	01/06/43	59°31'	108°36'	GILLIES CHANNEL
GILLILAND, ALFRED	ARMY	RFN	UNKNOWN	04/07/42	59°37'	108°50'	GILLILAND LAKE
GILLINGHAM, CHARLES A.	ARMY	SGT	PRINCE ALBERT	08/08/44	54°48'	102°51'	GILLINGHAM LAKE
GILSON, JOHN	RCAF	PO	SCOTT	28/04/44	55°34'	103°29'	GILSON LAKE
GIPES, LEWIS D.	ARMY	RFN	DIVISION 17	08/04/45	56°05'	104°12'	GIPES LAKE
GIRARD, JOSEPH	RCAF	SGT	SHELLBROOK	28/10/44	59°23'	106°41'	GIRARD RAPIDS
GIRARD, MARCEL M. C.	ARMY	RFN	FIFE LAKE	16/02/45	49°03'	105°27'	GIRARD CREEK
GIRARD, RENE P.	ARMY	PTE	ALIDA	28/11/45	55°50'	104°49'	GIRARD LAKE
GISLASON, JON	ARMY	RFW	ELFROS	06/06/44	56°13'	102°16'	GISLASON CREEK
GLANSBERG, MAURICE	ARMY	RFN	REGINA	09/07/44	55°58'	107°56'	GLANSBERG LAKE
GLASCOCK, ORVAL K.	RCAF	FS	SHAMROCK	27/04/43	54°12'	107°55'	GLASCOCK LAKE
GLASS, ERNEST I.	RCAF	FS	MOOSOMIN	02/01/44	54°23'	106°24'	GLASS LAKE
GLAUSER, ELWOOD A.	RCAF	WO1	DELISLE	14/11/43	59°31'	108°25'	GLAUSER LAKE
GLAVIN, JOHN A.	ARMY	A L SGT	LAKENHEATH	20/04/45	57°56'	109°49'	GLAVIN LAKE
GLAZEBROOK, JACK K.	RCAF	WO2	SASKATOON	26/02/43	59°33'	108°27'	GLAZEBROOK LAKE
GLEASON, LAWRENCE H.	RCAF	PO	CANORA	13/02/43	59°05'	102°30'	GLEASON LAKE
GLEW, GORDON W.	ARMY	PTE	ESTEVAN	17/08/44	54°11'	107°15'	GLEW LAKE
GLOECKLER, JOHN E.	RCAF	FO	SASKATOON	01/08/44	56°19'	103°25'	GLOECKLER LAKE
GLOVER, CHARLES G.	RCAF	WO2	WINDTHORST	06/09/43	55°43'	104°12'	GLOVER LAKE
GLOVER, CHARLES WILLIAM	RAF	FO	KELVINGTON	01/05/40	55°36'	104°34'	GLOVER PENINSULA
GNIUS, MIKE	RCAF	FO	REGINA	20/01/44	59°39'	103°10'	GNIUS LAKE
GOCHAGAR, FRANK	ARMY	A CPL	EDENWOLD	28/08/44	55°45'	104°58'	GOCHAGER LAKE
GODFREY, EARLE DOUGLAS	RAF	FO	SASKATOON	04/09/39	59°55'	109°00'	GODFREY LAKE
GODFREY, HERBERT L.	ARMY	L CPL	INDIAN HEAD	21/07/44	59°23'	105°52'	GODFREY BAY
GOEHRING, GORDON G.	RCAF	SGT	REGINA	12/12/44	59°32'	108°21'	GOEHRING LAKE
GOERTZEN, ISAAC W.	ARMY	PTE	PENN	27/05/44	58°02'	104°40'	GOERTZEN LAKE
GOLDING, JOHN J.	RCAF	SGT	MEADOW LAKE	11/01/44	56°39'	109°39'	GOLDING LAKE
GOODFELLOW, LLOYD T.	RCAF	WO2	SASKATOON	24/08/42	55°45'	106°54'	GOODFELLOW LAKE
GORDON, CYRIL JAMES A.	NAVY	L SBA	WEBB	20/09/43	55°50'	106°28'	GORDON LAKE
GORDON, MILTON G.	RCAF	FS	WEBB	06/06/43	55°47'	106°32'	GORDON BAY
GORIEU, RAYMOND A.A.	RCAF	FS	DOMREMY	30/06/42	55°00'	104°23'	GORIEU LAKE
GOSLING, LESLIE C.	RCAF	FL	NORTH BATTLEFORD	19/07/43	55°03'	104°43'	GOSLING LAKE
GOULD, HOWARD J.	RCAF	FO	MARYFIELD	18/10/43	56°47'	109°15'	GOULD RAPIDS
GOULD, JAY R.	RCAF	FS	SASKATOON	16/11/42	55°55'	103°27'	GOULD LAKE
GOURLAY, JOHN	ARMY	LIEUT	SASKATOON	02/05/45	57°07'	107°26'	GOURLAY LAKE
GOW, GORDON M.	ARMY	PTE	MANKOTA	01/10/45	58°06'	103°16'	GOW ISLAND
GOW, JAMES R.	ARMY	TPR	DIVISION 14	25/04/45	56°28'	104°29'	GOW LAKE
GOWRIE, CHESTER B.	RCAF	WO2	TRAMPING LAKE	20/12/43	55°47'	104°20'	GOWRIE BAY
GOYER, JOSEPH A.	RCAF	PO	BENGOUGH	03/02/44	59°58'	102°34'	GOYER LAKE
GRABOWSKI, JOSEPH	RCAF	PO	CHOICELAND	04/11/44	59°40'	102°04'	GRABOWSKI LAKE
GRAHAM, ARCHIBALD	RCAF	LAC	ASSINIBOIA	21/05/45	57°02'	105°51'	GRAHAM LAKE
GRAHAM, JAMES	RCAF	FS	REGINA	16/03/45	55°58'	107°03'	GRAHAM LAKE
GRAHAM, JAMES CRAIG	RCAF	PO	MOOSE JAW	29/01/44	59°20'	104°46'	GRAHAM FALLS
GRAHAM, JOHN J.	ARMY	PTE	LEROY	15/07/45	59°07'	108°04'	GRAHAM LAKE
GRAHAM, KENNETH L.	ARMY	A MAJ	MAPLE CREEK	01/11/44	58°27'	102°04'	GRAHAM LAKE
GRAHAM, LLOYD M.	ARMY	CPL	SHELLBROOK	06/09/44	59°08'	103°12'	GRAHAM BAY
GRAHAM, RICHARD R.	RCAF	PO	LIVELONG	30/07/42	56°28'	103°00'	GRAHAM ISLAND
GRAHAM, ROBERT	RCAF	PO	MOOSE JAW	05/03/43	59°20'	104°46'	GRAHAM BAY
GRAMIAK, MIKE J.	ARMY	PTE	BATTLEFORD	21/07/43	56°53'	102°55'	GRAMIAK LAKE
GRAMSON, WALTER J.	RCAF	PO	DELISLE	29/06/44	60°00'	102°43'	GRAMSON LAKE
GRANBOIS, MAURICE E.	RCAF	WO2	HALBRITE	21/02/45			PENDING
GRANBOIS, WALLACE L.	RCAF	PO	HALBRITE	23/04/44	57°52'	106°46'	GRANBOIS LAKE
GRANGER, ALBERT A.	ARMY	PTE	ESTEVAN	19/12/41	58°33'	105°12'	GRANGER LAKE
GRANT, BRUCE A.	RCAF	FO	REGINA	29/03/43	54°40'	102°08'	GRANT BAY
GRANT, CHARLES	RCAF	PO	CLEEVES	11/03/44	55°25'	107°28'	GRANT CREEK
GRANT, DUNCAN M.	RCAF	FL	WATROUS	28/09/43	55°17'	104°12'	GRANT BAY
GRANT, ROBERT GRIERSON	NAVY	SIG	REGINA	24/11/44	58°25'	103°05'	GRANT ISLAND
GRANT, WALTER R.	RCAF	PO	SASKATOON	19/02/45	57°21'	104°09'	GRANT LAKE
GRANT, WILLIAM P.	RCAF	SGT	SASKATOON	29/06/41			PENDING
GRAY, GORDON TILFORD	NAVY	LDG STO	SYLVANIA	18/03/45	55°28'	109°23'	GRAY CREEK
GRAY, JOHN S.W.	RCAF	LAC	WEYBURN	09/12/41	55°55'	104°13'	GRAY BAY
GRAYSON, CHARLES D.	ARMY	LIEUT	MOOSE JAW	20/07/44	56°17'	104°37'	GRAYSON LAKE
GREEN, ARTHUR S.	RCAF	WO2	DELISLE	24/05/43			PENDING
GREEN, CYRIL V.	ARMY	PTE	DIVISION 7	14/08/44	59°45'	109°22'	GREEN ISLAND
GREEN, FREDERICK A.	ARMY	PTE	PRINCE ALBERT	28/12/43	59°43'	108°12'	GREEN LAKE
GREEN, RALPH L.	RCAF	FO	VANGUARD	25/07/44	59°38'	108°44'	GREEN LAKE
GREEN, ROBERT C.	RCAF	SGT	ELBOW	23/08/44	58°28'	105°12'	GREEN BAY
GREENFIELD, FREDERICK	RCAF	LAC	MADISON	14/08/41	57°54'	107°50'	GREENFIELD RAPIDS
GREENWAY, JOHN K.	RCAF	FO	LLOYDMINSTER	03/06/44	58°23'	103°23'	GREENWAY ISLAND
GREENWAY, ROBERT S.E.	RCAF	FO	SIMPSON	15/02/43	59°03'	102°04'	GREENWAY BAY
GREENWAY, WILLIAM	ARMY	PTE	KINDERSLEY	21/01/43	58°25'	103°23'	GREENWAY PENINSULA
GREER, ROBERT L.	RCAF	LAC	ROULEAU	01/12/41	59°32'	108°28'	GREER LAKE
GREGORY, BRUCE D.	RCAF	SGT	RAVENSCRAG	04/12/42	55°10'	106°08'	GREGORY LAKE
GREGORY, RICHARD J.	RCAF	WO1	BENTS	05/10/44	56°41'	108°51'	GREGORY BAY
GRENNAN, GERALD B.	RCAF	WO1	REGINA	24/09/43	55°25'	104°02'	GRENNAN ISLAND
GREST, RALPH N.	RCAF	FO	HUMBOLDT	03/12/43	57°05'	105°40'	GREST BAY
GREY-NOBLE, HENRY	RCAF	FS	ANEROID	26/01/42	55°13'	104°46'	GREY-NOBLE ISLAND
GRICE, IVOR C.	RCAF	WO2	HUMBOLDT	02/03/43	59°28'	109°57'	GRICE LAKE
GRICE, MELVILLE J.	ARMY	PTE	KELVINGTON	09/08/44	57°58'	103°57'	GRICE LAKE
GRIFF, NICHOLAS F.	ARMY	GNR	BUCHANAN	02/09/43	59°20'	105°48'	GRIFF LAKE
GRIFFITHS, EDWARD H.	ARMY	BDR	STONY BEACH	05/09/44	56°51'	103°22'	GRIFFITHS BAY
GRIFFITHS, ROBERT T.	RCAF	FS	SASKATOON	23/09/43	59°22'	109°52'	GRIFFITHS CREEK
GRIGGS, THOMAS E.	RCAF	WO2	TISDALE	21/07/43	59°40'	109°16'	GRIGGS BAY
GRIMMER, JACK	ARMY	SGT	DIVISION 5	14/08/44	56°31'	104°34'	GRIMMER LAKE
GRINDLE, CLIFFORD M.	ARMY	PTE	OUTLOOK	24/10/44	59°53'	106°12'	GRINDLE LAKE
GRINDLEY, PHILIP S.	RCAF	WO2	MOOSE JAW	31/05/43	55°12'	102°20'	GRINDLEY LAKE
GRISWOLD, GEORGE F.	ARMY	RFN	SALTCOATS	06/06/44	59°39'	108°23'	GRISWOLD LAKE
GRITZFELDT, GEORGE F.	ARMY	PTE	STRASBOURG	09/09/44	56°10'	108°05'	GRITZFELDT LAKE
GROMNICKI, TONY	ARMY	RFN	STENEN	09/06/44	55°31'	106°05'	GROMNICKI LAKE
GROOMES, WILLIAM A.	ARMY	LIEUT	MOOSE JAW	04/01/45	57°53'	109°53'	GROOMES LAKE
GROPP, NORMAN A.	ARMY	LIEUT	MAPLE CREEK	05/08/44	55°00'	105°32'	GROPP BAY
GRUBB, CYRIL	ARMY	PTE	BALCARRES	02/10/44	55°22'	108°18'	GRUBB LAKE
GRUCHY, CHARLES A.	RCAF	FS	STRASBOURG	17/01/43	59°25'	108°54'	GRUCHY POINT
GRYGAR, THEODORE A.	ARMY	PTE	YORKTON	01/12/44	57°47'	109°28'	GRYGAR LAKE
GUEST, ROBERT C.L.	ARMY	CPL	YORKTON	25/04/45	59°42'	108°51'	GUEST LAKE
GUILBAULT, JOSEPH RENE C.	NAVY	AB	KELVINGTON	07/05/44	55°51'	108°06'	GUILBAULT LAKE
GULAK, JOHN E.	ARMY	GNR	DNEIPER	08/09/44	56°20'	103°07'	GULAK LAKE

NAME	BRANCH	RANK	HOMETOWN	CASUALTY DATE	LATITUDE	LONGITUDE	GEO-MEMORIAL
GULUTZAN, ALEX	ARMY	PTE	DIVISION 9	09/08/44	56°18'	105°21'	GULUTZAN LAKE
GUNDERSON, ELDON A.	ARMY	PTE	MACKLIN	21/05/45	59°28'	105°35'	GUNDERSON LAKE
GUNDERSON, GILBERT J.	ARMY	PTE	MACKLIN	08/12/44	59°38'	103°49'	GUNDERSON LAKE
GUNN, FRANCIS W.	RCAF	PO	CARROT RIVER	25/04/44	59°38'	108°51'	GUNN LAKE
GUNN, ROBERT JOSEPH	RCAF	FO	WILKIE	06/12/42			PENDING
GUNTER, HARRY W.	ARMY	RFN	HILLANDALE	09/10/44	57°42'	108°37'	GUNTER LAKE
GUPPY, FREDERICK J.S.	RCAF	FO	SASKATOON	02/10/43	59°20'	104°55'	GUPPY LAKE
GURNEY, ROBERT J.	ARMY	RFN	PRINCE ALBERT	09/06/44	58°28'	103°00'	GURNEY ISLAND
GUSTAFSON, ROY G.H.	RCAF	FS	AVONLEA	07/10/43	58°21'	102°03'	GUSTAFSON LAKE
GUSTILOV, WILLIAM	ARMY	RFN	REGINA	18/02/45	59°59'	109°01'	GUSTILOV LAKE
GUTHRIE, ARTHUR F.	ARMY	LIEUT	MOOSE JAW	13/10/44	58°56'	108°12'	GUTHRIE BAY
HAALAND, CLEMENT B.	RCAF	PO	WATROUS	25/07/44	58°00'	108°22'	HAALAND LAKE
HABKIRK, ROBERT E.	RCAF	LAC	PRINCE ALBERT	14/12/42	58°38'	102°33'	HABKIRK LAKE
HACKETT, BOYD J.	ARMY	TPR	ASQUITH	23/08/44	59°29'	105°18'	HACKETT LAKE
HADLEY, KEITH B.	RCAF	FO	PRINCE ALBERT	25/04/44	55°40'	105°47'	HADLEY ISLAND
HADLEY, NEVILLE H.	ARMY	A CAPT	PRINCE ALBERT	28/08/44	55°38'	105°52'	HADLEY BAY
HAGAN, ROBERT E.	RCAF	FS	WOLSELEY	22/05/43	54°07'	101°52'	HAGAN LAKE
HAGERTY, NORMAN E.	RCAF	PO	BELLE PLAINE	21/07/44	55°37'	105°40'	HAGERTY ISLAND
HAGLUND, VICTOR A.	RCAF	SGT	CADILLAC	02/03/45	58°08'	102°24'	HAGLUND LAKE
HAGUE, ALBERT F.	RCAF	FO	REGINA	23/11/43	54°52'	104°38'	HAGUE CREEK
HAILSTONE, WILLIAM C.	RCAF	FO	REGINA	13/07/43	55°48'	104°33'	HAILSTONE LAKE
HALE, EARL ROBERT	RAF	PO	LEMSFORD	13/08/40	55°21'	104°31'	HALE LAKE
HALE, FRANCIS J.	ARMY	PTE	TISDALE	30/09/42	58°16'	108°51'	HALE LAKE
HALIKOWSKI, ADOLPH	ARMY	RFN	DIVISION 15	21/06/44	55°37'	102°42'	HALIKOWSKI BAY
HALIKOWSKI, JOSEPH W.	RCAF	WO2	REYNAUD	03/04/43	55°39'	102°41'	HALIKOWSKI LAKE
HALL, STANLEY G.	RCAF	PO	SHAUNAVON	25/11/44	55°18'	105°42'	HALL POINT
HALLIDAY, FRANK W.R.	ARMY	PTE	CHRISTOPHER LAKE	28/03/45	59°37'	109°39'	HALLIDAY LAKE
HALLIDAY, GEORGE A.	ARMY	PTE	SHELLBROOK	27/08/44	57°49'	105°17'	HALLIDAY LAKE
HALLIDAY, ROBERT HARMON	ARMY	L CPL	PRONGUA	04/06/44	52°32'	101°50'	HALLIDAY LAKE
HALLIDAY, WILLIAM J.	ARMY	CPL	PRONGUA	25/10/44	52°32'	101°50'	HALLIDAY LAKE
HAM, JAMES A.	ARMY	PTE	TISDALE	27/08/44	54°38'	102°08'	HAM ISLAND
HAMBLY, ROSS S.	RCAF	SGT	SYLVANIA	18/09/41	54°41'	102°14'	HAMBLY LAKE
HAMILL, ROSS C.	RCAF	FL	WHITEWOOD	15/03/45	59°55'	103°25'	HAMILL LAKE
HAMILTON, HUGH B.	RCAF	PO	NORTH BATTLEFORD	26/08/44	55°14'	105°03'	HAMILTON BAY
HAMILTON, JAMES D.	RCAF	FS	KENASTON	23/06/43	58°18'	104°11'	HAMILTON LAKE
HAMILTON, WILLIAM P.	RCAF	WO2	BALCARRES	25/02/44	57°34'	104°33'	HAMILTON LAKE
HAMLYN-LOVIS, CHARLES	RCAF	FO	MOOSE JAW	18/02/45	56°50'	106°57'	HAMLYN-LOVIS LAKE
HAMPTON, WILLIAM G.	RCAF	PO	GOVAN	24/03/44	59°59'	106°34'	HAMPTON LAKE
HAMSON, JOSEPH E.R.	ARMY	BDR	INDIAN HEAD	23/07/44	59°56'	103°39'	HAMSON LAKE
HANBIDGE, RONALD D.K.	RCAF	FO	KERROBERT	08/01/45	56°50'	106°30'	HANBIDGE LAKE
HANIS, GEORGE V.	ARMY	TPR	STOCKHOLM	24/05/44	59°02'	102°03'	HANIS LAKE
HANISHEWSKI, JOSEPH	ARMY	PTE	RAMA	24/07/44	55°49'	106°16'	HANISHEWSKI LAKE
HANLEY, JOHN A.	ARMY	CAPT	HARRIS	30/05/44	56°12'	102°33'	HANLEY LAKE
HANNAH, HAROLD ALLAN	RCAF	FO	MOOSE JAW	27/01/45	59°06'	103°34'	HANNAH LAKE
HANNAH, LLOYD A.	RCAF	FO	MOOSE JAW	14/10/44	59°06'	103°34'	HANNAH LAKE
HANNAH, ROBERT S.	RCAF	WO2	FROBISHER	25/02/43	58°50'	103°42'	HANNAH RAPIDS
HANNAY, ALBERT E.	RCAF	FS	MCGEE	12/03/43	54°41'	102°17'	HANNAY ISLAND
HANS, STANLEY W.	RCAF	FS	CARON	25/05/44	60°01'	105°18'	HANS LAKE
HANSEN, AKSEL	ARMY	PTE	DIVISION 14	21/04/45	59°11'	102°55'	HANSEN LAKE
HANSEN, ELLIS M.	ARMY	PTE	RABBIT LAKE	13/12/44	56°28'	102°01'	HANSEN LAKE
HANSFORD, ALBERT H.	RCAF	FS	HUDSON BAY	01/10/42	56°36'	104°22'	HANSFORD BAY
HANSLEY, EDWARD B.	ARMY	L CPL	DIVISION 17	09/03/45	58°47'	109°19'	HANSLEY LAKE
HANSON, ALFRED G.	RCAF	LAC	PRINCE ALBERT	21/05/41	59°17'	105°54'	HANSON CREEK
HANSON, NORMAN C.	ARMY	SPR	PREECEVILLE	06/08/44	59°30'	108°40'	HANSON BAY
HANSON, ROBERT J.	ARMY	TPR	REGINA	05/09/44	56°55'	102°44'	HANSON CREEK
HARBO, EDWARD	RCAF	FO	SPY HILL	07/09/43	57°45'	109°23'	HARBO LAKE
HARBOR, NORMAN S.	RCAF	FS	HANLEY	28/10/44	59°35'	108°27'	HARBOR LAKE
HARBOTTLE, CECIL T.	RCAF	SGT	GLENAVON	11/10/41	59°32'	108°34'	HARBOTTLE LAKE
HARDEN, LLOYD E.	ARMY	PTE	RIVERHURST	26/02/45	59°02'	107°09'	HARDEN LAKE
HARDIE, WILLIS	ARMY	PTE	DAFOE	08/08/44	59°19'	105°50'	HARDIE LAKE
HARDING, OLIVER	RCAF	FS	HODGEVILLE	21/02/45	56°41'	108°31'	HARDING BAY
HARDY, DOUGLAS R.	RCAF	FO	REGINA	12/11/44	59°35'	104°20'	HARDY BAY
HARESIGN, SIDNEY	ARMY	PTE	MOOSE JAW	28/09/44	56°52'	105°56'	HARESIGN LAKE
HARKETT, WILLIAM	ARMY	PTE	MOOSE JAW	23/05/44	56°48'	104°08'	HARKETT LAKE
HARKNESS, WILBERT R.N.	ARMY	GNR	INDIAN HEAD	23/07/44	59°22'	108°54'	HARKNESS ISLANDS
HARMAN, ERNEST A.W.	ARMY	PTE	QU'APPELLE	19/08/42	55°17'	104°53'	HARMAN ISLAND
HARMON, LLOYD E.	RCAF	LAC	WATROUS	02/06/43	59°43'	109°41'	HARMON LAKE
HARPER, ALAN B.	RCAF	FS	KAMSACK	23/06/44	59°24'	106°17'	HARPER LAKES
HARPER, GEORGE B.	ARMY	LIEUT	WEYBURN	06/11/42	55°21'	102°07'	HARPER LAKE
HARPER, MILTON A.	RCAF	PO	KAMSACK	20/12/42	59°24'	106°17'	HARPER LAKES
HARPER, PHILIP	ARMY	PTE	TOGO	28/08/44	54°52'	103°01'	HARPER ISLAND
HARPER, ROBERT J.	ARMY	RFN	PLEASANTDALE	08/06/44	59°22'	103°56'	HARPER LAKE
HARRINGTON, JOHN	RCAF	WO2	GLENSIDE	12/06/43	56°23'	108°32'	HARRINGTON ISLAND
HARRINGTON, WILLIAM	ARMY	PTE	DIVISION 10	28/12/43	59°19'	105°26'	HARRINGTON LAKE
HARRIS, ARTHUR D.	ARMY	SGT	ELFROS	16/12/43	59°22'	103°54'	HARRIS LAKE
HARRIS, EMERSON P.	RCAF	LAC	SPEERS	23/03/42	58°47'	109°56'	HARRIS LAKE
HARRIS, JOHN C.	RCAF	FS	ROSETOWN	17/02/42			PENDING
HARRIS, WILLIAM S.	RCAF	WO2	YORKTON	15/04/43	54°54'	104°47'	HARRIS ISLANDS
HARRISON, ALLEN C.	ARMY	TPR	GLEN KERR	24/11/45	58°16'	103°36'	HARRISON PENINSULA
HARRISON, CLIFFORD R.	ARMY	TPR	DIVISION 10	09/08/44	58°17'	103°36'	HARRISON LAKES
HARRISON, FRANCIS G.	ARMY	CPL	REGINA	01/05/41	57°49'	109°28'	HARRISON LAKE
HARRISON, HAROLD H.	RCAF	FS	MARYFIELD	14/07/42	58°19'	103°55'	HARRISON ISLAND
HARRISON, JOHN W.	RCAF	PO	NIPAWIN	12/11/43	59°28'	104°43'	HARRISON BAY
HARRISON, RAYMOND O.	ARMY	CPL	HARDY	29/07/45	55°31'	102°07'	HARRISON BAY
HARRISON, RICHARD	ARMY	PTE	STONE	11/12/44	56°56'	103°19'	HARRISON ISLAND
HARRISON, STEWART	RCAF	FS	NORTH BATTLEFORD	24/07/43	55°04'	102°58'	HARRISON LAKE
HARRY, WILLIAM BRUCE	ARMY	SGT	PRINCE ALBERT	17/08/44	55°30'	107°24'	HARRY LAKE
HART, ELTON B.	RCAF	FL	LEWVAN	05/06/44	54°53'	104°37'	HART POINT
HART, RONALD JOSEPH	RCA	GNR	MELVILLE	29/04/45			PENDING
HARTLE, JOHN J.	ARMY	A SGT	LEROY	14/08/44	58°02'	102°54'	HARTLE LAKE
HARTLEY, NEAL C.	ARMY	RFN	RICHARD	09/06/44	54°56'	103°40'	HARTLEY LAKE
HARTNEY, DANIEL J.	RCAF	WO1	DRINKWATER	03/01/43	58°37'	106°14'	HARTNEY LAKE
HARVEY, JACK A.	RCAF	FO	MILDEN	21/07/44	59°20'	106°34'	HARVEY LAKE
HARVEY, PEACH B.	ARMY	PTE	EYEBROW	24/05/44	55°16'	102°40'	HARVEY LAKE
HARVEY, WILLIAM M.	ARMY	TPR	WROXTON	11/06/44	59°20'	103°54'	HARVEY LAKE
HASTIE, JACK R.	RCAF	FL	WEBB	09/07/43	56°08'	107°30'	HASTIE LAKE
HATCH, ALLAN E.	RCAF	FS	LEROY	13/05/43	55°34'	104°06'	HATCH LAKE
HATLE, CLIFFORD O.	RCAF	FL	DIVISION 4	17/04/43	59°59'	103°27'	HATLE LAKE
HAUFF, RUEBEN C.	ARMY	PTE	MAIDSTONE	16/12/43	59°28'	104°56'	HAUFF LAKE
HAUG, DONALD J.	RCAF	WO2	BALGONIE	10/11/43	59°44'	105°42'	HAUG LAKE
HAUGEN, WILLARD M.	RCAF	FS	STRONGFIELD	18/08/43	55°33'	104°49'	HAUGEN LAKE
HAUK, NORMAN A.	ARMY	CPL	UNKNOWN	06/06/44	59°52'	108°55'	HAUK LAKE
HAVARD, DONALD IVOR	RCAF	FS	ADANAC	14/05/43	54°57'	103°44'	HAVARD LAKE
HAWES, FREDERICK C.	RCAF	SGT	SASKATOON	02/06/43	55°50'	108°00'	HAWES LAKE
HAWKINS, GERALD	ARMY	CPL	LLOYDMINSTER	07/09/44	55°43'	105°46'	HAWKINS LAKE
HAWKINS, WALTER	RCAF	WO1	NAICAM	15/02/44	55°47'	104°32'	HAWKINS PENINSULA
HAWMAN, FREDERICK R.	ARMY	CPL	ARCOLA	06/03/45	54°57'	102°12'	HAWMAN LAKE
HAWRYLUK, THEODORE M.	RCAF	FO	NIPAWIN	06/10/43	54°54'	108°12'	HAWRYLUK CREEK
HAY, GLEN J.	RCAF	FO	LOON LAKE	11/05/45	59°25'	108°48'	HAY LAKE
HAY, STANLEY A.	RCAF	FO	ROWLETTA	14/02/45	55°26'	104°38'	HAY LAKE
HAYMAN, HENRY J.	ARMY	TPR	WADENA	07/03/45	55°42'	104°50'	HAYMAN LAKE
HAYNES, JOHN S.	RCAF	FO	LLOYDMINSTER	19/08/42	59°59'	107°20'	HAYNES LAKE
HAYWARD, WILLIAM A.	ARMY	PTE	DIVISION 5	30/05/44	56°26'	103°19'	HAYWARD RAPIDS
HAYWORTH, WILLIAM A.	RCAF	PO	REGINA	20/05/42	55°15'	104°27'	HAYWORTH ISLAND
HAZELTON, LAWRENCE W.F.	ARMY	RFN	REGINA	18/06/44	59°48'	109°55'	HAZELTON LAKE
HAZLE, OLIVER BAKER	NAVY	STO14	READLYN	01/09/43	55°07'	108°03'	HAZLE LAKE
HEAD, DONALD W.	ARMY	C CPL	SHIPMAN	25/04/44	59°40'	109°27'	HEAD BAY
HEAD, PERRY W.	ARMY	A CPL	ARBORFIELD	15/10/44	59°39'	109°27'	HEAD LAKE
HEALY, ROGER C.	RCAF	LAC	RADVILLE	18/02/45	55°24'	104°08'	HEALY ISLAND
HEARD, STANLEY M.	RCAF	FL	PIAPOT	18/08/43	59°20'	106°04'	HEARD LAKE
HEARN, EDGAR W.	RCAF	CPL	STENEN	24/02/46	55°28'	108°25'	HEARN LAKE
HEATHERINGTON, JOHN T.	NAVY	STO 1	REGINA	29/04/44	59°25'	108°48'	HEATHERINGTON LAKE
HEBERT, JOSEPH R.	RCAF	PO	REGINA	13/03/42	55°41'	103°24'	HEBERT ISLAND
HEDMAN, IRA H.	ARMY	PTE	TISDALE	21/08/44	57°09'	103°08'	HEDMAN LAKE
HEDEN, PHILIP G.	RCAF	PO	HALBRITE	29/07/43	59°08'	103°53'	HEDEN LAKE
HEIBERG, KENNETH G.	NAVY	PO	LANG	13/09/42	53°59'	104°35'	HEIBERG LAKE
HEIN, JOHN	RCAF	PO	ARTLAND	20/02/44	59°54'	103°25'	HEIN LAKE
HEINEN, ALBERT J.	ARMY	SPR	WILKIE	11/09/44	59°21'	108°54'	HEINEN BAY

Name	Branch	Rank	Hometown	Casualty Date	Latitude	Longitude	Geo-memorial	Name	Branch	Rank	Hometown	Casualty Date	Latitude	Longitude	Geo-memorial
HEINEN, FRANK W.	RCAF	PO	WILKIE	27/01/44	55°47'	108°08'	HEINEN LAKE	HINE, RAYMOND E.	RCAF	PO	OSAGE	17/12/44	55°31'	104°49'	HINE LAKE
HEINZ, JOSEPH	ARMY	PTE	BIENFAIT	19/08/42	58°13'	102°36'	HEINZ LAKE	HINDMARSH, FELIX C.	RCAF	PO	EDAM	12/04/44	55°05'	104°59'	HINDMARSH ISLAND
HEINZ, THEODORE	ARMY	CPL	BIENFAIT	20/07/44	58°13'	102°36'	HEINZ LAKE	HINTZ, FREDERICK	ARMY	RFN	ROSTHERN	25/09/44	55°06'	103°39'	HINTZ LAKE
HEINZIG, PAUL	RCE	SPR	YELLOW GRASS	04/11/44			PENDING	HISLOP, IVAN N.	RCAF	WO2	ARCOLA	11/07/43	59°24'	108°41'	HISLOP LAKE
HEINZMAN, WALTER C.	ARMY	L CPL	WEYBURN	19/08/42	59°27'	105°50'	HEINZMAN LAKE	HOAR, WILLIAM G.	RCAF	FO	CALDER	29/03/43	59°35'	104°24'	HOAR BAY
HEISE, HERMAN C.	ARMY	PTE	DUNDURN	03/03/45	56°46'	109°55'	HEISE LAKE	HOAR, WILLIAM J.	RCAF	WO2	PRINCE ALBERT	28/09/43	54°02'	101°49'	HOAR LAKE
HEISLER, GEORGE P.	ARMY	L CPL	VIBANK	08/03/44	59°26'	104°41'	HEISLER LAKE	HOBSON, JOHN K.	RCAF	PO	SASKATOON	10/08/42	56°49'	106°11'	HOBSON LAKE
HEKELAAR, HARRY	ARMY	PTE	MESKANAW	04/04/45	57°57'	108°44'	HEKELAAR LAKE	HOCKLEY, VICTOR S.	ARMY	PTE	CRESTWYND	29/07/43	56°29'	104°56'	HOCKLEY LAKE
HEMERY, ALBERT A.	RCAF	FS	SASKATOON	20/04/42	59°59'	105°56'	HEMERY LAKE	HODGE, ROY C.	ARMY	PTE	GRENFELL	19/06/45	57°48'	109°24'	HODGE LAKE
HEMING, CECIL D.	RCAF	PO	PELLY	17/04/43	58°24'	102°49'	HEMING BAY	HODGES, REGINALD F.	RCAF	SGT	KAMSACK	15/02/44	57°20'	104°50'	HODGES LAKE
HEMING, GEORGE C.	RCAF	FS	MOOSE JAW	17/04/43	54°07'	106°41'	HEMING LAKE	HODGES, ROBERT B.	RCAF	WO1	KAMSACK	07/06/43	55°28'	106°03'	HODGES LAKE
HEMMING, GORDON W.	RCAF	SGT	WYNYARD	25/04/44	55°39'	104°25'	HEMMING LAKE	HODGSON, JAMES L.S.	ARMY	RFN	ST. LOUIS	06/06/44	58°10'	105°05'	HODGSON LAKE
HEMSWORTH, JAMES T.	RCAF	PO	GULL LAKE	06/04/44	60°00'	104°35'	HEMSWORTH ISLAND	HODGSON, KENNETH	RCAF	SGT	RENOWN	04/05/43	56°30'	102°57'	HODGSON ISLAND
HENDERSON, BERTRAM H.	ARMY	RFN	PRINCE ALBERT	27/10/44	56°40'	103°45'	HENDERSON LAKE	HOEY, JAMES W.D.	RCAF	WO2	KELSO	25/06/43	59°34'	108°29'	HOEY LAKE
HENDERSON, CHARLES O.	ARMY	SGT	UNKNOWN	11/03/43			PENDING	HOFER, RICHARD H.	ARMY	TPR	LEADER	16/04/45	59°32'	108°30'	HOFER ISLAND
HENDERSON, DONALD F.	RCAF	SGT	SASKATOON	14/06/41	57°09'	107°26'	HENDERSON LAKE	HOFFMAN, ALBERT S.	ARMY	SPR	DIVISION 15	01/05/45	54°58'	102°00'	HOFFMAN ISLAND
HENDERSON, GERALD W.	RCAF	PO	KINLEY	03/01/44			PENDING	HOGANSON, HARRY L.	ARMY	CPL	NORTH BATTLEFORD	04/12/44	55°37'	106°12'	HOGANSON LAKE
HENNING, GRANT L.	RCAF	FS	MACKLIN	21/11/42	54°11'	107°40'	HENNING LAKE	HOIDAS, IRVIN F.	RCAF	PO	SASKATOON	20/05/42	59°56'	107°49'	HOIDAS LAKE
HENRY, GEORGE EDGAR	RCAF	FO	ISLAND FALLS	18/09/44	55°51'	104°04'	HENRY ISLAND	HOLDEN, ERNEST L.	RCAF	FL	MOOSE JAW	26/04/43	59°24'	108°45'	HOLDEN LAKE
HENSCHEL, WALTER A.	RCAF	FS	CABRI	20/12/42	55°43'	104°20'	HENSCHEL LAKE	HOLDEN, WILLIAM	RCAF	PO	SENLAC	05/05/43	56°09'	106°43'	HOLDEN LAKE
HENSON, GEORGE K.	RCAF	SGT	SASKATOON	13/08/41	57°08'	107°18'	HENSON LAKE	HOLLINGDALE, GEORGE L.	ARMY	PTE	ESTEVAN	16/08/44	54°34'	102°57'	HOLLINGDALE LAKE
HEPBURN, ELMER J.	RCAF	FO	MELVILLE	07/10/43	55°32'	104°07'	HEPBURN FALLS	HOLLINGSHEAD, KENNETH	ARMY	PTE	NEILBURG	27/02/45	56°05'	104°39'	HOLLINGSHEAD LAKE
HEPFNER, LAMBERT	ARMY	GNR	RICHMOUND	21/05/44	59°25'	105°59'	HEPFNER LAKE	HOLLINS, CHRISTOPHER W.	ARMY	MAJ	DIVISION 17	05/04/45	58°23'	108°57'	HOLLINS LAKE
HEPP, FRANK	ARMY	PTE	DIVISION 16	01/03/45	55°05'	103°14'	HEPP LAKE	HOLLOWELL, DONALD T.	RCAF	PO	WOLSELEY	19/03/43	55°34'	105°45'	HOLLOWELL LAKE
HEPPLER, ZEIGFRIED	ARMY	RFN	MELVILLE	02/09/44	56°13'	106°13'	HEPPLER LAKE	HOLLOWELL, ROBERT S.	RCAF	PO	WOLSELEY	01/06/43	55°33'	105°45'	HOLLOWELL ISLAND
HERBERT, HORACE M.R.	RCAF	PO	KELVINGTON	23/04/44	56°22'	107°58'	HERBERT BAY	HOLMAN, SIDNEY	ARMY	Q M S	REGINA	09/10/44	55°36'	105°04'	HOLMAN LAKE
HERLEN, ERNST O.	RCAF	PO	SASKATOON	09/06/44	54°19'	108°12'	HERLEN RIVER	HOLMES, EARL IRA	NAVY		WALDECK	13/09/42	55°08'	109°47'	HOLMES CREEK
HERMAN, GEORGE P.	RCAF	WO2	NETHERHILL	18/11/43	57°54'	107°57'	HERMAN RAPIDS	HOLMES A'COURT, WALTER	RCAF	FO	PRINCE ALBERT	02/01/44	56°15'	105°02'	HOLMES A'COURT LAKE
HERMAN, JOHN W.	ARMY	CPL	HAFFORD	16/12/43	55°51'	106°53'	HERMAN BAY	HOLMLUND, CHESTER A.	RCAF	PO	GLENSIDE	25/02/45	56°18'	106°41'	HOLMLUND LAKE
HERRICK, BERTRUM E.	ARMY	PTE	SHAUNAVON	23/01/45	55°06'	104°17'	HERRICK ISLAND	HOLTBY, ROBERT A.	RCAF	FS	MARSHALL	29/12/43	59°10'	102°21'	HOLTBY LAKE
HETHERINGTON, GEORGE	RCAF	FO	REGINA	17/12/44	56°46'	103°08'	HETHERINGTON LAKE	HOLUKOFF, PETER S.	ARMY	PTE	KAMSACK	18/10/44	56°58'	102°15'	HOLUKOFF ISLAND
HETHERINGTON, WILLIAM	RCAF	FS	REGINA	30/07/43	55°18'	104°04'	HETHERINGTON LAKES	HOLYER, JABEZ G.	ARMY	PTE	GRASSDALE	02/08/44	57°08'	107°51'	HOLYER LAKE
HEWETSON, WILLIAM R.	RCAF	PO	SASKATOON	29/01/44	56°14'	105°39'	HEWETSON LAKE	HOLYOAK, EDWIN H.	ARMY	PTE	SEMANS	28/07/44	60°01'	109°23'	HOLYOAK LAKE
HEWITT, GEORGE	ARMY	SGT	BRIGHTHOLME	05/07/44	54°27'	105°59'	HEWITT BAY	HONSVALL, ARTHUR	ARMY	PTE	TOMPKINS	23/11/44	59°23'	105°54'	HONSVALL LAKE
HEWITT, JAMES B.	ARMY	GNR	KELSO	26/12/44	55°27'	102°02'	HEWITT NARROWS	HOOD, DONALD A.	ARMY	PTE	HUDSON BAY	27/02/45	57°13'	103°54'	HOOD BAY
HEWSON, WARREN E.	ARMY	PTE	TISDALE	27/10/40	59°41'	105°49'	HEWSON LAKE	HOOD, FLOYD S.	ARMY	A S SGT	KELLIHER	16/06/43	55°39'	105°01'	HOOD CREEK
HICKS, KENNETH B.	RCAF	PO	PLATO	08/03/45	55°45'	105°53'	HICKS ISLAND	HOOKER, REX M.	ARMY	L BDR	DIVISION I	01/05/45	58°13'	102°45'	HOOKER LAKE
HICKS, STANLEY H.	RCAF	FS	ROULEAU	25/06/43	59°46'	108°08'	HICKS LAKE	HOOPER, JOHN	RCAF	SGT	CEYLON	24/05/43	56°28'	102°28'	HOOPER LAKE
HICKS, WILFRED N.	ARMY	L SGT	DIVISION 7	13/06/44	58°51'	103°22'	HICKS LAKE	HOPE, DONALD J.	RCAF	FO	YELLOW GRASS	22/02/44	55°09'	104°53'	HOPE ISLAND
HICKSON, JOHN W.	RCAF	PO	KINDERSLEY	08/03/45	55°22'	104°21'	HICKSON ISLAND	HOPE, KENNETH E.	RCAF	SGT	SUTHERLAND	24/08/42	55°59'	104°47'	HOPE LAKE
HIDLEBAUGH, DAVID M.	ARMY	CPL	SNOWDEN	04/07/44	55°30'	104°26'	HIDLEBAUGH LAKE	HOPKINS, HAROLD H.	ARMY	C Q M S	SASKATOON	08/06/43	54°26'	105°08'	HOPKINS LAKE
HIEBERT, THEODOR R.	RCAF	AC2	SASKATOON	02/05/41	58°59'	107°03'	HIEBERT LAKE	HOPKINS, OLIVER H.	ARMY	LIEUT	DIVISION 4	01/07/44	56°56'	103°16'	HOPKINS BAY
HILBACH, HERBERT H.H.	ARMY	RFN	KERROBERT	22/04/45	56°34'	107°04'	HILBACH LAKE	HOPKINS, RALPH BRUCE	RCAF	FO	NORTH BATTLEFORD	27/06/45			PENDING
HILL, DONALD M.M.	ARMY	PTE	CHRISTOPHER LAKE	15/01/44	59°35'	108°27'	HILL BAY	HOPPER, CLIFFORD	ARMY	L SGT	DIVISION 14	01/09/44	55°07'	103°35'	HOPPER LAKE
HILL, EDWARD H.	RCAF	FO	LUCKY LAKE	10/10/42	59°29'	108°13'	HILL LAKE	HOPTON, CLAYTON P.	RCAF	LAC	CABRI	12/12/40	55°21'	104°24'	HOPTON ISLAND
HILL, EDWIN	ARMY	AR QM2	FORT QU'APPELLE	04/05/45	59°52'	107°47'	HILL RIVER	HORAN, ERNEST B.	ARMY	TPR	SASKATOON	20/05/44	59°55'	107°01'	HORAN LAKE
HILL, FREDERICK W.	RCAF	WO1	BLAINE LAKE	22/11/43	59°23'	108°44'	HILL CREEK	HORN, JOHN	RCAF	FO	REGINA	29/01/44	54°55'	104°07'	HORN BAY
HILL, GEORGE W.	ARMY	SPR	DIVISION 10	11/12/44	59°18'	106°05'	HILL BAY	HORN, LAWRENCE A.B.	RCAF	FS	REGINA	24/08/42	55°49'	104°31'	HORN ISLAND
HILL, JAMES B.	RCAF	FO	BOHARM	26/10/44	56°45'	108°49'	HILL ISLAND	HORNOI, JAMES	RCAF	FO	REGINA	08/01/45	55°33'	108°16'	HORNOI BAY
HILL, JAMES B.H.	RCAF	FS	NIPAWIN	18/01/42	56°11'	104°33'	HILL LAKE	HORNSETH, ALVIN M.	RCAF	FS	KANDAHAR	12/08/42	55°37'	104°06'	HORNSETH LAKE
HILL, JOHN J.	RCAF	FS	PRINCE ALBERT	10/06/43	59°17'	106°08'	HILL POINT	HORST, GEORGE	RCAF	LAC	ROSTHERN	30/10/44	54°32'	107°07'	HORST BAY
HILL, LAWRENCE STANLEY	RCAF	FO	LUCKY LAKE	28/12/40	59°29'	108°13'	HILL LAKE	HORST, JOHN	ARMY	CPL	ROSTHERN	08/06/44	55°11'	103°37'	HORST LAKE
HILL, WILLIAM A.	ARMY	PTE	DIVISION 16	05/10/45	56°06'	102°01'	HILL LAKE	HORTON, DONALD E.	RCAF	PO	HUMBOLDT	17/06/44	57°48'	103°44'	HORTON ISLAND
HILL, WILTON H.	RCAF	FS	SASKATOON	13/05/43			PENDING	HORTON, HILLSON M.	ARMY	A L CPL	BRIERCREST	01/05/43	56°53'	102°43'	HORTON BAY
HILLERT, WILFRED D.	ARMY	PTE	SASKATOON	04/02/41	59°40'	107°11'	HILLERT LAKE	HORVATH, ALEXANDER J.	ARMY	PTE	PLUNKETT	21/08/44	56°51'	103°27'	HORVATH LAKE
HILLIER, HERBERT F.	ARMY	A CPL	SOUTHEY	11/10/44	56°37'	102°08'	HILLIER LAKE	HOULDING, ELWOOD C.	RCAF	SGT	SASKATOON	14/01/44	55°04'	104°04'	HOULDING LAKE
HILLIER, RICHARD	ARMY	PTE	SOUTHEY	10/10/44	56°54'	103°38'	HILLIER BAY	HOURD, EARL	ARMY	L CPL	BENDER	29/08/44	57°36'	102°29'	HOURD ISLAND
HILLIS, WILLIAM	ARMY	PTE	SEMANS	14/10/44	55°16'	104°55'	HILLIS ISLAND	HOWARD, WILLIAM R.	RCAF	FS	MILESTONE	07/05/42	57°44'	102°02'	HOWARD ISLAND
HILLMAN, DONALD E.	RCAF	FL	ELROSE	24/06/44	55°32'	106°29'	HILLMAN BAY	HOWE, MARTIN C.	RCAF	FS	LAFLECHE	01/04/42	54°29'	109°40'	HOWE BAY
HILLMAN, JAMES G.	RCAF	FO	ELROSE	25/02/44	55°34'	106°28'	HILLMAN ISLAND	HOWES, DOUGLAS G.	ARMY	SIGMN	SASKATOON	26/07/44	56°01'	104°46'	HOWES LAKE
HILLS, GLENN L.	ARMY	RFN	DIVISION 17	18/06/44	57°34'	103°57'	HILLS LAKE	HOWITSON, GEORGE A.	RCAF	SGT	WILKIE	22/11/43	55°32'	104°18'	HOWITSON LAKE
HILLS, JAMES O.	RCAF	FS	DILKE	23/06/43	59°42'	105°38'	HILLS LAKE	HOWLAND, FREDERICK C.	ARMY	SPR	REGINA	13/03/45	59°27'	108°39'	HOWLAND LAKE
HILLS, WILLIAM J.	RCAF	WO2	PERDUE	26/05/43	57°51'	102°02'	HILLS POINT	HOWLETT, ARCHIE P.	ARMY	PTE	WYMARK	22/10/44	54°25'	102°44'	HOWLETT CREEK
HILSENTEGER, ALEXANDER	ARMY	PTE	REGINA	07/06/44	55°09'	102°26'	HILSENTEGER LAKE	HOWLETT, CHARLES J. M.	RCAF	SGT	ORKNEY	11/11/41	55°17'	104°41'	HOWLETT ISLAND

Name	Branch	Rank	Hometown	Casualty Date	Latitude	Longitude	Geo-Memorial
HOZEMPA, PETER A.	ARMY	RFN	GLENAVON	30/10/44	58°58'	106°46'	HOZEMPA LAKE
HUARD, CLIFFORD E.	ARMY	A SGT	LASHBURN	08/06/44	57°54'	105°09'	HUARD LAKE
HUBER, WALTER L.	ARMY	TPR	SERATH	12/05/45	55°22'	102°11'	HUBER LAKE
HUDDLESTON, LESLIE E.L.	RCAF	FS	REGINA	03/11/42	56°06'	108°37'	HUDDLESTON LAKE
HUGGINS, JOHN R.	ARMY	TPR	FORT SAN	01/11/43	57°54'	103°52'	HUGGINS LAKE
HUGHES, ALBERT	ARMY	PTE	TOMPKINS	13/04/45	59°36'	109°29'	HUGHES CREEK
HUGHES, EDWARD F.	ARMY	PTE	LEMBERG	24/07/44	56°58'	103°08'	HUGHES BAY
HUGHES, GERALD C.	RCAF	WO1	REGINA	19/08/43	57°40'	105°14'	HUGHES LAKE
HUGHES, WALTER W.	RCAF	SGT	LOCKWOOD	17/12/41	59°16'	106°29'	HUGHES ISLAND
HUGLI, WILLIAM P.	RCAF	FO	REGINA	25/04/44	59°54'	102°16'	HUGLI LAKE
HULL, WILBERT A.	ARMY	PTE	NOTTINGHAM	23/05/44	58°09	102°28'	HULL LAKE
HUME, RAYMOND G.	RCAF	FS	RICHARD	21/04/43	55°10'	101°57'	HUME LAKE
HUNT, ANDREW R.	ARMY	PTE	LINTLAW	20/07/44	55°25'	103°09'	HUNT ISLAND
HUNT, BRUCE A.	ARMY	SPR	RADVILLE	27/02/43	59°28'	106°22'	HUNT LAKE
HUNT, CALVIN R.	ARMY	A L SGT	VALPARAISO	25/04/45	59°39'	108°15'	HUNT LAKE
HUNT, JACK	RCAF	FL	SWIFT CURRENT	29/11/44	55°26'	106°09'	HUNT BAY
HUNT, LESLIE W.	RCAF	FL	KINISTINO	04/07/43	54°59'	104°53'	HUNT BAY
HUNT, WILLIAM E. D.	NAVY	STO 1	SASKATOON	13/09/42	59°28'	106°25'	HUNT FALLS
HUNTER, DAVID R.	RCAF	FO	SUTHERLAND	21/01/44	55°26'	104°08'	HUNTER FALLS
HUNTER, HARVEY M.	ARMY	PTE	SASKATOON	28/08/41	59°40'	109°04'	HUNTER BAY
HUNTER, JAMES M.	RCAF	FS	MACNUTT	11/01/44	57°29'	104°15'	HUNTER LAKE
HUNTER, RAY L.	RCAF	FO	HANLEY	09/07/43	55°59'	104°12'	HUNTER ISLAND
HUNTER, RAYMOND O.	RCAF	FO	HAZENMORE	09/10/44	55°54'	106°18'	HUNTER LAKE
HUNTER, THOMAS M.M.	RCAF	FS	MELFORT	01/10/42	57°37'	102°39'	HUNTER POINT
HUNTER, WILLIAM L.	RCAF	PO	REGINA	22/11/43	59°23'	108°49'	HUNTER LAKE
HUNTINGTON, HARRY A.	RCAF	FS	NUT MOUNTAIN	17/04/43	60°01'	107°40'	HUNTINGTON LAKE
HUNTLEY, WILLIAM	ARMY	PTE	INDIAN HEAD	20/07/44	57°19'	106°14'	HUNTLEY LAKE
HURL, WILLIAM L.	RCAF	WO2	MARQUIS	19/03/43	55°09'	104°55'	HURL ISLAND
HUSAK, PETER	ARMY	PTE	ARRAN	07/03/45	55°55'	104°51'	HUSAK LAKE
HUTTON, EDSEL RAYMOND	RCAF	FS	RED EARTH	28/09/42	59°34'	108°07'	HUTTON LAKE
HUTCHINGS, CYRIL G.	RCAF	FO	BIGGAR	29/09/44	55°52'	104°16'	HUTCHINGS LAKE
HYDICHUK, MATHEW	ARMY	PTE	OXBOW	23/08/44	58°03'	102°46'	HYDICHUK LAKE
HYDICHUK, PETER	ARMY	A CPL	DIVISION 9	31/03/45	56°57'	102°14'	HYDICHUK ISLAND
IBBOTSON, THOMAS K.	RCAF	FL	RADISSON	01/08/43	56°38'	108°42'	IBBOTSON ISLAND
ILLINGWORTH, CHARLES G.	ARMY	PTE	NORTH BATTLEFORD	03/12/44	52°34'	108°02'	ILLINGWORTH ISLAND
ILLINGWORTH, HAROLD	ARMY	TPR	NORTH BATTLEFORD	27/02/45	52°34'	108°02'	ILLINGWORTH ISLAND
IMRIE, JAMES G.	ARMY	PTE	HERBERT	12/01/45	59°59'	102°51'	IMRIE LAKE
INCH, JAMES H.	RCAF	WO2	REGINA	16/08/44	55°08'	104°10'	INCH LAKE
INGELL, LESLIE R.	RCAF	PO	MACRORIE	25/03/44	59°21'	102°43'	INGELL LAKE
INGLEBY, HARRY	RCAF	SGT	MOOSE JAW	12/08/41	54°45'	107°59'	INGLEBY LAKE
INGRAM, JAMES W.	ARMY	PTE	PALMER	20/09/44	56°25'	105°15'	INGRAM LAKES
INMAN, GUY W.	RCAF	LAC	PAYNTON	27/03/43	55°25'	104°06'	INMAN CHANNEL
INNES, GORDON A.	RCAF	FS	REGINA	03/09/43	60°00'	102°37'	INNES LAKE
IRELAND, PERCY J.	RCAF	SGT	SILVER PARK	08/04/43	57°56'	102°48'	IRELAND LAKE
IRVINE, LEONARD CLAYTON	NAVY	AB	SASKATOON	29/04/44	56°59'	103°42'	IRVINE ISLAND
IRVINE, ROBERT C.	ARMY	MAJ	REGINA	30/04/44	56°58'	102°45'	IRVINE CREEK
IRVINE, WALTER H.	RCAF	FS	SASKATOON	29/08/42	56°21'	106°55'	IRVINE BAY
IRWIN, WESLEY G.	ARMY	SGT	PRINCE ALBERT	23/10/44	57°04'	107°26'	IRWIN LAKE
ISBISTER, ARCHIE	ARMY	RFN	MONT NEBO	06/06/44	52°32'	101°46'	ISBISTER LAKE
ISBISTER, RUSSEL R.	ARMY	RFN	MONT NEBO	06/06/44	56°26'	102°03'	ISBISTER LAKE
ISBISTER, VERN C.	ARMY	RFN	MONT NEBO	08/06/44	56°26'	102°02'	ISBISTER ISLAND
ISFAN, JOHN T.	RCAF	FO	DYSART	22/05/44	59°19'	106°18'	ISFAN LAKE
ISMOND, CLIFFORD G.	ARMY	PTE	WEYBURN	12/03/42	55°51'	104°38'	ISMOND LAKE
ISRALSON, GLEN H.	RCAF	FS	HANLEY	11/03/42	57°04'	107°40'	ISRALSON LAKE
IVISON, ROBERT	ARMY	CPL	SASKATOON	20/05/44	58°15'	103°36'	IVISON BAY
JACKMAN, JOHN C.	RCAF	FO	DAFOE	07/02/45	54°24'	108°12'	JACKMAN LAKE
JACKSON, EARL MORSE	RCAF	SGT	SHELL LAKE	27/02/42	55°28'	105°38'	JACKSON LAKE
JACKSON, FRANK T.	ARMY	PTE	KINLEY	21/07/44	57°46'	103°34'	JACKSON LAKE
JACKSON, KENNETH R.	RCAF	FS	SASKATOON	19/08/42			PENDING
JACKSON, KENNETH R.	ARMY	CPL	VALPARAISO	29/09/45	58°44'	109°41'	JACKSON LAKE
JACKSON, LEONARD M.	RCAF	WO2	NIPAWIN	06/01/44	55°06'	105°04'	JACKSON ISLANDS
JACKSON, WALLACE H.	RCAF	FS	ASQUITH	04/06/42	59°52'	107°47'	JACKSON LAKE
JACOBSON, JOHANNES	ARMY	RFN	SMEATON	15/08/44	57°06'	103°10'	JACOBSON LAKE
JACQUES, ALBERT L.	ARMY	CPL	PRINCE ALBERT	29/08/44	55°03'	103°37'	JACQUES LAKE
JAEGER, DONALD A.	ARMY	PTE	REGINA	05/10/44	59°26'	105°58'	JAEGER LAKE
JAHNKE, WALTER R.A.	RCAF	LAC	REGINA	15/09/42	59°25'	108°40'	JAHNKE LAKE
JAMES, ARCHIBALD H.J.	ARMY	SGT	ROULEAU	09/10/44	57°43'	106°32'	JAMES LAKE
JAMES, ROBERT B.	RCAF	SGT	SWIFT CURRENT	10/09/41	58°14'	109°29'	JAMES CREEK
JAMES, ROBERT F.	RCAF	FS	REGINA	14/12/42	50°58'	108°01'	JAMES CREEK
JANKE, ARTHUR	ARMY	SPR	DIVISION I	10/08/44	59°25'	106°22'	JANKE LAKE
JANS, WILLIAM FREDERICK	NAVY	AB	LASHBURN	17/08/44	55°10'	108°08'	JANS BAY
JANSEN, HJALMAR	ARMY	PTE	BLUE sBELL	17/12/45	57°44'	105°37'	JANSEN LAKES
JANSONN, LARS C.	RCAF	LAC	CRESTWYND	30/10/44	55°07'	104°10'	JANSONN LAKE
JANTZ, HARRY E.	ARMY	A COMS	DRAKE	18/12/44	59°39'	106°55'	JANTZ LAKE
JANZEN, LESLIE H.	RCAF	PO	ERWOOD	18/12/44	59°15'	103°30'	JANZEN LAKE
JARVIS, RALPH H.	RCAF	FS	KENASTON	25/07/43	54°27'	108°15'	JARVIS LAKE
JASCHINSKY, BENEDICT B.	ARMY	RFN	AVONLEA	27/10/44	57°01'	106°04'	JASCHINSKY LAKE
JASIN, WILLIAM	ARMY	PTE	GRENFELL	19/08/42	60°01'	102°23'	JASIN LAKE
JASPER, HARVEY B.	RCAF	FL	SASKATOON	17/05/40	57°57'	104°20'	JASPER LAKE
JEANNOTTE, OMER A.	ARMY	PTE	CUT KNIFE	26/09/44	59°27'	105°27'	JEANNOTTE LAKE
JEANNOTTE, REYNOLD J.	NAVY	TEL	SASKATOON	09/07/44	55°40'	108°34'	JEANNOTTE LAKE
JENSEN, WILLARD D.	ARMY	PTE	DIVISION 5	19/09/44	56°03'	107°24'	JENSEN LAKE
JEPSON, ALAN A.	RCAF	WO2	ATWATER	22/05/44	55°21'	104°52'	JEPSON LAKES
JEWELL, FRANK	ARMY	PTE	WEYBURN	19/08/42	59°36'	109°16'	JEWELL POINT
JEWELL, HARRY R.	ARMY	SGT	WEYBURN	12/08/44	56°48'	104°15'	JEWELL LAKE
JEWISON, ARTHUR B.	ARMY	RFN	MELFORT	12/09/44	57°53'	103°00'	JEWISON LAKE
JINKS, RONALD E.	ARMY	SGT	MOOSE JAW	15/08/44	56°37'	105°44'	JINKS LAKE
JIRA, ALFRED G.	RCAF	FL	CALDER	21/01/44	54°54'	104°04'	JIRA LAKE
JOHANNSEN, ANDREW	ARMY	AR SSGT	SALTCOATS	23/02/44	58°55'	106°05'	JOHANNSEN LAKE
JOHANNSEN, QUINTEN M.	ARMY	PTE	RAYMORE	30/04/45	55°38'	103°47'	JOHANNSEN LAKE
JOHANNSON, SIGURDUR	ARMY	L CPL	UNKNOWN	23/08/44			PENDING
JOHNS, IRVING L.	RCAF	FS	HENRIBOURG	26/01/45	57°33'	106°38'	JOHNS ISLAND
JOHNS, ROYCE A.	RCAF	FO	SASKATOON	05/10/44	55°11'	108°27'	JOHNS LAKE
JOHNSON, CHRISTIAN F.	ARMY	TPR	BERNARD	11/09/44			PENDING
JOHNSON, CLARENCE L.	ARMY	PTE	DIVISION I	22/09/44	55°34'	102°38'	JOHNSON PENINSULA
JOHNSON, DENNIS W.	RCAF	FS	MOOSE JAW	05/05/43	55°24'	106°24'	JOHNSON LAKE
JOHNSON, DONALD N.	ARMY	GNR	MELVILLE	21/07/44	56°56'	103°02'	JOHNSON BAY
JOHNSON, FUSI E.	RCAF	WO2	TESSIER	25/03/44			PENDING
JOHNSON, HAROLD C.	RCAF	WO2	WELDON	25/02/43			PENDING
JOHNSON, HARRY L.	RCAF	FS	REGINA	16/06/42	57°48'	102°14'	JOHNSON ISLAND
JOHNSON, IRWIN P.	ARMY	L BDR	MELVILLE	30/05/44	56°57'	103°02'	JOHNSON PENINSULA
JOHNSON, ISAAC B.	ARMY	SPR	FILLMORE	28/02/45	59°22'	106°18'	JOHNSON BAY
JOHNSON, LEONARD J.	RCAF	FS	HOFFER	30/07/43	57°05'	105°36'	JOHNSON ISLAND
JOHNSON, LORN W.	ARMY	PTE	BULYEA	19/12/41	55°38'	104°41'	JOHNSON BAY
JOHNSON, OSCAR E.	ARMY	PTE	DIVISION 5	04/01/45	59°14'	103°54'	JOHNSON LAKE
JOHNSON, RUSSELL J.	ARMY	TPR	FILLMORE	15/09/44	55°29'	102°22'	JOHNSON BAY
JOHNSON, WILLIAM A.	RCAF	WO1	LASHBURN	14/03/45			PENDING
JOHNSON, WILLIAM G.W.	RCAF	FO	MELVILLE	23/05/44			PENDING
JOHNSON, WILLIAM Q.	RCAF	PO	LANGENBURG	24/05/43	57°26'	104°11'	JOHNSON LAKE
JOHNSTON, ERNEST G.	RCAF	WO2	BETHUNE	25/11/43	57°40'	104°43'	JOHNSTON CREEK
JOHNSTON, GARTH G.	ARMY	A CPL	BROWNLEE	10/10/44	55°16'	104°43'	JOHNSTON PENINSULA
JOHNSTON, GREGG M.	RCAF	PO	ROSETOWN	18/08/43	59°39'	106°25'	JOHNSTON FALLS
JOHNSTON, HOWARD R. F.	RCAF	SGT	SASKATOON	19/08/41			PENDING
JOHNSTON, JAMES A.	ARMY	L CPL	MOOSE JAW	08/07/44	59°14'	103°41'	JOHNSTON BAY
JOHNSTON, KENNETH L.	RCAF	FL	NOKOMIS	18/09/42	57°21'	109°04'	JOHNSTON LAKE
JOHNSTON, ROBERT A.	ARMY	C S M	PONTEIX	31/08/44	54°28'	109°23'	JOHNSTON LAKE
JOHNSTON, RUSSELL F.	ARMY	PTE	SWIFT CURRENT	03/04/42	55°19'	104°33'	JOHNSTON LAKE
JOHNSTON, STANLEY J.	ARMY	RFN	KISBEY	06/06/44	58°54'	102°04'	JOHNSTON LAKE
JOHNSTON, WILLIAM L.	ARMY	CPL	ZEALANDIA	13/01/44			PENDING
JOHNSTON, WILLIAM O.	ARMY	A CPL	SASKATOON	24/11/43	58°16'	104°46'	JOHNSTON LAKE
JOHNSTONE, ERLE E.E.	RCAF	PO	UNKNOWN	20/07/42			PENDING
JOHNSTONE, GEORGE P.	RCAF	FO	REGINA	18/11/39	58°47'	106°49'	JOHNSTONE CREEK
JOHNSTONE, JOHN E.	ARMY	PTE	DIVISION 14	19/08/42	56°12'	104°36'	JOHNSTONE LAKE
JOHNSTONE, RALPH A.	RCAF	FO	MOOSE JAW	27/07/44	55°58'	107°37'	JOHNSTONE LAKE
JOHNSTONE, RONALD E.	RCAF	PO	YELLOW GRASS	30/01/44	56°53'	106°19'	JOHNSTONE LAKE
JOLLEY, JOHN P.	RCAF	FS	REGINA	15/10/42	58°17'	109°10'	JOLLEY LAKE
JOLLY, RAYMOND E.	RCAF	LAC	WEYBURN	14/12/43	55°56'	104°14'	JOLLY PENINSULA
JONES, ARCHIE W.	RCAF	LAC	INVERMAY	14/10/42	55°54'	107°10'	JONES PENINSULA

Name	Branch	Rank	Hometown	Casualty Date	Latitude	Longitude	Geo-Memorial
JONES, ARDIN LESTER	ARMY	SIG	SYLVANIA	20/01/44	59°34'	108°01'	JONES FALLS
JONES, ARTHUR H.	RCAF	FS	SOMME	16/03/45	54°57'	102°09'	JONES BAY
JONES, EARL FREDERICK	ARMY	PTE	RABBIT LAKE	26/02/45	59°37'	103°50'	JONES LAKE
JONES, EDWARD J.	ARMY	TPR	DIVISION I	15/08/44	55°19'	102°04'	JONES LAKE
JONES, EMERSON W.	ARMY	GNR	GLASNEVIN	29/06/44	55°24'	103°10'	JONES BAY
JONES, EVERETT R.O.	ARMY	TPR	BROCK	11/09/44	56°31'	103°00'	JONES PENINSULA
JONES, HECTOR L.	ARMY	A MAJ	REGINA	09/10/44	59°51'	108°58'	JONES BAY
JONES, HOWARD K.	RCAF	FO	YELLOW GRASS	21/06/44	56°17'	105°44'	JONES RAPIDS
JONES, JOHN	ARMY	PTE	INVERMAY	29/10/44	56°24'	103°45'	JONES LAKE
JONES, JOHN M.	ARMY	TPR	DIVISION 17	20/10/44	59°35'	108°03'	JONES LAKE
JONES, JOSEPH	RCAF	SGT	WEIRDALE	29/11/42	55°13'	104°54'	JONES ISLAND
JONES, MARSHALL L.	RCAF	FO	MOOSE JAW	31/01/44	55°21'	106°42'	JONES ISLAND
JONES, MAURICE C.P.	RCAF	FO	MOOSE JAW	16/11/43	55°13'	106°44'	JONES CREEK
JONES, PAUL R.	RCAF	PO	ST. WALBURG	14/10/44			PENDING
JONES, RAYMOND E.	ARMY	L CPL	QUILL LAKE	18/07/41	59°35'	103°49'	JONES CREEK
JONES, RICHARD V.	ARMY	SGT	BIENFAIT	17/04/45	55°42'	104°26'	JONES RIVER
JONES, ROBERT	RCAF	FS	ABBEY	19/08/42			PENDING
JONES, RONALD M.	RCAF	FO	REGINA	24/11/44	57°18'	107°01'	JONES PENINSULA
JONES, WILFRED A.	RCAF	GC	DIVISION 6	02/05/44	55°53'	106°37'	JONES BAY
JONES, WILLIAM G.	RCAF	LAC	CHOICELAND	01/01/044			PENDING
JONES, WILLIAM J.	RCAF	PO	SASKATOON	14/10/42	54°57'	104°18'	JONES CHANNEL
JORDAN, THOMAS L.	RCAF	WO2	MORSE	06/02/44	59°57'	109°13'	JORDAN LAKE
JORGENSEN, STANLEY J.	RCAF	SGT	SCEPTRE	17/04/43	54°35'	101°56'	JORGENSEN LAKE
JOSEPHSON, SVEIN	RCAF	PO	WYNYARD	03/09/43	56°35'	108°12'	JOSEPHSON LAKE
JOYCE, FREDERICK J.	RCAF	LAC	SASKATOON	14/11/42	59°26'	108°39'	JOYCE LAKE
JUDIESCH, THOMAS C.	RCAF	FS	MELFORT	07/02/43	59°30'	108°25'	JUDIESCH LAKE
JUGGINS, WILLIAM C.	NAVY	OS	LLOYDMINSTER	17/12/42	55°07'	108°35'	JUGGINS CREEK
JUNTUNEN, WILLIAM	ARMY	RFN	DIVISION 11	09/04/45	57°23'	102°02'	JUNTUNEN LAKE
KADMAN, JOHN A.	ARMY	RFN	WHITEWOOD	19/02/45	59°33'	108°56'	KADMAN LAKE
KAIN, GEORGE D.	RCAF	FO	OXBOW	23/08/43	54°53'	104°05'	KAIN LAKE
KAKAKAWAY, ALBERT	ARMY	TPR	KAMSACK	11/10/42	56°42'	107°49'	KAKAKAWAY LAKE
KALHEIM, BEN I.	RCAF	FO	WILKIE	30/08/44	58°52'	102°01'	KALHEIM LAKE
KALLICHUK, EDDY	ARMY	RFN	DIVISION 6	07/06/44	59°21'	106°13'	KALLICHUK LAKE
KALLN, ROY L.	ARMY	PTE	REGINA	17/04/45	58°26'	108°06'	KALLN LAKE
KAMMERER, GEORGE F.M.	ARMY	PTE	PUNNICHY	19/08/42	55°37'	104°47'	KAMMERER LAKE
KANTEN, ROY E.	ARMY	RFN	LISIEUX	25/10/45	60°00'	103°36'	KANTEN LAKE
KARALOFF, JOHN S.	ARMY	GDSM	BLAINE LAKE	10/12/43	54°24'	106°09'	KARALOFF LAKE
KARCZA, GEORGE	RCAF	FS	MOOSE JAW	27/08/43	55°17'	104°54'	KARCZA ISLAND
KAROS, STEPHEN	ARMY	L BDR	DIVISION 11	31/08/44	56°50'	102°10'	KAROS LAKE
KARPINKA, WALTER	ARMY	TPR	SASKATOON	26/05/44	56°54'	106°09'	KARPINKA LAKE
KASPER, RUSSELL R.	ARMY	CPL	LEADER	31/08/44	59°36'	103°40'	KASPER LAKE
KATO, WILLIAM G.	ARMY	TPR	DIVISION 6	08/08/44	55°20'	104°04'	KATO LAKE
KAUN, LEWIS C.	ARMY	PTE	MIDDLE LAKE	05/03/45	56°38'	105°33'	KAUN LAKE
KAVANAGH, JOHN P.	RCAF	PO	LAKE LENORE	09/03/43	55°36'	105°02'	KAVANAGH LAKE
KEALY, JOHN O.	ARMY	LIEUT	NORTH BATTLEFORD	17/05/44	59°39'	105°26'	KEALY LAKE
KEDDY, STEWART	ARMY	A CAP3	SUTHERLAND	16/01/44	59°28'	108°35'	KEDDY BAY
KEEFE, ERNEST J.	RCAF	FO	SHAUNAVON	28/06/44	57°38'	104°39'	KEEFE LAKE
KEELER, ERVIN L.	RCAF	FO	SASKATOON	30/01/44	58°32'	102°55'	KEELER PENINSULA
KEEP, ALBERT R.	ARMY	PTE	FOAM LAKE	25/09/43	55°07'	102°15'	KEEP LAKE
KEEPING, ARTHUR T.	RCAF	PO	CODETTE	02/11/44	58°04'	102°27'	KEEPING LAKE
KEEPING, JOHN R.	RCAF	FS	CODETTE	20/05/43	57°29'	106°25'	KEEPING ISLAND
KEEWATIN, MAURICE W.	ARMY	PTE	BALCARRES	28/08/44	56°20'	106°31'	KEEWATIN RAPIDS
KEIL, GEORGE A.	RCAF	FS	TOGO	20/10/42	59°25'	106°00'	KEIL LAKE
KELLER, FREDERICK	ARMY	L CPL	PRINCE ALBERT	15/08/44	55°17'	104°51'	KELLER ISLAND
KELLOGG, JAMES C.	ARMY	L CPL	DIVISION 17	18/07/44	56°33'	104°45'	KELLOGG LAKE
KELLOUGH, HOWARD J.	RCAF	SGT	SASKATOON	28/06/41	57°15'	102°29'	KELLOUGH ISLAND
KELLY, ALBERT	ARMY	PTE	FORT QU'APPELLE	20/07/44	58°13'	104°28'	KELLY BAY
KELLY, ANGUS C.	RCAF	FS	HAWARDEN	29/07/42	56°19'	108°04'	KELLY ISLAND
KELSEY, LORNE STANLEY	NAVY	AB	CHOICELAND	14/10/43	56°59'	103°58'	KELSEY LAKE
KEMP, DENNIS S.	RCAF	FO	PRINCE ALBERT	15/02/45	55°40'	104°16'	KEMP LAKE
KEMP, SIDNEY L.	ARMY	LIEUT	YORKTON	08/02/45	56°30'	105°21'	KEMP BAY
KEMPTON, LEONARD G.	ARMY	LIEUT	WEYBURN	19/08/42	55°59'	104°31'	KEMPTON LAKE
KEMPTON, MAURICE M.	RCAF	FO	MOOSE JAW	13/02/43	58°14'	103°00'	KEMPTON BAY
KENDEL, EWALD G.	RCAF	FO	MACNUTT	21/01/43	58°31'	103°07'	KENDEL ISLAND
KENNARD, JOHN EDWARD	ARMY	PTE	CUPAR	15/12/43	59°18'	106°16'	KENNARD LAKE
KENNARD, KENNETH	RCAF	FS	VICEROY	23/02/41			PENDING
KENNEDY, ELMER E.	RCAF	FO	RIDGEDALE	05/05/43	51°47'	106°45'	KENNEDY ISLANDS
KENNEDY, MAYNARD C.	ARMY	PTE	MAIDSTONE	11/09/44	57°33'	108°56'	KENNEDY LAKE
KENNY, WILLIAM B.	RCAF	WO2	WOLSELEY	27/02/43	55°04'	104°10'	KENNY LAKE
KERCHER, EDWIN R.	ARMY	LIEUT	WEYBURN	05/08/44	57°41'	106°30'	KERCHER LAKE
KERR, RICHARD I.	ARMY	PTE	CARLYLE	20/08/42	55°56'	104°41'	KERR BAY
KERR, RICHARD K.	ARMY	LIEUT	ASSINIBOIA	08/04/45	54°32'	102°36'	KERR LAKE
KERSLAKE, WALTER	RCAF	PO	WINDTHORST	22/10/43	58°16'	102°41'	KERSLAKE LAKE
KESTER, DOUGLAS J.	RCAF	SGT	SASKATOON	15/02/43	59°54'	108°57'	KESTER LAKE
KEWEN, THOMAS C.	RCAF	FO	SASKATOON	09/08/44	58°11'	103°51'	KEWEN LAKE
KEYES, ROBERT J.	RCAF	FO	REGINA	13/02/43	59°53'	108°10'	KEYES LAKE
KIBZEY, JOHN	ARMY	PTE	BIENFAIT	12/04/45	54°56'	102°26'	KIBZEY LAKE
KIDD, FRANCIS	ARMY	TPR	EVESHAM	25/06/44	58°00'	103°52'	KIDD LAKE
KIDD, JOHN A.B.	RCAF	PO	WAPELLA	24/08/43	54°58'	104°08'	KIDD LAKE
KIDD, LEONARD D.	RCAF	PO	HUMBOLDT	07/07/44	55°12'	105°03'	KIDD ISLAND
KIDNEY, A.E.	RCAF	SGT	SYLVANIA	11/08/44	52°22'	102°28'	KIDNEY LAKE
KILGAARD, ERIC	ARMY	A SGT	SASKATOON	17/03/41	57°15'	108°52'	KILGAARD LAKE
KILLIAN, CARMAN D.	ARMY	L SGT	LINTLAW	20/07/44	52°32'	101°55'	KILLIAN LAKE
KIMBER, MICHAEL P.	RCAF	FS	BLAINE LAKE	25/06/43	60°01'	108°22'	KIMBER LAKES
KINAKIN, MIKE M.	ARMY	TPR	KAMSACK	04/09/44	52°50'	101°48'	KINAKIN CREEK
KINDRACHUK, WILLIAM	ARMY	PTE	SPEERS	10/10/44	57°35'	104°34'	KINDRACHUK LAKES
KING, ALBERT EDWARD	NAVY	RA 5	SASKATOON	07/05/44	55°33'	106°13'	KING LAKE
KING, CONWELL O.	ARMY	PTE	MILDRED	11/02/45	56°31'	102°01'	KING ISLAND
KING, FERDINAND J.	ARMY	PTE	MILDRED	17/10/44	59°15'	103°45'	KING ISLAND
KING, GEORGE M.	RCAF	FS	SUMMERBERRY	22/09/43	59°18'	106°11'	KING CREEK
KING, LORNE J.	ARMY	PTE	REGINA BEACH	19/08/42	56°50'	102°12'	KING BAY
KING, MORLEY M.	ARMY	SPR	FLEMING	24/05/45	59°47'	109°05'	KING LAKE
KINGSLEY, WILLIAM C.	RCAF	FO	BIRCH HILLS	04/03/44	58°34'	102°07'	KINGSLEY LAKE
KINGSTON, PHILIP A.	RCAF	PO	REGINA	17/06/44	58°58'	102°30'	KINGSTON LAKE
KINNEE, RONALD A.	RCAF	FS	CARLYLE	15/09/42	55°09'	104°21'	KINNEE LAKE
KINSMAN, BENNETT G.	RCAF	PO	MACRORIE	31/12/44	58°40'	102°27'	KINSMAN LAKE
KIPPAN, LLOYD D.	RCAF	SGT	SEMANS	17/12/41	55°14'	104°08'	KIPPAN LAKE
KIRK, RAYMOND A.	RCAF	FS	YORKTON	24/08/43	54°09'	101°55'	KIRK ISLAND
KIRKPATRICK, FRANK G.	ARMY	CPL	TRUAX	07/07/44	57°54'	104°39'	KIRKPATRICK LAKE
KIRKPATRICK, ROY N.	RCAF	PO	CABRI	23/04/44	55°33'	106°23'	KIRKPATRICK LAKE
KIRKVOLD, LLOYD E.	ARMY	GDSM	KISBEY	29/05/45	56°14'	106°32'	KIRKVOLD LAKE
KIRSCH, LAWRENCE V.	RCAF	FL	YORKTON	15/09/46	57°56'	105°16'	KIRSCH LAKE
KITCHEMONIA, RUSSELL J.	ARMY	TPR	KAMSACK	12/10/44	55°42'	105°02'	KITCHEMONIA LAKE
KLASSEN, PETER J.	ARMY	PTE	SWIFT CURRENT	14/09/44	56°54'	102°02'	KLASSEN LAKE
KLEIN, ADAM	ARMY	PTE	REGINA BEACH	18/01/45	56°50'	102°28'	KLEIN ISLAND
KLEIN, ANTHONY	ARMY	PTE	LLOYDMINSTER	04/10/44	53°24'	108°01'	KLEIN LAKE
KLEIN, IRVINE G.	RCAF	PO	ESK	15/03/44	58°01'	103°08'	KLEIN LAKE
KLEMMER, FRANK	ARMY	LT	OLIVER	05/09/44	58°21'	102°43'	KLEMMER LAKE
KLIMAN, IRA I.	RCAF	WO1	REGINA	07/05/43	55°46'	104°23'	KLIMAN LAKE
KLINE, SOLOMAN	ARMY	PTE	ITUNA	08/07/44	59°36'	105°40'	KLINE LAKE
KLYNE, LAWRENCE	ARMY	PTE	DIVISION 16	19/02/45	56°24'	103°18'	KLYNE LAKE
KNIGHT, CECIL D.	ARMY	GDSM	AYLESBURY	26/04/45	55°59'	103°41'	KNIGHT BAY
KNIGHT, HAROLD C.	ARMY	RFN	HILLMOND	02/04/45	58°47'	109°02'	KNIGHT LAKE
KNIGHT, WILLIAM J.	ARMY	L CPL	ESTEVAN	19/08/42	55°39'	104°07'	KNIGHT LAKE
KNOBEL, NORMAN P.	ARMY	PTE	PRELATE	20/07/44	56°43'	104°28'	KNOBEL LAKE
KNOKE, JOSEPH	RCAF	PO	UNITY	05/12/44	58°43'	103°14'	KNOKE LAKE
KNOWLES, DOUGLAS B.	ARMY	LIEUT	UNITY	23/10/44	56°03'	104°34'	KNOWLES LAKE
KNOX, CHESTER D.	RCAF	PO	RITCHIE	03/07/44	55°53'	107°03'	KNOX BAY
KNOX, LLOYD E.	ARMY	PTE	DIVISION 2	01/08/44	57°22'	102°24'	KNOX ISLAND
KNUTSON, PALMER C.	ARMY	PTE	NAICAM	17/08/45	56°27'	102°36'	KNUTSON LAKE
KNUTSON, VINCENT H.	RCAF	FS	LAC VERT	23/02/43	57°03'	108°38'	KNUTSON LAKE
KNUUTTILA, ARNE G.	RCAF	FS	TANTALLON	01/09/43	54°11'	106°47'	KNUUTTILA LAKE
KOEHLER, WILLIAM G.	RCAF	LAC	LAKE VALLEY	26/05/43	59°58'	109°10'	KOEHLER LAKE
KOEPKE, JOHN B.	RCAF	SGT	REGINA	13/07/43	54°25'	107°21'	KOEPKE BAY
KOESTER, JAMES VICTOR	ARMY	LT	UNKNOWN	30/03/45	59°52'	108°49'	KOESTER LAKE
KOHN, BENJAMIN L.	RCAF	FS	REGINA	06/09/42	59°17'	102°29'	KOHN LAKE
KOLINIAK, NICK	ARMY	GNR	MAYFAIR	24/05/44	56°12'	103°35'	KOLINIAK LAKE
KOMARNISKI, ALEXANDER	ARMY	PTE	CUDWORTH	08/08/44	55°52'	106°00'	KOMARNISKI LAKE

Name	Branch	Rank	Hometown	Casualty Date	Latitude	Longitude	Geo-Memorial
KOMMES, JOHN J.	RCAF	FO	REGINA	25/07/44	58°26'	102°27'	KOMMES LAKE
KONKOL, JOHN	ARMY	GNR	CANORA	25/05/42	59°22'	105°58'	KONKOL LAKE
KONOPADA, MIKE	ARMY	PTE	FORT PELLY	16/01/45	55°46'	104°50'	KONOPADA LAKE
KONSMO, OLE BURNETT	NAVY	CK S	SHELL LAKE	18/03/45	59°27'	108°04'	KONSMO ISLAND
KOOP, BERNARD	ARMY	RFN	DIVISION 11	14/08/44	57°41'	108°57'	KOOP LAKE
KOPCHUK, JOHN	RCAF	FS	MELVILLE	22/06/43	57°00'	107°50'	KOPCHUK LAKE
KORNASH, EDWARD L.	ARMY	PTE	NORTH BATTLEFORD	06/05/44	59°54'	109°57'	KORNASH LAKE
KOROL, STAFFAN	ARMY	PTE	RENOWN	04/02/44	60°01'	103°41'	KOROL LAKE
KORPACH, THOMAS	ARMY	A CPL	GLASLYN	04/07/44	55°00'	104°02'	KORPACH LAKE
KORTES, GEORGE J.P.	ARMY	GNR	SASKATOON	17/04/45	59°59'	106°42'	KORTES LAKE
KOSHNEY, ALBERT A.	ARMY	PTE	GULL LAKE	06/08/44	59°26'	105°48'	KOSHNEY LAKE
KOSOWAN, JAMES J.G.	ARMY	RFN	KALYNA	10/04/45	59°26'	106°28'	KOSOWAN LAKE
KOSTENKO, NICHOLAS	NAVY	TEL	SASKATOON	13/09/42	59°26'	106°15'	KOSTENKO LAKE
KOSTENLY, JOSEPH L.	ARMY	PTE	WISHART	17/01/44	59°18'	105°53'	KOSTENLY LAKE
KOSTYSHYN, WILLIAM M.	RCAF	FS	MELVILLE	27/07/42	56°35'	105°12'	KOSTYSHYN LAKE
KOTCHOREK, ROBERT B.	ARMY	A L CPL	JANSEN	01/04/44	55°32'	104°53'	KOTCHOREK LAKE
KOTELMACH, P.S.	RCAF	LAC	KRYDOR	07/08/42	56°39'	105°28'	KOTELMACH LAKE
KOWALCHUK, WASYL	ARMY	RFN	NOBLEVILLE	18/02/45	57°18'	105°23'	KOWALCHUK LAKE
KOWALSKI, JOHN	RCAF	SGT	ESTEVAN	01/03/43			PENDING
KOWALSKI, LOUIS	RCAF	FS	ESTEVAN	11/03/42	57°14'	102°47'	KOWALSKI BAY
KOWALSKY, EMIL	ARMY	PTE	SINNETT	11/12/43	55°41'	104°53'	KOWALSKY LAKE
KOWBEL, HARRY	NAVY	AB	SASKATOON	25/06/40	59°21'	106°32'	KOWBEL LAKE
KRAKAUER, CHARLES	ARMY	CAPT	DIVISION 14	22/12/43	55°42'	105°29'	KRAKAUER LAKE
KRASIUN, G.	RCAF	CPL	KAYVILLE	09/06/46	56°42'	105°19'	KRASIUN LAKE
KRATCHKOWSKY, GUST	ARMY	PTE	HYAS	01/12/44	57°32'	105°28'	KRATCHKOWSKY LAKE
KRAUCHI, GEORGE E.	ARMY	GDSM	LOON LAKE	10/04/45	57°56'	102°11'	KRAUCHI PENINSULA
KRAUS, JOHN E.	ARMY	PTE	PRINCE ALBERT	13/08/44	55°42'	103°53'	KRAUS LAKE
KRISLOCK, BERNARD M.	ARMY	PTE	MELVILLE	09/02/45	56°28'	107°22'	KRISLOCK LAKE
KROEKER, CORNELIUS	ARMY	PTE	DIVISION 7	22/12/43	56°56'	102°10'	KROEKER ISLANDS
KROEKER, WALTER	RCAF	FL	LANGHAM	05/04/45	58°17'	102°56'	KROEKER LAKE
KRUGER, CARL W.	RCAF	FO	NEUDORF	31/03/44	55°45'	104°48'	KRUGER LAKE
KRUPSKI, JOHN M.	ARMY	GNR	LEMBERG	04/02/45	56°46'	107°40'	KRUPSKI LAKE
KRYSOWATY, JOHN	ARMY	SPR	DAVIDSON	18/05/44	59°24'	106°15'	KRYSOWATY LAKE
KUBIAN, KIZER	ARMY	PTE	LAMPMAN	20/07/44	55°15'	104°45'	KUBIAN ISLAND
KUKELKO, FRANK	ARMY	PTE	MARYFIELD	08/08/44	58°21'	103°03'	KUKELKO ISLAND
KULYK, NICK	RCAF	SGT	INSINGER	10/03/43	56°37'	105°29'	KULYK LAKE
KUNTZ, HARRY	ARMY	GNR	DIVISION 2	04/08/44	59°38'	105°43'	KUNTZ LAKE
KUNZ, JAMES J.	RCAF	WO2	SANDWITH	14/07/43	55°53'	108°14'	KUNZ CREEK
KURKOWSKY, MICHAEL	ARMY	PTE	STENEN	21/07/44	55°59'	104°50'	KURKOWSKY LAKE
KURULAK, HARRY	ARMY	PTE	DIVISION 14	27/07/44	55°17'	103°53'	KURULAK LAKE
KVAM, HAROLD	ARMY	PTE	SWIFT CURRENT	20/07/44	59°30'	108°30'	KVAM LAKE
KVAMME, CLARENCE J.	ARMY	CPL	VICEROY	30/08/44	57°58'	107°13'	KVAMME LAKE
KVAMSING, WALDEMAR	ARMY	PTE	ROSTHERN	28/01/44	55°03'	103°39'	KVAMSING LAKE
KVAPILIK, THOMAS G.	RCAF	LAC	LIMERICK	13/12/42	56°37'	106°45'	KVAPILIK LAKE
KWAS, MICHAEL	RCAF	PO	MELVILLE	28/01/44	54°58'	104°22'	KWAS CREEK
KWIATKOSKI, WALTER	ARMY	GNR	DIVISION 10	15/10/44	55°39'	104°50'	KWIATKOSKI LAKE
KYLE, CHARLES H.	RCAF	PO	MOOSE JAW	13/06/44	59°27'	104°45'	KYLE BAY
KYLE, KENNETH HARVEY	NAVY	AB	MOOSE JAW	22/10/40	55°10'	108°03'	KYLE LAKE
KYLE, VERGE A.	ARMY	TPR	CADILLAC	09/12/43	58°17'	102°05'	KYLE LAKE
KYLER, ROBERT W.	ARMY	PTE	SILVER PARK	20/09/44	59°59'	106°24'	KYLER LAKE
LABACH, PETER	RCAF	PO	ST. JULIEN	16/02/44	58°08'	102°51'	LABACH LAKE
LABBEE, GEORGE J.	ARMY	PTE	RADVILLE	25/07/44	55°43'	102°32'	LABBEE LAKE
LABIUK, GEORGE	RCAF	FS	KALYNA	23/06/43	54°24'	106°07'	LABIUK LAKE
LABRECQUE, HERVÉ A.	ARMY	RFN	ROSETOWN	08/06/44	55°30'	104°57'	LABRECQUE BAY
LACEY, WILLIAM M.	RCAF	FO	DRIVER	13/06/44	54°59'	104°14'	LACEY LAKE
LACINA, EMANUEL G.	RCAF	SGT	LENEY	12/03/43	59°58'	109°36'	LACINA LAKE
LACUSTA, FRED	ARMY	PTE	FURNESS	22/04/43	60°02'	105°09'	LACUSTA LAKE
LAING, KEITH N.	RCAF	FO	SASKATOON	26/08/43			PENDING
LAING, LESLIE N.	RCAF	FL	SASKATOON	15/03/45	55°52'	104°39'	LAING ISLAND
LAIRD, DAVID A.	RCAF	PO	SCOTSGUARD	22/03/44	55°21'	105°44'	LAIRD BAY
LAKE, WILLIAM V.	ARMY	PTE	DIVISION 13	16/04/44	59°10'	103°40'	LAKE ISLAND
LALOND, CLAYTON G.	ARMY	PTE	SPEERS	26/04/45	56°20'	102°35'	LALOND LAKE
LALONDE, JOSEPH L.E.	ARMY	SGT	DIVISION 16	14/03/45	56°19'	102°37'	LALONDE BAY
LAMBERT, MILFORD A.	RCAF	SGT	WELWYN	11/04/43	59°17'	106°12'	LAMBERT BAY
LAMBTON, CHARLES H.	ARMY	PTE	LANIGAN	10/12/43	57°20'	105°15'	LAMBTON LAKE
LAMONT, CLAIR W.	ARMY	GNR	WELWYN	25/07/44	55°27'	104°24'	LAMONT BAY
LAMPIN, FRANK E.	RCAF	FO	REGINA	14/01/44	58°09'	103°54'	LAMPIN LAKE
LANCELEY, CHARLES HENRY	RCAF	FSGT	CUPAR	08/09/42	55°07'	105°01'	LANCELEY ISLAND
LAND, EARL L.	ARMY	PTE	PADDOCKWOOD	25/09/44	59°36'	109°44'	LAND LAKE
LAND, ROBERT J.	RCAF	FL	LUSELAND	14/01/45	55°25'	104°42'	LAND LAKE
LANDRY, LUCIEN	ARMY	PTE	REGINA	26/08/45	59°27'	106°15'	LANDRY LAKE
LANDRY, STANLEY J.	ARMY	PTE	MEADOW LAKE	15/12/44	54°35'	108°39'	LANDRY CREEK
LANEGRAFF, ERNEST W.	RCAF	LAC	MEADOW LAKE	27/10/42	59°24'	106°00'	LANEGRAFF LAKE
LANES, ERNEST C.	ARMY	PTE	SHELLBROOK	16/12/43	55°50'	105°55'	LANES LAKE
LANG, REGINALD T.	ARMY	MAJ	SASKATOON	17/12/43	56°46'	107°21'	LANG LAKE
LANGLEY, WILLIAM H.	RCAF	SGT	WEYBURN	10/11/42	59°16'	105°48'	LANGLEY CREEK
LARANCE, CHARLES A.	ARMY	PTE	DIVISION 16	16/09/44	60°02'	108°12'	LARANCE LAKE
LARIVIERE, GERARD A.	ARMY	SPR	GRAVELBOURG	20/11/44	59°28'	106°14'	LARIVIERE LAKE
LARIVIERE, JOSEPH E.	ARMY	PTE	PRINCE ALBERT	16/05/42	55°08'	103°09'	LARIVIERE LAKE
LAROCQUE, JAMES W.	ARMY	A CPL	REGINA	07/11/41	59°23'	105°49'	LAROCQUE BAY
LARSEN, ARNOLD W.	RCAF	FO	CLIMAX	26/08/44	58°04'	103°05'	LARSEN LAKE
LARSEN, PEDER	ARMY	SGT	ALIDA	01/02/43	55°58'	106°10'	LARSEN LAKE
LARSON, ALFRED P.	RCAF	WO2	NORTHGATE	12/03/43	57°12'	107°55'	LARSON LAKE
LARSON, CLARENCE F.	RCAF	WO1	TISDALE	04/01/44	55°47'	105°42'	LARSON LAKE
LARSON, CLIFFORD J.	ARMY	SPR	DIVISION 7	10/08/44	59°18'	106°04'	LARSON RIVER
LARSON, IVAR	RCAF	SGT	EASTEND	23/04/44	59°43'	109°54'	LARSON LAKES
LARSON, LARS E.	ARMY	PTE	BROADVIEW	26/01/45	56°58'	103°13'	LARSON BAY
LARSON, RICHARD H.	RCAF	PO	DINSMORE	17/11/43			PENDING
LARTER, WILLIAM J.	ARMY	ARM SGT	BELLE PLAINE	30/12/43	58°12'	109°59'	LARTER CREEK
LASBY, LAWRENCE E.	RCAF	PO	REGINA	14/12/42	58°28'	103°44'	LASBY LAKE
LASKY, DENNIS	ARMY	PTE	SASKATOON	09/11/44	56°59'	106°05'	LASKY LAKE
LAST, CECIL R.	ARMY	PTE	CREELMAN	19/08/42	57°04'	107°54'	LAST LAKE
LATHAM, PERCY F.	ARMY	SGT	MOOSE JAW	30/05/44	59°59'	103°54'	LATHAM LAKE
LATURNUS, ANDREW	RCAF	PO	REVENUE	13/05/44	57°22'	108°32'	LATURNUS LAKE
LATURNUS, EDWARD	ARMY	PTE	REVENUE	26/10/44	56°10'	104°36'	LATURNUS ISLAND
LAUGHTON, WILFRED	ARMY	TPR	MOOSE JAW	17/08/44	56°54'	105°49'	LAUGHTON LAKE
LAURIE, STEWART	ARMY	PTE	DIVISION 9	19/08/42	59°08'	103°34'	LAURIE ISLAND
LAVALLIE, HARRY	ARMY	PTE	MAPLE CREEK	28/05/43	57°44'	108°13'	LAVALLIE LAKE
LAVERDIERE, ANDRE C.	ARMY	PTE	GRAVELBOURG	06/10/44	57°11'	106°06'	LAVERDIERE CREEK
LAVIGNE, JOSEPH E.R.	RCAF	SGT	MELFORT	09/01/43	57°14'	102°55'	LAVIGNE LAKE
LAW, HAROLD N.	RCAF	WO2	REGINA	27/07/42	59°21'	106°24'	LAW LAKE
LAWLEY, EDWARD D.	RCAF	LAC	SASKATOON	15/09/42	59°50'	108°49'	LAWLEY BAY
LAWRENCE, REGINALD M.	RCAF	FS	MAPLE CREEK	15/04/42	57°29'	105°46'	LAWRENCE LAKE
LAWRENCE, ROBERT E.	ARMY	GNR	KENNEDY	25/07/44	55°46'	102°08'	LAWRENCE BAY
LAWRENCE, THOMAS E.	NAVY	AB	SASKATOON	24/11/44	56°58'	103°43'	LAWRENCE ISLAND
LAWRYSYN, WILLIAM	ARMY	L SGT	DIVISION 5	30/03/45	58°53'	106°27'	LAWRYSYN LAKE
LAWSON, JAMES B.	ARMY	MAJ	REGINA	01/09/44	55°14'	104°16'	LAWSON LAKE
LAWTON, DARWIN C.	RCAF	PO	SASKATOON	15/03/45	58°32'	102°33'	LAWTON LAKE
LAXDAL, HUGH L.	RCAF	SGT	SALTCOATS	01/08/42	55°57'	106°13'	LAXDAL LAKE
LAXDAL, RUDOLPH J.	ARMY	A L CPL	DAFOE	17/09/41	56°55'	102°22'	LAXDAL ISLAND
LAY, PETER C.E.	RCAF	FO	REGINA	16/08/40	58°18'	102°10'	LAY LAKE
LAYCOCK, MAURICE P.	RCAF	FO	FAIRY GLEN	28/10/44	54°08'	104°47'	LAYCOCK LAKE
LAZENBY, HUGH G.	ARMY	PTE	GLENBAIN	10/08/44	57°46'	107°54'	LAZENBY LAKE
LEACH, ROBERT	ARMY	SPR	DIVISION 6	24/07/40	54°58'	102°26'	LEACH LAKE
LEACH, RONALD W.	RCAF	FS	INDIAN HEAD	16/03/42	56°33'	103°48'	LEACH ISLAND
LEADBEATER, GORDON B.	RCAF	SGT	PELLY	24/05/43	57°09'	107°28'	LEADBEATER LAKE
LEADLEY, HENRY R.	RCAF	SGT	MANOR	27/01/43	54°21'	106°04'	LEADLEY LAKE
LEARN, KEITH G.	RCAF	FO	TOGO	02/04/44	55°25'	107°34'	LEARN LAKE
LEASK, JAMES J.	ARMY	RFN	WEYBURN	06/06/44	59°43'	108°53'	LEASK LAKE
LEAVITT, ROBERT F.	RCAF	FL	REGINA	21/09/41	57°16'	107°01'	LEAVITT LAKE
LE BARRE, ROWLAND F.	ARMY	PTE	PLEASANTDALE	03/10/44	54°54'	102°16'	LE BARRE LAKE
LEBLANC, JOSEPH A.I.	RCAF	FS	DIVISION 13	28/07/43	56°55'	102°11'	LEBLANC ISLAND
LEBLANC, OVIDE J.	ARMY	SPR	WEIRDALE	28/10/44	59°21'	106°08'	LEBLANC LAKE
LEBLANC, PETER JOSEPH	ARMY	PTE	WEYBURN	19/08/42	55°06'	107°25'	LEBLANC BAY
LEBOLDUS, JOHN A.	RCAF	FS	VIBANK	24/11/43	56°16'	107°53'	LEBOLDUS CHANNEL
LEBOLDUS, MARTIN B.	ARMY	SGT	VIBANK	20/02/44	56°15'	107°52'	LEBOLDUS ISLANDS
LEBOLDUS, PETER J.	RCAF	FO	VIBANK	13/02/43	56°15'	107°51'	LEBOLDUS LAKE
LECKIE, NORMAN A.	RCAF	FS	SHEHO	06/04/42	55°21'	104°43'	LECKIE LAKE

Name	Branch	Rank	Hometown	Casualty Date	Latitude	Longitude	Geo-Memorial
LECKIE, ROBERT C.	RCAF	FO	PORTREEVE	15/06/44	58°21'	102°40'	LECKIE LAKE
LEDERHOUSE, LEO D.	ARMY	PTE	PRINCE ALBERT	13/10/44	54°56'	102°06'	LEDERHOUSE LAKE
LEDFORD, WILLIAM H.	RCAF	WO1	SASKATOON	28/08/43	59°52'	102°10'	LEDFORD LAKE
LEDINGHAM, ROBERT A.	RCAF	PO	MOOSE JAW	10/08/43	60°01'	107°48'	LEDINGHAM LAKE
LEDOUX, GILBERT	ARMY	PTE	BATTLEFORD	20/01/45	56°54'	106°21'	LEDOUX LAKE
LE DREW, DONALD A.P.	RCAF	PO	REGINA	22/03/44	58°34'	103°55'	LE DREW LAKE
LEE, AISEL A.	ARMY	L SGT	AVONLEA	29/12/44	56°28'	103°55'	LEE BAY
LEE, CHARLES C.	RCAF	FS	REGINA	18/08/42	55°12'	104°17'	LEE LAKE
LEE, HOWARD O.	RCAF	FS	REGINA	14/07/43			PENDING
LEFURGEY, ARCHIE W.	RCAF	FS	REGINA	07/08/42	55°10'	105°01'	LEFURGEY ISLAND
LEHMAN, BRUCE E.	RCAF	SGT	REGINA	22/01/44	60°00'	105°24'	LEHMAN LAKE
LEHMAN, THOMAS M.	ARMY	A SGT	MAYFAIR	02/03/45	55°23'	104°10'	LEHMAN RAPIDS
LEIBEL, WILLIAM	ARMY	RFN	DENZIL	27/03/44	59°35'	108°41'	LEIBEL LAKE
LEJOUR, ALBERT J.	ARMY	PTE	LESTOCK	13/12/43	58°29'	103°03'	LEJOUR ISLAND
LELAND, KENNETH E.	ARMY	PTE	WELDON	15/08/44	55°33'	103°57'	LELAND LAKE
LEMKE, FRITZ M.	ARMY	PTE	BRUNO	10/04/45	56°34'	102°20'	LEMKE BAY
LEMPEREUR, GEORGE M.	ARMY	CPL	PRINCE ALBERT	18/10/44	55°51'	103°19'	LEMPEREUR LAKE
LENICHEK, VICTOR R.	RCAF	FS	WOLSELEY	27/07/42	57°07'	107°29'	LENICHEK LAKE
LENIUK, JOHN	ARMY	PTE	CARMEL	24/07/43	59°28'	104°39'	LENIUK LAKE
LENSON, DONALD	ARMY	L CPL	DIVISION I	21/12/42	60°01'	109°41'	LENSON LAKES
LENZ, LAMBERT W.	RCAF	WO1	MUENSTER	29/07/44	59°31'	108°27'	LENZ ISLAND
LEPP, ARTHUR S.	ARMY	TPR	CHELAN	02/10/43	55°13'	103°58'	LEPP LAKE
LEROY, ALBERT	ARMY		VISCOUNT	05/09/44			PENDING
LESKIW, ANTHONY	NAVY	OS	SASKATOON	20/10/40	54°35'	102°38'	LESKIW LAKE
LESKIW, JOHN	ARMY	RFN	REGINA	06/06/44	59°18'	103°49'	LESKIW BAY
LESTER, HAROLD ROBERT	NAVY	O TEL	LAURA	01/05/41	55°13'	108°59'	LESTER CREEK
LETHRIDGE, JOHN W.	RCAF	PO	LIMERICK	27/04/44	59°59'	103°21'	LETHRIDGE LAKE
LEVESQUE, HENRY J.	ARMY	SIGMN	PRUD'HOMME	23/04/45	56°33'	102°36'	LEVESQUE BAY
LEVINE, DAVID	RCAF	FS	SWIFT CURRENT	12/12/44	55°51'	107°25'	LEVINE LAKE
LEWIS, BERNARD ARTHUR	NAVY	CM GNR	UNKNOWN	22/10/40			PENDING
LEWIS, DAVID E.K.	RCAF	LAC	SWIFT CURRENT	19/04/44	56°09'	104°55'	LEWIS LAKE
LEWIS, GILBERT A.	RCAF	PO	KINDERSLEY	13/05/44	56°13'	106°33'	LEWIS FALLS
LEWIS, RAYMOND D.	RCAF	FS	MELFORT	10/04/43	56°21'	105°42'	LEWIS RAPIDS
LEWIS, STANLEY W.	ARMY	PTE	ASSINIBOIA	13/12/44	59°33'	103°52'	LEWIS BAY
LIDDLE, HARVEY J.	ARMY	CPL	MOOSE JAW	24/12/44	55°36'	104°05'	LIDDLE LAKE
LIGGINS, WILLIAM	ARMY	PTE	MAZENOD	02/05/42	56°28'	106°54'	LIGGINS LAKE
LIGHT, ALAN S.	RCAF	LAC	BATTLEFORD	05/06/42	59°40'	104°19'	LIGHT BAY
LIGHTLE, HOWARD A.	RCAF	LAC	MOOSE JAW	14/12/42	56°46'	103°40'	LIGHTLE BAY
LINDENBACH, PHILIP J.	ARMY	PTE	REGINA	21/07/44	56°15'	108°35'	LINDENBACH LAKE
LINDER, JOHN W.	ARMY	A CPL	WAWOTA	25/09/44	55°20'	104°17'	LINDER LAKE
LINDOFF, ELMER A.	ARMY	GNR	STOCKHOLM	26/10/44	56°03'	104°37'	LINDOFF LAKE
LINDSAY, FRANK D.	RCAF	FS	SASKATOON	06/06/44	56°04'	103°54'	LINDSAY LAKE
LINDSTAD, OLE P.	ARMY	GNR	DUBUC	13/06/42	59°27'	105°45'	LINDSTAD LAKE
LINDSTROM, ALVIN G.	ARMY	PTE	PREECEVILLE	24/03/45	59°59'	106°03'	LINDSTROM LAKE
LINDSTROM, LLOYD L.	ARMY	GDSM	WADENA	28/08/44	55°22'	103°27'	LINDSTROM LAKE
LINKLATER, RAYMOND E.	RCAF	FO	BURNHAM	15/07/44	58°46'	102°31'	LINKLATER BAY
LINN, HUBERT J.	RCAF	PO	MARIENTHAL	30/08/44	57°57'	103°31'	LINN ISLAND
LINNELL, LLOYD M.	RCAF	SL	WEYBURN	29/01/44	59°59'	108°19'	LINNELL LAKE
LINTON, LEONARD T.	RCAF	PO	DOUGLASTON	20/02/44	60°00'	103°17'	LINTON LAKE
LINTON, ROSS F.	RCAF	PO	WOLSELEY	02/12/43	55°18'	104°30'	LINTON LAKE
LINWOOD, WILLIAM	RCAF	FS	SASKATOON	30/06/42	60°00'	107°48'	LINWOOD LAKE
LITOWSKI, NICK	ARMY	PTE	KINDERSLEY	15/06/44	59°57'	108°21'	LITOWSKI LAKE
LITTLE, ASHLEY L.	RCAF	LAC	DINSMORE	25/02/42	59°15'	105°41'	LITTLE CREEK
LITTLE, DOUGLAS M.	ARMY	SIGMN	DIVISION 14	09/06/44	59°26'	103°55'	LITTLE LAKE
LITTLE, ROBERT J.	RCAF	LAC	CARON	09/10/42	59°45'	108°14'	LITTLE LAKE
LITTLE, SHELDON BOYD	NAVY	STO	BIGGAR	22/12/46	56°55'	103°43'	LITTLE ISLAND
LITTLECROW, HAROLD C.	ARMY	SPR	PRINCE ALBERT	26/07/44	59°25'	106°05'	LITTLECROW LAKE
LLOYD, CHARLES H.O.	ARMY	L SGT	REGINA	06/04/45	55°01'	103°00'	LLOYD LAKE
LOBB, THOMAS E.	ARMY	PTE	BEATTY	24/09/44	55°20'	103°30'	LOBB LAKE
LOBBAN, GEORGE H.	ARMY	A CPL	REGINA	08/10/44	59°41'	109°35'	LOBBAN LAKE
LOCKE, HUGH F.	RCAF	FS	RIVERHURST	10/11/42	59°15'	107°15'	LOCKE LAKE
LOCKER, ROBERT LORNE	RCAF	WO1	HUDSON BAY	18/04/43	58°38'	105°56'	LOCKER LAKE
LOCKHART, ALFRED C.	ARMY	PTE	MERVIN	06/04/44	58°52'	109°09'	LOCKHART LAKE
LOCKINGER, FREDERICK W.	ARMY	L CPL	WATSON	13/04/45	59°53'	108°39'	LOCKINGER LAKE

Name	Branch	Rank	Hometown	Casualty Date	Latitude	Longitude	Geo-Memorial
LOCKWOOD, DUANE F.	RCAF	AC1	PINKHAM	19/08/44			PENDING
LOCKWOOD, HAROLD L.	NAVY	OS	MOOSE JAW	07/05/44	55°36'	109°17'	LOCKWOOD LAKE
LOCKWOOD, MERTON R.	RCAF	WO2	PINKHAM	30/11/42	57°13'	105°17'	LOCKWOOD LAKE
LOEWEN, DALE H.	RCAF	FO	SCOTT	28/04/44	55°34'	103°05'	LOEWEN ISLAND
LOEWEN, HENRY	RCAF	SGT	ROKEBY	30/10/44	56°54'	108°06'	LOEWEN LAKE
LOEWEN, JOHN	ARMY	CFN	HERBERT	04/08/44	56°52'	102°16'	LOEWEN BAY
LOEWEN, JOHN D.	ARMY	CFN	LAWSON	07/07/44	59°14'	103°50'	LOEWEN LAKE
LOFVENDAHL, JOHN	ARMY	SGT	DIVISION 5	01/09/44	55°46'	104°42'	LOFVENDAHL LAKE
LOGAN, LLOYD C.	ARMY	PTE	VALOR	21/07/45	59°59'	105°42'	LOGAN LAKE
LONG, ALBERT MORGAN	RCAF	PO	PRINCE ALBERT	06/07/43	54°57'	102°22'	LONG BAY
LONG, ALFRED J.	RCAF	WO2	SASKATOON	24/02/44	59°45'	103°50'	LONG CHANNEL
LONG, ARTHUR B.	RCAF	FO	SASKATOON	15/08/43	57°28'	104°09'	LONG LAKE
LONG, LINDSAY	RCAF	AC2	WISHART	26/12/41	57°27'	106°25'	LONG ISLAND
LONG, MICHAEL L.V.	RCAF	SGT	SASKATOON	14/01/45	59°45'	103°50'	LONG CHANNEL
LOOYSEN, DANIEL D.	ARMY	PTE	REGINA	29/12/44	58°00'	107°08'	LOOYSEN LAKE
LOPPE, ERVIN A.	RCAF	SGT	OXBOW	09/08/43	56°08'	104°05'	LOPPE LAKE
LORANGER, NORMAN A.	RCAF	FO	CUT KNIFE	08/05/44	57°58'	103°22'	BAY & ISLAND
LORANGER, WALTER G.	ARMY	PTE	CUT KNIFE	23/10/44	57°58'	103°22'	BAY & ISLAND
LORENSEN, CLARENCE W.	ARMY	TPR	MACDOWALL	02/04/45	55°47'	106°00'	LORENSEN LAKE
LORENZ, CARL E.	ARMY	CFN	HUMBOLDT	24/10/45	57°54'	104°29'	LORENZ LAKE
LORENZ, SYLVESTER H.	RCAF	PO	ST. WALBURG	10/05/45	54°03'	104°59'	LORENZ LAKE
LORIMER, DONALD R.	RCAF	PO	ROSE VALLEY	01/12/42	55°08'	107°02'	LORIMER LAKE
LORNSON, ARTHUR C.	RCAF	WO2	MONTMARTRE	18/06/44	55°37'	104°07'	LORNSON LAKE
LOSZCHUK, PETER	RCAF	FO	FILLMORE	30/08/44	56°59'	106°22'	LOSZCHUK LAKE
LOVE, JOHN V.	ARMY	MAJ	YORKTON	06/06/44	57°11'	103°52'	LOVE LAKE
LOVE, LAWRENCE W.	RCAF	PO	REGINA	17/06/44	55°05'	104°59'	LOVE ISLAND
LOVELL, HERBERT M.	ARMY	LIEUT	KELVINGTON	06/04/45	55°07'	103°15'	LOVELL LAKE
LOVERICK, ALFRED	ARMY	PTE	DIVISION 6	24/07/44	56°58'	103°30'	LOVERICK LAKE
LOVERIDGE, DENIS L.	RCAF	FO	REGINA	08/09/44	56°45'	107°20'	LOVERIDGE LAKE
LOVING, LESLIE R.B.	RCAF	FL	REGINA	05/11/44	55°19'	104°34'	LOVING LAKE
LOWDERMILK, AUSTIN H.	ARMY	PTE	KENASTON	22/12/44	56°45'	102°17'	LOWDERMILK BAY
LOWE, EDWARD C.H.	ARMY	LIEUT	MOOSE JAW	21/10/44	59°21'	103°10'	LOWE ISLAND
LOWE, LESLIE A.R.	RCAF	WO2	CARROT RIVER	13/04/44	55°07'	102°30'	LOWE BAY
LOWERY, HAROLD J.	ARMY	PTE	GARRICK	17/02/44	60°00'	106°27'	LOWERY LAKES
LOWICK, MORTON A.	RCAF	PO	FOSTERTON	29/07/44	56°21'	106°52'	LOWICK LAKE
LOWTHER, DAVID W.	RCAF	WO2	TUXFORD	03/03/43	54°09'	107°51'	LOWTHER LAKE
LOWTHER, JOHN C.	RCAF	FO	TUXFORD	28/09/43	54°09'	107°51'	LOWTHER LAKE
LOWTHER, ROY W.	RCAF	PO	MELFORT	19/04/44	57°36'	102°26'	LOWTHER ISLAND
LOYNS, RONALD H.	RCAF	FS	SASKATOON	19/08/42	54°03'	103°02'	LOYNS LAKE
LUCAS, HAROLD F.	ARMY	PTE	DIVISION 14	11/08/42	55°07'	104°19'	LUCAS LAKE
LUCIE, BENJAMIN	ARMY	PTE	MEADOW LAKE	01/10/44	57°40'	103°52'	LUCIE LAKE
LUCYK, STEVEN W.	RCAF	WO2	KRYDOR	03/11/43	55°17'	104°09'	LUCYK LAKE
LUFFMAN, GEORGE H.	ARMY	LIEUT	DIVISION 13	01/08/44	59°19'	103°19'	LUFFMAN LAKE
LUFFMAN, HAROLD W.	ARMY	PTE	KISBEY	29/08/44	58°50'	106°29'	LUFFMAN LAKE
LUNDQUIST, ARNOLD F.	ARMY	TPR	GARRICK	22/06/45	57°38'	105°27'	LUNDQUIST LAKE
LUNNIN, THOMAS H.	RCAF	PO	OSAGE	19/07/44	56°41'	106°20'	LUNNIN LAKE
LUNT, WALLACE E.	ARMY	PTE	DIVISION 17	24/09/44	59°59'	105°22'	LUNT LAKE
LUPICHUCK, FRANK	ARMY	PTE	TOGO	13/09/44	55°54'	104°55'	LUPICHUK LAKE
LUSSIER, ANTONIN R.	ARMY	PTE	NUT MOUNTAIN	05/03/44	55°35'	104°47'	LUSSIER LAKE
LUST, RONALD	ARMY	SGT	REGINA	16/09/44	55°50'	104°11'	LUST LAKE
LUTCHER, HENRY H.	ARMY	PTE	YORKTON	28/10/44	59°33'	105°51'	LUTCHER LAKES
LUTEN, LEO O.	RCAF	AC1	RADVILLE	15/09/42	60°00'	109°32'	LUTEN LAKE
LUTHER, NORMAN C.G.	RCAF	WO1	SINTALUTA	30/06/43	55°45'	104°11'	LUTHER LAKE
LUTZKO, HENRY	ARMY	L CPL	GOODEVE	16/08/44	55°49'	104°41'	LUTZKO LAKE
LYLE, HORACE KEITH	RCAF	FO	UNKNOWN	08/12/44	57°24'	103°09'	LYLE LAKE
LYLE, ROBERT S.	RCAF	WO1	ETHELTON	18/08/44	55°46'	105°07'	LYLE POINT
LYNDS, ALFRED G.	RCAF	FS	MILLERDALE	05/08/42	59°25'	106°39'	LYNDS LAKE
LYNN, WILLIAM H.	ARMY	RFN	STRASBOURG	17/11/44	58°49'	107°50'	LYNN LAKE
MACALLISTER, GORDON D.	RCAF	WC	REGINA	26/02/42	55°40'	106°54'	MACALLISTER LAKE
MACARTNEY, ARTHUR S.	ARMY	SGMN	UNKNOWN	08/08/44	59°42'	105°58'	MACARTNEY LAKE
MACDONALD, ANGUS L.	ARMY	SPR	EARL GREY	25/12/44	59°16'	106°14'	MACDONALD POINT
MACDONALD, CLIFFORD A.	ARMY	BDR	JASMIN	07/06/44	59°57'	108°39'	MACDONALD BAY
MACDONALD, COLIN	ARMY	PTE	NIPAWIN	19/08/42	59°21'	103°06'	MACDONALD LAKE
MACDONALD, DONALD	ARMY	PTE	LLOYMINSTER	23/05/44	56°45'	108°21'	MACDONALD CREEK

234

Name	Branch	Rank	Hometown	Casualty Date	Latitude	Longitude	Geo-memorial
MACDONALD, DOUGLAS A.	RCAF	FL	ROCKGLEN	02/01/44	55°54'	104°57'	MACDONALD ISLAND
MACDONALD, GLEN R.	ARMY	L SGT	REGINA	15/11/43	56°49'	102°20'	MACDONALD PENINSULA
MACDONALD, JOHN E.	RCAF	FL	REGINA	06/06/41	54°59'	102°32'	MACDONALD LAKE
MACDONALD, JOSEPH R.G.	RCAF	FS	KINDERSLEY	26/07/43	56°12'	106°33'	MACDONALD FALLS
MACDONALD, RONALD D.J.	RCAF	LAC	STOCKHOLM	05/06/42	57°21'	104°20'	MACDONALD LAKE
MACDONALD, WILLIAM C.	RCAF	LAC	REGINA	08/07/42	59°41'	108°04'	MACDONALD RIVER
MACDONALD, WILLIAM J.	ARMY	A CPL	PRINCE ALBERT	12/04/45	56°29'	105°14'	MACDONALD BAY
MACDONELL, CHARLES B.	RCAF	PO	EDAM	15/01/45	55°06'	104°58'	MACDONELL ISLAND
MACDONNELL, JOHN K.	RCAF	FO	KANDAHAR	21/09/44	54°00'	105°16'	MACDONNELL LAKE
MACDOUGALL, ROBERT H.	ARMY	L CPL	REGINA	18/09/44	55°32'	105°45'	MACDOUGALL BAY
MACEACHERN, HERBERT G.	ARMY	RFN	REGINA	13/06/44	56°57'	103°24'	MACEACHERN BAY
MACFIE, JAMES E.	ARMY	L BDR	WAITVILLE	24/12/44	55°14'	102°36'	MACFIE LAKE
MACGILLIVRAY, DONALD	RCAF	SGT	SILVER PARK	13/04/43	59°22'	105°42'	MACGILLIVRAY LAKE
MACGILLIVRAY, ROBERT	RCAF	PO	SILVER PARK	08/02/44			PENDING
MACGREGOR, MELVIN W.	ARMY	PTE	INDIAN HEAD	15/08/44	59°34'	105°53'	MACGREGOR LAKE
MACGUIRE, FRANK	RCAF	AC2	MOOSE JAW	21/11/40	57°01'	106°38'	MACGUIRE LAKE
MACK, FREDERICK C.	RCAF	LAC	MCELHANNEY	24/07/43	59°24'	106°05'	MACK BAY
MACKAY, HAROLD N.	ARMY	CPL	CEYLON	14/08/41	55°34'	104°40'	MACKAY BAY
MACKAY, JAMES	RCAF	FO	DODSLAND	16/12/43			PENDING
MACKAY, WILLIAM J.	RCAF	WO2	SASKATOON	03/04/43	57°04'	109°11'	MACKAY CREEK
MACKENZIE, DAVID V.	RCAF	LAC	MOOSE JAW	12/04/44	57°19'	107°50'	MACKENZIE LAKE
MACKENZIE, NORMAN A.F.	RCAF	WO2	NORTH BATTLEFORD	27/04/44	59°57'	109°10'	MACKENZIE LAKE
MACKENZIE, WILLIAM L.	ARMY	TPR	QUILL LAKE	23/08/44	59°53'	103°17'	MACKENZIE CREEK
MACKEY, HAROLD D.	RCAF	FL	REGINA	10/04/45	59°54'	108°04'	MACKEY LAKE
MACKIE, CLIFFORD	ARMY	PTE	PRINCE ALBERT	27/07/44	56°31'	102°27'	MACKIE RAPIDS
MACKIE, GEORGE F.S.	RCAF	PO	SASKATOON	08/01/42	56°55'	108°52'	MACKIE RAPIDS
MACKIE, HAROLD W.	ARMY	PTE	MOOSE JAW	20/07/44	56°21'	105°29'	MACKIE LAKE
MACLACHLAN, ALBERT J.	RCAF	FS	WATROUS	12/06/43	59°24'	105°43'	MACLACHLAN LAKE
MACLACHLAN, ROBERT B.	RCAF	PO	REGINA	06/07/42	55°03'	104°29'	MACLACHLAN LAKE
MACLEAN, JOHN MURDO	NAVY	STO 2	REGINA	24/08/41	56°53'	103°32'	MACLEAN BAY
MACLEAN, NORMAN D.	ARMY	SIGMN	MEDSTEAD	14/07/44	59°44'	108°07'	MACLEAN LAKE
MACLEAN, WILLIAM O.	RCAF	PO	REGINA	03/01/43	57°54'	106°36'	MACLEAN ISLANDS
MACLENNAN, BRUCE	RCAF	PO	GULL LAKE	31/03/45	54°27'	106°19'	MACLENNAN LAKE
MACMILLAN, WILLIAM R.E.	NAVY	STO M	SASKATOON	31/12/42	56°51'	103°32'	MACMILLAN LAKE
MACMURCHY, EDWARD D.	RCAF	FO	VISCOUNT	27/09/43	52°21'	103°14'	MACMURCHY LAKE
MACNAIR, ELMOR J.A.	RCAF	FO	SASKATOON	12/09/44	55°09'	105°06'	MACNAIR ISLAND
MACNEIL, RODERICK A.	ARMY	PTE	REGINA	20/07/44	56°18'	105°26'	MACNEIL LAKE
MACPHERSON, IAN EDGAR	ARMY	CAPT	REGINA	18/04/44	55°21'	104°28'	MACPHERSON BAY
MACPHERSON, JAMES H.	ARMY	GNR	PRINCE ALBERT	29/11/40	59°33'	108°12'	MACPHERSON LAKE
MACRAE, WILLIAM JOHN	RAF	FO	REGINA	08/03/40	59°36'	108°03'	MACRAE LAKE
MADDEN, NEIL P.	ARMY	L SGT	REGINA	08/07/44	59°43'	109°38'	MADDEN LAKE
MADDEN, WILLIAM J.	ARMY	PTE	REGINA	19/08/42	55°29'	103°29'	MADDEN LAKE
MADOLE, CARL HUBERT	NAVY	OS	REGINA	13/09/42	56°16'	105°10'	MADOLE LAKE
MAGNES, HAROLD J.	RAF	FO	LOCKWOOD	09/11/43			PENDING
MAGUIRE, CLARENCE A.	ARMY	SIGMN	SASKATOON	26/07/44	55°23'	102°48'	MAGUIRE LAKE
MAIER, JOHN J.	ARMY	PTE	CUDWORTH	17/09/44	58°04'	108°06'	MAIER LAKE
MAIN, JAMES E.	ARMY	SGT	WOLSELEY	14/08/44	56°02'	103°50'	MAIN LAKE
MAIN, LENNOX C.	RCAF	PO	ABBEY	03/10/43	54°56'	104°25'	MAIN ISLAND
MAKSEMUIK, WILLIAM	ARMY	PTE	NIPAWIN	24/04/45	57°55'	109°06'	MAKSEMUIK LAKE
MALCHOW, MERTON W.	ARMY	PTE	CANTUAR	11/08/40	55°31'	104°07'	MALCHOW LAKE
MALINOSKI, JOHN J.	ARMY	RFN	WISHART	18/06/44	59°18'	106°34'	MALINOSKI LAKE
MALLEN, WILLIAM B.	RCAF	FO	REGINA	21/02/45	58°25'	103°02'	MALLEN LAKE
MALLETT, GEORGE E.	ARMY	L CPL	WISETON	07/05/45	56°50'	102°53'	MALLETT LAKE
MALLORY, LESLIE A.	RCAF	WO2	SHAUNAVON	24/08/43	55°08'	105°01'	MALLORY ISLAND
MALLOY, DEAN M.	ARMY	PTE	SASKATOON	07/06/44	56°59'	103°27'	MALLOY LAKE
MALONEY, JAMES J.	ARMY	PTE	MOSSBANK	31/03/45	55°17'	104°32'	MALONEY LAKE
MANDEL, JACOB B.	ARMY	CAPT	ESTEVAN	14/08/44	55°06'	105°01'	MANDEL ISLAND
MANDIN, EMILE F.B.	RCAF	FS	DUCK LAKE	09/06/42	57°46'	108°17'	MANDIN LAKE
MANG, RONALD F.	RCAF	PO	EDENWOLD	13/07/43	54°59'	104°29'	MANG LAKE
MANN, EDWARD J.	RCAF	FO	REGINA	29/07/44	57°37'	105°29'	MANN LAKE
MANN, RONALD P.	RCAF	SGT	NORTH PORTAL	30/11/41	59°52'	109°50'	MANN NARROWS
MANN, WALTER E.	RCAF	FS	REGINA	13/05/43	56°06'	108°07'	MANN CREEK
MANSON, JOHN G.	RCAF	PO	MOOSE JAW	18/04/44	58°36'	103°16'	MANSON LAKE
MANSON, MERLIN J.	ARMY	L CPL	PONTEIX	04/06/44	55°03'	102°18'	MANSON BAY
MANSON, PAUL R.	ARMY	PTE	WINTON	16/07/44	56°15'	102°42'	MANSON LAKE
MANTLE, E. FRANK	ARMY	MAJ	REGINA	01/08/44	55°41'	107°32'	MANTLE LAKES
MANTYSAARI, RALPH A.	ARMY	A CPL	WAPELLA	02/03/45	55°03'	107°49'	MANTYSAARI LAKE
MARCHANT, JAMES E.	RCAF	FS	CLAIR	04/12/43	59°16'	106°27'	MARCHANT ISLAND
MARCHANT, JOHN P.	RCAF	FO	CLAIR	25/03/45	59°44'	106°00'	MARCHANT LAKE
MARDER, MOIE	RCAF	FO	UNKNOWN	30/01/44	52°25'	102°02'	MARDER LAKE
MAREAN, FRED A.	RCAF	FS	ESTLIN	12/03/43	57°37'	105°29'	MAREAN LAKE
MARGETTS, RALPH	ARMY	PTE	MANOR	19/08/42	59°34'	106°00'	MARGETTS LAKE
MARK, STANLEY R.	ARMY	BDR	KAMSACK	24/08/44	56°24'	105°28'	MARK LAKE
MARQUARDT, EDWARD G.	ARMY	SIGMN	ARTLAND	08/08/44	57°22'	102°00'	MARQUARDT LAKE
MARSHALL, GEORGE C.	RCAF	PO	ST. WALBURG	26/10/43	55°06'	105°02'	MARSHALL ISLAND
MARSHALL, LAWRENCE	RCAF	PO	LUSELAND	24/03/44			PENDING
MARSHALL, THOMAS C.	ARMY	PTE	DIVISION 9	01/03/45	57°13'	104°46'	MARSHALL LAKE
MARSHALL, WILLIAM J.	RCAF	FS	HARRIS	13/04/42			PENDING
MARSIN, JOHN A.	ARMY	BDR	REGINA	24/05/44	58°17'	107°54'	MARSIN RIVER
MARTEN, LIONEL CUTHBERT	ARMY	PTE	UNKNOWN	19/08/42	55°23'	104°13'	MARTEN BAY
MARTIN, BERNHARD W.	RCAF	FO	GOLDEN PRAIRIE	03/02/45	55°10'	106°14'	MARTIN RAPIDS
MARTIN, DAVID J.	ARMY	SGT	RENOWN	24/05/44	59°11'	103°38'	MARTIN BAY
MARTIN, EDWARD	RCAF	FO	UNKNOWN	04/01/46			PENDING
MARTIN, IRWIN A.	RCAF	FS	HERSCHEL	02/10/43			PENDING
MARTIN, IVAN W.	RCAF	PO	HORSHAM	16/03/44	57°32'	106°47'	MARTIN RIVER
MARTIN, JOHN L.	RCAF	FO	PHIPPEN	14/01/44	55°12'	104°51'	MARTIN ISLAND
MARTIN, LESLIE C.	RCAF	FO	CARON	03/04/45	55°47'	107°45'	MARTIN BAY
MARTIN, LOUIS G.	ARMY	SGT	BIG RIVER	09/01/44	55°56'	108°57'	MARTIN CREEK
MARTIN, MAURICE A.	RCAF	PO	DELISLE	16/02/44	57°19'	105°39'	MARTIN LAKE
MARTIN, ROY S.	ARMY	A BDR	DIVISION 12	16/06/45	59°11'	103°39'	MARTIN ISLAND
MARTIN, VICTOR L.	RCAF	FO	NUT MOUNTAIN	17/01/43	54°49'	102°18'	MARTIN LAKE
MARTIN, WALTER K.	RCAF	WO2	REGINA	01/11/42	56°00'	107°00'	MARTIN LAKE
MARTIN, WILFRED BERNARD	RCAF	FS	DAYLESFORD	04/05/44	58°11'	107°25'	BERNARD LAKE
MARTINSON, DOUGLAS S.	RCAF	FO	NORTH BATTLEFORD	11/11/44	56°39'	109°42'	MARTINSON LAKE
MARTYNUIK, STEVE	ARMY	PTE	BIENFAIT	20/07/44	59°42'	106°02'	MARTYNUIK LAKE
MARYNOWSKI, MICHAEL E.	RCAF	FO	PAYNTON	16/12/43	57°57'	109°07'	MARYNOWSKI LAKE
MASON, ALEXANDER	ARMY	PTE	MAPLE CREEK	17/01/45	58°09'	102°00'	MASON LAKE
MASON, EARL W.	RCAF	PO	ELROSE	15/09/41	54°55'	102°50'	MASON ISLAND
MASON, GORDON W.	RCAF	FL	REGINA	31/05/43	55°37'	104°38'	MASON BAY
MASON, ROBERT H.	ARMY	PTE	MOOSOMIN	26/10/44	55°29'	102°15'	MASON LAKE
MASSEY, NORMAN E.	ARMY	GDSM	SHELLBROOK	14/08/44	55°03'	103°57'	MASSEY LAKE
MASSON, JOHN M.	ARMY	PTE	DIVISION 13	06/07/43	55°29'	104°28'	MASSON LAKE
MATHESON, C. RUSSELL	ARMY	C Q M S	PRINCE ALBERT	26/10/43	54°48'	102°30'	MATHESON LAKE
MATHESON, DONALD J.	ARMY	LIEUT	REGINA	26/08/44	59°58'	107°49'	MATHESON LAKE
MATHEWS, THOMAS D.	RCAF	AC2	SHELLBROOK	24/02/43	56°07'	108°26'	MATHEWS CREEK
MATHISON, EARL D.	RCAF	PO	BOUNTY	01/01/45	58°29'	104°54'	MATHISON LAKE
MATHISON, ROY C.	ARMY	LIEUT	BOUNTY	04/05/45	55°39'	104°16'	MATHISON ISLAND
MATKIN, FREDERICK J.	RCAF	FS	LEADER	08/09/41	54°23'	108°25'	MATKIN LAKE
MATTHEWS, GEORGE R.	ARMY	MAJ	ESTEVAN	20/07/44	58°47'	102°22'	MATTHEWS BAY
MATWIY, JOHN	ARMY	PTE	YORKTON	21/08/45	56°41'	102°15'	MATWIY LAKE
MATYAS, FRANK E.	ARMY	RFN	LEMBERG	09/06/44	56°29'	107°42'	MATYAS LAKE
MAUNDER, JAMES E.	ARMY	RFN	EYEBROW	13/10/44	59°42'	108°38'	MAUNDER LAKE
MAVOR, GRAHAM R.	ARMY	CPL	DIVISION 4	19/08/42	59°40'	106°04'	MAVOR LAKE
MAXMEN, STANLEY R.	RCAF	SGT	MOOSE JAW	28/07/42	59°21'	104°45'	MAXMEN LAKE
MAY, DAVID A.	ARMY	CAPT	NIPAWIN	27/02/43	55°56'	107°10'	MAY BAY
MAY, JAMES	RCAF	PO	REGINA	20/02/44	57°51'	104°58'	MAY CREEK
MAY, KENNETH A.	ARMY	GNR	HARRIS	23/02/45	59°24'	105°16'	MAY LAKE
MAYER, ALFRED P.	ARMY	TPR	REGINA	13/02/45	55°11'	102°27'	MAYER LAKE
MAYNARD, DOUGLAS L.	ARMY	GNR	YORKTON	17/11/44	59°25'	108°41'	MAYNARD LAKE
MAYO, JAMES G.	ARMY	RFN	FORGET	04/07/44	59°43'	109°23'	MAYO BAY
MCADAM, WILLIAM H.	RCAF	SGT	BROMHEAD	15/08/41	56°08'	109°54'	MCADAM LAKE
MCALISTER, WILLIAM J.	NAVY	AB	ESTON	22/10/40	55°37'	109°40'	MCALISTER LAKE
MCALPINE, JOHN B.	ARMY	PTE	MOOSE JAW	28/07/44	56°54'	104°29'	MCALPINE LAKE
MCANDREW, COLIN J.	ARMY	TPR	MARCHANTGROVE	06/06/44	56°15'	102°34'	MCANDREW LAKE
MCANEELEY, EMMITT F.	RCAF	WO2	HUMBOLDT	20/02/44	56°27'	108°47'	MCANEELEY LAKE
MCARTER, GLENVILLE	RCAF	WO2	SASKATOON	03/09/42	56°52'	108°15'	MCARTER LAKE
MCARTHUR, DANIEL	ARMY	PTE	MOOSE MOUNTAIN	03/03/45	55°41'	102°13'	MCARTHUR BAY
MCARTHUR, DUNCAN A.	ARMY	PTE	RUNCIMAN	28/08/44	55°15'	102°24'	MCARTHUR LAKE

Name	Branch	Rank	Hometown	Casualty Date	Latitude	Longitude	Geo-Memorial
MCARTHUR, EDWARD	ARMY	PTE	MOOSE MOUNTAIN	03/05/43	58°53'	102°02'	MCARTHUR BAY
MCARTHUR, JAMES B.	RCAF	PO	INDIAN HEAD	13/07/43	57°50'	104°36'	MCARTHUR CREEK
MCAVOY, JAMES M.	ARMY	C S M	WEYBURN	19/08/42	55°51'	104°47'	MCAVOY LAKE
MCBEATH, THOMAS A.	RCAF	PO	PRINCE ALBERT	03/04/45	56°43'	109°05'	MCBEATH LAKE
MCBLAIN, MALCOLM T.	ARMY	RFN	KEATLEY	27/10/44	59°53'	109°44'	MCBLAIN LAKE
MCBRIDE, GORDON J.	ARMY	RFN	PRINCE ALBERT	06/06/44	54°51'	102°46'	MCBRIDE LAKE
MCBRIDE, JOHN D.	RCAF	FO	PRINCE ALBERT	03/04/43	59°21'	106°04'	MCBRIDE BAY
MCBRIDE, LESLIE B.	RCAF	FS	SEMANS	01/09/43	55°45'	104°30'	MCBRIDE RAPIDS
MCBURNEY, H.R.	RCAF	FL	SASKATOON	25/05/40	60°00'	109°25'	MCBURNEY LAKE
MCCAFFREY, ARTHUR	ARMY	TPR	PERDUE	06/06/44	56°15'	102°47'	MCCAFFREY BAY
MCCAFFREY, JOHN H.A.	RCAF	PO	MELVILLE	29/07/44	55°23'	104°36'	MCCAFFREY LAKE
MCCALL, ROY C.	ARMY	CPL	MONTMARTRE	02/09/44	55°09'	102°23'	MCCALL LAKE
							PENDING
MCCALLUM, JOHN F.	RCAF	FS	SASKATOON	24/10/42			
MCCALLUM, WILBERT J.	ARMY	L CPL	UNITY	11/09/44	57°12'	102°38'	MCCALLUM ISLAND
MCCANN, DANIEL A.	RCAF	WO1	MOOSE JAW	06/04/42	56°25'	108°07'	MCCANN ISLAND
MCCLEAN, DELMAR J.R.	ARMY	PTE	GLASLYN	26/02/45	58°15'	103°53'	MCCLEAN LAKE
MCCLELLAN, JOHN FORBES	NAVY	AB	ASQUITH	06/02/43	56°59'	103°47'	MCCLELLAN ISLAND
MCCLELLAND, WILLIAM G.	RCAF	WO1	NORTH PORTAL	08/06/44	59°22'	105°36'	MCCLELLAND LAKE
MCCLURE, JAMES E.	RCAF	WO2	WILKIE	15/07/44	54°23'	106°06'	MCCLURE LAKE
MCCOMB, GEORGE M.	ARMY	TPR	ASQUITH	25/05/44	55°32'	104°50'	MCCOMB LAKE
MCCOMBIE, JOHN S.	ARMY	L SGT	TISDALE	09/04/45	59°27'	106°46'	MCCOMBIE LAKE
MCCONECHY, DONALD H.	RCAF	WO2	PADDOCKWOOD	13/07/43	59°46'	107°46'	MCCONECHY LAKE
MCCONVILLE, JAMES A.	ARMY	GNR	PONTEIX	26/04/41	59°29'	106°18'	MCCONVILLE LAKE
MCCORKLE, DONALD F.	RCAF	PO	PANGMAN	03/06/44	57°02'	107°23'	MCCORKLE LAKE
MCCORMICK, JOHN GIBNEY	RCAF	FO	KELVINGTON	24/07/43	55°06'	101°58'	MCCORMICK LAKE
MCCORMICK, JOSEPH	RCAF	LAC	KELVINGTON	27/07/41	55°06'	101°58'	MCCORMICK LAKE
MCCORMICK, JOSEPH ROY	ARMY	FS	MOOSE JAW	02/03/43	56°19'	103°48'	MCCORMICK BAY
MCCOURT, JAMES H.	ARMY	PTE	MONT NEBO	03/02/45	59°55'	109°45'	MCCOURT LAKE
							PENDING
MCCOWAN, JAMES G.	RCAF	LAC	SUMMERBERRY	11/05/42			
MCCOY, ALFRED E.	RCAF	FS	SASKATOON	09/05/42	56°10'	108°45'	MCCOY LAKE
MCCOY, HAROLD	ARMY	PTE	SASKATOON	25/05/44	55°50'	103°40'	MCCOY LAKE
MCCRADY, ALEXANDER C.	RCAF	FO	MILESTONE	08/11/42	58°45'	108°42'	MCCRADY LAKE
MCCREA, MAURICE P.	ARMY	PTE	ARBORFIELD	25/02/45	56°21'	104°32'	MCCREA LAKE
MCCREA, SIDNEY B.	ARMY	L CPL	DIVISION I	23/02/45	57°27'	102°34'	MCCREA ISLAND
MCCRINDLE, WILLIAM D.	NAVY	AB	PONTRILAS	29/04/44	56°26'	102°50'	MCCRINDLE LAKE
MCCUAIG, RUSSELL K.	RCAF	AC1	BIGGAR	01/07/40	56°05'	103°42'	MCCUAIG BAY
MCCULLOCH, KARL E.	ARMY	LT COL	SASKATOON	18/10/44	55°34'	103°41'	MCCULLOCH LAKE
MCCULLOCH, ROBERT L.	RCAF	FS	SHAUNAVON	22/09/42	55°07'	105°02'	MCCULLOCH ISLAND
MCDONALD, BERNARD J.	ARMY	PTE	SASKATOON	19/01/45	58°53'	104°47'	MCDONALD CREEK
MCDONALD, CLIFFORD A.	ARMY	BDR	TATE	07/06/44	59°57'	108°39'	MCDONALD BAY
MCDONALD, DANIEL	RCAF	LAC	REGINA	20/09/45	55°59'	107°09'	MCDONALD LAKE
MCDONALD, DONALD A.	RCAF	WO2	HUMBOLDT	21/01/44	52°25'	103°20'	MCDONALD LAKE
MCDONALD, DONALD S.	RCAF	PO	MOOSE JAW	11/10/41	57°54'	102°25'	MCDONALD LAKE
MCDONALD, GORDON C.	RCAF	PO	ESTON	25/08/42	56°31'	104°14'	MCDONALD PENINSULA
MCDONALD, IVAN G.	ARMY	PTE	LACADENA	21/09/44	58°48'	105°08'	MCDONALD LAKE
MCDONALD, JOHN D.	RCAF	FS	PRINCE ALBERT	09/11/42	59°32'	108°02'	MCDONALD RAPIDS
MCDONALD, JUSTIN A.	ARMY	CAPT	PRINCE ALBERT	06/11/40	56°15'	104°41'	MCDONALD LAKE
MCDONALD, MARTIN J.	RCAF	FO	LAFLECHE	13/06/44	57°12'	105°35'	MCDONALD LAKE
MCDONALD, MELVYN A.	RCAF	PO	BALCARRES	05/04/43	57°39'	106°43'	MCDONALD RIVER
MCDONALD, RONALD J.	NAVY	AB	SASKATOON	06/02/43	59°23'	106°43'	MCDONALD FALLS
MCDONALD, STAFFORD A.	ARMY	TPR	ELROSE	02/10/44	59°04'	108°27'	MCDONALD LAKE
MCDONALD, WILLIAM R.C.	RCAF	PO	MELVILLE	15/07/42	55°41'	106°30'	MCDONALD BAY
MCDONELL, JOHN A.	ARMY	TPR	CARLYLE	28/10/44	55°23'	104°40'	MCDONELL LAKE
MCDOUGALL, ALEXANDER	ARMY	PTE	WAPELLA	18/10/44	56°55'	103°09'	MCDOUGALL BAY
MCDOUGALL, LAWRENCE J.	RCAF	PO	AVONLEA	03/03/43			PENDING
MCDOUGALL, REGINALD E.	RCAF	FO	REGINA	22/05/44	57°31'	105°16'	MCDOUGALL LAKE
MCDOUGALL, WALTER J.	ARMY	LIEUT	REGINA	16/08/44	59°58'	109°41'	MCDOUGALL LAKE
MCDOWELL, KENNETH L.	RCAF	WO1	REGINA	17/05/42	57°39'	104°12'	MCDOWELL LAKE
MCEACHERN, GERALD J.	RCAF	WO1	REGINA	19/05/43	57°57'	109°33'	MCEACHERN LAKE
MCEACHERN, REGINALD M.	RCAF	FS	REGINA	21/10/43	55°57'	107°24'	MCEACHERN LAKE
MCEWEN, JOHN F.	RCAF	WO2	RIVERHURST	22/10/43	59°14'	106°13'	MCEWEN LAKE
MCEWEN, LAWRENCE D.	RCAF	FS	ERNFOLD	14/05/43	56°09'	104°51'	MCEWEN LAKE
MCFARLANE, ARTHUR W.	ARMY	SPR	GAINSBOROUGH	21/07/44	59°22'	106°22'	MCFARLANE BAY
MCGILLIVRAY, ALLAN E.	ARMY	PTE	WILKIE	04/03/45	58°55'	102°30'	MCGILLIVRAY LAKE
MCGILLIVRAY, EARL L.	RCAF	SGT	CENTRAL BUTTE	29/11/42	57°23'	105°49'	MCGILLIVRAY LAKE
MCGINNIS, WILLIAM J.	ARMY	PTE	NOKOMIS	25/04/44	59°19'	105°29'	MCGINNIS LAKE
MCGOWN, LAUGHLIN L.	ARMY	RFN	RUNCIMAN	06/06/44	54°40'	102°06'	MCGOWN ISLAND
MCGRATH, JOHN F.	RCAF	FL	BATTLEFORD	21/07/42	56°49'	108°37'	MCGRATH CREEK
MCGRATH, JOSEPH	NAVY	AB	KINDERSLEY	28/08/43	59°52'	108°09'	MCGRATH LAKE
MCGRAW, ANDREW F.	ARMY	BDR	WHITEWOOD	07/06/44	59°37'	108°53'	MCGRAW LAKE
MCGREGOR, ALEXANDER M.	RCAF	PO	REGINA	19/04/44	53°51'	102°05'	MCGREGOR LAKES
MCGREGOR, DAVID B.	RCAF	WO	REGINA	08/06/42	53°51'	102°05'	MCGREGOR LAKES
MCGREGOR, JACK A.	RCAF	PO	REGINA	13/06/42	57°15'	105°00'	MCGREGOR LAKE
MCGUGAN, FRANCIS R.R.	ARMY	SL	WEYBURN	21/04/44	57°04'	105°31'	MCGUGAN ISLAND
MCGUIGAN, WILLIAM H.	RCAF	SGT	MEADOW LAKE	29/05/44	55°29'	105°09'	MCGUIGAN LAKE
MCGUNIGAL, PHILIP ARTHUR	ARMY	A BDR	ARBORFIELD	04/09/44	55°48'	105°22'	MCGUNIGAL LAKE
MCHARG, VERNON F.	RCAF	FS	WATSON	26/01/43	59°41'	104°03'	MCHARG LAKE
MCILVENNA, PERCY	ARMY	CPL	ESTEVAN	07/08/44	54°39'	102°50'	MCILVENNA BAY
MCINTYRE, CLAYTON B.	ARMY	GNR	STENEN	11/11/42	59°43'	102°17'	MCINTYRE LAKE
MCINTYRE, GORDON A.	RCAF	FO	MARRIOTT	19/10/45			PENDING
MCINTYRE, JACK E.	RCAF	PO	BIGGAR	13/05/44			
MCINTYRE, JAMES R.	ARMY	SGT	SHAUNAVON	19/08/42	55°17'	105°50'	MCINTYRE LAKE
MCINTYRE, WILLIAM	ARMY	RFN	PADDOCKWOOD	09/06/44	59°43'	108°16'	MCINTYRE LAKE
MCINTYRE, WILLIAM CLARK	ARMY	LCPL	BJORKDALE	16/10/45	54°52'	103°10'	MCINTYRE ISLAND
MCIVER, ALBERT E.	RCAF	LAC	WOLSELEY	26/04/42	56°03'	103°44'	MCIVER CHANNEL
MCIVER, HENRY C.	RCAF	FL	MEADOW LAKE	13/06/44	59°24'	106°09'	MCIVER LAKE
MCIVOR, CLIFFORD D.	RCAF	FO	REGINA	27/04/44	57°17'	107°16'	MCIVOR LAKE
MCKAGUE, CARMAN C.	ARMY	PTE	SYLVANIA	05/12/45	56°30'	103°41'	MCKAGUE LAKE
MCKAY, ALEXANDER	ARMY	LIEUT	NORTH BATTLEFORD	20/09/44	59°34'	108°16'	MCKAY BAY
MCKAY, DONALD M.	ARMY	TPR	DIVISION 5	02/11/44	56°52'	103°24'	MCKAY ISLAND
MCKAY, HARRY R.	RCAF	FS	BIGGAR	04/02/43	-		PENDING
MCKAY, MELVIN	ARMY	RFN	CARLYLE	19/02/45	56°30'	106°56'	MCKAY LAKE
MCKAY, WILLIAM L.	ARMY	PTE	DIVISION 16	22/07/44	59°34'	108°14'	MCKAY CREEK
MCKECHNIE, MORTON HUGH	NAVY	AB	REGINA	13/09/42	56°28'	105°29'	MCKECHNIE LAKE
MCKEE, FERRIS R.	ARMY	TPR	CREELMAN	19/09/44	54°18'	105°47'	MCKEE BAY
MCKEE, WILLIAM E.	RCAF	SGT	BRACKEN	27/09/43	55°02'	104°11'	MCKEE LAKE
MCKEE, GORDON KENNETH	ARMY	SGT	CREELMAN	18/10/43	55°08'	105°01'	MCKEE ISLAND
MCKEEN, LEONARD I.	ARMY	RFN	PRINCE ALBERT	11/06/44	56°41'	103°50'	MCKEEN LAKE
MCKENNA, ROBERT J.	ARMY	A CPL	CLOAN	28/08/44	55°04'	104°25'	MCKENNA LAKE
MCKENZIE, CECIL M.	RCAF	LAC	PAYNTON	29/03/43			PENDING
MCKENZIE, DANIEL N.	RCAF	FO	DAHINDA	25/05/44	59°25'	107°06'	MCKENZIE LAKE
MCKENZIE, GEORGE A.	ARMY	TPR	MARSHALL	16/08/44	56°23'	103°50'	MCKENZIE LAKE
MCKENZIE, GORDON J.	RCAF	FO	FROUDE	18/09/44	55°12'	104°58'	MCKENZIE ISLAND
MCKENZIE, JACK WILLIAM	ARMY	PTE	PRINCE ALBERT	08/02/44	56°24'	106°27'	MCKENZIE FALLS
MCKENZIE, JOHN A.	ARMY	A CPL	MAPLE CREEK	08/08/44	56°55'	103°52'	MCKENZIE RAPIDS
MCKENZIE, JOHN M.	RCAF	FS	GOODWATER	11/12/41	57°38'	104°15'	MCKENZIE LAKE
MCKENZIE, WILLIAM J.	ARMY	GNR	MOOSE JAW	06/09/44	59°34'	109°34'	MCKENZIE POINT
MCKIE, ALEXANDER	ARMY	A SGT	CABRI	23/10/44	57°15'	107°29'	MCKIE LAKE
MCKILLOP, NORMAN C.	RCAF	FO	MOOSE JAW	12/09/44	55°34'	106°19'	MCKILLOP LAKE
MCKNIGHT, JUSTIN E.	ARMY	PTE	MISTATIM	08/09/43	56°34'	103°43'	MCKNIGHT LAKE
MCLACHLAN, DANIEL	ARMY	SGT	LLOYDMINSTER	08/04/45	53°15'	108°39'	MCLACHLAN CREEK
MCLACHLAN, DONALD P.	RCAF	FS	HERSCHEL	09/03/43			PENDING
MCLACHLAN, GEORGE H.	NAVY	STO2	ASSINIBOIA	25/06/40			PENDING
MCLAREN, JACK	RCAF	PO	MAIDSTONE	14/10/42	60°00'	105°46'	MCLAREN LAKE
MCLAREN, LEWIS W.	ARMY	PTE	MAIDSTONE	21/12/43	57°05'	104°31'	MCLAREN LAKE
MCLAUGHLIN, RUSSELL L.	NAVY	PO WT9	PLENTY	19/05/45	56°50'	103°59'	MCLAUGHLIN LAKE
MCLAY, DONALD C.	RCAF	LAC	MOOSE JAW	01/08/44	56°57'	107°37'	MCLAY LAKE
MCLEAN, EARL F.	ARMY	RFN	SHAUNAVON	26/02/45	59°37'	108°03'	MCLEAN FALLS
MCLEAN, JOHN S.	ARMY	PTE	MCKAGUE	02/09/44	57°52'	102°17'	MCLEAN BAY
MCLEAN, LAURENCE M.	RCAF	WO1	PUNNICHY	06/01/43	55°25'	106°44'	MCLEAN BAY
MCLEAN, LESLIE	RCAF	PO	WAPELLA	05/07/44	57°41'	104°21'	MCLEAN LAKE
MCLEAN, NEIL C.	ARMY	PTE	MELFORT	24/09/44	57°30'	102°45'	MCLEAN CHANNEL
MCLEAN, ROY V.	RCAF	SGT	BETHUNE	21/02/43	57°40'	104°47'	MCLEAN CREEK
MCLELLAN, CHARLES	ARMY	PTE	DIVISION 14	24/09/44	56°21'	104°34'	MCLELLAN LAKES
MCLENNAN, ALEXANDER C.	ARMY	PTE	NORTH BATTLEFORD	28/11/49	56°26'	103°36'	MCLENNAN LAKES
MCLENNAN, JAMES E.	ARMY	L CPL	PRINCE ALBERT	08/08/44	56°42'	103°33'	MCLENNAN CREEK
MCLEOD, ALBERT A.	ARMY	GNR	LORLIE	19/06/45	56°51'	107°06'	MCLEOD FALLS
MCLEOD, HAROLD D.	RCAF	PO	UNKNOWN	05/03/45			PENDING

Name	Branch	Rank	Hometown	Casualty Date	Latitude	Longitude	Geo-Memorial
MCLEOD, HENRY W.	RCAF	SL	REGINA	27/09/44	57°44'	105°02'	MCLEOD CREEK
MCLEOD, JAMES N.	RCAF	FL	REGINA	31/12/44	58°47'	102°27'	MCLEOD ISLAND
MCLEOD, RALPH J.	ARMY	A L SGT	NORTH BATTLEFORD	25/09/44	56°45'	103°57'	MCLEOD LAKE
MCLINTOCK, WILLIAM S.	RCAF	FO	REGINA	21/09/44	60°00'	103°23'	MCLINTOCK LAKE
MCLURG, JOHN SPERRY	ARMY	L/CPL	UNKNOWN	16/08/44	55°05'	102°54'	MCLURG LAKE
MCMAHON, JACK B. M.	NAVY	STO 1 4	MELFORT	16/07/44	55°43'	108°25'	MCMAHON LAKE
MCMAHON, JOHN F.	RCAF	LAC	GOVAN	24/04/42	58°21'	104°04'	MCMAHON LAKES
MCMASTER, JAMES H.	RCAF	FS	REGINA	21/10/43	54°56'	102°34'	MCMASTER LAKE
MCMECHAN, IAN K.	ARMY	SGT	COLEVILLE	25/10/44	55°36'	105°06'	MCMECHAN LAKE
MCMILLAN, ALBERT J.	ARMY	RFN	MCLEAN	06/06/44	55°44'	105°09'	MCMILLAN LAKE
MCMILLAN, ARCHIBALD K.	RCAF	PO	SASKATOON	24/03/45			PENDING
MCMILLAN, CLARENCE O.	RCAF	FS	MANKOTA	01/07/44	57°07'	105°42'	MCMILLAN LAKES
MCMILLAN, GEORGE A.	ARMY	PTE	MCLEAN	28/08/44	56°47'	102°53'	MCMILLAN CREEK
MCMILLAN, GLEN A.	RCAF	WO1	ANTLER	13/05/43	55°48'	104°49'	MCMILLAN ISLAND
MCMORRIS, JOSEPH K.	RCAF	FO	LEWVAN	01/12/43	55°24'	104°24'	MCMORRIS BAY
MCMURCHY, WILLIAM A.	RCAF	FO	VONDA	26/07/42	56°19'	107°52'	MCMURCHY LAKE
MCMURDO, MELVIN E.	RCAF	SGT	TISDALE	17/04/41	54°31'	102°06'	MCMURDO LAKE
MCNABB, JOHN G.	ARMY	RFN	BIRCH HILLS	11/06/44	57°50'	104°35'	MCNABB LAKE
MCNEIL, ARCHIBALD H.S.	ARMY	SGT	SASKATOON	20/09/44	59°27'	108°37'	MCNEIL LAKE
MCNICHOL, DAVID L.	RCAF	FS	NOKOMIS	25/08/43	59°40'	105°44'	MCNICHOL LAKE
MCNICHOL, GLEN A.	RCAF	PO	RICHLEA	17/04/43	57°19'	107°35'	MCNICHOL LAKE
MCNICHOL, ROBERT H.	ARMY	GNR	NOKOMIS	05/08/44	55°29'	104°40'	MCNICHOL LAKE
MCNIE, DONALD C.	RCAF	PO	REGINA	03/02/45	59°27'	108°49'	MCNIE LAKE
MCNULTY, THOMAS N.	RCAF	FO	SASKATOON	10/10/44	56°34'	108°16'	MCNULTY LAKE
MCORMOND, CHARLES R.	RCAF	PO	SUTHERLAND	13/06/44	54°07'	102°33'	MCORMOND LAKE
MCPHEE, ALLEN J.	RCAF	WO2	UNKNOWN	14/07/42			PENDING
MCPHERSON, JAMES F.	ARMY	TPR	ROKEBY	24/09/44	59°25'	103°15'	MCPHERSON LAKE
MCPHERSON, JOSEPH C.	RCAF	FS	WAWOTA	03/06/42	57°28'	104°15'	MCPHERSON LAKE
MCQUILLIN, GEORGE A.	RCAF	FO	DIVISION 16	14/01/43	60°01'	102°26'	MCQUILLIN LAKES
MCRAE, CHRISTOPHER F.	RCAF	FS	PARKMAN	23/09/43	58°24'	102°53'	MCRAE ISLAND
MCRAE, RODERICK H.	RCAF	FS	MOOSOMIN	11/06/44	56°05'	105°48'	MCRAE LAKE
MCRAE, WILLIAM GORDON	RCAF	FL	PARKMAN	26/03/45	58°25'	102°50'	MCRAE BAY
MCRITCHIE, RONALD E.	RCAF	SGT	WEYBURN	14/09/42	59°44'	105°35'	MCRITCHIE LAKE
MCROBB, JAMES K.	RCAF	FO	REGINA	29/07/44	53°46'	107°15'	MCROBB LAKE
MCROBBIE, WILLIAM	ARMY	PTE	BROADVIEW	02/03/45	54°39'	101°52'	MCROBBIE LAKE
MCSHERRY, LESLIE ANDREW	RAF	FO	MOOSE JAW	08/04/40	52°30'	101°46'	MCSHERRY LAKE
MCTAGGART, DAVID A.	NAVY	TEL	MOOSE JAW	22/10/40	58°02'	108°25'	MCTAGGART LAKE
MCTAGGART, WESLEY A.	ARMY	WO2	UNKNOWN	05/05/45	56°53'	102°16'	MCTAGGERT ISLAND
MCTAVISH, ARCHIBALD S.	RCAF	FO	REGINA	07/08/44	57°38'	106°03'	MCTAVISH CREEK
MCWILLIAMS, GILBERT	ARMY	PTE	PRINCE ALBERT	05/08/43	57°08'	103°41'	MCWILLIAMS CREEK
MCWILLIAMS, RAY E.	ARMY	TPR	LOREBURN	12/10/44	55°07'	102°21'	MCWILLIAMS LAKES
MEAD, ANTHONY	ARMY	RFN	DIVISION 3	17/09/44	59°38'	108°47'	MEAD LAKE
MEALING, KENNETH	ARMY	PTE	KELLIHER	01/08/44	59°17'	106°39'	MEALING POINT
MEANEY, WILLIAM P.	ARMY	SPR	REGINA	23/12/43	54°39'	102°17'	MEANEY LAKE
MEANWELL, VICTOR	RCAF	FS	COURVAL	30/11/42	57°35'	108°39'	MEANWELL LAKE
MEEKER, CLARENCE A.	ARMY	PTE	PIERCELAND	21/07/44	55°18'	103°58'	MEEKER LAKE
MEERSMAN, ALFONS	ARMY	SPR	DIVISION 16	23/07/44	59°23'	106°09'	MEERSMAN LAKE
MEIER, PAUL H.	ARMY	LIEUT	LEADER	26/02/45	59°39'	103°47'	MEIER LAKE
MEILI, ERNEST O.	ARMY	GNR	COURVAL	14/01/44	56°39'	104°02'	MEILI LAKE
MELANSON, GEORGE A.	ARMY	PTE	BROADVIEW	13/10/44	55°38'	105°55'	MELANSON LAKE
MELBY, PALMER J.	ARMY	SPR	BIRCH HILLS	11/09/44	59°20'	106°29'	MELBY LAKE
MELENCHUK, JOHN	ARMY	TPR	DYSART	13/09/42	59°27'	106°29'	MELENCHUK LAKE
MELNICK, NICHOLAS	RCAF	FO	VISCOUNT	11/04/44	54°12'	102°12'	MELNICK LAKE
MENEILLY, JAMES A.	RCAF	CPL	BIGGAR	10/01/43	56°47'	107°50'	MENEILLY LAKE
MERK, GEORGE ADAM	NAVY	STWD	REGINA	21/08/44	55°44'	108°08'	MERK LAKE
MERKLEY, ALBERT J.	ARMY	PTE	MOOSE JAW	23/07/44	56°07'	103°19'	MERKLEY LAKE
MERLE, GEORGE P.F.	RCAF	SGT	REGINA	07/10/42	54°10'	101°58'	MERLE BAY
MERRITT, JOHN P.	RCAF	PO	MAJOR	31/03/44	58°51'	103°30'	MERRITT LAKE
MERRITT, KENNETH F.	ARMY	TPR	CABRI	10/08/44	56°13'	102°44'	MERRITT ISLAND
MESHKE, LESTER G.	ARMY	PTE	CRAIK	12/01/45	57°22'	102°57'	MESHKE CREEK
MESSENGER, ROBERT F.	RCAF	AC2	CABRI	10/09/43	57°55'	109°19'	MESSENGER LAKE
MESSUM, STANLEY E.	RCAF	FO	LLOYDMINSTER	06/04/44	58°57'	103°25'	MESSUM LAKE
METCALFE, DONALD IRVING	NAVY	EA A3	KELVINGTON	29/04/44	56°48'	103°58'	METCALFE LAKE
METKA, JOSEPH	RCAF	PO	MOOSE JAW	26/02/44	58°20'	102°16'	METKA LAKE
MEYERS, ALFRED P.	ARMY	SIGNM	MELVILLE	24/10/44	56°58'	103°11'	MEYERS BAY
MEYERS, PHILIP	ARMY	GNR	MELVILLE	05/09/44	56°50'	103°05'	MEYERS ISLAND
MICHAEL, JOHN EDWARD	NAVY	AB	DIVISION 16	10/06/45	56°53'	103°37'	MICHAEL BAY
MICHAUD, HERBERT	ARMY	GNR	REGINA	28/08/44	56°04'	106°52'	MICHAUD BAY
MIDDLEMAS, ROBERT J.	RCAF	WO2	REGINA	24/03/44	54°58'	104°16'	MIDDLEMAS LAKE
MIDDLEMISS, KENNETH R.	RCAF	PO	HEARNE	15/01/44	59°47'	103°56'	MIDDLEMISS LAKE
MIDDLEMISS, WALTER R.	ARMY	PTE	YORKTON	02/03/45	54°42'	102°51'	MIDDLEMISS BAY
MIDDLETON, ISAAC C.	ARMY	CPL	VISCOUNT	03/03/45	59°13'	103°39'	MIDDLETON LAKE
MIDDLETON, JOSEPH J.	ARMY	PTE	YORKTON	15/08/44	57°26'	104°27'	MIDDLETON LAKE
MIEYETTE, LLOYD	RCAF	WO1	MELVILLE	16/09/43	59°59'	107°57'	MIEYETTE LAKE
MIKO, JOSEPH	ARMY	PTE	DIVISION 15	06/06/44	53°53'	107°43'	MIKO LAKE
MILLAR, GEORGE R.	RCAF	FS	BETHUNE	16/02/42	55°19'	102°57'	MILLAR LAKE
MILLARD, HENRY A.	ARMY	A CPL	MEDSTEAD	05/07/44	58°09'	108°34'	MILLARD LAKE
MILLER, ALFRED S.	RCAF	FS	SINNETT	12/02/44	56°48'	105°11'	MILLER ISLAND
MILLER, ERWIN H.	ARMY	L CPL	BIRMINGHAM	28/08/44	59°17'	103°48'	MILLER ISLAND
MILLER, HERMAN E.	ARMY	PTE	DAHINDA	15/09/44	56°55'	103°32'	MILLER BAY
MILLER, JACOB	ARMY	PTE	BATEMAN	11/10/42	56°54'	103°32'	MILLER ISLAND
MILLER, JOSEPH M.	RCAF	FS	MARCHWELL	25/07/44	57°11'	104°15'	MILLER LAKES
MILLER, LLOYD G.	ARMY	SIGMN	DELISLE	23/07/44	59°29'	108°20'	MILLER CREEK
MILLER, LOWELL H.	ARMY	GDSM	HUDSON BAY	24/02/45	58°52'	106°00'	MILLER CREEK
MILLER, SPRAGUE M.	ARMY	PTE	SPRINGWATER	13/09/44	56°39'	104°57'	MILLER RAPIDS
MILLER, THEODORE A.	ARMY	CAPT	WEYBURN	15/08/44	58°57'	102°00'	MILLER LAKE
MILLER, WILLIAM G.	RCAF	PO	LLOYDMINSTER	05/03/45	55°17'	103°52'	MILLER CHANNEL
MILLER, WILLIAM L.	ARMY	L CPL	YORKTON	17/01/45	55°24'	106°19'	MILLER BAY
MILLIKEN, DOUGLAS W.	RCAF	WO2	SASKATOON	04/12/43	55°12'	104°59'	MILLIKEN ISLAND
MILLIKEN, PETER S.	RCAF	FL	SASKATOON	23/06/44	58°00'	104°07'	MILLIKEN CREEK
MILLSON, HAROLD R.	RCAF	FS	MILESTONE	03/03/43	56°44'	106°10'	MILLSON LAKE
MILMINE, JOHN M.	RCAF	PO	KIPLING	01/07/41	59°38'	108°24'	MILMINE LAKE
MILNE, WILLIAM S.	RCAF	FS	REGINA	29/11/42	56°25'	103°07'	MILNE LAKE
MILNER, HOWARD A.	ARMY	CPL	MOOSOMIN	29/08/44	55°36'	104°52'	MILNER LAKE
MILWARD, LEO V.	RCAF	PO	REGINA	31/03/44	59°24'	108°56'	MILWARD LAKE
MINERS, HAROLD M.	RCAF	SGT	SASKATOON	07/07/42	55°36'	106°20'	MINERS LAKE
MINOR, NORMAN G.	RCAF	SGT	REGINA	09/10/43	57°56'	103°46'	MINOR BAY
MIREAU, ALBERT O.	RCAF	SGT	HARRIS	02/06/42	56°56'	106°36'	MIREAU LAKE
MITCHELL, DAVID C.	ARMY	RFN	DIVISION 17	08/06/44	58°20'	104°37'	MITCHELL ISLAND
MITCHELL, DONALD A.	RCAF	FS	GRENFELL	28/09/42	59°44'	109°36'	MITCHELL LAKE
MITCHELL, JOHN M.	RCAF	FL	BIGGAR	07/05/44	55°04'	104°21'	MITCHELL LAKE
MITCHELL, JOHN R.K.	ARMY	TPR	DIVISION 16	24/05/44	58°16'	104°38'	MITCHELL BAY
MITCHELL, JOHN W.	RCAF	FO	SASKATOON	21/08/44			PENDING
MITCHELL, PETER J.F.	RCAF	PO	MANOR	23/10/44	57°09'	107°10'	MITCHELL LAKE
MITCHELL, PHILIP H.	RCAF	WO2	LLOYDMINSTER	26/02/43	54°34'	102°59'	PHILMITCHELL LAKE
MITCHELL, ROBERT G.	RCAF	PO	ESTEVAN	17/07/41	58°55'	105°49'	MITCHELL CREEK
MITCHELL, RUSSELL T.	RCAF	SGT	STRASBOURG	15/12/41	57°53'	104°06'	MITCHELL LAKE
MITCHELL, WALTER L.	RCAF	WO1	PRINCE ALBERT	29/06/44	59°48'	109°04'	MITCHELL BAY
MITCHELL, WILLIAM A.	RCAF	LAC	TOMPKINS	23/01/44	55°20'	107°38'	MITCHELL LAKE
MITCHELL, WILLIAM D.	RCAF	WO1	PRINCE ALBERT	24/05/44	59°37'	107°17'	MITCHELL RAPIDS
MOE, ROALD A.	ARMY	PTE	SPALDING	02/03/45	57°18'	107°12'	MOE LAKE
MOEN, RONALD O.	RCAF	FO	SASKATOON	12/08/44	58°38'	102°42'	MOEN LAKE
MOFFAT, MALCOLM M.	ARMY	PTE	BETHUNE	07/02/45	58°17'	103°42'	MOFFATT LAKE
MOFFATT, WILLIAM F.	ARMY	PTE	MOOSOMIN	14/12/44	59°42'	106°54'	MOFFATT LAKE
MOGALKI, ROY E.	RCAF	FS	GOODWATER	31/03/44	53°46'	107°27'	MOGALKI LAKE
MOGEY, HAROLD FREDERICK	ARMY	CPT	REGINA	28/10/44	55°46'	107°31'	MOGEY LAKE
MOHR, LESLIE ADAM	NAVY	AB	REGINA	26/06/42	56°02'	104°24'	MOHR LAKE
MOIR, ALLAN R.	ARMY	PTE	REGINA	09/04/44	55°49'	104°47'	MOIR LAKE
MOLDENHAUER, JOHN R.	ARMY	PTE	COLONSAY	14/08/44	56°57'	103°10'	MOLDENHAUER LAKE
MOLLARD, LLOYD B.	RCAF	FO	PRINCE ALBERT	15/07/44	59°48'	109°32'	MOLLARD LAKE
MOLLER, ROY W.	RCAF	FS	DUBUC	05/03/44	54°23'	101°51'	MOLLER LAKE
MOLLISON, GEORGE W.	ARMY	C CPL	GOVAN	29/03/45	57°05'	103°10'	MOLLISON LAKE
MOLONEY, DAVID T.	ARMY	A L CPL	DIVISION 16	09/06/44	54°39'	108°33'	MOLONEY CREEK
MOLOSKI, HARVEY T.	ARMY	RFN	ESTERHAZY	17/02/45	55°37'	106°14'	MOLOSKI LAKE
MOLSBERRY, CLARKE B.	ARMY	PTE	LOON LAKE	26/10/44	56°07'	104°23'	MOLSBERRY LAKE
MONCRIEFF, STANLEY R.	RCAF	WO2	SENLAC	26/11/43	55°09'	104°17'	MONCRIEFF LAKE
MONSON, MERVAL T.	ARMY	A L BDR	PLENTY	24/04/44	55°33'	103°40'	MONSON LAKE
MOON, DAVID C.G.	ARMY	L CPL	REGINA	28/12/43	57°31'	105°35'	MOON LAKE

Name	Branch	Rank	Hometown	Casualty Date	Latitude	Longitude	Geo-Memorial
MOONEY, CLARENCE R.	RCAF	LAC	REGINA	19/05/45	55°15'	105°07'	MOONEY BAY
MOORE, CLAUDE R.	RCAF	LAC	WILKIE	16/09/41			PENDING
MOORE, EARL F.	ARMY	SGT	MOOSE JAW	24/11/43	58°16'	102°30'	MOORE LAKE
MOORE, GEORGE N.	RCAF	FS	WILKIE	16/04/42			PENDING
MOORE, GORDON L.	ARMY	GNR	DIVISION 12	26/04/44	59°27'	108°32'	MOORE CREEK
MOORE, HAROLD E.	RCAF	SGT	LAWSON	11/09/41	55°12'	105°10'	MOORE ISLAND
MOORE, JAMES R.	RCAF	FS	HEARNE	17/10/42	55°50'	107°42'	MOORE LAKE
MOORE, KENNETH A.	ARMY	PTE	ROULEAU	31/08/44	55°19'	104°32'	MOORE LAKE
MOORE, KENNETH T.	ARMY	PTE	NORTH BATTLEFORD	17/09/44	59°51'	108°34'	MOORE RAPIDS
MOORE, LLOYD GEORGE	NAVY	AB	REGINA	20/09/43	54°07'	102°21'	MOORE BAY
MOORE, LORNE J.	RCAF	FS	REGINA	23/10/44	57°27'	105°03'	MOORE LAKES
MOORE, ROBERT F.	ARMY	TPR	LINTLAW	06/06/44	59°02'	108°02'	MOORE LAKE
MOORE, ROGER	RCAF	FS	KINLEY	07/09/43			PENDING
MOORE, THEODORE B.T.	RCAF	PO	TANTALLON	16/09/42	58°31'	103°12'	MOORE POINT
MOORHEAD, DONALD R.	ARMY	CPL	MAPLE CREEK	06/06/44	49°53'	109°16'	MOORHEAD CREEK
MORIN, EUGENE	ARMY	PTE	MEADOW LAKE	18/11/44	57°16'	106°04'	MORIN RIVER
MORIN, NAPOLEON	ARMY	RFN	CUMBERLAND HOUSE	11/06/44	58°11'	103°11'	MORIN ISLAND
MORIN, NORMAN J.	ARMY	RFN	MEADOW LAKE	09/06/44	57°18'	106°03'	MORIN LAKE
MORLIDGE, ARTHUR B.	RCAF	FO	LLOYDMINSTER	02/10/42	59°50'	108°33'	MORLIDGE LAKE
MORPHY, JOHN N.	ARMY	TPR	VISCOUNT	06/09/44	56°50'	108°54'	MORPHY LAKE
MORRIS, ALAN H. A.	RCAF	WO	NOKOMIS	21/03/44	55°17'	104°12'	MORRIS RAPIDS
MORRIS, BLAKE	NAVY	AB	REGINA	10/05/41	56°59'	103°33'	MORRIS LAKE
MORRIS, ERNEST H.	ARMY	SPR	SASKATOON	17/08/42	59°42'	107°52'	MORRIS LAKE
MORRIS, FREDERICK E.	ARMY	PTE	PUNNICHY	01/05/41	56°50'	102°25'	MORRIS ISLAND
MORRIS, GEORGE T.	RCAF	FS	BALCARRES	12/07/42	57°26'	106°11'	MORRIS BAY
MORRISON, DONALD B.	ARMY	RFN	SYLVANIA	04/07/44	58°41'	108°06'	MORRISON LAKE
MORRISON, EARL W.	ARMY	A L CPL	MELFORT	27/05/44	57°31'	106°19'	MORRISON ISLAND
MORRISON, EWEN	NAVY	LDG SMN	YORKTON	24/11/44	56°49'	103°44'	MORRISON ISLAND
MORRISON, FRANK T.	ARMY	L CPL	COOKSON	31/03/45	56°50'	102°03'	MORRISON LAKE
MORRISON, JOHN D.	RCAF	SGT	BALCARRES	24/08/44			PENDING
MORRISON, JOHN D.	RCAF	SL	REGINA	24/03/42	56°12'	102°16'	MORRISON BAY
MORRISON, WESLEY K.	ARMY	RFN	CARLYLE	08/06/44	58°46'	102°04'	MORRISON LAKE
MORRISON, WILLIAM M.	RCAF	LAC	PENSE	25/07/42	57°30'	105°04'	MORRISON CREEK
MORROW, GEORGE D.H.	RCAF	SGT	BIG BEAVER	08/09/43	57°41'	108°44'	MORROW LAKE
MORTENSON, THEODORE R.	ARMY	PTE	MOOSE JAW	20/07/44	56°36'	102°14'	MORTENSON LAKE
MORTON, WILLIAM A.	ARMY	GNR	MELFORT	09/03/45	57°24'	102°42'	MORTON ISLAND
MOSS, CLAUDE A.	RCAF	FO	SASKATOON	05/07/44	57°15'	107°49'	MOSS LAKE
MOSSING, FREDERICK W.	RCAF	FL	REGINA	12/05/45	55°21'	104°38'	MOSSING LAKE
MOSTOWAY, HARRY	ARMY	GNR	WROXTON	31/05/44	55°58'	104°44'	MOSTOWAY LAKE
MOUNTNEY, IRWIN R.	ARMY	PTE	WALDRON	27/04/43	55°42'	105°07'	MOUNTNEY LAKE
MOWER, WILMORE H.	ARMY	GNR	HAZEL DELL	16/10/43	55°55'	105°00'	MOWER LAKE
MOYSEY, NOEL H.	RCAF	FO	ESTON	13/08/44	55°14'	105°02'	MOYSEY ISLAND
MUCHA, WILLIAM	ARMY	SIGMN	BETHUNE	31/10/44	59°47'	107°45'	MUCHA LAKE
MUDFORD, VERNON	RCAF	PO	MANKOTA	09/05/44	59°23'	108°53'	MUDFORD ISLAND
MUIRHEAD, HARVEY D.	RCAF	WO1	ESTEVAN	17/02/43	59°40'	109°31'	MUIRHEAD LAKE
MUIRHEAD, WILLIAM J.	ARMY	L CPL	ESTEVAN	20/07/44	54°13'	107°30'	MUIRHEAD LAKE
MULLEN, ALBERT L.	RCAF	SGT	REGINA	31/01/44	55°16'	104°41'	MULLEN ISLANDS
MULLEN, GILBERT A.	ARMY	PTE	MELFORT	10/06/44	58°10'	102°22'	MULLEN LAKE
MULLIGAN, ALBERT E.	ARMY	PTE	SASKATOON	23/06/44	55°15'	103°28'	MULLIGAN LAKE
MULLINS, FREDERICK E.	ARMY	LIEUT	VERA	29/09/44	58°09'	104°51'	MULLINS LAKE
MULLIS, EARL A.	RCAF	FS	TYNER	21/03/42	59°33'	106°07'	MULLIS LAKE
MULLOCK, ROBERT	ARMY	PTE	SOMME	17/10/44	55°28'	104°51'	MULLOCK LAKE
MUNN, WILLIAM F.	RCAF	PO	REGINA	25/04/42	59°42'	109°10'	MUNN LAKE
MUNNS, DOUGLAS C.	ARMY	SPR	SASKATOON	23/09/44	59°23'	106°09'	MUNNS LAKE
MUNRO, ALLAN	ARMY	CPL	LUCKY LAKE	27/10/44	56°47'	102°24'	MUNRO BAY
MUNRO, GEORGE	ARMY	PTE	AVONLEA	05/07/43	57°58'	103°32'	MUNRO ISLAND
MUNRO, HECTOR W.	RCAF	FO	SHEHO	24/11/43	55°43'	103°31'	MUNRO LAKE
MUNROE, DOUGLAS T.	ARMY	PTE	GIBBS	28/08/44	55°17'	105°23'	MUNROE PENINSULA
MURDOCK, RAYMOND H.	RCAF	FS	CLAIR	22/07/43	59°30'	106°27'	MURDOCK LAKE
MURPHY, MERTON B.	RCAF	FS	PAYNTON	18/08/43	55°06'	105°14'	MURPHY ISLANDS
MURPHY, WILLIAM A.	RCAF	FS	SASKATOON	12/03/42			PENDING
MURRAY, DAVID W.	ARMY	SGT	ESTEVAN	27/07/44	55°14'	105°02'	MURRAY ISLAND
MURRAY, LEWIS B.	RCAF	WO2	YORKTON	02/01/43	55°07'	105°01'	MURRAY BAY
MUSIC, FREDERICK W.	RCAF	FS	REGINA	02/03/43	56°09'	107°11'	MUSIC LAKE
MUSTARD, JOHN G.	ARMY	TPR	TISDALE	20/02/45	59°30'	108°04'	MUSTARD LAKE
MYDASKI, STANLEY	RCAF	WO1	MITCHELLTON	15/03/44	59°39'	106°19'	MYDASKI LAKE
MYERS, JAMES G.	ARMY	CPL	SASKATOON	21/05/44	57°24'	105°05'	MYERS LAKE
MYERS, MARQUIS DE	ARMY	SGT	REGINA	10/09/44	54°59'	103°14'	MYERS LAKE
MYERS, THEODORE W.	RCAF	WO2	WEYBURN	02/01/44	59°50'	109°31'	MYERS LAKE
MYLREA, RUSSELL EDWARD	NAVY	STO 1	ROSETOWN	22/10/40	55°39'	106°19'	MYLREA LAKE
NAIRN, LLOYD S.	RCAF	FO	REGINA	15/06/44	55°34'	103°10'	NAIRN ISLAND
NEALE, DOUGLAS	RCAF	FS	BATTLEFORD	13/03/43	55°22'	106°20'	NEALE LAKE
NEIL, JOHN V.	ARMY	A CPL	PRINCE ALBERT	08/08/44	56°58'	105°05'	NEIL LAKE
NEIL, ROSS M.	RCAF	FS	SASKATOON	27/06/42	59°24'	106°27'	NEIL LAKE
NEIL, RUSSELL J.	ARMY	L SGT	PRINCE ALBERT	10/08/44	59°23'	107°28'	NEIL BAY
NEILLY, ROY W.	ARMY	PTE	LOON LAKE	09/10/44	59°59'	105°08'	NEILLY LAKE
NEILSON, CLARENCE R.	ARMY	RFN	BIG RIVER	08/07/44	59°33'	109°45'	NEILSON LAKE
NEILSON, VERNON A.	ARMY	CPL	SWIFT CURRENT	08/02/45	55°36'	105°10'	NEILSON LAKE
NELAN, JOHN J.	ARMY	SPR	SASKATOON	01/05/45	59°29'	106°17'	NELAN ISLAND
NELLIGAN, ALLAN N.	RCAF	FL	LASHBURN	28/10/44	56°45'	106°56'	NELLIGAN LAKE
NELMS, EDWARD J.	RCAF	FS	REGINA	15/06/42	60°00'	102°41'	NELMS LAKE
NELSON, BJORN R.	RCAF	WO1	FORGET	04/03/45	57°07'	104°37'	NELSON LAKE
NELSON, CHARLES P.R.	ARMY	C S M	RICHARD	08/06/44	59°42'	108°28'	NELSON BAY
NELSON, DANIEL H.	ARMY	PTE	NAICAM	01/08/43	59°37'	104°59'	NELSON PENINSULA
NELSON, JACK A.	ARMY	C S M	PRINCE ALBERT	08/04/45	55°59'	104°36'	NELSON LAKE
NELSON, JACK N.	RCAF	FL	TISDALE	29/12/43	52°28'	102°05'	NELSON CREEK
NELSON, JOHN A.	RCAF	LAC	COLFAX	26/08/43	57°03'	105°40'	NELSON BAY
NELSON, ORVIN K.	RCAF	FO	SASKATOON	21/01/44			PENDING
NELSON, RAYMOND M.	ARMY	RFN	GRAINLAND	12/06/44	55°12'	104°49'	NELSON ISLAND
NESBITT, J.E.	RCAF	AC1	SASKATOON	10/06/40	55°18'	104°32'	NESBITT LAKE
NESBITT, JOHN WATSON	NAVY	O SIG	TESSIER	13/07/45	56°57'	103°41'	NESBITT ISLAND
NESS, OLAV A.	RCAF	FO	STURGIS	18/03/42	59°21'	109°53'	NESS BAY
NEUFELD, EDWARD H.	RCAF	FO	ST. BOSWELLS	12/10/45	58°41'	102°15'	NEUFELD LAKE
NEUFELD, JOHN	ARMY	PTE	HERBERT	01/10/44	60°00'	105°31'	NEUFELD LAKE
NEUFELD, LESLIE A.	ARMY	PTE	NIPAWIN	10/06/44	55°29'	104°32'	NEUFELD BAY
NEUFELD, THEODORE	ARMY	GNR	WINGARD	17/11/43	59°18'	106°10'	NEUFELD CREEK
NEVILLE, ANDREW C.	RCAF	SGT	NORTH BATTLEFORD	24/02/44	56°43'	106°23'	NEVILLE LAKE
NEWBURG, EARL LLOYD	RCAF	FS	MOOSE JAW	27/04/43	55°50'	104°13'	NEWBURG BAY
NEWCOMBE, DONALD F.	RCAF	WO1	SASKATOON	27/08/43	56°48'	107°51'	NEWCOMBE LAKE
NEWMAN, FRANCIS EDWIN	RCAF	PO	FORWARD	21/02/45	55°00'	101°56'	NEWMAN LAKE
NEYRINCK, GEORGE E.L.	ARMY	PTE	NORTH BATTLEFORD	21/07/44	55°57'	104°21'	NEYRINCK LAKE
NICHOL, EVERETT C.	ARMY	SGT	TRUAX	25/05/44	54°54'	102°19'	NICHOL LAKE
NICHOL, JAMES A.	ARMY	RFN	NORTH BATTLEFORD	09/07/44	58°10'	105°18'	NICHOL LAKE
NICHOL, WALTER W.	RCAF	FO	BATEMAN	16/05/43	55°31'	108°21'	NICHOL ISLAND
NICHOL, WILLIAM B.	RCAF	WO2	ZEHNER	13/05/43	55°54'	106°25'	NICHOL LAKE
NICHOLSON, ALBERT H.	ARMY	PTE	MAIDSTONE	01/01/44	55°09'	103°31'	NICHOLSON LAKE
NICHOLSON, DAVID A.	ARMY	L SGT	DIVISION 14	17/08/44	58°12'	104°17'	NICHOLSON ISLAND
NICHOLSON, NORMAN W.	ARMY	GNR	REGINA	03/01/43	56°46'	103°03'	NICHOLSON BAY
NICOL, JAMES C.	RCAF	FS	SPRUCE HOME	01/06/43	59°28'	109°44'	NICOL ISLAND
NIKIRK, CHARLES E.	ARMY	A CPL	KERROBERT	24/05/44	56°02'	107°44'	NIKIRK LAKE
NISBET, GEORGE D.	RCAF	SGT	CONQUEST	24/05/43			PENDING
NISBET, ROBERT A.	RCAF	FO	ARDATH	03/02/45	60°00'	108°12'	NISBET LAKE
NIVEN, CHARLES M.	RCAF	FS	BALDWINTON	04/09/43	54°24'	108°28'	NIVEN LAKE
NOBLE, ARTHUR W.	ARMY	RFN	GLASLYN	09/07/44	56°24'	103°09'	NOBLE BAY
NOKUSIS, MAURICE E.	ARMY	RFN	FILE HILLS	08/07/44	56°43'	107°50'	NOKUSIS LAKE
NORDBYE, GORDON L.	RCAF	FS	AYLESBURY	08/06/44	59°04'	103°30'	NORDBYE LAKE
NOREN, P. O. KENNETH	RCAF	FS	KIPLING	08/07/44	52°15'	103°13'	NOREN LAKE
NORGANG, JOSEPH	ARMY	PTE	CUPAR	16/09/44	59°29'	106°00'	NORGANG LAKE
NORMAN, FRANKLIN C.	ARMY	PTE	DAVIDSON	03/03/45	56°43'	104°12'	NORMAN LAKE
NORRIS, R.J.	ARMY	PTE	UNKNOWN	25/07/44	55°36'	104°34'	NORRIS BAY
NORTON, TRUEMAN	ARMY	PTE	ESTEVAN	19/08/42	54°14'	107°32'	NORTON LAKE
NORWOOD, HAROLD F.	ARMY	PTE	REGINA	15/04/45	58°43'	106°55'	NORWOOD LAKE
NOVA, ANDREW	RCAF	FO	MELVILLE	14/01/44	54°03'	106°44'	NOVA LAKE
NOWOSAD, AUGUST	RCAF	PO	VONDA	25/10/41	58°22'	103°11'	NOWOSAD ISLAND
NOYES, ROBERT E.	ARMY	L CPL	DIVISION I	28/08/44	53°58'	104°57'	NOYES LAKE
NUGENT, EDWIN A.	ARMY	PTE	DELISLE	09/04/45	55°42'	104°06'	NUGENT LAKE
NYBERG, ERNEST	ARMY	A C S M	LOON LAKE	18/06/44	56°48'	103°45'	NYBERG BAY
NYSTROM, OLOF E.	ARMY	PTE	KANDAHAR	25/08/44	60°00'	108°31'	NYSTROM LAKES

NAME	BRANCH	RANK	HOMETOWN	CASUALTY DATE	LATITUDE	LONGITUDE	GEO-MEMORIAL
OAKS, WILLIAM C.	ARMY	CPL	SASKATOON	09/12/43	56°59'	106°29'	OAKS LAKE
OATWAY, JOHN E.	RCAF	FS	PHIPPEN	28/09/42	54°33'	102°56'	OATWAY LAKE
OBACK, ADOLPH	ARMY	PTE	BIENFAIT	08/09/44	58°20'	102°35'	OBACK LAKE
OBEIRNE, WILLIAM F.H.	RCAF	PO	INDIAN HEAD	27/01/44	56°21'	107°43'	OBEIRNE LAKE
O'BRIEN, GEORGE W.	ARMY	PTE	MOOSE JAW	30/05/41	56°21'	103°49'	O'BRIEN LAKE
O'BRIEN, JOHN E.	RCAF	PO	REGINA	12/09/44	59°23'	106°20'	O'BRIEN LAKE
O'BRIEN, ROBERT H.	RCAF	FS	SASKATOON	19/03/43			PENDING
OBST, DANNY	ARMY	L SGT	YELLOW GRASS	01/11/44	58°51'	103°35'	OBST LAKE
O'CONNELL, GEORGE F.L.	RCAF	FS	KEELER	22/06/44	56°29'	102°01'	O'CONNELL LAKE
O'CONNELL, THOMAS H.	RCAF	FO	REGINA	17/04/43	55°53'	104°03'	O'CONNELL LAKE
O'CONNOR, CHARLES JOSEPH	RCAF	FS	REGINA	08/07/44	54°14'	105°53'	O'CONNOR LAKE
O'CONNOR, STAFFORD T.	RCAF	FS	CEYLON	04/05/43	54°28'	105°35'	O'CONNOR BAY
ODDAN, HAROLD E.	RCAF	FO	LLOYDMINSTER	13/05/44	54°39'	102°22'	ODDAN LAKE
O'DELL, WILLIAM H.	ARMY	LIEUT	MOOSE JAW	20/07/44	53°56'	104°30'	O'DELL LAKE
O'DONNELL, FRANCIS T.	ARMY	TPR	MAPLE CREEK	30/07/44	57°16'	107°10'	O'DONNELL ISLAND
OGILVY, JAMES S.	RCAF	FS	MOOSE JAW	16/07/43	59°46'	109°20'	OGILVY BAY
OGILVY, STUART T.	RCAF	LAC	MOOSE JAW	07/12/40	59°44'	109°23'	OGILVY ISLAND
OGLOFF, GEORGE W.	ARMY	PTE	ARRAN	15/04/44	56°20'	102°49'	OGLOFF BAY
O'GRADY, JOHN E.	RCAF	FO	SASKATOON	06/12/42	56°26'	107°38'	O'GRADY LAKE
OGSTON, CHARLES	ARMY	L CPL	CRAIK	03/10/44	56°40'	109°53'	OGSTON LAKE
OKEMASIS, JOSEPH	ARMY	PTE	MUSKEG LAKE	07/12/43	59°23'	104°39'	OKEMASIS LAKE
OLDFORD, LESLIE	RCAF	SGT	REGINA	23/08/42	56°30'	105°21'	OLDFORD LAKE
OLFMAN, SOLOMON	ARMY	GNR	KAMSACK	31/07/42	55°50'	107°25'	OLFMAN CREEK
OLIPHANT, JOHN P.G.	ARMY	SGT	CONNELL CREEK	15/07/45	59°26'	107°53'	OLIPHANT LAKE
OLLIS, LAWRENCE E.	ARMY	GNR	NORTH MAKWA	05/03/45	54°12'	106°51'	OLLIS LAKE
OLLIS, REGINALD K.	RCAF	PO	NORTH MAKWA	22/04/43	54°12'	106°51'	OLLIS LAKE
OLMSTEAD, LESLIE J.	RCAF	SGT	STOUGHTON	17/10/44	59°44'	106°51'	OLMSTEAD LAKE
OLNEY, ELMER F.	ARMY	TPR	CARIEVALE	03/10/44	59°25'	105°03'	OLNEY LAKE
OLSON, ANDREW G.	RCAF	PO	SWIFT CURRENT	21/09/43	55°53'	105°30'	OLSON LAKE
OLSON, CARL G.	ARMY	GNR	AMIENS	29/04/45	56°57'	102°01'	OLSON LAKE
OLSON, DONALD B.	RCAF	FO	LLOYDMINSTER	14/02/45	59°44'	108°50'	OLSON BAY
OLSON, LLOYD ALLYN	NAVY	TEL	SASKATOON	02/09/44	56°48'	103°39'	OLSON BAY
OLSON, OLE ADRIAN	NAVY	STO 1	ROBSART	22/10/40	56°53'	103°38'	OLSON PENINSULA
OLSON, OLE L.	ARMY	SPR	INVERMAY	26/04/45	59°18'	106°53'	OLSON ISLAND
OLSON, OMAR E.	RCAF	LAC	DELISLE	15/06/42	56°55'	108°44'	OLSON RAPIDS
OLSVIK, DAVID O.	RCAF	FO	PARKSIDE	20/02/44	56°17'	107°39'	OLSVIK LAKE
OOMS, FERDINAND F.L.	ARMY	GNR	KENOSEE	13/07/41	58°19'	102°25'	OOMS LAKE
OPRUK, PETER	RCAF	FO	CALDER	06/06/43	59°56'	108°43'	OPRUK LAKE
ORBAN, F.A.	ARMY	TPR	UNKNOWN	12/08/44	55°42'	104°32'	ORBAN LAKE
ORIORDAN, TERENCE T.	ARMY	TPR	ARBORFIELD	17/02/44	57°40'	103°47'	ORIORDAN LAKE
ORMISTON, WILLIAM D.	ARMY	CAPT	REGINA	21/02/45	58°56'	105°32'	ORMISTON LAKE
ORR, DONALD H.	RCAF	FO	MOOSE JAW	18/08/43	58°57'	104°47'	ORR LAKE
ORR, JAMES S.	RCAF	FS	LAURA	01/09/42	57°22'	108°53'	ORR PENINSULA
ORR, JOHN E.	ARMY	CAPT	MOOSE JAW	09/10/44	55°50'	105°54'	ORR LAKE
ORR, RUBEN S.	RCAF	WO2	VERA	26/11/43	54°56'	104°56'	ORR ISLAND
ORTON, NELSON R.	RCAF	PO	BIRCH HILLS	22/03/45	55°40'	105°55'	ORTON LAKE
OSBORNE, ALLAN J.	ARMY	GNR	DIVISION 8	24/08/44	57°24'	105°08'	OSBORNE LAKE
OSHOWY, FRANK J.	ARMY	GNR	HEADLANDS	30/05/44	59°57'	107°46'	OSHOWY LAKE
OSIPOFF, GEORGE A.	ARMY	A SGT	REGINA	09/08/44	56°31'	102°05'	OSIPOFF LAKE
OSTEN, MAX M.	RCAF	PO	HUDSON BAY	05/05/42	54°05'	106°44'	OSTEN LAKE
OSWALD, HENRY C.	RCAF	SGT	KENDAL	26/02/44	59°48'	109°50'	OSWALD LAKE
OTT, JOHN	RCAF	FS	BENGOUGH	24/09/42	59°23'	104°47'	OTT LAKE
OUELLETTE, WALTER J.	ARMY	SGT	SASKATOON	28/12/43	55°25'	102°10'	OUELLETTE LAKE
OUROM, RICHARD K.	RCAF	FO	BATTRUM	28/04/45	55°35'	103°12'	OUROM LAKE
OVERLAND, JOHN S.	RCAF	SGT	PREECEVILLE	12/12/44	59°35'	106°14'	OVERLAND LAKE
OWENS, ALLAN R.	ARMY	RFN	LUCKY LAKE	11/06/44	59°23'	105°50'	OWENS LAKE
PACHAL, OTTO C.	ARMY	PTE	KIPLING	26/02/45	55°21'	106°24'	PACHAL LAKE
PADGET, RICHARD E.	RCAF	FO	SASKATOON	16/02/44	59°34'	108°32'	PADGET BAY
PAGAN, ARTHUR R.	RCAF	FO	SASKATOON	15/07/43	54°19'	108°16'	PAGAN LAKE
PAGE, WILLIAM FISHER	NAVY	SL S2	YORKTON	22/05/41	55°53'	108°18'	PAGE ISLAND
PAGE, WILLIAM LEONARD	NAVY	SL	REGINA	20/09/43	52°57'	108°07'	PAGE CREEK
PAGEN, GORDON L.	ARMY	PTE	DIVISION 5	26/02/45	57°38'	106°59'	PAGEN LAKE
PAINTER, HERBERT F.	ARMY	PTE	YORKTON	19/02/45	55°43'	104°51'	PAINTER CREEK
PAINTON, ROBERT JAMES	ARMY	LT	ESTON	13/09/44	58°23'	102°32'	PAINTON LAKE
PAISLEY, GEORGE H.	ARMY	PTE	NIPAWIN	15/08/44	59°19'	105°02'	PAISLEY LAKE
PALMER, BRINSLEY G.H.	RCAF	WO1	SASKATOON	25/04/44	55°43'	104°09'	PALMER LAKE
PALMER, HUGH F.	ARMY	PTE	QUILL LAKE	20/07/44	59°24'	102°38'	PALMER LAKE
PALMER, JOHN	RCAF	WO2	EATONIA	13/05/43	59°39'	108°45'	PALMER LAKE
PANASUK, NICK	ARMY	GNR	DIVISION 16	27/09/44	59°58'	109°44'	PANASUK LAKE
PAPIC, JOHN R.	ARMY	PTE	DIVISION 3	19/08/42	59°38'	108°31'	PAPIC LAKE
PARADIS, MARC J.	ARMY	A L SGT	BALDWINTON	03/03/45	60°01'	108°09'	PARADIS LAKE
PARENTEAU, WALTER J.	ARMY	PTE	REYNAUD	19/12/41	55°04'	102°41'	PARENTEAU LAKE
PARISIAN, RAYMOND	ARMY	PTE	QU'APPELLE	28/08/44	58°47'	106°42'	PARISIAN LAKE
PARK, EDWIN E.F.	RCAF	PO	SASKATOON	09/05/44	57°56'	104°12'	PARK CREEK
PARK, GILBERT E.	RCAF	LAC	REGINA	15/05/43	55°07'	103°49'	PARK LAKE
PARK, JAMES W.	ARMY	TPR	BROADACRES	09/02/45	59°28'	108°24'	PARK LAKE
PARKER, ARTHUR L.	ARMY	TPR	SASKATOON	25/07/44	58°07'	105°32'	PARKER LAKE
PARKER, BRUCE A.	RCAF	FO	SASKATOON	12/12/44	57°05'	104°12'	PARKER LAKE
PARKER, GORDON C.	ARMY	CPL	HUMBOLDT	11/12/43	58°14'	103°32'	PARKER ISLAND
PARKER, REGINALD F.	ARMY	CAPT	SASKATOON	20/07/44	59°29'	108°15'	PARKER BAY
PARKER, SAMUEL R.	RCAF	FS	REGINA	07/09/43	54°44'	102°13'	PARKER ISLAND
PARKER, VERNICE J.	RCAF	SGT	REGINA	07/04/41	56°48'	108°39'	PARKER BAY
PARKER, VICTOR CLARENCE	NAVY	AB	SASKATOON	17/12/44	59°28'	108°11'	PARKER POINT
PARKER, WILLIAM G.	RCAF	FS	WELWYN	03/10/43	57°02'	105°34'	PARKER BAY
PARKHURST, ALLAN E.	ARMY	PTE	FAIRY GLEN	26/07/43	59°59'	104°24'	PARKHURST PENINSULA
PARKS, ROWLAND I.	RCAF	PO	HANLEY	17/03/45	55°42'	104°09'	PARKS ISLAND
PARKS, WILLIAM R.	RCAF	PO	PRINCE ALBERT	18/12/43	56°03'	104°42'	PARKS LAKE
PARKUNOW, THOMAS J.	ARMY	RFN	BIGGAR	23/04/45	56°53'	102°59'	PARKUNOW LAKE
PARR, CECIL H.	ARMY	SGT	WOLSELEY	02/08/44	54°32'	105°24'	PARR LAKE
PARRISH, JOHN	ARMY	PTE	BATTLEFORD	18/09/44	56°47'	103°19'	PARRISH LAKE
PARRY, ALBERT	ARMY	PTE	DIVISION 16	06/07/44	57°54'	109°16'	PARRY LAKE
PARTINGTON, RICHARD	NAVY	LDG SMN	SASKATOON	16/04/45	56°11'	104°12'	PARTINGTON LAKE
PARTRIDGE, HENRY A.	RCAF	PO	WATSON	05/03/43	59°41'	107°46'	PARTRIDGE LAKE
PARTRIDGE, WILLIAM N.	RCAF	PO	HAZLET	14/05/43	56°02'	108°29'	PARTRIDGE CREEK
PASTERFIELD, WILLIAM E.N.	RAF	PO	CRAIK	25/04/42	56°48'	103°49'	PASTERFIELD LAKE
PATERSON, ALEXANDER G.	RCAF	FS	WINDTHORST	06/12/42	57°41'	104°13'	PATERSON LAKE
PATERSON, JOSEPH F.	RCAF	FO	SASKATOON	30/12/42	56°58'	102°53'	PATERSON BAY
PATERSON, STEWARD T.	RCAF	FS	SASKATOON	09/05/42	55°36'	104°40'	PATERSON LAKE
PATTERSON, LEO HARKNESS	RCAF	WO2	MELFORT	28/01/44	57°39'	102°38'	PATTERSON ISLAND
PATTERSON, ROBERT A.	RCAF	FS	MOSSBANK	22/11/42	59°16'	105°43'	PATTERSON CREEK
PATTERSON, VERNON F.	RCAF	FL	MOOSE JAW	20/11/42	55°47'	107°33'	PATTERSON LAKE
PATTISON, RAYMOND C.	ARMY	TPR	MEDSTEAD	08/07/44	51°16'	104°14'	PATTISON LAKE
PATTON, THOMAS P.	ARMY	PTE	REGINA	21/07/44	56°22'	102°07'	PATTON BAY
PATTYSON, LEONARD W.	RCAF	FO	REGINA	24/07/44	58°50'	104°58'	PATTYSON LAKE
PATZER, EDWIN F.	RCAF	FO	YORKTON	21/05/45	57°06'	108°24'	PATZER LAKE
PAUL, GEORGE W.	RCAF	PO	LANG	15/05/43	59°38'	108°57'	PAUL LAKE
PAUL, JOSEPH P.	ARMY	TPR	FOX VALLEY	20/08/42	56°22'	103°51'	PAUL LAKE
PAUL, MAYNARD A.	ARMY	PTE	KISBEY	02/01/42	58°13'	103°05'	PAUL ISLAND
PAUL, PETER	ARMY	RFN	LLOYDMINSTER	27/08/44	56°48'	103°30'	PAUL BAY
PAUL, ROBERT A.	RCAF	PO	MOOSE JAW	25/03/45	55°50'	106°10'	PAUL LAKE
PAWLITZA, ELVYN J.	RCAF	FO	ABBEY	13/06/44	53°58'	107°29'	PAWLITZA LAKE
PAWLIUK, JOHN	RCAF	LAC	WAKAW	06/09/43	57°50'	104°51'	PAWLIUK LAKE
PAYN, ROBERT L.	RCAF	PO	LIMERICK	24/03/42	56°06'	103°46'	PAYN CREEK
PAYNE, RICHARD J.	ARMY	RFN	MONT NEBO	06/09/44	58°21'	108°41'	PAYNE LAKE
PEACH, ROBERT T.	ARMY	RFN	PLATO	19/08/44	59°39'	105°42'	PEACH LAKE
PEAKER, GEORGE E.	RCAF	FO	SASKATOON	19/03/45	56°03'	107°46'	PEAKER LAKE
PEARCE, DAVID L.	ARMY	GNR	LANCER	24/11/43	54°33'	103°01'	PEARCE BAY
PEARCE, DOUGLAS	RCAF	FS	PARKMAN	28/06/42	55°58'	106°16'	PEARCE LAKE
PEARCE, GORDON A.	RCAF	FS	REGINA	02/07/42	57°45'	102°44'	PEARCE LAKE
PEARCE, WILFRED A.	ARMY	A CAPT	SASKATOON	25/09/44	56°35'	103°23'	PEARCE BAY
PEARSON, AXEL P.	ARMY	A SGT	KELLIHER	18/08/44	59°29'	105°28'	PEARSON LAKE
PEARSON, PERCY A.	ARMY	A CPL	WYNYARD	06/10/44	55°01'	102°24'	PEARSON LAKE
PEART, EDWARD B.	RCAF	FS	REGINA	25/06/43	55°00'	104°28'	PEART LAKE
PEAT, WALTER	ARMY	RFN	NORTH BATTLEFORD	08/07/44	55°17'	104°15'	PEAT LAKE
PEDDIE, ROY NORMAN	NAVY	STWD	ARBORFIELD	16/04/45	59°22'	106°41'	PEDDIE LAKE
PEDERSEN, HAROLD	ARMY	PTE	DIVISION 14	05/07/43	59°28'	108°17'	PEDERSEN ISLAND
PEDERSEN, WALTER C.	RCAF	FS	DIVISION 14	14/09/42	55°32'	106°46'	PEDERSEN LAKE
PEDERSON, GORDON O.	ARMY	GDSM	ABBEY	20/09/44	59°03'	108°55'	PEDERSON LAKE

Name	Branch	Rank	Hometown	Casualty Date	Latitude	Longitude	Geo-Memorial
PEEBLES, ROY	ARMY	RFN	MOOSE JAW	06/06/44	59°28'	108°40'	PEEBLES LAKE
PEIRSON, ROBERT S.	ARMY	CFN	INVERMAY	03/05/45	56°22'	102°54'	PEIRSON LAKE
PELKEY, CHARLES E.	RCAF	CPL	ALAMEDA	02/06/45	59°38'	104°01'	PELKEY LAKE
PELLANT, JAMES W.	RCAF	PO	GRONLID	21/03/45	57°56'	102°54'	PELLANT LAKE
PELLERIN, LORENZO	ARMY	RFN	ALBERTVILLE	04/07/44	59°24'	105°10'	PELLERIN LAKE
PELLETIER, JOHN	ARMY	L CPL	LINTLAW	25/07/44	57°38'	106°10'	PELLETIER ISLAND
PELLETIER, JOSEPH	ARMY	RFN	FORT QU'APPELLE	06/06/44	54°58'	102°52'	PELLETIER LAKE
PELLTIER, ANTON	ARMY	RFN	DIVISION 10	06/06/44	59°22'	103°12'	PELLTIER BAY
PELTIER, JOHN	ARMY	GNR	LEBRET	21/05/44	55°34'	105°04'	PELTIER LAKE
PENDLETON, WILLIAM	ARMY	L CPL	BROOKSBY	28/10/44	56°58'	104°42'	PENDLETON LAKE
PENNER, ALVIN H.	RCAF	FS	LAIRD	30/03/43	59°10'	104°24'	PENNER LAKE
PENNER, FRANK	ARMY	PTE	WYMARK	15/12/44	56°25'	103°46'	PENNER LAKE
PENNER, ISAAC A.	RCAF	SGT	NIPAWIN	27/04/43	55°22'	104°24'	PENNER ISLAND
PENNEY, WILLIAM F.	RCAF	FS	INCHKEITH	01/08/42	55°26'	104°01'	PENNEY LAKE
PENNYCOOK, ELMER J.	ARMY	L CPL	CARROT RIVER	01/05/44	58°15'	102°50'	PENNYCOOK LAKE
PERCY, ROBERT A.	ARMY	L CPL	SASKATOON	17/09/44	55°13'	104°47'	PERCY ISLAND
PEREPELITZ, FRED	ARMY	PTE	PREECEVILLE	19/09/44	55°50'	104°34'	PEREPELITZ LAKE
PERNEROWSKI, ERNEST J.	ARMY	PTE	SASKATOON	28/04/44	56°46'	103°24'	PERNEROWSKI LAKE
PERPELUK, STEVE	ARMY	PTE	WROXTON	17/08/44	55°56'	104°44'	PERPELUK LAKE
PERPETE, MAXIMIN	ARMY	CPL	FORGET	20/07/44	57°20'	106°11'	PERPETE LAKE
PERRON, ANTOINE J.E.	RCAF	FS	MONTMARTRE	25/07/43	59°32'	106°04'	PERRON LAKE
PERRON, GAETAN M.	ARMY	PTE	MONTMARTRE	10/04/45	56°57'	103°21'	PERRON ISLAND
PERRY, JOHN	ARMY	RFN	PRINCE ALBERT	13/06/44	59°44'	108°29'	PERRY LAKE
PERRY, SHELDON W.W.	RCAF	FL	PELLY	20/01/44	55°24'	106°27'	PERRY BAY
PERWIZNUIK, JOHN	ARMY	A CPL	MOOSE JAW	08/10/44	56°54'	105°30'	PERWIZNUIK LAKE
PETCH, JAMES W.	ARMY	PTE	MORIN CREEK	22/03/42	55°09'	104°06'	PETCH LAKE
PETE, MIKE	ARMY	RFN	PRINCE ALBERT	21/02/45	55°45'	103°14'	PETE LAKE
PETERS, ALBERT J.	ARMY	RFN	REGINA	08/06/44	59°47'	109°37'	PETERS BAY
PETERS, ARTHUR K.	ARMY	PTE	SUPERB	15/08/44	59°29'	108°22'	PETERS ISLAND
PETERS, FRANCIS L.	ARMY	MAJ	BATTLEFORD	06/06/44	56°50'	103°46'	PETERS LAKE
PETERS, HARRY S.	ARMY	L CPL	MARKINCH	08/06/44	59°35'	107°52'	PETERS BAY
PETERS, HERBERT P.	RCAF	SL	ROSTHERN	05/11/43	55°09'	104°37'	PETERS ISLAND
PETERS, KEITH A.	RCAF	FS	LAFLECHE	05/10/42	59°48'	108°10'	PETERS FALLS
PETERS, ROY D.	RCAF	SGT	HERBERT	27/07/42	54°58'	104°32'	PETERS BAY
PETERSON, ALFRED S.	ARMY	TPR	HANLEY	09/08/44	59°46'	102°26'	PETERSON CREEK
PETERSON, JOHN A.	RCAF	FL	ABBEY	19/01/42	57°46'	105°51'	PETERSON CREEK
PETERSON, LLOYD H.	RCAF	FS	THEODORE	13/02/43			PENDING
PETERSON, OTTO J.	RCAF	FO	LLOYDMINSTER	27/09/40	54°27'	106°00'	PETERSON BAY
PETERSON, WALLACE R.	ARMY	PTE	RADVILLE	25/07/44	56°19'	103°54'	PETERSON CREEK
PETTINGALE, STANLEY L.	RCAF	FO	SASKATOON	12/08/43	55°38'	106°46'	PETTINGALE LAKE
PHANEUF, EUGENE J.	ARMY	RFN	ESTEVAN	12/10/44	54°52'	102°48'	PHANEUF LAKE
PHILLIPS, ALEXANDER R.	ARMY	LCPL	EATONIA	02/12/44	57°44'	102°16'	PHILLIPS ISLAND
PHILLIPS, CLIFFORD S.	RCAF	FO	VALPARAISO	13/05/44	54°57'	102°14'	PHILLIPS LAKE
PHILLIPS, MICHEAL	ARMY	PTE	WEYBURN	29/08/45	57°50'	104°37'	PHILLIPS CREEK
PHILLIPS, THOMAS	ARMY	RFN	ESTON	15/09/44	58°42'	103°45'	PHILLIPS LAKE
PHILLIPS, WINSTON S.M.	RCAF	PO	MCCORD	08/08/44	57°22'	106°00'	PHILLIPS LAKE
PHOENIX, OWEN H.	RCAF	FS	REGINA	26/07/43	59°26'	104°57'	PHOENIX LAKE
PICK, CLARENCE F.	RCAF	FS	VALLEY CENTRE	26/08/43	59°14'	105°00'	PICK ISLAND
PICKEL, GORDON E.	RCAF	FS	MAIDSTONE	12/07/42	52°24'	103°18'	PICKEL LAKE
PICKFORD, RAYMOND E.	ARMY	PTE	BROADVIEW	19/08/42	57°13'	108°49'	PICKFORD LAKE
PIGGOTT, JOHN E.	RCAF	PO	SASKATOON	03/04/42	57°05'	107°23'	PIGGOTT LAKE
PIKET, JACOB	RCAF	SGT	REGINA	12/05/43	55°11'	104°13'	PIKET LAKE
PILLING, JOHN	ARMY	CPL	KINISTINO	06/06/44	55°36'	103°44'	PILLING LAKE
PINKNEY, CHARLES F.	ARMY	PTE	ESTEVAN	19/08/42	54°03'	105°05'	PINKNEY LAKE
PIOTROFSKY, PAUL	RCAF	LAC	REGINA	02/05/43	59°33'	104°10'	PIOTROFSKY LAKE
PIPER, FREDERICK J.	RCAF	PO	TUXFORD	18/08/43	59°41'	107°55'	PIPER LAKE
PIPRELL, GORDON L.	RCAF	FO	BORDEN	30/08/44	54°09'	104°54'	PIPRELL LAKE
PIRIE, JAMES A.	RCAF	FS	PENNANT	30/05/43	59°15'	104°14'	PIRIE LAKE
PIXLEY, ASA N.	RCAF	WO1	SNOWDEN	18/04/45	59°48'	104°20'	PIXLEY BAY
PIXLEY, FREDERICK J.	ARMY	PTE	HANLEY	04/08/44	55°22'	103°24'	PIXLEY LAKE
PLATANA, DANIEL D.	RCAF	FO	REGINA	15/07/44	55°10'	104°10'	PLATANA LAKE
PLATT, GEORGE	ARMY	CAPT	SASKATOON	17/06/45	56°21'	102°41'	PLATT LAKE
PLATT, ORVILLE I.	RCAF	SGT	WOLSELEY	17/07/41	59°16'	105°43'	PLATT CREEK
POEGAL, DONALD L.	RCAF	LAC	NADEAUVILLE	09/01/41	59°41'	104°50'	POEGAL LAKE
POITRAS, EDWARD	ARMY	PTE	FORT QU'APPELLE	19/08/42	58°35'	105°35'	POITRAS LAKE
POLGREEN, FRANCES E.	ARMY	LT N S	REGINA	11/05/43	59°47'	103°13'	POLGREEN LAKE
POLISHAK, GUST J.	ARMY	RFN	MELVILLE	06/10/44	55°32'	105°10'	POLISHAK LAKE
POLLOCK, ROBERT J.	RCAF	FS	CANORA	03/09/42	55°26'	102°57'	POLLOCK LAKE
POLLON, CLIFFORD S.A.	ARMY	PTE	PELLY	14/08/45	56°22'	103°08'	POLLON LAKE
POLLON, ERNEST S.	RCAF	WO2	UNKNOWN	26/05/43			PENDING
POLOWICH, MICHAEL L.	RCAF	LAC	WATSON	29/01/43	59°28'	108°12'	POLOWICH BAY
POOLE, EARL J.W.	ARMY	PTE	STOUGHTON	19/08/42	55°56'	104°32'	POOLE LAKE
POPPLEWELL, CHETWIN H.	RCAF	FO	DINSMORE	29/09/43	56°24'	108°11'	POPPLEWELL ISLAND
PORTEN, JACK M.F.	ARMY	PTE	LEROY	08/09/46	59°21'	105°02'	PORTEN LAKE
PORTER, CHARLES R.	RCAF	FO	TURTLEFORD	25/04/44			PENDING
PORTER, PERCY E.	ARMY	PTE	MELFORT	04/12/44	57°40'	102°42'	PORTER BAY
PORTMAN, HERBERT G.	RCAF	FO	SASKATOON	17/02/44	60°02'	109°13'	PORTMAN LAKE
POSTHUMUS, BERENT	ARMY	RFN	ROSE VALLEY	12/10/44	51°18'	104°10'	POSTHUMUS LAKE
POTT, ZINA	ARMY	GDSM	SHELL LAKE	09/03/45	59°41'	102°24'	POTT BAY
POTTER, JOHN F.	RCAF	FO	REGINA	11/04/44	56°44'	107°38'	POTTER LAKE
POTTER, WILLIAM D.	RCAF	FO	SASKATOON	14/05/44	55°24'	104°17'	POTTER RAPIDS
POTTLE, ASTON J.W.	RCAF	FS	MOOSE JAW	15/05/42	59°55'	104°18'	POTTLE ISLAND
POULIN, EUGENE	ARMY	PTE	DIVISION 15	17/09/44	55°32'	106°11'	POULIN LAKE
POULIN, FERNAND	ARMY	SPR	DOLLARD	07/01/46	57°54'	107°15'	POULIN BAY
POULIN, WILLIAM	RCAF	FS	DODSLAND	01/09/43	54°05'	101°51'	POULIN LAKE
POULTON, ALAN R.	ARMY	TPR	CANWOOD	20/11/43	57°50'	104°27'	POULTON LAKE
POULTON, JOHN D.	ARMY	LIEUT	NORTH BATTLEFORD	10/04/42	55°27'	104°54'	POULTON LAKE
POURBAIX, ALBERT E.	RCAF	FO	LAMPMAN	25/04/43	56°25'	108°43'	POURBAIX LAKE
POVOL, ERVIN	ARMY	CPL	DIVISION 2	09/06/44	54°52'	103°59'	POVOL LAKE
POW, DAVID E.	ARMY	PTE	ESTEVAN	22/08/42	55°09'	104°51'	POW ISLAND
POW, JOHN W.	ARMY	RFN	KHEDIVE	28/08/44	58°13'	103°37'	POW BAY
POW, LESLIE G.D.	RCAF	FO	WOLSELEY	25/11/44	55°33'	103°10'	POW LAKE
POWDRILL, ROSS	RCAF	FL	MOOSE JAW	08/06/44	55°05'	104°32'	POWDRILL LAKE
PRATT, DAVID	RCAF	FO	TUFFNELL	28/05/43	56°14'	107°32'	PRATT RAPIDS
PRATT, RALPH W.	RCAF	SGT	IMPERIAL	06/02/44	59°28'	105°48'	PRATT LAKE
PRENTICE, ARTHUR H.	ARMY	GNR	GRENFELL	08/08/44	54°57'	102°01'	PRENTICE LAKE
PRESCOTT, HOWARD	ARMY	PTE	BROADACRES	01/11/44	55°45'	105°41'	PRESCOTT LAKE
PRESTON, DAVID P.	ARMY	SGT	MAPLE CREEK	30/04/45	55°19'	103°03'	PRESTON LAKE
PRESTON, JOHN A.	RCAF	PO	MOOSOMIN	26/06/42	57°36'	104°10'	PRESTON CREEK
PRICE, ARTHUR	ARMY	RFN	NORTH BATTLEFORD	08/07/44	56°28'	102°58'	PRICE ISLAND
PRICE, GEORGE A.	ARMY	PTE	LLOYDMINSTER	09/08/44	56°54'	103°41'	PRICE LAKE
PRIEST, THOMAS	RAF		LLOYDMINSTER	10/01/42	56°46'	102°32'	PRIEST POINT
PRIME, GORDON O.	RCAF	SGT	KYLE	11/08/44	59°04'	105°43'	PRIME ISLAND
PRING, CLIFFORD R.	RCAF	FO	YOUNG	28/07/44	59°43'	109°06'	PRING LAKE
PRINGLE, BERTRAM H.	RCAF	FO	HARRIS	05/11/43	55°09'	107°51'	PRINGLE LAKE
PRITCHARD, WILLIAM D.	ARMY	PTE	DIVISION 9	27/07/44	56°45'	103°33'	PRITCHARD LAKE
PRITCHETT, WALTER L.	ARMY	PTE	TRUAX	05/03/45	57°50'	107°09'	PRITCHETT LAKE
PROBERT, KENNETH F.	RCAF	FO	MOOSE JAW	11/04/44	54°35'	101°54'	PROBERT LAKE
PROCTOR, LEONARD D.	RCAF	FO	BIGGAR	22/03/44	55°25'	101°58'	PROCTOR NARROWS
PROKOPCHUK, SAM	ARMY	PTE	DIVISION 9	27/02/45	59°26'	105°54'	PROKOPCHUK LAKE
PRONGUA, CHARLES V.	ARMY	PTE	IBSTONE	17/10/44	55°07'	103°12'	PRONGUA LAKE
PROPP, FREDERICK E.	ARMY	LIEUT	RUNNYMEDE	20/12/44	55°42'	104°09'	PROPP LAKE
PROSOFSKY, ALFRED W.	RCAF	PO	REGINA	29/07/44	59°44'	107°53'	PROSOFSKY LAKE
PROUDFOOT, WILLIAM W.	RCAF	FO	REGINA	13/06/44	56°57'	108°25'	PROUDFOOT LAKE
PROUDLOCK, THOMAS H.	RCAF	PO	KINDERSLEY	26/03/44	60°00'	108°24'	PROUDLOCK LAKE
PROWSE, LEMUEL E.	RCAF	FL	BENGOUGH	10/05/45	52°10'	103°31'	PROWSE LAKE
PRUDEN, JAMES D.	ARMY	PTE	BIG RIVER	25/07/44	57°33'	109°36'	PRUDEN RAPIDS
PULLEY, ROBERT J.	ARMY	LIEUT	SASKATOON	20/07/44	59°36'	109°50'	PULLEY LAKE
PURCELL, JOHN G.	RCAF	SGT	DIVISION 10	16/02/42	59°44'	107°49'	PURCELL LAKE
PURDEY, GEORGE W.	ARMY	L SGT	WAPELLA	14/08/44	56°33'	103°36'	PURDEY LAKE
PURDY, CLIFFORD IRWIN	NAVY	CODER	NORTH BATTLEFORD	13/04/45	55°46'	108°09'	PURDY LAKE
PURMAL, CHARLES S.	ARMY	RFN	DIVISION 5	24/04/45	55°25'	104°26'	PURMAL BAY
PURVIS, DONALD E.	ARMY	A L SGT	ESTEVAN	20/07/44	54°05'	106°39'	PURVIS LAKE
PURVIS, JAMES	ARMY	PTE	LLOYDMINSTER	23/08/44	56°53'	103°33'	PURVIS BAY
PUTNAM, MAX E.	RCAF	FS	WATSON	26/01/43	55°50'	105°29'	PUTNAM LAKE
PYETT, FREDERICK E.	ARMY	PTE	SASKATOON	18/10/44	57°26'	103°38'	PYETT LAKE
PYLYPOW, STEVE	ARMY	PTE	GLASLYN	28/01/45	56°26'	105°51'	PYLYPOW LAKE
QUICKFALL, CLARKE E.	RCAF	FS	KINDERSLEY	01/12/43	59°58'	108°01'	QUICKFALL LAKE

Name	Branch	Rank	Hometown	Casualty Date	Latitude	Longitude	Geo-memorial
QUINLAN, JOHN M.	RCAF	PO	PRINCE ALBERT	04/03/44	55°14'	104°57'	QUINLAN ISLAND
QUINNELL, CLARENCE L.	ARMY	TPR	STAR CITY	10/08/44	60°01'	109°39'	QUINNELL LAKE
RABINOVITCH, SAMUEL	RCAF	AC2	KELLIHER	28/05/42	57°52'	105°36'	RABINOVITCH LAKE
RACHKEWICH, HARRY	ARMY	RFN	CHELAN	18/07/44	55°33'	105°23'	RACHKEWICH LAKE
RADCLIFFE, COLIN J.	ARMY	A MAJ	REGINA	28/07/45	55°58'	104°58'	RADCLIFFE LAKE
RAE, DONALD A.	RCAF	PO	REGINA	14/01/44	56°03'	107°52'	RAE LAKE
RAE, GEORGE A.	RCAF	PO	PRINCE ALBERT	08/07/44	59°38'	108°49'	RAE BAY
RAIBL, HERBERT M.	RCAF	AC2	REGINA	06/04/40	59°11'	105°54'	RAIBL LAKES
RAINVILLE, JULES	ARMY	L SGT	WILLOW BUNCH	02/05/43	57°45'	106°25'	RAINVILLE LAKE
RAMAGE, LAWRENCE H.	RCAF	WO2	STAR CITY	20/10/43	59°44'	109°34'	RAMAGE LAKE
RAMSDELL, RONALD F.	ARMY	CPL	MOOSE JAW	09/08/44	60°00'	107°34'	RAMSDELL CREEK
RAMSEY, DONALD R.	ARMY	LIEUT	CARNDUFF	28/03/44	54°27'	105°58'	RAMSEY BAY
RANGER, RAYMOND	RCAF	FS	COLEVILLE	04/10/43	60°00'	109°19'	RANGER LAKE
RANKIN, JOHN M.	RCAF	LAC	PADDOCKWOOD	24/09/42	55°31'	106°51'	RANKIN LAKE
RANSCHAERT, LESLIE	ARMY	TPR	YORKTON	07/12/44	56°48'	102°15'	RANSCHAERT LAKE
RASMUSSEN, FLOYD R.	ARMY	GDSM	VALBRAND	14/08/44	59°29'	105°10'	RASMUSSEN LAKE
RATHBONE, JOHN C. H.	NAVY	SA	REGINA	09/08/44	55°28'	108°18'	RATHBONE LAKE
RATTEE, WILLIAM V.	RCAF	FS	MOOSE JAW	23/03/43	56°55'	107°28'	RATTEE LAKE
RAY, CLARENCE DAN	ARMY	LIEUT	TISDALE	20/04/45	55°32'	102°52'	RAY BAY
RAYNER, ROBERT FRANK	NAVY	AB	NORTH BATTLEFORD	24/11/44	59°21'	106°41'	RAYNER LAKE
REA, JOSEPH H.	ARMY	PTE	SHAUNAVON	02/12/45	59°20'	106°01'	REA LAKE
READ, FREDERICK W.	RCAF	FS	BETHUNE	19/11/42	57°47'	105°07'	READ LAKE
READ, KENNETH N.	RCAF	FS	SASKATOON	21/12/42	59°20'	105°31'	READ LAKE
REBBECK, ALFRED J.	ARMY	PTE	SOUTH FORK	21/09/44	55°23'	104°17'	REBBECK LAKE
REDMAN, EARLE	RCAF	PO	MELFORT	03/04/43	57°54'	103°04'	REDMAN LAKE
REDMOND, JACK E.	RCAF	SGT	MAPLE CREEK	20/12/43	54°26'	108°21'	REDMOND LAKE
REDWOOD, GEORGE C.	ARMY	A L CPL	BIENFAIT	28/08/42	55°32'	105°42'	REDWOOD LAKE
REED, ALEXANDER J.	RCAF	FS	TURTLEFORD	17/04/42	55°23'	104°11'	REED ISLAND
REED, CLIFFORD H.	RCAF	WO2	REGINA	16/01/43	56°41'	102°47'	REED LAKE
REED, HOWARD M.	RCAF	SGT	ALAMEDA	13/04/44	55°21'	104°27'	REED PENINSULA
REED, RAYMOND A.	RCAF	PO	ALAMEDA	05/08/44	55°22'	104°10'	REED RAPIDS
REGAMBAL, BEN L.	ARMY	PTE	OUTLOOK	08/08/44	58°26'	102°10'	REGAMBAL LAKE
REGIMBAL, ALFRED E.	RCAF	SGT	WOOD MOUNTAIN	17/02/41	55°27'	106°35'	REGIMBAL ISLAND
REGIMBAL, WILFRED H.	RCAF	FO	WOOD MOUNTAIN	02/11/44	55°25'	106°33'	REGIMBAL BAY
REHILL, DON R.	RCAF	PO	KAMSACK	04/07/42	59°24'	106°32'	REHILL LAKE
REID, DANIEL T.	ARMY	L CPL	EASTEND	18/10/44	58°42'	102°03'	REID BAY
REID, GEORGE L.	ARMY	LIEUT	MOOSE JAW	12/08/44	55°33'	104°35'	REID ISLAND
REID, JOHN B.	RCAF	FS	DILKE	18/04/43	55°36'	108°16'	REID BAY
REID, ROBERT F.	ARMY	PTE	MOOSE JAW	20/05/44	56°47'	102°55'	REID ISLAND
REID, ROBERT L.	ARMY	PTE	MELFORT	20/07/44	57°19'	102°40'	REID CHANNEL
REID, WILLIAM JOHN	ARMY	SGT	NUT MOUNTAIN	16/01/44	59°45'	103°58'	REID LAKE
REID, WILLIAM JOHN	RCAF	FS	CYMRIC	14/05/43	54°59'	102°51'	REID LAKE
REID, WILLIAM V.F.	RCAF	FO	UNKNOWN	16/03/44			PENDING
REILANDER, ALOYIS V.	RCAF	SL	REGINA	15/02/44	54°55'	105°03'	REILANDER CREEK
REIMER, ALVIN W.	RCAF	FS	FORT QU'APPELLE	12/01/42	55°47'	107°29'	REIMER LAKE
REISNER, RUSSELL M.	RCAF	FO	LIMERICK	20/05/43	57°47'	103°35'	REISNER LAKE
REIST, CHARLES A.	RCAF	SGT	MOOSE JAW	07/08/43	59°48'	107°30'	REIST LAKE
REITENBACH, JOSEPH	ARMY	PTE	HUBBARD	07/05/44	58°10'	102°35'	REITENBACH LAKE
REITER, ANTON	ARMY	PTE	TRAMPING LAKE	24/11/43	55°34'	105°51'	REITER LAKE
REITH, ROBERT M.	ARMY	RFN	STENEN	04/07/44	58°25'	106°06'	REITH LAKE
REITLO, CLIFFORD L.	RCAF	FO	PREECEVILLE	06/03/45	59°45'	103°33'	REITLO LAKE
RENAUD, LEO E.	ARMY	RFN	MARCELIN	18/10/44	60°01'	107°04'	RENAUD LAKE
RENNIE, ROBERT E.	RCAF		GULL LAKE	06/11/44			PENDING
RENOUF, JOHN S.	RCAF	FO	CUPAR	23/03/43	59°31'	107°55'	RENOUF LAKE
RENTON, ALBERT	RCAF	FO	REGINA	15/07/43	55°28'	104°23'	RENTON LAKE
RENWICK, CLIFFORD W.	RCAF	FS	FAIRMOUNT	24/09/43	59°57'	109°59'	RENWICK LAKE
RENZ, ALBERT	ARMY	PTE	UNKNOWN	20/09/44	55°44'	105°26'	RENZ LAKE
RETZER, WALTER P.	RCAF	FO	BULYEA	13/01/45	55°09'	108°56'	RETZER LAKE
REVELL, ROBERT W.	RCAF	WO2	NORTH BATTLEFORD	27/09/43	59°49'	105°40'	REVELL LAKE
REYNOLDS, BERNARD W.	RCAF	FS	LAKE LENORE	10/07/42	56°41'	102°31'	REYNOLDS ISLAND
REYNOLDS, CHARLES F.	ARMY	A SGT	LESLIE	06/02/44	59°51'	102°45'	REYNOLDS PENINSULA
REYNOLDS, DONALD D.	ARMY	LIEUT	BIGGAR	06/04/44	57°56'	102°45'	REYNOLDS LAKE
REYNOLDS, GEORGE G.	ARMY	CAPT	REGINA	23/07/44	54°56'	102°14'	REYNOLDS LAKE
REYNOLDS, JOSEPH B.	RCAF	FL	LAKE LENORE	18/02/41	56°39'	102°29'	REYNOLDS PENINSULA
REYNOLDS, VERNON E.	RCAF	SGT	PUNNICHY	04/01/42	55°20'	105°30'	REYNOLDS BAY
RHEILANDER, ROBERT	ARMY	PTE	REGINA	12/08/43	59°24'	105°57'	RHEILANDER LAKE
RHIND, EDWARD	RCAF	FO	SASKATOON	05/10/45	55°19'	104°51'	RHIND ISLAND
RHODES, KENNETH E.	RCAF	PO	CANORA	01/07/44	55°13'	104°14'	RHODES LAKE
RIACH, DOUGLAS	RCAF	FO	NOKOMIS	20/02/44	59°45'	109°15'	RIACH BAY
RICE, KENNETH M.	ARMY	GNR	DIVISION 14	06/09/44	56°51'	103°46'	RICE LAKE
RICHARDSON, ALBERT G.	ARMY	RFN	GILROY	06/10/44	58°28'	102°54'	RICHARDSON BAY
RICHARDSON, ARTHUR A.	ARMY	TPR	CARRUTHERS	01/03/44	59°43'	108°16'	RICHARDSON LAKE
RICHARDSON, HENRY D.	RCAF	LAC	SASKATOON	22/08/41			PENDING
RICHARDSON, JOHN G.	RCAF	FL	SASKATOON	17/11/40	59°50'	107°57'	RICHARDSON RAPIDS
RICHARDSON, WALTER A.	ARMY	A CAPT	MOOSE JAW	01/08/44	58°41'	103°56'	RICHARDSON LAKE
RICHES, WILLIAM A.	ARMY	LIEUT	ABERDEEN	29/08/44	59°46'	102°15'	RICHES LAKE
RICHIE, CALVIN	RCAF	FS	REGINA	05/06/43	59°06'	105°47'	RICHIE LAKE
RICHMOND, HERBERT D.	ARMY	PTE	OGEMA	19/08/42	57°48'	104°32'	RICHMOND LAKE
RICHMOND, KENNETH L.	RCAF	SGT	LEROSS	19/07/43	59°54'	109°49'	RICHMOND NARROWS
RICHTER, GEORGE W.	ARMY	L CPL	DISLEY	05/03/45	55°26'	104°54'	RICHTER LAKE
RIECKE, HARRY CARL	NAVY	PO	WEYBURN	20/02/43	54°34'	103°03'	RIECKE LAKE
RIEGER, PAUL	ARMY	PTE	LANDIS	28/10/44	55°53'	107°40'	REIGER BAY
RIEHL, JOHN	ARMY	RFN	PRELATE	25/06/45	56°39'	104°45'	RIEHL LAKE
RIES, EMIL P.	ARMY	PTE	CRAVEN	18/09/44	57°27'	107°53'	RIES LAKE
RIGDEN, STANLEY J.	RCAF	SGT	TUXFORD	28/04/44	59°42'	104°02'	RIGDEN LAKE
RIGGS, LEONARD E.	RCAF	FS	BALDWINTON	02/01/45	59°50'	104°34'	RIGGS LAKE
RILEY, WILLIAM D.	RCAF	LAC	REGINA	15/12/41	59°54'	104°33'	RILEY LAKE
RING, RALPH J.	ARMY	TPR	VISCOUNT	24/05/44	57°29'	106°13'	RING ISLAND
RINK, WENDEL	RCAF	FO	KENDAL	11/03/45	55°33'	104°06'	RINK LAKE
RIPLEY, EARL T.	ARMY	PTE	GLENBAIN	26/07/44	54°57'	102°29'	RIPLEY LAKE
RITHALER, GEORGE	ARMY	GNR	DIVISION 5	20/02/45	55°32'	105°01'	RITHALER LAKE
ROADHOUSE, GEORGE L.	ARMY	L CPL	EVESHAM	05/12/44	55°32'	105°52'	ROADHOUSE LAKE
ROBB, GEORGE BARCLAY	RCAF	FS	EXPANSE	07/09/42	54°29'	105°08'	ROBB LAKE
ROBB, ROBERT B.	ARMY	CPL	EXPANSE	20/07/44	54°29'	105°08'	ROBB LAKE
ROBBESTAD, LAIF H.C.	ARMY	PTE	TURTLEFORD	09/10/44	55°14'	102°28'	ROBBESTAD LAKE
ROBERTS, DENNIS E.	RCAF	FO	SASKATOON	01/06/44	54°12'	107°39'	ROBERTS LAKE
ROBERTS, GEORGE A.	RCAF	FO	REGINA	04/03/44	57°38'	105°58'	ROBERTS LAKE
ROBERTS, GEORGE W.	RCAF	FS	SASKATOON	03/09/42	56°09'	104°38'	ROBERTS ISLAND
ROBERTS, KENNETH	ARMY	A CPL	MOOSE JAW	14/08/44	58°14'	102°17'	ROBERTS LAKE
ROBERTS, LEON J.	RCAF	FO	PARKSIDE	22/10/43	59°29'	107°58'	ROBERTS LAKE
ROBERTS, MAURICE L.	RCAF	WO2	CLAIR	07/11/42	55°02'	102°13'	ROBERTS BAY
ROBERTS, RAYMOND LESLIE	NAVY	AB	MOOSE JAW	29/04/44	56°56'	103°33'	ROBERTS LAKE
ROBERTS, WILLIAM H.	ARMY	RFN	DIVISION 17	08/07/44	59°40'	109°25'	ROBERTS LAKE
ROBERTSON, CLIFFORD C.	RCAF	FS	PRINCE ALBERT	02/11/44	59°47'	109°00'	ROBERTSON BAY
ROBERTSON, DONALD L.	RCAF	FS	HAZLET	03/04/43	55°24'	106°00'	ROBERTSON ISLAND
ROBERTSON, DONALD M.	NAVY	AB	WATROUS	12/04/41	56°50'	103°43'	ROBERTSON POINT
ROBERTSON, DONALD R.	RCAF	FS	SASKATOON	10/10/42			PENDING
ROBERTSON, DOUGLAS P.	NAVY	STO PO	SASKATOON	08/08/44	54°54'	103°25'	ROBERTSON ISLAND
ROBERTSON, FORBES	RCAF	PO	SASKATOON	29/04/43	55°47'	104°47'	ROBERTSON BAY
ROBERTSON, GEORGE M.	RCAF	FS	WAPELLA	02/04/42	57°45'	104°03'	ROBERTSON BAY
ROBERTSON, IAN ANDERSON	NAVY	AB	SONNINGDALE	29/04/44	56°50'	103°38'	ROBERTSON ISLANDS
ROBERTSON, JOHN W.	RCAF	WO2	ARELEE	23/06/43			PENDING
ROBERTSON, MURRAY T.	RCAF	LAC	REGINA	25/04/44	55°57'	107°31'	ROBERTSON LAKE
ROBERTSON, THEODORE M.	NAVY	CH STO	SWIFT CURRENT	20/09/43	56°50'	103°42'	ROBERTSON PENINSULA
ROBERTSON, WILLIAM D.	NAVY	STO 1	SWIFT CURRENT	22/10/40	56°49'	103°43'	ROBERTSON NARROWS
ROBINSON, CECIL R.	RCAF	FS	WALPOLE	26/06/42	55°55'	106°17'	ROBINSON LAKE
ROBINSON, GEORGE C.	RCAF	FO	REGINA	18/08/43	57°15'	102°41'	ROBINSON BAY
ROBINSON, HAROLD R.	ARMY	LIEUT	SASKATOON	13/10/44	59°36'	108°24'	ROBINSON ISLAND
ROBINSON, HARVEY B.	ARMY	PTE	ESTEVAN	06/11/44	54°43'	102°51'	ROBINSON POINT
ROBINSON, JOHN E.	RCAF	WO1	ARCOLA	06/03/43	57°13'	104°08'	ROBINSON LAKE
ROBINSON, WESLEY C.	ARMY	SGT	DIVISION 2	25/04/45	56°21'	103°46'	ROBINSON ISLAND
ROCHON, ALDEN J.	ARMY	PTE	MONTMARTRE	19/08/42	54°39'	101°56'	ROCHON LAKE
ROCHVILLE, WILFRED J.	ARMY	PTE	REGINA	28/02/41	56°11'	107°21'	ROCHVILLE LAKE
RODGERS, NATHAN	ARMY	GNR	DIVISION 14	03/11/44	55°38'	105°59'	RODGERS LAKE
RODMAN, GLEN R.	RCAF	SGT	IMPERIAL	16/12/44	59°26'	108°37'	RODMAN LAKE
RODSETH, JOHN N.	NAVY	AB	DINSMORE	08/08/44	56°20'	105°20'	RODSETH LAKE
ROGAL, JOSEPH M.	RCAF	WO2	GRIFFIN	27/03/43	52°25'	103°11'	ROGAL LAKE
ROGERS, CALVIN C.	ARMY	RFN	DAVIDSON	31/10/44	56°17'	103°45'	ROGERS LAKE

Name	Branch	Rank	Hometown	Casualty Date	Latitude	Longitude	Geo-Memorial
ROGERS, CLIFFORD R.	ARMY	PTE	WEYBURN	25/11/42	55°30'	105°50'	ROGERS BAY
ROGERS, MAURICE B.	ARMY	GNR	EDGELEY	10/08/44	59°31'	108°57'	ROGERS LAKE
ROGERS, SIDNEY J.	RCAF	PO	BUCHANAN	26/02/44	57°32'	106°12'	ROGERS ISLAND
ROMANIUK, LLOYD L.	ARMY	PTE	DIVISION 14	25/10/44	55°36'	105°47'	ROMANIUK LAKE
ROMULD, HAROLD M.	RCAF	FO	DUNBLANE	17/06/44	55°35'	103°06'	ROMULD ISLAND
RONDOW, WILLIAM	ARMY	CPL	MOOSE JAW	23/09/44	56°23'	105°34'	RONDOW LAKE
RONEY, LILLIAN L.	ARMY	PTE	IMPERIAL	14/08/42	56°17'	108°21'	RONEY BAY
ROOKE, CLARENCE J.	RCAF	CPL	CUPAR	19/05/42	59°37'	107°52'	ROOKE LAKE
ROOP, ALVIN V.	ARMY	GDSM	REGINA	28/04/45	56°27'	106°41'	ROOP LAKE
ROPER, ALBERT G.	ARMY	TPR	VISCOUNT	01/09/44	56°32'	105°37'	ROPER ISLAND
ROPER, ERNEST A.	ARMY	PTE	VISCOUNT	21/07/44	56°28'	105°41'	ROPER BAY
ROSE, CLAYTON J.	ARMY	SGT	UNKNOWN	17/09/44	58°37'	102°37'	ROSE LAKE
ROSE, CLIFFORD W.	RCAF	PO	KAMSACK	19/04/44	59°35'	107°41'	ROSE LAKE
ROSENFELT, ADAM	ARMY	A CPL	WOODROW	23/07/44	58°14'	106°53'	ROSENFELT LAKE
ROSIE, GEORGE	NAVY	L STO M	BETHUNE	15/11/42	59°23'	106°38'	ROSIE LAKE
ROSINSKI, BALIESLAW P.	ARMY	PTE	INVERMAY	14/09/44	59°19'	105°46'	ROSINSKI LAKE
ROSS, ALEXANDER	ARMY	SGT	DIVISION 6	13/09/44	59°23'	107°46'	ROSS ISLAND
ROSS, ALLEN R.	RCAF	FS	PRINCE ALBERT	17/04/43	59°43'	109°46'	ROSS LAKE
ROSS, CARMAN V.	RCAF	PO	FRONTIER	28/05/44	57°13'	105°10'	ROSS LAKE
ROSS, HORACE R.	RCAF	WO2	PITMAN	03/09/43	55°52'	107°15'	ROSS BAY
ROSS, JAMES D.	RCAF	SGT	ASSINIBOIA	06/01/41	58°28'	103°17'	ROSS CHANNEL
ROSS, JOHN	RCAF	FS	REGINA	27/07/42	55°57'	107°33'	ROSS LAKE
ROSS, PATRICK LEO	NAVY	O SIG	SASKATOON	05/11/40	56°59'	103°54'	ROSS LAKE
ROSS, ROMAN	ARMY	PTE	LORLIE	26/02/46	59°51'	103°23'	ROSS LAKE
ROSS, STANLEY G.M.	RCAF	PO	REGINA	19/07/44	57°39'	106°03'	ROSS CREEK
ROSS, VICTOR	ARMY	PTE	MEADOW LAKE	25/12/41	54°34'	108°33'	ROSS CREEK
ROSS, WILLIAM GARFIELD	NAVY	STO PO	REGINA	25/06/40	56°46'	103°33'	ROSS RIVER
ROTARIU, GEORGE	ARMY	PTE	WOOD MOUNTAIN	01/10/44	58°14'	106°10'	ROTARIU LAKE
ROULSTON, LORNE E.	ARMY	PTE	MARCHWELL	20/10/44	59°30'	105°45'	ROULSTON LAKE
ROURKE, THOMAS JAMES	NAVY	MM	SASKATOON	14/04/43	54°47'	102°57'	ROURKE LAKE
ROUSE, CHARLES J.	RCAF	FO	MILDEN	06/03/45			PENDING
ROUSELL, ORVAL S.	ARMY	PTE	JUNIATA	12/10/44	59°59'	107°53'	ROUSELL LAKE
ROWAN, THOMAS S.	ARMY	GNR	REGINA	04/11/44	57°34'	106°48'	ROWAN LAKE
ROWE, TERRY FAULKNER	ARMY	LT	PRINCE ALBERT	06/02/44	55°11'	104°54'	ROWE LAKE
ROZELL, GLEN E.	RCAF	FS	SASKATOON	21/07/43	57°27'	109°31'	ROZELL LAKE
RUBIN, HECTOR B.	RCAF	FL	KAMSACK	21/03/43	55°17'	104°40'	RUBIN ISLAND
RUDE, GORDON J.	RCAF	PO	LAKE ALMA	31/03/45	54°48'	107°55'	RUDE LAKE
RUDOLPH, LEO	ARMY	A SGT	ROSTHERN	27/10/44	56°35'	102°25'	RUDOLPH LAKE
RUDOLPH, WILLIAM	ARMY	L CPL	ROSTHERN	23/09/44	55°50'	106°01'	RUDOLPH LAKE
RUMPEL, REINHOLD P.	ARMY	SIGNM	STRASBOURG	30/11/42	58°18'	106°34'	RUMPEL LAKE
RUPERT, EARL	ARMY	SGT	MELFORT	20/07/43	58°34'	102°34'	RUPERT LAKE
RUPERT, KENNETH M.	RCAF	FS	MELFORT	26/04/45	56°54'	105°03'	RUPERT LAKE
RUSHMER, JOHN S.	ARMY	PTE	CODETTE	19/08/42	57°38'	106°24'	RUSHMER CHANNEL
RUSHMER, MATTHEW	ARMY	A L SGT	DIVISION 14	15/09/44	57°40'	106°16'	RUSHMER PENINSULA
RUSHTON, NICHOLAS C.	RCAF	SGT	SWIFT CURRENT	16/05/44	55°01'	102°27'	RUSHTON LAKE
RUSSELL, HENRY M.	RCAF	FS	LAFLECHE	27/08/42	54°55'	102°12'	RUSSELL LAKE
RUSSELL, HUGH J.	ARMY	LIEUT	MAPLE CREEK	31/08/44	56°46'	103°44'	RUSSELL ISLAND
RUSSELL, JOSEPH V.	RCAF	FL	SPEERS	21/02/44	55°20'	104°39'	RUSSELL BAY
RUSSELL, LAWRENCE ELGIN	ARMY	CPL	ELFROS	22/02/45	57°26'	105°22'	RUSSELL LAKE
RUSSELL, MAXWELL A.	RCAF	FO	LAFLECHE	26/06/43	54°55'	102°12'	RUSSELL LAKE
RUSSELL, WILLIAM F.	RCAF	PO	MARRIOTT	25/03/44			PENDING
RUSTAD, ALVIN M.	ARMY	L CPL	ROSE VALLEY	06/06/44	55°02'	103°49'	RUSTAD LAKE
RUTHERFORD, THOMAS	RCAF	FO	HODGEVILLE	10/04/44	57°22'	103°19'	RUTHERFORD LAKE
RUTZKI, JOHN	RCAF	FS	MCKIM	27/04/44	59°44'	106°16'	RUTZKI LAKE
RYAN, FRANK J. T.	ARMY	SGT	CUDWORTH	06/07/45	55°49'	104°07'	RYAN ISLAND
RYAN, JAMES W.	ARMY	PTE	BROADVIEW	23/10/44	56°50'	103°03'	RYAN BAY
RYAN, LAWRENCE D.	RCAF	FS	LUSELAND	05/04/43	57°23'	104°49'	RYAN LAKE
RYCKMAN, FRANK	ARMY	RFN	CARIEVALE	08/06/44	59°48'	106°24'	RYCKMAN BAY
RYCKMAN, SIDNEY T.	ARMY	L CPL	CARIEVALE	19/02/45	58°39'	106°47'	RYCKMAN LAKE
SABINE, EUGENE P.	RCAF	PO	ETHELTON	25/05/44	57°06'	109°52'	SABINE LAKE
SABISTON, WILLIAM W.G.	ARMY	CPL	MILDMAY PARK	26/06/44	56°00'	104°32'	SABISTON LAKE
SACKNEY, JOSEPH R.	ARMY	PTE	SHEHO	05/05/42	55°58'	104°55'	SACKNEY LAKE
SAHLI, GEORGE K.	ARMY	GNR	DIVISION 13	25/12/44	55°05'	102°55'	SAHLI LAKE
SAINT, JOHN W.	ARMY	GNR	DIVISION 5	08/08/44	56°08'	105°07'	SAINT LAKE
SALABA, ALEXANDER J.	RCAF	FO	WILLOW BUNCH	02/01/44	57°45'	103°41'	SALABA LAKE
SALESKI, JOHN P.	ARMY	PTE	WINDTHORST	21/07/44	56°30'	109°24'	SALESKI LAKE
SALMOND, GEORGE	ARMY	L SGT	ESTEVAN	19/08/42	54°29'	105°07'	SALMOND LAKE
SAMSON, ALFRED F.	ARMY	RFN	ALBERTVILLE	04/07/44	58°10'	104°37'	SAMSON LAKE
SANDERSON, EARL A.	RCAF	FL	SPRUCE LAKE	14/01/44	58°08'	106°52'	SANDERSON LAKE
SANDERSON, FRANK G.	RCAF	SGT	AVONLEA	20/01/44	59°44'	107°38'	SANDERSON RIVER
SANDERSON, GEORGE F.	RCAF	PO	AVONLEA	03/06/42	59°44'	107°38'	SANDERSON RIVER
SANDERSON, ROBERT C.	ARMY	A CPL	MAPLE CREEK	08/06/43	56°54'	103°27'	SANDERSON BAY
SANDERSON, ROBERT L.	RCAF	PO	ELSTOW	10/02/44			PENDING
SANDO, NELS M.	ARMY	PTE	STURGIS	16/09/44	57°31'	108°29'	SANDO LAKE
SANDOMIRSKY, MARVIN M.	RCAF	WO2	REGINA	03/03/45	55°48'	104°14'	SANDOMIRSKY ISLAND
SANGRET, AUGUST	ARMY	PTE	BATTLEFORD	29/04/43			PENDING
SANTO, FRANK R.	RCAF	WO1	BENDER	05/05/43	55°36'	106°27'	SANTO ISLAND
SANTO, JOHN A.	RCAF	PO	BENDER	01/08/44	55°40'	106°22'	SANTO BAY
SANTY, SAMUEL F.	RCAF	WO2	MOOSE JAW	16/09/42	60°00'	104°09'	SANTY LAKE
SAPSFORD, JOHN A.	ARMY	SPR	DIVISION 17	28/02/45	59°27'	107°50'	SAPSFORD LAKE
SARGINSON, LORNE H.	ARMY	PTE	KELLIHER	22/01/45	54°42'	103°10'	SARGINSON LAKE
SARKA, KENNETH F.	ARMY	TPR	ASSINIBOIA	02/07/42	60°00'	102°24'	SARKA LAKE
SARUK, MICHAEL A.	RCAF	WO2	ALVENA	23/05/44	59°50'	102°59'	SARUK LAKE
SAUNDERS, ANDREW L.	RCAF	LAC	BORDEN	28/12/42	57°38'	104°29'	SAUNDERS LAKE
SAUNDERS, WILLIAM L.	RCAF	FL	FORT QU'APPELLE	03/12/44	55°46'	107°06'	SAUNDERS CREEK
SAUTER, ERNEST R.	ARMY	PTE	FAIRLIGHT	19/10/42	55°17'	104°44'	SAUTER BAY
SAVA, JOSEPH	ARMY	PTE	ESTEVAN	20/07/44	58°40'	102°18'	SAVA LAKE
SAWATZKY, JOHN	ARMY	RFN	OSLER	09/06/44	58°03'	104°39'	SAWATZKY LAKE
SAWATZKY, JOHN	ARMY	A CPL	PETAIGAN	28/04/45	56°35'	103°54'	SAWATZKY RAPIDS
SAWDEN, CHARLES E.	ARMY	PTE	CONSUL	19/08/42	55°11'	106°14'	SAWDEN LAKE
SAYERS, GEORGE W.	ARMY	PTE	BATTLEFORD	22/12/42	57°15'	105°18'	SAYERS LAKE
SAYESE, JAMES A.	ARMY	A CPL	PRINCE ALBERT	14/08/44	55°37'	103°50'	SAYESE LAKE
SCALES, ALFRED ERIC	NAVY	OS	REGINA	05/05/43	54°05'	105°27'	SCALES LAKE
SCHAFF, LEONARD	RCAF	FS	BURSTALL	14/10/44	59°30'	106°30'	SCHAFF LAKE
SCHAFFER, ROY J.	ARMY	PTE	REGINA	13/12/44	56°45'	103°36'	SCHAFFER LAKE
SCHARFE, PITMAN E.	ARMY	LIEUT	UNKNOWN	06/01/45	59°29'	105°33'	SCHARFE LAKE
SCHEIDEL, NICK P.	ARMY	RFN	SASKATOON	21/02/45	56°49'	103°15'	SCHEIDEL LAKE
SCHERR, ALEXANDER	ARMY	PTE	DIVISION 13	14/08/44	55°19'	102°54'	SCHERR LAKE
SCHIELE, ADOLPH	ARMY	PTE	REVENUE	05/08/44	58°16'	108°56'	SCHIELE BAY
SCHJEFTE, OSCAR	ARMY	A CPL	TRIBUNE	31/07/44	57°13'	106°48'	SCHJEFTE LAKE
SCHLEMKO, GABRIEL F.	ARMY	GNR	SCOTSGUARD	01/10/41	56°58'	107°07'	SCHLEMKO LAKE
SCHMIDT, WALTER B.	ARMY	A CPL	CONSUL	14/03/45	55°02'	102°17'	SCHMIDT BAY
SCHMIDT, WILLIAM C.	ARMY	PTE	REGINA	22/08/44	59°51'	107°38'	SCHMIDT BAY
SCHMITZ, DONALD J.E.	RCAF	PO	HUMBOLDT	05/06/44	56°03'	106°35'	SCHMITZ LAKE
SCHNEIDER, DOUGLAS O.	RCAF	FS	REGINA	24/10/44	57°50'	105°07'	SCHNEIDER LAKE
SCHNEIDER, MAX	ARMY	RFN	REGINA	28/11/45	56°10'	108°34'	SCHNEIDER LAKE
SCHOLEY, CHARLES L.	RCAF	SGT	RYERSON	01/06/42	59°31'	106°26'	SCHOLEY LAKE
SCHOTTS, PERCY H.	ARMY	PTE	SIMPSON	08/08/44	55°05'	102°13'	SCHOTTS LAKE
SCHULL, FREDERICK H.	RCAF	FS	MOOSE JAW	27/06/43	59°20'	106°32'	SCHULL LAKE
SCHULTZ, ELMER J.	RCAF	FS	HUBBARD	24/07/43	56°33'	103°35'	SCHULTZ RAPIDS
SCHURMAN, GEORGE W.	ARMY	PTE	DENZIL	07/02/45	59°40'	106°00'	SCHURMAN LAKE
SCHUTTE, EDMUND R.	ARMY	RFN	DIVISION 16	15/08/44	56°24'	102°30'	SCHUTTE BAY
SCHWAB, JOHN H.	RCAF	PO	REGINA	04/06/43	56°35'	102°10'	SCHWAB LAKE
SCHWANDT, EDWARD G.	ARMY	LIEUT	STRASBOURG	27/08/44	60°00'	102°17'	SCHWANDT RIVER
SCHWEITZER, JACOB A.	RCAF	FS	REGINA	28/04/42	59°34'	107°49'	SCHWEITZER BAY
SCIBAN, HENRY ALBERT	NAVY	AB	SASKATOON	25/06/40	59°16'	106°21'	SCIBAN BAY
SCOBIE, LEWIS W.	RCAF	SGT	ROSETOWN	11/10/42	59°41'	109°16'	SCOBIE PENINSULA
SCOLLON, VIVIAN M.	ARMY	CPL	LLOYDMINSTER	26/04/44	56°38'	105°05'	SCOLLON RAPIDS
SCOTT, ARCHIBALD B.	ARMY	PTE	SOMME	01/05/45	56°48'	102°35'	SCOTT CREEK
SCOTT, DONALD J.	ARMY	MAJ	CUPAR	08/08/44	59°44'	108°02'	SCOTT BAY
SCOTT, DONALD J.	RCAF	WO2	STALWART	26/05/44	55°10'	102°14'	SCOTT LAKE
SCOTT, FOSTER W.J.	RCAF	PO	NORTH BATTLEFORD	12/08/41	57°14'	103°12'	SCOTT RAPIDS
SCOTT, HENRY H.	ARMY	PTE	REGINA	30/10/41	56°48'	102°34'	SCOTT BAY
SCOTT, JOHN H.	RCAF	SGT	MOOSE JAW	21/11/40	56°04'	105°35'	SCOTT RAPIDS
SCOTT, RICHARD A.	ARMY	LIEUT	DIVISION 5	02/05/43	59°56'	108°11'	SCOTT ISLAND
SCOTT, ROBERT B.	RCAF	PO	HORIZON	10/10/44	57°04'	105°28'	SCOTT ISLAND
SCOTT, ROBERT I.	RCAF	FO	GLEN EWEN	09/02/43			PENDING
SCOTT, ROBERT T.	RCAF	SGT	HORIZON	11/03/42	57°02'	105°32'	SCOTT BAY

Name	Branch	Rank	Hometown	Casualty Date	Latitude	Longitude	Geo-Memorial
SCOTT, THOMAS F.	RCAF	SGT	BIGGAR	28/05/44	55°45'	104°15'	SCOTT LAKE
SCOTT, WILLIAM L.	RCAF	WO1	YORKTON	28/06/42	57°50'	106°45'	SCOTT CREEK
SCRAMSTED, ALLAN L.	ARMY	GNR	DUNLOP	01/04/44	55°22'	104°47'	SCRAMSTED LAKE
SCRIMES, FRANK J.B.	RCAF	FS	REGINA	02/06/42	58°34'	103°26'	SCRIMES LAKE
SCUTT, LEONARD A.	RCAF	FO	MELAVAL	23/06/44	57°38'	103°37'	SCUTT LAKE
SEABY, FRANCIS E.	RCAF	FO	INDIAN HEAD	05/03/45	57°41'	106°07'	SEABY LAKE
SEAKER, RONALD A.	RCAF	WO1	REGINA	16/03/43	55°15'	104°47'	SEAKER ISLAND
SEALEY, WALTER BERTIE	NAVY	AB	SASKATOON	24/11/44	54°16'	104°36'	SEALEY LAKE
SEBELIUS, CECIL L.	RCAF	SGT	VANTAGE	22/06/43	59°46'	108°33'	SEBELIUS LAKE
SEBESTYEN, DENIS	RCAF	PO	SASKATOON	01/07/44	56°43'	108°47'	SEBESTYEN ISLAND
SEE, DOUGLAS R.	RCAF	FS	DIVISION 14	10/08/43	56°38'	106°10'	SEE LAKE
SEEMAN, THEODORE A.	RCAF	FO	THEODORE	28/07/46	59°46'	106°15'	SEEMAN LAKE
SEIVEWRIGHT, JOHN E.	ARMY	PTE	ARCOLA	01/09/44	54°43'	102°44'	SEIVEWRIGHT ISLAND
SIEVEWRIGHT, STANLEY C.	ARMY	CPL	ARCOLA	15/08/44	55°51'	104°10'	SIEVEWRIGHT LAKE
SELBY, JOHN M.	ARMY	TPR	MOOSE JAW	04/01/45	55°41'	104°56'	SELBY PENINSULA
SELLS, RICHARD V.	ARMY	L CPL	GULL LAKE	03/03/45	59°32'	108°27'	SELLS LAKE
SELMES, ALBERT J.	ARMY	PTE	SASKATOON	24/06/45	56°40'	106°33'	SELMES LAKE
SENTON, CLAUDE	RCAF	PO	SIMPSON	24/05/44	60°00'	108°02'	SENTON LAKE
SENYK, STEVEN	NAVY	STO 2	SWIFT CURRENT	25/06/40	55°30'	107°01'	SENYK LAKE
SERGENT, JOSEPH R.L.	RCAF	FO	MEADOW LAKE	17/04/43	54°33'	108°37'	SERGENT LAKE
SERHON, DAN	ARMY	PTE	RAMA	26/01/44	57°01'	107°42'	SERHON LAKE
SERNOWSKI, WILLIAM	ARMY	PTE	DIVISION 15	31/03/45	58°11'	104°46'	SERNOWSKI LAKE
SERWATKA, PETER	ARMY	PTE	GLASLYN	20/07/44	59°00'	109°35'	SERWATKA CREEK
SERWATKEWICH, JOSEPH	ARMY	RFN	ITUNA	06/06/44	56°50'	102°16'	SERWATKEWICH LAKE
SETTEE, ALEXANDER	ARMY	FUS	CUMBERLAND HOUSE	03/09/44	53°26'	108°12'	SETTEE BAY
SEVERSON, NORMAN A.	ARMY	SGT	EDAM	31/10/44	56°05'	104°02'	SEVERSON LAKE
SEYMOUR, JOHN H.	RCAF	FO	SASKATOON	22/01/44	56°20'	107°27'	SEYMOUR LAKE
SHANNON, IRL W.	ARMY	SPR	BIRCH HILLS	26/08/44	59°22'	106°53'	SHANNON LAKE
SHARP, ANDREW	RCAF	FO	BIGGAR	08/11/44	55°36'	108°20'	SHARP ISLAND
SHARP, BENJAMIN	ARMY	A L SGT	SASKATOON	20/12/43	59°24'	108°38'	SHARP BAY
SHARPE, GEORGE A.	ARMY	TPR	YORKTON	19/12/44	55°26'	105°07'	SHARPE LAKES
SHARPE, NORMAN R.	ARMY	A CAPT	MOOSE JAW	15/09/44	56°45'	103°20'	SHARPE LAKE
SHASKO, PETER	ARMY	SPR	RUNNYMEDE	05/01/42	59°16'	106°47'	SHASKO BAY
SHAW, CLARENCE H.F.	ARMY	A CPL	MOOSE JAW	28/05/42	59°47'	109°22'	SHAW LAKE
SHAW, DENIS T.	RCAF	FS	REGINA	31/07/43	59°43'	109°21'	SHAW ISLAND
SHAW, DENZIL F.	ARMY	TPR	SEMANS	24/05/44	56°45'	102°29'	SHAW ISLAND
SHAW, ROBERT S.	RCAF	FO	GAINSBOROUGH	04/11/42	55°30'	108°24'	SHAW BAY
SHAW, WILLIAM K.	ARMY	CPL	SWIFT CURRENT	09/04/45	49°44'	109°41'	SHAW CREEK
SHEA, EDGAR N.	ARMY	SPR	SPRING WATER	26/08/44	59°27'	106°50'	SHEA BAY
SHEA, EDWARD L.	RCAF	FO	NETHERHILL	05/11/44	60°00'	108°33'	SHEA LAKE
SHEA, OMAR C.	ARMY	Q M S	REGINA	01/05/44	58°11'	109°53'	SHEA CREEK
SHEA, WALTER A.	ARMY	A SGT	MOOSE JAW	09/04/45	56°18'	106°33'	SHEA RIVER
SHELDON, PERCY	ARMY	GNR	OLD WIVES	23/10/42	56°49'	104°34'	SHELDON LAKE
SHEPHERD, ALFRED A.	RCAF	FO	HUMBOLDT	31/07/43	57°06'	102°51'	SHEPHERD LAKE
SHEPHERD, JOHN C.	ARMY	TPR	KELVINGTON	14/08/44	58°54'	103°56'	SHEPHERD CREEK
SHEPHERD, WILLIAM J.	ARMY	BDR	MOOSOMIN	19/06/44	57°53'	107°44'	SHEPHERD RAPIDS
SHEPLEY, ROBERT A.	ARMY	RFN	DIVISION 16	13/08/44	60°00'	104°19'	SHEPLEY ISLAND
SHEWCHUK, VICTOR	ARMY	PTE	VONDA	05/08/44	59°53'	109°35'	SHEWCHUK LAKE
SHIELS, ROBERT K.	ARMY	RFN	DIVISION 8	10/07/44	57°59'	109°44'	SHIELS LAKE
SHIER, RUSSELL R.M.	ARMY	TPR	WELDON	02/05/45	59°59'	104°31'	SHIER ISLAND
SHINNAN, ROBERT G.	ARMY	CAPT	REGINA	09/06/44	54°58'	109°33'	SHINNAN ISLAND
SHKWAROK, JOSEPH	ARMY	SPR	SHELL LAKE	05/02/43	54°44'	102°28'	SHKWAROK LAKE
SHOEMAKER, DONALD A.	ARMY	RFN	HANDSWORTH	03/08/44	55°17'	104°33'	SHOEMAKER LAKE
SHNIER, CLIFFORD	RCAF	PO	UNKNOWN	30/07/43	54°54'	102°50'	SCHNIER ISLAND
SHOLTE, GORDON E.	RCAF	FO	VESPER	29/07/44	57°44'	109°28'	SHOLTE LAKE
SHORT, ROBERT P.	RCAF	CPL	SASKATOON	17/01/43	59°35'	108°51'	SHORT LAKE
SHORTEN, ALBERT G.	RCAF	WO2	REGINA	13/03/43	59°50'	108°01'	SHORTEN LAKE
SHORTRIDGE, RAYMOND F.	RCAF	FS	PRINCE ALBERT	24/08/43	55°30'	104°22'	SHORTRIDGE LAKE
SHULTS, RUSSELL H.	RCAF	LAC	NIPAWIN	14/12/42	59°56'	108°36'	SHULTS LAKE
SHUTTLEWORTH, DOUGLAS	RCAF	FL	REGINA	18/08/43	54°38'	102°41'	SHUTTLEWORTH LAKE
SIEBEN, JOSEPH G.	RCAF	PO	COSINE	02/02/44	57°45'	109°26'	SIEBEN LAKE
SIEGEL, OTTO	ARMY	GNR	LUSELAND	13/08/44	55°23'	103°04'	SIEGEL LAKE
SIEMENS, ARCHIE H.	RCAF	PO	SASKATOON	22/06/44	56°02'	106°41'	SIEMENS LAKE
SILL, RUSSELL L.	ARMY	PTE	KUROKI	02/03/43	57°19'	107°15'	SILL LAKE
SILVERTHORN, ALLAN M.	RCAF	FO	DILKE	19/06/45	58°54'	109°22'	SILVERTHORN LAKE
SILVESTER, NORMAN E.	ARMY	RFN	CHAPLIN	09/07/44	59°43'	108°36'	SILVESTER LAKE
SILVIUS, KAY K.	ARMY	TPR	FAIRLIGHT	02/08/44	57°26'	108°15'	SILVIUS LAKE
SIM, JAMES W.	ARMY	L BDR	SASKATOON	06/09/45	55°27'	104°42'	SIM LAKE
SIM, LAWRENCE E.	ARMY	RFN	REGINA	06/06/44			PENDING
SIMMER, JOHN R.	ARMY	PTE	TRIBUNE	12/11/44	56°23'	105°28'	SIMMER LAKE
SIMONS, CLINTON LEROY	NAVY	O SIG	SWIFT CURRENT	13/09/42	59°30'	106°11'	SIMONS LAKE
SIMONSON, ERNEST S.	RCAF	FO	SWIFT CURRENT	10/07/44	57°12'	109°39'	SIMONSON LAKE
SIMONSON, ROY E.	RCAF	FO	MOOSE JAW	16/06/44	56°45'	109°29'	SIMONSON RAPIDS
SIMONSON, VERNON L.	RCAF	FS	SWIFT CURRENT	01/08/42	57°24'	102°25'	SIMONSON ISLAND
SIMPKINS, EDWARD W.	ARMY	A CAPT	SASKATOON	17/07/44	56°49'	103°14'	SIMPKINS LAKE
SIMPSON, ALEXANDER J.	RCAF	FS	OXBOW	22/05/43	59°25'	106°52'	SIMPSON LAKE
SIMPSON, DAVID C.	RAF		PRINCE ALBERT	16/10/41			PENDING
SIMPSON, GEORGE B.	RCAF	FS	GAINSBOROUGH	15/08/42	55°14'	105°08'	SIMPSON ISLAND
SINCLAIR, EARL S.	ARMY	TPR	CHIPPERFIELD	06/06/44	56°53'	108°56'	SINCLAIR LAKE
SINCLAIR, ELIE V.	ARMY	L SGT	REGINA	09/06/44	54°23'	102°50'	SINCLAIR CREEK
SINCLAIR, WILLIAM D.	ARMY	PTE	PUNNICHY	11/04/44	57°16'	103°50'	SINCLAIR LAKE
SINGH, JAMES	ARMY	RFN	UNKNOWN	12/10/44	54°20'	104°59'	SINGH LAKE
SINGLETON, ALFRED H.	ARMY	CAPT	ROULEAU	14/05/43	56°11'	108°14'	SINGLETON LAKE
SITTER, CLEMENCE J.	ARMY	TPR	KENDAL STATION	19/10/44	59°22'	105°02'	SITTER LAKE
SKALICKY, ALPHONSE L.	ARMY	L CPL	DIVISION 15	14/04/45	55°58'	104°26'	SKALICKY LAKE
SKEATES, CLIFFORD E.	RCAF	LAC	ABBEY	04/06/44	59°21'	108°49'	SKEATES ISLAND
SKINNER, EDWIN ALFRED	NAVY	PO	SASKATOON	02/01/46	56°56'	103°58'	SKINNER LAKE
SKLARCHUK, EDWARD R.	RCAF	WO2	NORTH BATTLEFORD	03/08/43	55°17'	106°15'	SKLARCHUK LAKE
SKWARCHUK, JOHN	ARMY	RFN	DEVIL LAKE	04/07/44	55°31'	105°34'	SKWARCHUK LAKE
SKWARCHUK, METRO	ARMY	TPR	DEVIL LAKE	06/06/44	57°59'	107°54'	SKWARCHUK LAKE
SLABICK, JOHN J.	RCAF	WO2	ESTEVAN	24/02/43	55°36'	104°28'	SLABICK LAKE
SLANEY, GEORGE E.	ARMY	L CPL	MOOSE JAW	25/09/44	55°50'	104°38'	SLANEY LAKE
SLUGOSKI, JOSEPH	RCAF	WO1	YORKTON	04/02/43	59°44'	106°12'	SLUGOSKI LAKE
SMAILES, FREDERICK J.	ARMY	A CPL	OGEMA	17/08/44	55°38'	102°12'	SMAILES ISLAND
SMALL, FREDERICK G.	RCAF	FO	REGINA	09/10/43	56°05'	106°57'	SMALL ISLAND
SMALL, HARRY E.	ARMY	RFN	SASKATOON	12/09/44	59°02'	108°25'	SMALL BAY
SMALLEY, KENNETH G.	RCAF	FS	HUMBOLDT	09/10/43	56°40'	106°19'	SMALLEY LAKE
SMALLWOOD, GEORGE K.	ARMY	PTE	STOUGHTON	22/07/44	53°37'	104°25'	SMALLWOOD LAKE
SMITH, ALLAN E.	ARMY	LIEUT	REGINA	08/07/44	59°53'	108°29'	ALLANSMITH RIVER
SMITH, ARTHUR A.	ARMY	TPR	SASKATOON	24/05/44	58°27'	105°16'	SMITH ISLAND
SMITH, ARTHUR P.L.	RCAF	PO	CUPAR	24/04/42	57°51'	102°11'	SMITH CHANNEL
SMITH, ARTHUR S.	ARMY	RFN	DIVISION 8	06/06/44	58°26'	105°14'	SMITH PENINSULA
SMITH, CHARLES	ARMY	L CPL	REGINA	19/12/41	59°29'	108°31'	SMITH LAKE
SMITH, CHARLES DUNSMORE	NAVY	OS	OGEMA	25/06/40	54°56'	102°59'	DUNSMORE BAY
SMITH, CHARLES J.	RCAF	FS	REGINA	30/01/43	55°47'	106°06'	SMITH BAY
SMITH, DAVID J.	ARMY	PTE	DEER RIDGE	04/05/45	56°40'	108°28'	SMITH BAY
SMITH, DEAN W.	RCAF	WO2	REGINA	07/02/43	56°16'	104°27'	SMITH NARROWS
SMITH, DONALD A.	ARMY	TPR	SWIFT CURRENT	16/08/44	59°44'	109°05'	SMITH POINT
SMITH, DONALD H.	RCAF	SGT	ELFROS	12/04/43			PENDING
SMITH, DONALD J.	RCAF	FO	NAICAM	16/05/43	57°36'	103°43'	SMITH RIDGE
SMITH, ERIC G.	RCAF	FS	SECRETAN	16/06/44			PENDING
SMITH, FREDERICK W.	RCAF	FS	SASKATOON	03/10/43			PENDING
SMITH, GEORGE E.	RCAF	PO	REGINA	06/12/44			PENDING
SMITH, GEORGE E.	RCAF	FS	REGINA	13/07/44	55°31'	104°39'	SMITH BAY
SMITH, GEORGE G.	ARMY	SGT	REGINA	01/07/40			PENDING
SMITH, GEORGE J.	RCAF	FL	VERWOOD	01/05/44	55°57'	106°45'	SMITH LAKE
SMITH, GILBERT J.	RCAF	LAC	ELFROS	28/01/45			PENDING
SMITH, JACOB C.	ARMY	PTE	MELFORT	06/03/45	58°27'	102°22'	SMITH LAKE
SMITH, JAMES A.	RCAF	FO	REGINA	27/06/43	55°41'	106°30'	SMITH PENINSULA
SMITH, JAMES D.	RCAF	PO	MOOSE JAW	18/12/44	55°46'	107°07'	SMITH RAPIDS
SMITH, JAMES F.	RCAF	WO2	MOOSE JAW	08/04/43	55°30'	106°29'	SMITH CHANNEL
SMITH, JERROLD ALPINE	RCAF	PO	REGINA	10/08/42	57°12'	107°29'	JERROLD LAKE
SMITH, JOHN D.	ARMY	SIGMN	MELFORT	12/12/45	59°24'	107°49'	SMITH PENINSULA
SMITH, JOHN E.G.	ARMY	PTE	CLIMAX	29/09/44	56°47'	102°33'	SMITH PENINSULA
SMITH, LEONARD L.	ARMY	PTE	CHELAN	19/08/42	59°25'	107°11'	SMITH RAPIDS
SMITH, LESLIE G.	ARMY	SAP	LEASK	11/09/44	59°22'	106°47'	SMITH RIVER
SMITH, LESLIE G.	RCAF	FS	REGINA	24/05/43			PENDING
SMITH, LLOYD HENRY	RCAF	PO	STURGIS	31/03/44	57°58'	106°46'	LLOYDSMITH LAKE

Name	Branch	Rank	Hometown	Casualty Date	Latitude	Longitude	Geo-Memorial
SMITH, LLOYD HILBERT	RCAF	FO	WEYBURN	10/05/42	55°44'	107°39'	SMITH CREEK
SMITH, ROBERT C.	RCAF	SGT	DAVIDSON	03/11/43	56°53'	102°33'	SMITH RIVER
SMITH, ROBERT C.	ARMY	PTE	CLIMAX	19/12/41			PENDING
SMITH, ROBERT G.	RCAF	FO	MOOSE JAW	05/03/45	55°47'	107°07'	SMITH FALLS
SMITH, ROBERT L.	ARMY	PTE	GLENAVON	21/07/44	51°00'	108°04'	SMITH CREEK
SMITH, ROY HAMILTON	RCAF	FS	MELVILLE	23/08/43	57°29'	104°17'	SMITH CREEK
SMITH, RUSSELL C.	RCAF	WO1	KAMSACK	15/04/42	58°35'	103°48'	SMITH BAY
SMITH, SAMUEL N.J.	ARMY	L SGT	DIVISION 15	19/08/42	56°41'	108°27'	SMITH RIVER
SMITH, SIDNEY H. P. L.	RCAF	FS	CUPAR	07/07/45	58°39'	109°16'	SMITH POINT
SMITH, THOMAS E.	RCAF	AC2	TESSIER	07/07/42			PENDING
SMITH, VERNON B.	RCAF	PO	REGINA	15/02/45	55°31'	104°39'	SMITH BAY
SMITH, WILFRID B.	RCAF	SGT	HAWARDEN	29/05/41			PENDING
SMITH-JONES, HENRY V.	RCAF	FS	REGINA	29/04/43	55°33'	106°00'	SMITH-JONES LAKE
SMITH-WINDSOR, GRENVILLE	RCAF	PO	CUPAR	26/06/42	59°24'	107°48'	SMITH-WINDSOR ISLANDS
SMYSNIUK, NICK	ARMY	PTE	ITUNA	21/07/44	59°37'	108°36'	SMYSNIUK LAKE
SMYTH, DAVID B.	RCAF	FS	KISBEY	15/10/42	55°13'	106°33'	SMYTH LAKE
SMYTH, MICHAEL S.	RCAF	PO	STRASBOURG	25/07/43	56°25'	107°51'	SMYTH LAKE
SMYTHE, LORNE N.	ARMY	L CPL	WEIRDALE	17/12/44	59°37'	109°55'	SMYTHE LAKE
SNOOK, ALBERT V.	RCAF	FO	WYNOT	20/10/43	59°41'	109°23'	SNOOK LAKE
SNOWFIELD, DARYL LESLIE	NAVY	OS	REGINA	18/01/44	54°03'	105°24'	SNOWFIELD LAKES
SOEDER, GLEN A.	RCAF	FS	SASKATOON	18/09/42	54°35'	102°03'	SOEDER ISLAND
SOEDER, WILLIAM E.P.	RCAF	FO	SASKATOON	31/03/44	54°35'	102°03'	SOEDER BAY
SOHOROWICH, JOHN	ARMY	L CPL	TISDALE	05/10/44	57°18'	102°01'	SOHOROWICH LAKE
SOLBERG, OLUF	ARMY	PTE	DIVISION 7	08/08/44	52°37'	104°43'	SOLBERG LAKE
SOLMES, MORTON	ARMY	PTE	DIVISION 12	27/09/44	55°35'	104°08'	SOLMES LAKE
SOLOMKA, NICHOLAS	RCAF	FO	SASKATOON	06/08/43	57°04'	107°36'	SOLOMKA LAKES
SOLYMOS, BARTHOLOMEW	ARMY	TPR	MAIDSTONE	25/07/44	55°47'	104°10'	SOLYMOS LAKE
SOMERVILLE, ALFRED J.	ARMY	PTE	MCLEAN	20/07/41	59°30'	105°03'	SOMERVILLE LAKE
SOMMERFELD, SAMUEL W.	NAVY	AB	SASKATOON	29/04/44	56°21'	105°27'	SOMMERFELD LAKE
SORENSON, MELVIN	ARMY	PTE	PADDOCKWOOD	16/07/43	55°03'	102°33'	SORENSON LAKE
SOROSKI, BILLY W.	RCAF	WO1	SASKATOON	19/09/44	55°33'	104°04'	SOROSKI LAKE
SOTKOWY, STANLEY W.	RCAF	FS	SUMMERBERRY	17/12/42	55°36'	104°24'	SOTKOWY LAKE
SOUTAR, JAMES R.F.	RCAF	PO	SHAUNAVON	18/08/42	55°11'	105°07'	SOUTAR ISLAND
SOUTH, THOMAS E.	ARMY	A L CPL	PRINCE ALBERT	02/03/44	59°33'	108°18'	SOUTH BAY
SPARKES, DOUGLAS G.	RCAF	SGT	REGINA	30/08/44	59°57'	108°34'	SPARKES LAKE
SPARKS, WILMOT A.	RCAF	PO	SASKATOON	28/08/44	55°33'	104°39'	SPARKS ISLAND
SPARLING, LAWSON F.	RCAF	WO2	AYLSHAM	26/06/43	59°23'	104°37'	SPARLING LAKE
SPEIRS, DAVID A.	ARMY	PTE	SHAUNAVON	09/10/44	55°15'	105°02'	SPEIRS ISLAND
SPENCE, CHESTER C.	ARMY	TPR	EDAM	17/09/44	53°28'	108°06'	SPENCE BAY
SPENCER, GORDON L.	RCAF	SGT	FORT QU'APPELLE	17/10/44	54°17'	109°41'	SPENCER CREEK
SPENCER, HERBERT	ARMY	PTE	DIVISION 5	02/02/43	54°58'	104°12'	SPENCER BAY
SPENCER, JAMES D.	RCAF	PO	WEIRDALE	07/05/44	54°09'	106°54'	SPENCER LAKE
SPERLING, JOHN P.	RCAF	CPL	CHAMBERLAIN	14/02/43	59°30'	105°34'	SPERLING LAKE
SPRATT, FREDERICK	ARMY	TPR	ROULEAU	30/05/44	59°33'	102°03'	SPRATT LAKE
SPRING, KENNETH L.	RCAF	WO2	REGINA	12/06/43	59°24'	108°55'	SPRING LAKE
SPRINGER, ARTHUR	ARMY	PTE	MEETING LAKE	20/12/44	58°05'	108°37'	SPRINGER LAKE
SPRINGSTEIN, NORMAN R.	RCAF	PO	MERID	28/12/44	57°23'	107°56'	SPRINGSTEIN LAKE
ST. GERMAIN, EMILE	ARMY	PTE	ST. LAURENT GRANDIN	21/10/44	59°37'	108°02'	ST. GERMAIN LAKE
ST. JOHN, RAY	ARMY	L CPL	HERBERT	25/10/44	55°06'	103°28'	ST. JOHN LAKE
ST. PIERRE, ARMAND L.	RCAF	PO	PRINCE ALBERT	09/02/45	55°45'	104°26'	ST. PIERRE LAKE
STACK, JAMES S.O.	ARMY	RFN	DIVISION 5	04/07/44	55°42'	105°10'	STACK LAKE
STACKHOUSE, DONALD G.	ARMY	A CPL	REGINA	31/05/44	56°32'	103°16'	STACKHOUSE BAY
STAINGER, WILLIAM G.	ARMY	PTE	INDIAN HEAD	19/08/42	59°54'	103°07'	STAINGER LAKE
STALLARD, THOMAS N.	ARMY	RFN	GLEN ELDER	22/12/41	59°17'	105°26'	STALLARD LAKE
STANDING, THOMAS	NAVY	LDG SMN	SASKATOON	22/10/40	54°49'	101°58'	STANDING LAKE
STAPLEFORD, ERNEST B.	RCAF	FL	MOOSE JAW	26/03/43	55°31'	105°08'	STAPLEFORD LAKE
STAPLES, DONALD A.	RCAF	FO	REGINA	02/11/44	57°38'	102°52'	STAPLES LAKE
STAPLES, JOHN W.	RCAF	PO	ROSETOWN	03/07/44	55°16'	104°43'	STAPLES BAY
STARFIELD, KARL G.	ARMY	TPR	RIVERHURST	15/07/44	55°17'	104°45'	STARFIELD ISLAND
STAUBLE, WESTON B.	RCAF	WO2	ALSASK	29/03/43	57°34'	106°34'	STAUBLE ISLAND
STAWNYCHKA, MIROSLAW	ARMY	PTE	CANORA	20/12/44	56°53'	102°05'	STAWNYCHKA LAKE
STEAD, GEORGE T.	RCAF	LAC	BIGGAR	24/07/43	59°22'	108°50'	STEAD ISLAND
STEADMAN, AUBREY D.	RCAF	WO2	REGINA	07/09/43	56°54'	107°00'	STEADMAN LAKE
STEEDEN, STANLEY E.	RCAF	LAC	COLONSAY	24/05/44	59°22'	108°52'	STEEDEN ISLAND
STEELE, CHARLES W.	ARMY	LT COL	WEYBURN	18/07/44	58°24'	102°00'	STEELE LAKE
STEELE, DONALD T.	RCAF	FL	CARNDUFF	09/03/45	59°35'	107°49'	STEELE BAY
STEELE, GEORGE W.	ARMY	GNR	WHITEWOOD	10/05/45	56°53'	103°21'	STEELE BAY
STEELE, JOHN D.	RCAF	WO2	ARCOLA	09/04/43	55°12'	104°05'	STEELE LAKE
STEIN, ARTHUR G.	RCAF	FO	NEUDORF	29/07/44	55°28'	105°41'	STEIN LAKE
STEINHAUER, GEORGE H.	ARMY	PTE	MORSE	31/03/42	59°20'	105°21'	STEINHAUER LAKE
STEMPEL, LAWRENCE S.	RCAF	LAC	SASKATOON	29/11/39	55°46'	104°10'	STEMPEL LAKE
STENHOUSE, JAMES K.	RCAF	PO	REKNOWN	20/06/44	57°50'	107°32'	STENHOUSE LAKE
STENHOUSE, ROBERT C.	RCAF	CPL	PORTREEVE	18/03/45	59°18'	102°43'	STENHOUSE LAKE
STEPHEN, DONALD	NAVY	L TEL	UNKNOWN	21/08/44			PENDING
STEPHENS, CHARLES H.	ARMY	CPL	REGINA	26/02/45	56°58'	102°55'	STEPHENS BAY
STEPHENS, JAMES T.	ARMY	RFN	REGINA	31/10/44	59°35'	108°05'	STEPHENS LAKE
STEPHENS, ROGER L.	ARMY	CAPT	OXBOW	06/08/44	55°36'	103°32'	STEPHENS LAKE
STEPHENS, WILLIAM D.	NAVY	LS	SASKATOON	10/02/42	54°57'	104°24'	STEPHENS BAY
STEVENSON, BERT L.	RCAF	FS	SASKATOON	08/01/45	57°59'	103°56'	STEVENSON RIVER
STEVENSON, GEORGE D.	ARMY	PTE	REGINA	24/02/41	56°57'	102°41'	STEVENSON LAKE
STEVENSON, HOWARD M.	ARMY	LIEUT	MOOSE JAW	16/07/44	58°47'	102°27'	STEVENSON ISLAND
STEVENSON, JOHN	ARMY	SIGMN	REGINA	05/08/42	56°56'	102°42'	STEVENSON BAY
STEVENSON, ROBERT G.	NAVY	STO 1	HUDSON BAY	18/03/45	55°57'	104°12'	STEVENSON ISLAND
STEWARDSON, ELDON S.	ARMY	SGT	SWIFT CURRENT	01/11/44	57°51'	107°25'	STEWARDSON LAKE
STEWART, ERNEST D.	ARMY	L CPL	BAILDON	16/08/44	54°40'	103°12'	STEWART LAKE
STEWART, ERNEST G.	ARMY	CPL	RALPH	21/07/44	52°24'	102°07'	STEWART CREEK
STEWART, HOWARD M.	RCAF	PO	ST. WALBURG	16/02/44	55°34'	105°33'	STEWART LAKE
STEWART, JAMES M.	ARMY	A MAJ	NORTH BATTLEFORD	29/09/44	55°22'	104°28'	STEWART BAY
STEWART, LORNE G.	RCAF	SGT	OXBOW	05/07/43	59°20'	108°55'	STEWART POINT
STEWART, MELVIN H.	ARMY	CPL	MOOSE JAW	20/07/44	59°43'	109°09'	STEWART LAKE
STEWART, NORMAN H.	ARMY	PTE	ASQUITH	21/12/43	55°24'	103°57'	STEWART ISLAND
STEWART, ROBERT W.	RCAF	FS	DYSART	15/12/42	59°30'	108°03'	STEWART FALLS
STEWART, RODGER A.	ARMY	RFN	WATSON	16/08/44	56°05'	104°55'	STEWART RAPIDS
STEWART, THOMAS J.	ARMY	A SGT	ASSINIBOIA	17/09/44	56°58'	103°48'	STEWART BAY
STEWART, WALTER F.	RCAF	FO	OXBOW	14/07/43	57°24'	106°20'	STEWART CHANNEL
STEWART, WILLIAM B.	ARMY	LIEUT	ASSINIBOIA	29/08/44	53°44'	104°21'	STEWART CREEK
STICKLEY, DAVID W.	ARMY	PTE	TISDALE	18/09/44	54°06'	104°40'	STICKLEY LAKE
STILBORN, JOHN H.	RCAF	PO	DUFF	13/12/42	55°08'	104°01'	STILBORN LAKE
STILBORN, KENNETH E.	RCAF	FS	LEMBERG	13/11/42	56°33'	102°05'	STILBORN BAY
STINCHCOMBE, ARTHUR R.	NAVY	O TEL	REGINA	01/05/41	56°23'	105°24'	STINCHCOMBE LAKE
STINSON, OLIVER M.	ARMY	PTE	DIVISION 17	15/06/44	59°41'	102°21'	STINSON ISLAND
STIRLING, ALBERT W.	ARMY	BDR	READLYN	10/08/44	55°31'	105°12'	STIRLING LAKE
STOCK, MORLEY B.	RCAF	FO	REGINA	18/02/45	55°53'	104°08'	STOCK LAKE
STOIK, HENRY J.	RCAF	CPL	NORTH BATTLEFORD	14/05/44	59°34'	108°33'	STOIK ISLAND
STOLAR, HOWARD	ARMY	SPR	WILLOWBROOK	06/06/44	59°23'	106°57'	STOLAR LAKE
STOLL, ERNEST F. J.	RCAF	PO	REGINA	25/08/42	55°31'	104°13'	STOLL LAKE
STOLL, VICTOR W.	ARMY	PTE	GRENFELL	02/05/45	55°31'	104°12'	STOLL LAKE
STORK, CLARENCE A.	ARMY	A SGT	EASTEND	04/08/44	59°35'	104°25'	STORK ISLAND
STOROZUK, MICHEAL	ARMY	SPR	BURROWS	26/08/44	59°22'	106°45'	STOROZUK LAKE
STOVER, HAROLD D.	ARMY	CFN	MOOSE JAW	13/01/45	56°20'	105°47'	STOVER LAKE
STRATTON, GEORGE F.	ARMY	A L CPL	REGINA	01/08/44	55°31'	105°05'	STRATTON LAKE
STRATTON, W.J.	ARMY	PTE	UNKNOWN	02/07/44	56°18'	103°21'	STRATTON CREEK
STRATYCHUK, STEVE	ARMY	GNR	UNKNOWN	26/02/45	59°27'	106°33'	STRATYCHUK LAKE
STREISEL, GEORGE S.	RCAF	WO2	KILLALY	24/05/44	58°12'	106°14'	STREISEL LAKE
STRINGER, RONALD H.	RCAF	SL	WILLOWS	21/01/45	54°33'	102°39'	STRINGER LAKE
STROME, FRANK G.	ARMY	GNR	WATSON	21/07/43	59°29'	108°01'	STROME LAKE
STRONG, CLARENCE O.	ARMY	LIEUT	ALAMEDA	08/08/44	58°13'	103°03'	STRONG ISLAND
STROUTS, HARLEY R.	RCAF	PO	HANLEY	12/04/42	57°06'	107°22'	STROUTS LAKE
STRUMM, MAYNARD L.	RCAF	PO	SASKATOON	14/07/44	57°51'	104°05'	STRUMM LAKE
STUART, GEORGE A.	NAVY	AB	MOOSE JAW	21/08/44	56°53'	103°56'	STUART RAPIDS
STUART, PETER D.G.	RCAF	PO	PUNNICHY	29/08/41	56°34'	105°39'	STUART ISLAND
STUSIAK, NICHOLAS	RCAF	FO	BIENFAIT	27/05/44	55°42'	105°22'	STUSIAK LAKE
SUMMERS, ARTHUR B.	RCAF	FL	YORKTON	09/02/45	57°58'	107°22'	SUMMERS LAKE
SUNSTRUM, MICHAEL J.	RCAF	FO	NAICAM	17/01/43	55°55'	104°40'	SUNSTRUM LAKE
SURBEY, VINCENT J.	RCAF	SGT	SASKATOON	25/08/43	55°11'	102°00'	SURBEY LAKE
SUTHERBY, CHARLES A.L.	RCAF	FS	YELLOW GRASS	29/08/42	56°43'	102°04'	SUTHERBY LAKE
SUTHERLAND, WILLIAM R.	RCAF	SGT	SASKATOON	24/06/41	59°43'	107°46'	SUTHERLAND BAY
SUTTILL, WILLIAM	RCAF	FS	LESTOCK	10/12/42	55°10'	104°40'	SUTTILL BAY

Name	Branch	Rank	Hometown	Casualty Date	Latitude	Longitude	Geo-Memorial
SUTTON, ARTHUR WILLIAM	NAVY	L	SASKATOON	24/01/45	57°54'	107°23'	SUTTON LAKE
SUTTON, CYRIL B.	RCAF	PO	MARSHALL	04/08/44	56°56'	102°24'	SUTTON ISLAND
SVEINSON, HELGI S.	RCAF	FS	WYNYARD	02/10/42	57°10'	108°50'	SVEINSON LAKE
SWALM, EARL C.	ARMY	PTE	KINDERSLEY	22/09/44	60°00'	109°29'	SWALM LAKE
SWANSON, WILLIAM C.O.	ARMY	PTE	CRANE VALLEY	20/07/44	56°10'	106°20'	SWANSON LAKE
SWEENEY, JAMES W.J.	ARMY	RFN	BIG RIVER	02/11/44	56°08'	102°27'	SWEENEY BAY
SWEENEY, WILFRED	RCAF	SGT	WEYBURN	23/11/43	52°24'	102°29'	SWEENEY LAKE
SWEET, JOHN A.	ARMY	A L SGT	DIVISION I	19/09/44	55°10'	104°03'	SWEET LAKE
SWEETING, RICHARD G.	ARMY	L CPL	GULL LAKE	13/09/45	59°35'	105°35'	SWEETING LAKE
SWIDERSKI, LOUIS T.	ARMY	PTE	BIENFAIT	20/07/44	54°18'	107°51'	SWIDERSKI LAKE
SWITZER, STUART A.	RCAF	WO2	WAPELLA	16/03/43	59°40'	109°43'	SWITZER LAKE
SYLVESTER, CLARENCE E.	ARMY	L BDR	MOOSE JAW	07/07/44	56°30'	103°55'	SYLVESTER ISLAND
SYLVESTER, VICTOR T.	RCAF	PO	MOOSE JAW	03/08/43	56°08'	106°37'	SYLVESTER CREEK
SYMONS, FRANCIS R.	RCAF	PO	BATTLEFORD	03/01/45	58°21'	102°54'	SYMONS ISLAND
SYMONS, VERNON H.	ARMY	PTE	ESTEVAN	04/05/44	54°09'	106°55'	SYMONS LAKE
SYNTAK, CASMIER	ARMY	PTE	CUT KNIFE	11/02/45	55°25'	103°03'	SYNTAK LAKE
SZUSZWAL, NICK	NAVY	AB	SASKATOON	03/12/44	56°27'	105°21'	SZUSZWAL LAKE
TABBERNOR, STANLEY E.	ARMY	RFN	PRINCE ALBERT	12/08/44	55°39'	103°17'	TABBERNOR LAKE
TAGSETH, MELVIN C.	RCAF	SGT	LESLIE	13/08/41	55°11'	104°16'	TAGSETH LAKE
TAIT, ANDREW	ARMY	PTE	FORT QU'APPELLE	04/07/44	55°56'	106°55'	TAIT BAY
TAIT, FRANCIS A.	RCAF	FS	DILKE	28/01/42	55°12'	104°35'	TAIT ISLAND
TALKINGTON, RICHARD	ARMY	CPL	BROADVIEW	04/04/43	59°27'	106°41'	TALKINGTON LAKE
TALMAN, RICHARD E.	RCAF	SGT	FERTILE	26/05/43	55°42'	104°23'	TALMAN LAKE
TANAKA, MINORU	ARMY	TPR	WYMARK	20/02/45	60°00'	103°52'	TANAKA LAKE
TARASOFF, FREDERICK	NAVY	AB	SASKATOON	20/03/43	56°19'	105°17'	TARASOFF LAKE
TATE, LESLIE J.	ARMY	TPR	MACDOWALL	02/08/44	55°55'	104°28'	TATE LAKE
TATHAM, GEORGE B.	RCAF	SGT	KELLIHER	28/06/42	54°01'	106°47'	TATHAM LAKE
TATLOW, RAYMOND	ARMY	GNR	LOVE	28/02/45	58°06'	102°56'	TATLOW LAKE
TAYLOR, CHARLES M.	ARMY	PTE	MEADOW LAKE	08/08/44	54°36'	108°40'	TAYLOR CREEK
TAYLOR, CLIFFORD E.	ARMY	L CPL	REGINA	18/08/44	59°23'	105°46'	TAYLOR BAY
TAYLOR, DONALD D.M.	RCAF	CPL	SWIFT CURRENT	07/11/44	56°48'	107°34'	TAYLOR ISLAND
TAYLOR, HAROLD B.	ARMY	SGT	REWARD	06/10/44	59°30'	108°17'	TAYLOR LAKE
TAYLOR, JEFFREY J.	ARMY	TPR	NORTH BATTLEFORD	02/02/44	56°12'	104°50'	TAYLOR CREEK
TAYLOR, JOHN A.	RCAF	PO	BIRCH HILLS	16/12/43	55°36'	104°42'	TAYLOR ISLAND
TAYLOR, ROBERT	RCAF	PO	DUNCAIRN	16/03/45	55°46'	107°08'	TAYLOR LAKE
TAYLOR, ROBERT F.	ARMY	GNR	PRINCE ALBERT	07/06/44	56°12'	104°49'	TAYLOR BAY
TAYLOR, VERNON E.	ARMY	PTE	ABBEY	23/07/44	56°26'	103°56'	TAYLOR LAKE
TAYLOR, WALTER D.	ARMY	PTE	WEYBURN	19/08/42	55°40'	102°07'	TAYLOR BAY
TAYLOR, WILBURN M.	RCAF	FO	SASKATOON	08/08/44			PENDING
TAYLOR, WILLIAM	RCAF	FO	NOTTINGHAM	15/03/44	57°24'	105°22'	TAYLOR BAY
TAYLOR, WILLIAM B.	RCAF	PO	ARCOLA	04/07/43	57°06'	104°08'	TAYLOR LAKE
TEALE, RALPH	ARMY	RFN	VALPARAISO	02/11/44	58°42'	109°55'	TEALE LAKE
TELFER, ROBERT L.	RCAF	WO1	HUMBOLDT	28/08/42	55°25'	104°40'	TELFER LAKE
TEMPLE, LESLIE P.C.	ARMY	GNR	GRENFELL	13/04/45	59°29'	104°33'	TEMPLE LAKE
TENEYCKE, CHARLES H.D.	ARMY	PTE	WALLWORT	09/04/42	55°26'	104°55'	TENEYCKE LAKE
TENKLEI, EDWARD S.	ARMY	SGT	REGINA	05/04/45	55°54'	103°38'	TENKLEI LAKE
THACKERAY, COLIN	ARMY	PTE	GOODWATER	11/12/44	57°17'	102°01'	THACKERAY ISLAND
THEAKER, THOMAS K.	RCAF	WO1	WILCOX	21/04/45	55°58'	104°04'	THEAKER BAY
THIBAULT, GASTON	ARMY	RFN	UNKNOWN	25/09/44	59°48'	108°59'	THIBAULT LAKE
THIBEAULT, JOHN O.	ARMY	PTE	BIG RIVER	03/01/45	56°30'	103°39'	THIBEAULT LAKE
THOMAS, DONALD	ARMY	RFN	FORT QU'APPELLE	06/06/44	56°33'	106°16'	THOMAS FALLS
THOMAS, EDWARD	RCAF	FS	QU'APPELLE	14/06/42	57°29'	105°10'	THOMAS CREEK
THOMAS, GEORGE W.	ARMY	LIEUT	REGINA	10/06/44	59°48'	107°58'	THOMAS LAKE
THOMAS, MAX	RCAF	FO	ROCKGLEN	15/09/46	55°17'	104°28'	THOMAS LAKE
THOMAS, NORMAN L.W.	ARMY	A L CPL	MOOSOMIN	29/06/41	56°55'	103°02'	THOMAS LAKE
THOMPSON, ALAN EDWARD	RAF	SL	SASKATOON	07/08/43	55°59'	105°24'	THOMPSON LAKE
THOMPSON, ALEXANDER	ARMY	A CPL	ROKEBY	31/01/44	58°05'	104°15'	THOMPSON BAY
THOMPSON, ARCHIBALD W.	ARMY	PTE	HERBERT	01/04/45	59°25'	108°53'	THOMPSON CREEK
THOMPSON, CLAYTON T.	ARMY	L CPL	DISLEY	22/04/45	59°28'	108°47'	THOMPSON LAKE
THOMPSON, CLIFFORD A.	RCAF	PO	CARNDUFF	30/07/44	57°01'	104°04'	THOMPSON LAKE
THOMPSON, EDWARD W.	ARMY	SGT	SASKATOON	16/08/44	56°42'	104°09'	THOMPSON RAPIDS
THOMPSON, GEORGE W.	RCAF	WO2	MELVILLE	09/10/43	57°20'	104°16'	THOMPSON RIVER
THOMPSON, GILBERT	ARMY	RFN	REGINA	06/06/44	59°41'	109°50'	THOMPSON BAY
THOMPSON, GORDON E.	ARMY	PTE	TISDALE	09/12/43	56°43'	109°16'	THOMPSON CREEK

Name	Branch	Rank	Hometown	Casualty Date	Latitude	Longitude	Geo-Memorial
THOMPSON, GORDON W.	RCAF	FS	ZEALANDIA	30/05/43			PENDING
THOMPSON, HUGH V.	ARMY	CPL	MAIDSTONE	10/06/44	53°17'	108°42'	THOMPSON LAKES
THOMPSON, JOHN	NAVY	CK S	PRINCE ALBERT	08/08/44	55°00'	108°22'	THOMPSON CREEK
THOMPSON, JOHN A.	ARMY	RFN	REGINA	08/06/44	58°07'	104°12'	THOMPSON LAKES
THOMPSON, JOHN B.	RCAF	PO	SASKATOON	27/09/41			PENDING
THOMPSON, NORMAN R.	RCAF	WO2	SASKATOON	21/01/43			PENDING
THOMPSON, ORVAL M.	ARMY	PTE	WAPELLA	18/07/44	56°53'	102°47'	THOMPSON LAKE
THOMPSON, PETER	NAVY	TEL	KINDERSLEY	03/07/44	56°25'	107°36'	THOMPSON LAKE
THOMPSON, RAYMOND F.	RCAF	FO	REGINA	14/03/45	55°50'	107°11'	THOMPSON INLET
THOMPSON, ROBERT A.	ARMY	PTE	ROCHE PERCEE	20/07/44	55°20'	105°14'	THOMPSON PENINSULA
THOMPSON, ROBERT J.	ARMY	RFN	LAFLECHE	08/07/44	56°52'	103°40'	THOMPSON BAY
THOMPSON, RODERICK J.	RCAF	PO	FIELDING	24/03/44	56°21'	103°53'	THOMPSON FALLS
THOMPSON, ROLLA L.	ARMY	RFN	STOCKHOLM	18/02/45	56°53'	102°44'	THOMPSON CREEK
THOMPSON, STANLEY C.	RCAF	FS	DAVIDSON	27/10/41	53°39'	104°27'	THOMPSON CREEK
THOMPSON, WILLIAM B.C.	RCAF	PO	MOOSOMIN	01/01/43	57°39'	104°48'	THOMPSON CREEK
THOMSON, ERNEST T.	ARMY	SPR	DIVISION 11	03/10/45	59°17'	106°37'	THOMSON ISLAND
THOMSON, NORMAN W.	ARMY	PTE	ESTEVAN	19/08/42	55°53'	102°03'	THOMSON BAY
THOMSON, RICHARD K.	RCAF	FO	SASKATOON	31/03/44			PENDING
THOMSON, THOMAS D.	RCAF	PO	MOOSE JAW	17/01/44	59°06'	109°07'	THOMSON BAY
THORELL, OLE H.	ARMY	RFN	WADENA	26/02/45	59°37'	105°45'	THORELL LAKE
THORNTON, HARVEY	RCAF	WO2	NORTH BATTLEFORD	20/03/44	55°34'	105°00'	THORNTON LAKE
THORPE, HARRY	ARMY	GNR	WAPELLA	21/07/44	55°27'	104°20'	THORPE BAY
THORSON, MILO N.	ARMY	RFN	DOLLARD	29/03/45	55°18'	105°14'	THORSON ISLAND
THRIFT, JOHN H.	RCAF	FO	ESTEVAN	26/01/42	58°44'	103°24'	THRIFT LAKE
TIGHE, FRANCIS W.	ARMY	PTE	LIMERICK	09/04/41	57°43'	103°11'	TIGHE LAKE
TILSON, ALBERT	ARMY	L CPL	REGINA	27/10/44	57°13'	106°44'	TILSON LAKE
TINDALL, CHARLES ARTHUR	RCAF	FO	WATSON	13/08/43			PENDING
TINDALL, EVERETT W.	ARMY	GNR	WATSON	05/07/43	59°59'	103°16'	TINDALL LAKE
TOCHER, JAMES	ARMY	L CPL	MOOSOMIN	21/07/44	55°20'	102°19'	TOCHER LAKE
TOCKER, HARRY R.	ARMY	PTE	GROVE PARK	24/05/44	56°49'	109°07'	TOCKER LAKE
TODD, ARTHUR F.	RCAF	FS	ZELMA	06/09/43			PENDING
TODD, JOHN E.	RCAF	LAC	SEMANS	07/08/42	59°31'	108°29'	TODD ISLAND
TODOS, WILLIAM	NAVY	AB	ITUNA	22/10/40	59°20'	106°40'	TODOS LAKE
TOLAND, GERALD THOMAS	RAF	WC	YORKTON	27/02/41	55°16'	104°50'	TOLAND BAY
TOLAND, KEITH LEONARD	ARMY	CPL	YORKTON	05/12/41	55°16'	104°52'	TOLAND ISLAND
TOMBLIN, THOMAS E.C.	ARMY	TPR	WYNYARD	15/08/44	57°21'	105°11'	TOMBLIN LAKE
TOMCZAK, MARCEL E.	RCAF	FO	SASKATOON	26/07/43	57°02'	109°05'	TOMCZAK LAKE
TOMSETT, MARTIN E.	RCAF	FL	REGINA	26/07/41	56°23'	106°43'	TOMSETT LAKE
TOPPING, FREDERICK WILLS	RCAF	PO	PRINCE ALBERT	31/03/44	58°36'	103°45'	TOPPING ISLAND
TOPPING, WILLIAM F.	RCAF	FS	FINDLATER	12/03/43	59°22'	106°21'	TOPPING BAY
TOPPINGS, IRVING J.	RCAF	FO	INCHKEITH	31/03/44	55°55'	105°21'	TOPPINGS LAKE
TORKELSON, DONALD L.	RCAF	WO2	BENGOUGH	25/06/42	55°31'	106°12'	TORKELSON LAKE
TORONCZUK, C.	RCAF	FS	RADVILLE	10/08/42	55°19'	106°15'	TORONCZUK LAKE
TORRANCE, HAZEN D.	ARMY	PTE	SWIFT CURRENT	06/02/45	55°39'	105°07'	TORRANCE LAKE
TORRANS, JAMES R.	ARMY	PTE	SWIFT CURRENT	26/13/44	56°50'	105°50'	TORRANS LAKE
TORWALT, RHEINHOLD	ARMY	PTE	JANSEN	24/07/41	58°18'	103°53'	TORWALT LAKE
TOTH, LESLIE WILFRED	RCAF	FSGT	STOCKHOLM	24/11/44	54°25'	107°26'	TOTH BAY
TOWNSEND, JOHN F.	ARMY	CPL	NIPAWIN	22/08/44	62°42'	95°20'	TOWNSEND LAKE
TOWNSEND, PHILIP E.T.	RCAF	PO	BALGONIE	01/03/43	57°38'	104°44'	TOWNSEND LAKE
TOWNSEND, ROBERT W.E.	RCAF	FS	TISDALE	29/07/44	52°29'	101°45'	TOWNSEND LAKE
TRAILL, WESLEY A.R.	ARMY	L CPL	PRINCE ALBERT	25/09/44	55°24'	103°46'	TRAILL BAY
TRAINOR, JAMES B.	ARMY	TPR	ST. WALBURG	31/08/44	59°54'	109°17'	TRAINOR LAKE
TRAPP, BYRON A.	RCAF	PO	HARRIS	21/06/42	55°45'	103°11'	TRAPP CREEK
TRASK, CYRIL R.	RCAF	PO	MEADOW LAKE	05/03/43	54°41'	108°47'	TRASK LAKE
TRASK, MARION E.	RCAF	WO1	HANLEY	14/05/44	56°00'	103°45'	TRASK BAY
TRASK, WOODROW A.	RCAF	WO1	HANLEY	09/15/45	59°15'	105°41'	TRASK CREEK
TRELEAVEN, GARNET C.	ARMY	CPL	NUT MOUNTAIN	23/07/44	57°19'	105°13'	TRELEAVEN LAKE
TRENT, FREDERICK B.	RCAF	PO	PATHLOW	22/03/45	54°58'	102°25'	TRENT LAKE
TRICKER, EDWARD H.	ARMY	RFN	NORTH BATTLEFORD	12/12/44	55°59'	104°27'	TRICKER LAKE
TRICKETT, DOUGLAS H.	RCAF	FL	MCLEAN	25/07/44	52°28'	101°52'	TRICKETT LAKE
TRITHART, NORMAN W.	ARMY	SPR	KIPLING	21/10/44	59°24'	106°49'	TRITHART LAKE
TROMBURG, FRED A.	ARMY	SGT	DIVISION I	19/08/42	58°34'	103°41'	TROMBURG BAY
TROVILLO, FRANK L.	RCAF	WO1	SASKATOON	25/04/43	59°42'	109°27'	TROVILLO LAKE
TUCKER, JOHN R.	RCAF	PO	WELWYN	26/07/42	57°53'	102°03'	TUCKER ISLAND

Name	Branch	Rank	Hometown	Casualty Date	Latitude	Longitude	Geo-Memorial
TUFTS, HARRY W.R.	RCAF	FS	YORKTON	17/06/44	57°45'	108°29'	TUFTS LAKE
TULL, ERNEST S.	ARMY	PTE	BANKEND	01/01/44	59°17'	104°45'	TULL LAKE
TULLOCH, ARCHIE	RCAF	FO	CRAIK	20/07/44	59°22'	108°51'	TULLOCH ISLANDS
TULLOCH, STEWART	RCAF	FO	CRAIK	02/12/44	59°22'	108°51'	TULLOCH ISLANDS
TUMA, CHARLES	RCAF	PO	CHURCHBRIDGE	04/02/43	58°38'	109°14'	TUMA LAKE
TURCOTTE, GABRIEL J.	ARMY	SPR	DIVISION 14	28/10/44	59°22'	106°35'	TURCOTTE LAKE
TURCOTTE, GARNET H.	RCAF	WO2	DIVISION 2	10/12/42	55°39'	104°49'	TURCOTTE CREEK
TURNBULL, JAMES O.	RCAF	LAC	WILKIE	10/01/43			PENDING
TURNER, ALFRED G.	RCAF	WO1	CHICKNEY	02/11/42	57°23'	106°39'	TURNER ISLAND
TURNER, JAMES M.	RCAF	LAC	CENTRAL BUTTE	06/09/42	55°55'	107°29'	TURNER LAKE
TURTLE, EDGAR L.	RCAF	FL	MARSHALL	15/09/46	57°35'	102°23'	TURTLE ISLAND
TURVEY, FREDERICK W.	RCAF	FO	MARSHALL	06/10/42	54°29'	109°54'	TURVEY LAKE
TWIGGE, GERALD A.	RCAF	PO	MARYFIELD	29/01/44	54°30'	103°13'	TWIGGE LAKE
TYACKE, JOHN W.	ARMY	PTE	SILVER PARK	08/12/43	54°13'	102°37'	TYACKE LAKE
TYCOLES, ELMER L.	RCAF	WO2	KAMSACK	24/12/43	59°24'	104°41'	TYCOLES LAKE
TYDEMAN, THOMAS	ARMY	A CPL	ST. WALBURG	28/07/43	56°13'	104°23'	TYDEMAN LAKE
TYMAN, DONALD D.J.	ARMY	PTE	REGINA	19/08/42	55°15'	104°02'	TYMAN LAKE
TYREMAN, NORMAN R.	ARMY	A CPL	TISDALE	11/02/45	54°57'	102°23'	TYREMAN LAKE
TYRRELL, ARNOLD J.	RCAF	FO	QU'APPELLE	04/02/45			PENDING
ULBRICHT, GUSTAVE	ARMY	FUS	DIVISION 8	25/09/44	59°35'	105°41'	ULBRICHT LAKE
ULLEY, ALFRED G.	ARMY	GNR	WISHART	03/10/44	59°30'	108°55'	ULLEY ISLAND
UMPHERVILLE, COLIN	ARMY	RFN	GRONLID	15/11/42	58°06'	103°46'	UMPHERVILLE RIVER
UMPHERVILLE, JERRY	ARMY	PTE	DIVISION 14	17/09/44	57°53'	104°19'	UMPHERVILLE LAKE
UMPHERVILLE, ROBERT M.	ARMY	PTE	GRONLID	17/05/44	56°24'	103°44'	UMPHERVILLE LAKE
UNDERDAHL, GEORGE T.	ARMY	PTE	MAPLE CREEK	19/08/42	49°26'	109°51'	UNDERDAHL CREEK
UNGER, ABRAHAM	NAVY	AS	MCMAHON	25/10/44	59°48'	109°58'	UNGER LAKE
UNSER, A.N.	RCAF	FO	HAZENMORE	15/08/44	54°42'	103°12'	UNSER LAKE
URBAN, LUDVICK	ARMY	RFN	DIVISION 5	09/06/44	57°35'	106°02'	URBAN LAKE
URTON, JOSEPH R.	ARMY	PTE	MOOSE JAW	25/10/41	58°47'	107°31'	URTON LAKE
UZELMAN, P.	RCAF	PO	REVENUE	23/12/44	57°10'	107°20'	UZELMAN LAKE
VAGG, ROBERT A.J.	RCAF	FO	REGINA	12/02/44	54°44'	103°19'	VAGG LAKE
VALLANCE, JOHN	RCAF	PO	REGINA	21/04/43	59°27'	106°52'	VALLANCE LAKE
VALLIERE, JOSEPH A.	ARMY	A CPL	DIVISION 17	05/04/45	59°40'	108°58'	VALLIERE LAKE
VAN DE VEEN, JACOB	ARMY	RFN	PARKSIDE	08/07/44	57°18'	109°49'	VAN DE VEEN LAKE
VAN NES, HENRY	ARMY	PTE	HUDSON BAY	27/02/45	55°10'	107°08'	VAN NES LAKE
VANCE, ELMER R.	RCAF	PO	BETHUNE	21/04/43	54°49'	103°39'	VANCE LAKE
VAREY, ROBERT F.	RCAF	FS	ELSTOW	04/02/42	54°36'	105°45'	VAREY LAKE
VASS, DANIEL P.	ARMY	SGT	CARNDUFF	21/12/43	54°56'	102°08'	VASS LAKE
VAUDNER, WILSON A.	RCAF	FS	ASSINIBOIA	19/06/45	57°54'	109°28'	VAUDNER LAKE
VENN, FREDERICK A.	ARMY	PTE	ORMISTON	20/08/42	54°31'	105°18'	VENN LAKE
VERAAS, AUDFINN	RCAF	FS	STRONGFIELD	30/07/43	59°59'	108°52'	VERAAS LAKE
VEREGIN, HOWARD P.	RCAF	SGT	ARELEE	23/08/44	59°54'	108°06'	VEREGIN LAKE
VERES, STEPHEN J.	RCAF	FS	PLUNKETT	12/06/45	57°04'	108°35'	VERES LAKE
VERMEERSCH, RAYMOND J.A.	ARMY	PTE	LANGENBURG	21/10/44	57°35'	109°30'	VERMEERSCH LAKE
VINCENT, ERIC C.	ARMY	RFN	DIVISION 16	01/09/44	55°15'	103°30'	VINCENT LAKE
VINCENT, HOWARD J.	RCAF	SGT	CANORA	10/08/42	59°22'	106°48'	VINCENT LAKE
VINEY, FREDERICK H.	RCAF	FO	ABBEY	16/08/43	54°48'	103°18'	VINEY LAKE
VOAKES, FREDERICK J.	ARMY	A SGT	LANGBANK	10/03/45	55°09'	107°07'	VOAKES LAKE
VOGEL, FRANZ	ARMY	PTE	DIVISION 17	09/08/44	55°52'	104°54'	VOGEL LAKE
VOGELSANG, EDWARD W.	RCAF	FO	SASKATOON	08/01/43	57°10'	108°48'	VOGELSANG LAKE
VOLLHOFFER, TITUS	RCAF	AC1	SOUTHEY	24/07/43	57°35'	104°54'	VOLLHOFFER LAKE
VOLLMAN, JOHN M.	ARMY	A CPL	BALGONIE	19/12/44	57°21'	104°01'	VOLLMAN LAKE
VON ESCHEN, GEORGE O.	ARMY	PTE	FOXFORD	26/02/45	54°25'	106°57'	VON ESCHEN BAY
WACHNOW, MORLEY B.	ARMY	SGT	NORTH BATTLEFORD	28/07/44	59°51'	109°42'	WACHNOW LAKE
WADDINGTON, HARRY E.	ARMY	A SGT	REGINA	18/07/44	57°13'	105°24'	WADDINGTON LAKE
WAGAR, DONALD E.	ARMY	RFN	HANLEY	08/07/44	57°18'	109°47'	WAGAR LAKE
WAGNER, EDWIN	ARMY	A CPL	PLUNKETT	26/02/45	58°03'	102°42'	WAGNER LAKE
WAKEFIELD, CLIFFORD H.	ARMY	BDR	WYNYARD	22/05/43	57°26'	103°50'	WAKEFIELD LAKES
WAKEFIELD, JOHN H.	ARMY	CPL	DIVISION 17	21/02/44	55°56'	104°01'	WAKEFIELD LAKE
WAKEMAN, WILLIAM A.	RCAF	FS	PUNNICHY	13/10/42	59°30'	105°58'	WAKEMAN LAKE
WALDRON, ARTHUR G.	ARMY	LIEUT	LASHBURN	09/06/44	58°02'	108°44'	WALDRON LAKE
WALEN, GEORGE	RCAF	FS	SASKATOON	05/03/43	55°08'	104°38'	WALEN LAKE
WALES, DOUGLAS	ARMY	RFN	PLEASANTDALE	17/06/44	57°29'	109°47'	WALES LAKE
WALKER, BRUCE D.	RCAF	FO	KISBEY	08/08/44	59°23'	103°50'	WALKER LAKE
WALKER, CLIFFORD	ARMY	PTE	GOVAN	19/08/42	59°24'	103°48'	WALKER BAY
WALKER, HUGH M.	ARMY	LIEUT	CANORA	06/06/44	55°36'	104°45'	WALKER BAY
WALKER, NORMAN S.	ARMY	RFN	BALCARRES	08/07/44	56°34'	106°15'	WALKER CREEK
WALKER, RALPH	ARMY	SPR	GLENBUSH	02/05/45	54°58'	102°16'	WALKER LAKE
WALKER, WILLIAM A.	RCAF	FS	KISBEY	17/03/42	57°18'	104°40'	WALKER RIVER
WALKLEY, FRANK	ARMY	GNR	INDIAN HEAD	13/10/44	56°21'	107°36'	WALKLEY LAKE
WALL, ADOLPH L.	RCAF	PO	STOCKHOLM	09/10/44	56°23'	107°51'	WALL LAKE
WALL, ALEXANDER	ARMY	A SGT	HAGUE	23/05/44	56°27'	102°11'	WALL ISLAND
WALLACE, CLARENCE B.	RCAF	SGT	STONY BEACH	08/01/44	57°46'	102°14'	WALLACE ISLAND
WALLACE, DON	RCAF	FL	LANG	14/06/44	59°27'	108°01'	WALLACE BAY
WALLACE, JOHN	RCAF	FS	LANG	02/12/43	59°27'	108°01'	WALLACE BAY
WALLACE, PETER WILLIAM	NAVY	AB	SASKATOON	29/04/44	56°52'	103°44'	WALLACE BAY
WALLACE, RALPH G.	ARMY	PTE	CHAMBERLAIN	20/07/44	56°48'	102°08'	WALLACE CREEK
WALLACE, ROBERT A.	ARMY	PTE	ESTEVAN	19/08/42	56°31'	106°58'	WALLACE LAKE
WALLACE, ROBERT NOBLE	RCAF	FSGT	NOKOMIS	28/09/43	55°27'	105°54'	WALLACE ISLAND
WALLACE, W.W.	RCAF	FS	FILLMORE	30/01/43	57°02'	105°27'	WALLACE BAY
WALLAND, ALLAN C.	RCAF	SGT	WATROUS	08/11/42	59°22'	104°41'	WALLAND LAKE
WALLIS, PETER	ARMY	L CPL	KENASTON	22/01/45	56°34'	109°40'	WALLIS BAY
WALSH, JOHN A.	ARMY	PTE	GRAVELBOURG	29/07/45	56°56'	103°41'	WALSH BAY
WALSH, PATRICK C.	RCAF	FS	YORKTON	29/03/42	58°59'	103°24'	WALSH LAKE
WALSH, PATRICK DOUGLAS	NAVY	LDG S36	JASMIN	20/09/43	55°36'	106°07'	WALSH LAKE
WALSH, WARD E.	ARMY	RFN	TISDALE	24/07/44	57°09'	102°06'	WALSH ISLAND
WALTON, JOHN W.	ARMY	R Q M S	MOOSOMIN	02/05/42	55°30'	108°21'	WALTON BAY
WANAMAKER, WILLIAM J.	ARMY	CPL	DIVISION 14	23/08/44	55°51'	106°18'	WANAMAKER LAKE
WANNER, ANTON	ARMY	PTE	LAMPMAN	11/01/45	54°25'	105°56'	WANNER LAKE
WARD, CLARENCE H.	ARMY	L CPL	REGINA	27/07/44	54°56'	101°57'	WARD LAKE
WARD, COURTNEY	ARMY		BANGOR	17/09/44			PENDING
WARD, DENYS FRANCIS H.	ARMY	CAPT.	SASKATOON	24/07/43	58°37'	104°40'	WARD CREEK
WARD, FRANCIS H.	ARMY	RFN	DIVISION 17	11/06/44	58°35'	104°35'	WARD LAKES
WARD, JOHN L.	RCAF	FS	BATTLEFORD	28/02/43	55°21'	101°58'	WARD BAY
WARNE, ALFRED R.	ARMY	CPL	MACOUN	25/07/44	54°21'	104°06'	WARNE LAKE
WARNE, THOMAS H.	RCAF	WO2	KENNEDY	18/02/43	55°15'	104°59'	WARNE ISLAND
WARNER, JOHN D.	ARMY	BDR	BALCARRES	22/05/44	57°08'	103°56'	WARNER LAKE
WARNER, RALPH G.	ARMY	GNR	KENNEDY	05/09/43	56°54'	109°01'	WARNER RAPIDS
WARNES, ALLAN E.	ARMY	LIEUT	BLADWORTH	24/05/44	57°26'	107°15'	WARNES LAKE
WARNOCK, GEORGE R.	RCAF	PO	REWARD	04/05/44	55°29'	104°44'	WARNOCK LAKE
WARR, LESLIE M.	ARMY	L CPL	SASKATOON	24/12/41	57°20'	107°18'	WARR LAKE
WARREN, BERTRAM G.	RCAF	FS	LUCKY LAKE	24/08/43	57°14'	107°40'	WARREN LAKE
WARREN, EARLE F.	RCAF	FO	RADVILLE	07/05/44	59°50'	102°48'	WARREN LAKE
WARREN, JOSEPH H.	RCAF	PO	MOOSE JAW	22/04/43	57°05'	109°11'	WARREN RAPIDS
WARREN, ROY E.	RCAF	FO	YORKTON	11/06/44	58°49'	102°29'	WARREN BAY
WARREN, SIDNEY G.	ARMY	PTE	KELLIHER	14/12/44	56°31'	103°58'	WARREN LAKE
WARWICK, CLAUDE CARL	NAVY	AB	REGINA	01/03/45	59°20'	106°55'	WARWICK RAPIDS
WASDEN, HAROLD D.	ARMY	PTE	MILDRED	11/12/44	59°58'	109°34'	WASDEN LAKE
WASEND, HAROLD	ARMY	PTE	DIVISION 16	16/12/43	59°31'	105°16'	WASEND LAKE
WASKOWICH, PAUL	ARMY	PTE	CHELAN	04/05/44	57°37'	105°56'	WASKOWICH LAKE
WASYLUK, PETER	ARMY	PTE	DIVISION 15	15/08/44	54°30'	106°05'	WASYLUK BAY
WATERBURY, ORVILLE R.	RCAF	FL	PRINCE ALBERT	12/03/43	58°10'	104°22'	WATERBURY LAKE
WATERS, NORMAN J.	RCAF	WO2	LIPTON	26/05/43	55°50'	105°19'	WATERS LAKE
WATSON, HENRY H.	RCAF	LAC	MAPLE CREEK	24/09/44	57°26'	105°14'	WATSON LAKE
WATSON, JOHN S.	ARMY	PTE	WYNYARD	14/12/44	58°39'	102°48'	WATSON LAKE
WATSON, RICHARD H.	ARMY	PTE	VANTAGE	05/01/44	56°57'	103°42'	WATSON ISLAND
WATSON, ROBERT J.	ARMY	PTE	DUMMER	16/08/44	56°57'	103°42'	WATSON NARROWS
WATSON, WILLIAM J.	RCAF	FO	SASKATOON	04/12/44	55°40'	105°31'	WATSON BAY
WATT, A.	RCAF	PO	ATWATER	15/08/44	54°21'	108°16'	WATT LAKE
WATT, ALEXANDER S.	RCAF	FS	REGINA	25/09/42	56°31'	103°10'	WATT ISLAND
WATTS, TERENCE G.N.	ARMY	SGT	REGINA	28/12/43	55°45'	105°03'	WATTS LAKE
WAY, HERBERT H.	RCAF	SGT	DINSMORE	26/05/42	57°17'	104°34'	WAY LAKE
WAY, JAMES O.	RCAF	WO2	REDVERS	17/04/43	59°35'	108°22'	WAY LAKE
WAYNERT, ELVIN T.	ARMY	GNR	WHITEWOOD	15/03/45	59°34'	108°47'	WAYNERT LAKE
WEATHERUP, ROBERT G.	ARMY	PTE	REGINA	29/08/45	57°29'	103°03'	WEATHERUP LAKE
WEAVER, HAROLD D.	RCAF	SGT	SASKATOON	20/09/41	57°18'	102°28'	WEAVER ISLAND
WEBB, DAVID ARTHUR	RCAF	PO	FAIRMOUNT	21/09/44	52°25'	102°30'	ARTHUR LAKE
WEBB, EDWARD V.	RCAF	WO1	MOOSE JAW	25/04/44	56°08'	105°23'	WEBB BAY

Name	Branch	Rank	Hometown	Casualty Date	Latitude	Longitude	Geo-Memorial
WEBB, EDWIN E.	ARMY	A L CPL	BROWNING	24/05/44	55°39'	106°02'	WEBB LAKE
WEBB, WILLIAM M.	RCAF	PO	BROADVIEW	23/09/42	57°34'	104°32'	WEBB RIVER
WEBER, FREDRICK G.	ARMY	RFN	AVONLEA	06/06/44	55°10'	107°29'	WEBER ISLAND
WEBER, MARTIN P.F.	ARMY	PTE	MUENSTER	08/08/44	59°47'	109°42'	WEBER LAKE
WEBER, WILFRED E.	RCAF	FO	YELLOW GRASS	05/03/45	55°10'	107°27'	WEBER BAY
WEBLEY, LESLIE C.E.	RCAF	FS	ASSINIBOIA	09/05/44	55°54'	105°30'	WEBLEY LAKE
WEDGEWOOD, ARTHUR J.	ARMY	PTE	WELWYN	28/07/44	56°39'	108°49'	WEDGEWOOD LAKE
WEEDON, JAMES F.G.	RCAF	PO	PADDOCKWOOD	01/11/44	57°09'	107°20'	WEEDON LAKE
WEERES, ORVILLE H.	ARMY	PTE	ARDILL	02/05/42	58°24'	107°04'	WEERES LAKE
WEIGHTMAN, OLIVER J.	ARMY	RFN	KISBEY	18/05/44			PENDING
WEISBRODT, JOHN W.	ARMY	GNR	SOUTHEY	25/09/43	59°28'	105°54'	WEISBRODT LAKE
WEISS, ROSS	RCAF	FS	GIRVIN	02/03/43	55°07'	104°35'	WEISS LAKE
WELK, JOHN G.	RCAF	FO	CHURCHBRIDGE	16/01/45	55°30'	104°55'	WELK LAKE
WELLBELOVE, JOHN A.	ARMY	LIEUT	ESTON	25/09/44	58°37'	102°58'	WELLBELOVE BAY
WELLS, ALBERT E.	RCAF	FS	RUNCIMAN	08/01/45	52°24'	103°17'	WELLS LAKE
WELLS, JOSEPH J.	ARMY	PTE	DIVISION 16	20/12/43	54°53'	102°38'	WELLS LAKE
WELLS, ROBERT S.	ARMY	MAJ	WEYBURN	20/07/44	55°33'	105°37'	WELLS LAKE
WELSH, DOUGLAS	ARMY	L SGT	BROADVIEW	23/07/44	56°59'	103°05'	WELSH ISLAND
WELSH, GERALD A.	RCAF	FS	SASKATOON	31/05/42	59°20'	109°03'	WELSH ISLAND
WELSH, JOHN V.	RCAF	WO2	REGINA	18/12/42	56°26'	105°28'	WELSH BAY
WELSH, LAWRENCE R.	RCAF	PO	REGINA	21/11/44	56°26'	105°35'	WELSH RAPIDS
WENAUS, ORVILLE E.	RCAF	AC2	VERWOOD	31/12/42	56°05'	107°20'	WENAUS LAKE
WENGER, JOHN	RCAF	FO	REGINA	08/07/44	57°32'	109°35'	WENGER LAKE
WENZEL, CLARENCE G.	RCAF	PO	LEADER	26/04/44	56°28'	107°41'	WENZEL LAKE
WERRY, ELMOR W.	RCAF	CPL	REWARD	09/12/42	59°33'	103°36'	WERRY LAKE
WERT, CLARENCE M.	RCAF	PO	MAIDSTONE	21/11/44	54°50'	104°44'	WERT LAKE
WEST, ROBERT G.	RCAF	SL	MOOSE JAW	23/06/44	57°50'	108°19'	WEST LAKE
WEST, STEVEN R.	ARMY	RFN	ESTON	25/09/44	55°19'	104°34'	WEST LAKE
WEST, WILLIAM D.	ARMY	L CPL	LESLIE	09/10/44	56°51'	103°20'	WEST LAKE
WESTERN, EARLE J.	ARMY	LIEUT	REGINA	05/10/44	55°54'	105°37'	WESTERN ISLAND
WESTGATE, MARION M.	RCAF	NS	REGINA	27/10/43	57°22'	107°45'	WESTGATE LAKE
WESTHAVER, HAROLD A.	RCAF	FO	REGINA	15/02/43	57°58'	106°19'	WESTHAVER LAKE
WESTLAKE, HAROLD E.	ARMY	TPR	MOSSBANK	28/04/43	59°32'	108°38'	WESTLAKE LAKE
WESTLAKE, JOHN M.	RCAF	FO	MOOSE JAW	18/04/44	56°24'	103°14'	WESTLAKE ISLAND
WETTON, GEORGE A.	ARMY	L CPL	SOMME	21/12/44	54°54'	102°38'	WETTON LAKE
WHALEY, SAMUEL K.	RCAF	AC2	DENHOLM	23/04/42	59°57'	106°05'	WHALEY BAY
WHEELER, FREDERICK I.	ARMY	PTE	ARCHERWILL	14/08/44	58°36'	103°07'	WHEELER LAKE
WHEELER, MENNO	ARMY	L CPL	LANGHAM	19/07/44	58°34'	103°05'	WHEELER PENINSULA
WHEELER, WILLIAM B.	RCAF	FS	SASKATOON	25/07/43	55°46'	104°54'	WHEELER LAKE
WHETTER, MARTIN F.	ARMY	S SGT	WATSON	05/05/45	55°57'	104°41'	WHETTER LAKE
WHIDDEN, CHARLES A.	RCAF	SGT	BEECHY	04/11/41	59°55'	106°20'	WHIDDEN ISLAND
WHIGHAM, ROBERT B.	ARMY	PTE	MURRAYDALE	16/12/43	58°48'	104°25'	WHIGHAM LAKE
WHITBREAD, SYDNEY	ARMY	PTE	TISDALE	28/10/42	54°59'	102°25'	WHITBREAD LAKE
WHITE, CAPTAIN C.	RCAF	SGT	GULL LAKE	13/06/44			PENDING
WHITE, ASHLEY B.	RCAF	FS	NORTH BATTLEFORD	22/10/43			PENDING
WHITE, HOWARD K.	ARMY	TPR	MAPLE CREEK	10/12/43	56°55'	103°27'	WHITE BAY
WHITE, JOHN W.F.	ARMY	SGT	DIVISION 15	15/04/44	55°55'	107°23'	WHITE INLET
WHITE, JOSEPH J.	RCAF	SL	REGINA	23/10/42	57°10'	109°15'	WHITE CREEK
WHITE, LLOYD E.	RCAF	FS	SASKATOON	15/10/42			PENDING
WHITE, ROBERT BORDEN	NAVY	STO 1	MAPLE CREEK	19/09/41	56°58'	103°46'	WHITE ISLAND
WHITE, WILLIAM C.	ARMY	LIEUT	REGINA	08/07/44	59°39'	109°43'	WHITE BAY
WHITE, WILLIAM H.	RCAF	AC1	CARNDUFF	03/05/42	57°14'	104°27'	WHITE LAKE
WHITE, WILLIAM L.C.	ARMY	A CAPT	MAPLE CREEK	08/07/44	55°55'	106°22'	WHITE LAKE
WHITEHEAD, ARTHUR JOHN	NAVY	AB	MOOSE JAW	24/11/44	54°49'	101°54'	WHITEHEAD LAKE
WHITEHEAD, LAUREL M.	RCAF	WO2	MORTLACH	23/07/45	59°58'	107°56'	WHITEHEAD LAKE
WHITFORD, DAVID	ARMY	PTE	SWEETGRASS	23/07/44	57°46'	104°38'	WHITFORD LAKE
WHITFORD, HAROLD K.	ARMY	PTE	BATTLEFORD	21/11/44	55°34'	103°18'	WHITFORD BAY
WHITFORD, WALTER	ARMY	TPR	MAIDSTONE	12/10/44	58°01'	104°29'	WHITFORD RIVER
WHITLEY, ROBERT N.	RCAF	FO	REGINA	22/10/44	55°14'	104°55'	WHITLEY ISLAND
WHITTAKER, JOHN M.	RCAF	WO2	MOOSE JAW	27/05/43	59°30'	105°31'	WHITTAKER LAKE
WHYTE, DAVID A.	RCAF	LAC	NIPAWIN	07/07/43	54°50'	104°54'	WHYTE LAKE
WHYTE, P.A.	RCAF	PO	SASKATOON	15/08/44	59°39'	108°42'	WHYTE BAY
WICK, STANLEY A.	RCAF	PO	CONQUEST	24/03/44	55°30'	104°07'	WICK RAPIDS
WICK, WILBUR W.	ARMY	PTE	SASKATOON	05/11/43	59°37'	108°49'	WICK LAKE
WICKENKAMP, ESTELLES A.	RAF	PO	STENEN	07/04/40	57°29'	109°38'	WICKENKAMP LAKE
WIEGAND, GOTTLIEB	ARMY	PTE	YOUNG	22/04/45	56°28'	109°40'	WIEGAND LAKE
WIGGINS, DONALD N.	ARMY	TPR	CENTRAL BUTTE	26/02/45	54°51'	108°06'	WIGGINS BAY
WILD, ALLEN	ARMY	SGT	REGINA	22/08/44	55°07'	102°36'	WILD LAKE
WILDE, CHARLES G.	RCAF	FS	RICHMOUND	03/07/42	50°28'	109°54'	WILDE HILLS
WILDE, CLARENCE E.	RCAF	SGT	KINLEY	02/01/43	55°14'	104°51'	WILDE ISLAND
WILDE, RICHARD N.	RCAF	AC1	RICHMOUND	08/07/41	55°07'	104°59'	WILDE BAY
WILDEY, NORMAN R.	ARMY	A CPL	BIRCH HILLS	25/09/44	55°54'	106°	WILDEY LAKE
WILDFONG, GORDON W.	RCAF	WO2	CUT KNIFE	16/03/44	54°49'	102°27'	WILDFONG LAKE
WILEY, JAMES W.	RCAF	FO	VISCOUNT	25/11/43	57°36'	102°41'	WILEY BAY
WILKEN, GARNET W.	RCAF	FS	YELLOW GRASS	09/11/42	59°15'	102°06'	WILKEN LAKE
WILKES, ALBERT	ARMY	L CPL	FROUDE	17/09/44	57°30'	109°44'	WILKES LAKE
WILKINS, ROBERT S.	ARMY	PTE	REGINA	08/05/45	56°39'	102°08'	WILKINS LAKE
WILKINSON, BERNARD E.	RCAF	SGT	SASKATOON	15/02/43	55°22'	105°21'	WILKINSON LAKE
WILKINSON, EINAR THOR	RAF	FO	CANORA	14/02/41	57°25'	102°02'	WILKINSON LAKE
WILLIAMS, CAMERON C.	ARMY	LIEUT	REGINA	02/11/44	53°58'	104°23'	WILLIAMS LAKE
WILLIAMS, CHARLES F.	RCAF	FS	SASKATOON	06/07/42			PENDING
WILLIAMS, EDWARD F.	RCAF	PO	GARDEN HEAD	12/01/45	57°23'	104°49'	WILLIAMS LAKE
WILLIAMS, JAMES R.	RCAF	FS	ENID	28/04/45	55°55'	109°03'	WILLIAMS CREEK
WILLIAMS, JAMES WILLIAM	ARMY	L CPL	PONTRILAS	27/02/45	54°40'	103°35'	WILLIAMS ISLAND
WILLIAMS, JOHN A.	ARMY	TPR	LANIGAN	21/07/44	54°36'	102°28'	WILLIAMS CREEK
WILLIAMS, JOHN K.D.	RCAF	PO	SASKATOON	30/06/41	54°55'	102°20'	WILLIAMS BAY
WILLIAMS, ROLAND W.	RCAF	FO	UNITY	18/04/45	57°52'	107°14'	WILLIAMS RIVER
WILLIAMS, WILLIAM G.	ARMY	SGT	MOOSE JAW	06/06/44	58°46'	103°25'	WILLIAMS LAKE
WILLIS, ARTHUR E.	ARMY	TPR	MOOSE JAW	08/08/44	56°15'	105°53'	WILLIS LAKE
WILLISON, RAYMOND P.	RCAF	FO	MOOSE JAW	09/11/44	56°04'	102°29'	WILLISON RAPIDS
WILLS, JACK G.	RCAF	FO	SASKATOON	21/09/44	56°02'	107°53'	WILLS LAKE
WILSON, DAVID W.	ARMY	PTE	CODERRE	02/01/45	59°07'	108°23'	WILSON CREEK
WILSON, DOUGLAS GORDON	ARMY	PTE	QUILL LAKE	08/12/44	54°56'	104°08'	WILSON ISLANDS
WILSON, GEORGE S.	ARMY	RFN	YORKTON	10/04/45	59°37'	109°17'	WILSON RIVER
WILSON, GEORGE W.	RCAF	SGT	PLEASANTDALE	15/09/42			PENDING
WILSON, HOWARD W.	ARMY	RFN	SHAUNAVON	06/07/44	56°55'	103°21'	WILSON ISLAND
WILSON, HUGH	ARMY	SGT	QU'APPELLE	26/10/43	59°51'	103°38'	WILSON LAKE
WILSON, JAMES H.	RCAF	FO	MOOSE JAW	31/03/44	55°44'	106°47'	WILSON PENINSULA
WILSON, JOHN G.	ARMY	PTE	MOSSBANK	09/08/44	56°56'	103°50'	WILSON PENINSULA
WILSON, KEITH D.	ARMY	CAPT	REGINA	25/06/44	59°40'	108°10'	WILSON LAKE
WILSON, KENNETH WILLIAM	ARMY	PTE	WATSON	20/12/43			PENDING
WILSON, KEVIN D.	RCAF	FO	LIMERICK	27/06/43	57°16'	105°31'	WILSON LAKE
WILSON, ROBERT HARVEY	NAVY	AB	REGINA	07/05/44	56°57'	103°49'	WILSON BAY
WILSON, ROBERT PERRY	RCAF	PO	NEILBURG	27/01/44	58°08'	106°33'	WILSON LAKE
WILSON, ROSS MACRAE	NAVY	SL	REGINA	08/09/42	54°47'	102°04'	WILSON LAKE
WILSON, RUSSELL G.	RCAF	WO2	TISDALE	22/11/43	57°23'	102°42'	WILSON ISLAND
WILSON, THOMAS H.	RCAF	FO	PARKMAN	08/06/44	57°04'	105°22'	WILSON BAY
WILSON, THOMAS O.	RCAF	WO2	CRAIK	20/02/44	55°44'	106°03'	WILSON ISLAND
WILSON, WILLIAM D.	ARMY	SPR	SASKATOON	27/05/45	54°58'	109°34'	WILSON POINT
WILSON, WILLIAM R.	RCAF	FS	MOOSE JAW	14/01/44	54°37'	102°12'	WILSON ISLAND
WILSON, WILLIAM T.	RCAF	PO	YORKTON	16/01/45	59°39'	109°22'	WILSON LAKES
WILT, FRANCIS E.	RCAF	SGT	STELCAM	29/02/44	56°43'	105°15'	WILT LAKE
WILTSE, THOMAS E.	RCAF	PO	READLYN	21/08/44	59°41'	108°35'	WILTSE RIVER
WING, KENNETH C.	RCAF	FO	NORTH BATTLEFORD	07/12/44	52°56'	108°05'	WING LAKE
WINN, HARRY	ARMY	CPL	ESTEVAN	25/07/44	54°41'	102°48'	WINN ISLAND
WINN, JOHN T.	ARMY	PTE	ESTEVAN	19/08/42	54°40'	102°49'	WINN BAY
WINTERBURN, CLARENCE	ARMY	TPR	PRINCE ALBERT	26/09/44	55°56'	103°18'	WINTERBURN LAKE
WINTERINGHAM, JOHN G.	ARMY	TPR	ESTEVAN	19/12/44	54°48'	102°52'	WINTERINGHAM LAKE
WINTHROPE, WILLIAM J.	NAVY	SG L	SASKATOON	28/03/42	54°11'	106°57'	WINTHROPE LAKE
WIRTH, CARL J.	ARMY	CPL	REGINA	15/08/44	57°05'	107°30'	WIRTH LAKE
WITOSHYNSKI, NICK	ARMY	PTE	DIVISION 16	28/12/43	58°52'	109°06'	WITOSHYNSKI LAKE
WITT, JAMES J.	ARMY	RFN	BELLE PLAINE	09/06/44	59°42'	108°54'	WITT LAKE
WIUM, GUNNAR	ARMY	L CPL	DIVISION 15	13/07/44	55°25'	104°12'	WIUM BAY
WIVCHARUK, JOHN	ARMY	RFN	BLAINE LAKE	13/12/44	59°44'	108°48'	WIVCHARUK LAKE
WLADYKA, EDWARD	ARMY	RFN	WATROUS	06/06/44	55°40'	104°47'	WLADYKA FALLS
WOOD, FREDDIE F.	ARMY	PTE	MOOSE JAW	08/08/44	56°55'	102°41'	WOOD BAY
WOOD, HUGH R.	RCAF	PO	SASKATOON	18/04/45			PENDING
WOOD, JOHN J.	ARMY	PTE	MEOTA	17/12/44	56°10'	104°40'	WOOD BAY

Name	Branch	Rank	Hometown	Casualty Date	Latitude	Longitude	Geo-Memorial
WOOD, JOHN W.	RCAF	PO	GLASLYN	11/11/41	57°04'	107°14'	WOOD CREEK
WOOD, RONALD M.	RCAF	FS	WILLOW BUNCH	21/02/45			PENDING
WOOD, STANLEY A.	RCAF	SGT	UNKNOWN	20/10/43			PENDING
WOOD, STANLEY E.	NAVY	AB	OGEMA	22/10/40	55°05'	105°19'	WOOD CREEK
WOOD, WILLIAM G.	RCAF	SGT	BRANCEPETH	23/05/43	59°43'	105°27'	WOOD ISLAND
WOODARD, THOMAS HAROLD	RCAF	PO	WEYBURN	12/04/44	54°08'	102°13'	WOODARD BAY
WOODHAMS, GEORGE T.J.	RCAF	SGT	HURONVILLE	25/08/41	55°35'	104°43'	WOODHAMS CREEK
WOODHEAD, ROBERT M.	RCAF	PO	WAPELLA	27/05/42	52°49'	103°35'	WOODHEAD LAKE
WOODLEY, DONALD S.	RCAF	FS	SASKATOON	08/04/42	56°30'	102°11'	WOODLEY LAKE
WOODMAN, DONALD FRANK	NAVY	TEL	SASKATOON	13/07/45	56°53'	103°46'	WOODMAN BAY
WOODMAN, EDWARD G.	ARMY	CAPT	REGINA	07/12/44	59°59'	105°35'	WOODMAN LAKE
WOODS, HARVEY G.	ARMY	PTE	MOOSE RANGE	56°17'	103°17'		WOODS LAKE
WOODWARD, RODNEY T.	NAVY	AB	MOOSE JAW	19/07/40	57°52'	102°43'	WOODWARD RIVER
WOODWARD, SIDNEY	ARMY	CPL	KAMSACK	04/09/44	59°15'	106°03'	WOODWARD LAKE
WOOLARD, ROBERT A.	ARMY	LIEUT	STAR CITY	19/08/42	54°18'	108°39'	WOOLARD LAKE
WOOLHETHER, SPENCER E.	RCAF	PO	DAHINDA	22/03/44	59°21'	105°24'	WOOLHETHER LAKE
WORDEN, EDWIN O.	ARMY	L SGT	BROADVIEW	08/04/45	57°43'	108°04'	WORDEN LAKE
WORMWORTH, THOMAS C.	NAVY	AB	SWIFT CURRENT	17/12/40	54°59'	102°12'	WORMWORTH LAKE
WOTHERSPOON, ALBERT E.	RCAF	PO	LANGENBURG	17/03/45	54°48'	108°57'	WOTHERSPOON LAKE
WRENSHALL, BERNARD H.	RCAF	FO	MILDEN	08/08/44	60°00'	105°26'	WRENSHALL LAKE
WRIGHT, DAVID M.	ARMY	TPR	ASSINIBOIA	16/07/44	59°28'	103°56'	WRIGHT BAY
WRIGHT, DONALD L.	RCAF	WO2	SASKATOON	26/12/43	57°48'	104°03'	WRIGHT RIVER
WRIGHT, JOHN E.	RCAF	FO	DENHOLM	04/03/44	56°19'	102°01'	WRIGHT ISLAND
WRIGHT, RONALD H.	ARMY	PTE	QUILL LAKE	20/12/44	59°33'	103°26'	WRIGHT LAKE
WRIGHT, WILLIAM W.	RCAF	WO2	NORTH BATTLEFORD	13/07/43	54°52'	103°05'	WRIGHT LAKE
WUNDER, PETER A.	ARMY	GNR	FOAM LAKE	21/05/44	55°10'	102°05'	WUNDER LAKE
WUNSCH, ALFRED B.	ARMY	L SGT	MORSE	24/09/44	55°59'	104°53'	WUNSCH LAKE
WURTZ, ANDREW H.	ARMY	PTE	KELVINGTON	02/09/44	54°56'	102°46'	WURTZ LAKE
WYCHERLEY, RONALD N.	RCAF	PO	SASKATOON	15/01/42	56°11'	107°48'	WYCHERLEY LAKE
WYKES, RICHARD C.	ARMY	GNR	PRINCE ALBERT	19/04/45	55°32'	103°33'	WYKES LAKE
WYLIE, CHARLES B.	RCAF	FS	INSTOW	05/08/44	55°08'	107°12'	WYLIE CREEK
WYLIE, RICHARD B.	RCAF	SL	ESTEVAN	03/06/41	54°09'	106°52'	WYLIE LAKE
WYLLIE, JOHN F.	RCAF	FO	PRINCE ALBERT	13/06/44	54°48'	102°49'	WYLLIE LAKE
WYMAN, MERRIT M.	RCAF	LAC	SASKATOON	01/10/41	55°11'	104°15'	WYMAN LAKE
WYSOSKI, WALTER P.	ARMY	A CPL	OAKSHELA	01/01/45	55°31'	106°55'	WYSOSKI LAKE
YACKLE, JOHN R.	ARMY	PTE	AVONHURST	02/03/45	57°06'	107°51'	YACKLE LAKE
YAHOLNITSKY, NESTER	ARMY	PTE	YORKTON	23/09/44	56°34'	103°44'	YAHOLNITSKY LAKE
YAHOLNITSKY, WALTER L.	RCAF	WO2	MIKADO	09/04/43	54°53'	104°49'	YAHOLNITSKY CREEK
YALOWEGA, JOHN	ARMY	PTE	DIVISION 14	09/08/44	57°48'	104°53'	YALOWEGA LAKE
YASKOWICH, WALTER L.	ARMY	SPR	WYNYARD	11/05/44	54°57'	102°07'	YASKOWICH LAKE
YATES, ALBERT C.	RCAF	FS	REGINA	10/09/42	55°31'	108°19'	YATES BAY
YAWORSKI, ADOLF E.	RCAF	WO2	RAMA	25/03/44	56°00'	103°41'	YAWORSKI ISLAND
YAWORSKI, NICHOLAS	ARMY	PTE	MACNUTT	09/08/44	58°52'	106°38'	YAWORSKI LAKE
YEO, DANIEL	ARMY	C S M	SMEATON	06/06/44	57°27'	103°16'	YEO LAKE
YOST, GLENN F.	ARMY	PTE	DORINTOSH	22/07/44	55°34'	106°38'	YOST LAKE
YOUNG, ALFRED	NAVY	AB	REGINA	22/10/40	55°25'	104°51'	YOUNG PENINSULA
YOUNG, GEORGE M.	ARMY	GDSM	REGINA	26/02/45	54°57'	102°13'	YOUNG LAKE
YOUNG, HAROLD G.	ARMY	SIGMN	PAYNTON	09/12/44	55°56'	104°37'	YOUNG ISLAND
YOUNG, JAMES R.	RCAF	FS	VISCOUNT	02/05/42			PENDING
YOUNG, JOSEPH P.	RCAF	PO	REGINA	23/05/44	57°48'	105°31'	YOUNG LAKE
YOUNG, KENNETH I.	RCAF	WO2	WYNYARD	25/02/43	56°04'	104°44'	YOUNG LAKE
YOUNG, LEWIS E.	ARMY	PTE	MEADOW LAKE	07/05/44	54°38'	108°34'	YOUNG CREEK
YOUNG, MARTIN	ARMY	PTE	BRANCEPETH	24/09/44	58°20'	103°18'	YOUNG ISLAND
YOUNG, RALPH	ARMY	PTE	DIVISION 17	16/01/44	53°27'	108°13'	YOUNG BAY
YOUNG, STANFORD G.	RCAF	PO	REGINA	31/08/43	55°57'	107°30'	YOUNG LAKE
YUNKER, BERNARD	RCAF	FL	BALGONIE	05/07/44	57°09'	107°32'	YUNKER LAKE
YURCHISON, WILLIAM	RCAF	FO	PELLY	05/11/43	57°23'	104°05'	YURCHISON LAKE
YURKOWSKI, JOSEPH S.	RCAF	SGT	LANIGAN	23/07/42	58°44'	105°08'	YURKOWSKI LAKE
ZACHARIAS, HENRY J.	RCAF	FS	HERBERT	22/01/44	55°51'	104°15'	ZACHARIAS LAKE
ZACHER, FRANK X.	ARMY	L CPL	ODESSA	13/08/42	57°15'	103°25'	ZACHER LAKE
ZADWORNY, THADDEUS J.	RCAF	FO	ITUNA	22/05/44	57°07'	107°36'	ZADWORNY LAKE
ZAHARIK, JACOB	ARMY	CPL	REGINA	23/01/45	56°04'	106°29'	ZAHARIK LAKE
ZALESCHUK, DEMETRO	RCAF	FS	ROSTHERN	17/04/43	56°34'	102°14'	ZALESCHUK LAKE
ZANDER, DONALD	RCAF	FS	HANDEL	31/08/43	56°39'	108°05'	ZANDER LAKE
ZAPFE, MERTON E.	RCAF	FS	SASKATOON	24/05/43	52°28'	101°39'	ZAPFE LAKE
ZAPFE, WILLARD C.	RCAF	FO	SASKATOON	23/03/43	59°22'	108°52'	ZAPFE ISLAND
ZBARSKY, RALPH	NAVY	AB	SASKATOON	16/04/45	55°53'	105°14'	ZBARSKY BAY
ZBYTNUIK, TONY	RCAF	PO	KAMSACK	18/04/44	55°26'	107°37'	ZBYTNUIK LAKE
ZEMLAK, MIKE	ARMY	PTE	WISHART	09/10/44	59°36'	109°01'	ZEMLAK LAKE
ZENTNER, WILLIAM J.	ARMY	PTE	LANGENBURG	08/02/45	57°32'	103°51'	ZENTNER LAKE
ZIGOLYK, PEAT	ARMY	PTE	BLAINE LAKE	24/07/44	57°02'	103°23'	ZIGOLYK LAKE
ZILLINSKY, ANDREW	ARMY	A CPL	WATROUS	08/08/44	56°46'	102°27'	ZILLINSKY ISLAND
ZIMMER, IGNATIUS J.	RCAF	LAC	CUDWORTH	24/01/44	57°09'	105°46'	ZIMMER LAKE
ZIMMER, RONALD	ARMY	SGT	VISCOUNT	02/01/44	55°06'	104°52'	ZIMMER ISLAND
ZIP, JOHN A.	ARMY	RFN	TWAY	02/19/45	55°54'	104°03'	ZIP LAKE
ZIPORKIN, JACK	NAVY	AB	REGINA	03/12/42	54°51'	102°41'	ZIPORKIN LAKE
ZORA, JOHN E.	RCAF	LAC	REGINA	07/05/43	59°34'	108°25'	ZORA LAKE
ZULAUF, TOBIAS	ARMY	PTE	FOX VALLEY	01/14/45	55°53'	104°51'	ZULAUF LAKE
ZUNTI, JAMES JOSEPH	RCAF	WO2	LUSELAND	11/23/43	55°26'	104°47'	ZUNTI LAKE

248

Selected Bibliography

Air Force Association of Canada. "RCAF Personnel: Honours and Awards, 1939-1945." <www.airforce.ca>.

Allison, Les and Harry Hayward. *They Shall Grow Not Old: A Book of Remembrance.* Brandon: Commonwealth Air Training Plan Museum, 1992.

Brickhill, Paul. *The Dam Busters.* London: Pan Books, 1972 (first published 1951).

British.Forces.Com. "The Fall of Hong Kong." <british.forces.com>.

Buchanan, Lt.Col. G.B. *The March of the Prairie Men: The History of the South Saskatchewan Regiment.* Ottawa: Queen's Printers, 1956.

Brown, Gordon, and Terry Copp. *Look to Your Front: Regina Rifles, A Regiment at War, 1944-45.* Laurier Centre for Military Strategic and Disarament Studies, Wilfrid Laurier University, 2001.

Cuthand, Doug, and Michele Kiss, Directors. *Nikiskisinan: We Remember Them.* Videocassette. Tri-Media Productions, n.d.

Commonwealth War Graves Commission. "Debt of Honour Register." <yard.ccfa.gov.uk>.

Dunsmore, Spencer. *Above and Beyond: The Canadians' War in the Air, 1939-45.* Toronto: McClelland & Stewart, 1996.

—-,*Wings For Victory: The Remarkable Story of the British Commonwealth Air Training Plan in Canada.* Toronto: McClelland & Stewart, 1994.

—-, and William Carter. *Reap the Whirlwind: The Untold Story of 6 Group, Canada's Bomber Force of World War II.* Toronto: McClelland & Stewart, 1991.

Falconer, Jonathan. *The Bomber Command Handbook, 1939-1945.* Thrupp-Stroud, Gloucestershire: Sutton Publishing, 1998.

Hendrie, Andrew. *Canadian Squadrons in Coastal Command.* St. Catharines, Ontario: Vanwell Publishing Limited, 1997.

Hodgson, David. *Letters from a Bomber Pilot.* London: Thames Methuen, 1985.

Maple Leaf Up. "The Canadian Army Overseas, 1939-1945." <www.mapleleafup.org>.

Margolian, Howard. *Conduct Unbecoming: The Story of the Murder of Canadian prisoners of War in Normandy.* Toronto: University of Toronto Press, 1998.

McAndrew, Bill. *Canadians and the Italian Campaign: 1943-45.* Montreal: Editions Art Global, 1996.

McKee, Fraser, and Robert Darlington. *The Canadian Naval Chronicle, 1939-1945: The Successes and Losses of the Canadian Navy in World War II.* St. Catharines, Ontario: Vanwell Publishing Limited, 1996.

Middlebrook, Martin, and Chris Everitt. *The Bomber Command War Diaries: An Operational Reference Book, 1939-1945.* London: Penguin, 1990.

Royal Air Force. "The Battle of Britain." <www.raf.mod.uk>.

Royal Canadian Air Force. "Aircraft of the Canadian Forces." <www.rcaf.com/aircraft>.

Schull, Joseph. *Far Distant Ships: An Official Account of Canadian Naval Operations in World War II*. Toronto: Stoddart, 1987.

"South Saskatchewan Regiment." <cap.estevan.sk.ca/ssr>.

Stacey, Colonel C.P. *The Victory Campaign: The Operations in North-West Europe 1944-45*. Vol. 3 of *The Official History of the Canadian Army in the Second World War*. 3 vols. Ottawa: Department of National Defence, 1960.

Tripp, F.R. *Canada's Army in World War II: Badges and Histories of the Corps and Regiments*. Toronto: The Unitrade Press, 1983.

Veterans Affairs Canada. "Canada-Italy, 1943-1945." <www.vac-acc.gc.ca>.

—-,"Canadian Virtual War Memorial." <www.vac-acc.gc.ca>.

Wings For Freedom. "Squadrons & Units." <www.rcaf.com>.

Wyatt, Bernie. *Maximum Effort: The Big Bombing Raids*. Erin, Ontario: The Boston Mills Press, 1986.